CANADIAN
TRANSPORTATION
ECONOMICS

A. W. Currie

UNIVERSITY OF TORONTO PRESS

Preface

In 1925, when he was Chancellor of the Exchequer, Winston Churchill commented that aviation was changing so rapidly that one needed wings to keep up with it. This remark is still true and applies to other modes of transport as well as aircraft.

Nevertheless, the purpose of this book is not to forecast future trends or even to describe in detail the technological changes which have occurred in the last few years. The author's objective is to describe and analyse the economics of transport in Canada whether by rail, highway, inland and coastal waterways, the high seas, air, or pipeline. He has tried to avoid setting himself up as a one-man royal commission empowered to reform the business of transport. At the same time he has taken pains not to become embroiled too deeply in economic theory.

The general plan of this book is similar to the author's *Economics of Canadian Transportation* which was first published in 1954. Since then, transportation has changed so rapidly that over one-third of the old book had to be discarded, nearly half had to be drastically revised, and minor changes had to be made on most of the remaining pages. Moreover, substantial amounts of new material had to be added. The changes were so extensive that both publisher and author felt a new book was justified.

The author hopes that this new publication, like its predecessors, will prove of interest to employees of railways, steamship companies, airlines, and pipelines, to operators of motor vehicles, to shippers, consignees, and other businessmen, to professional economists, and to citizens generally. In other words, the author has attempted to keep in mind the differing needs of several classes of readers. At the risk of boring a few of them with tiresome details, he has purposely included what may appeal to others. The rates, fares, and other prices given in the book are those in effect at the date of the case in question and may not be currently applicable to traffic.

June 1967   A. W. C.

Contents

CANADIAN TRANSPORTATION ECONOMICS

1

Transportation
in the Canadian Economy

THE HISTORY of transportation in Canada has been written often and well.[1] Nothing can be gained by rethreshing old straw but a brief prospectus seems to be called for in order to sketch the background for succeeding chapters. From the earliest days of settlement, the governing bodies of the country have taken an active part in providing and regulating transportation by water, highway, rail, and, more recently, by air and pipeline. Generally the public has insisted that these facilities be operated on a commercial basis, i.e., that receipts from the users of the service cover the operating costs, return on the investment, taxes, and other expenses. In some instances the welfare of the public, the broad benefit to the nation as a whole, is considered to outweigh deficits on the facility. Then cost-revenue relationships are overlooked and losses regarded with equanimity. A fundamental and persistent problem in the history of Canadian transportation is the interplay of two radically different concepts: straight business principles on the one hand and such matters as national unity, the movement of trade through Canadian ports, the opening up of new areas, defence, and avoiding the ruination of national credit on the other.

To 1896

By the early thirties of the nineteenth century public funds, largely borrowed in Great Britain, had built 6,000 miles of post and military roads, the Lachine, the Rideau, and the Welland canals. These facilities were constructed for the purposes of defence, the administration of justice, and internal economic development. In the later thirties and forties more canals were built along the St. Lawrence in the hope of attracting through Canadian channels and Canadian ports the rapidly growing traffic of the American Middle West and reproducing within Canada the prosperity brought to New York State by the Erie Canal.

Although the first steam railway in what is now the Dominion was opened in 1836, the building of railways proceeded at a snail's pace until the 1850s. Various municipalities and the colonial governments gave cash grants to local lines. These subsidies, while generous in the light of existing taxing and borrowing capacity, were not large in total. Private capitalists hoped for personal profits from constructing and operating the early railway mileage, including the Grand Trunk. The public on the other hand did not look for a financial return on its investment in canals. As railways proved their worth by the speed, economy, and dependability of their service, public expenditures on canals and roads gradually declined.

When the scattered colonies in British North America began seriously to consider forming themselves into a larger and stronger unit, they realized that cheap, reliable, year-round transportation was essential if they were to be effectively bound together socially, politically, and economically. Consequently, the promise of railway construction formed an integral part of the Confederation scheme of 1867. Transportation was also important later when Prince Edward Island, British Columbia, and Newfoundland entered the Dominion.

The obligation to the Maritime Provinces was acted upon by building, entirely at public cost, the Intercolonial and the Prince Edward Island Railway and ferry, and by not requiring that the rate level be high enough to cover fully the interest on the public's investment. The terms of union between British Columbia and the new Dominion were fulfilled by constructing the Canadian Pacific Railway. This company "was brought into existence and carried through its early difficulties by direct Government support and large financial assistance from public funds. As a result of this support and assistance, coupled with the rapid growth of Canadian population and wealth, and its own wise and prudent management, the Canadian Pacific has 'made good.' It has raised without further Government help, hundreds of millions of new capital."[2] It used these funds and its own reinvested earnings to improve its way, structures, and equipment, to erect hotels, and to build or purchase branch lines as well as inland-waterway and ocean steamships. Meanwhile both the Grand Trunk and the Intercolonial had extended their facilities, partly by construction and partly by consolidating the small lines which had been built for local purposes.

By 1896 in the thickly settled parts of Canada east of the Great Lakes, the railway network was approaching its present mileage. West of Lakehead only one through line and a few branches were in operation. With the exception of the Intercolonial, all the companies were privately managed. From provincial and federal governments the railways received assistance which was substantial especially if measured by the low national income which prevailed throughout the long depression of the eighties and nineties. It is particularly worthy of note that this aid was given outright. It was paid in cash or land, and, excluding the Intercolonial, the recipients had no further claim on the public treasury and expected to conduct their affairs solely with a view to corporate profit.

The need for more transportation facilities was so strong that the necessity for public control appeared at the time to be relatively unimportant. In 1874 the broad scheme of the Classification was adopted from England and the principles behind the present (standard mileage) class rates and commodity tariffs were formulated. For all practical purposes the railways themselves determined the level of freight rates, the charges for individual shipments, and the quality of their service. The public had to rely on competition between different companies and between railways and steamships adequately to protect the interest of all.

Canals and inland waterways, though they still performed a valuable function, were not significantly improved between 1860 and 1896. Such highways as existed were as a rule unbelievably bad. With the exception of a few toll roads they were financed by local units of government from their general tax revenues. They were primarily intended to give access to the land abutting upon them.

1896–1917

Between roughly 1896 and 1914 Canada experienced unprecedented prosperity. By 1905 she had committed herself to building two new transcontinental railways, the Canadian Northern and the Grand Trunk Pacific. The Dominion government undertook to construct the National Transcontinental from Winnipeg across Northern Ontario, Quebec, and New Brunswick to Moncton and to lease it to the Grand Trunk Pacific. All these lines, including the many miles of branches laid down by the Canadian Pacific throughout the West, were expected to pay their own way. On the other hand when the Government improved the navigable waterway along the St. Lawrence and the Great Lakes and began construction of a new Welland Canal, it abandoned the cost-revenue approach entirely. By abolishing canal tolls in 1903, the Dominion forsook an old but half-hearted attempt to have users pay at least part of the cost of the canal system. Highways, which were scarcely any better than in the previous century, continued to be financed in the same manner as schools, fire departments, and other non-commercial public enterprises.

The additions to the railway network were made for two main reasons: to settle Canada's undeveloped agricultural land and exploit her minerals and lumber and to direct the flow of Canadian trade throughout the length of the Dominion. These objectives could not be attained unless the charges for carrying primary products were low enough to permit traffic to move in volume. In 1897 the Dominion under the Crow's Nest Pass Agreement and in 1901 the province of Manitoba under the so-called Manitoba Agreement subsidized certain railways in return for concessions in freight tolls. The reductions brought about by these arrangements were voluntarily accepted by other railway companies operating in the territories covered by the agreements. In consequence reductions in rates which governments had paid one company to introduce on the lines it then operated were voluntarily extended by every carrier to all of the rapidly growing mileages.

In order to improve the machinery for controlling rates and service on railways and to deal with allegations of unjust discrimination between persons, places, and classes of freight, the government established the Board of Railway Commissioners which took office in 1904. Thus the period from 1896 to 1914 was notable for rapid, almost frenzied, extensions of railway mileage, for reductions in rates on primary products and settlers' effects, and for comprehensive schemes for regulating rail carriers.

The most conspicuous feature of Canadian transportation history during the six years after 1914 was the collapse of the Grand Trunk, Grand Trunk Pacific, and Canadian Northern as privately owned enterprises. None of these railways could pay its own way under a level of freight tolls which was set on the requirements of the Canadian Pacific. In other words the expectation that these railways would have adequate revenues from rates and fares to meet all their expenses proved to be not well founded.

The common stock of the Canadian Northern and the Grand Trunk Pacific represented practically no cash investment. Thus while in outward form these two companies were private concerns, substantially both of them were the financial responsibilities of national and provincial governments. Whereas the Canadian Pacific had been generously aided at its inception and then left to look after itself, the new lines involved the government in a succession of obligations. None of these had apparently been anticipated when the first steps toward building the lines were taken. If noticed at all, the dangers had been discounted. Viewed fifty years later, the government's policy after 1900 saddled the country not only with privately owned railway systems that could not finance themselves, but with mileage which often duplicated services already in operation. The decisions are understandable only in the light of the unbridled optimism of the early years of the present century, and of the fact that railways then had a virtual monopoly of all land transportation. No one could have foreseen that war would break out before the new companies had completed their main lines and established their earning power.

Because the Dominion was already responsible for most of the money spent on constructing the roads, it was natural that it should be directly concerned when they got into trouble. Moreover, some of the provincial governments had obligated themselves so heavily for bond guarantees that they might have been seriously embarrassed if suddenly called upon to carry out their promises. Since its incorporation, the Grand Trunk had never been a real success though it had managed to struggle along. Its remaining strength was, however, progressively undermined by the losses on its western subsidiary, the Grand Trunk Pacific.

Royal Commission of 1917

This complex and cheerless situation was considered by a Royal Commission appointed in 1917. Two of the three Commissioners recommended, and the government accepted the proposal, that the Canadian Northern, the Grand Trunk, and the Grand Trunk Pacific Railways should be consolidated with the Intercolonial, the National Transcontinental, and other lines wholly owned by the government into a single system, later called the Canadian National Railways. The Commission made clear beyond any shadow of doubt that the government-owned railways were to be run as a straight commercial concern. Unfortunately, while the government of the day accepted the proposal of the majority of the Commissioners regarding operation by a separate corporation, it failed properly to buttress it against political or non-economic influences. For instance, the Commission proposed that the Board of Trustees which was to manage the system should be permanent and self-perpetuating. Instead the Board of Directors (as this body was called when appointed) had fifteen members who were "selected on a basis of regional representation—a method which necessarily gave weight to other considerations as well as those of business capacity or technical qualifications."[3] Moreover Sir Henry Thornton, whose particular policies are outlined later, was an expansionist. Thus the groundwork was laid for departing from business principles in the administration of the Canadian National.

Meanwhile on account of the inflation which took place during and immediately after the war, the Board of Railway Commissioners allowed the railways to increase their tolls considerably. The Manitoba and Crow's Nest Pass agreements were both abrogated, the first by the

Board, the second by the government under the War Measures Act and later by amending the Railway Act. When dealing with these rate cases, the Board had to concern itself with such questions as how much net revenue the railways should be allowed for interest and dividends, whether the rate level should be set by the financial requirements of the high or of the low cost road, and how promptly rates should be brought in line with changing costs of operation on the one hand and the market value of the goods being shipped on the other. The advances which the Board allowed were niggardly with the result that, while the Canadian Pacific had ample revenue to cover its requirements, the railways then being incorporated in the present Canadian National were being operated at substantial deficits. In essence, the Board, with the government's approval, set up the Canadian Pacific as the yardstick for rate-making purposes. It was to be operated as a commercial enterprise but the Canadian National with its heavy indebtedness would have to justify itself on the grounds of being a pioneering road, serving all regions, and contributing to national unity.[4]

1920–9

In the 1920s public investment in transportation facilities, temporarily suspended during hostilities, again reached prodigious amounts. The Dominion poured money into the Canadian National to rehabilitate and unify the various individual and often competing companies which had been thrown together between 1917 and 1923, and to bring its physical assets up to the standard of the Canadian Pacific. The Dominion was also compelled to advance funds to meet operating deficits on the System. It completed the Hudson Bay Railway on which work had started before the war. It greatly improved the accommodation for shipping at Halifax, Saint John, and Montreal and constructed new harbour facilities at Vancouver, New Westminster, Victoria, and Prince Rupert. It finished the new Welland Ship Canal. All this physical plant was built with the triple objective of reducing the cost of transportation, opening up the country, and keeping trade flowing along Canadian routes rather than through the United States. Meanwhile, the Canadian Pacific was embarking on an ambitious but well-rounded plan for keeping its railways up to date, building branch lines, erecting hotels, and modernizing its fleet of steamships.

Provincial governments tended to withdraw from further investment in railways after 1920 for the Dominion government assumed their former obligations to the Canadian Northern and Grand Trunk Pacific. Although Ontario and British Columbia had their own local railways and

Newfoundland took over a bankrupt private line, the chief provincial expenditures were on highways. Operators of passenger automobiles, trucks, and buses demanded hard-surfaced roads with gentle curves and gradients, well marked, and open throughout the year. The municipalities which had formerly been responsible for roads and bridges were unable or unwilling to finance expensive modern highways.

The provincial governments, however, could collect revenue from substantially all users of the highways through the medium of a tax on gasoline and various licence fees. This source of revenue proved so lucrative and the demand for better roads so insistent that the network of provincial highways grew by leaps and bounds. With the insignificant exception of a few toll roads, for the first time in Canadian history the way was open for providing highways on a commercial basis. Revenues could be collected from motorists in proportion to their use of the facilities while expenditures for maintaining highways and for interest on highway debt could be kept within the income from licences and gasoline taxes. Though provincial departments of highways do not conduct a business in the ordinary sense of the term, their operations approximate those of commercial enterprises.

Early in the 1920s railway rates as a whole were cut back from their postwar peak. In 1922 the Crow's Nest Pass Agreement which had been abrogated during the war was suspended by legislation for a further period of two years except that the rates on grain and grain products from the West to Lakehead were restored to the 1899 level. In 1925 Parliament extended this arrangement without limit of time. The original Agreement legally covered only the lines operated by the Canadian Pacific in 1897. The new legislation applied the low rates on grain to the entire railway mileage in the West. On the other hand it cancelled the statutory rates on various settlers' effects. Subsequently, the Board of Railway Commissioners ordered the 1899 tolls to apply, with some modification, on grain westbound through Pacific coast ports for export. The fundamental reason for continuing the Agreement in modified form was political. The Royal Commission of 1951 phrased it: "abandonment [of the Agreement] would mean that Parliament no longer looks upon Western Canada's production of grain for export as an industry requiring special consideration as in the national interest."[5]

The Maritime Provinces derived little benefit from the reduction of grain rates in the West. Moreover they were suffering from a secular decline in prosperity and alleged that railway rates were responsible for their business depression. A Royal Commission under the chairmanship of Sir Andrew Rae Duncan, appointed in 1925, recommended a reduction of 20 per cent in the current tolls within the Maritime Provinces.

The Commission gave three reasons for its recommendations: "(1) pre-Confederation promises made to the Maritime Provinces to enable them to obtain entry into the markets of Central Canada; (2) the greater increases in rates on the Intercolonial Railway since 1912 as compared with increases in the rest of Canada, and (3) the circuity of the route taken by the Intercolonial Railway [for reasons of national defence]."[6] The recommendations of the Duncan Commission as adopted by Parliament did not materially affect the earning power of railways since the government paid 20 per cent of the normal toll and the shipper the remainder. None the less the legislation interfered in the national interest with railway tolls which had presumably been set purely for business reasons.

Depression

In the 1930s during the world-wide depression in industry and trade, the Canadian Pacific had to forgo dividends on its common and even on its preference stock. In four years, 1932–5, its earnings failed to cover fixed charges which had to be met from reserves. The deficit on the Canadian National grew to the point where it practically equalled all the federal income tax. Capital investment in railways virtually ceased. The provinces continued to spend money on the construction and maintenance of highways though on a much smaller scale than before. As a public relief project the Dominion began building part of a trans-Canada highway and a national airway but its projects for new canals and harbour works had been completed before the onset of the depression. The Canadian Pacific had either finished the programme of investment it had started, or curtailed it because of the financial stringency. In a word, the provision of physical facilities for the movement of passengers and freight, a conspicuous feature of our economic history for over a century, had temporarily halted.

After 1929 prices and wages declined. Nevertheless, the general rate level was not significantly changed as it had been in 1897, 1901, 1922, and 1927 to stimulate expansion in the country as a whole or in particular sections of it. Users of the railways apparently recognized that industry and agriculture were so badly depressed that reductions in railway tolls would plainly be incapable of bringing about revival. Lower freight tolls would not lead to any significant increase in the volume of freight hauled and hence would not increase the net revenues of the railways which were already inadequate. Moreover, the railways feared that if they voluntarily cut their rate level they would have difficulty getting it raised again.

Royal Commission, 1931–2

The morass in which both the publicly and the privately owned systems found themselves led to the appointment of another Royal Commission, this one under the chairmanship of Sir Lyman Poore Duff. The Commission was particularly impressed by "the red thread of extravagance" in the administration of the Canadian National, by the existence of railway lines which duplicated each other or which had insufficient traffic to cover their operating expenses, and by economically wasteful competition between the two large systems. The Commission proposed radical changes in the constitution of the governing body of the Canadian National and voluntary co-operation between the two roads with a view to cutting out unnecessary waste while retaining the virtues of free competition.

In some respects the Commission attempted to put the Canadian National back on a commercial basis, as the Royal Commission of 1917 had intended. At the same time it tried to protect the Canadian Pacific from unfair competition by the publicly owned road. It did not, however, reduce the excessive capitalization of the Canadian National to the point where the System could be expected to pay its operating expenses and interest. So in the main it gave its blessing to current practice. The privately owned system was to approach the problems of transportation from the standpoint of profit and loss but the success of the National System was not to be appraised by ordinary commercial standards.

1932–9

A most significant change in Canadian transportation was the rapid growth in the volume of goods moving over the highways as compared with traffic by rail. This shift was due to the fine new highways and secondary roads, the low initial cost of new or second-hand vehicles, the lack of suitable alternative employment for many operators, and the absence of legislative restrictions on admission to the industry except as regards safety. Furthermore the right of way (the highway) was provided by provinces and paid for by users on a more or less pay-as-you-go basis by means of gasoline taxes. Operators of motor vehicles paid for highways in almost direct proportion to their use of them. They were not burdened with fixed charges which went on regardless of use and which nearly prostrated the railways.

In 1933 Parliament passed legislation to protect the public against arbitrary abandonment of lines by railway companies. In 1938 it authorized railways to publish agreed charges, subject to the approval of the Board of Railway Commissioners, with the object of enabling them better to meet competition from trucks. In order to provide as far as possible for an integrated, smoothly working mechanism embracing all forms of transport, the Board was directed to co-ordinate and harmonize the operations of all agencies of transport within its jurisdiction. It was given power to license package freighters along the Great Lakes, the St. Lawrence, the Mackenzie and its tributaries. It might also set tolls for the carriage of freight on these waterways with the exception of bulk cargoes on the Great Lakes and the St. Lawrence. It was to issue certificates of public convenience and necessity to airlines and to set their tolls.[7] In view of the Board's new duties, its name was altered to the Board of Transport Commissioners.

On the whole the decade of the 1930s was a period of retrenchment for railways, of growing control over inland-water navigation and airlines, and of efforts at adjustment between competing transportation agencies. The decade also saw the inauguration of regular services across Canada by air as well as a remarkable expansion in non-scheduled commercial flying into areas which were isolated as long as only surface transport was available. In 1937, Trans-Canada Air Lines, a subsidiary of Canadian National Railways, began to fly the transcontinental route and Canada's share of trans-border services with the United States. In 1964 its name was changed to Air Canada. Most of the companies giving air services in a generally north and south direction within Canada were gradually acquired by the Canadian Pacific Air Lines, a subsidiary of the Canadian Pacific Railway. Subsequently, several other companies entered the business of connecting northern communities with thickly settled areas. Meanwhile, Canadian Pacific Air Lines was flying across the Pacific, and to Amsterdam, Lisbon, and Rome. In 1958 it got the right to make one daily flight each way between Vancouver, Toronto and Montreal. Nine years later it was allowed 25 per cent of the transcontinental market for air travel within Canada. So, in airlines, as in railways, some services are operated by the Government and others by private capitalists. Whereas public ownership of a trans-continental railway was undertaken more or less of necessity, public ownership of an airline was deliberate.

For the most part airlines were able to meet their operating expenses from their own revenues: wages and salaries, fuel, repairs, depreciation, and interest out of receipts from passengers, express, and the carriage of air mail. They contributed relatively little toward the maintenance of public airports, the operation of navigation aids, the supply of weather information, or interest on the ground facilities which they used. Thus they are on a commercial basis only within a very narrow meaning of the term.

War and Postwar

During World War II, railways assumed the main burden of carrying munitions, troops, civilians engaged in war work, foodstuffs for our servicemen abroad, and supplies for the civilians and troops of other Allied countries. Railway traffic, military and civilian, reached the highest level in Canadian history. Under the price and wage control measures introduced late in 1941, tolls for the services which railways rendered to shippers and passengers, the price of the materials and equipment they purchased, and the wages of the men they employed were all frozen. Railway operating expenses swelled, but this was almost entirely because more supplies and workers were needed to handle the enormous volume of traffic. Increased operating expenses were easily absorbed by the higher gross revenues arising from the amount of business done. Net revenues were ample to provide for the usual operating expenses, depreciation (which was introduced for the first time on Canadian railways), taxes, interest, reserves, and deferred maintenance. The Canadian National had large surpluses even after meeting all the interest on its huge indebtedness. The Canadian Pacific resumed dividends, though at lower rates than in the twenties and materially reduced bonded indebtedness. Thus during the war years both major railways operated on a cash nexus.

Late in 1945 and throughout 1946, the railway situation deteriorated. Costs of operation rose after the end of hostilities and especially following the general lifting of price and wage controls in 1946. But rates and fares remained at their old levels. Highway carriers again became strong competitors of the railways for certain types of business. Net revenues of the railways began to fall sharply from their wartime peaks. Accordingly, they were forced to apply to the Board of Transport Commissioners for a general increase in tolls, the first since 1920.

The increases authorized by the Board in 1948 proved inadequate to meet the financial requirements of the carriers. Wage rates, material prices, and, after 1957, interest rates continued to rise. Therefore, other increases in freight rates were necessary. But the Board could not raise rates on export grain in Western Canada (Crow's Nest Pass rates) because they were legally held down to the level of September, 1899. Besides, by 1955 and certainly by 1958, it was becoming clear that for all practical purposes many non-statutory railway rates, as well as passenger fares, had nearly reached their economic ceiling. They could not be increased further without diverting traffic to competing agencies or choking off long-hauled freight because shippers were unable to pay higher transportation costs and still sell their goods in distant competitive markets. The possibility of increase was still further reduced when the prices of some agricultural products began slowly to recede from their postwar peaks or were in danger of doing so. As soon as some freight rates reach their economic ceiling, it becomes apparently unfair and even oppressive to raise other tolls whose economic ceiling may be higher. Regions complain about being put under what they regard as serious economic disabilities. Thus, while theoretically it may be true that some rates can be raised by sizable amounts before they reach their economic ceiling, the level that is politically practical is somewhat lower.

Royal Commission, 1951

Even by the end of 1948, shortly after the Board of Transport Commissioners had brought down its first important postwar decision on the general level of rates, dissatisfaction was widespread among shippers, especially in the West and the Maritimes. So the St. Laurent Government appointed a royal commission under the chairmanship of the Hon. W. F. A. Turgeon to review the entire problem. In its report, made in 1951, the commission declared that rates must be just and reasonable not only to the railways but also to shippers and consignees.

The task of the Board in fixing, determining and enforcing just and reasonable rates, involves a duty to both the railways and the public; the Board must therefore be in a position that will enable it to determine, in so far as possible, the balance which will bring about this desired end. But since economic conditions may be such that different considerations exist under one state of affairs than under another, it is not proper to lay down the priority which should be given to the principles which should guide the Board. The Canadian Pacific by its proposed amendment [for a rate base and a fair return] asks that priority be given to the principle of a fair return on investment; yet experience has shown that such a factor may not be the guiding factor, it may be one which in times of economic depression must give way to other considerations. The procedure of rate making must be flexible, and this flexibility now exists under the Railway Act.[8]

The Commission made no provision for protecting railways against political pressure to build new or abandon old lines. It said that "the day of ill conceived and therefore excessive construction seems to have gone by, and our people can feel reasonably assured that from now on no railway ventures will be undertaken excepting after thorough investigation of each project, and always with due regard to the financial commitments involved."[9] Similarly "railways should be allowed to practice . . . economies in cases where operations are shown to have become sub-

stantially unnecessary or to be definitely unprofitable, especially . . .
when it is shown that reasonable service can be assured by other agencies."[10] In other words in constructing and abandoning lines the cash
nexus and not public benefit is to be paramount.

On the matter of co-operation between the two major railways, the
Royal Commission of 1951 seems to have favoured every effort at
further economies because it recommended continuance of the legislation and improvement in the annual report submitted to Parliament. Yet
it rejected all of the more drastic proposals for introducing savings and
warned against the danger of short-sighted economies. For various reasons the Commission rejected the claim of the Canadian Pacific that the
Crow's Nest Pass rates on export grain in the West were unremunerative. Whether these reasons were sound is not, at the moment, important.
The significant thing for our purposes is that the Commission refused to
go along with the Canadian Pacific in what virtually amounted to a
demand for higher freight tolls on grain. The Commission left it up to
Parliament to decide what was national policy.

In short, the main body of the report of the Royal Commission of
1951 displays the confusion of objective which has characterized the
history of transportation in Canada almost from the beginning. The
Commission does not seem to have considered all the implications
involved in the question: are transportation services to be regarded as
business institutions like department stores, factories, or farms, or are
they to be looked upon as almost eleemosynary agencies wherein the
cost-revenue relationship is subordinate to the welfare of the public?
Substantially, the Commission concluded with the idea that railways are
to be run like the post office, that they are to make a profit if they can
but that the objective in setting tolls is to cover costs and also help the
country's economic life.

The basic problem facing the Commission and the equivocal conclusion reached in the main body of the report were seen clearly by Commissioner Angus.[11] His general thesis was that the Canadian Pacific was
entitled to an opportunity to earn a fair return on its railway investment.
If this should prove to be impossible, the suggestions he made with
respect to rate base, rate of return, varying the rate of return with different stages in the business cycle, and so on would have the advantage
of placing in their true light any subsidies which Parliament might be
prepared to grant at any time in order to relieve the burden on freight
rates. In short, Dr. Angus wanted the Canadian Pacific run as a commercial enterprise and advocated legislation which would give it a
chance to succeed on such a basis. If it could not thrive on this theory

because of the opposition of certain regions of the country to reasonable tolls, then Dr. Angus would leave the door open for subsidies. But the legislative changes he proposed would have the advantage of making clear what subsidies needed to be paid.

As for the Canadian National, Dr. Angus thought that it should be expected to do the best it could at rates fair to the Canadian Pacific. It would have to operate certain properties and provide certain services irrespective of their commercial merits. It was not possible to establish comparability between the two major railways, either to excite emulation or make one railway a check on the other. Still, the capital structure of the Canadian National could be made equal to the earning power of the railway capitalized at a low rate of interest. It could consist of bonds in the hands of the public and of equity securities in the hands of the Government. The management might be allowed considerable freedom in building a surplus or reserve.

1951–61

Although the Turgeon Commission took a rather narrow approach to the current railway problem, the St. Laurent Government lost no time in embodying its main recommendations into law. For instance, it laid down what it called a national freight-rates policy for Canada whereby rates on any class or kind of freight should be equalized across Canada. Equalization was not to apply, however, on freight within the Atlantic Provinces, on export, import, and competitive traffic, or on export grain from Western Canada. Other parts of the legislation "tidied up" the Railway Act but the general approach of the Government was the same as that of two of the three commissioners, that is, all except Dr. Angus. All that was required, in their view, was some adjustment in the existing regulations governing freight rates in order to deal with a long list of complaints from shippers and the provincial governments which acted for them. No drastic reorganization of the transportation set-up was called for.

For a short time this theory worked tolerably well. Then the Korean War touched off a series of wage boosts and led to a sharp rise in the cost of supplies. Business recessions in 1954 and 1957 reduced railway revenues below expectations. Hence the railways were forced to apply for further increases in the general level of rates. The Crow's Nest and related rates were excluded from all increases. On many kinds of traffic, higher rates drove business to competitors. As a result, the increases authorized by the Board of Transport Commissioners could be applied to a smaller and smaller proportion of the total traffic. The fourteen general increases approved in the years 1948-58 permitted rates to be raised by 155 per cent. Though the shortcomings of statistics make it difficult to state precisely the amount of the increases actually achieved, they were of the order of 55 per cent. Also, because each general increase could be effectively applied to a smaller base of traffic, each successive increase had to be for a higher percentage than the one that preceded it in order to provide a given amount of net revenue. Further, the Western and Atlantic Provinces continued to argue that the burden of the increases fell mainly on them for, so they said, the St. Lawrence Valley escaped higher railway tolls on account of the greater pervasiveness of water and highway competition in that area. Moreover, the railways were feeling the pinch of the low statutory and related rates on the movement of export grain. The out-of-pocket cost of handling this traffic was rising and competition tended to prevent the railways from offsetting their losses on grain by higher tolls on other classes of freight.

Early in 1959, when the railways applied to the Board of Transport Commissioners for a further increase of 12 per cent (subject to the usual exceptions), the Government of Mr. Diefenbaker took three steps. First, it appointed a Royal Commission under the chairmanship of the Hon. C. P. McTague, former chief justice of Ontario and, after his illness and resignation, under M. A. MacPherson of Regina, a former attorney-general of Saskatchewan who had represented his province in all the postwar rate cases. Second, it forbade the Board from authorizing any further increases in the general level of rates pending receipt of the MacPherson Report. Third, it passed the Freight Rates Reduction Act. This gave the railways a subsidy of $20 million for the fiscal year ending March 31, 1960, and provided for a roll-back in freight rates. This roll-back cut the increase that was allowed in December, 1958, from 17 to 10 per cent and later to 8 per cent. The roll-back did not apply to competitive rates, international traffic, export rates on grain and grain products from Western Canada, and passenger fares.

After these steps, the Diefenbaker Government obviously hoped that it need take no further action until the MacPherson Report had laid down a long-run programme for dealing with the railway problem. In the summer of 1960, however, railways and unions became locked in another wage dispute. The railways asserted that since their hands were tied because of the freeze on freight rates, they could consent to only a small increase in wage rates. When the men threatened to go on strike early in December, 1960, the Government passed legislation forbidding any strike on the railways until after May 15, 1961, and freezing wages to their current level. The Cabinet hoped to have the MacPherson Report before May and in fact, it did receive the first volume in March.

Then it decided that it would have to await the second volume before implementing any of its proposals. This decision apparently left the railways to work out their own destiny.

As things turned out, the Government soon had to intervene again. Wage negotiations were resumed in anticipation of the expiration of the legislation which froze wage rates until May 15, 1961. The railways again pleaded inability to pay higher wages as long as the Government forbade any general increase in tolls by the Board of Transport Commissioners. The men were unwilling to accept the relatively small increase accepted by the carriers and planned to strike on May 16. At the last moment the railways agreed with the men's request. Shortly thereafter the Government undertook to add $50 million to the subsidy already received by the railways under the roll-back. Both subsidies were continued even after the second volume of the MacPherson Report was received in December, 1960. In short, the Diefenbaker Government did little to deal with the railway problem beyond the payment of subsidies.

It is true that subsidies are nothing new in Canadian railway history; however, those of 1958–66 were unusual for several reasons. Excluding deficits on the Canadian National, they were larger than in any equal period of time. Most of the amount, or $50 million, was not tied to any particular service performed by railways, whereas formerly subsidies (except for deficits on publicly-owned lines) had always been related to a specific project such as new construction or a reduction in certain defined rates. Of course, it can be argued that the subsidies of 1958–66 prevented increases in the general level of rates and therefore were for a specific purpose. In this event, however, they were unfair to carriers by highway and inland waterway. Inasmuch as part of the subsidies were paid to fend off a threatened railway strike, they could be said to constitute a subsidy to labour, though the Government denied this was the case. Certainly continuation of subsidies that were not directly related to specific projects was contrary to the proposals of the MacPherson Commission made first in March, 1961, and repeated in December. Finally, the subsidies constituted a major departure from the principle that railways should be run as business enterprises.

Royal Commission, 1961: General Recommendations

The MacPherson Commission worked on the premise that competition was now a major factor in Canadian transportation. It said that the current troubles of the railways stemmed largely from burdens imposed on them when they held a virtual monopoly of inland transportation. The Commission's principal concern was to remove the burden of past obligations. By making the necessary changes in law and altering public attitudes, it hoped that the railways would be able effectively to meet competition from other forms of transport. At the same time the commission was anxious that the changes would not take place so rapidly that maladjustments in the economy would result. A transitional period was required during which subsidies were needed. But the amount of public assistance was, for the most part, to be reduced from year to year as maladjustments were corrected.

The Commission found four major areas—uneconomic passenger services, unprofitable branch lines, statutory and related rates on grain, and statutory free transportation—where obligations associated with public regulation and attitudes inhibited the railways' competitive ability and inflicted a burden on the users of railway services. Consequently, subsidies were called for in these areas until such time as the obligations were removed. Because details of the recommendations in each of these areas will be dealt with in the appropriate chapters later, only a brief summary is called for at this point.

According to the commission, uneconomic passenger services existed over the length and breadth of the nation but with different degrees of intensity. It thought that, given a reasonable amount of public co-operation, the railways should be able to eliminate non-paying passenger trains within five years. During this period they should get an adjustment grant of $62 million in 1961. This amount would decline in regular stages to $12.4 million in 1965 and to nothing thereafter, except in cases where no alternative form of transport was available. In the latter event the subsidy should be made annually by Parliament on the recommendation of the Board of Transport Commissioners. The subsidies, which the Commission circumlocutiously called adjustment grants, would be tied strictly to the operating deficits in the passenger service without anything for interest on the investment in the locomotives, cars, stations, yards, etc., used in that service. Thus, by making railways share in the burden of passenger-train losses, the Commission hoped they would be motivated to cut back on such services as quickly as possible. It is to be noted that the Commission did not visualize the abandonment of all passenger trains, at least in the immediate future. Some trains such those between Montreal and Toronto might continue to meet their operating expenses and make some contribution to interest for many years to come. Meanwhile, local trains on branch lines, already poorly patronized, would be withdrawn fairly quickly.

Abandonment would be facilitated if the Commission's proposal for a change in the law were accepted by the Government. The current practice was for the Board to weigh the inconvenience to the public occasioned by the abandonment against the financial losses experienced by the railway through the continuance of the service. The Commission would permit the railways to remove any uneconomic passenger service except when the Board was satisfied that no reasonable alternative public highway existed.

The second area where the railways had to provide service which handicapped them in their ability to meet competition was over light density lines. Ultimately, rail plant would have to be rationalized by the elimination of unprofitable branches. But an abruptly implemented programme of rail line abandonment would cause dislocations which would not be in the interests of the economy as a whole. Hence subsidies were necessary over a period of time, estimated at fifteen years, sufficient to enable the adjustments to be made both in the railway investment and in investment, such as grain elevators, which is tied to rail. Accordingly, the Commission recommended that the government should provide a fund of not more than $13 million a year to be administered by the Board of Transport Commissioners. The Board would assign priorities for abandonment so that investment could be scaled down in some orderly fashion. As more and more uneconomic branches were eliminated, the need for the public to bear the losses would diminish. Immediately, the fund would relieve railways and railway users of the burden of uneconomic lines. Eventually, it would bring railway plant down to the place where it would be economically viable.

The export grain traffic was another field where railways should be relieved of some of their burdens. The techniques used by the railways for arriving at the cost of handling export grain in Western Canada had been examined with great care by the Commission, by its staff, and by experts called by the provinces and the railways. Although recognizing that an element of judgment was necessarily involved in all such analyses, five of the six commissioners felt that the cost of moving this traffic had been determined with an acceptable degree of precision. Commissioner René Gobiel of Quebec City disagreed with his colleagues on this point, though he went along with his colleagues on the estimated losses on passenger service and uneconomic branch lines. The majority found that on the basis of the costs of 1958, revenue from statutory and related rates fell short of the expenses incurred in moving this traffic by $11 million on each railway. Since the rates had their origin and were perpetuated by an act of Parliament, it was the responsibility of Parliament to ensure that railways received sufficient remuneration for the work performed, including a reasonable return on the investment needed to move such traffic. The Commission did not consider that its terms of reference required it to make any judgement about the level of the statutory rate or any change in it. But two commissioners—Mr. Herbert Anscomb of Victoria and Mr. Archibald H. Balch of Ottawa—said that Parliament should review conditions in agriculture, and when the industry was able, it should raise the statutory rates to relieve taxpayers of the burden of the subsidy.

Statutory free transportation was another place where railways were burdened with costs that ought to be borne by the public exchequer. Over the years, a large number of people had become entitled to free travel by rail. The Commission did not object to railways honouring their retired employees with passes nor giving passes to their active employees who were travelling by rail for business or pleasure. It felt, however, that when Parliament authorized free transportation to senators, members, deputy ministers, and other public officials, then Parliament and not the railways should pay for such travel.

In its second volume the Commission recommended abolition of the subsidy of 20 per cent on local traffic within Nova Scotia, New Brunswick, and Prince Edward Island, while retaining it in Newfoundland because highways and highway transport were not well developed in that province. The MacPherson Commission would also retain the subsidy of 30 per cent on the Maritime portion of the rate on traffic from any place east of Lévis to any place in Canada west thereof. It would make the subsidy payable to any common carrier, whether by rail, road, or water. Similarly, it proposed that the subsidy on the carriage of feed grain from the Prairies to Eastern Canada and British Columbia should be paid to carriers other than railways. It recommended that the so-called bridge subsidy across Northern Ontario should be abolished because it had proved inequitable.

Finally, the MacPherson Commission proposed that railways be relieved of some of the legal rigidities of filing rates with the Board and it stressed the importance of cost in setting individual rates. On the first of these two points the Commission seems to have thought that it was breaking new ground, whereas in fact it was only following current practice because for years the board had winked at enforcing the strict letter of the law requiring notice of increases and decreases in tolls.

The Commission believed that the remedies it suggested would "help to ensure that the railways will take their proper place in a Canadian transportation system designed to encourage and facilitate national unity and national development in the highest degree. Relief from obligations of the past and the burden associated with these obligations—eased in the short run and removed in the long run—should permit the railways to adapt successfully to the increasingly competitive environment."[12]

Careful examination of the MacPherson Report suggests that the Commission hoped that its recommendations, if implemented, would make the railways pay their own way without government aid. The main exception was on export grain where the adjustment grant—as usual the Commission sedulously avoided the word subsidy—would presumably be permanent. Clearly the Commission, like Dr. Angus, believed that railways were entitled to earn a fair return on their investment and if this should prove impossible they might be subsidized. It also believed that subsidies must be related to specific objectives and that, if possible, they should be reduced as the need for them disappeared. Of course, for political reasons the Commission did not stress the economic viability of the railways, particularly of the Canadian Pacific, as much as the desirability of keeping low rates on export grain and providing for the orderly rationalization of plant in the public interest. Still, it is obvious that the MacPherson Commission was greatly impressed by the need to put railways on a business basis.

The National Transportation Act, 1967

For numerous reasons, chiefly associated with party politics, it was not until early February, 1967, that Parliament finally passed legislation based on the MacPherson Report of 1961. On the face of things, Parliament carried out the main thesis of the report, which was that every mode of transport should be operated on business principles. At the same time the new National Transportation Act qualified the thesis to such an extent that the nation remained in the position of regarding transport as an instrument of national policy as well as a business. To begin with, the Act set forth the broad policy:

It is hereby declared that an economic, efficient and adequate transportation system making the best use of all available modes of transportation at the lowest total cost is essential to protect the interests of the users of transportation and to maintain the economic well-being and growth of Canada, and that these objectives are most likely to be achieved when all modes of transport are able to compete under conditions ensuring that having due regard to national policy and to legal and constitutional requirements (a) regulation of all modes of transport will not be of such a nature as to restrict the ability of any mode of transport to compete freely with any other modes of transport; (b) each mode of transport, so far as practicable, bears a fair proportion of the real costs of the resources, facilities and services provided that mode of transport at public expense; (c) each mode of transport, so far as practicable, receives compensation for the resources, facilities and services that it is required to provide as an imposed public duty; and (d) each mode of transport so far as practicable carries traffic to or from any point in Canada under tolls and conditions that do not constitute (i) an unfair disadvantage in respect of any such traffic beyond that disadvantage inherent in the location or volume of the traffic, the scale of operation connected therewith or the type of traffic or service involved, or (*ii*) an undue obstacle to the interchange of commodities between points in Canada or unreasonable discouragement to the development of primary or secondary industries or to export trade in or from any region of Canada or to the movement of commodities through Canadian ports; and this Act is enacted in accordance with and for the attainment of so much of these objectives as fall within the purview of subject matters under the jurisdiction of Parliament relating to transportation.

The first step in carrying out this policy ought to have been the immediate lifting of the "freeze" or "roll-back" on freight rates that had been in effect since 1960 and accelerating the programmes for the abandonment of non-paying passenger trains and branch lines. This was impracticable for both political and economic reasons. A sudden increase in rates after six years of relative stability would handicap trade, industry, and agriculture. It would also tend to add to the cost of living which had been rising for several years. Moreover, it was argued that higher rates and an accelerated programme for abandoning lines and passenger trains would prove more burdensome to the Western and Atlantic Provinces than to Ontario and Quebec.

Accordingly, the legislation of 1967 continued the subsidies under the Freight Rates Reduction Act (the "roll-back"), federal assistance in anticipation of the implementation of the final recommendations of the MacPherson Report, the Maritime Freight Rates Act, and some minor items. The aid, which totalled $110 million in 1967, was to be reduced by $14 million or 12½ per cent a year until it would finally disappear at the end of 1974. Payment of these subsidies would reduce the need for higher freight rates but not preclude them. Indeed, railways may have to raise a good many of their tolls, or at least try to do so, if wage rates, interest charges, and the cost of supplies continued to rise.

The general aid outlined above may, however, be eliminated by 1970 or 1971. The National Transportation Act provides that, following recommendations of the Canadian Transport Commission which it created, the federal government may subsidize the continued operation of non-paying branch lines and passenger trains. The total of this "tied" aid in any given year is to be deducted from the amount of the "general" aid described in the preceding paragraph. When the total of tied aid exceeds the total of general aid, the latter will become a dead letter. Details on federal aid to unprofitable passenger trains and branches will be given in subsequent chapters.

In addition to the power of the new Transport Commission to defer the rationalization of plant and have the federal government pay all or most of the losses sustained by the railways, the Act states that the Governor-in-Council (the Cabinet) may designate branch lines that shall not be abandoned, or designate areas where no abandonments may be authorized, within such periods as the Governor-in-Council may prescribe. During these periods the railways concerned will be entitled to receive a subsidy from the Dominion to cover their operating losses on the lines in question. Losses on commuter services are payable as the Cabinet sees fit. In short, the legislation contains provisions for the protection, at public expense, of communities, shippers, and consignees which might be adversely affected by the sudden withdrawal of rail services.

Even before the new legislation became law, the Government announced that it had ordered the Board of Transport Commissioners not to authorize the abandonment of about 17,000 miles of line in Western Canada prior to the end of 1974. This left 1,839 miles of "unprotected mileage" or roughly 10 per cent of the total mileage of main track in Alberta, Saskatchewan, and Manitoba. At the time of the "freeze order" the two major railways had filed applications to abandon a total of 4,224 miles in these provinces.

The National Transportation Act set aside the recommendations of the MacPherson Commission on transport in the Atlantic Provinces pending the receipt of a report by a firm of consulting engineers. As will be explained in chapter 5, the Commission's proposals would not stand up under careful analysis. The engineers' study was completed in June, 1967.

The MacPherson Commission had also proposed that the Dominion subsidize railways for the difference between their receipts from the carriage of grain exported from Western Canada and the cost of handling this traffic. The Minister of Transport stated that the study of costs submitted to the Commission was out of date because it was based on data for 1958. Furthermore, the costs of constructing and operating grain elevators and of moving grain by rail were being reduced by technological advances. Finally, the volume of traffic, notably of grain and potash, over rail lines in Western Canada had been rising steadily ever since the MacPherson Commission had reported. The government proposed that the Canadian Transport Commission should review the cost of handling export grain and recommend what subsidies, if any, the railways should receive for moving grain to so-called export positions at Lakehead and at Canada's Pacific ports. This plan was defeated by a single vote when the House of Commons sitting in Committee of the Whole dealt with details of the legislation.

Though the new legislation excluded any reference to a possible subsidy to railways for carrying Western grain for export, it did extend the statutory provisions covering the rates on such traffic. Rates to Lakehead —the original Crow's Nest Pass rates—were already set by law. Rates on grain exported through ports on Canada's Pacific coast, which had been published by order of the Board of Railway Commissioners on substantially the same basis as the corresponding tolls eastbound, were now made statutory. So were "At and East" grain rates, i.e., those on grain brought down the Lakes to ports on Georgian Bay or the Lower Lakes and then moved to Montreal, Halifax, Saint John, and other ports in Canada for export.

The legislation of 1967 contained the same provisions on maximum and minimum rates as had been proposed by the MacPherson Commission. Maximum rates applied only to captive shippers, those who had no practicable alternative to rail transport. Minimum rates had to be compensatory; they must cover the variable costs of handling the traffic in question. Between these upper and lower limits, railways were to have more freedom than formerly to quote rates as they saw fit.

The Canadian Transport Commission which was set up by the legislation was to take over the functions of the Board of Transport Commissioners, the Air Transport Board, and the Canadian Maritime Commission. It was "to perform . . . [its] functions with the object of co-ordinating and harmonizing the operations of all carriers engaged in transport by railways, water, aircraft, extra-provincial motor vehicle transport and commodity pipelines." It was to do research in both a broader and more intensive manner than hitherto done by the previously existing boards. In particular, it was to

"inquire into and report to the Minister upon measures to assist in a sound economic development of the various modes of transport over which Parliament has jurisdiction . . . upon possible financial measures required for direct assistance to any mode of transport . . . [including] the Canadian merchant marine . . . establish general economic standards and criteria to be used in the determination of federal investment in equipment and facilities as between various modes of transport and within individual modes . . . inquire into . . . the overall balance between expenditure programs of government departments or agencies for the provision of transport facilities . . . and participate in the work of intergovernmental, national or international organizations dealing with any form of transport under the jurisdiction of Parliament."

The National Transportation Act—only the highlights of the legislation have been given—shows the same balancing of objectives as in the past. Modes of transport are simultaneously to be economically viable organizations and means for carrying out national objectives. The Canadian Transport Commission is to promote sound economic development and recommend direct financial assistance by the government. Plant is to be rationalized but at a sufficiently slow rate that no area or producer is to be seriously hurt. At worst, he will suffer only if he has been unable to make a satisfactory adjustment during the time between the Commission's investigation of the unprofitability of a branch or passenger train and its final abandonment. Moreover, throughout the entire legislation runs a common thread: the need to satisfy the political and economic aspirations of various parts of Canada.

The Basic Problem in Canadian Transportation

The author has tried to summarize the history of Canadian transportation in terms of the interrelationship of the profit motive and the desire to benefit the country at large. He believes this interrelationship mainly explains the development and policies of Canadian transportation. We expect carriers on inland waters and in the air to pay their own operating expenses but make inadequate charges for the use of the enormously expensive canals, airports, and navigation aids which are supplied at public expense. For many years the provinces and the municipalities supplied highways without direct charge to the users of them. Recently, provincial governments have aimed to collect enough through taxes levied directly on the users of the facilities to pay the expenses they incur for roads. Local roads and city streets are still maintained out of general tax revenues but the proper allocation of the costs of provincial highways among owners of private passenger-cars, buses, and commercial trucks is not yet satisfactorily determined.

Our policy for railways is not clear. After receiving generous assistance of its initial transcontinental line, the Canadian Pacific has been able to prosper from the charges it makes for service rendered shippers, consignees, and passengers. But it fears that the economic environment in which it operates will become so unfavourable that in future years it will be unable to raise the capital funds which are necessary for modernizing its plant. It also fears that its financial needs may be sacrificed to political pressures of one sort or another. Alternately, it is afraid that by accepting too many government subsidies it may become an impotent bondslave of the government of the day. In the past the Canadian Pacific was a national asset of tremendous value. It is capable of fulfilling the same role in future, provided always that its financial integrity is not sacrificed to regional pressures for lower rates.

The government-owned system inherited many lines which had never paid and yet could not be abandoned. A declaration that it must stand on its own feet financially would be ineffectual unless, by good luck or exceptionally accurate forecasting, the annual fixed charges it was expected to pay just equalled its net revenue over a period of years. If the commercial revenues of the publicly owned enterprise failed to cover its expenses, the government could not wash its hand of the whole affair; it would still have to provide cash to cover the deficit. Nevertheless there is some psychological value in stating that the Canadian National Railways is to be run on ordinary business principles, that it ought to meet its fixed charges every year, that if it fails to do so the management should be called strictly to task, and that the government should not, by interfering with the level of freight rates or by foisting more unprofitable lines on the unfortunate system, keep it perpetually in the poorhouse.

Throughout our transportation history we have not been able permanently to resolve the conflict between preserving private enterprise and using public funds to carry out national objectives. Yet we have always been supplied with safe, efficient, and low cost service. Perhaps it is impossible to settle even in such a narrow field as transportation the basic problem of modern economic society, the problem of how far governments should interfere in economic affairs. The problem is much broader than capitalism versus socialism, or public versus private ownership. The same question constantly recurs in the United States where all railways are privately owned. It is "whether, because of the general and widespread benefits which transportation confers on the community and nation, it is desirable to include transportation services in the same category as general government services . . . or whether it would be more desirable for transportation to be financed by the user, as is the case with other goods and services, since transportation constitutes an integral part of the cost of production and distribution."[13]

2

The Rate Structure Surveyed

FREIGHT RATES[1] are the prices charged by a railway for its freight services. Each railway must be prepared to quote a price for the transport of every kind of goods that can be transported by rail from each of the stations in Canada to every other station in Canada and the United States. Before the history of rate-making and a detailed analysis of principles can be effectively dealt with, it is necessary to see the broad picture. For reasons to be given in full later, railways charge different prices for hauling different kinds of goods. Over the years railways have published thousands of tariffs or price lists for moving freight. Tariffs may be grouped under class rates, commodity tariffs, statutory rates on grain and grain products, competitive tariffs, agreed charges, and tariffs for international, overhead, export, and import traffic. Each of these kinds of tariff requires explanation.

Mileage class rates, formerly called standard mileage class rates, apply when no other tariff covers the movement. Every commodity moving by rail is listed in a book called the Classification which is described in chapter 7. Since it would be impracticable to set a rate for each commodity, carriers divide articles into several groups or classes. Up to March 1, 1955, the classes were numbered 1 to 10. On that date the former Class 1 became Class 100. Each of the other new classes was numbered on the basis of the relationship between the rate on that class in the standard mileage class rate scale and the rate on the former Class 1 in the same scale. For example, as rates on Class 2 were 85 per cent of the rates on Class 1, former Class 2 became Class 85. Old Classes 3 to 8 became 70, 55, 45, 40, 33, and 30. Former Class 9 (livestock) is now 40 for horses and mules, and 33 for cattle, calves, hogs, and sheep, while old Class 10 is now Class 27. A few articles formerly carried at multiples of First, such as Christmas tree lighting outfits at D-1 (double First), are now called by the appropriate percentage, i.e., 200. One advantage of the new numbering system was that it readily permitted the introduction of additional classes. By 1957 there were classes for scrap iron and steel, in carloads (20), for cordwood, slabs, edgings, and other mill refuse (10), and for potatoes (30). Except on the White Pass and Yukon Route, the Classification has been uniform throughout Canada for many years.

The rates applicable on each of the various classes are worked out from a table called the (standard) mileage class rate scale, which is approved by the Board. This gives the rate in cents per hundred pounds for each class for various lengths of haul. From July 1, 1927, to July 1, 1949, different standard mileage class rates applied in the following class-rate regions:

(1) Maritime, consisting of Nova Scotia, New Brunswick, Prince Edward Island, that part of Quebec lying east of Lévis and Diamond (opposite Quebec City) as well as Newfoundland after it joined Confederation on March 31, 1949;

(2) Ontario-Quebec, the area between Lévis, Windsor, Sudbury, Sault Ste. Marie, Capreol, and Cochrane, Ontario;

(3) Superior, or Algoma as it was called by officials of the Canadian Pacific, from Sudbury, Capreol, and Cochrane to Port Arthur and Armstrong (which is on the northern line of the Canadian National and the same distance east of Winnipeg as Port Arthur);

(4) Prairie, from Lakehead and Armstrong to the Rocky Mountains;

(5) Pacific, which included almost all British Columbia.

In 1949, as a result of the decision of the Board of Transport Commissioners in the so-called Mountain Differential Case, class rates in the Pacific region were reduced to the Prairie level. In 1951, following the report of the Royal Commission of that year, an amendment to the Railway Act declared it "to be the national freight rates policy that, subject to [certain exceptions], every railway company shall, so far as is reasonably possible, in respect of all freight traffic of the same description, and carried on or upon the like cars or conveyances, passing over all lines or routes of the company in Canada, charge tolls to all persons at the same rate, whether by weight, mileage or otherwise." The same legislation directed the Board to carry out this policy of equalization except as related to "(a) joint international rates . . . ; (b) rates on export and import traffic through Canadian ports, where in practice such rates bear a fixed and long-standing relationship with rates on similar traffic through ports in the United States; (c) competitive rates; (d) agreed charges; (e) rates over the White Pass and Yukon route; (f) rates [under] the *Maritime Freight Rates Act* . . . ; or (*g*) where the Board considers that an exception should be made."

In 1953, as a first step in carrying out this national transportation policy, the Board ordered standard mileage class rates west of Lakehead to be reduced by 5 per cent and permitted the corresponding rates in the Ontario-Quebec region to be increased by not more than 10 per cent. On March 1, 1955, complete identity of these scales was achieved and the Superior or Algoma scale was also brought into line. As a result the mileage class rates are uniform throughout all Canada west of Lévis except over the White Pass and Yukon.

The legislation on equalization specifically exempted the Maritime region from its provisions. Under the Maritime Freight Rates Act of 1927 the Dominion government undertook to pay 20 per cent of the charge for hauling freight within this region, with the shipper or consignee paying the remainder. In 1957, the Government's share of the toll on freight from the Maritimes into Central Canada was increased to 30 per cent of the Maritime portion of such haul. For example, on a shipment from Halifax to Toronto, the general principle is that the normal rate from Halifax to Lévis is reduced by 30 per cent and added to the normal rate from Lévis to Toronto. These provisions may, however, be modified within two years after the passage of the legislation of 1967 and as a result of the recommendations of a firm of consultants which studied the problem.

Equalization also had the effect of abolishing all distributing class rates except east of Lévis. Long ago railways began publishing these low rates apparently on the theory that the greater volume of traffic to and from wholesale centres warranted lower tolls or that they should meet competition from water carriers. In Ontario-Quebec the original "town tariff" rates caused much dissatisfaction. They varied from place to place without obvious reason. International rates between Buffalo, Detroit, and Port Huron over Canadian railways and to these stations from points within Ontario were lower than rates to adjacent places within Canada such as Niagara Falls, Bridgeburg, Windsor, and Sarnia. These complaints were dealt with by the Board of Railway Commissioners in 1907. The Board put Canadian rates on a lower and more uniform basis, and in Schedule A of its judgment named Montreal and about 50 stations in Southern Ontario which were entitled to town tariff rates. Later, Schedule A was extended to include Parry Sound, North Bay, Sudbury, and Sault Ste. Marie.[2] Town tariff rates were below standard mileage class rates by varying percentages, usually 20 or more.[3] In 1952 the Board suggested that Schedule A or town tariff rates be brought up to approximately 85 per cent of the standard mileage class rates and, as explained, they officially disappeared on March 1, 1955. Town tariff rates are published for wholesale centres in the Maritimes along the same general principles as formerly applied in Southern Ontario.

In Western Canada distributing class rates, which corresponded to the town tariff rates in the East, were given to 33 wholesale centres.[4] Western distributing class rates were almost uniformly 15 per cent below standard. Formerly, in determining distributing class rates between Fort William, Port Arthur, and Winnipeg, the actual distance of 420 miles was assumed to be 290 miles. This "constructive mileage" gave to Winnipeg and points west thereof lower rates on this kind of traffic than they would otherwise have enjoyed.[5] A similar arrangement applied on freight moving inland from Churchill, Manitoba, and from Vancouver, New Westminster, Victoria, and Prince Rupert. These constructive mileages and indeed all the distributing class rates in Western Canada were abolished when equalization of mileage class rates became effective in 1955.

Standard mileage class rates and even distributing class rates were often too high to allow low-valued goods, such as farm products, lumber, and minerals, to move in volume and be sold in distant markets. To develop this kind of traffic, railways published a variety of commodity tariffs.[6] These have been continued partly because of competition from truckers, mainly to assist primary producers in selling in other parts of Canada.

Prior to 1951 much controversy developed over the relative levels of commodity tariffs east and west of the Great Lakes. Under the national freight rates policy of equalization west of Lévis, some of the old commodity scales, e.g., those on livestock and potatoes, were easily integrated into the mileage class rate structure. Moreover, commodity scales were made uniform on building brick and tile, common clay, gravel, and so on.[7]. The Board hoped that, in accordance with the legislation of 1951, it could publish uniform scales for coal, lumber, pulpwood, and grain for domestic use. This proved impracticable, mainly because any new scales would seriously upset trade relationships which had developed over many decades under the old scales. In 1967 the efforts at equalization were officially abandoned. In the Atlantic region, i.e., all Canada east of Lévis, the old Ontario-Quebec scales, less 20 per cent, continued to apply despite the policy of equalization. They were, however, subject to changes in the general level of rates. This arrangement may be changed as a result of a study of transportation in the Maritimes which was completed in 1967.

Over the years 1897-9, by authority of the Crow's Nest Pass Agreement of 1897, reductions were made in rates on settlers' requirements, such as building materials, furniture, and farm implements, moving west of Lakehead and on grain and flour, the staple products of the West, being hauled eastward to Lakehead. The Agreement has been altered by subsequent legislation so that it now covers only grain and grain products. In order to prevent the unjust discrimination or undue preference which arose when rates on grain eastbound were held down by statute while those on grain westbound remained at their normal level, in the 1920s the Board of Railway Commissioners reduced the rates on grain and grain products moving westward for export through ports on Canada's Pacific coast. By legislation passed in 1967, these decisions of the Board were written into the law so that they became statutory too. Simultaneously, the rates on export grain from ports on Georgian Bay and elsewhere on the Lower Lakes to Montreal, Saint John, Halifax and other ports in Canada were brought within the statute. The MacPherson Commission found that railways carried export grain at a loss and proposed subsidies to make up the deficiency between the cost of handling this product and the amount charged shippers. In 1967 Parliament decided to defer consideration of this matter. Rates on export grain constitute an important segment of the rate structure whether viewed from the standpoint of the grain-grower or of the carriers.

Railways publish numerous tariffs to meet competition from trucks and ships plying inland and coastal waters. Most of these tariffs are in the St. Lawrence Lowlands where water competition is pervasive and highway competition is keen. There are, nevertheless, numerous competitive tariffs in the Maritimes, on the Prairies, and in British Columbia.

Actual and potential competition between Eastern Canada and the Pacific coast via the Panama Canal has led railways to publish low transcontinental rates between Montreal, Toronto, and other Eastern points, and Vancouver. Also, by shipping their goods via the Panama Canal, European manufacturers were often able to undercut the prices of Canadian-made goods along the Pacific coast. When this occurred, Canadian railways lost traffic on the finished goods, on the raw materials, and on the consumers' products which Canadian factory workers could not buy because they had less employment. Transport economists refer to this as market competition. To prevent further losses of traffic, Canadian railways reduced some of their transcontinental rates.

Furthermore in an effort to meet competition from truckers, Canadian railways publish agreed charges. They feel that they can offer lower tolls than the (standard) mileage class rates to any shipper or group of shippers who will agree to send all or most of their traffic by rail. Agreed charges have become popular with both major railways and with many shippers. In consequence, the volume of traffic moving under them has been growing.

On account of the close economic interrelationships of Canada and the United States, the volume of international traffic is great and special tariffs have been introduced to deal with it. Besides, some traffic moves between two stations in the same country but over rails located in the other country. This so-called "overhead" traffic includes freight between Detroit and Buffalo over lines across the peninsula of Western Ontario, and traffic between Montreal and Saint John, New Brunswick, across Maine. By an informal but well established arrangement between the Board of Transport Commissioners and its predecessor on the one hand and the Interstate Commerce Commission on the other, rates on overhead traffic are controlled by the regulatory authority of the country where the traffic originates and terminates. Finally, Canadian railways publish export and import rates as described later in this chapter.

Rates between Class-Rate Regions

Prior to equalization, each rate-making region, such as the Maritimes, Ontario-Quebec, and the Prairies, had its own scales of class, distributing, and commodity rates. Railways also had to quote rates on traffic moving between regions, such as, between Halifax, Toronto, and Winnipeg. There was no theoretical reason why a scale of rates could not be devised to cover very long hauls, even hauls from coast to coast. However, there were many practical difficulties.

The first difficulty was that the level of rates applicable to, say, first class traffic was different in the West than in the East. Second, the relationship between classes differed. For example, in the East the fifth class rate was commonly one-half of first for the same distance, whereas in the West fourth was one-half of the first, and fifth was 45 per cent of first. Even so, the fifth class rate in the West for a given distance was usually higher than the fifth class rate in the East for the same length of haul. This was the result of the generally higher level of all class scales in the West. Moreover, some commodity scales which were the same East and West for distances up to 200 miles were lower in the West for distances of 500 miles and over. These dissimilarities were the outgrowth of allegedly higher operating costs in the West and the need for comparatively low tolls per ton-mile on very long hauls if Western producers were to be able to sell in distant markets. If they could not ship because of high rates on long hauls, the railways would lose traffic and revenue which they might otherwise have secured.

A further difficulty was that if one were to add one scale to another in order to arrive at the rate on a shipment from, say, Toronto to Estevan, Sask., one would get an abnormally high rate relative to distance. This was true because, as we shall see, the cost per ton-mile and therefore the rates are quite high for short hauls. As distance increases, the ton-mile cost and the ton-mile rate decline. In other words, while the total cost and the rate increase with distance, they do not increase in strict proportion to distance. To add the rate in one scale to the rate in another in order to get the through rate means, in effect, that one assumes that the shipment goes through two short and relatively costly hauls when in fact it goes through only one long haul. Besides, if the total charge for the long haul gets too high, the movement of freight will be inhibited. The shipper may decide not to send the goods at all because, after paying the railway, he cannot make a profit. In this event the railway loses some traffic which it might have got if the rate it published bore a more reasonable relationship to distance and the cost of moving the traffic.

For these reasons a system of proportionals or arbitraries was devised. The through rate was compiled by taking the normal class rate to a given intermediate city, called a breaking point, and then adding an arbitrary, which broadly varied with distance, for the additional haul beyond the breaking point. The amount of the arbitrary would be lower, often much lower, than the normal rate applicable to local movements beyond the breaking point. This was done because an arbitrary was considered to be part of a through rate. It is used only in conjunction with another rate to establish a through rate from origin to destination. Therefore it must take account of the economies which a railway obtains, per ton-mile, by hauling goods for a longer distance. In Canada arbitraries were formerly used in setting all rates between Ontario-Quebec on the one hand and either the West or the Maritimes on the other. They were also used at both ends of the haul, so to speak, when freight moved between the Maritimes and the West.

Equalization eliminated the need for arbitraries on class traffic between Ontario-Quebec, Superior territory, and the West because it required that, as far as possible, rate scales should be uniform throughout this wide area. But since equalization did not apply to the Atlantic Provinces or so-called "select territory," arbitraries still apply on traffic to and from that area.[8] They also apply on traffic between Ontario-Quebec and the West which does not come under an equalized scale.

The "key" arbitrary on traffic to and from the Atlantic Provinces is the rate between Montreal and Saint John, N. B. On March 1, 1955, when the equalized class scales came into effect in most of Canada, the Board set the key rate at 64 cents per hundred pounds on Class 100 traffic eastbound because this was the rate just prior to equalization. It also set the rate on eastbound traffic from Montreal to other places in the Atlantic Provinces in accordance with established practice and as shown in Table 1. The westbound rate, which is also given, is much lower than

TABLE 1
Arbitraries on Maritime Traffic Above Montreal
Class 100 Rates as of March 1, 1955 in cents per 100 pounds

	Eastern Canada*		Western Canada*	
	Eastbound	Westbound	Eastbound	Westbound
Saint John, N.B.	64	38	48	25
Halifax, N.S.	73	38	56	25
Mulgrave, N.S.	77	46	64	31
Sydney and Bridgewater, N.S.	82	46	73	31
Liverpool, N.S.	100	62	88	50
Middleton, Lockeport, Shelburne	113	62	104	65
Bridgetown, N.S.	128	62	121	75
Yarmouth, N.S.	128	78	121	75
Port aux Basques, Nfld.	111	68	100	54
Cornerbrook, Nfld.	141	92	129	78
Grand Falls, Nfld.	170	116	159	102
St. John's, Nfld.	216	152	205	138

* Eastern Canada means west of Montreal and East of Lakehead and Armstrong, Ont. Western Canada means west of Lakehead and Armstrong.

the corresponding rate in the opposite direction because of the subsidy paid under the Maritime Freight Rates Act. The rates on traffic other than Class 100 were adjusted in the same way as in the standard class scale, i.e., 85, 70, 55, etc. The entire province of New Brunswick has the same rates as Saint John, while small towns in Nova Scotia and Newfoundland are grouped with the nearest city in the table for rate-making purposes. All places between Montreal and the western edge of Maritimes Region, i.e., as far east as Lévis, Diamond Junction, and Boundary, P.Q., have the same rates as Montreal. All stations in the province of Quebec east of Lévis, roughly all those in the Gaspé Peninsula, are included in select territory for rate-making purposes.

Then the Board decided that traffic between the Atlantic Provinces and points in Ontario lying between Lakehead and Grafton (78 miles due east of Toronto) should pay the normal class rate to and from Montreal plus the arbitrary beyond. Thus, the Class 100 rate from Brantford would be the normal rate from that city to Montreal plus the arbitrary of 64 cents per 100 pounds to Saint John with appropriate adjustments to other places east of Lévis and on other classes of freight.

Rates on traffic west of Montreal and east of Grafton on the one hand

and select territory on the other had to be "graded in" to produce a more or less symmetrical alignment of rates to distance and to the rates which applied between the Maritimes and Montreal on the one hand and Toronto on the other. Grading in was necessary in order to avoid the distortion that occurs when the relatively high rates on short hauls are applied to places just beyond the breaking point. More specifically, in the absence of any adjustment, in 1955 the rate from a point 20 miles west of Montreal to Saint John would have been 50 cents on Class 100 for the first 20 miles plus the arbitrary of 64 cents beyond Montreal. This would give a total charge of 114 cents for a haul of 502 miles. This works out to 4.54 cents per ton-mile and compares with 64 cents for 482 miles or 2.55 cents per ton-mile over the distance covered by the arbitrary. Obviously it is inequitable to charge about 78 per cent more per ton-mile just because of the extra haul of 20 miles. Hence, the rate for 502 miles had to be reduced or graded in so that it bore a tolerably close relationship to distance and to the costs incurred by the railway in handling the traffic. Similar "fits" had to be made for other places west of Montreal until, in the Board's opinion, a total rate made up of the class rate from stations west of Grafton to Montreal plus the arbitrary to or from Montreal bore a respectable relationship to the cost of hauling freight over the distance in question.

Despite grading in or fitting, some anomalies remain. These are inevitable, for if they were eliminated entirely the rate structure would become even more complicated than it is and shippers would lose the benefit of the greater simplicity which the use of arbitraries is designed to achieve. Anomalies exist on the edges of all rate-making territories. For example, the rate from Quebec City to Halifax is higher than from Lévis to the same destination, even though Lévis is just across the St. Lawrence from Quebec City. The explanation is that Lévis comes within the provisions of the Maritime Freight Rates Act, whereas Quebec City does not.

Rates on traffic moving between Ontario-Quebec and the West are based on one of several principles. Equalized scales apply wherever published, e.g., on class traffic. Where such scales are not applicable, the rate from Ontario-Quebec to the West is the normal rate to Fort William, Port Arthur, West Fort William, and Armstrong, plus an arbitrary beyond. This arbitrary broadly varies with distance. On traffic in the reverse direction, the arbitrary applies to Lakehead and Armstrong, and the normal rate east thereof. For reasons to be given shortly, all stations between Windsor and Montreal generally pay the same rates on traffic to and from Western Canada. On grain exported from the West to Lakehead or forwarded from ports on Georgian Bay and the Lower Lakes to

Montreal, Halifax, Saint John, etc., statutory rates apply. Finally, there are several agreed charges and other competitive tariffs designed to meet the competition of truckers hauling traffic between Lakehead and points on the Prairies, which originates in, or is destined for, places in southern Ontario. Rates on traffic between British Columbia and Ontario-Quebec come under equalized scales, arbitraries, or special transcontinental rates that were introduced to meet potential or actual competition by water between Montreal and Vancouver or to meet market competition from suppliers across the Atlantic or on the eastern seaboard of the United States.

As a rule, railways charge the same tolls on traffic between the West and all stations between Windsor and Montreal. This uniformity of treatment grew out of water competition. In the late nineteenth and early twentieth centuries small sailing vessels and steamships called at many lake ports which are now rarely used. In water transport the terminal charges are high relative to the cost of moving between one port and another. It involves a lot more time, trouble, and expense to berth a vessel, load and off-load cargo, take on fuel, etc., than to do the corresponding jobs on a shipment by rail. On the other hand, line-haul costs by water are much lower than by land because shipowners, unlike railways, do not have to acquire a right of way or build and maintain a roadbed. Hence, because of the nature of their costs, rates by water transport are likely to be the same to or from ports a few dozen miles apart.

Moreover, in the early days competition between carriers on the Great Lakes was intense. Whenever any rate got out of line with rates from other ports, competition soon brought it back to the common level. In the end, ships charged the same rate per hundred pounds on package freight, that is, on all cargo except grain, iron ore, and other commodities handled in bulk, which was forwarded to the West regardless of the originating port on Georgian Bay, the Lower Lakes, or the upper St. Lawrence. Of necessity, railway managers were forced to follow the practice of shipping lines in order to get a fair share of the traffic in manufactured goods and other relatively valuable articles bound for the West.

In recent years truckers have hauled goods to ports such as Sarnia, Toronto, and Hamilton from inland centres like Stratford, London, Kitchener, and Peterborough. These goods are then sent by ship to Lakehead. In this way truckers have perpetuated the effect of the water competition which prevailed when so many small ports were in use. In addition, numerous manufacturing cities in southern Ontario compete among themselves and with Montreal for the trade of the West. When the question of equalization came up, these places favoured continuation of the policy of uniformity of rates on traffic to the West, whether by rail or water, because this practice put them all on the same footing as far as rates were concerned. They considered that the policy of equalization, insofar as it related to shipments to the West, would run counter to their interests because it would disturb relationships which were long standing and had proved mutually satisfactory to manufacturers, railways, and shipping lines. In short, they raised objections when the Board started to consider how it could relate class rates more closely with distance, as Parliament had required it to do under equalization.

Then there was an additional difficulty. The rail distance to the West from Windsor, Chatham, London, and many other places in south-western Ontario is less via the United States than via Canada north of Lake Superior. If rates from these cities were based strictly on distance, that is, if they were equalized, their rates through Canada would have to be raised and Canadian railways would lose business to lines in the United States.

In the end the Board made a compromise between long-established practice and the new rule of law. In effect, it took advantage of the provision in the law that allowed it to make an exception to equalization "where the Board considers that an exception should be made." Its compromise was that stations which were more distant from the West than Toronto would retain the same rate as Toronto on traffic to the West. In this way the Board preserved uniformity of rates on Western traffic for all cities between Windsor and Montreal. It also provided that stations that were closer to the West via Canadian lines than Toronto would have lower rates than Toronto. Their rates would vary with distance in accordance with the class rate scale. This ruling benefited such places as Parry Sound, Sudbury, and Sault Ste. Marie which are on relatively direct lines between Toronto and the West. It also gave lower rates to Renfrew, Fitzroy, and places west thereof in the Ottawa Valley.

Expressed in different terms, all the area bounded by Sault Ste. Marie, Sudbury, Windsor, and Montreal—an area which some railwayman with a flair for language and a limited knowledge of geometry called the triangle—formerly had the same rates on traffic to the West. After March 1, 1955, the lower part of the triangle retained uniform rates but the upper parts got the benefit in rates of their proximity to the West relative to Toronto. This principle applied to places in the former Algoma or Superior territory as well as in the triangle as such. In other words, Toronto and all places that are closer to the West than Toronto use the new or equalized class rate scale on shipments of goods coming under that scale and destined for the West. All places in the old triangle between Windsor and Montreal which are farther from the west than

Toronto, now take the same rate as Toronto. Equalization cut out the system of arbitraries which formerly applied on traffic moving under class rates between Eastern and Western Canada.

Equalization also resulted in the elimination of the constructive mileage between Lakehead and Winnipeg, between Armstrong (the station on the former National Transcontinental Railway which is the same distance east of Winnipeg as Lakehead) and Winnipeg, and inland from Churchill, Victoria, Vancouver, New Westminster, and Prince Rupert. At the same time a sort of constructive mileage was created between Victoria and Vancouver. Because of the relatively low cost of transport by water, the actual distance between these two cities (86 miles) was reduced to 43 miles for the purpose of making through rates.

In order to simplify the exposition, the preceding paragraphs were sometimes made to read as if traffic moved only from the triangle and Superior territory into the West. Of course, it moves in the opposite direction too. The same principles apply in both directions, and this was true both before and after equalization. Between 1951 and 1966 when the bridge subsidy of $7 million per annum was in effect, rates on all non-competitive freight hauled north of Lake Superior were reduced by amounts which, in the aggregate, amounted to the subsidy. The subsidy was reduced to $4 million in 1967, $2 million in 1968, and is to be abolished in 1969. It was not paid on traffic moving by water. Water rates will be dealt with shortly.

Prior to equalization, freight between the West and Quebec City moved under standard mileage class rates or distributing rates to Lakehead or Armstrong plus arbitraries beyond. After equalization Quebec City was given the same rate as Toronto. This rate was carried back to the Oskelanea River, a few miles west of Parent, where the rail mileage to Winnipeg is the same as the rail mileage from Toronto to Winnipeg. Stations west of this river took the appropriate rates under the new class rate scale and, of course, the arbitraries disappeared.

Rates between the West on the one hand, and stations east and south of Montreal but west of Lévis, Diamond Junction, and Boundary on the other are calculated by taking the appropriate rate to or from Montreal and adding an arbitrary. Admittedly this is a departure from the strict mileage class scale which should apply under equalization. The exception can be justified because the amount of traffic is not great, the area affected is relatively small, and the arrangement fits in well with what prevails between the West and Maritime or select territory. It will be realized that the legislation that directed the Board to equalize the rate structure did not apply to rates under the Maritime Freight Rates Act. Accordingly, the old system of arbitraries still applies on traffic between this region and the West. Table 1 shows the arbitraries on Class 100 which applied from various places on March 1, 1955. They are lower on westbound than on eastbound traffic because of the subsidy of 30 per cent of the Maritime portion of the rate which is paid by the Dominion. It will also be noted that as a rule the arbitraries to Western Canada are lower than the corresponding toll to Eastern Canada. This takes account of the tapering, i.e., the tendency of the cost of rail transport per ton-mile to decline a little as the length of haul increases. Moreover, if rates were to increase in strict proportion to distance, they would sooner or later become so high that manufacturers in the Maritimes would be unable to sell at a profit in Western Canada, particularly in competition with suppliers in the St. Lawrence Lowlands who are closer to the market in the West.

Freight between Eastern and Western Canada may move by water along the Great Lakes and connecting rivers as well as by an all-rail route. Railways give faster, more dependable service than water carriers and so the latter have to quote slightly lower rates if they wish to stay in business. In other words, the rates quoted by lake carriers are at certain differentials below the rates all-rail and the rates rail-water-rail, i.e., where transport by water comes between two movements by rail. The differentials vary with the class of freight and the place of origin or destination in the East. In 1964 on Class 100 the water-rail rate per hundred pounds was 9 cents below the rail-water-rail and 34 cents below all-rail in those cases where the Eastern terminus was east of the Detroit River. The corresponding figures for Class 27 were 2 and 9 cents. On traffic between ports on the Detroit and St. Clair rivers on the one hand and Western Canada on the other, the differentials of water-rail below rail-lake-rail were 19 and 5 cents on Classes 100 and 27, respectively. They were 44 and 12 cents under all-rail on the same two classes. In all cases the rates on other classes were fitted in between the extremes that have been given for two classes of freight and sets of termini. Lake carriers are free to depart from these differentials on bulk cargoes, such as grain and iron ore, and on any kind of freight which does not move by rail at one or both ends of the movement by water. This last exemption is of growing importance because trucking companies, some of them owned by operators of inland shipping concerns, are bringing freight to, say, Toronto at one end and hauling it away from Fort William at the other, and vice versa.

International Rates

Owing to the large amount of traffic between Eastern United States and Canada and the fact that American railways penetrate Canada and vice versa, joint through rates are published on almost every kind of freight. Goods moving in either direction are typically classified according to the so-called Official Classification which has been agreed upon by railways operating in that part of the United States north of the Ohio and Potomac rivers and east of the Mississippi. Class rates for this traffic are related to the distance between points in Canada and stations in the United States in the same general manner as those for traffic moving over hauls of the same length entirely within the United States. Commodity rates between Eastern Canada and Eastern United States are built up on various bases. As a rule they are arranged so that Canadian exporters can compete on equitable terms with American producers selling in the same market in the United States.

Relatively few through rates have been published between Eastern Canada and the southern and western states. The volume of our trade with Southern Territory (south of the Potomac and Ohio and east of the Mississippi) and with Western Territory (west of the Mississippi) is comparatively small. Moreover, it is not easy to negotiate rates with the several railways which necessarily participate in any movement between these areas and Canada. Whatever trade does take place moves at regular United States rates to the international boundary and at the normal Canadian rates beyond. A few commodity rates have been worked out and the American Classification applies.

The amount of trade between Western Canada and the United States is not nearly so large as between the eastern portions of the two countries. Instead of general agreements between railways for low through rates, it is therefore the practice to quote rates which are merely the sum of the locals. Thus the toll from Winnipeg to St. Paul, Minn., is the sum of the local rate to Emerson on the 49th Parallel plus the local rate from Emerson to St. Paul. On some traffic to and from stations on or near the Pacific coast, Canadian and American railways publish joint rates in order more effectively to meet competition from coastal steamships.

Rates on traffic between stations in Canada and points in the United States in either direction must be filed with the Board of Transport Commissioners and the Interstate Commerce Commission. The Board controls the rate over such portion of the through route as lies within Canada, and the Commission has jurisdiction over the United States portion. Neither authority has power to compel railways to agree to joint international rates. Rates on traffic between two points in the United States through Canada, e.g., Detroit to Buffalo through St. Thomas, Ont., must be filed with both official bodies. Technically the Dominion Board has jurisdiction over the rates on that part of the route lying within Canada. In practice it allows the Interstate Commerce Commission to fix the entire rate. On traffic between two points in Canada through the United States, such as between Montreal and Saint John across Maine, or Winnipeg and Port Arthur via the Canadian National line south of Lake of the Woods, the Board by custom, though perhaps not by law, has full control.

International rates have given rise to several complaints by Canadians. Shippers and consignees on the Prairies want joint international rates which are lower than the sum of the locals. While publication of such rates between all points in Canada and all stations in the United States might be desirable, it cannot be brought about by legislation or regulation in Canada for the simple reason that we cannot compel United States carriers to agree to such rates. Occasionally the sum of the locals between Canadian points through the United States is less than the through rates within Canada.[9]

Whenever the Interstate Commerce Commission changes rates within the United States (including the American portion of hauls between Canada and the United States), the practice of the Board of Transport Commissioners since its inception has been almost automatically to permit the same increases or decreases on the Canadian portion of the international haul. Increases made in this way by the Board are published without allowing Canadians the right to be heard and without investigating whether Canadian railways actually need the extra revenue. The Board's action is apparently unfair to shippers and consignees of freight moving across the boundary and derogates from our right as a sovereign nation to set rates on all traffic movements in Canadian territory, whether they are part of a through international haul or not. But the alternative is even less satisfactory. If Canadian railways did not increase their rates on lumber from Vancouver to Boston simultaneously with the American railroads' increase on lumber from Seattle to Boston, mill owners at Seattle would complain of loss of markets and unjust discrimination. Railways in the United States want to protect shippers along their lines and their own revenues. Hence they would withdraw their concurrence in the joint international rate from Vancouver to Boston. The rate which would then apply on the latter haul would be a relatively high one, namely, the sum of the local rates. Canadian shippers would be cut out of the Boston market and would be worse off than if Canadian railways had advanced their rates as the Americans had done.

Furthermore, freight originating in Trois Rivières, Que., destined for Buffalo, N.Y., may be hauled by a Canadian railway and delivered to American lines at Montreal, Prescott, or Black Rock on the Niagara frontier. Through rates by the various routes are equal to begin with. If an increase were permitted on only the United States portion of these through rates, the increase in cents per hundred pounds would not be the same over the various routes because the mileage within the United States differs. The total charge and therefore the relationship between the various gateways would be disturbed and the flow of trade across the international border thrown into confusion. These examples could be multiplied many times. Consequently the Royal Commission of 1951 refused to recommend any change in the Board's practice on international rates.[10] Later, the Board of Transport Commissioners, after lengthy hearings, decided that there was no practical way of dealing with the problem.[11]

Export and Import Rates

In North American railway parlance, the term international rates relates to export and import traffic between Canada and the United States. Therefore, it excludes overhead traffic where the movement is between two parts of the same country across part of the territory of the second. The words international traffic also exclude traffic between Canada and the United States and countries overseas. This is called export and import or, more simply, port traffic. Expressed in different terms, international traffic is basically an all-rail movement between two neighbouring countries. Port traffic involves a movement by water overseas as well as by rail within North America. But freight going partly by rail and partly by water between two ports on the Great Lakes, on inland rivers, and between the mainland of Canada and Prince Edward Island, Newfoundland, Vancouver Island, etc., is domestic traffic.

Various ports and the railways which serve them compete intensively for overseas traffic. New York City has the advantages of size, a large domestic market, good access to the Great Lakes Basin, a head start, and steamship lines serving every important port in the world. Other ports on the Atlantic coast of North America are less favoured. As early as the 1860s railways with their termini at these ports cut tolls, whereupon the lines serving New York reduced their rates. After a series of rate wars, the structure became stabilized. Export rates to Philadelphia were 2 cents per hundred pounds on freight generally and 1 cent less on grain and grain products than they were to New York. On this basis New York was content to let Philadelphia get its "fair share" of ocean trade. In the course of time, however, railroads in the United States began to publish the same class rates on export and import traffic through all ports on the Atlantic seaboard of that country.

Rates on export and import traffic published by Canadian railways are designed (*a*) to keep Canadian ports on a parity with the American ports with which they compete, and (*b*) to recognize the shorter rail haul to ports on the lower St. Lawrence River than to ports along the seacoast of either Canada or the United States. The history of these rates is tangled, but the situation set up by the Board of Transport Commissioners in 1956 is shown in Table 2.

TABLE 2
Export and Import Rates (Overseas)
Class Rates

To	From	Are Equal to the Rates	
		From	To
(*a*) Saint John	Windsor, Ont.[2]	Detroit	New York
Halifax			
Portland, Me.			
Boston			
New York			
Philadelphia			
Norfolk, Va.[3]			
Newport News, Va.[3]			
(*b*) Any of the above Ports	Armstrong Fort William Port Arthur	Duluth	New York
(*c*) Any of the above Ports	Sault Ste. Marie, Ont.	Sault Ste. Marie, Mich.	New York
(*d*) Montreal	All stations between Windsor and Saint John[2]	Two cents per 100 lbs. less than rates to Saint John	
(*e*) Quebec Sorel Trois Rivières	(*i*) All stations Toronto & west	same as Montreal	
	(*ii*) All stations east of Toronto	same as Saint John[4]	

[1]Rates include loading and unloading of cars at steamship piers served by railway tracks and charges for wharfage. Rates to and from Montreal and Quebec also include switching charges made by the National Harbours Board. This is done to keep these ports competitive with American ones.

[2]The Detroit–New York or Windsor–Saint John rate is taken as 100 per cent. Then the rate comes down (or goes up) by one percentage point for each 30 miles by which the distance between the station of origin and Saint John is less (or greater) than the shortest rail distance between Windsor and Saint John (1,040 miles). Because of competition over the shorter route via US railroads to New York City, rates from Hamilton, Hagersville, and stations in the Niagara Peninsula are the same as the rates from Toronto to Saint John.

[3]Rates to Norfolk and Newport News are confined to points in Canada on and west of the lines from Toronto to North Bay.

[4]Subject to the rates from Toronto being applied as a maximum from intermediate stations.

Commodity export and import rates (except on grain) vary from one commodity to another and from time to time, depending on competition between railways serving different ports and between railways, motor trucks, and occasionally water-lines. On bulk grain several sets of rates apply. Let us first take the rates on grain which originates in Western Canada, is brought by ship from Lakehead to Bay ports (Midland, Port McNicoll, Collingwood, Owen Sound) as well as to Goderich, Sarnia, Windsor, Port Colborne, Toronto, Kingston, and Prescott, and which is then sent by rail to Montreal, Halifax, Saint John, West Saint John or to ports such as Trois Rivières, Quebec City, and Baie Comeau on the Gulf and River St. Lawrence below Montreal. Under the National Transport Act of 1967 (sec. 329) these ex-lake or "At and East" rates were frozen to the level prevailing prior to 1961 and are subsidized by the Dominion. They are the same as the rates prior to 1961 on ex-lake grain landed at Buffalo and sent on to New York City except that (a) rates from ports on Georgian Bay, etc. (but not from Prescott) to Montreal, Trois Rivières, etc. are one-half cent per bushel lower than to Saint John, and (b) from Prescott, Montreal, etc., to Saint John, etc., are one and one-half cents below those from Bay ports to the same destinations. In other words, within broad limits these grain rates recognized the effect of distance.

Other rates on grain are published to apply from Fort William, Port Arthur, and Armstrong all-rail to Montreal, Saint John, and other Atlantic ports and are not held down by the statute passed in 1967. Rates on grain moved all-rail from Fort William, etc., to New York, Philadelphia, and Baltimore are the same as all-rail from Duluth to New York. Finally, rates on export grain that originates at local stations in Ontario and Quebec are not statutory and are related to the rates between Chicago and New York. Export rates are also published on grain products, flaxseed (linseed) and its products, soybeans and soybean products, but the arrangements are too complicated to permit succinct description.

Instead of using these export or import rates, the shipper has the option of sending his freight to, or bringing it from, the seaport at the local or domestic rate applicable to the traffic in question. In this event, he has to make his own arrangements for loading or unloading his freight between the railway car and the shed alongside ship. Local rates are almost always at a higher level per mile than export and import tolls, but on relatively short hauls to Canadian ports the sum of the local rate and the cost of terminal handling is sometimes less than the published export or import rate. When this occurs, the local rate plus terminal handling constitutes the maximum that may be charged on overseas trade.

Rates on export and import traffic through Canadian ports (except on export grain) are altered in precisely the same way as export and import rates in the United States, but domestic rates within Canada were not raised as rapidly after 1945 as domestic rates in the United States. This situation created certain distortions in rates on traffic being exported from Toronto via Halifax and Saint John. Before the Royal Commission of 1951 the Maritimes Board of Trade wanted the distortions removed, especially in order to comply with the government policy of encouraging traffic through all Canadian ocean ports. The railways opposed the request because lowering export and import tolls through Halifax and Saint John would disturb long-standing and mutually satisfactory inter-relationships between various ports in Canada and the United States. American carriers could retaliate by withdrawing the joint rates on exports and imports to and from the United States via Saint John, Halifax, and Montreal. As a result Canadian ports would suffer. Consequently the Royal Commission rejected the Maritime request.[12]

Because of the growth of trucking and the use of containers between New York and Toronto and other places in southern Ontario, Canadian railways have had to reduce some of their export and import rates. Competition between railways and trucks from these same centres in Ontario to Saint John and Halifax is sometimes not very potent. Consequently, Canadian railways leave these tolls at their old level which is, of course, higher than the competitive rates via New York. As a result the ports on Canada's Atlantic coast often criticize Canadian railways for their apparent failure to protect our shipping interests in Halifax and Saint John.

From Western Canada export commodity rates are published to Montreal, Saint John, and Halifax on varying bases, the ruling factor always being competition with rates via United States ports. Export class and commodity rates are also published from Eastern Canada, the Prairies, and interior British Columbia to Vancouver, New Westminster, Victoria, and Prince Rupert. Most of these export and import rates (except on grain) are equal to the tolls between the same points of origin and Portland, Ore., and Seattle.

Tariffs in General

Freight tariffs are voluminous and complicated. Over 600 important tariffs are in common use, not to mention numerous joint tariffs with United States railways. Tariffs must be frequently changed in order to meet the needs of shippers and the forces of competition. Supplements are filed with the Board of Transport Commissioners every business day of the year and total roughly 40,000 annually. From time to time a very large number of rates have had to be changed as a result of general increases or decreases. In order that railways may get the higher revenues or that shippers may benefit from lower tolls without delay, railways have issued correction sheets which state that whenever the rate in the old tariff is, say, 60 cents and the authorized increase is 20 per cent, the new rate will be 72 cents. As a rule fractions of a cent are treated by dropping changes of less than one-half cent and adding a full cent for fractions of one-half cent or over. As soon as possible after the general increase or decrease, all the relevant tariffs are reprinted to show the correct rates.

The legislation of 1967 makes it possible for railways to publish rates without getting the prior consent of the Board, provided they do not exceed the allowable amount on captive shippers nor fall below a reasonably compensatory level in the case of competitive traffic. This legislative change will not, however, reduce the number of rates which must be filed with the Board. Filing is necessary in order to keep the new Canadian Transport Commission informed of what is going on. More important, filing makes it possible for the Commission to state precisely what rate legally applied at a given time. This allows an aggrieved shipper to learn the correct charge for the carriage of his freight.

No shipper, consignee, or local railway agent needs to know more than a small fraction of the total number of tariffs on file with the Commission. But the principles upon which rates are based must be understood before the picture of transportation in Canada may be fairly viewed.

3

The General Rate Level

ONE OF THE THORNIEST PROBLEMS in the economics of rail transport has been the general level of rates. Earlier works by this author have set forth in some detail the applications made by railways to the Board of Transport (or Railway) Commissioners for authority to increase substantially all their tolls at one time. For reasons to be given shortly, Canadian railways, like those in the United States, are facing mounting difficulties in effectively applying general or across-the-board increases. Therefore, they are being compelled to make selective increases. They must raise rates on those kinds of freight that will stand higher charges rather than get authority to raise tolls generally. Yet regardless of whether the increases are general or selective, the Board will have to determine the financial requirements of the railways and for that purpose it will follow the principles which it had evolved by 1958.

On the face of things, the legislation of 1967 should either have outlawed general rate cases or given the new Canadian Transport Commission specific directions about how to handle them. In fact, the law did neither. This was because, with the exception of the years 1851–80, the Railway Act has never stipulated a general rate of return and, though the charter of the Canadian Pacific (1880) allowed 10 per cent, the clause has always been a dead letter. All increases in the general level authorized by the Board were based on the premise that inasmuch as it had the undoubted right to increase one or more rates at a time, it had authority to change them all simultaneously (except the Crow's Nest Pass rates). There was no need to amend a law which contained no specific provision regarding general rate cases.

The legislation of 1967 avoided reference to general rate cases for another and more fundamental reason. In all the postwar cases, rates on export grain from Western Canada were excluded. So were rates on export, import, international, port, and overhead traffic where, by custom, Canadian railways changed their rates at the same time and in the same degree as carriers in the United States. In addition, many rates had to be exempted from the general increase because of the fear, and often the reality, that the general increase would drive traffic off the rails to truckers and inland ships. This effect tended to become more serious as time went on. In order to get a given quantum of increased revenue, say $100 million, railways had to ask for steadily rising percentages of general increase because these increases could be applied to a shrinking volume of traffic. Though the Board could grant authority to increase many rates by a given percentage, railways found that, in practice, they had carefully to select those kinds of traffic on which they could effectively apply the increase. In a word, general increases became selective increases. Figuratively speaking, railways were using a steam shovel to eat their porridge: changing circumstances forced them to use a spoon.

Increases of these higher percentages or, what is the same thing, small increases made in quick succession, led people to assume that railways were primarily responsible for inflation in commodity prices and to argue that the higher tolls bore more severely on some parts of Canada than on others. Political and regional opposition grew in intensity until finally, in 1960, the Diefenbaker government forbade all general increases. The Pearson government continued the freeze until 1967. There seemed little point in getting the Board to authorize a general increase in tolls if governments were going to prevent it coming into force.

What is more, by 1960 shippers and provincial governments were prepared to accept the view that railways were no longer in a position to raise their rates so as to get an exorbitant or even an adequate return on investment. At the same time railways thought they would be at least as well off financially if they had greater freedom to meet competition by adjusting individual rates whenever possible, rather than go through the time-consuming process of getting authority to raise rates generally only to discover in the end that the increases had to be selective, not general. Shippers were prepared to allow this freedom, subject to two conditions: First, shippers who had no alternative means of transport, i.e., those who were captive to the rails, wanted protection against excessive charges; rail users wanted to make sure that every rate quoted by a railway was reasonably compensatory to it. If railways were permitted to publish rates below the cost of handling the traffic in question, they would have to recoup their losses by charging more on other traffic, notably on freight that can be economically moved only by rail. Moreover, non-compensatory rates would be unfair to competitors of railways. There was also a risk that railways might destroy some of their competitors by slashing tolls and then exploit their virtual monopoly. In brief, the shortcomings of general rate cases led to selective increases plus new rules of rate-making to cover captive shippers and competitive traffic.

Even though general rate cases may be things of the past, it still remains true that railways must get enough revenue to cover all their operating expenses, such as wages, diesel fuel, repair parts, stationery, rails, ties, and the like. In addition, they must secure enough revenue after their operating expenses to meet their taxes, interest, and, if privately owned, their dividends. Unless they do so, they will be forced to pay substandard wages, neglect the maintenance of their track and rolling stock, cut down on the quality of their service, and generally deprive shippers and travellers of decent accommodation. Alternatively, they will need to rely on government subsidies. A fair return to employees on railways and to investors in them is essential from the standpoint of the welfare of users of railway facilities. The general rate cases of 1948–58 provide the criteria by which a fair return can be measured. This is true even though the fair return is unlikely to be secured by percentage increases in rates generally.

This chapter deals with four questions: Why are railways in economic difficulties? What are the peculiar problems faced by each of Canada's major railways, the Canadian Pacific and the Canadian National? What are the criteria of an adequate level of rates which may be attained either by making individual adjustments in rates or by general increases? How does equalization affect the general picture? Though equalization was written out of the law in 1967, regional pressures are so strong in Canada that railways cannot afford to stir up too much animosity in regions which, for one reason or another, feel they are being unfairly treated. Subsequent chapters will deal with two other significant factors in the general rate level, the statutory or Crow's Nest Pass rates on export grain and the Maritime Freight Rates Act.

Problems of Railways Generally

Many of the difficulties faced by railways are self-evident. Others will be elaborated in later chapters. Competition is clearly a factor. Railway rates and fares must not get out of line with tolls set by other modes of transport. Railways compete with highway carriers almost everywhere in Canada: they are in competition with ships along the Great Lakes and St. Lawrence River, throughout most of the Maritimes and Newfoundland, and for traffic between Montreal and Canada's west coast. Pipelines for natural gas and petroleum, and power lines for hydro-electricity reduce the demand for coal which typically moves by rail. Civil aviation is a strong competitor for passengers and potentially for cargo. Of course, railways gain something from this competition for they move some of the construction materials and operating supplies used by their competitors. Also, they benefit from the industrial expansion and the higher standards of living resulting from these faster and more economical methods of transport. Yet on the whole competition clearly has a detrimental effect on the net income of railways.

Besides competition, the most efficient use of raw materials and the better location of plants reduce the demand for railway services. Society is spending a larger proportion of its income on services such as entertainment, care of the body, education, social welfare, and private transport (automobiles). This means that a relatively smaller proportion is spent on physical goods and, therefore, on the transportation of property by common carriers. The share of the Gross National Product received by railways tended steadily downward from about 7 per cent in the early 1920s to 6 per cent in the late twenties and thirties to 4 per cent in 1948, and thereafter. Some allowance has to be made for the lag in the rise of railway rates behind wage rates.

After 1945 railways undoubtedly benefited from the rapid growth of Canada's population, the discovery of new resources, and the steady rise in the standard of living. Yet the gains were not as large as might have been expected because much of the traffic, being of high value in relation to bulk, was exposed to competition from truckers. In addition, much of the new business required special equipment to handle it and was concentrated on lines which were becoming congested. Relatively little was moved over branch lines which had excess capacity and were barely meeting the out-of-pocket costs of keeping them open. Furthermore, progressive urbanization involves shortening the length of haul on many commodities and thereby enlarging the field of operation for truckers rather than for railways.

Two other factors clearly affect the future of Canadian railways. They have been hampered by the difficulty of reducing the quality and amount of services that do not pay their own way and by the practices of labour unions. Though shippers and travellers may not use a branch line except perhaps when alternative agencies are weather-bound, they will protest bitterly when the railway tries to abandon an unprofitable branch. Labour unions have been instrumental in making railway wage rates uniform across Canada, in limiting hours of labour, getting holidays with pay, preventing one occupational group from taking over the duties of another, raising wages to keep pace with the rising cost of living, and in attempting to get Canadian railway wages up to the United States level. Railways, perhaps even more than other industries, have lost some of their freedom to reduce wages or prevent increases in them. Moreover, employees are naturally reluctant to give up their jobs, seniority rights, and homes because railway managers think they can save money for their company by abandoning a branch or terminal, cancelling a passenger train, or introducing a technological improvement such as an automated marshalling yard. The process of adjusting the work force to new operating conditions is distressing to labour as well as time-consuming, exasperating, and often expensive (at least in the short run) to railway executives. In a word, the labour problems associated with rationalization of plant are far from simple.

Canadian railways must also face up to acute problems of regionalism within Canada. After 1945 the governments of all the provinces except Ontario and Quebec opposed every application made by railways for general increases in rates. Members of Parliament, including those from the provinces in the St. Lawrence Lowlands, appear to vie with each other in trying to prove that their particular regions bear a disproportionate share of the cost of operating railways. Similarly, they demand that more government money be spent on harbours, the St. Lawrence Seaway, and airports within their constituency. While such expenditures may be justified in the long run and in the overall picture, they often have the effect of depriving railways of traffic which they badly need to make ends meet financially. Moreover, people demand the continuance of unprofitable branch lines and non-paying passenger trains which are a fiscal drain on the railways. Railways cannot afford to ignore or ridicule the existence of these pressures. If they did so, they would find that even more money would be spent by provincial governments on highways and even more stringent provisions included in the Railway Act with the object of protecting the public against allegedly high rates, poor service, and arbitrary decisions on the abandonment of non-paying branches by railway officials. The National Transportation Act of 1967 will probably have the effect of reducing this pressure because branch lines may be subsidized by the Dominion.

Outlook for the Canadian Pacific

The economic viability of railways, long important in Canada, constituted the main theme of the submissions made by the Canadian Pacific to the Board of Transport Commissioners in all the postwar rate cases and to the Royal Commissions of 1951 and 1961. During the war and the preceding depression the Company had to postpone all but the most essential projects for the expansion and modernization of its plant. After the war it had to catch up on deferments which had been forced upon it. Moreover, so the Company felt, Canada is still a growing country and its expanding industries and commerce will require not only increased transportation services but also improved standards of service. Although since about 1930 the Canadian Pacific has generally steered clear of building new branch lines, it has had to build automated hump yards, lay heavier rail and ballast, extend passing tracks, use more centralized traffic control, convert from steam to diesel locomotives, and so forth. These expenditures are essential if the Railway is effectively to reduce its cost of operation to meet the strong competition which it now encounters and to provide the quality of transportation service the public is entitled to. And this necessitates the raising of more and more capital.

The problem of raising capital has been complicated by the relations between the Canadian Pacific and the Canadian National. The latter has no apparent difficulty in raising money for it can draw on the long purse of the state. The Commission of 1931–2 stated that Parliament had voted money to the National System freely if not lavishly. No evidence was submitted to any Board or Royal Commission since 1933 to show either that the management of the Canadian National had been extravagant, that Parliament had failed to exercise proper restraint upon the railway estimates placed before it, or that the two roads had been engaging in "general competitive folly."[1] On the contrary, up to about 1960 officials of both railways asserted that the Canadian National-Canadian Pacific Act of 1933 had been very valuable in preventing wasteful competition. The legislation was repealed in 1967 because both railways wanted a basic rearrangement of passenger-train services between the cities covered by agreements under the Act and because the new legislation contained provisions for joint use of unprofitable branch lines. Despite these changes in attitude and legislation, the Canadian Pacific is still apprehensive that any recapitalization of the Canadian National will imperil the financial stability of the privately owned railway and indeed of private enterprise generally.

To sum up, the Canadian Pacific must raise large amounts of capital to modernize its physical plant. Theoretically it can obtain funds by any or all of the following means: investing depreciation reserves, retaining and reinvesting profits, selling new securities to the general public, and obtaining government loans. Under conventional accounting methods, depreciation is based on the original cost of the asset. On account of the rapid rise in material prices after 1945 depreciation reserves were insufficient to replace the assets against which reserves were originally set up. Although new assets bought with depreciation allowances may have longer lives, lower costs of maintenance, or greater productivity than the original assets, depreciation reserves were still inadequate. In 1949 this situation, which was common to all businesses, was eased by a change in income tax regulations, but the Railway did not change its methods of accounting until 1954.

Ploughing back earnings might be the most satisfactory source of capital were it not for several facts. Railway net earnings are not likely to be large enough to give the Canadian Pacific all the capital it requires from this source. This is because of the apparently insatiable demands of railways for funds, the failure of railways to share in general business prosperity as fully as rapidly-expanding industries like electronics and petro-chemicals, and the vulnerability of rail net income to recessions in general business. Moreover, investors are normally unwilling to buy new stock unless they are receiving good cash dividends on the stock they already hold or believe that its market price will rise fairly steadily. The directors of a company have to take care that they do not plough back so much of their net earnings into the company that by paying little or no dividends, they dry up the sale of new securities to the public.[2] Finally, paying corporation income taxes on profits before reinvesting them in the business is an expensive way of raising money. Even so, reinvestment has the advantage that the company incurs no contractual obligation to pay interest annually or repay principal at some future time.

The Canadian Pacific receives very substantial profits from its subsidiary, the Consolidated Mining and Smelting Company of Canada, and from mineral rights, chiefly in oil fields in Alberta. These funds are theoretically available for reinvesting in railway property. But shareholders may protest if the money they should have been getting from highly profitable ventures is diverted into relatively unprofitable railway assets. They may be particularly annoyed because the diversion can be made by directors virtually without the consent of the shareholders.[3]

A railway may raise capital from bonds and stocks. Bonds, if well secured, are easier and cheaper to sell than stock and over the years interest payments will be less than dividends. On the other hand bonds must be repaid at maturity and the interest on them must be paid on its due date otherwise the company is bankrupt technically and usually practically as well. As a result companies try to avoid issuing bonds to a larger total nominal amount than they can pay interest on in the poorest business year which they anticipate. In other words the minimum annual net operating earnings after wages, raw materials, depreciation, property taxes, etc., combined with the rate of interest, set the maximum or outside limit to the amount which a corporation can safely borrow. In view of the secular decline in their net operating revenue and in particular of the variability in their net revenues because of the business cycle, railway managements are convinced that they should not increase their debt beyond its present ratio to total investment. What is more, after about 1957 the going rate of interest on newly issued bonds of public utilities rose from roughly 3 to nearly 6 per cent.

Equipment trust notes appear to be a particularly attractive type of borrowing instrument. In a broad sense they are used in the same way as the purchase of a house on mortgage or of an automobile on the instalment plan. The rolling stock pledged to secure the notes has an average service life approximately twice as long as the notes themselves. Expressed in different terms, the notes are paid off faster than the equipment depreciates in value. Consequently, it can at any time be sold for an amount large enough to redeem the notes and pay the costs of seizure. The equipment is reasonably well standardized and would find many prospective purchasers among other railways. Moreover, it must be kept in good repair, otherwise it is of no use to the leasing railway and will not be accepted in interchange by other systems. On some of its equipment trust issues the Canadian Pacific has pledged as additional security 4 per cent debenture stock of a higher nominal value than the notes themselves.

During the 1940s the generally prevailing cost of money was unusually low and equipment trust notes could be sold at interest rates of 2 per cent per annum or less. Even so, the Railway disliked the prospect of adding to its total indebtedness and its annual fixed charges by the sale of more notes. It claimed that since the notes must be repaid within a relatively short time—fifteen or twenty years—these notes become in reality a revolving fund. What is more, this method of finance cannot be used for reducing grades, installing signals, improving terminals, or for any purpose except that of procuring equipment. At best, it can supply only part of the financial requirements of railways. After about 1957 the interest rate on equipment trust notes began to rise.

Another and in general by far the most desirable source of funds for a railway is the sale of new stock. Shares have no maturity date and, while the investor must foresee a reasonable rate of return on his money over a period of time, he is prepared to forgo dividends should the company not have enough money to declare them. Stock gives a corporation a flexibility not possessed by other types of securities. Because railway net income is vulnerable to declines in the prosperity of general business, the sale of stock is strongly favoured by railway managements. Unfortunately the public is sceptical of the future of railways. Institutional investors with very large sums to invest, such as insurance companies, are either selling their holdings of railway securities or refusing to buy more. The psychology of investors is one of the vitally important factors bearing on future transportation policy. The present attitude may change, of course, and the Canadian Pacific has argued that it would change if the legislation it proposed were accepted by Parliament. The receipt by the Corporation of non-rail income, especially from mineral rights, has often had a buoyant effect on the price of its stock.

The final source of funds for capital investment is government loans, or else securities sold to the public by the Canadian Pacific with the unconditional guarantee of the Dominion for interest or principal or both. While the Canadian Pacific accepted such loans during the depression of the 1930s, it argued before the Royal Commission of 1951 that it could not accept further loans and still remain a private enterprise. At times, it has also been reluctant to accept government aid in other or non-capital forms. For example, it proposed to the Royal Commission of 1961 that the losses which it experienced, so it said, in the carriage of export grain at statutory rates should be offset by a credit on its corporate income tax. The MacPherson Commission rejected this plan, mainly because it would be of no benefit to the railway if the volume of its traffic were low and it had no taxable income. The railway did, however, accept the subsidy to provide a roll-back in freight rates and further subsidies in anticipation of those recommended by the MacPherson Commission. However, this financial aid was for operating expenses, losses on non-paying branch lines, etc., and not for investment in fixed assets. Within limits, the financial position of the Canadian Pacific Railway Company is being saved by its net earnings from non-rail sources, now rolled together in Canadian Pacific Investments, Ltd., rather than from rail property as such.

Outlook for the Canadian National

The Canadian National Railways has been a national undertaking, though up to a point it is expected to behave as a commercial enterprise. Much of its mileage has no other *raison d'être* than a political one. National policy determined the capitalization of the System because the government did not allow the privately owned systems to go into bankruptcy as they normally would have done. Even while the Royal Commission of 1951 was holding its hearings, the former Newfoundland Railway was entrusted for operation to the Canadian National, which estimated that its losses annually on this railway would average $10 million. In 1918–20, 1929, and 1950, various other, relatively short railways had also been unloaded on the unfortunate Canadian National.[4] Moreover the national policy of basing freight rates on the financial needs of the Canadian Pacific necessarily resulted in heavy deficits on the Canadian National. This policy may be justified in the national interest. It keeps tolls lower than they would otherwise be and helps the exchange of goods at home and their export abroad. It prevents shareholders of the Canadian Pacific from receiving the unreasonably high return which they theoretically would get if the Board of Transport Commissioners used the high cost Canadian National as the standard for rate-making purposes. Using the Canadian Pacific as a base condemns the Canadian National to heavy deficits except under unusual conditions such as those prevailing during the war.

The proper balancing of national and commercial considerations is of fundamental importance to the Canadian National and in national transportation policy. If the objective of the System is chiefly to serve the nation, recurring deficits may be no more objectionable than are "losses" on the post office or on education. Theoretically it might extend lines into new territories, continue to operate any number of non-paying branches, give more luxurious and frequent service than is strictly required by the needs of trade, and yet not be overly concerned about losses. Although waste should never be tolerated, particular policies would be judged not only by whether the revenue received would at least cover the expenditure made but by whether something of value to the general public would accrue to offset any monetary loss. On the other hand, if the Canadian National were to be operated solely as a business enterprise every policy of the management would have to be judged from a purely dollar-and-cents point of view. Old lines would be abandoned and new ones constructed on precisely the same principles as those followed by the privately owned and operated railway. The important point is that standards for judging performance should be no different for a public than for a privately owned system.

The impression one gets from reading the evidence before the two postwar Royal Commissions and before the Board of Transport Commissioners in various rate cases is that the Canadian National would like to operate as a purely business enterprise but knows that it is still dependent on Parliamentary grants for capital purposes and for covering unavoidable deficits in operations. In any event, one hears less than formerly of the Railway being judged mainly by its ability to open up new parts of Canada, of embalming all the errors of private enterprise, or of waiting for the population of the country to increase to the point where it will be able to carry the large mileage of railway lines.

The Yardstick Railway

In several of the general rate cases after 1945 argument arose over which of the two major Canadian railways should be used as the standard for rate-making purposes. Although several railways other than the two large transcontinental systems operate in Canada, they serve relatively small sections of the country, are branches of American systems, or are owned by provincial governments. Since it would be impracticable to have different levels of rates for two railways with differing financial needs, the financial requirements of either the Canadian National or the Canadian Pacific must be the guide or yardstick.

This question can be regarded as settled. Directives of the Cabinet, decisions of the Board of Transport Commissioners, recommendations of the Royal Commission of 1951, and the legislation of 1967 all set the Canadian Pacific as the yardstick.[5] When the Canadian Transport Commission sets compensatory rates, it is to have regard "to all relevant factors and to compute the costs of capital as proper for the Canadian Pacific Railway." As already explained, adoption of this principle contributes toward higher deficits on the Canadian National and toward a lower level of tolls than if rates were set to meet the financial requirements of the publicly owned system.

Operating Costs

Once the yardstick had been chosen, the Board had to determine the total financial requirements of the yardstick company. These included the expenses of operating the railway under honest, economical, and efficient management, plus taxes, interest, dividends, and surplus. Having determined the total amount of revenue which the yardstick carrier required, the Board had to set the general rate level. In doing so, it had to take care that the total revenue that was needed was secured from shippers and consignees in such a way that the overall burden was minimized and that various classes of railway patrons were treated equitably.

In the postwar rate cases both the Board and opponents of the increases have paid for more attention to financial requirements than to operating costs. Even so, in 1949 the Board complained that the railways presented no evidence to show what portion, if any, of the increase in labour costs of 17 cents an hour was proper and necessary.[6] The railways took pains in subsequent cases to forestall a possible repetition of this criticism.

As a rule, regulatory authorities will not allow public utilities to put up prices in anticipation of higher costs not yet actually incurred. But in 1958 the Board and the Cabinet both permitted an increase in freight rates even though the railways, at the date of the decisions, had not yet formally agreed with the unions to raise wage rates.

In at least five of the eight postwar rate cases, provincial witnesses alleged that the Canadian Pacific was spending excessive amounts on maintenance, departing from the accounting practices of the Interstate Commerce Commission which were generally accepted by Canadian railways, or executing quasi-capital works under the guise of maintenance.[7] To the extent that railways were guilty of any juggling of their accounts, they inflated their operating costs and so got higher freight rates than they should have. The Board's staff carefully investigated the books of the Canadian Pacific and as a result gave it a "clean bill of health" both on the principles which it had adopted and on the system of internal checks undertaken to ensure that the actual entries in the books conformed with the principles.[8] Then effective January 1, 1956, following recommendations of the Royal Commission of 1951, the Board laid down a uniform system of accounts and required Canadian railways to adhere to it.[9] Ten years later the MacPherson Commission proposed that the Board "be directed to review the whole Classification of Accounts at intervals not longer than every two years, in order to assure that technological application and operating re-organization shall be accurately reflected in the Accounts."[10] This proposal was incorporated into law.

Technological Advances

It is obvious that improvements in operating efficiency provide railways with an opportunity to offset rising wage rates and material prices and so reduce the need for higher tolls. In 1948 and 1956-7 provincial counsel called attention to marked advances in efficiency, as measured by several widely accepted indices. Inasmuch as railways were expected to make further technological gains, counsel contended that freight rates should not be raised while the programme of dieselization was going on.

The two major railways agreed with the provinces on the fact that they had benefited from the use of diesel rather than steam power, from better methods of repairing cars and maintaining roadway, and so on. The Canadian Pacific asserted, however, that it could continue to improve its performance only if it could secure large amounts of additional capital, and it could not raise the necessary funds unless the level of freight rates was high enough to give it a reasonable return on its present investment. Statisticians of the Canadian Pacific found that, bearing in mind differences in wage rate, material prices, and volume of traffic, modernization had cut the railway's operating costs by about 18.5 per cent over the year 1947-56. More savings were possible but, the Board declared, "unfortunately past experience has indicated that savings from dieselization are being more than offset by increases in other costs, notably labour and material costs, instead of being made available in part to users of railway services in the form of lower rates and to shareholders in the form of higher net income. Such savings have to date only been instrumental in holding down what would otherwise have been greater increases in unit operating costs, and the Board cannot give weight to this 'savings factor' in advance of actual results and forecasts showing a levelling-out or reversal of the upward trend of expenses in relation to revenues."[11]

Depreciation

Any physical asset, no matter how well it is kept in working order, eventually wears out. It may not disappear entirely: some scrap value commonly remains but it becomes so expensive to repair and operate that it is cheaper for the owner to buy a new asset to do the same work. Depreciation provides for the loss of serviceability which occurs despite proper repair and maintenance. Part of the original cost of the asset (less scrap value) is included in operating costs each year and the same amount is simultaneously credited to the reserve for depreciation. When the asset is actually taken out of service, i.e., discarded, its cost (less scrap value) is eliminated from captial investment and charged against the depreciation reserve which has been set up to meet this contingency. In this way a business provides for the loss of serviceability which takes place over the life of a physical asset.

Up to 1949, all Canadian businesses computed depreciation on the straight line basis, that is, the original cost (less scrap value) was charged off in equal annual amounts over the anticipated life of the asset. The only exception was the Canadian Pacific which preferred to base its depreciation charges on use, that is, on the number of locomotive-miles, car-miles, or gross ton-miles in the case of locomotives, passenger- and freight-train cars, and other depreciable property. Whereas under the straight line method, annual depreciation charges are the same whether business is good or bad, under "user" these charges are higher in periods of great activity than when business is slack. The Canadian Pacific emphasized the obvious advantages of varying annual depreciation charges with the business cycle and its gross revenues. It also pointed out that in some depression years of the 1930s the Interstate Commerce Commission had to permit railways in the United States to forgo depreciation entirely because their gross revenues were inadequate to cover straight line depreciation as well as other operating expenses.

On the other hand provincial counsel stressed the fact that straight line depreciation was the universal practice in business, except on the Canadian Pacific. They also objected to freight users being charged what they regarded as an excessive amount of depreciation merely because business was good. All parties agreed that if the rates of depreciation were accurately set, the same total charge would be made over the service life of the asset. They disagreed on whether the annual depreciation charges should be constant or vary with traffic volume. Although the Board permits a railway to adopt "user" in its own accounts if it wishes to do so, it has persistently required that, for the purpose of arriving at the general rate level, the amount of depreciation which may be included in the accounts of the yardstick company shall be ascertained by the straight line method.[12]

Income Tax

Besides the operating expenses just mentioned, the Canadian Pacific, the yardstick railway, must meet its financial charges including income taxes, interest, and dividends. In the first postwar rate case, the provinces contended that income tax should be taken out of whatever remained after operating expenses, interest and other taxes had been paid. They said, in effect, that income tax should come out of the pockets of the railway owners. Instead, the Board ruled that taxes on income, like taxes on real property, were an expense of doing business and should be passed on to railway patrons. This ruling accorded with precedent and the Railway Act,[13] and was followed in all later cases.

Controversy over income tax was revived in 1956–7. Because of the rise in prices after 1945, all businesses, including railways, found that when an asset wore out and had to be replaced by a new one, the amount against the old asset in the depreciation reserve, having been based on original cost, was much less than the cost of the replacement asset which had to be purchased at current prices. The problem of the inadequacy of depreciation reserves was partly solved when the government gave businesses the opportunity to use a new method of calculating depreciation for the purpose of arriving at taxable income.

Formerly, under the regulations of the Department of National Revenue, the annual depreciation charge was computed by dividing the original cost of the asset (less salvage value) by its service life in years. For example, an asset which cost $1,000, possessed no salvage or scrap value, and had an estimated useful life of twenty years, would be depreciated at the rate of 5 per cent or $50 a year. Under regulations which became effective January 1, 1949, the Department of National Revenue permitted use of the diminishing balance method of depreciation or capital cost allowances which now became the preferred term. On the asset described above, the depreciation rate would be 10 per cent calculated on the balance remaining after the depreciation of the previous years had been deducted from original cost. In our example, the capital cost allowance in the first year would be $100 (10 per cent of $1,000); in the second year it would be $90 (10 per cent of the original cost less the first year's depreciation or $1,000 less $100); in the third year $81 which is 10 per cent of $1,000 original cost minus accumulated capital cost allowance of $190; and so on. In the seventh and eighth years the capital cost allowances under the new scheme would be approximately $53 and $47, or roughly the same as the old depreciation charge ($50). Capital cost allowances could theoretically be continued indefinitely because the original cost of the asset less accumulated reserve would never reach zero. Consequently, provision is made in the law for charging against operating expenses the undepreciated value which remains in the account when the asset in question is actually retired.

The essential point is that the diminishing balance method permits heavier charges to operating expenses in the early years of the life of an asset than does the older method. As the asset becomes older, the position is reversed. The new charge for capital cost allowance is less than what the old charge for depreciation would have been. Different total charges to operating expenses for loss in serviceability of assets brings about differences in net corporate income and hence in corporate income tax. One of the purposes of the new scheme was to reduce income tax payments when assets were new and thereby increase the amount of corporate income after taxes. With more cash on hand, corporations would be encouraged to buy new equipment. Their purchases would stimulate business prosperity and they would not be handicapped, as they alleged they had been, by the inadequacy of their depreciation reserves.

Now it is clear that if under the new scheme income tax payments are to be less when assets are new than they would have been under the old regulations of the Department of National Revenue, they will be higher later on. In our example, income tax payments could be expected to increase after the seventh year. To meet this situation the Canadian Pacific set up a Tax Equalization Reserve. Among its financial requirements for current years it planned to include an item for the higher amounts of income tax which it expected it would have to pay later on.

The provinces attacked this proposal largely on the ground that if a taxpayer rapidly expanded his business, the high capital cost allowances on newly acquired assets would offset or more than offset the reduced capital cost allowances on assets which had been in use for several years. Consequently, the Reserve would either never be needed or would be required at such a remote date that it should be ignored in arriving at the present level of freight rates. The Reserve was also based on the theory that rates of corporate income tax would never be changed. Besides, if the Railway ceased to earn any taxable income, it would have no need for an Income Tax Reserve.

On the other hand, witnesses for the Canadian Pacific were confident that the Reserve was not for a remote contingency but was a realistic deferred liability. The record showed that the Company's capital expenditures had not been uniformly high or even constant and that income tax rates had not remained unchanged. The income tax regulations might result in the Company's having to pay large amounts in a poor business year when it would not be able to protect itself by raising freight rates. Until the Reserve was used to meet the income tax liability, it would constitute an interest-free loan. If it should happen that radically altered conditions eliminated the need for the Reserve, its disposition would be subject to control by the Board of Transport Commissioners. Unless the Board so determined, the funds which had been accumulated in the Reserve would not be available for distribution to shareholders. Meanwhile, they would reduce the Company's need for funds from outside sources to meet the cost of capital expansion. This need had been acute for several years and was expected to continue.

After carefully weighing these arguments, the Board allowed the Canadian Pacific to include the annual additions to the Tax Equalization Reserve among its financial requirements. The eight provinces appealed the Board's ruling on this matter to the Cabinet which, on April 29, 1958, over-ruled the Board. In other words, the Canadian Pacific is not allowed to include income taxes as an expense in rate cases beyond the amount which it actually pays or expects to pay in a given year.[14]

Other Income

The Canadian Pacific is more than just a railway. It is a holding company with large and profitable investments in the Consolidated Mining and Smelting Company, Trans-Canada Pipe Lines, Rio Algom Mines, MacMillan Bloedel (lumber), and several other concerns. Moreover, it owns ocean, inland, and coastal ships, hotels, commercial telegraphs, and Canadian Pacific Air Lines. These holdings are not part and parcel of the Railway, though of course they are useful to it. According to the provinces in the *Twenty-one Per Cent Case*, 1948, net receipts from all these sources, the so-called "other income," should be added to the operating revenue of the Railway per se in order to determine the financial need of the carrier. The railways objected to the provincial claim, in part because the Board's jurisdiction was limited by the provisions of the Railway Act which did not cover the enterprises (except telegraphs) which provided the other income.

The Board excluded "other income" because unless it did so a highly undesirable situation might arise. "If the income from profitable outside investments is to be used to reduce what would otherwise be just and reasonable rates, then it may well be argued that if net losses were made in any such undertakings the users of the railway transportation services might be called upon to pay higher rates to recoup such losses." Railways other than the Canadian National and Canadian Pacific were interested in the application and these for the most part have no other income. It would be unfair to fix rates for them on the basis of the other income of the two large transcontinental systems.[15] The Board pointed out that in other cases it had excluded "other income."[16]

Income Tax on Other Income

According to the Canadian Pacific, income tax on the entire corporate income of the company should be a charge against railway operating expenses. The Company has a common treasury for all its various enterprises. Its whole corporate revenue, including railway operating income and "other income," goes into this common treasury and from it all disbursements are made. On occasions, the Company said, it has found it necessary to resort to "other income" to help it meet its railway operating requirements. So long as this situation continued, all the income tax paid by the corporation should be included among railway expenses. Besides, the Company claimed, it was impossible to segregate the income tax into two component parts, viz., that portion derived from income on railway operations as against that portion derived from ancillary services and investments and referred to as "other income." The Board ruled that "as other income is not to be taken into account in fixing . . . rates for transportation services, it would be most unfair to those who have to pay the rates, to include as an operating expense of the Canadian Pacific such income tax as may be payable in respect of other income."[17] Therefore the Board divided the income tax between rail and non-rail, that is, between what should be borne out of freight rates and what should not.

Interest and Dividends

A similar problem of division arose over the interest and dividends payable by the holding company. In the first postwar rate case (1948), the Company argued that all the fixed charges and dividends of the Corporation should be met out of railway revenues and freight rates. The "other income" of the Company had contributed large sums to the common treasury. Part of these sums was not paid out as dividends but was used to pay off some of the bonded debt of the Company and thereby reduce the amount of interest which must be met by users of that property of the Company devoted to railway transportation. Since railway users benefited from lower interest payments because of "other income," it was proper that they should bear the interest and dividends on the entire capitalization. The provincial governments took exception to this view. They contended that if, as the Canadian Pacific had argued, "other income" should not be taken into account for the purpose of setting freight rates, then interest and dividends on the investment which gave rise to the "other income'" should also be excluded.

The Board found itself in some difficulty in dealing with this point. Because of the close relationship of railway transportation and other enterprises of the Canadian Pacific, the Board was not able to calculate with any degree of satisfaction what the amount of fixed charges attributable to non-transportation enterprises, if any, might be. Consequently, it allowed the entire corporate interest and dividends as a charge against railway rates. This point was one of those referred to the Cabinet, which stated that it was favourably impressed with the desirability of having some part of the Corporation's financial needs borne by its non-rail operations. In the ensuing case before the Board, the provinces argued that the Corporation's interest and dividends should be apportioned between rail and non-rail on the basis of relative investment in the two kinds of property. Later, one province wanted the apportionment made on the basis of relative earnings from the two sources. The Board rejected this plan because to have all these payments thrown upon non-rail operations would be unrealistic if at some future time the railway properties had no net earnings before interest.

The Canadian Pacific's solution was fundamentally different. Rail earnings should provide a dividend of 4 per cent on all the Corporation's preference stock, 5 per cent on all its ordinary, and a surplus to come and go on. "Other income" would permit the Company to pay more than 5 per cent on its common stock and so lift its price high enough to enable the Company to sell equity securities and use the proceeds of their sale for the modernization of rail property. The Board accepted this principle and set the surplus at about 2 per cent of the investment in rail property and, of course, it divided the Corporation's interest charges between rail and non-rail in proportion to the investment in each.[18] It used this "formula" with some modifications in all subsequent postwar rate cases.

Surplus

In 1948 the Canadian Pacific asked that the rate level be set high enough to cover some "additions and betterments" which it itemized. It contended that its finances were not strong enough to allow it to raise money by the sale of stocks and bonds in the open market. Because of rapidly rising prices, the depreciation currently being charged against operations was inadequate to provide for replacing fixed assets when they wore out. Shippers should provide some of the capital which was necessary to keep the plant modernized and capable of rendering the quality of service which they expected and were entitled to. Respondents declared that it was the duty of investors to supply the capital for investment in property. It was unreasonable to ask shippers to supply money to buy assets and then ask them to pay depreciation, repairs, and a fair rate of return upon those assets.

The Board did not deal directly with these arguments but ruled that a "railway company, as in the case of other enterprises, should have something in addition to 'come and go on,' to provide for contingencies and to help equalize the result of poor years with good years." It should also "have something, if necessity arises, to put back into the railway operation undertaking for the improvement of the services which it is required to furnish. That is, apart from major capital requirements."[19]

In 1952 new jargon was advanced. Canadian Pacific witnesses, disliking the word surplus since it did not convey the idea of a requirement that must be included in setting the freight level, preferred such expressions as undistributed profits, retained earnings, something left over after provision for fixed charges and dividends, something to come and go on, a little fat in years of prosperity, and a reserve for a rainy day. The Board agreed that the principle purpose of the surplus was to lend stability to an enterprise, to beget confidence in prospective investors, and to attract capital when a public sale of securities was desirable. While the amount of surplus was not susceptible of accurate determination, surplus was usually if not invariably found in efficiently operated companies.

Canadian Pacific's witnesses also asked that the surplus of $15,235,-000 which the Board had allowed in previous cases should be increased by nearly 30 per cent. It was true that since 1947 the Company's average annual surplus was less than $2 million. Even so, it should have the same opportunity as unregulated companies of building up, in the current cycle of prosperity, substantial surpluses against the day of reduced earnings.

The Board felt that a larger allowance for surplus would unduly and unnecessarily raise freight rates. A corporation which had consistently paid a good rate of return to its shareholders was not in the same need of an annual addition to surplus as one which had an inferior dividend record. But the Canadian Pacific was doing better every year, and the Board said that there was less need for surplus as a means of attracting capital than formerly. At the same time the Board refused to cut down the amount of surplus which it currently allowed merely because, for one reason or another, the yardstick railway was unable to earn all the allowable amount. To reduce the permissive amount would be unfair to the smaller railways and to the Canadian National, which would lack a reasonable chance to meet their fixed charges.[20]

The Formula

To recapitulate: The Board laid down a permissive level of income for the yardstick railway. It took into account passenger receipts and incidental railway earnings. Then it tried to set freight rates at such a level that, if all went well, the Canadian Pacific would be able to meet its operating expenses (including depreciation) and taxes, the rail portion of the Corporation's fixed charges, 4 per cent on its preference and 5 per cent on its paid-up ordinary stock, and a surplus which it set at about 2 per cent on the total investment in rail property. In 1957 the Board made an additional allowance for requirements of $2.4 million, as explained later.

The allowable amounts for fixed charges and dividends have varied from time to time on account of changes in the financial structure of the Company and fluctuations in rates on foreign exchange. The significant statistics are shown in Table 3.

TABLE 3

	1948 Million	1950 Million	1958 Million
Fixed charges	$18.0	$11.7	$13.0
Dividends on preference and ordinary stock	21.3	20.6	20.6
Surplus	15.2	15.2	15.2
Additional allowance			2.6
TOTAL	54.5	47.6	51.3

SOURCE: *Eleven Per Cent Case*, (1957) 74 C. R. T. C. 209, 227; 46 J. O. R. R. no. 19A, 1, 19-20: *Fifteen Per Cent Case*, (1958) 76 C. R. T. C. 53, 60; 47 J. O. R. R. no. 19 A, 1, 9.

The Final Computation

After making adjustments in operating expenses, providing for income tax, and allowing for the so-called financial requirements, the Board had to estimate the net rail income for the "constructive year," that is, for all or part of the year during which the increase, if any, would apply. In formulating its estimate of future income, the Board had the assistance of its own experienced advisers, and of expert witnesses called by the provinces and the railways. Inevitably, opinions differed, but as the Board usually had before it the actual results for part of the constructive year, it needed to forecast for only the remaining months.

Table 4, based on that in the *Fifteen Per Cent Case*, 1958 and for the constructive year 1957, shows how the Board pulled together the various detailed estimates in order to arrive at its conclusion regarding the amount of additional revenue which was required. When this table was compiled, the Board had actual data to the end of October.

TABLE 4

Permissive level of net rail income as shown in Table 3			$51,253,000
Net rail income for constructive year		$48,160,000	
Allowance for excess of straight line over user depreciation	$377,000		
Less income tax (47½%)	179,000		
Decrease in net rail income		198,000	47,908,000
Deficiency in net rail income			$ 3,345,000
Allowance for income tax (47½%) on additional revenue yield requirement			3,027,000
Revenue yield requirement from increased rates			$6,372,000

SOURCE: *Fifteen Per Cent Case*, (1958) 76 C.R.T.C. 53, 71; 47 J.O.R.R. no. 19A, 1, 23.

None of the additional revenues needed by the Canadian Pacific could be secured from grain and grain products subject to statutory and related rates nor from international, overhead, import-export, and similar traffic, which are excluded from general rate cases for reasons given earlier. The Board decided to allow an increase of 7 cents per ton on coal (except lignite) and coke. It set the anticipated increased revenue from this source at $385,000 in the constructive year. It subtracted this last amount from the revenue yield requirement as shown in the table. The resultant figure ($5,918,000) was the amount which had to be collected from the traffic which was subject to the increase.

Finally, the Board estimated that rates on the traffic (except coal and coke) covered by the application would have to be raised 3.6 per cent to yield $5,918,000. Any increase allowed in this *Fifteen Per Cent Case*, 1958, would have to include increases already allowed in the two preceding cases, the *Seven and Eleven Per Cent Cases*, 1956–7, which were part of the same original application. As the two earlier cases had raised rates by 11 per cent, a further increase of 3.6 per cent would make the increase, including the earlier ones, total 15 per cent (11 plus 3.6 per cent of 11).

In the immediate postwar rate cases the Board was able to apply to substantially all the traffic (except coal and coke) covered by the application any percentage increase which it felt to be necessary. By the mid-1950s competition from other agencies of transportation had become so keen that the Board had to recognize that the necessary increase in gross revenue could be obtained only by applying different percentage increases to competitive rates, agreed charges, and non-competitive rates. In many instances, no increase at all could be made to "stick." In other cases, application of the full amount of the increase authorized by the Board or even part of it would prevent movement because shippers could not afford to pay the higher rate and still sell in distant markets in competition with more favourably located suppliers. Thus railways were suffering from loss of business to competitors and from market competition. A freight traffic manager of the Canadian Pacific called this attrition and erosion.

Proposed Changes in the Formula

A most important fact is that at no time since 1945 has the Canadian Pacific been able to earn the full permissive income allowed by the Board under the formula. This situation has been brought about by competition, the continuous increases in wages and material costs, the time lag between increases in operating expenses and related increases in freight rates, and so on. In other words, the Railway has been unable to reach the level of earnings which the Board, not to mention the railways themselves, thought to be just and reasonable. Besides, the more or less continual battle between the railways and eight provincial governments before the Board of Transport Commissioners was costly and exasperating for all parties and bad for the carriers' public relations.

In the late 1950s railway executives and the Board expressed dissatisfaction with the formula and the Board officially asked interested parties to suggest improvements. Both railways requested that the process of getting the Board's permission to raise the general rate level either be abolished or greatly simplified. They said they should be free to alter rates promptly to keep them more closely in line with unavoidable increases in operating costs. They recognized that they must avoid rates which create undue preference or unjust discrimination for any class of traffic or group of shippers. For this reason they did not expect to have the same degree of freedom to alter prices as is normally possessed by businesses outside the field of public utilities. Nevertheless, they felt that they should not be hamstrung in setting rates as they had been in the past. Alternatively, the Canadian Pacific would introduce an entirely new formula, the rate base-rate of return method which will be discussed shortly. Later, counsel for the Canadian Pacific argued that the Board should take into account the cost of raising new money, i.e., the marginal cost, estimated at 10 per cent. The formula was based on historical cost, on what it had cost to raise funds by bonds and shares when railways were well regarded by investors, when their earnings were buoyant, and when interest rates were relatively low. Conditions had altered, and while the Canadian Pacific and shippers still benefited from the favourable terms of sale of bonds and shares over the previous eighty years, the Company had to pay the high current rates if it hoped to attract new funds. As it stood, the formula did not recognize this fact.

Counsel for the Canadian National generally supported this point of view. In addition, he demanded that the formula should give more weight to the financial requirements of the publicly owned system.

For their part, the provinces considered that no change in the formula was necessary except that the Board should eliminate an allowance of $2.4 million which it has permitted to be transferred on January 1, 1956, from non-rail to net rail investment of the yardstick railway under the uniform classification of accounts. The proposals of the provinces can hardly be called a significant contribution to a complex problem.

As it turned out, the Board was not at all receptive to the suggestions it had invited.[21] In 1958 it rejected the provincial request for disallowance of $2.4 million. It largely ignored the request of the Canadian National that it be used as the yardstick equally with the Canadian Pacific. Finally, it turned down the latter's claim that the record of earnings of a railway company should be looked at in precisely the same light as that of other undertakings, even though they competed for new funds in the same capital market. The Board said that rates arrived at under the formula had not prevented the Canadian Pacific from maintaining its credit in the financial world. The level of freight rates had not, in the Board's view, contributed to whatever lack of attraction the company's ordinary stock may have had for the investing public. The price of the stock thad fluctuated a good deal since 1946, and many factors besides freight rates seem to have influenced this fluctuation. Moreover, the effect on the future market price of the stock of a higher level of permissive earnings was conjectural. The Board concluded by stating that although it was concerned about the suitability of the formula to a changed situation, it was not convinced that it needed any major alteration. After all, it was only one of the steps in the determination of a just and reasonable level of rates.

It is perhaps not unfair to suggest that the Board saw the weaknesses of the formula, could think of no improvements itself, and so asked for suggestions. When it got no proposals that seemed worthwhile, it decided that, everything considered, the formula was still acceptable. The MacPherson Commission advised that the formula and general rate cases be scrapped, recommended that railways be given greater freedom in meeting competition in the hope that they would cover their financial requirements, and proposed legislation designed to protect captive shippers and prevent non-compensatory rates.

Rate Base-Rate of Return

Because the Canadian Pacific felt that the existing formula did not provide it with a fair rate of return, it advocated adoption of a quite different doctrine. This required that the regulatory authority determine the fair valuation of the physical property used in the service of transportation and set a fair return on this base. Fundamentally, the Canadian Pacific's plan was that used in the United States for many years and applied to companies supplying gas, water, electrical energy, telephone services, and urban and intercity transport.

In 1948 and 1949 the Board of Transport Commissioners rejected the Canadian Pacific's plan. The Board felt that while it might have some regard to such a scheme, the Railway Act did not lay down what it was to take into account in setting the general level. A valuation had never been undertaken for Canada. In a word, it refused to be drawn into an extensive and complicated question.[22]

Then the Railway requested the Royal Commission of 1951 to recommend an amendment to the Railway Act whereby "rates shall not be deemed to be just and reasonable unless, taken as a whole, they are sufficient to provide a fair return upon the investment in the railway property of the Canadian Pacific Railway Company and the Board may from time to time determine the investment in railway property upon which the return is to be calculated and the rate of such return."[23] The Company said that if in the public interest it was to continue as a privately owned system, its capital must be protected and additional capital attracted. It considered that the "requirements" method used in recent cases was unfair since it did not take into account surplus earnings which had been ploughed back by shareholders and on which they were entitled to a return. The method was too uncertain and contentious to be equitable. Use of a rate base would eliminate disputes over treatment of "other income" and the apportionment of interest and dividends between railway and non-railway operations. Consequently the Board would be able to deal with general rate cases more expeditiously.

The Royal Commission stated that the purpose of the proposed amendment seemed to be to safeguard the position of the Canadian Pacific as a free enterprise but it thought it inadvisable to recommend writing the proposal into law. In the first place the Board of Transport Commissioners had laid down that no order would be made that would imperil capital funds invested in transportation. It had at least recognized the principle of a fair return, a reasonable surplus, and rates sufficient to attract capital and maintain credit.[24] Second, fair return on property investment might be one of the tests of a reasonable general rate level; it must not be either the sole or the guiding test. Third, the procedure of rate making must be left flexible: the experience of the United States showed that a statutory floor was impossible of achievement in periods of economic distress; adoption of the proposed amendment would tend to make the Board mere computers of a rate base and rate of return, and calculators of the amount of increases necessary to bring about that rate of return. In any event the Board had authority under existing legislation to fix tolls on the rate base-rate of return method. Therefore, the Royal Commission felt that no amendment to the Railway Act was required.

With its proposal virtually rejected by the Royal Commission, the Railway renewed its plea before the Board in 1952 and again in 1954. The Canadian Pacific and the provinces refurbished their old arguments. The Canadian National, though it joined its privately owned competitor in requesting higher tolls whenever these were necessitated by higher operating expenses, said that it was neutral on the rate base-rate of return method. Provincial counsel said they were aghast at the increase in rates which would be necessary if the Canadian Pacific were to get what it wanted under the new scheme. Some witnesses stated that competition had become sufficiently intense and widespread to insure they would be automatically protected against freight rates which might otherwise bear too heavily on them. On the contrary other shippers said that the net effect of the plan would be to set the maxima or ceiling (the standard mileage class rates) so high that railways would be free to set substantially every rate wherever they pleased. In other words, the proposal provided the railways with a huge "playground" for making rates to suit themselves, subject only to the prohibition against unjust discrimination and undue prejudice.

Following the advice of a firm of chartered accountants whom it engaged, the Board set the value of the Canadian Pacific's net rail investment on December 31, 1951, at $1,140,214,801. The Board said that it would see that the Railway kept this figure up to date by adding the value of additions and betterments to property and deducting for annual depreciation charges and for abandonments. Still, it was not to be regarded as a rate base as the Canadian Pacific used the term. The Board said it would calculate the rate of return and use the resultant figure as one of the "end" tests in considering the reasonableness of a permissive level of rates. In the Board's words, fair return on property investment may be one of the tests: it must not be the sole or guiding test.[25] Besides, the United States was in the process of modifying, if not totally abandoning the rate base method.[26]

Horizontal Increases

Having determined how much more revenue the Canadian Pacific needed to meet its financial requirements and having excluded the statutory rates on grain, export-import rates, etc., the Board then had to decide how much particular rates had to be raised. The simplest way of doing this was to raise all the remaining rates by the same percentage, i.e., by a horizontal increase. In 1948 the provinces argued that raising rates which were already high by the same percentage as rates forced down by truck and water competition would accentuate regional discrepancies and aggravate inequalities in rate levels. This contention was rejected by the Board. Before the Royal Commission of 1951 the provinces enlarged on their objections to increases "across-the-board" which discriminated against interline hauls where the joint or combination rate was higher than the rate for the same distance over the lines of a single railway company. Horizontal increases would also distort the normal class arbitraries above recognized base points. Further, after a horizontal increase a manufacturer or farmer at a distance from the market had to pay more money for his transportation than one near the market. The cost of putting some portions of the supply on the market was increased more than that for other portions. Specifically, if the rate from B to A was 50 cents and from C to A was $1.00 and if the horizontal increase was 20 per cent, B paid ten cents more and C paid 20 cents more than before. Thus, nearby producers benefited from the increases because their distant competitors were placed at a disadvantage in selling in the common market.

This argument did not necessarily work only to the advantage of suppliers in the St. Lawrence Lowlands, as counsel for the West argued. Higher freight rates may have protected manufacturers in the Maritimes, the West, or British Columbia who sold to nearby consumers. But on account of the increase in freight rates, these manufacturers might have to pay higher prices for raw materials and equipment than their competitors in the St. Lawrence Lowlands. In any event, consumers had to pay more than formerly for their manufactured goods.

Counsel for the West and the Maritimes quoted decisions of the Interstate Commerce Commission in which percentage increases were limited in various ways. In rebuttal, the railways quoted other decisions in which the same Commission had approved of horizontal increases. Furthermore, because general rate increases are necessitated by rises in wage rates and the cost of supplies, it is reasonable to assume, so railways argued, that the cost of handling long-haul and short-haul traffic has risen by the same percentage. Consequently, all freight rates should rise by the same proportion. What is more, if maxima were set on long-haul rates, as the provinces had suggested, charges for the short-haul would have to be raised very high in order to provide carriers with the gross revenue needed to meet their requirements. Sooner or later, the railways said, they would reach the point where they could not add to their revenues by raising rates over short distances because high rates would drive business to highway carriers. They already had to publish many truck-competitive rates. Raising rates on short-haul traffic by relatively more than on long-haul business would drive still more business to trucks.

Railways said they found horizontal increases an expeditious means of covering increased operating costs. If they had to devise and publish an elaborate scheme for varying the increases by commodities or by length of haul, they would expose themselves to attack by every group of shippers which felt that the proposed plan discriminated against them as compared with some other shippers. In consequence, the effective date of the increase would be postponed. The delays, which were already great, would become disastrous, since during the deferment of the final decision they would have to continue paying the higher operating costs.

Railways felt sure that for every long-haul shipper or consignee who might benefit from the application of maxima increases instead of horizontal ones, a short-haul shipper would object. Superficially, this struggle over the uniform percentage increase was a conflict between shippers and railways. Fundamentally, it was between classes of shippers. Counsel for railway patrons who were distant from their markets and sources of supply appeared before the Royal Commission but the more favourably located patrons were unrepresented. Hence railways were forced into the position of advancing the arguments favourable to short-haul shippers and consignees. Railways made it clear, however, that their primary interest was in so adjusting freight rates as to get gross revenues adequate to meet their financial requirements.

Railways also asserted that during a period of rising prices market patterns are not disturbed by imposing the same percentage increase on all rates, provided the rate increases are no higher than the general rise in prices. Even with an increase in tolls of 100 per cent, the position of the distant supplier is not worsened provided his selling price has also doubled. Railways explained the shippers' protests by suggesting that during the long time lag of freight rate increases behind commodity prices, producers had become accustomed to exceptional profits. They had been selling goods at higher prices without having to pay any more for transportation. Naturally they felt they were being hurt when they lost this exceptional advantage, that is, when freight rates were later raised to bring them more closely in line with commodity prices and operating costs.

The Royal Commission of 1951 expressed its sympathy with the views of both parties but obviously found difficulty in finding a satisfactory alternative to horizontal increases. It did call attention to various possibilities: a lower percentage increase on commodities moved long distances than on short-haul freight, smaller increases on low valued goods than on more valuable articles, increases subject to a maximum of so many cents per hundred pounds, and flat increases which were so many cents per hundred pounds regardless of length of haul.[27] The Royal Commission refused to recommend the statutory prohibition of horizontal increases as some provinces had requested but it declared that in future general rate cases, carriers should make studies of traffic conditions in all their implications and should present to the Board proposals for one or more of the alternatives to horizontal increases. The railways should pay special attention to long-haul traffic and to basic or primary commodities. The new statistical techniques in connection with the waybill study would help in providing railways and the Board with the information necessary for a choice of one or other of the alternatives which would still give carriers adequate revenue. If railways failed to adopt the approach recommended, it ought to be the duty of the Board to see that they did so.[28]

In subsequent rate cases the railways stated they were at a loss about how to carry out the admonition of the Royal Commission. Provincial counsel fulminated but did not come up with a practical alternative either. Railways stated that in the past they had always been ready to deal promptly with the complaint of any shipper who felt he had been injured by a horizontal increase. The fact that few such complaints had been lodged suggested that the tried and recognized procedure was generally satisfactory. When the railways proposed a flat increase instead of a horizontal one on livestock, Alberta, previously a strong opponent of horizontal increases, objected. A flat additional charge would tend to increase the movement of live animals out of the province instead of encouraging processing within Alberta. "This example of conflicting interests shows how difficult it is to deal with exceptions in a general revenue case," according to the Board.[29]

In other cases the Board dealt with complaints about horizontal increases from canners of vegetables and fish meal, lumbermen, a stove manufacturer, the Maritime steel industry, and companies mining lignite coal in Western Canada and base metals in British Columbia.[30] In general, the Board found it impossible to make exceptions. The gist of the matter was that, despite some drawbacks, the horizontal method of getting revenue worked tolerably well as long as the increases could be applied over a broad segment of rail traffic. But now that erosion and attrition were such powerful factors, horizontal increases tended, as a practical matter, to become selective. The MacPherson Commission recognized this point by its recommendations on rates.

Equalization

Equalization of freight rates is concerned chiefly with the effort of Western Canada to overcome its transportation disabilities. Prior to roughly 1900, the prevailing level of rates in the West was much higher than in Eastern Canada. The extent of the difference was reduced in the *Western Rates Case*, 1914, in some of the general rate cases towards the end and immediately after World War I, and in the *Mountain Differential Case*, 1949. More especially, rates on grain under the Crow's Nest Pass Agreement and related decisions of the Board gave the West the advantage of low tolls on its chief staple export.

Yet, when all this had been done, there still remained some differences in standard mileage class rates, distributing tariffs, and commodity mileage scales. It is impossible to say what the difference was in dollars and cents. No one knew how much traffic moved under each of the various scales. Some commodity mileage scales in the West were higher than in the East for short distances and lower for longer ones in which, so the railways claimed, Western shippers were mainly interested. Numerous other differences will become apparent in the course of the next few pages. The main point is that over the years a sense of injustice had developed in the West over the level of freight tolls in that area compared with those on the same kinds of freight moving in Southern Ontario and Quebec. Therefore all four Western provinces united, first in demanding that the government appoint a Royal Commission to investigate this and other matters, and then in presenting their views on equalization to that body.

The Maritime Provinces, on the contrary, opposed equalization on the grounds that it could not be achieved and that if it were attempted, it would lower net revenues and bring about such increases in tolls that, even with their statutory protection under the Maritime Freight Rates Act, they might be worse off than formerly. The Canadian National conceded the desirability of equalizing class rates, distributing or town tariffs, and distance commodity scales but said it was impracticable to equalize specific commodity rates and competitive rates. The Canadian Pacific took much the same view, though its studies of equalization were not complete. It insisted that the Crow's Nest Pass rates would have to be allowed to find their proper level if true equalization were to be secured. It stated that the constructive mileage on traffic between Fort William and Winnipeg and the corresponding adjustments from Churchill and the Pacific coast would all have to go. Both railways wanted equalization effected without detriment to their net revenue.

Despite the differences in view as expressed in evidence before it, the Royal Commission said that because of the substantial unanimity of opinion on equalization and the terms of the Order-in-Council requiring the Board to make a General Investigation, the broad principle should be accepted. But the Order-in-Council did not make equalization mandatory. It merely directed an investigation "with a view to the establishment of a fair and reasonable rates structure, which will, under substantially similar circumstances and conditions, be equal in its application to all persons and localities." By holding that circumstances were dissimilar, the Board could perpetuate the existing structure. In any event a directive to the Board did not bind the Royal Commission.

Although the Commission would allow many exceptions to equalization, such as international, export, import, competitive, and statutory grain rates, it recommended that the Railway Act be amended, as it subsequently was,[31] and that the Board be required to effect and maintain uniformity in rates throughout Canada. This "national policy" on transportation was objected to by members of Parliament from the Maritimes, chiefly on the ground that their tolls might be increased and their statutory advantages whittled down. As finally passed, the legislation protected the Maritime position. In effect equalization was not to apply on traffic east of Lévis and Megantic.

It will be noted that equalization in the literal sense was not recommended by the Commission, nor is it attainable. If absolute equality were ordered, a reduction in rates on hardware between Toronto and Montreal to meet water competition would bring about a corresponding reduction in the rates on hardware between Halifax and Truro, Winnipeg and Regina, and every other two places in Canada. This kind of equalization would ruin the railways and utterly confound the established channels of trade within Canada. Therefore only a modified kind of equalization could be proposed.

When equalization came before the Board in January, 1951, the Chief Commissioner pointed out that the new legislation definitely changed the practice of the past and placed with the Board the initiative for accomplishing the purposes of the national policy on freight rates. The General Investigation of 1927 had been largely a matter of complaint and answer, whereas in 1952 the Board was starting off with a new mandate under the direction of Parliament to initiate an equalized rate structure.[32]

The new mandate proved short-lived. The Board soon found that agreement over the proposed rate scales would take longer than anticipated. In 1952 it said that it expected to have class rates equalized by January 1, 1954. In 1953 it postponed the effective date another year, but as a first step toward complete equalization it lowered class rates in Western Canada by 5 per cent while raising those in the East 10 per cent. Finally, effective March 1, 1955, it ordered that standard mileage class rates be made identical throughout Canada except on the White Pass and Yukon Route and in the Maritimes.

The rate of taper in the new rate scales was more pronounced than in the Board's original plan or in the scales currently in force. In other words, rates did not increase as rapidly with distance as formerly. It was expected that the new arrangement would benefit Western Canada more than the East because as a rule consumers and producers in the West are farther from sources of supply and from markets than those east of the Great Lakes. On the other hand the West would lose the constructive mileage, the use of a sort of artificial mileage of 290 for the purpose of computing rates instead of the actual mileage of 420 between Lakehead and Winnipeg. This constructive mileage, which also applies inland from ports on Canada's Pacific coast and from Churchill, Man., was important chiefly to Winnipeg. As the distance from ports lengthens, the value of constructive mileage declines in much the same way as a "free lift" of five miles in an automobile is important to a man who is walking ten miles but not to the man who has to walk nearly 200. Apparently Winnipeg believed that the general reduction in tolls in the West relative to those in the East which would be brought about by equalization and the psychological satisfaction of the final removal of the long-standing discontent over regional differences would compensate for loss of constructive mileage. Oddly enough, the Board's equalization plan partially restored a sort of constructive mileage which had long prevailed between Vancouver and Victoria, B.C. Until the Board's decision removing the mountain differential in 1949, these two cities had enjoyed identical rates on all long distance traffic. Thereafter, the distance (about 83 miles) between the two cities was taken into account in setting all rates. The Board proposed that under equalization this distance should be cut to 42 miles for rate-making purposes. The Board also departed from equalization in setting rates between Western Canada and the so-called triangle in southern Ontario as explained in chapter 2.

After dealing with standard mileage class rates, the Board turned its attention to other aspects of equalization. In September, 1957, it promulgated equalized commodity mileage scales on building brick and tile, sand, gravel and crushed stone, common clay, cinders, furnace slag, and cobble or rubble stone.[33] In the same Order it directed that commodity mileage scales on certain kinds of freight be abolished and that these goods thereafter be shipped under class rates. This had the effect of equalizing rates across Canada on cordwood, edgings, mill refuse, slabs, and sawdust, which were to be carried at Class 10, on scrap iron or steel (Class 20), on livestock (Class 40 for horses, mules and ponies; Class 33 for cattle, calves, sheep and hogs), and on potatoes (Class 30). In 1960 it deferred consideration of equalized rates on 76 commodities including anthracite coal, cement, sugar beet pulp, gluestock, lumber, and pulpwood.[34]

Meanwhile the Board had considered rates on domestic grain and grain products within Western Canada. This case was exceptionally complicated because the proposed scales were tied up with (a) the railways' need for additional revenue to cover their total financial requirements and the sensitivity of the West to higher tolls on its main export; (b) the submission of British Columbia that domestic grain rates in that province should, as a matter of law, be reduced to the level of the export grain rate at Vancouver, involving a cut of about 63 per cent; (c) a rather similar complaint by Vancouver that rates on domestic grain from the Prairies to British Columbia should be made upon the same basis as the statutory (Crow's Nest) rates from the Prairies to Lakehead, which would involve a reduction of roughly 67 per cent; (d) a submission by

British Columbia and Manitoba that, since domestic grain rates in the West were unjust and unreasonable, they should be cut by 30 per cent; and (e) the proposal of the railways that these rates be raised by 20 per cent "so as to place them more nearly in a proper position in the general rate structure."

Partly on account of what it called "the contradictory and interlocking nature of the proceedings," the Board made a careful study of its own. It compared the average weight per car, average length of haul, average revenue per ton-mile and average revenue per car-mile for dry onions, wooden shingles, nickel ore concentrates, plywood, canned foods, nails and wire, and so forth with similar data for grain. The Board concluded that the existing level of domestic grain rates in Western Canada did "not result in an unreasonably low return to the railways from a revenue standpoint." These rates had been subject to some, but not all, of the postwar general increases. As for the corresponding rates in the East, the Board said it lacked information on the volume of grain moved at competitive tolls. Presumably it had in mind both competition from trucks within Ontario and from American railroads between Buffalo and New York. Rates over these lines have, in the past, held down the amount which Canadian railways can charge on Western grain landed at ports on Georgian Bay and the Lower Lakes and sent on to Montreal, Halifax, etc., for export overseas. These tolls are commonly called ex-lake or "At and East" rates. The upshot of the Board's deliberations was that equalization was not imposed on domestic grain.[35] In 1967 At and East rates, but not those on domestic or locally-raised grain within Eastern Canada, were set by statute at the level which prevailed in 1961 and are subsidized by the Dominion.

Obviously equalization has not proved a success. It came too late for that. If it had been introduced after the Board's General Investigation of 1926–7, it would have helped allay the sense of grievance over freight rates that has existed in the West and in British Columbia for many years. Besides, in 1927 equalization could have been applied to the Maritimes which were then confident that with the aid of the Maritime Freight Rates Act they could profitably sell goods in Central Canada. Finally, the proportion of traffic moved under standard mileage class rates and distributing or "town" tariffs in 1927 was high enough to make it worthwhile for the Board to go ahead with the time-consuming work of equalizing scales on a basis that was fair to the railways and equitable to shippers in all parts of Canada.

By 1951, efforts at equalization were balked by several factors. First, as time went on, it became progressively harder to disturb trade relationships which had become adjusted, if not frozen, to a given scale of rates.

Second, highway competition had become intense, especially on high-rated goods that typically moved under class, not commodity, rates. Consequently, the proportion of classified traffic which was 21 per cent of all revenues in 1951 fell to 5 per cent in 1961. The decline would have been greater except for the Board's programme, described above, of substituting class rates for commodity rates on brick, stone, cordwood, scrap iron, etc., and for the change in the mixing rule in Western Canada, as explained in Chapter 6. If the figures are adjusted for these factors—as they ought to be in order to compare like with like—the decline in class traffic is even greater than the percentage shows. Another point, perhaps of some significance, is that membership of the Board of Transport Commissioners changed almost entirely during the 1950s. The new members may not have fully shared in the views of the Chief Commissioner in 1951. Finally, the West may have decided that the solution to its economic difficulties lay less in getting the same rates as other parts of Canada than in promoting the growth of highway transport, expanding the sales of Canadian grain abroad, developing secondary manufacturing within the area, and so on.

At all events the Royal Commission of 1961 stated that "the new approach [equalization] emphasized the disregard of the cost of service principle in the pricing of railway services" and quoted the Board to the effect that equalization called for "equality of tolls . . . even although the circumstances and conditions (for example, costs of railway operation, density of traffic) are not substantially similar."[36] Up to a point this is true. What the MacPherson Commission failed to stress was that within limits costs were overlooked in the interests of fairness and national unity.

The MacPherson Commission failed to express any clear opinion whether equalization should be retained, extended, or abolished. Yet the tenor of its report was that national transportation policy should be to rely mainly on cost. On the face of it, this would mean the restoration of the mountain differential, probably higher rates on the Prairies than in the East, and certainly higher tolls in the Maritimes and Newfoundland where rail costs per ton-mile are notoriously higher than the national average. Probably, the Commission should have put in a caveat about the restoration of regional differences. In any case it obviously hoped that competition from highway carriers would keep rail rates down and perhaps equalize them. It expected that haulage by road, already pervasive in the St. Lawrence Lowlands and significant elsewhere, would expand both geographically and vertically, that is, spread more evenly throughout the entire country, extend through longer hauls, and broaden out from more to less valuable goods. In short, so it would appear, the

Commission hoped that competition would accomplish regional equality of treatment which had not yet been secured by legislation except to a limited degree. Where this kind of competition was not likely to occur for many years because of the poor quality of the roads, as in Newfoundland, the Royal Commission would subsidize railway rates in order to lower the cost of transport to the shipper.

It seems to the author that both Royal Commissions proceeded on unsound premises. The first, that of 1951, underestimated the growing strength of competition and therefore its scheme of equalization by law had very limited results. The second Royal Commission, in 1961, saw the significance of competition but wrongfully assumed that it would soon be of approximately equal strength across the Dominion. This may eventually be true if strength is measured by the proportion of total ton-miles moving by highway, but it is not likely to be true if strength is measured by equality of cost and rates of road transport. The price of vehicles and fuel as well as the cost of roads relative to vehicle-miles or ton-miles will likely continue to be higher in the Prairie and Seaboard provinces than in Quebec and Ontario. If provincial governments carry out the recommendation of the MacPherson Commission that they recover the cost of roads from highway users, then it follows that taxes on each vehicle and on each gallon of fuel will be higher in eight provinces than in the two central ones. Of course, it is possible that some governments will decide to shift a large part of the costs of road transport to the general taxpayer by collecting inadequate revenue from highway users to meet the costs of its roads. In this way they may keep trucking rates lower than they would otherwise be, but hardly as low as in Ontario and Quebec because the tax on motor vehicles and fuel is only a fairly small part of the total costs of running a truck. Moreover, a policy of abnormally low rates on trucks and motor fuel would be directly contrary to one of the main objectives of the MacPherson Commission and the National Transportation Policy as laid down by Parliament in 1967. As far as practicable, users should pay the full costs of the services supplied to them, whether by governments or private business.

It is also possible that the Atlantic and Western Provinces will give up their persistent attempts to use freight rates as a means of offsetting their geographic and economic disabilities. They may turn their attention toward direct aid to farmers and fishermen, financial assistance to manufacturing and mining, etc. Alternatively, they will demand subsidies for the continued operation of unprofitable branch lines and passenger trains. By failing to take a definite stand on equalization and at the same time advocating a drastic rationalization of plant, the MacPherson Commission may have merely substituted one kind of regional complaint for another.

Provinces which complain of unfair treatment in some freight rates, commonly overlook their advantages in other freight rates. The Atlantic Provinces have the Maritime Freight Rates Act; southern Ontario and Quebec the greater effectiveness of competition from carriers by water and highway; the Prairie Provinces have the Crow's Nest and related rates; British Columbia has low transcontinental tolls, while the higher costs of constructing and operating railways in mountainous territory are "smeared" across the entire country.

To sum up, the National Transportation Act of 1967 clearly implied, in some of its sections, that rates should be based on cost and that railways should be allowed to rationalize their plant in order to bring their costs in line with their revenues. But other sections of the legislation provided that railways be paid subsidies which, to begin with, would be general and then eventually would be tied to the continued operation of uneconomic branch lines and passenger trains. Thus, several sections of the Act are basically inconsistent with each other. Finally, by failing to lay down better guidelines for the determination of the general level of rates, the legislation left several critical questions in substantially the same position as they were in 1958. The new Canadian Transport Commission, like the old Board of Transport Commissioners, will have to determine the financial requirements of the railways and, in addition, decide whether any further revenues which they need will be secured by selective increases or by an attempt to raise rates generally.

4

Rates on Export Grain

FREIGHT RATES on grain exported from Western Canada would be important in Canadian transportation even though Parliament never passed a statute that directly affected them. Large sections of the Canadian Prairies are climatically suited only for the growth of cereals and for grass for cattle and sheep. After the end of World War II, the overall dependence on wheat was lessened by the discovery of petroleum, natural gas, and potash, the steady development of mixed farming in parts of Manitoba and southern Alberta, the expansion of manufacturing in Winnipeg and elsewhere, and the exploitation of the mineral, forestry, and fishery resources of the adjacent parts of the Shield. Even so, wheat is still the mainstay of large areas, particularly in Saskatchewan. When our policy on freight rates was being formulated, it was the basis of the economy of the entire area.

In the production of wheat, the Canadian West has several advantages: intelligent farmers, fertile soils, level fields which permit the use of tractors and other power-driven machinery, and efficient transport. On the other hand, the average amount of precipitation, never much above the minimum for the growth of wheat, may fall below this level from time to time. When precipitation is subnormal, yields decline and, though quality normally improves, this fact is little consolation to the farmer whose crop is so poor that it will not pay him to harvest it. Because wheat is produced in many parts of the world besides Canada, the world price may be low notwithstanding a poor crop in the Dominion. The converse is also true: a big Canadian crop may coincide with a high world price. Hence, as a result of climatic and worldwide economic conditions, the money incomes of farmers in Western Canada are unstable from year to year.

This instability in income is aggravated by the comparatively high and fixed cost of transport and of handling grain in elevators. Broadly speaking, these charges are deducted from the world price before arriving at the net price on the farm. Let us suppose that the world price, usually taken as the price in Liverpool, is $2.00 a bushel and that the cost of transport, etc., is 35 cents a bushel. If the price in Liverpool falls by 10 per cent, that is, from $2.00 to $1.80, the net to the Canadian farmer will shrink from $2.00 minus 35 cents to $1.80 minus 35 cents. Thus, the farmer gets $1.45 instead of $1.65. The decline in his net return is 12.12 per cent as a result of a drop of 10 per cent in Liverpool. If the fall in the world price is 50 per cent, the decline in the farmer's net will be nearly 67 per cent. In other words, the comparative rigidity of the cost of moving grain from the farm to the world market results in any decline in world price impinging with greater severity on the net return to wheat-growers.

Western Canadians also point out that they are farther removed from cheap ocean transport than other large wheat exporters. The Argentine, Australia, and India have relatively short hauls by rail and then long, but cheap, transport across the high seas. The grain exporting areas of the United States are closer to Lakehead (central Minnesota to Duluth) or the Pacific coast (the "Inland Empire" around Spokane to Seattle) than Canadian wheatfields are to Fort William, Port Arthur, and Vancouver. That part of the Laurentian Shield which lies directly west of Lake Superior is relatively narrow inland from Duluth but broad to the west of Fort William. The Rocky Mountain Plateau is comparatively wide in the United States but pinches out north of the border. Admittedly, the Canadian West gains from being able to use fairly cheap water transport along the Great Lakes and St. Lawrence River. It also benefits from the short haul across the north Atlantic. This advantage is not as great as might appear at first sight because ocean shipping is typically much cheaper per ton-mile than transport by rail. So, taking one thing with another, Canadian grain-growers suffer from their inland or land-locked position relative to their competitors in the United States or the southern hemisphere.

The dependence of the Canadian West on rail transport has been reduced by some changes in technology and increased by others. In the main, railways are financially more interested in the size of the crop than they are with either its quality or its price. Nevertheless, they always hope that farmers will get a good price for their grain, for if they do, they will be able to buy more machinery, household furniture, clothing and "store goods" of all kinds than if prices were depressed. Unfortunately for the railways, the growth of highway transport has deprived them of much of the business which is induced by good prices for grain. They have lost what they regard as the cream of their business and so are financially less able to carry grain at low, or skim milk, rates.

On the other hand, technological change has certainly stimulated the movement of some kinds of freight, even by rail. The shift from horse-drawn to power-driven machinery has led to the movement of gasoline and diesel fuel by rail, highway, and pipeline. But farmers are now dependent for power on products raised off the farm, rather than on horses, hay, and oats which were formerly produced on the farm itself. Freight rates on the new machinery and on the fossil fuels required to operate it are comparatively rigid from one year to the next. This increases the pressure on the farmer whenever the price of grain declines or he experiences a bad crop. The pressure leads him to protest against any increases whatsoever in freight rates.

What is more, the new equipment permits each farmer to cultivate a larger area than before. It has reduced the number of people living on farms and thereby cut down the overall consumption of foodstuffs, clothing, household equipment, and the like. This factor has, of course, been offset by an improved standard of living which has raised the level of consumption per capita and by the growth of urban population.

In order to minimize their losses in traffic and revenues brought about by changing techniques in raising grain and by highway transport, railways have tried to reduce their costs. Their efforts in some directions, such as closing redundant stations and introducing diesel locomotives, could progress without significant opposition from the public. But cost-reducing measures in other directions, notably the abandonment of non-paying branch lines, have been bitterly opposed.

In sum, railways have been unable to hang on to the better-paying classes of freight and have been left to perform the task of carrying grain at comparatively low tolls between country elevators and terminals at Lakehead and Vancouver. They might be able to handle grain on a profitable basis if wages and costs of railway equipment and supplies had remained at the level of the 1940s or if, notwithstanding inflation, they had been able to rationalize their plant so as to reduce their costs drastically. Despite a broadening in the economy of the Prairie Provinces since 1945, grain-growing with all its basic uncertainties continues to be the staple of large parts of the West and the rates on grain remain one of Canada's major problems in transport.

Crow's Nest Pass Agreement, 1897

Although rail connections between the West and the eastern parts of

Canada were completed in the early 1880s, the development of Western Canada languished. Population remained sparse, the price of grain in world markets was relatively depressed, and yields were reduced by drought and grasshoppers. Most of all, the Prairies lacked varieties of grain which would give heavy yields per acre in an area with rather low and uncertain rainfall and which would mature in the comparatively short period that was free from killing frost. Yet as so often happens, criticism was not directed toward this basic and long-run problem but to those things which could be quickly changed.

In 1897 the Crow's Nest Pass Agreement was signed by the Dominion government and the Canadian Pacific.[1] This Agreement granted the Railway a cash bonus amounting eventually to about $3,400,000 for the construction of a railway from Lethbridge through Crowsnest Pass to Nelson, B.C. In return the Company undertook to reduce by 3 cents per hundred pounds the then existing rates on grain and flour from all points in the West to Fort William, Port Arthur, and points east thereof, by September 1, 1899. From Brandon, which was roughly the centre of wheat production at the time, this reduction amounted to 19 per cent. In addition, on various commodities from Eastern Canada westbound, the Railway cut rates by various percentages: fresh fruit 33⅓, coal-oil (kerosene) 20; cordage, implements, pipe, horseshoes, wire, building materials, livestock, and furniture 10. Finally the Company conveyed certain coal-bearing lands in southern British Columbia to the Dominion for the purpose of securing a sufficient and suitable supply of coal to the public at reasonable prices. In brief, in return for a cash subsidy, the Canadian Pacific reduced freight rates on the chief export of the region and on settlers' requirements inbound. The concessions were made without any time limit.

The Agreement has occupied such a large place in the controversies over railway rates in Canada that in the course of time the reasons for its adoption have often become distorted. Sir William Van Horne, then general manager of the Canadian Pacific, has been credited with enormous vision because he saw that low rates would induce new settlement, increase the volume and the profitability of the Railway's traffic, and enormously enhance the value of the Company's extensive holdings of land. Alternatively, he has been called stupid because he failed to see that operating costs might rise and therefore it was foolish to agree to cut rates without limit of time. With other purposes in mind, some speakers have lauded the Laurier Government for its magnificent foresight in making sure that the West would get the benefit of low rates on its chief export in perpetuity. Railway and Government have both been credited with nation-building on a grand scale.

The fact is that the subsidy permitted the Canadian Pacific to build a line of railway which it had planned for some time. The branch would open up valuable mineral areas in southern British Columbia and would prevent the district from becoming economically tributary to the American lines which were entering from the south. The development of the district would provide a welcome nearby market for ranchers in Alberta. The Province of Manitoba proposed to aid construction of a direct line from Winnipeg to Duluth unless the Canadian Pacific reduced rates. This threat must have had an influence on executives in Montreal. Besides, the Railway was showing signs of growing prosperity and was financially in a better position than formerly to take a chance on reducing rates in order to stimulate business. Still, the Railway's chief motive seems to have been to get a line into southern British Columbia as cheaply and quickly as it could.

On the part of the Government, there was undoubtedly a desire to open up an important mining area by a Canadian line and the wish to be reasonably friendly with the financial interests controlling the Canadian Pacific. More particularly, the proprietors of the Toronto *Globe* who were very influential with the government stood to benefit materially from the development of southern British Columbia. The *Manitoba Free Press* openly accused Mr. Robert Jaffray and Senator G. A. Cox of the *Globe* of being "at the head of a syndicate that have taken over the charter of the British Columbia Southern Railway which controls several million acres of land including coal deposits of the Crow's Nest Pass and are now negotiating with the Government for the construction of the road." The *Globe* did not deny the fact, contenting itself with defending the proposed agreement on the grounds of public policy.

Manitoba Agreement

In 1901, only four years after the Crow's Nest Pass Agreement was signed, it became a dead letter for all practical purposes. This was because farmers in Manitoba, at this time virtually the only grain-growing area in the West, wanted still lower rates on grain. Local merchants pointed out that the reduction in rates on settlers' effects inbound tended to favour Montreal and Toronto as distributing centres rather than Winnipeg. The province as a whole, still resentful of the virtual monopoly which the Canadian Pacific had possessed, disliked giving it another grant. Manitoba was convinced that only a competing railway to Lakehead would solve her problem. In 1901 the province leased the facilities in Canada (355 miles) of the bankrupt Northern Pacific and by agreement assigned the lease to the Canadian Northern.[2] The latter road was the child not merely of William Mackenzie and Donald Mann but of a growing financial clique in Toronto centring round the Canadian Bank of Commerce in opposition to the well-established Canadian Pacific– Bank of Montreal group in Montreal. The Canadian Northern consolidated the Northern Pacific lines with its own original nucleus, the Manitoba Railway and Canal Company, running from Dauphin to Portage la Prairie. It then built a road into Port Arthur. Manitoba guaranteed the bonds on all these lines, and the railway agreed to reduce the existing rate on grain from Manitoba to Lake Superior by more than 4 cents per hundred pounds and the rates on all other freight in both directions by more than 15 per cent of the rates then in force.[3]

For a time the Canadian Pacific refused to reduce its rates to the level of those on the Canadian Northern. The latter had neither branch lines, equipment, nor elevators to move a considerable volume of grain and thus its competition was ineffective. However, because complaints of gross injustice arose from farmers not on Canadian Northern lines, in 1903 the Manitoba Government got the Canadian Pacific to reduce its rates on grain from Winnipeg to Lakehead by three cents, provided the reductions of the Canadian Northern on grain were limited to the same amount. Then the Canadian Pacific voluntarily cut the rate on grain from what is now Saskatchewan and Alberta by two cents and on other commodities by $7\frac{1}{2}$ per cent. Finally, in 1910, to prevent unjust discrimination, the Board of Railway Commissioners ordered rates in Alberta and Saskatchewan to be reduced by another $7\frac{1}{2}$ per cent, thus equalizing the scales across the Prairies.[4]

One important trend from 1897 to 1903 was the reduction in the rates on wheat and settlers' effects as a result of agreements between railways and governments. In both the Manitoba and the Crow's Nest Pass agreements one railway company received a subsidy but its competitors had to meet the reductions even though they received no *quid pro quo*. Railways voluntarily cut the rates on some commodities with the object of encouraging development in the West, increasing the volume of their traffic, and adding to the sale value of their land grants. In particular they reduced rates on farm implements from Lakehead to most points in the West below the agreed rates. Thus, west of the Great Lakes, the carriers adopted a definite policy of maintaining the class rates but of cutting charges on the chief article of export, on settlers' effects, and on agricultural machinery. Dominion and provincial governments and railways had a common policy of fitting the rate structure to the needs of the developing West.

During the first decade of the twentieth century Western Canada enjoyed unexampled prosperity. The price level was rising. Money was cheap and Canadians could borrow on easy terms for investment in railways, farms, and factories. While borrowing large sums from Britain, Canadians took advantage of the most advanced agricultural methods and machinery from the United States where climatic and economic conditions were similar to those in Canada. By 1900 the American West was fairly well filled up and settlers from Europe were readily turned to Canada by the lure of free land. An immigration policy, intelligently conceived and aggressively administered by the federal government and the railways, took every advantage of favourable general conditions. New types of grain suitable to the peculiar climatic conditions of the West were developed. Yields per acre were consistently good and foodstuffs were easily sold in Europe.

Undoubtedly low rates on export grain were a powerful but by no means the determining factor in the prosperity. It is significant that after about 1900 cost of transferring grain from the West to Liverpool was reduced at almost every stage—at local and especially at terminal elevators (through improvements in equipment for handling grain and in elevator construction), on the Great Lakes, and on the high seas.[5] These lower costs gave the farmer a relatively higher net return than formerly, thus accelerating the pace of settlement.

During this period the West cried for more railways and equipment. Owing to widespread prosperity, complaints about the level of rates ceased. The railway network was steadily extended, usually in anticipation of settlement. The Canadian Pacific built new branches at an average annual rate of over 380 miles for the years 1898 to 1915 inclusive, or more than a mile a day every day for eighteen years. It double-tracked some Western mileage and built facilities to handle grain cheaply from ports on Georgian Bay to Montreal. Simultaneously the Canadian Northern pushed its lines throughout the Prairies. The Grand Trunk Pacific was constructed between Prince Rupert and Winnipeg and thence, as the National Transcontinental, to Quebec City and Moncton. The purpose of the extension east of Winnipeg was to give a direct rail route from the Prairies to the Atlantic so that Canadian grain could be exported through Canadian and not through United States ports. Finally, American railroad executives, especially Mr. James J. Hill, were casting covetous glances at Canada and there were rumours that Hill's Great Northern would build still another complete line in Canada from the Great Lakes to the Pacific.

In spite of all this actual and proposed construction, there were many complaints that rail facilities were not being provided quickly enough. Furthermore, objections were raised to the fact that much of the land owned by the Canadian Pacific throughout the Prairies was exempt from taxation. Yet, on the whole, the period from 1903 to 1915 was one of expanding railway facilities in the West, rather than a time when the level of rates formed an important matter of public interest.

Wartime Increases

By early 1917 the war began to have a pronounced effect on Canadian railways. Owing to the lack of any comprehensive system of price and wage control, its urgent demands steadily increased wages and commodity prices. Railway operating expenses increased much more rapidly than net railway revenues and so in 1917 all the companies applied for an immediate increase of 15 per cent in freight rates and passenger fares.

On the basis of the evidence presented before it, the Board readily concluded that there could "be no question in view of the actual results, that railways require greater revenues and must have them if proper efficiency is to be maintained and the demand of the country for transportation at all adequately met."[6]

The Board then had to face the problem of the Manitoba and Crow's Nest Pass agreements. It felt that, however justified special agreements on rates might be, they should not be used to create or perpetuate unjust discrimination which was forbidden by the Railway Act. From this point of view the agreements might be set aside. But the Railway Act specifically exempted "Special Acts" from the Board's jurisdiction. The Board decided that the Manitoba Agreement, being the act of a provincial legislature, was not a "Special Act" within the meaning of the Railway Act. Consequently, it had the legal authority to raise rates above the level provided in it. On the other hand, the Crow's Nest Pass Agremeent, which had been confirmed by the Dominion Parliament, did bind the Board and so it limited the size of the increase which it could legally authorize on grain from Western Canada and on settlers' needs inbound.

In the end, the Board raised most rates by 15 per cent but made numerous modifications in order not to disturb existing trade relationships any more than necessary, especially between different parts of the country. In the West rates on grain were raised 2 cents per hundred pounds or roughly 10 per cent, thus keeping them below the Crow's Nest Pass level. The new rates were to be effective on February 1, 1918, but shippers of wheat, coarse grains, lumber, livestock, and some other commodities were so vigorous in their complaints that the Board postponed the increases until March 15 and on grain until June 1. The postponements left the Grand Trunk and Canadian Northern without some revenue which they sorely needed. Meanwhile, the Canadian Pacific was able to earn a higher rate of return on its capitalization than the government considered reasonable. Consequently, it had to submit to special taxes levied by Order-in-Council passed under authority of the War Measures Act. When this authority expired one year after the armistice, the Canadian Pacific came within the provisions of the Income War Tax Act.

In 1918 the general level of railway tolls was raised by 25 per cent and in 1920 by a further 40 per cent.[7] In consequence, rates reached the highest level authorized in Canada up to that time. Moreover, on July 27, 1918, the government exercised its authority under the War Measures Act to pass an Order-in-Council permitting rates on export grain to be raised above the level set by the Crow's Nest Pass Agreement.

above
Crow's Nest
See Roche
p. 129
q 130

Immediate Postwar Reductions

reductions

Late in 1920 prices of commodities crashed and a severe but, as it happened, relatively short depression occurred. In order to ease the strain on business and to bring rates more in line with what the traffic was able to bear, the railways voluntarily made a number of important reductions, notably on grain, livestock, hay, lumber, wool, and hides. In July, 1921, railways in Canada and the United States cut wages and in August the Board held informal discussions with the railways on rate reductions. The Canadian Pacific argued that lower rates would imperil payment of dividends on its ordinary shares, while the other railroads feared they would be unable to cover their operating expenses. As things turned out, prices of materials and rates of wages continued to decline and the Canadian Pacific had better net earnings than it expected. Accordingly, the Board reduced rates effective December 1, 1921. The reductions were made in a complicated way but, taking one thing with another, ranged between 10 and 15 per cent.

CPR
against

Special Committee, 1922

After December 1, 1921, no important changes in rates were made until July, 1922. In order to explain these, it is necessary to go back to the discussions in Parliament during the sessions of 1918 and 1919 relating to the revision and consolidation of the Railway Act of 1907. It will be recalled that the Cabinet, acting under the authority of the War Measures Act of 1914, had passed an Order-in-Council virtually exempting the Board of Railway Commissioners from the restrictions of the Crow's Nest Pass Agreement which, as a "Special Act" within the meaning of the Railway Act, would otherwise have prevented the Board from raising rates above those set out in the Crow's Nest Pass Agreement.

In the session of 1918 the House of Commons passed a Railway Consolidation Bill which made no reference whatever to Special Acts. In the Senate the leader of the government party moved that the powers of the Board should not be restricted by the provisions of any Special Act heretofore enacted or by any agreement heretofore or hereafter made. This amendment would give the Board complete control over freight rates and permanently abrogate the Crow's Nest Pass and Manitoba agreements. But Senator Watson from Portage la Prairie, acting at the instance of the Government of Manitoba, strenuously objected to the proposed amendment.

The Railway Consolidation Bill, not having been passed in the 1918 session, came up again in 1919. This time the Commons specifically stipulated that the Board should not excuse any allegation of unjust discrimination on the ground that it was justified or required by any special agreement. Again Senator Watson objected. Eventually the Senate agreed to accept the Commons' proposal but with the proviso, later accepted by the Commons, that the removal of the restrictions on the Board's power should remain in force for a period of only three years. In other words, until July 6, 1922, but not thereafter, rates might be above the level of the Crow's Nest Pass Agreement or any other "Special Act."

Early in the session of 1922, in view of the approaching expiration of the suspension of the Agreement, the government, instead of doing the logical thing of referring the matter to the Board of Railway Commissioners, appointed a "Special Committee of the House on Railway Transportation Costs." The personnel of the Committee was impressive but the practice of referring such complicated technical matters as freight rates to an unskilled political body cannot be too strongly condemned. The only reason for a committee in this case was that the West had completely lost faith in the Railway Commission, largely because of the injudicious public addresses of Chief Commissioner F. B. Carvell. He had told the West its rates were already low enough, had defended the Canadian Pacific, criticized the projected Hudson Bay Railway on which the West had set its heart, and had attacked railway labour.

In the hearings before the Committee the railways argued that they had already voluntarily made several reductions in rates on farm products and that rates in general had been reduced by the Board's order of December 1, 1921. In particular they emphasized that the complete restoration of the Crow's Nest Pass Agreement would seriously deplete their revenues at a time when railway operating costs were still high. They claimed that although the Agreement applied only to the limited number of commodities named in it and legally would be restricted to Canadian Pacific lines in existence in 1897, nonetheless, restoration of the Agreement would force down practically all rates across Canada, for the Board was legally obliged to prevent unjust discrimination between commodities and localities and thus would have to reduce many other rates in all parts of the country.

On the other side of the case, the agricultural interests contended that the Agreement was a legally binding contract. Although the Canadian Pacific had taken the subsidy, the West had never received any protection under the contract. As soon as the maxima came to be charged, the Canadian Pacific complained and was relieved of its obligations. Moreover, restoration of the 1899 rates was essential if the West was to get necessary relief from depressed agricultural conditions.

In any event the problem was decided from the standpoint of politics rather than economics. The Liberal Government, lacking a clear majority of seats in the Commons, was dependent on the Progressive party, a farmers' bloc of 65 members, for support. Moreover, the Liberal party was itself divided between a protectionist and a low-tariff group. In the end the Special Committee recommended that the Agreement be suspended for a further period of two years except that the rates on grain and flour should be restored at once to the level set by the Crow's Nest Pass Agreement. This proposal was accepted by Parliament[8] and shortly thereafter the budget was passed with some Progressive support, notwithstanding that it did not go nearly so far in lowering tariffs as most farmers in the West had hoped for.

To outline the political reasons for the restoration is not to suggest that economic arguments could not be made to justify the Government's action. Relief to agriculture and the fact that the benefits from lower rates on grain would be shared by all Canada, including railways, through a revival in general business, could be urged as reasons for the restoration of the Agreement. But these economic arguments could easily be honoured beyond their deserts. The Agreement gave the West a legal claim for rates lower than it could have secured on clear economic principles and the political circumstances of the moment favoured the attainment of the West's desires.

At about this time a new factor entered. The original Crow's Nest Pass Agreement applied only to traffic through Lakehead, but with the opening of the Panama Canal, Vancouver had become an important exporting centre and was anxious to extend its tributary area further backward into the plains. Hence Premier John Oliver appeared before the Special Committee to argue for the same basis of rates in British

Columbia as on the Prairies. He demanded the application of the Crow's Nest Pass rates westbound through Vancouver and the abolition of the mountain differential. He said the latter was a violation of the spirit of Confederation. His province had joined the Dominion only on condition that a transcontinental railway line be built and this implied the same rates all across the country. If for sake of argument, Premier Oliver continued, the Board was right in finding that Canadian Pacific costs in the mountains were higher, mile for mile, than on the Prairies, costs on the Canadian National (the former Canadian Northern) were no more because its route avoided stiff grades and expensive tunnels. The Province should not be made indefinitely to pay for the Canadian Pacific's mistake in choosing the less favourable route. Notwithstanding Premier Oliver's pleas, the Special Committee of 1922 did not specifically consider British Columbia's claims for equalization of rates. Indeed the Committee's recommendation that Crow's Nest rates on grain and flour eastbound be restored put British Columbia under a greater relative handicap than before.

Reductions, 1922

In the meantime the Board had been giving further study to the general level of freight rates particularly in the light of the Order-in-Council of 1920 (P.C. 2434) which directed it to consider the financial requirements of the Canadian Pacific alone and to equalize freight rates across Canada. By the time the Board was ready to hand down its judgment on June 30, 1922, it had before it the evidence submitted by the railways before the Special Committee of the House. There the railways had proposed reductions on several basic commodities totalling $8,340,000. Instead of accepting this proposal the Government, for reasons already given, enforced the Crow's Nest rates on grain. In consequence gross revenues would decline by something less than $7,200,000. Deducting the latter sum from the total reduction voluntarily offered, left about $1,200,000 still available for reductions in rates. The Board calculated that this amount would be the equivalent of a reduction of 7½ per cent on the rates then in effect on freight other than grain under the Crow's Nest Pass Agreement as amended. So the Board reduced rates by this amount. It will be noted that, instead of dealing in detail with the financial conditions of the Canadian Pacific, the Board took as the basis of its rate adjustments the amount of the reductions offered to the parliamentary committee by the Company.

The Board repeated many of its early statements about differences in operating conditions in the East, on the Prairies, and in the mountains.[9]

It also referred to the controlling effect of competition with American railroads and Great Lakes steamships in Eastern Canada. It rejected British Columbia's argument that, by charging higher tolls in that province, the Canadian Pacific was breaking the contract made between that Company and the Dominion in 1881. The province had not been a party to the contract and hence had no standing in court as regards any breach of it. Nevertheless, the Board did reduce the standard mileage class rates in British Columbia to bring them more closely to the level on the Prairies.

Export Grain Westbound

British Columbia and Alberta appealed this decision to the Cabinet on the ground that the Board had not dealt specifically with the rates on grain for export through Vancouver and other Pacific coast ports. The Cabinet referred the case back to the board[10] which subsequently explained that after the parliamentary restoration of the Crow's Nest rates in 1922, it had realized that complaints of unjust discrimination against Vancouver would arise and hence had reduced rates westbound by 20 per cent.[11] Now British Columbia and Alberta were requesting the application of the Crow's Nest rates westbound.

In dealing with this request the Board pointed out the intimate connection between United States and Canadian export rates. It emphasized the importance of port competition for Canadian and American grain being exported through Montreal, Portland, Boston, New York, Baltimore, Philadelphia, Newport News, and Galveston. The Board had to keep this competition in mind in setting export grain rates within Canada.

Although the two Western provinces wanted the Crow's Nest rates applied to export wheat westbound, the Board felt that rates set by Parliament for particular reasons and under special conditions were not to be taken as a basis or standard for other rates. Except for the Crow's Nest rates on grain, all tolls were to be set by the Board in full exercise of its jurisdiction to fix just and reasonable tolls.

The majority decision of the Board was to arrive at rates on grain being exported through Vancouver by taking the mileage and rates on grain from Port McNicoll on Georgian Bay to Montreal and adding thereto the mileage and rates from a number of points in the West to Lakehead. This gave the actual rail rate from these specific points to Montreal after eliminating the lake movement where rates were set by competitive forces and not by the Board. To simplify matters, the Board took Cantaur, Sask., as the basis for rates. It is mid-way between Fort

William and Vancouver on the main line of the Canadian Pacific. Its export rate to Vancouver was about 10 per cent more than its rate to Fort William plus the rate from Port McNicoll to Montreal. Accordingly the Board, while denying the letter of the Crow's Nest Pass rates through Vancouver, reduced them by 10 per cent. Commissioner Oliver, dissenting, said that it was more realistic to ignore the charge from ports on Georgian Bay to Montreal. Accordingly, he would take the railway station equidistant between Vancouver and Fort William and scale the rates down equally in both directions from there, provided costs of operation were identical along both routes. An expert inquiry would be needed to determine a fair allowance for hauling grain through the mountains. Hence, Commissioner Oliver did not find it necessary exactly to define the rates westbound over the Canadian Pacific from the prairies to Vancouver.

Crow's Nest Pass Rates, 1924-5

Although the decision of the majority of the Board to reduce export grain rates westbound by 10 per cent went immediately into effect, the question of the Crow's Nest Pass Agreement was by no means settled. The two-year exemption of the limitation of the Agreement on the powers of the Board was due to expire on July 6, 1924. Early in that year the railways petitioned the Cabinet for a further suspension of the entire Act. They claimed that operating costs were 140 per cent higher than in 1897. Great disparities would result from the restoration of the Agreement since the Canadian Pacific intended to apply it only to its mileage in operation in 1897 and to the products enumerated. The Canadian National would have to meet these rates at competitive points. Like the Canadian Pacific, it could ill afford a loss in revenue.

Counsel for the West argued, however, that the contract between the Canadian Pacific and the people should be enforced. The Agreement had been suspended only because of temporary wartime conditions. Until 1922 it had never afforded the West any protection because the maximum had never been charged except between 1897, the date of the Crow's Nest Pass Agreement, and 1902, when the Manitoba Agreement came into effect. Toward the end of World War I when rates were again raised to the level of the Crow's Nest Pass Agreement, the Canadian Pacific had complained and the Agreement had been abrogated.

Meanwhile the general political situation, always significant where freight rates on grain are concerned, had become clarified. The Liberals had arrived at a more complete understanding with the Progressives. The retirement of Sir Lomer Gouin, who led the protectionist Liberals, had left the lower tariff group more largely in control of the party. Nevertheless on the freight rate question the wishes of the Progressives, most of whom came from the Prairie Provinces, could not be ignored. Hence the Liberals took no action. And so on July 7, 1924, the Crow's Nest Pass Agreement was restored in its entirety, i.e., not only on grain and flour eastbound from the West for export but westbound on the various settlers' needs originally stipulated.

In anticipation of this possibility the Canadian Pacific had filed with the Board tariffs based on the Crow's Nest scale. These new rates applied only to Canadian Pacific lines in both Eastern and Western Canada as they existed in 1897. The Canadian National filed similar rates at competitive points, both roads retaining existing schedules at points not on the 1897 lines of the Canadian Pacific. The result was chaos in the rate structure. Manufacturers of similar products only a few miles apart paid quite different rates to the West because one place was on a Canadian Pacific line which existed in 1897 and the other was not. It was inevitable that complaints should pour into the Government from all parts of the country. These were turned over to the Board of Railway Commissioners, the Government contending that it was the duty of the Board to consider charges of unjust discrimination.

In its decision,[12] October 14, 1924, the majority of the Board, after extensive citations, held that their powers were not circumscribed by the Agreement; that the Crow's Nest rates were fixed by agreement and not by statute; that an agreement did not bind the Board; and that it was not to be allowed indirectly to control rates on competitive lines of a railway not a party to it. The Board's function was to determine just and reasonble rates. In a word, the Board restored the rates in effect prior to July 7, 1924. This decision was directly contrary to the board's own ruling in 1917. Two commissioners, Dr. McLean, who had been on the Board at the earlier date, and Commissioner Oliver, dissented.

The decision of the majority raised a storm of protest in the West which had, of course, lost the actual benefit of the low Crow's Nest rates on commodities from the East and the potential gain from further reductions which might have to be made to eliminate the unjust discrimination which these rates inevitably entailed. Manitoba, Saskatchewan, and Alberta got leave to appeal to the Supreme Court. Meanwhile, the Cabinet on December 25, 1924 (P.C. 2220), suspended the operation of the Board's order of October 14 pending the decision of the Supreme Court. Thus the full Agreement was brought back into operation on the Canadian Pacific lines as they existed in 1897 and at competitive points on other railways. The situation which had held from July 7 to October 14 was reinstated.

On February 26, 1925, the Supreme Court rendered its decision on the several questions of law which had been submitted to it.[13] Briefly, the Court ruled that: (1) as a matter of law the Board of Railway Commissioners is not empowered to authorize rates in excess of the maximum rates referred to in the Crow's Nest Pass Act; (2) the Crow's Nest rates apply only between points which are on the lines of the Canadian Pacific as they existed at the date (1897) of making the Agreement. "Parliament, having by statute assumed the obligations under the Agreement, must change or amend them by statute."

The court's opinion threw the whole matter back into the political arena. By this time the political power of the western Progressives was well recognized and the insistence, if not the justice, of their cause appreciated in all parts of Canada. Without much discussion Parliament approved legislation[14] which, while it suspended the Agreement indefinitely, continued the Crow's Nest rates on grain and flour through Fort William and applied them from every point in the West eastbound to Lakehead, not merely from points on the 1897 lines of the Canadian Pacific. The Minister of Railways and Canals explained that railways could not stand the application of the Crow's Nest rates in their entirety. Since unjust discrimination is forbidden by the Railway Act, the Board of Railway Commissioners could not use these statutory rates on grain as criteria for the reasonableness of other rates in Canada.

The Minister stated that by this legislation the East got freedom from discrimination. The West got the Crow's Nest rates on grain on all lines between British Columbia and Lakehead, a total of over 17,000 miles, instead of fewer than 3,000 miles of the Canadian Pacific line in 1897. Members of Parliament from British Columbia objected that there was discrimination against that province, but Government spokesmen declared that the Agreement had not affected British Columbia before and did not now.

Order 36769

On June 5, 1925, the Cabinet directed the Board of Railway Commissioners to make a general investigation of the entire freight-rate structure of the country. In particular, it ordered the Board to consider the encouragement of the movement of freight through Canadian ports and to deal with the increase in traffic westward and eastward through Pacific ports owing to the expansion of trade with the Orient and the opening of the Panama Canal.

In November, 1924, some months before the General Investigation was ordered, a newly appointed Chief Commissioner and another member of the Board held a session in Vancouver to discuss routine matters. By their leave, at the last moment there was added to the agenda a petition from the province of British Columbia that there be applied to the movement of grain westbound through Vancouver the Crow's Nest basis of rates that were applicable to traffic eastbound through Fort William. After receiving a certain amount of testimony the two commissioners reserved judgment. Nearly a year later, in August, 1925, Vancouver shipping interests protested against the delay in handing down an opinion on the case. On September 2 the Board voted 3 to 2 to consider this case as part of the General Investigation. Later on the same day the two commissioners who had sat in Vancouver issued Order 36769 applying the Crow's Nest Pass rates to grain westbound for export. Two other commissioners called the action of their colleagues "incredible and grotesque."[15] Shipping interests in the East appealed the Order to the full Board which, by the time of the hearing on the appeal and thanks to a new appointment, had its full complement of six members. The Board divided evenly on the appeal and so, in accordance with normal legal procedure, the Order stood.

Then the three westernmost provinces protested that railways were not conforming with the Order. The Canadian Pacific was basing its rates on grain from Calgary to Vancouver not on its own direct mileage (642), but on the longer mileage via the Canadian National from Edmonton to Vancouver (766). As a result, a station on the Canadian Pacific 876 miles from Vancouver took the same rate as one 1000 miles from Fort William. Complainants said this practice was in direct contravention of Order 36769 which required that Crow's Nest rates be applied on the same basis on export grain westbound as eastbound.

The Board heard the appeal in February, 1926, but withheld judgment until completion of the General Investigation. It also refused leave to British Columbia to prosecute the Canadian Pacific for failure to obey the Order. The Supreme Court rejected a complaint from Alberta that railways were breaking the law. Finally, Alberta and Saskatchewan appealed to the Cabinet which declared that "Order 36769 was clear and unambiguous and need not be varied or added to."[16]

Rates on Export Grain, 1927–60

The upshot of the long and bitter controversy of the 1920s was that rates on grain exported from Western Canada through Lakehead were held down by acts of Parliament to the level prevailing in 1899. Rates on grain exported through Canada's ports on the Pacific coast were kept at roughly the same level by order of the Board of Railway Commissioners.

Since 1899 rates of wages have risen, materials cost more, traffic has grown in volume, numerous technological improvements have taken place, interest rates declined and then rose; yet rates on export grain are unchanged. On no other commodity in Canada and probably in no other part of the world are rates held down by statute to the level prevailing in the nineteenth century. Furthermore, though grain rates were originally applicable on westbound grain over 3,000 track-miles of one company, today they apply in both directions and over 17,000 track-miles of the Canadian Pacific, Canadian National, and Northern Alberta railways. They have sometimes held down the rates on domestic grain in the West and apply to more grain products than originally.[17] They may have been responsible for increasing the tolls on all other commodities in Canada.

Carriers recognize the importance of having the rates on grain as low as possible because Canadian grain growers suffer from the geographical disability of being landlocked. At the same time railways emphasize that rates ought to be high enough to give them a fair remuneration for the work they do. They had complained about the low statutory and related rates in the 1920s and 1930s but, as railway executives said later, they learned to live with them. As long as these rates covered out-of-pocket costs and made some contribution to overhead, railways did not suffer too much. By carrying a large volume of export grain at a low net yield per ton-mile, they got a tolerably large aggregate contribution to the common costs of running the railway. Moreover, under any given set of circumstances, low rates on grain increased the net returns of farmers, added to their disposable incomes, and increased the sales of farm implements, foodstuffs, clothing, and household appliances. The freight rates on these other goods were fully compensatory, and so railways were able to make up for the comparatively low net revenue per ton-mile on grain by hauling large quantities of other freight at a fairly good level of net revenue per ton-mile.

After World War II this situation rapidly worsened. Wages and other costs of operating a railway skyrocketed relative to prewar days. Soon it became doubtful, and finally it was certain, that rates on export grain were not high enough to cover the out-of-pocket costs of handling this traffic. Besides, competition had cut down both the volume of other kinds of freight and the rates which railways could charge for hauling it. It was no longer practicable to offset low rates on export grain by getting higher revenues from other kinds of traffic. Under the circumstances, the Canadian Pacific had no alternative but to demand higher revenue from Western export grain.

The Railway argued before the Royal Commission of 1951 and the Board of Transport Commissioners that over the years the rates on export grain got more and more out of line with the price of wheat.[18] In 1897 when the Agreement was made and in 1899 when the reductions were completed, the average price of wheat in the West was 99 and 70 cents per bushel. In 1922 and 1925 when Parliament confirmed its control of freight rates on grain, wheat sold at between $1.50 and $2.00 per bushel. In 1932 it was down to less than 55 cents. For the five crop years ending July 31, 1950, however, Western farmers were paid $1.75 per bushel. Accordingly they were able to stand a considerable increase in rates without hindering economic development. In 1951 the Vice-President (Traffic) of the Canadian Pacific thought that doubling the export grain rates would not be unreasonable in view of the increases in grain prices.[19]

The Canadian Pacific admitted that it was possible that national policy required special assistance to producers of grain on the Prairies. If that were the case, assistance should not be given at the cost of other users of railway services by charging them higher tolls, or at the cost of Railway by lowering its dividends and the rate of return on its investment in rail property. The Railway was determined not to accept any subsidy itself. It wanted to remain a privately owned enterprise and it argued vigorously that acceptance of subsidies was entirely inconsistent with private enterprise. So it seemed to follow that any subsidy would have to be paid directly to grain-growers. This, in turn, raised administrative difficulties allied with paying relatively small amounts to thousands of individual farmers scattered across the Prairies.

Throughout the years, and especially before the Royal Commission of 1951, the West has contended that the Crow's Nest Pass Agreement is the Magna Carta of its economic life. Western prosperity depends on there being low rates on the chief article of export. Without favourable rates the three million Canadians on the plains would be reduced to relative beggary. The West asserts that the rates were introduced as a result of a legally binding contract voluntarily entered into by the Canadian Pacific. The Railway received the consideration, a cash subsidy, stipulated in the Agreement besides coal-bearing lands. By means of the subsidy the Canadian Pacific got a line which stopped further American economic penetration into the wealthy area of southern British Columbia. At the time the contract was made the Railway believed the subsidy it received was adequate compensation for the reductions in rates. The West got no benefit from these reductions between 1903 and 1918 since throughout that period tolls were below the Crow's Nest level. While it may be true that the Canadian Pacific now regards the Agreement of 1897 as improvident, contracts are not set aside just because conditions have altered. The Company, says the West, bound itself to maintain these rates in perpetuity and ought to be held to its bargain.

The answer of the Canadian Pacific is that Parliament abrogated the Agreement in 1918, 1922, and 1925. Legislation relieved the Company of its obligation to maintain reduced rates on certain traffic westbound from Lakehead. However, it extended the rates on grain and flour from points on the Canadian Pacific lines in existence in 1897 to all the Company's lines west of Fort William whenever built. By the legislation of 1925 the Crow's Nest Pass rates were made applicable to the western lines of railways other than the Canadian Pacific. By decision of the Board, they cover export grain westbound through Pacific coast ports. Thus, so the Canadian Pacific argues, the legal contentions of the West collapse. Moreover, it points out that the contract is no longer burdensome merely on the Canadian Pacific: it is a dead weight on all railways in Western Canada and on shippers of commodities other than grain.

The Prairie Provinces do not rest their case on legal arguments alone. They contend that on economic grounds the Agreement of 1897 was sound since it involved simultaneous reductions in tolls on settlers' needs inbound and on the chief export of the region. The Agreement was clearly directed, so the Royal Commission of 1951 was told, toward the furtherance of economic development in the Prairie region and toward the linking of that development with the Eastern Canadian economy.

According to the West, the considerations which, at the turn of the century, gave rise to parliamentary action with respect to grain rates are as valid today as then. In fact, experience has demonstrated and emphasized the importance of an additional relevant circumstance, the inherent instability of an economy so dependent on the vagaries of nature. In the Western view, stability of transportation costs at the lowest possible level is absolutely essential to the survival of the wheat economy. The rate concessions are, in short, still basic to Western prosperity for they are needed to assist in reducing the barrier between the producing plains and the markets of the world. For many years the railways published as low rates on grain in Eastern Canada as in the West. The Eastern rates applied to both domestic and ex-lake grain, i.e., to grain which was grown and consumed locally in Ontario and Quebec and to that which came mainly from the West to ports on Georgian Bay and was then sent by rail to Montreal, Saint John, or Halifax for export. The existence of these low rates, some of them brought about by competition with lake carriers but all voluntarily made by railways, was quoted throughout the West as proof of the reasonableness of Crow's Nest Pass rates. Eastern rates vary from time to time, however, and the fact that they have sometimes been higher than the statutory Western rates reduces the soundness of the argument from the Western point of view.

The Canadian National did not take any positive position on the Crow's Nest Pass rates before the Royal Commission of 1951. Its only statement on them related to this principle of regulation. There was "some merit to the suggestion that all rates should be placed under the jurisdiction of the Board of Transport Commissioners.[20] On the other hand, the West opposed taking rates on export grain away from direct control by Parliament. According to a witness before the Royal Commission, western farmers felt that Parliament was better able to discover what was "just and reasonable" with respect to grain rates, in an over-all sense, than any board or tribunal, however eminent its personnel.

The Canadian Pacific Railway had prepared on elaborate study of its costs of handling grain in the West. For 1948, the loss was somewhere between $13,769,000 and $16,947,000. The exact deficiency could not be accurately determined. The Prairie Provinces wanted to cross-examine the experts who had prepared the Railway's estimate and to make a study of their own covering more than one year. The Commission felt that contentious accounting in a matter of great complexity would be so time-consuming and expensive that no one would be satisfied. The Crow's Nest Pass rates gave the West protection similar to the Maritime Freight Rates Act and to the economic forces holding down freight rates in the St. Lawrence Valley and on transcontinental traffic.

Though the Royal Commission would recommend no immediate change in legislation, it made it clear that nobody had asked that the current level of grain rates should never be changed. All that had been requested was that the rates should remain in the direct control of Parliament. In brief, the Commission acquiesced in the view that "Parliament itself should make whatever changes in these rates, upward or downward, it may appear just and reasonable to make as time goes on."[22]

After 1951 the statutory and related rates came under fire from several directions. Chief Justice Gordon McG. Sloan of British Columbia said in 1954, when he acted as arbitrator in a labour dispute, that these rates were one of the causes preventing railways from paying their employees the same amount of fringe benefits as employees in other industries.[23] In 1958 the Canadian Pacific stated before the Board of Transport Commissioners that over one-quarter of the revenue tonmiles on that Railway had been "carved out" of the rate structure by the statutory and related rates. Witnesses for the Canadian Federation of Agriculture and similar organizations stated that because farm income was declining agriculture could not support higher tolls. Replying to this testimony, counsel for the Canadian Pacific said that in view of the low statutory rates on grain it was "sheer effrontery for agricultural people to complain."[24] In the same case counsel for British Columbia referred to the "biggest distortion" in the freight-rate structure brought about by the Crow's Nest rates and to the changes in wage rates, prices, and interest rates which had taken place since the Royal Commission had reported in 1951.[25]

Royal Commission of 1961

Shortly after this Commission was appointed, Prime Minister Diefenbaker declared that it was not to deal with the Crow's Nest Pass rates. But when the Commission met, the Chairman, then Mr. C. P. McTague, formerly chief justice of Ontario, ruled that what had been said in the House of Commons was irrelevant to the point at issue. The Commission was bound only by its terms of reference and under these terms it was legally obliged to look at the statutory and related rates.

Before the earlier Royal Commission, that of 1951, the Canadian Pacific had advocated increasing the rates on export grain in the West and it had categorically rejected a subsidy payable to the railways. Now it recognized that grain rates could not be increased without detrimentally affecting the Canadian economy. Therefore, some public aid was needed to keep grain rates at their existing level. However, the Railway was still steadfastly opposed to accepting any direct subsidy itself and suggested that the aid take the form of a reduction in the amount of corporate income tax which it would otherwise have to pay. Somewhat similar concessions were being made in Canada on new mines, petroleum companies, and shipbuilding. Reductions in income tax were also being used in Britain and the United States to assist specified industries.

Alternatively, the Railway said that the subsidy should go directly to the farmers. They would be charged a freight rate which would cover the full cost of handling the traffic by rail. Then they could claim a rebate from the Government for the difference between the rate they had paid and the statutory and related rate. Reversing its position of ten years earlier, the Canadian Pacific now believed these rebates could be made without undue expense for auditing and without serious danger of fraud.

The Railway lost some of its enthusiasm for this scheme when the Canadian Truckers Association proposed that the farmer be allowed the same rebate if he shipped his grain by truck instead of rail. In the

United States grain for export is hauled over the roads for 1,000 miles or more to ports on the Gulf of Mexico and Lake Michigan. This movement is largely back-haul at low rates in trucks which carry full loads of citrus fruits and agricultural implements in the reverse direction. In addition, some grain is handled by truckers who buy it from farmers, haul it to a terminal elevator, sell it for as much as they can, and make a profit out of the difference between the purchase and sales prices. This would not be permitted in Canada for all our export wheat must be sold through the Canadian Wheat Board, a government agency. Furthermore, in Canada long-haul trucking of grain is impracticable because rail rates on this product are so low. Even if doubled, as the Canadian Pacific once proposed, they would still be less than in the United States. Trucking costs are also a little higher in Canada than farther south. Our grain-growing areas are farther away from ocean and lake ports. Our terminal elevators are not equipped for handling grain brought by truck and even if they were, delivery by both truck and railway box car might result in congestion and higher handling charges at our ports. Congestion and delay are especially serious at Lakehead because of the relatively short time between harvest and the close of navigation.

Although the long-haul movement of export grain is not yet economic in Canada, conditions may change. Naturally, the railways want to hang on to the grain traffic as long as they can make money from its carriage. Not paying the subsidy to truckers would be a means of holding traffic to the rails. Even so, the Canadian Pacific disliked the idea of taking money from the government. Representatives of some farm organizations said their members were equally reluctant to accept a subsidy because it suggested that grain growing was an economic weakling. One of the humours of the situation was that both sides to the dispute agreed on the necessity for aid but neither seemed willing to take it.

The Canadian National fully supported the Canadian Pacific on the need for some sort of assistance to cover the total cost of handling export grain in the West. Its position was in marked contrast to its lukewarm support ten years earlier and suggests how much more serious the problem had become in the intervening years. Each railway had prepared its own elaborate study of the cost of handling grain. The two studies, though not identical, followed the same general lines as described more fully in the chapter entitled "Rates on Particular Commodities." Although the studies cost about $500,000 each, the expenditure would have proved an excellent investment if railways had got a large annual subsidy on grain beginning in 1967. But even without this financial aid, the studies yielded a good return since the same methods could fairly readily be adapted to other kinds of freight.

Witnesses appearing before the MacPherson Commission on behalf of the grain trade, Alberta, and Manitoba (Saskatchewan took a position of neutrality) attacked many details of the cost study. For example, they squabbled with both railways over the time it took to shunt cars in yards and the mileage required to place empty cars in position for loading beside country elevators. More particularly, they quarrelled about "solely related" lines, that is, the mileage of lines which owed their continued existence entirely to the movement of grain. According to the railways, all the interest charges on these lines should be assessed against grain. None of it should be charged against the comparatively minor quantities of other freight which these lines sometimes carried. Further argument developed over whether the appropriate rate of interest to be allowed on the total investment in track, cars, locomotives, etc., used to handle grain should be the rate which the Canadian Pacific was currently earning on all its investment in rail property, or the rate which it ought to earn if it were to meet all its financial requirements as laid down by the Board of Transport Commissioners. Some witnesses for the grain trade denied that export grain was carried at a loss and said that the real trouble lay in excessive mileages of branch lines, unprofitable passenger-train services, competitive rates, and agreed charges. One or two witnesses asserted that the real trouble was competition between the railways and the real solution was unification and public ownership of both big systems.

In the end the MacPherson Commission recommended that "upon submission and approval of reports of the variable cost of moving grain and of the revenue therefrom for the previous year, the railways be granted annually a sum of money equal to the shortfall of revenues on variable expense plus $9 million in the case of the Canadian Pacific Railway and $7.3 million . . . [for] the Canadian National Railways. . . . When the process of rationalizing plant by the elimination of [unprofitable] rail lines . . . has substantially progressed, or when it appears that there has been any substantial change in the overhead costs of the railways, the constant costs of the railways should be re-evaluated"[26] and the amount of the subsidies adjusted accordingly. The Commission was of the opinion that the total of the subsidies which it recommended for the Canadian Pacific would, as long as the costs and conditions of transport remained as they were in 1958, "place export grain traffic in a position comparable to other segments of traffic in the light of the permissive level of earnings. Making adjustments necessary due to the different financial structure of the Canadian

National Railways, the payment recommended . . . as a contribution on behalf of the export grain traffic to overheads is $7.3 million."[27]

In essence, the commission recommended a subsidy made up of two parts: (a) an amount sufficient to cover the difference between variable or out-of-pocket expenses of handling export grain in the West and the revenues received from shippers, and (b) the proper contribution of export grain to the fixed or overhead cost of operating each railway. With costs and operating conditions as they were in 1958, each railway would get $11 million from the Dominion. Basically, the MacPherson Commission would see to it that the two major railways would get the same gross revenues from handling export grain as they would have got if the freight rates on it could have been set in the light of purely commercial considerations.

Legislation, 1967

For various reasons, parliamentary consideration of the MacPherson Report was deferred for over five years after its completion. In 1966 the Minister of Transport, Mr. J. W. Pickersgill, stated that the estimates made by the Commission were badly out of date since they were based on data for 1958. One of the earliest responsibilities of the new Canadian Transport Commission would be to make another analysis of these costs. Its study was to be completed within three years.

Mr. Pickersgill went on to say that rather spectacular improvements were being made in methods of handling grain in country and terminal elevators as well as on railways. These included replacing all the older and smaller elevators with larger structures having the best facilities for handling grain at low cost, notably by spouting it on fast-moving, endless belts. The new facilities would probably be "flat" so that grain would be stored in great bins fairly close to the ground rather than being elevated high up in the "sentinels of the plains." Other economies will result from the better location of elevators and perhaps through what the British call liner trains and the Americans multiple car shipments. Instead of a way-freight picking up and setting off a few cars at every station, almost every day, it would wait until a huge elevator had loaded perhaps twenty cars. Periodically, perhaps once a week, it would pick up all these cars and leave the required empties. By calling at four or five large elevators or towns, the train would soon be complete. Then, subject to a wide variety of operating conditions, it could move quickly and economically to Lakehead or Vancouver. In effect, the retail peddling of loaded and empty cars would be replaced by handling in wholesale lots. Every improvement would reduce the need for subsidies on the movement of export grain.[28] Hence, in the Minister's opinion, a new study was required to see what aid, if any, was required.

During the debate on this proposal, members from the West made it clear that they resented having to accept a subsidy on the carriage of their main export. They believed that grain could be moved at a profit even at the statutory rates, provided the elevator system was modernized, railways made full use of modern technology in the use of locomotives and cars, in the operation of hump yards, centralized traffic control, and the like, and provided one railway could have running rights over the tracks of another in order to shorten its haul and save money. They also pointed out that the volume of traffic on Western lines had been growing rapidly because of the discovery of potash, the expansion of base-metal mining in adjacent parts of the Shield, heavy yields of grain, and the clearing of more acreage in the Park Belt, which is the lightly wooded area lying just north of the lands which were originally covered by grass alone. According to these Members of Parliament, the expansion of traffic would reduce the cost per ton-mile below the level of the statutory rates. These members tacitly assumed that the reductions in operating costs which they anticipated would not be offset, or more than offset, by rising rates of wages, interest, and costs of railway equipment.

In the end, the Government's plan was defeated by a single vote. A review of the costs of handling export grain by the Transport Commission or even by a Royal Commission may be revived at a subsequent session of the House of Commons. Meanwhile, Parliament has not left railways unprotected against the financial losses which they said they were experiencing on export grain. The legislation provided for an overall subsidy of $110 million to the railways in 1967. This amount will be cut back by $12\frac{1}{2}$ per cent per annum until the payment in a given year is exceeded by subsidies payable under other provisions of the National Transportation Act. In its final form the specific, or tied, subsidies related only to unprofitable branch lines and passenger trains. In its original form they also covered the traffic in export grain. Thus for the next few years the railways will be getting in general form, the overall subsidy, what they would otherwise have got in specific form, a subsidy tied to grain. In short, the problem of providing the railways with adequate revenues for handling grain is deferred until such time as the annual reductions in the general subsidy plus the tied subsidies on branch lines and passenger trains again put the railways on a starvation diet, financially speaking.

The legislation of 1967 extended the coverage of the statutory rates on grain. Prior to this date, the only grain rates in this category were those on the movement to Lakehead. They were covered by the Crow's Nest Pass Act of 1897 as modified by an amendment to the Railway Act in 1925. The corresponding rates on grain exported westward through Canada's Pacific ports had been set by the Board of Transport Commissioners under Order 36769, also in 1925. The Board was unlikely to raise these rates because it was obliged under the Railway Act to forbid unjust discrimination and under the National Transportation Act to see that "each mode of transport . . . carries traffic . . . under tolls and conditions that do not constitute (*i*) an unfair disadvantage . . . beyond the disadvantage inherent in the location or volume of the traffic . . . or (*ii*) an undue obstacle to the interchange of commodities between points in Canada or unreasonable discouragement to the development of primary or secondary industries or to export trade in or from any region of Canada or to the movement of commodities through Canadian ports." In the absence of any other legal stipulations, the Canadian Transport Commission might have raised the westbound rates on export grain by ruling that higher tolls would not infringe any of the stipulations quoted above. In order to plug up this loophole, small though it might be, the Act made these tolls statutory (sec. 328).

The Crow's Nest Pass Agreement, even after the amendment of 1925, applied to grain and grain products to Lakehead whether for export or for domestic consumption anywhere in Canada. By contrast, the rates under Order 36769, even after confirmation by the National Transportation Act of 1967, covered only grain for export. Grain from Western Canada to Canada's Pacific coast for making bread and pastry or for feeding to livestock or poultry within Canada is charged at domestic rates. Of course, domestic rates also apply to Western grain when it moves eastward of Lakehead for local use, e.g., from Goderich to London, or from Midland to Peterborough. But mile for mile the rate on Western grain consumed in Eastern Canada is less than the rate on domestic grain used in Vancouver. This is because for a substantial part of the total haul, namely, from point of origin on the Prairies to Lakehead, the grain is handled at the low rates under the Crow's Nest Pass Agreement, whereas grain for use in, say, Vancouver, pays domestic rates for the entire haul. What is more, a railway charges two quite different rates for performing substantially the same service. From the same country elevator in the West it may haul one car of wheat to Vancouver for export at the low rate applicable under Order 36769 and another car in the same train from the same point to Vancouver at the higher domestic rate. Frequent complaint was made about this situation[29] but the Board of Transport Commissioners allowed it to continue on the theory that the export of grain was part of a through movement to a destination overseas. Hence, the rates charged for this haul did not constitute a standard for judging the reasonableness of the rates on a haul that was entirely confined to two places within Canada. Domestic rates on grain were subject to almost all the postwar increases while export rates were held down either by statute or by Order 36769. As a result, the discrepancy between domestic and export rates between the West and Vancouver became greater as time went on.

The legislation of 1967 took this situation into account. Under sec. 471, "not later than six months after . . . [the setting up of the Canadian Transport Commission] or the coming into force of this section, which-ever last occurs, the Commission shall undertake a study of the differ-ences between rates on grain moving for export to ports in British Columbia and rates on grain moving otherwise to such ports, and shall report to the Governor in Council for such action as he deems desirable or expedient in the public interest."

Prior to 1967, the Board of Transport Commissioners set "At and East" grain rates in the same manner as all other tariffs except those cov-ered by the Crow's Nest Pass and related rates. At and East rates cover grain brought by ships from Lakehead to Midland, Goderich, etc., and moved thence by rail to Montreal, Halifax, and so on. As a rule, the Board tried to keep these rates at such a level that the traffic would move through ports in Canada rather than by water to Buffalo and then by rail or water (the Erie Canal) to New York. Thus in a broad sense At and East rates were competitive.

In 1961, however, the Board decided to leave the rates at their current level pending final disposition of the recommendations of the MacPher-son Commission.[30] Moreover, the volume of this ex-lake traffic had seriously declined following the opening of the St. Lawrence Seaway. The legislation of 1967 (sec. 329) continued the freeze and provided that the federal government would subsidize this movement on substantially the same basis as the government had originally planned for grain ex-ported from the West, taken as a whole.

(1) In this section, (a) 'Eastern port' means any of the ports of Halifax, Saint John, West Saint John and Montreal and any of the ports on the St. Lawrence River to the east of Montreal; (b) 'Eastern rates' [commonly called At and East rates] means (i) in relation to grain, the freight rates applying on the 30th day of November, 1960, to the movement of grain in bulk for export from any inland point to an Eastern port, and (ii) in relation to flour, the freight rates applying on the 30th day of September, 1966, . . .;

(c) 'inland point' means, (i) in relation to grain, any of the railway points along Georgian Bay, along Lake Huron or along any waterways directly or indirectly connecting with Lake Huron and not being farther east than Prescott, but including Prescott, and (ii) in relation to flour, any point in Canada east of the 90th degree of west longtitude [which is a few miles west of Fort William].

(2) For the purpose of encouraging the continued use of the Eastern ports for the export of grain and flour, (a) rates for grain moving in bulk [and on flour] for export to any Eastern port from any inland point over any line of a railway company subject to the jurisdiction of Parliament shall be maintained at the level of rates applying [on the dates given above].

(3) The Commission shall from time to time determine in respect of . . . [the movements described above] a level of rates consistent with section 334 [which requires that every toll cover at least the variable cost of the movement] and shall cause such rates to be published in the *Canada Gazette*.

(4) The Governor in Council may, on the recommendation of the [Canadian Transport] Commission, authorize the Minister of Finance to pay out of the Consolidated Revenue Fund to a railway company . . . [that handles any traffic described above] an amount equal to the difference [if any] between (a) the total amount received by the company in respect of that year for the carriage of such grain or flour, and (b) the total amount that the company would have received in respect of that year had the grain or flour been carried at the rates determined and published by the Commission under subsection (3) instead of at the Eastern rates.

Until such time as the Commission determines the level of rates under subsection (3), the existing rates shall be deemed to be compensatory as required by sec. 334.

5

The Maritime Freight Rates Act

LIKE the Crow's Nest Pass and related rates on grain, the Maritime Freight Rates Act is a prominent feature in the national rate structure. By the early 1920s the Maritime Provinces were becoming disgruntled with the economic benefits they were deriving from the Canadian union, particularly with regard to transportation. They contended that they had entered Confederation under protest, that they had given up control of their own provincial customs tariffs which had been their chief source of revenue, and that the tariff of the Dominion government had fostered manufacturing development in the St. Lawrence Valley and destroyed it in the Maritimes. Although the Intercolonial Railway had been built as agreed to in the British North America Act, for strategic reasons it had been located far back from the United States boundary. Its route was circuitous and the districts it served produced little local traffic. For these reasons the cost of operating the road should be borne in large part by the Dominion and not by the Maritimes alone. As long as the Intercolonial was operated by a department of the government, its freight rates had been kept low. Since 1912 rates had been increased to a greater extent in the Maritimes than elsewhere in Canada.

The Maritimes also believed that their ports of Halifax and Saint John had not received a reasonable portion of the export grain traffic of the West. Leading Canadian statesmen, in urging the Maritime Provinces to enter Confederation, had asserted that the Intercolonial would afford to Canadian merchandise an outlet and inlet on the Atlantic Ocean available all year round. To Maritime merchants, traders and manufacturers, the Railway would open up a large market in the St. Lawrence Valley. The new market was an important consideration since the population of the Maritimes was small and their trade was threatened by discontinuance on the part of the United States of the reciprocal trade arrangements that had prevailed from 1854 to 1866. Moreover, in order further to develop Canadian trade through Saint John and Halifax, early in the twentieth century the Government had built a railway by almost direct line from Winnipeg to Quebec City, and thence to Moncton. Unfortunately, the development of Canada's Atlantic ports had languished.

The general economic difficulties within the Maritimes, the high level of tolls compared with 1912, and the slow progress of Atlantic ports inevitably led the Maritime Provinces to demand some adjustments in freight rates. To deal with these questions, in 1925 the Dominion appointed a Royal Commission under the chairmanship of a British industrialist, Sir Andrew Rae Duncan.

The Duncan Report

The Duncan Commission proposed larger money grants from the federal to the provincial governments, customs duties on American coal so as to provide a larger market for the Maritime product within Canada, subsidies to by-product coke ovens which used Nova Scotia coal, and so on. The Commission found that because the former Intercolonial had been located near the Gulf of St. Lawrence for military and not for economic reasons, it was about 250 miles longer than it should have been.[1] Hence, "to the extent that commercial considerations had been subordinated to national, imperial and strategic elements," the cost of the circuitous route "should be borne by the Dominion and not by the traffic that might pass over the line." Although this principle had been followed until 1912, since then rates in the Maritimes had been raised more than elsewhere in Canada. They had gone up from 100 to 192; in other parts of the country the cumulative increase was from 100 to roughly 155.[2]

The upshot of the Royal Commission's deliberations was the recommendation, shortly afterwards implemented by the Dominion government in the Maritime Freight Rates Act,[3] that an immediate reduction of 20 per cent (so that 192 would become approximately 155) be made on all rates charged on traffic which both originates and terminates in the Maritimes and on the Maritime portion of the through rate on all traffic which originates within the region (except import traffic) and which is destined for stations outside the region. All existing freight tariffs were to be cancelled and the Board of Railway Commissioners was to substitute therefor tariffs showing a reduction of 20 per cent below the rates previously existing. The difference between the rates published in the old and in the new tariffs, or 20 per cent, was to be paid by the federal government to the railways. The revised tolls were to become effective on July 1, 1927, the sixtieth anniversary of Confederation. They were to continue in effect as long as the costs of railway operation in Canada remained approximately the same as at the date of the Act but the Board might increase or reduce such tolls from time to time to meet increases or reductions, as the case might be, in such costs of operation. The Board was also to adjust or vary such substituted tolls from time to time as new industries or traffic conditions might arise but always in conformity with the intent of the Act.

The Act defined preferred movements and select territory. Preferred movements comprised (a) local traffic all-rail, between points in select territory; (b) traffic moving westward outbound all-rail from points in select territory to points beyond in Canada, e.g., Moncton to Montreal, the 20 per cent reduction being based on the proportion of mileage in select territory to the total mileage and toll involved;[4] (c) traffic moving outward for export by rail and sea from ports in select territory, the reduction applying on the Canadian rail portion of the through rate (from Fredericton to Liverpool via Saint John, for instance, the reduction applies on the Fredericton–Saint John part of the route); (d) traffic moving on railway-owned car ferries (e.g., traffic moving from Tormentine to Borden–mainland to Prince Edward Island) was to be treated as rail traffic for the purposes of the Act. On the other hand preferred movements were *not* to include (a) traffic inward or outward all-rail from or to the United States; (b) traffic moving inward, eastbound within Canada from points not in select territory to points so located, e.g. Toronto to Moncton; (c) import traffic to Canada from points overseas, e.g. Liverpool to Moncton or to Toronto; (d) passenger and express.

Select territory included rather more than the three Maritime provinces of Nova Scotia, New Brunswick, and Prince Edward Island because it took in that section of the province of Quebec lying east of Diamond Junction and Lévis. Diamond Junction is the point where the Transcontinental met the old Intercolonial. Lévis, directly across the river from Quebec City, is the station where the Intercolonial terminated in 1879, before it purchased a line giving it access over its own rails into Montreal. Preferred rates in select territory were deemed to be statutory and not based on any principle of a fair return to the railway for services rendered in carrying such traffic. The Board was not to use these statutory rates as a measure of the reasonableness of other rates in Canada or vice versa. The Board was not to approve or allow any tariffs which might destroy or prejudicially affect the statutory advantages in rates to persons and industries in the Maritimes in favour of persons or industries located elsewhere than in the select territory. The Act was extended to Newfoundland when it joined Confederation on March 31, 1949. In 1957 it was further amended so that on traffic from select territory to other parts of Canada, the government's share of the Maritime portion of the toll became 30 per cent instead of 20.

Operation of the Act

Broadly speaking, trade in the Maritimes has continued to be depressed. Deep-seated problems of geography, history, and economics cannot be corrected by tinkering with freight tolls, and the Maritime Freight Rates Act failed to fulfil the hopes of its sponsors. There is little evidence to show that it significantly increased the sales of Maritime products in Central Canada. On the other hand the low tolls unquestionably encouraged local rail transportation within select territory. Simultaneously, they may have held back the growth of trucking.

Over the years the Act gave rise to knotty legal problems. Both the Board and the Supreme Court agreed that the Board's power to certify normal tolls, from which the statutory deduction was to be allowed, was not exhausted with initial certification. With the Board's permission, railways reduced rates in select territory to take account of newly established industries, of the need of existing industries to have better access to raw materials and markets, and of competition from water carriers and truckers. These reductions brought up the problem of whether railways were to continue to be reimbursed by the federal government and if so, whether they were to get 20 per cent of the normal toll or 20 per cent of the reduced rate. After the Board had twice changed its mind, the Supreme Court ruled that if, for example, the normal rate was $1.00 and the railway voluntarily reduced it to 65 cents to meet competition, it would still get the subsidy of 20 cents while charging the shipper 65 cents.[5]

Another, more important problem arose in the late thirties when railways reduced rates on potatoes to meet competition in the St. Lawrence Lowlands but did not simultaneously cut tolls on the same commodity in select territory. The Maritimes contended that competitive reductions in Ontario and Quebec should be matched by proportionate reductions in the Maritimes. They argued that the Act was designed to maintain a certain planned relation between the two areas. By reducing rates in one region and not in the other, railways prejudicially affected Maritime shippers in contravention of the legislation. The advantages which the Act was designed to give the Maritimes were being "whittled away" by competitive rate reductions outside select territory. Railways answered that they must meet these competing rates. If they did not do so, they would lose the business which would go by truck and the Maritimes would be adversely affected anyway. In fact the railways are really benefiting the Maritimes for giving these special rates reduces the overhead to be borne by others including the Maritimes.[6]

The Board accepted the Maritime view that the Act required it not to approve or allow tariffs which destroyed or prejudicially affected the statutory advantages to the Maritimes.[7] Whether a tariff had such a result was a question of fact. On the issue of fact the Board decided against the applicant and so concluded that truck-compelled rates on potatoes in Ontario ought not to be disallowed. The Board said it had not been established that in the matter of potato shipments in Ontario the whole difference had arisen through motor competition with the railways. Variations in price and in the quantity of potatoes moving from the Maritimes to Ontario were attributable to crop conditions from year to year and numerous economic causes. The Board was not satisfied that the competitive tariff on potatoes had either destroyed or prejudicially affected the advantages provided to shippers in select territory under the Act. Cancelling potato rates in Ontario would not improve the position of Maritime shippers to any degree and would only result in depriving railways of the small portion of the traffic of potatoes in Ontario which they had been able to retain under the substantially reduced rates. On appeal, the Supreme Court expressed confidence in the Board and decided against the Maritime shippers.[8]

Shippers in the Maritimes had the empty satisfaction that both the Supreme Court and the Board had held that rates outside select territory might be cancelled if they nullified the benefits to the Maritimes under the Act. At the same time they had to accept the bitter pill that it was practically impossible to prove prejudice as required by the Board because so many economic factors which might influence movement were involved. The difficulty faced by Maritime shippers was to segregate the transportation factor from the others and have it appear as the sole cause of the destruction of Maritime trade at a particular time and place. However, though legally the position of the Maritimes was weak, the fact remained that competitive rates tended to destroy rate relationships on which industry had been constructed and developed, and that industries located within the orbit of motor and water transportation have a distinct advantage over those which are located outside and are competing in the same market in the competitive zone.

A Royal Commission appointed by the province of Nova Scotia in 1934 could suggest no method for dealing effectively with the complaint.[9] The Rowell-Sirois Commission found itself "unable to accept the argument that, in the circumstances now existing, a railway rate differential in favour of a region must be maintained against all forms of competition and regardless of the costs of operation. This difficulty about the maintenance of these Maritime rates is a consequence of truck competition, and it can only be dealt with as part of the wider problems of transportation."[10] Though the Royal Commission of 1951 had power to make this broad study and heard testimony on the Act's shortcomings, it recommended only two minor changes.[11] In 1957, the Dominion began to pay 30 instead of 20 per cent of the Maritime portion of the rate on freight westbound from select territory to the St. Lawrence Lowlands and the West.

Royal Commission, 1961

The MacPherson Commission agreed with Maritime shippers that the Act had been of little practical advantage in enabling them to sell in the St. Lawrence Lowlands.[12] It quoted part of the report of the Duncan Commission as summarized in the preamble to the original Maritime Freight Rates Act (17 Geo. V, c. 44):

A balanced study of events and pronouncements prior to Confederation, and at its consummation, and of the lower level of rates which prevailed on the Intercolonial system prior to 1912, has . . . confirmed the representations submitted to the Commission on behalf of the Maritime Provinces, namely, that the Intercolonial Railway was designed . . . to afford to Maritime merchants, traders and manufacturers the larger market of the whole Canadian people instead of the restricted market of the Maritimes themselves.

Once this premise is accepted, it is hard to see, so the MacPherson Commission argued, how this objective could be reached to any significant extent by subsidizing all intra-Maritime traffic. In addition, the Commission believed that the subsidy had inhibited the growth of what it called carriage over the highways in select territory. Accordingly, the Commission recommended abolition of the subsidy on all intra-Maritime movements except in Newfoundland where there was, at the date of the report, no really pervasive competition to railway services.

The MacPherson Commission also proposed that subsidies payable under the Act should go to all types of carriage. In other words, they would be paid to operators of common carriers by highway and presumably by water as well as to the railways. While the Commission recognized that its recommendation would involve an administrative burden, it did not believe that the work of paying the subsidy and auditing the accounts of carriers would either be insuperable or unduly expensive. Subsidization would be confined to common carriers, spot checking was all that would be required, violation of the regulations would lead to the cancellation of all subsidies otherwise payable to the common carrier concerned, and only a small number of carriers (other than the railways) participated in the movement of freight westward from select territory.

The Commission did not deny that the new regulations, if accepted by the government, would hurt the railways. But it argued that the purpose of the original legislation was not to help the railways but to prevent them from imposing the full burden of their high costs on shippers of the region. Besides, as a general principle the government should not favour one mode of transport above another.

The Commission's logic is not above reproach. It argued that the Act had inhibited the growth of highway transport in the Maritime Provinces and yet proposed to retain it in Newfoundland, where high-way competition was feeble and presumably needed to be developed. If it is true that the Act prevented the growth of highway transport, one of the reasons must have been that the lower level of the subsidized rail rates discouraged truckers. It logically follows that abolition of the subsidy on intra-Maritime traffic by rail will lead to an increase in tolls payable by shippers. In effect, the Commission assumes, though without presenting any data to support its conclusion, that once the subsidy is cancelled, highway transport will expand to the point where it will cut tolls below the level charged by railways. If it is economically possible for highway carriers to operate under such tolls, it is hard to understand why they have not already done so.

What is more, after the Commission had asserted that the Government should treat all modes of transport in the same way, it proposed to subsidize common carriers by highway while denying the same aid to private truckers. It believed that policing the legislation would not be difficult because of the small number of participants in transport by highway from select territory to other parts of Canada. At the same time it failed to consider whether the number of common carrier truckers within Newfoundland would be large or small. If large, the Commission would have to admit that its premise that the Act had inhibited the growth of trucking was unsound. In that event, it would have to face up to the problem of auditing a considerable number of way-bills to prevent abuse of the subsidy. If, on the other hand, the Commission were to say that the number of intra-provincial truckers within Newfoundland was likely to be small, it would be carrying one of its theories through to its logical conclusion but hampering the economic growth of the Island and denying Newfoundland shippers

the benefits of highway transport. In any case, the Commission overlooked the possibility that private carriers, whether within Newfoundland
or on hauls from select territory westward into other parts of Canada,
would go through the formalities of becoming common carriers in order
to get the subsidies. It is easier to distinguish between private and
common carriers in theory than it is in practice.

Moreover, the MacPherson Commission's view of the Duncan Report
is based on too narrow and legalistic grounds. To be sure, the preamble
to the original Act refers only to interregional movements and the
promises made at Confederation about Maritime products getting access
to the larger markets of the St. Lawrence Lowlands. But elsewhere
the report talks of Maritime rates having risen faster since 1912 than
rates in other parts of Canada. Besides, the tenor of the report clearly
supports the position that the Maritime Provinces were an economically depressed area and that reduced rates within select territory
would improve its prospects. In the 1950s the area "opted out" of
equalization because it feared an increase in its rates, local as well
as interregional. One suspects that the relatively few manufacturers in
the Maritimes who hoped to sell in Central Canada were more active
in presenting their views to the MacPherson Commission than the large
number of suppliers and distributors who served local markets and who
benefited from the intra-regional subsidy under the act. Professor Roy E.
George of Dalhousie University has calculated that the average cost of
raw materials used in a typical factory in Nova Scotia is inflated by
about three-quarters of one per cent on account of higher transport
charges relative to the same kind of plant in Ontario or Quebec.[13]

Legislation, 1967

The proposals made by the MacPherson Commission on the Maritime
Freight Rates Act did not commend themselves to the Government in
Ottawa. Instead, the Minister of Transport proposed that all rates in
select territory be left undisturbed for two years pending receipt of a
report by a firm of engineering consultants. The National Transport Act
(sec. 335) confirmed this arrangement and made special reference to
rates on lumber, coal, and coke between two points in Canada, one or
both being in select territory.

The engineers proposed that subsidies payable under the Maritime
Freight Rates Act should go to carriers by highway and water as well as
by rail. They suggested that the Dominion government extend its
assistance for the construction of additional roads and harbours in the
Maritimes. On the other hand they rejected the Maritime request that a

new highway or corridor road be built with Canadian funds across Maine in order to provide more direct access between Montreal and Saint John.

In the author's view, the economy of the Atlantic Provinces would have benefited more if the sums spent to subsidize freight rates had been used in other directions. These include the modernization of the fishing industry, larger aid to the construction of highways, more assistance to either hydro-electric or thermal power plants, and research on the use of local resources. At the same time one must recognize how unlikely the Atlantic Provinces are to cheerfully give up the transportation subsidies they have enjoyed since 1927. This will be especially true if the federal government should find it necessary to subsidize the carriage of export grain from the West and keep tolls on the St. Lawrence Seaway at a level lower than necessary to amortize the cost of construction over the anticipated period of fifty years.

6

Rates on Particular Commodities

THE RATE to be charged for the carriage of a particular article between specific points is a fundamental problem in railway rate making. Conclusions regarding the propriety of any general level of rates must be translated into rates on particular hauls. The general level has less significance to the shipper or consignee than the definite amount which he has to pay for the carriage of his goods from one place to another. Usually he is more concerned with the relationship between the rates he is charged and those charged his competitors than he is with the general level of all rates. Further, the problem of competition between different transportation agencies and effectual co-ordination of them into an integrated transportation system resolves itself into setting individual rates and thus determining the relationship of the rates on particular shipments by carriers by rail, highway, water, and air.

Cost of Service

As a rule businesses set their prices on the basis of their costs. Economists and the general public sometimes lump the "bundle of concepts" relating to prices into a single convenient term, supply and demand. The use of this term merely pushes inquiry back one stage and raises further questions: What determines demand? What is the relation between the price per unit and the number of units of the good which will be taken off the market at that price? On the supply side, do costs of production per unit increase, decrease, or remain constant with changes in the total number of units produced? What costs are important in determining prices? Are they the costs of the exceptionally well managed or unusually well located firm, the costs of the firm which cannot profitably produce at current prices, or the costs of the concern whose total receipts at the going price per unit barely cover its expenses? What happens when elements of monopoly are present? All these and other related questions are quite obviously difficult to answer either in theory or in practice.

In general, under conditions of free competition the price of each article must be high enough to cover the cost of producing the most costly unit, or in economic language, the marginal unit, which the public requires to fill its demands at that price. The cost that really matters is the cost of producing the last or most expensive unit which the public will take off the market at a price just high enough to cover this cost. Producers whose costs are lower than those of the marginal unit need not sell for any less than their competitor at the margin for, once the goods come on the market, purchasers have no way of distinguishing between marginal and sub-marginal units and hence can be made to pay the same price for all. Because their costs are lower than the going price per unit and they need not sell for less, low cost producers get a differential return which is called, depending on its source, pure rent (from land) or pure profit (from management). Providing we clearly understand what we mean by the word "cost" and do not overlook the significance of the demand aspect, we can say with some accuracy that the price of any good is, in the long run, determined by its cost of production.

Although what has just been said is true for industry generally, it is not applicable to railways. In the past unrestrained competition between railway companies led to poor service, improperly maintained equipment and roadway, inadequate returns to investors and, perhaps most serious of all, unjust discrimination and undue preference. To prevent these evils—railway history is filled with rate wars—railways agreed among themselves to maintain rates and the public instituted regulation. Consequently an element of monopoly (one seller in a given market) or oligopoly (a few sellers in a single market) or in Canada duopoly (since this country has only two major railways) is normally present in rail service. Besides, a railway provides a great many services. The same locomotive may haul, and the same track may support, traffic in coal, livestock, sand, canned vegetables, explosives, miscellaneous merchandise, and passengers, mail, and express. It is very difficult to allocate the cost of operating the locomotive—fuel, lubricants, wages, depreciation, and interest—or the cost of the road bed, a bridge, or a repair shop over the variety of articles hauled.[1] "It is impossible to get at the exact cost of a particular movement in railway traffic. All that can be done is to approximate cost: and as emphasized by the experts . . . the element of opinion is very important."[2] Even if such costs could be determined, it might well be that rates set to include a full proportion of the total costs of operating the railway would be so high as to prohibit the movement of some goods, such as grain for export, which, from the point of view of the public it would be advantageous to move readily. Conversely, rates on valuable articles set on a cost basis would be much lower than the owners of them would be willing to pay and ship in quantity.

There are three other reasons why it is difficult to set rates by cost of production. Because a large share of all the costs of operating a railway is comparatively fixed, because total costs do not increase or decrease in exact proportion to changes in the volume of traffic, the cost of hauling a ton of freight cannot be determined until the end of the year or other fiscal period. The average cost per ton-mile can be arrived at only after the total expenses and the number of ton-miles hauled during the period are known. Obviously it would be impracticable for a railway to defer assessing and collecting tolls until after the business of the year had been completed.

The business cycle also has a bearing. The cost per unit and hence the freight rate might be high in periods of depression when business is peculiarly unable to pay high tolls. Conversely, costs and rates might be low in boom times when shippers and consignees could pay higher charges with less difficulty.[3]

Finally, operating conditions complicate the relationship between costs and rates. It costs substantially the same total amount to haul a fully laden as a partially filled car, or to move a train with ten cars behind the locomotive as one with thirty cars. The average lading per car and the number of cars per train will vary from day to day. Consequently costs per ton-mile and per car-mile fluctuate from one day to another. The only cost data which have much meaning for rate-making purposes are average costs taken over a sufficiently long period of time that daily variations are ironed out.

Nevertheless, although cost cannot be used as the basic factor in setting rates, it cannot be completely neglected. Total receipts, which are, obviously, the product of individual rates multiplied by the volume of traffic moved at these rates, must cover total costs including depreciation, interest, and dividends. Then, too, while the cost for any one commodity cannot be accurately ascertained, it is often possible to say within a reasonable margin of error that the cost of hauling one commodity amounts to so much more or less than the cost of handling another. By assuming that the rates on the one about which no complaint is made are fair and reasonable, the railway or the Board can arrive at the rate for the other with some approach to correctness. Further, some costs of moving traffic are directly related to the number of cars handled. These include the costs of billing, shunting, and depreciation on the car. With every increase in the number of tons in a car, costs per ton-mile of moving that shipment will tend to decline. Accordingly, without knowing except in a rough way how much it costs to haul a given commodity between two points, railways can afford to quote lower rates per ton-mile when the car is heavily laden than when it contains only a few tons of the same freight. Such prices are known as "incentive rates" because they encourage the shipper to load each car more heavily, and thereby make more effective use of the railway's total inventory of freight cars. Incentive rates have also often proved useful in allowing railways effectively to meet competition from trucks. Finally, out-of-pocket costs, the additional or extra cost incurred by taking an additional shipment, set a limit below which the rate on a particular shipment ought not to fall.

Decreasing Costs

Rate-making for individual commodities can be approached by looking at two principles in economics: decreasing costs and common costs. According to the former, cost *per unit* declines as the number of units produced increases. *Total* costs increase less rapidly than the number of units of output and thus cost *per unit* is reduced as production increases.

Some analysis of railway expenses will bring out the principle of decreasing costs more clearly.[4] Railway expenses fall into six groups: (*a*) interest on funded debt, rentals on leased lines, real estate and other taxes, dividends, and the like; (*b*) maintenance of way and structures, i.e., stations, bridges, fences, rails, ties, ballast, and so forth; (*c*) maintenance of equipment, e.g., locomotives, cars, and machinery in shops; (*d*) transportation expenses such as wages of train crews, locomotive fuel, and service at stations; (*e*) traffic expenses such as advertising, freight solicitation services, and traffic bureaus; (*f*) general expenses including the president's salary and the cost of the legal, accounting, and secretary's departments. The last five of these groups are collectively known as operating expenses.

After working through these elements of expense in some detail, Professor Jackman[5] and other transportation economists concluded that about 55 per cent of the operating expenses of a typical railway or 65 per cent of its total expenses went on despite any changes in the amount of traffic carried by the railway. In other words, only 45 per cent of the operating and 35 per cent of the total expenses would increase, or decrease, more or less directly with increases or decreases in the volume of traffic hauled over the railway.

Owing to the large proportion of expenses which was said to be relatively constant, additional freight can be hauled without an equivalent increase in expenses. This can be demonstrated by a simple example. Let us assume that a railway carries 100 units of freight and that its expenses are $100 of which $15 are for interest and taxes. Of the operating expenses ($85) 55 per cent ($46.75) are assumed to be constant, and 45 per cent ($38.25) variable with traffic volume. Suppose that the railway's business increases by 10 per cent. The variable operating expenses increase in direct proportion to the rise in volume, or 10 per cent ($3.83), but interest and similar charges as well as the constant proportion of operating expenses will be unchanged.[6] Total expenses are now $15.00 + $46.75 + $38.25 + $3.83, or $103.83 for 110 units of traffic. The average cost per unit, formerly $1, has declined to 94.4 cents $103.83 ÷ 110). The railway is operating under decreasing costs.

In the above example it was assumed that the additional freight was charged at the same rate per unit as the freight already being handled, so that gross railway revenue became $110. As a matter of fact it would pay the railway to cut its prices on the additional freight, if that business could not be secured at the charges currently in effect. The additional ten units cost only $3.83 in total or about 38 cents per unit to handle. This is usually referred to as the out-of-pocket cost. If the carrier cannot get the traffic on any better terms, it can profitably cut the current tolls to almost the out-of-pocket costs, though preferably it will get something more than this in order to add to its profits.

In connection with the principle of decreasing costs, four important qualifications should be noted. First, the railway may have to reduce its rates so much in order to get the extra business that the total receipts from the traffic at the new rates may be less than the increase in variable expenses incurred on account of the additional traffic. In other words, the new freight rate per unit may be less than the out-of-pocket cost per unit and so the carrier might have been better off if it had never bid for the extra business. Reduced rates for additional business may lead to cutting rates on some old business since railways must take care not to infringe the law prohibiting undue preference or unjust discrimination.

Second, the additional traffic may necessitate an increase in physical plant such as purchase of more cars and locomotives, expansion of terminal facilities, and laying down more main-line track. In that event charges for interest, maintenance of way and structures and of equipment—most of which we have assumed to be constant—may in fact increase. This possibility does not necessarily invalidate the principle of decreasing cost but it does mean that when the railway plant is already being used to capacity, any additional traffic can be handled only at very heavy out-of-pocket cost. More accurately speaking, the carrier may temporarily enter a stage of increasing cost. Under these circumstances the carrier will either charge exceptionally high rates on the additional business or it will raise the rates on traffic which is already being carried at rates which are close to the out-of-pocket costs for that traffic. If it selects the second alternative, it will choke off some of the less profitable traffic, and be able to confine itself to what pays better.

In practice, railways are rarely faced with either alternative because the likelihood of their operating at capacity for any length of time is comparatively remote. Railways, especially in Canada where density of traffic is less than in the United States, typically have a considerable amount of unused capacity. Furthermore, all of the facilities of a particular railway will not be used at capacity at the same time. One terminal may be congested while others have idle track and yard locomotives. Box cars may be scarce but empty refrigerator cars may be plentiful. In other words, a marked expansion in the volume of traffic will set up a series of bottlenecks. As soon as practicable, the railway will eliminate one bottleneck after another by purchasing new rolling stock, constructing new sidings, erecting signals, and so on. Over a period of years the plant will be enlarged to keep its overall capacity more or less in line with the volume of traffic being handled. Although in the short run investment costs can be regarded as fixed, in the very long run they will vary directly with traffic.

Third, the theory assumes that other things remain unchanged. Although cost per unit will normally decline as a result of more intensive use of plant, this decline may be offset by increases in costs in other directions, such as higher wages. On the other hand cost may be reduced by more efficient equipment, better operating methods, and technical improvements generally, quite apart from the intensity of use of plant. The term decreasing cost applies only to lower unit costs due to a more complete utilization of an existing plant. The doctrine assumes that all other factors affecting cost are unchanged during the period of time when the number of units of output is growing.

Joint and Common Costs

The other principle or economic "law" underlying the theory of freight rates on individual commodities is that of joint and common costs. Joint costs occur where it is physically impossible to produce one article without producing another. The classic example in textbooks is cotton lint and cotton seed. Total receipts from selling both products must in the long run be equal to the number of units sold multiplied by the marginal cost of production. Unless total receipts covered costs, farmers would not continue to produce the amount of cotton lint and seed which the public demands at going prices. Yet costs cannot be used to set the price of each of the articles because it is not possible to segregate the cost of producing one article from the cost of producing the other. The costs of production are incurred jointly and are not susceptible of division between the two articles.

For every one pound of lint which is raised, two pounds of seed are inevitably produced also. Thus for any given quantity of lint brought on the market, the amount of seed offered for sale is predetermined. For all practical purposes the supply of each of the articles on the market at any one time is fixed. Consequently the price which each will bring will be determined chiefly by the strength of the demand for that article. In short, when two articles are produced under conditions of joint cost, receipts from the sale of both must cover the total cost of producing the marginal unit times the number of units sold, but the price of either one of the joint articles is set chiefly by demand. In some instances, for example the pressing of cotton seed for the manufacture of oil, special expenses are incurred for this extra processing. The price of oil must at least cover this extra charge occasioned by it alone, otherwise the seed will not be processed. But the amount of contribution which cottonseed oil makes to the joint costs of production over and above its special cost is a function of demand.

This principle may be illustrated from other aspects of economic life. A retail butcher buys the carcass of a hog. If he were to offer all cuts of meat for sale at the same price per pound, he would find that the choice parts like bacon and ham would be quickly snapped up by housewives but that the less desirable ones, such as the hocks, would not sell. So he would not get sufficient revenue to cover the cost of the carcass. In order to dispose of the entire animal at one time and have his receipts cover his costs, the butcher will vary his prices by cuts. If he noticed that ham was selling rapidly whereas hocks were moving slowly at the price he was asking, he would raise the price of the one and lower that of the other. He would adjust his prices on the various cuts in accordance with the relative strength of the demand for them. At the same time he would try to make these changes so that the total receipts from all the cuts would cover the cost of the carcass plus the appropriate share of his costs of doing business such as heat, light, interest, depreciation, and wages.

Common costs arise when two or more products or services are produced by use, in the main, of the same means of production. A railway carries passengers and freight over the same rails, with the same fuel depots, the same despatchers, the same president, etc., and it has only one debt and one share capital. It also handles many kinds of freight—coal, wheat, potato chips, steel girders, toothpaste, oranges, sheep, and a host of other things—with the same rails, locomotives, marshalling yards, and so on. In all these cases costs are incurred in common for the various kinds of freight.

At the same time one must recognize that some railways carry only freight and a few haul only passengers. In these cases no expenses are incurred in common for passengers or freight. Some lines even haul only one class of freight, e.g., Minnesota iron ore to ports on Lake Superior, West Virginia coal to tidewater, or ferrous ore along the Quebec, North Shore and Labrador Railway. Such carriers will have no common costs, though they do have joint ones. The latter arise because cars which are filled with one kind of freight to be hauled in one direction must be hauled back empty in the opposite direction. Joint costs also arise on companies which carry a variety of traffic. For example, an increase in the volume of gasoline going by rail inevitably means an increase in the mileage of empty tank cars, for it is practically impossible to get a return shipment which will not be contaminated by the gasoline fumes within the car. Empty mileage cannot be entirely avoided even on so-called general purpose freight cars, such as box and flat cars. Back-loading may be achieved on some cars or for part of the distance, but the amount of empty movement relative to loaded is a major problem in operating a railway.

One should also note that some expenses, e.g., the maintenance of passenger coaches and of freight cars or the wages of freight- and passenger-train conductors or the loss and damage on particular classes of freight, are attributable to one particular kind of service and to no other. For reasons already given, rates and fares on each class of traffic, like the price of cottonseed oil, should be high enough to cover these exceptional expenses involved in handling passengers and each class of freight. Even so, if one takes the business of railway rate-making as a whole, the intriguing and difficult problem is that of common costs.

From a practical point of view the difference between joint and common costs may not be great. In both instances the proceeds from the sale of all services should equal the total costs of operating the railway including depreciation, interest, a fair rate of dividend, and a reasonable surplus to come and go on. The price or rate charged for carrying any class or kind of goods should cover the costs that can be directly attributed to it (including the cost of hauling back empty cars so that they may be loaded again) and make some contribution to the common costs of the railway. The size of this contribution to common costs varies with the demand for the service, that is, with the ability of shippers and consignees to pay a given level of tolls and still have the goods move in volume. Thus despite the technical differences between joint and common costs, the price-setter or rate-maker has had to pay rather more attention to the demand for a given service than to the cost of moving the particular class of passengers or kind of freight.

Value of Service

The importance of demand in setting many rail rates on individual commodities is so great that, even at the risk of some repetition, the matter must be elaborated. Although there are exceptions, the railway industry typically supplies several broad groups of service—for freight, passengers, mail, express and so on—and within each group it supplies a variety of individual services. For example, in freight service a railway carries some articles in carloads, others in small lots, some at high speeds and for long distances, others at low speeds and in short hauls; some goods are valuable in relation to their bulk, others are of little value per cubic foot or per pound. Yet most railway expenses such as interest, maintenance of equipment, fuel for locomotives, or the repairs on a bridge are incurred in common for different kinds of traffic.

At least until the early 1960s, statisticians found themselves unable to divide these common and joint costs among the different kinds of traffic without using more or less arbitrary assumptions. In consequence, their conclusions were usually suspect. Therefore, economists and traffic managers stressed the demand side of rate-making rather than cost. Of course they recognized that the freight rate on each individual service or group of services should always be high enough to cover the extra or out-of-pocket expenses incurred in connection with it but the proportion which each service will contribute to the common expenses will vary with intensity of demand. In economics this is the principle of value of service or charging what the traffic will bear.

The clause, "what the traffic will bear," is sometimes interpreted in a derogatory sense. Often it is taken to refer to the monopolistic practice of getting the highest possible rate or price from each unit of service. Actually the clause merely means that the price is set, by and large, by the value of the benefits which the railway user receives from shipping the commodity in question. These benefits are measured by what he is willing to pay and still ship the commodity in substantial quantities. Value of service is not measured by the largest possible amount per unit which can be collected before the article will cease to move at all but by what the shippers or consignees of it will pay and continue to use the railway regularly. Instead of stating the principle in the words "charging what the traffic will bear," it would be more accurate to say "not charging what the traffic will not bear."

If the carrier tries to charge more than the railway user can afford to pay,[7] the freight will not move. Let us assume that all the goods coming on a given market are carried by one railway and are of precisely the same quality. If for some reason or other the cost of production plus the cost of transport is very high, consumers will, as a rule, purchase only small quantities of the article. In that event, the suppliers and the railway will both lose business which they might otherwise have had. If the railway were to lower its tolls, the price in the market would decline, purchasers would buy more of the goods, and as a result both the producers and the railway would be better off.

Let us now suppose that *two* railways connect the suppliers with their market. One carrier, seeing how things stood, might decide to cut rates. By so doing it would gain in two ways: first, by the increased consumption at the market brought about by lower prices to consumers; and second, by capturing traffic from its rail competitor. Soon the other railway would probably cut rates to equal those of its competitor. Both companies would now share the traffic in much the same ratio as before. It is possible that they would both gain because consumption had increased and, while they get a smaller revenue per ton, they would be handling more tons. However, it is more likely that one road after the other might reduce rates below the going rate until eventually they would scarcely cover wages, fuel, and other such costs, leaving nothing for maintenance of equipment, interest, and so on. In that case, one or both lines would eventually become bankrupt. Foreseeing this disaster, both roads might sign an agreement to maintain rates at some reasonable level, a situation which economists and the general public would recognize as monopoly.

Alternatively, without any consultation with each other, each road would maintain rates. It would do this on the theory that if it cut tolls, its competitor would follow suit. In the long run neither road would be any farther ahead and if rate-cutting were carried too far, both might be ruined. This situation, little recognized by the public at large, is known to economists as duopoly or, if there are more than two roads, as monopolistic competition.

When there was only one road, it looked solely to the effect of rates on total sales in the market. When there were two roads competing with each other intensively on the basis of rates, they had to look at two factors: (*a*) the effect of freight rates on market price, consumption, and the total volume of traffic; and (*b*) the effect of rates on the relative amount of business handled by each line. But as soon as railways began to work together on rates, whether by formal agreement or implicitly, their primary consideration was what rate they ought to charge and still have the commodity move in such volume as to give them the maximum net profit. In other words, they reverted to the position of a single road, as far as rate-making was concerned, and mainly watched what the traffic would bear.

In recent years much traffic moves by truck. Where trucking is a factor, traffic managers for a railway have to bear in mind: (*a*) what the traffic will bear in the sense of how much consumers are willing to pay and still buy the goods; and (*b*) what the traffic will bear in the sense of how much railways can charge and still keep all or some of the traffic from truckers. In other words, the growth of trucking has tended to restore the situation which prevailed when two railways set their rates in competition with each other. Highway transport has added, or more accurately has restored, a second meaning to the doctrine of what the traffic will bear. At times, however, truckers base their rates on what the railways charge. In that event, the trucking rates are set on what the traffic will bear in the sense that term was used by the older economists and by railways when they had a virtual monopoly of inland transport. In other words, truckers and railways usually compete with each other on rates but sometimes act as duopolists.

Yet the principle of what the traffic will bear, even with recent modifications, is subject to an important qualification. A railway is entitled to a reasonably compensatory toll for the service it is prepared to render. This privilege has been affirmed in several rate cases. "If the nature or value of a commodity offered for transportation is such as to demand an unreasonably low rate, there is no legal obligation upon the carrier to meet this demand."[8] "Value of service to the shipper in a general sense is the ability to reach a market and make his commodity a subject of commerce. . . . In a more definite and accurate sense it consists in reaching a market at a profit, being in effect what the traffic will bear to be remunerative to the producer or dealer."[9] "Regardless of the value of the traffic, the carriers are entitled to rates which are reasonable for the services they perform."[10] The National Transportation Act of 1967 specifically forbids railways charging unremunerative tolls.

In sum, each rate must be high enough to cover the out-of-pocket expenses incurred for transporting the freight in question and make some contribution to joint or common costs. The amount of such contribution is governed by the value of service to the shipper. The Board stated in 1927 that "Cost of operation is, of course, an important factor, but the traffic department in establishing rates endeavour to make them such as will move traffic, having regard to competition, actual and market, without going into operating costs. In rate cases the cost question naturally arises in defense of the reasonableness of the rates which are attacked."[11]

Numerous problems associated with measuring value of service will be dealt with in the succeeding chapter. In general, it is determined by the value of the article being transported. Low valued articles such as firewood and gravel will not move in quantity at high freight rates. Shippers of high valued goods such as silk are able to stand high rates and still send their product in substantially undiminished volume. Thus rates on low valued, bulky articles may barely cover their out-of-pocket costs per unit whereas valuable ones will make a larger contribution per unit to the common costs. As everyone knows, retail merchants often find it is more profitable for them to cut prices and sell a large number of units at a low gross margin per unit than to maintain prices and sell only a few units at a large margin per unit. Like other businesses railways try to maximize their profits. Many years ago[12] railways discovered the same thing as the retailer: they could make more money by differentiating tolls, by charging according to what the traffic will bear, than by levying a uniform toll on all freight. The carriage of low valued articles at rates per unit which are just a little higher than out-of-pocket costs per unit may be profitable business for a railway. Despite the low rate per ton-mile, the total contribution which the units make to common costs may be substantial because of the large number hauled. High valued goods do not necessarily bring the most profit to the carrier because, while the toll per unit is high, the number of units transported is comparatively small.[13]

On the surface it may appear morally unjust to charge two commodities quite different tolls for a service which costs the railway very little more in one case than in the other. Yet when a carrier charges low rates on some goods which will not stand higher rates, it obtains from this traffic a contribution to common costs which it would not have got at all except for the fact that it gave such low rates. If the low tolls had not been offered, the shipper of the low valued freight could not have afforded to send the goods and the railway would not have received the contribution to common costs which it did. The common costs would be practically the same without this freight but there would be one significant difference: all these common costs would have to be borne by returns from the high valued goods alone. So the rates on these goods would have to be higher than they are. Low rates on low valued goods make it possible for the carrier to charge lower tolls on valuable articles than would otherwise have been feasible. The rates on valuable articles will be lower, not higher, on account of low rates on goods which will bear only low tolls.

An illustration from another field may be helpful. In operating a motion picture theatre some expenses, such as interest, depreciation, taxes on the building, heat, and light, remain the same whether the auditorium is partially or completely filled. Other costs, such as taxes on admission tickets, the royalty for the use of the film (in most large theatres but not always in smaller ones), and so forth, vary directly with the number of patrons. Still other expenses, such as wages for usherettes, vary to some extent with attendance but not in direct proportion to it.

During the afternoon performance, attendance is normally smaller than in the evening and the cost per patron is higher. The expenses which are fixed in total are spread out over fewer people thus resulting in higher cost per patron. The variable costs, i.e. those which vary directly with the number of patrons, are the same per customer at both performances. Despite the higher cost per patron in the afternoon than at night, the admission charge is normally less than it is later in the day. If a patron at the evening performance were to complain of being charged more than in the afternoon even though the cost per patron is less, the theatre manager might explain that if he charged the same price at both showings, attendance in the afternoon would decline greatly. For various social and business reasons most people prefer to go to a motion picture in the evening. But some people, who might not go in the evening at the high prices prevailing then, can be induced to attend in the afternoon by the offer of a ticket at a lower price. If they do come in the afternoon, the total receipts from their patronage will cover the out-of-pocket cost of running the performance in the afternoon and make some contribution to the fixed costs of the theatre. If the afternoon's receipts are not large enough to cover the out-of-pocket cost, the manager will of course cancel showings at that time.[14] The contribution which this afternoon performance makes to common costs reduces the amount of such costs which must be borne by patrons at the evening shows. As a result, the prices of admission to these later showings are lower, not higher, than they would have been if reduced prices had not been offered at other times of the day.

Of course the theatre manager may not be well enough versed in economics to explain all these matters. He knows that he makes the most money when every seat in his theatre is filled at every showing of the film. He knows that he cannot get full occupancy at afternoon performances unless he charges less than he does in the evening. He knows too that any receipts he gets in the afternoon above what he has to pay out for admission taxes, wages for projectionist, ticket-seller, usherettes, and so on will either add to his own profits or make it possible for him to charge less at the evening performances if it should be necessary for him to do so in order to get a full house then. If he could raise his prices and still get a full attendance at all showings, he would quickly increase them. In fact, this is what he does when a highly praised film is shown for the first time. Even at a single performance, he may charge different prices for loges, orchestra seats, and balconies though obviously the cost per patron is nearly the same in all cases. The theatre manager has found out by experience, or at least the industry has discovered empirically, what is the appropriate price to be charged at different showings and for the different seats in the same theatre. Though he may never have heard of the expression, he charges what the traffic will bear and still come to his theatre. His pricing policy in its essentials is identical with that of railways.

Many other businesses besides theatres, butcher shops, and railways experience joint costs and charge on the basis of value of service. Telephone companies, electric light and power concerns, resort hotels with "off season" rates, book publishers with *de luxe*, trade, book-club, and paper cover editions of the same book, and the medical profession follow a similar policy. The chief limitation on the still further extension of differential pricing is the difficulty of distinguishing consumers who are willing and able to pay high prices from those who are just on the margin of buying or of not buying at low prices. When a person is very hungry, he may be willing to pay 25 cents for a chocolate bar. In fact he need pay only the normal price. If the merchant knew when this customer entered his shop that he would pay 25 cents for a bar, he would doubtless raise his price to that amount. But as he cannot tell from the customer's appearance what he will pay, he can ask no more than the going price. Moreover, if the number of prospective purchasers at 25 cents a bar, could they be identified, were quite small relative to the total number of buyers, it would hardly be worthwhile for the merchant to try to differentiate.

The theatre operator can see that the person who is willing to pay, let us say, 75 cents to see a motion picture attends the afternoon performance and that only those who are willing to pay more are admitted in the evening. The butcher readily discriminates purchasers of ham and of sausage. Similarly in the freight business, the railway finds it easy to distinguish one commodity from another. Hence it can charge the shippers of goods what the commodity they are shipping will bear and still be transported in substantial amounts. In its passenger department, a railway can differentiate in fares between pullmans and coaches, for it can see that the traveller who has bought only a coach ticket does not ride in a pullman car. It cannot, however, distinguish between one coach passenger who might be willing to pay three cents a mile and another who will pay only two cents. For this reason the extent of differentiation is much less in passenger fares than in freight rates. To be able to distinguish between customers or goods on the basis of ability to pay is fundamental to the achievement of a successfully differentiated pricing structure.

Regardless of the business concerned, the lack of uniformity of prices for broadly similar services is known as differential pricing or discrimination. The economist uses the word discrimination in a technical rather than a popular sense. Discrimination may easily become unjust, unfair, and unreasonable but in its proper or economic connotation the word itself means merely that rates are adjusted to conditions of demand and not according to cost of service. The practical application of the theory of a differentiated pricing system is one of the primary responsibilities of a railway traffic manager.

Criticism of the Theory

Although the so-called classical theory of railway rates was never wholly free of criticism, it has been under intensive fire only since the 1930s. During the depression it was observed that railway managers were able to keep expenses for maintenance of way and structures, for maintenance of equipment, and for transportation at fairly uniform percentages of gross revenues. Experience showed that the proportion of the total expenses of the railway which was represented by variable expenses was much higher than formerly believed. Instead of being 45 per cent of the total, they seemed more in the neighbourhood of 70 or 75 per cent.[15] In the immediate postwar period when wage rates and prices of materials rose faster than the increases in tolls allowed by the Board, the proportion of operating expenses to gross revenues rose well above the previous ratio. Yet whenever gross revenues began to fall off, the head office would advise subordinate officials charged with the immediate responsibility for maintenance to cut expenses by postponing work.

Although expenditures are generally correlated with gross revenues, the relationship is not always identical. Programmes of maintenance are often undertaken in the spring on the assumption of a large gross revenue from handling the fall crop. If agricultural yields are poor, revenues will decline but too late in the year to allow railway managers to cancel financial obligations already incurred. Conversely, revenues in the last quarter of the year may exceed expectations and so the percentage will be abnormally depressed. Severe weather, floods, or a sudden increase in wage rates may throw the percentages out of line. Finally, the possibility of postponing some maintenance until a later year when wages or costs of materials are lower may allow a certain leeway in expenditures. Yet when all is said and done, it is surprising how close is the relationship between expenditures and revenues.

This conclusion does not support the older transportation economists who contended that the fixed or uncontrollable expenditures, those which did not vary in total with volume of traffic, constituted a high proportion of the total. Of course it is undeniably true that on light traffic lines there is a minimum below which it is absolutely impossible to cut expenses. But as the number of ton-miles per mile of line increases, expenditures on maintenance and transportation tend to grow in almost direct proportion to the increase in traffic. Over a few years capital investment increases owing to the necessity of heavier rails and bridges, more powerful locomotives, and more commodious yards, stations, and freight-houses. Once the investment is made it is not possible to cancel it immediately traffic falls off. Even so, over a period of time, railway managers keep investment somewhat closely in line with volume of traffic.

In short, recent analysts have placed less emphasis than their predecessors on the influence of fixed expenses and variable unit costs in the determination of railway rates. The trend in thinking has been toward giving more attention to average unit costs. "It follows that the bidding for competitive or additional traffic by quoting low carload rates based on variable costs may easily prove to be unprofitable because the cost of handling the added business is apt to be far more than the . . . out-of-pocket cost [estimated at 45 per cent by the older group of economists]. In fact, the added cost in the long run, may be almost the same as the average over-all cost. This is particularly true when the volume of traffic which is attracted by the low rates is considerable."[16]

Furthermore, in the 1930s economists began to see more clearly than formerly that the concept of variable cost had validity only when related to a certain period of time. An expense which may be fixed in the short run may, in the long run, vary with the volume of traffic. Mr. J. B. Eastman, one of the most experienced and able men ever to serve on the Interstate Commerce Commission, stressed the indefiniteness of the concept of out-of-pocket costs:

In the first place, what is a particular service? Do we mean the transportation of one particular carload of coal, all the coal in one trainload of coal, or all the coal carried by one railway in a year? The wages of the crew of a particular train might be unaffected by adding one more car of coal to the train, in which case train wages would not be out-of-pocket for the added car of coal. But if an entire train of coal were added to the traffic the wages of the crew would clearly be in the out-of-pocket group. If we have in mind all of the coal carried in a year, the wear and tear on the track would be an appreciable out-of-pocket cost.

To put the preceding thought in another way, the concept may be said to be indefinite because some expenses, while apparently not immediately connected with a given amount of added traffic, are, nevertheless, over a period of time proportionate to the volume of traffic. Thus, the repairs to a locomotive immediately caused by a given train run would be of a minor character, but after 100,000 miles had been run there would inevitably be heavy repairs, and hence one would say that such repairs should be included in the out-of-pocket group in the broad view of the matter. In a still broader view, one might include part of the interest on investment among out-of-pocket items, because the amount of equipment needed is largely dependent on the volume of movement, as are also certain maintenance of way expenses designed to adapt the track facilities to increased traffic.[17]

Commissioner Eastman mentioned other practical difficulties with the concept, particularly if it were applied to competitive business. He suggested that the adoption of this theory by one kind of carrier would prevent traffic going to a competing form of transportation which was inherently better fitted to handle it. Moreover, Commissioner Eastman said, for any one carrier the theory could easily be extended to cover more and more kinds of traffic with the result that eventually the net revenue of the carrier would be imperilled. He was unable to believe that the out-of-pocket cost of the great volume of traffic which had been attracted to railways by the application of this theory was anything like as low as the railways had contended.[18] In brief, Commissioner Eastman's views support the opinion of an official of the Canadian National that the concept of out-of-pocket costs is necessarily as flexible as the circumstances demand.[19]

Analysis of Costs

As already suggested, many efforts have been made throughout the years to ascertain the cost of moving particular classes of freight. For instance, about 1940 Dr. Ford K. Edwards, then chief cost analyst of the Interstate Commerce Commission, divided the total operating expenses of railways between passenger and freight departments in accordance with a formula used by the Commission. Then, in what has come to be known as Rail Form A,[20] he apportioned freight expenses by groups: running expenses; station expenses; expenses for special services such as the operation of grain elevators and for items such as

loss and damage on freight; general overhead including traffic solicitation, head office and legal expenses; rent of facilities used jointly
with other railways; and so on. Within each of the groups he broke
down or apportioned the expenses in a logical manner over car-miles,
gross ton-miles, or time. Then he used the unit costs to build up cost
scales. He made no attempt to segregate costs by particular types of
traffic such as grain, scrap iron, livestock, or cheese but knowing the
kind of car, average lading per car, and empty movement for any
commodity, he could construct an appropriate cost scale.

Previous costing studies had generally used a composite ton-mile,
a measure of service which took in all commodities and lengths of
haul. The Edwards scheme had several advantages. It recognized how
costs are affected by the weight of the payload within a car, the
amount of empty movement associated with particular kinds of traffic,
switching at intermediate terminals, the time taken for loading and
unloading, and many other details. The method was particularly useful
in comparing costs of handling traffic in different regions. Older methods
of analysis overlooked differences between one region and another in
the consist of traffic or the relative proportions of high-rated and
low-rated traffic, variations in length of haul, in the amount of empty
mileage, and so on. Edwards' plan allowed the analyst to take notice
of these variables and eliminate those which have really nothing to do
with regional differences in the cost of handling traffic. Thus, the
student was able to compare like with like. Moreover, he was able to
segregate the cost of main-line and of way-freight service. It was not
possible to make this division with previous methods and their value
was therefore reduced.

The Edwards' studies showed fairly clearly that there was less scope
for differential pricing than was formerly assumed. Moreover, Edwards'
techniques were imaginative, comprehensive, and as correct as anyone
could expect, having regard to the analytical apparatus which he had
at his command. Rail Form A is still being used for rate-making in the
United States. Nevertheless, a fundamental difficulty remained. No one
could be certain that Edwards' method of apportionment was the most
accurate that could be devised. The cost of maintaining roadbed may
vary with the number of trains, the number of cars, the gross weight of
loaded and empty cars passing over it, or a combination of all three.
It may also be related to the amount of precipitation or the nature of
the terrain over which the road is built. Various arguments could be
advanced by accountants and engineers for selecting one or other of
these bases. Yet in the last analysis their conclusions were largely
subjective.

A notable advance in costing for rate-making purposes was made in the late 1950s by means of multiple regression. The method was already well established in mathematics for the name was given to it by Sir Francis Galton (1822–1911). He studied the heights of fathers and of their sons in order to determine whether the heights of sons moved, or as he said regressed, toward the heights of the fathers. Although the term may at first confuse the uninitiated, regression has a very definite meaning for statisticians.

What the statisticians want to get is a formula which will most accurately show the relationship between two or more sets of variables. They record, for example, the average cost per mile of line of maintaining track in each of the roughly 30 divisions of the Canadian Pacific or the Canadian National. These costs will vary from one division to another. The problem is to find what causes the variation. If the statistician discovered that the cost of maintaining track rose or fell by one percentage point every time there was an increase or decrease of one per cent in gross ton-miles per mile of line, he could reasonably conclude that changes in the one factor were the direct cause of changes in the other. Then, knowing the number of gross ton-miles (i.e., the weight of cars and contents and the mileage they moved) of grain or livestock or patent medicines, he would be able to estimate with great accuracy how much of the total cost of maintaining track should be charged to each kind of traffic. Such a simple and perfect correlation of one variable with another would be most unusual. Commonly the statistician has to work with approximations.

Generally, after a statistician has collected his data, he plots them on a chart of the sort used in elementary geometry. He draws two lines at right angles to each other and then makes a scale—in our example track maintenance costs per mile of line—along the horizontal or x axis and makes another scale—for gross ton-miles per mile of line— along the vertical or y axis. His next step is to place a dot at the appropriate place on the chart where a line drawn at right angles to the x axis and at the proper place along its scale would intersect a similar line drawn at right angles from the y axis. The point of intersection or the dot would show the relationship between track maintenance costs and, say, gross ton-miles for that particular division. Similar dots would be spotted for each of the other divisions. In this way the statistician gets what he calls a scatter diagram.

His next problem is to draw a line, which may be straight, a curve, or some other pattern, which most nearly passes through all the points of intersection or dots. There are several ways of doing this. One is by visual observation, which is really guessing where the line ought to be.

A common, and far more accurate method, is that of least squares. Let us imagine that a trend line has already been drawn. Then the statistician draws a line from each of the dots or points to meet the trend line at right angles. The distance along each of the lines so drawn is called a deviation. The statistician computes the mathematical squares of each deviation (i.e., he multiplies the length of the deviation by itself), adds all the data for the squares both above and below the line, and finally divides this total by the number of observations, in our case 30 which is the number of railway divisions. If the trend line has been correctly placed, the averages of the squared values is a minimum. Squaring the deviations gives special emphasis to large deviations and avoids the nuisance that some deviations are positive (plus) and some are negative (minus quantities). A trend line drawn according to the least squares method is called a line of regression. As a rule any such line starts not at the junction of the x and the y axes but at some point above the x axis. When this happens, the line of regression has both a constant factor, shown by the distance above the x axis or horizontal line, and a slope, shown by the upward or downward inclination or slope of the trend line to the x axis. Expressed algebraically, the line is $y = a + bx$.

Once the statistician has a regression line on his scatter diagram or, better still, can fill in the data in the equation of such a line, he can say with some confidence that if the figure of gross ton-miles per mile of line for, say, wheat, is such and such, then the cost of maintaining track per mile which is attributable to wheat is so and so. The accuracy of the latter figure depends on how nearly the line of regression passes through all the points on the scatter diagram. In other words, accuracy depends on the closeness of the "fit" of the regression line or formula to the observed data. Statisticians have devised tests which measure this accuracy or, as they say, which will give the probable error of estimate.

The main limitation on using the method of least squares has been the number of calculations which have to be made to analyse even a simple set of data. In our example, we used figures for track maintenance per mile of line and gross ton-miles for about 30 divisions on each of two railways. We had to calculate deviations from the line of regression, square them, add the squares, and finally divide by the number of observations (30). Our work would have been enormously complicated if we had used four or five variables (e.g., train-miles, locomotive-miles, gross ton-miles, yard and train switching miles, and an index for relative gradients on various divisions) instead of only two (expenditures on track maintenance and gross ton-miles). Moreover, when we had completed our calculations, we could not be certain that we had made the best analysis. We might have got better results with different combinations of the above variables or conceivably with different variables altogether. Unfortunately, to test any hypothesis used to require a vast amount of work.

These two difficulties, namely, the physical labour of making numerous calculations and the problem of experimenting with new statistical raw material, have been overcome by the use of electronic computers. The work of programming, that is, of feeding the data into the machine so that it can effectively handle the figures, is time-consuming and calls for a high degree of skill. But once the electronic "brain" has the facts in its "memory," it can sort them out very rapidly. As a result, if the statistician is not satisfied with some fit or even if he is just curious to learn the result he would get from introducing a different factor, he can quickly adjust the machine so that it makes use of additional or substitute data. It will provide him with a formula and even a copy of the scatter diagram and regression line in less than a minute.

As already explained, the regression line may be straight, curved, or some other form. In technical lingo it may be linear, curvilinear, one-tailed, two-tailed, etc. Simple regression involves using only one specific variable to explain expenses. Multiple regression is the explicit use of two or more variables. The analyst of railway costs can carry out his observations over a number of different days, weeks, months, or years. In this case, his study is known as time-series analysis. He may also make observations of a number of economic factors at the same point in time. This cross-section analysis has the advantage that changes in wage rates and material prices do not create any problem as they do in time-series analysis. Furthermore, the analyst can compare data of different railway companies, but since such data are likely to be affected by the financial position of the firms and the policies of their executives, it is better to use data from the various divisions of the same railway.

The MacPherson Commission thought that multiple regression analysis constituted a major breakthrough in the problem of railway costing. One commissioner, René Gobiel of Quebec City, dissented from this view. Incidentally he was the only one who had had any previous experience with multiple regression.

In the author's opinion there is a danger that the new techniques, valuable as they are under certain conditions, will give rise to an exaggerated and unwarranted belief in the possibility of finding the correct cost of every movement by rail or even the total cost of handling certain classes of freight. Admittedly, the methods used to cost the movement of export grain in Western Canada stood up well under fire from numerous experts engaged by the grain trade and by the Royal Commission of 1961. Further improvements in the technique and especially some shortcuts in method can be expected. Yet it would be wrong to leave the reader with the impression that use of multiple regression analysis reduces railway costing to a mechanical routine and that rates can be set solely on the basis of cost. Demand or value of service is still significant in rate-making, and railway traffic men cannot afford to ignore it.

It must also be remembered that multiple regression has been used to analyse only part of the total costs of the railway, viz., shops and engine houses, power plants, despatching, station expenses, locomotive supplies, fences, snowsheds and signs, and water and fuel stations. Beyond this, some expenses can be assigned directly, such as loss and damage which is divided by kinds of freight, and grain doors which are panels of lumber or plywood which are fitted across the doorways of cars to prevent bulk grain from filtering out during transit.

Yet when all this has been done, there still remain certain fixed or constant costs which do not lend themselves to either regression analysis or to direct allocation. These costs include taxes on income and real estate, telegraph and telephone expenses incurred for the purposes of operating the railway, office expenses, pensions, and most of all, the cost of capital. These costs may be divided among various kinds of traffic in proportion to their ability to bear a certain amount of the overhead, or in the same ratio as the variable costs on different kinds of traffic, or may even be largely ignored on the theory that the traffic under study is incremental and that any contribution it makes to the overhead is so much to the good. On the other hand in the cost study on grain, the railways argued that costs of capital were "basic to the plant," that is, that certain branches had been constructed and much of the investment in main lines had been made primarily for grain. Therefore, so they argued, the grain traffic should bear all the costs of the investment in "solely-related lines" and its full share of the cost of the investment in other facilities.

As one of the experts employed by the MacPherson Commission explained, it is possible to contend that the grain trade is incapable of paying more than the bare variable costs. In that event all the fixed costs must be borne by other segments of the traffic. If this proves impossible, the size of the plant must be reduced. At the other extreme one can argue that the transportation of grain to export positions should make a large enough contribution to bring the railways' earnings up to a point sufficient to keep all their present facilities in existence.[21]

In the end the MacPherson Commission concluded that the cost of handling the grain traffic should include fully distributable costs, i.e., long-run variable costs plus a return on the investment. It then went on to say, in effect, that Canadian grain could not stand rates high enough to cover these costs. Hence, a subsidy was required on export grain that was subject to statutory and related rates. Details about the recommended subsidy were considered in connection with the Crow's Nest Pass Rates. The government planned to have the Canadian Transport Commission review the methods used by the railways in their studies, bring the statistics up to date, and recommend what subsidies, if any, should be paid railways for moving Western grain to export positions. This proposal was defeated in the House. Thus, railways and government were stimied, at least temporarily, in their effort to get parliamentary recognition for the new methods of finding costs. But the Board had already accepted the techniques when applied to finding losses on branch lines and on commuter passenger trains.

Principles of Rate-making and the Royal Commission of 1961

Besides hearing voluminous testimony on the costing of the grain traffic, the MacPherson Commission heard several witnesses expound their views on the general theory of rate-making and in its report it set forth its own ideas. Limitations of space prevent a full description of all the evidence. Since the views of the Commission are of a semi-official nature, the obvious approach would be to quote from its report. Unfortunately, the Commission's discussion of the theory is diffuse and sometimes contradictory. For example, on page 19 of volume *II* it says that "several of the most important decisions respecting any costing operation are matters of judgment and not of technique, and are likely to remain so." Forty pages later, it states that "the great strides made recently in the techniques applicable to the costing of rail movements give confidence and *precision* to the rate-makers." (Italics added). On page 61, it declares that "where price competition exists, the effective level of prices for transportation services is thus set at the level of the out-of-pocket costs of the *high*-cost carrier, or somewhat above." By page 70 the Commission seems to have changed its opinion for it reports that "if the trucking industry can haul at rates below the rail minimum, public policy should do nothing to hinder it—nor indeed will enlightened railway management." Speaking of maximum rate control the Commission says on page 96 that "the regulatory authority in acting as an appeal board provides a forum for the shipper who feels he is being unjustly treated" while on page 106 it says that it does "not see why the operation of the machinery [for maximum rate control] should require any public hearings whatsoever." Under these circumstances, the author is forced to prepare his own summary of the problem which the Royal Commission faced and its proposals for dealing with it.

In essence, the Commission was grappling with the problem of how to adapt the older or classical theory of rates to a changed set of economic conditions. When railways had a fairly complete monopoly of inland transport, their minimum rate was their out-of-pocket costs and their maximum on any kind of freight was set by its ability to pay a stipulated toll and still move in volume. Because value of service varied from one kind of traffic to another, the rate also varied. In some instances, the maximum was precisely the same as the fully-allocated costs which can be defined as the out-of-pocket costs of carrying a particular kind of traffic plus a full share of the common costs. In other cases the maximum was higher than fully-allocated costs. In some instances it was lower, though still high enough to equal the out-of-pocket. In all instances the amount of excess above out-of-pocket was determined by value of service. If the railway had not charged more than fully-allocated costs on the traffic which would stand such rates, it would have failed to meet all its common costs, because on some classes of freight it could charge little more than out-of-pocket on account of low value of service. It had to gain on the swings what it lost on the roundabouts.

For decades this system proved generally satisfactory. Under normal business conditions the railways got enough revenue to cover all their operating costs plus interest and a reasonable amount for dividends and surplus. Shippers of high valued goods and those who had no alternative means of transport did not complain too much about their relatively high rates because they could still sell in volume and, if sufficiently erudite, they could see that their rates, while high, were lower than they would have been if the railways had not quoted low tolls on traffic that could not bear any higher tolls. Shippers of low-valued goods were exceptionally pleased because their tolls enabled them profitably to sell in distant markets. All things considered, this method of rate-making served the national interest because the basic industries on which our prosperity then largely depended, such as agriculture, forestry, and mining, got comparatively low rates.

This neat and generally acceptable world of rates and traffic was upset by increased competition and by rising wage rates, interest charges, and material prices. For a time railways were able to adapt themselves reasonably well to the new conditions. Loss of traffic to competitors did not seem too disastrous during the 1930s when the depression was blamed for everything. Railways thrived during the war when motor traffic was handicapped by the rationing of fuel, the lack of new vehicles, and sometimes by the shortage of repair parts. By the time highway competition had reasserted its vigour, rapid technological improvements on railways tended, in part, to offset rising costs of operation and growing competition. By the late 1950s, however, railways had "milked" the high valued traffic for about all it would yield and they still lacked revenue to meet their financial requirements. Their only alternatives—short of government subsidies—were to prune their costs by the abandonment of unprofitable branches and passenger trains, or increase the tolls on those goods and in those areas where they still had most of the traffic to themselves. In practice this meant higher rates on bulky freight, such as forest, agricultural, and mineral products, and on long hauls. The new conditions apparently also meant that tolls in the west and British Columbia would rise relatively more than tolls in the St. Lawrence Lowlands. The same situation would have applied in the Atlantic Provinces but for the Maritime Freight Rates Act.

None of the witnesses testifying before the MacPherson Commission on this matter objected to railways publishing agreed charges and other competitive rates as long as these rates covered out-of-pocket or variable costs. Nor did they object to rates equal to fully-allocated costs on so-called captive traffic—the kinds of goods which can be sent only by rail by reason of bulkiness, distance from market, or lack of highway or water competition. What they did criticize were rates made in excess of fully-allocated costs on captive traffic which were made for the purpose of making up the difference between fully-allocated costs on competitive traffic and the rates actually charged on such traffic. Expressed in simpler but not wholly accurate language, they objected to railways using their "profits" from charging more than fully-allocated cost of captive traffic to make up for "losses" on competitive traffic. These witnesses were particularly upset because the captive traffic was mainly in the West and the competitive traffic, so they insisted, was largely in the St. Lawrence Lowlands.

Thus in the ten or fifteen years after 1945, changing economic circumstances and the fact that the general increases authorized by the Board could be applied only to a shrinking proportion of all rail traffic had served to aggravate, not to mitigate, the regional differences in the rate level. The policy of equalization introduced in 1951 did little to correct what witnesses before the MacPherson Commission on behalf of Manitoba, Alberta, British Columbia, the Saskatoon Chamber of Commerce, and the grain trade called distortions and inequities in the rate structure. Moreover, the periodic battles between the provinces and the railways over rates¯ had proved expensive and exasperating. Therefore, the provinces wanted to find a simpler and fairer method of setting rates than the existing one.

In the end the Commission chose a proposal advanced by witnesses for Manitoba. The regulatory authority should set maximum and minimum rates, and the railways should be free to set rates on the vast bulk of traffic which was carried at rates within this range. Broadly speaking, the maximum rate should be the long-run variable cost plus 150 per cent of that cost; the minimum should not be lower than the variable costs of the movement in question.

Legislation, 1967

The government accepted the Commission's general thesis, discarded some of the complexities or refinements which the Commission had proposed, and introduced others. The essence of the new legislation is that every rate must be compensatory. It must exceed the variable cost of the movement as determined by the Canadian Transport Commission. In determining this cost, the Commission is to have regard to all relevant factors and to compute the costs of capital on the basis of the Canadian Pacific. The Commission is to disallow noncompensatory rates. It must investigate minimum rates after complaint and may do so of its own motion.

The legislation also provides for the determination of maximum rates. These apply to so-called captive shippers, those who have no practical alternative to rail transport. A shipper who believes himself to be captive may ask the Canadian Transport Commission to indicate to him the probable range of rates he will be charged if he decides to take advantage of the legislation. Having learned the probable range, the shipper may still be dissatisfied with the rate currently quoted him by the railway. If so, he may ask the Commission to fix his rate which will be the variable cost plus 150 per cent of this cost, with some adjustments for carloads containing 50,000 pounds or over. Having been informed of the fixed rate, the shipper has 30 days within which to decide to continue the old rate, accept the new one fixed by the Board, or accept any lower rate arrived at by further negotiation between himself and the railway. In the event that he accepts the fixed rate, the shipper must send all his goods by rail for at least one year after the rate has been fixed. In order to ensure that the shipper adheres to his contract, the Commission has authority to examine his books and other records. If he has failed to meet his obligation to ship all his freight by rail, the Commission may cancel the fixed rate and the railway may recover the difference in the freight bill calculated on the fixed rate and on the rate in effect before it became operative, plus liquidated damages.

For the purpose of arriving at fixed rates, the Commission is to calculate costs on the basis of cars carrying 30,000 pounds of the freight in question. This weight was selected because it constitutes a substantial load moved by truck. In effect, the process of setting a fixed rate starts off with the conditions of transport used by the main competitor of the railway. Whenever more than 30,000 pounds of the commodity can be loaded in a standard-size freight car, the Commission will work out rates for a carload of 50,000 pounds. Many of the expenses of operating a railway, such as shunting in yards, billing, and interest and depreciation on cars, vary with the number of cars rather than with the weight of their load, whether net or tare. Under the new legislation, the railway must as a general rule pass on to captive shippers one-half of the savings which arise from heavier loading. Thus, one-half of the difference in cost between hauling a car loaded with 30,000 pounds and one loaded with 50,000 pounds is to be retained by the railway and one-half will show up in lower rates per hundred pounds payable by the captive shipper.

The legislation on maximum and minimum rates is subject to the Maritime Freight Rates Act and therefore the federal subsidy of 20 per cent applies on local traffic and 30 per cent applies on the Maritime portion of traffic from select territory to other parts of Canada. The Terms of Union with Newfoundland may also modify the legislation on maximum rates.

Within roughly four years after the legislation was proclaimed, that is, by late 1971, the Canadian Transport Commission is to report to the government on the operation of these provisions regarding maximum and minimum rates. It will also make recommendations which the government of the day will presumably take under advisement. In a sense the legislation on maximum and minimum rates is to be operative for an experimental period of four years.

In view of the novelty of the new regulations, the pertinent sections of the National Transportation Act are quoted in full:

334. (1) Except as otherwise provided by this Act all freight rates . . . [except statutory ones] shall be compensatory; and the Commission may require the company issuing a freight tariff to furnish to the Commission at the time of filing the tariff or at any time, any information required by the Commission to establish that the rates contained in the tariff are compensatory.

(2) A freight rate shall be deemed to be compensatory when it exceeds the variable cost of the movement of the traffic concerned as determined by the Commission.

(3) In determining for the purposes of this section the variable cost of any movement of traffic, the Commission shall (a) have regard to all items and factors prescribed by regulations of the Commission as being relevant in the determination of variable costs; and (b) compute the costs of capital in all cases by using the costs of capital approved by the Commission as proper for the Canadian Pacific Railway Company.

(4) The Commission may disallow any freight rate that after investigation the Commission determines is not compensatory.

(5) Where the Commission receives information by way of a complaint or otherwise containing *prima facie* evidence that a freight rate shown in a tariff filed with the Commission is not compensatory, the Commission shall conduct an investigation to determine if such rate is compensatory, and in any other case the Commission may, of its own motion, conduct such an investigation.

336. (1) A shipper of goods for which in respect of those goods there is no alternative, effective and competitive service by a common carrier other than a rail carrier or carriers or a combination of rail carriers may, if he is dissatisfied with the rate applicable to the carriage of those goods after negotiation with a rail carrier for an adjustment of the rate, apply to the Commission to have the probable range within which a fixed rate for the carriage of the goods would fall determined by the Commission; and the Commission shall inform the shipper of the range within which a fixed rate for the carriage of the goods would probably fall.

(2) After being informed . . . of the probable range . . . the shipper may apply to the Commission to fix a rate for the carriage of the goods, and the Commission may after such investigation as it deems necessary fix a rate equal to the variable cost of the carriage of the goods and an amount equal to one hundred and fifty per cent of the variable cost as the fixed rate applicable to the carriage of the goods . . . (hereinafter in this section referred to as the 'goods concerned').

(3) In determining the variable cost of the carriage of goods for the purposes of this section, the Commission shall (a) have regard to all items and factors prescribed by regulations of the Commission as being relevant in the determination of variable costs; (b) compute the costs of capital in all cases by using the costs of capital approved by the Commission as proper for the Canadian Pacific Railway Company; (c) calculate the cost of carriage of the goods concerned on the basis of carloads of thirty thousand pounds in the standard railway equipment for such goods; and (d) if the goods concerned may move between points in Canada by alternative routes of two or more railway companies, compute the variable cost on the basis of the lowest cost rail route.

(4) Where a fixed rate is made under this section, the Commission shall forthwith notify the shipper of the rate so fixed, and if within thirty days of the mailing of the notice to the shipper by the Commission, the shipper enters into a written undertaking with a railway company, in a form satisfactory to the Commission, to ship the goods concerned by rail in accordance with this section, the company shall file and publish a tariff

of the fixed rate which shall be effective upon such date as the Commission may, by order or regulation, direct.

(5) When a shipper enters into a written undertaking as provided in subsection (4), (a) the shipper shall cause to be shipped by rail, for a period of one year from the date the fixed rate takes effect and for so long thereafter as the fixed rate as originally fixed or as altered under paragraph (a) of subsection (7) remains in force, all shipments of the goods concerned except such shipments as the Commission may from time to time authorize to be shipped for experimental purposes by another mode of transport; and (b) the charges for any shipments of the goods concerned in the standard railway equipment for goods of that type shall be (i) except in any case under subparagraph (ii) or (iii), at the fixed rate on the basis of a minimum carload weight of thirty thousand pounds, and for shipments under thirty thousand pounds, at the prevailing rate under the tariffs of the company for goods of that type unless the shipper assumes the charges for a shipment of thirty thousand pounds at the fixed rate, (ii) except in any case coming under subparagraph (iii), if the carload weight of a single shipment of the goods is fifty thousand pounds or more, at a rate to be determined by deducting from the fixed rate an amount equal to one half the amount of the reduction in the variable cost of the shipment of the goods concerned below the amount of the variable cost with reference to which the fixed rate was established, but rates need be determined under this subparagraph only as required and then for minimum carload weights based on units of twenty thousand added to thirty thousand and a rate for a carload weight in excess of fifty thousand pounds and between any two minimum carload weights so established shall be the rate for the lower of such minimum carload weights, or (iii) at such rate less than the fixed rate, on the basis of such minimum carload weight, as the shipper may negotiate with a railway company at the time he enters into the written undertaking or at any time thereafter, and every such rate so negotiated shall be filed and published in accordance with regulations, orders or directions made by the Commission.

(6) The Commission may require any shipper for whom a rate has been fixed under this section to supply any information to the Commission, or make available for the inspection by the Commission, shipping books, shipping records and invoice records of every kind for the purpose of verifying that the shipper has complied with paragraph (a) of subsection (5); and where it is shown to the Commission that the shipper has contravened that paragraph, or where the shipper defaults in giving the Commission any information required by it, the Commission may authorize cancellation of the fixed rate in respect of the goods concerned.

(7) Where a fixed rate has been cancelled pursuant to . . . [the preceding subsection, the railway] company may recover from the shipper for all goods shipped at the maximum rate the difference between charges at the maximum rate and charges based on the rate in effect on such goods immediately before the effective date of the maximum rate, and, in addition, the company is entitled to liquidated damages at the rate of ten per cent of the maximum rate on all goods shipped by the shipper otherwise than in accordance with the provisions of the written undertaking . . .

(8) At any time after the expiration of one year from the date the fixed rate became effective . . . (a) the Commission may, upon being satisfied

of a change in the variable cost in relation to which a rate was fixed under this section, alter the fixed rate as the Commission may specify; (*b*) the shipper may give notice in writing to the Commission and to any railway company with whom he had shipped the goods concerned that the shipper no longer desires to be bound by the written undertaking . . . on and after a date specified in the notice, not being earlier than ten days from the date of the notice, and thereupon his undertaking is terminated as of the date so specified, and the fixed rate . . . cancelled . . .; and (*c*) where the Commission is satisfied that there is available to the shipper in respect of the goods concerned an alternative, effective and competitive service by a common carrier other than a rail carrier . . . the Commission by order may, upon application of a railway company, authorize the cancellation of the fixed rate as originally fixed or as altered under paragraph (*a*) . . . upon such date, not being earlier than ten days from the date of the order, as is stated in the order.

(9) An application under this section shall be in such form and contain such information as the Commission may . . . require and without limiting the generality of the foregoing, (*a*) an application . . . shall be accompanied by copies of all letters and documents exchanged between the shipper and any railway company in respect of the negotiations between . . . [them] for an adjustment in the rate applicable to the goods to be shipped or received by the shipper; and (*b*) in the case of an application under subsection (2) the shipper making the application shall pay to the Receiver General for the use of Her Majesty such fee, if any, as may be determined by the Commission but not exceeding in any event twenty-five dollars.

(10) This section is subject to the *Maritime Freight Rates Act* and Term 32 of the Terms of Union of Newfoundland with Canada.

(13) In this section 'shipper' means a person sending or desiring to send goods between points in Canada or who receives or desires to receive goods shipped between points in Canada.

(14) [Deals with adjustments necessitated by the bridge subsidy and its gradual removal].

(16) As soon as practicable after the expiration of four years from the coming into force of this section the Commission shall, after holding such public hearings as it may deem expedient and hearing the submissions of interested parties, report to the Governor in Council on the operation of this section and matters relevant thereto and, having regard to the national transportation policy, shall make such recommendations to the Governor in Council with respect to the operation of the section as the Commission considers desirable in the public interest.

387 A. (1) In computing the costs of the undertaking of the company for the purposes of . . . [setting rates under the preceding sections], there shall be included such allowance on a periodic basis (*a*) for depreciation, and (*b*) in respect of the cost of money expended, whether or not the expenditure was made out of borrowed money, as to the Commission seems reasonable in the circumstances.

(2) Without limiting the powers of the Commission under this Act to determine costs, (*a*) if the costs of a portion of the undertaking of the company or of a particular operation of the company are to be computed for a particular period, such of the costs of the whole undertaking of the

company or any other portion of such undertaking thereof as, in the opinion of the Commission, are reasonably attributable to that portion of the undertaking or to the particular operation, as the case may be, in respect of which the costs are being computed, may be included in such computation of costs, irrespective of when, or in what manner, or by whom such costs were incurred; and (b) if the costs of a portion of the undertaking of the company or of a particular operation of the company are to be computed in respect of future operations of the company, they shall be determined in accordance with estimates made on such basis as to the Commission seems reasonable in the circumstances.

(3) Any determination of costs by the Commission for any of the purposes of this Act is final and binding upon all parties interested and affected thereby.

387 B. (1) The Commission shall by regulation prescribe for any of the purposes of this Act the items and factors, including the factors of depreciation and the cost of capital as provided in subsection (1) of section 387 A, which shall be relevant in the determination of costs, and, to the extent that the Commission deems it proper and relevant to do so, the Commission shall have regard to the principles of costing adopted by the Royal Commission on Transportation appointed by Order-in-Council dated the 13th day of May, 1959 [the MacPherson Commission], in arriving at the conclusions contained in the report thereof, and to later developments in railway costing methods and techniques and to current conditions of railway operations.

(2) When the Commission proposes to amend any regulations made under subsection (1), the Commission shall give notice of the proposed amendment in the *Canada Gazette* and in such additional publications as it deems desirable, and any transportation company, organization, provincial authority or municipal authority in Canada may, within twenty days . . . (a) request the Commission to hold hearings on the matter of the proposed amendment; or (b) give notice to the Commission that it intends to submit to the Commission views and recommendations on the matter . . . in writing . . . [within] forty days . . .; and the proposed amendment shall be brought into force not earlier than sixty days from the day of the publication in the *Canada Gazette* unless . . . [hearings are held or written submissions received] and . . . the Commission may bring the proposed amendment into force, as originally proposed or as altered after such hearings, on a day fixed by the Commission.

(5) Where an amendment to a regulation made under this section is proposed by a person other than the Commission and the amendment has merit in the opinion of the Commission, the Commission shall circulate the proposal and replies thereto and, if the Commission considers it desirable to do so, . . . (a) bring the proposed amendment into force . . . not earlier than ninety days from the day that the proposed amendment was received by the Commission; or (b) hold hearings . . . and bring the proposed amendment into force, as originally proposed or as altered after such hearings, on a day fixed by the Commission.

387 C. Where information concerning the costs of a railway company or other information that is by its nature confidential is obtained from the company by the Commission in the course of any investigation under this

Act, such information shall not be published or revealed in such a manner as to be available for the use of any other person, unless in the opinion of the Commission such publication is necessary in the public interest.

Comments on the Legislation

The success of the legislation on minimum or compensatory rates for all shippers and maximum or fixed rates for captive shippers depends on a number of factors. First, experts employed by the railways will have to arrive at long-run variable costs and experts working for the Commission will have to test the statistical soundness of the probable ceiling and of the fixed rate correctly and expeditiously. The author doubts if they can do this, even with electronic machines. It is one thing to "cost" a wide range of operations like the movement of export grain: it is more complicated to determine the long-run variable cost for the particular haul and the fairly small volume of traffic which interests a particular shipper who has complained. In 1963 the Interstate Commerce Commission expressed the opinion that "the multiple regression formula proves little in the absence of corroborating evidence."[22] Railway officials assert, on the other hand, that they have been using costing for several years as a means of setting rates. They have confidence in various shortcut methods they have devised to overcome the time-consuming and rather expensive job of getting detailed figures for use in the electronic or mechanical brain. They plan to use cost data for setting rates on shipments which are charged something above the minimum and below the maximum rates as defined in the legislation. In short, costing will be applied to rate-making for the bulk of railway traffic carried at rates between the maximum and the minimum and on which the railways will have freedom to vary rates as conditions of traffic and cost of carriage require. Thus, according to the railways use of costing for maximum and minimum rates merely extends what railways have already been doing and will continue to do for their own purposes and for a broad spectrum of rates.

Another problem associated with the new legislation over maximum and minimum rates arises out of the fact that what constitutes variable costs depends on the time span. Admittedly, the recommendations of the MacPherson Commission refer to "long run" costs but these words will not preclude endless argument. Moreover, the legislation neglects to define variable costs. One expert employed by the Royal Commission foresaw this problem. Let us imagine, so he wrote,

a railway giving service only between two points and carrying a single commodity. Before going into business this railway must construct a roadbed and lay tracks. Provided that the road is built to carry a minimum amount of traffic, the normal profit on this investment and the depreciation on it form fixed costs, for they can be escaped only by abandoning the business. If the traffic increases, more expensive rail will be required. Therefore, to some extent the investment will vary with traffic. In addition to the track, the railway will require cars in which to carry the traffic and motive power to move it. The investment in these items, like the investment in heavier rail, will vary with traffic. As the traffic increases rolling stock will not be sold immediately to adjust to the new situation, but obviously investment in rolling stock can be adjusted downwards more readily than can investment in roadbed.

In addition to the investment in road and equipment, the railway must supply fuel to power the locomotives and a crew to operate the trains. In the case of the first of these, if there is greater or less traffic there will be more or less fuel required . . . The adjustment to changes in traffic volume will be almost instantaneous . . . Fuel would be a variable expense in the extremely short run. If the railway operation was sufficiently large that a great number of crews were available, crew wages would also be variable in the extremely short run, since crews could be laid-off and re-hired to adjust to changed requirements without affecting the efficient operation of the railway. If on the other hand, the railway operation was small, the cost of crew wages would not be as variable in the short run as would fuel costs. At some minimum point, crews would be required to stand idle (or at least would demand the equivalent in pay) since there would not be sufficient traffic to employ them full time, yet there would be too much traffic to be moved without them. Exactly the same effect is created when overtime is worked by a smaller crew at premium rates. The cost of wages would then be variable only in a longer run than fuel costs. However, some part of fuel costs and crew wages may appear fixed since the railway may wish to preserve regular service even with a small amount of traffic offered.

The most important cost to the railway for a specific movement is the marginal cost. That is the increase in variable cost caused by increased traffic. If the rate received is less than the marginal cost, the railway will be worse off the more traffic it receives. If the railway receives more than the marginal cost, it will be better off carrying the traffic than not, [because] some contribution will have been made towards paying the fixed costs . . . One of the problems of applying marginal costs [is that] there are a multitude of differing marginal costs . . . The degree to which adjustments are made in the plant will depend upon the timing as well as the amount of traffic which it is expected will be moved.[23]

In short, multiple regression and the concept of cost embodied in the legislation of 1967 run into the same problem that was mentioned earlier and which Commissioner Eastman foresaw. Railways do not deal with a determinable body of variable costs and another determinable body of costs called fixed. What is fixed and what is variable can be determined only by reference to time and to the volume of traffic under study. Thus multiple regression will give an answer that is acceptable to shippers and railways only when representatives of both groups agree on the precise meaning of certain words. Such agreement is unlikely and, though the Commission will be compelled by law to arrive at what variable costs are in any given case (and what 150 per cent of such costs are in other cases), the answer will still be suspect. The essence of the matter is that what constituted a just and reasonable rate under the legislation that was in effect prior to 1967 and what constitutes variable costs under the new legislation are both questions of human judgment. Statistical analysis will lend plausibility and perhaps even considerable support for the Commission's final decision but the answer to the long-standing riddle of what constitutes an economically sound railway rate still necessitates the judicious weighing of evidence and the exercise of wisdom.

Thoughtful and fair-minded members of the public recognize that judgment is involved in most aspects of life. It is exercised by the motorist driving along a highway, a housewife baking a pie, or a teacher marking an examination paper. Judgment must also be exercised by a Commission when it tries to determine the long-run variable cost of moving a given quantity of freight. Yet the public has a right to know whether the maker of the decision had sufficient data, whether he acted in a judicial manner, and whether his decisions are consistent with his opinions expressed in other more or less similar cases. One trouble with the new legislation is that complainants are denied the right to examine the figures for themselves and even pursue every detail of the method by means of cross-examination in open court. The railways are prepared to reveal to officials of the Canadian Transport Commission all their figures on costs and their methods of arriving at such costs. But, so they say, they cannot reveal such data to the public even when there is no competition for the traffic in question. The railways contend that shippers of traffic that is not captive to the rails and truckers competing for other business would be able to use the details on costing for captive traffic to calculate the railways' costs on other traffic with some precision. Then they would use these data either to beat down railway tolls on other, non-captive traffic or take business away from the rails by seeing where the railways were making money and then undercutting these rates. Railway executives claim that the mandatory sharing of all data on costs with the shipping public and with competitors is wrong in principle. It runs counter to the concept of free competition which, according to a main theme of the MacPherson Commission, should pervade the field of railway rates more in the future than it has in the past.[24] Once the doctrine of relative freedom from official control over all rates is accepted, the idea that a carrier, like any other business, should be allowed to "play his cards close to his chest" has to be accepted to, or so executives of Canadian railways have argued.

The trouble is that shippers may become unhappy about having to rely so much on the say-so of the Commission. They assert that they cannot judge the fairness of either a maximum or a minimum rate unless all the facts are spread on the transcript of the hearings before the Commission. As the National Transportation Act stands, the Commission has the power to withhold some data. Presumably it will do so at the request of the railways. This is contrary to the principles of British jurisprudence, though there are exceptions for heinous crimes and treason. Furthermore, experts employed by the Commission to check up on the costing methods of the railways cannot be put in the witness box for cross-examination.

Under the previous railway legislation, the shipper had, of course, to rely to a considerable extent on the fair-mindedness of members of the Board of Transport Commissioners. Even so, he or his counsel could argue from the mass of decisions which had been built up over the years. Under the legislation of 1967 they are more or less cast adrift. They have to work in the dark at least until a body of precedent has been accumulated. It is fair to add that this argument should not be pushed too far, otherwise Parliament could never introduce any innovations in statute or common law.

Some doubt has also been cast on whether the legislation on captive shippers has any practical value. No one appearing before the House of Commons Committee in 1967 could point a finger to any shipper or piece of traffic and say for certain whether it was captive or not. One Member of Parliament argued that shippers of farm machinery from Hamilton or Toronto, of nickel concentrates from Sudbury, and of potash from Saskatchewan would all be captive inasmuch as there was only one shipper of the commodity at the place named or even in the entire country. On the contrary, the President of the Canadian National contended that carriers by highway were always present, either potentially or actually. Moreover, each of the above shippers faced market competition, i.e., competition from suppliers elsewhere in Canada, or in the world, selling in the same market.

Inevitably, the Commission will have to interpret the meaning of the word "captive" and its decision will doubtless be confirmed or modified by the Supreme Court of Canada. It may be that the Commission will decide that there are no captive shippers within the meaning of the law. In other words, the authorities may find that competition extends to the point where every shipper has a practical alternative to rail transport.

General Comments

Although the MacPherson Commission stressed the importance of cost-oriented rates, it could not avoid references to demand. Indeed, it scolded railways for not placing equal emphasis on research on demand as on finding costs.[25] The legislation stresses cost but since it relates to only minimum and maximum rates, it leaves railways free to set most rates as they see fit. Before publishing rates on the great bulk of their traffic which will be carried at rates between minimum and maximum tolls, railways will unquestionably have regard to value of service. This is absolutely necessary because if railways were to set all their rates at the level of their variable costs, they would be unable to collect enough revenue to cover their non-variable expenses. If the Commission sets variable costs and hence minimum rates at a relatively low level, then railways will have to set other rates at a somewhat higher level than would have been the case if the Commission interpreted the meaning of variable costs in such a way that costs and hence minimum rates were rather higher. The author suspects that, notwithstanding the provisions in the law regarding setting minimum rates on the basis of costs, railways and the Commission will not ignore the effect of such rates on the movement of traffic.

The inescapable fact is that every railway rate is a balance between cost of service and value of service. This is true of all prices because cost and value of service essentially mean the same thing as supply and demand. As Alfred Marshall long ago explained: to argue which is more important, supply or demand, is like squabbling over which blade of a pair of scissors does the cutting. When railways had a large measure of monopoly, they could concentrate on demand—but they also had to watch cost in order to ensure that total revenues from all traffic covered all their costs and that no individual rate was below out-of-pocket. Nowadays, when railways face strong competition, demand has taken on a new dimension. It is measured less by the ability of the goods to bear higher tolls and still move in volume. It is now judged mainly by the likelihood of traffic moving by non-rail carriers. Unquestionably, on some traffic the upper limit is still set by the fact that any higher toll would make it impossible for the producer to sell in distant markets. More commonly, it is determined by the fact that higher tolls by rail would drive the business to other agencies of transport. Thus in many instances railway rates are set by the costs of handling the goods by highway carrier.

If one looks back over the history of railway rate-making, one observes an almost continuous tendency for greater emphasis to be placed on cost and, at the same time, a persistent tendency for value of service to reassert its influence. Part of the reason for this is that most people are suspicious of demand as a factor in pricing. Somehow or other, cost appeals to the popular sense of justice. Up to a point it is true to say that the recent emphasis on costing is the result of the desire of railways to keep up with the times by using electronic brains, and partly their hope that the use of cost will either justify the payment of government subsidies or make shippers more willing to pay higher rates to meet the higher costs of transport. In short, costing is good public relations for the railways and, subject to the roughly equal importance of demand, it is sound economics.

Within the last few years there has been a reversal of roles among railway users. At one time shippers of relatively valuable articles had to pay high tolls relative to those on low-valued goods. When they complained, they were told that by charging low rates on bulky articles which could not bear any higher rates, the railways got a substantial contribution to the common costs of operating the company. This contribution cut down the amount of common costs which had to be borne by valuable freight and so the tolls upon it, though high, were not as high as they would have been if the railways had not bid for low-valued goods. Western farmers and other long-distance shippers did not complain about this practice of rate-making as such, though they often did object to the relative level east and west of the Great Lakes. As producers, they gained from having low rates on their staple exports and they tended to overlook the relatively high tolls on valuable freight such as implements, clothing, some foodstuffs, and consumers' durables. People are always more conscious of their position as producers than as consumers. Accordingly, the Prairies and British Columbia were generally prepared to accept the older set-up in railway rates.

In recent years, especially in the 1950s, rates on high-valued goods moving by rail have tended to come down relative to rail rates on bulky goods. This has been the result of competition. Though the West complained that their rates on valuable goods were high relative to those in the St. Lawrence Lowlands, they were more or less reconciled to the situation by the hope that eventually they would enjoy as much highway competition as Southern Ontario and Quebec. In this event their rates on high-valued goods were bound to fall and they would enjoy a larger measure of equality in rates. This hope seems to have been shared by the MacPherson Commission as shown by its discussion of equalization.

The hope of more competition in every part of Canada is likely to prove well founded because of the steady improvement in the quality of roads and the use of equipment for clearing snow. But the expectation that highway costs will be roughly uniform is less sound, unless part of the cost of roads in the Atlantic and Western Provinces is borne by the general taxpayer and not by highway users as the MacPherson Commission advocated. What is far more certain is that, in order to approximate their financial requirements, railways will have to raise their rates on low-valued goods. Heretofore, rates on valuable articles have come down in the face of competition. This was fine as long as railways could get reasonably adequate returns on their investment or, in the case of the Canadian National, a subsidy from the federal government. But once costs rose above a certain level the Canadian Pacific was forced to bring up its low rates to more nearly meet the rates on valuable goods which had already come down. This process started when horizontal increases could be applied only to a shrinking proportion of the total traffic. It is bound to continue unless offset by generous government subsidies on various kinds of traffic in addition to export grain or unless wage rates, material prices, and interest rates fall, technological change or abandonment of service occur very rapidly, or the operating costs of all highway operators rise spectacularly.

If, as the author thinks, rates on captive or semi-captive traffic are certain to rise relative to the rates on competitive traffic, captive shippers are certain to complain. The logical answer to their complaints is to apply the same argument formerly used with shippers of valuable freight. Because the railway publishes low rates on traffic which will not bear higher tolls, it reduces the rates which it would otherwise have to charge on captive freight. What is more, the West has the low statutory rates on export grain, British Columbia has been relieved of the mountain differential which it used to claim was intolerable, absolutely crushing, and utterly unbearable, the St. Lawrence Lowlands have the benefit of much competition from truckers and inland ships, and the Atlantic Provinces have the protection of the Maritime Freight Rates Act. These are offsets to the allegedly high rates on captive traffic. The essential trouble is that the offsets are too often overlooked and the disabilities, unfortunate as they may be, are exaggerated out of their proper proportion. Moreover, people in one region are likely to complain because they lack the offsets to high freight rates which exist elsewhere in Canada. Shippers in one part of the country focus their attention on what others possess, while tending to ignore or at least grudgingly admitting that they have compensations in their own rates. In short, the problem of freight rates in Canada is not solely economic; it is partly political. Our railways are business enterprises; they are also instruments of national policy.

The simple fact is that the railway rate structure is undergoing radical change. As Pigou foresaw in 1891, differential pricing could be maintained only so long as railways were in a monopolistic position.[26] The traditional competition between railways and inland steamships was resolved when the latter accepted traffic at a differential below current railway tolls or the former ceased to bid for bulky low-grade freight on which steamships had a great competitive advantage. Unfortunately for the railways, their competition with airlines, pipelines, and above all motor vehicles has not stabilized and their rate structure is therefore unsteady. Railways complain they have lost the high-rated traffic, the cream which allowed them to carry the staples of the country at skim-milk prices. Yet to raise the tolls on basic commodities and on commodities from relatively remote areas would be to destroy the prosperity of large sections of Canada and precipitate a painful relocation of industry and population. These economic results may easily be exaggerated in public discussion but the political implications of trying to raise the low rates on grain, for instance, probably outweigh economic considerations. On the other hand, to raise rates on high valued goods while keeping the existing levels on staples would merely invite more competition from highway carriers and eventually more rate-cutting and loss of business to railways. Another alternative, cutting the existing, fairly high railway rates on valuable articles with the hope of recovering business lost to trucks, would merely aggravate the problem of road-rail competition.

Theoretically it might be possible to pass legislation requiring trucks and buses to charge the same tolls as railways. Such a law might help to stabilize rates and eliminate unjust discrimination. But in the long run such regulation, if carried to an extreme, would break down because the shipper might put his own vehicle on the highway rather than pay the charges of the common carrier and, of course, there is no effective way of regulating the tolls of private operators. To prohibit the operation of shipper-owned trucks or to forbid the operation of any trucks beyond a certain number of miles with the object of preserving intermediate and long distance traffic for the railways which can handle it profitably, would be to deny the public the economic advantages of a new transportation agency. In any event the regulation of highway traffic to protect the solvency of the railways or to preserve the present rate structure would run into constitutional difficulties. A final possibility is to encourage railways to purchase trucking companies. Such a trend is open to the objection that railways might throttle a competing medium of transportation.

The gist of the matter is that no simple juggling of the rate structure or legislative enactments will suffice to solve the financial difficulties of the railways. The differentiated rate structure is slowly crumbling under pressure from competitive transportation agencies. In the past the railway pricing system performed two economic functions: it increased the net revenue of the carriers beyond what it would have been if the service rendered had been charged for at uniform prices; and more or less incidentally, it promoted the welfare of the nation. In particular it was designed to assist in the achievement of certain national objectives such as the movement of traffic through Canadian ports and the stimulation of the export trade. The fundamental problem today is how to adjust rates without disturbing any more than necessary the social and economic benefits which have proceeded from the highly differentiated rate structure of the past. Britain, the United States, Canada, and other countries with well-established railway networks and a rapidly developing system of highway transport all face this problem. All of them are grappling for a solution.

7

The Classification

An explanation of why railways do not charge the same rate for handling all articles was developed in the preceding chapter. Of course, railways cannot carry differentiation to the point of setting a separate rate for each and every commodity carried. Consequently they group articles into a limited number of classes for the purposes of rate-making. In addition, Canadian railways have numerous commodity rates. These latter tolls apply to individual commodities and were introduced because the appropriate rate under the classification was higher than the commodity in question could bear and still move in large volume. Besides, railways have competitive tariffs.

Procedure

Essentially, a freight classification is an alphabetical list of articles, together with the "rating" which each commodity takes. The "rating" is the class or group into which the article is placed for the purpose of quoting freight charges. The "rate" is the charge, usually in cents per hundred pounds, for transporting a commodity or class of freight between various points. Ratings are found in the classification; rates in freight tariffs.[1]

In order to determine the rate on any shipment, the shipper or consignee would do well, first, to consult the Pick Up and Delivery tariff, sometimes called the P. & D., or Collection and Delivery tariff. This publication applies to a large number of commodities which typically move in small quantities. The first part contains an alphabetical list of the various commodities in less than carload lots to which this tariff applies. The name of each article is followed by the column (One, Two, Three, or Four) to which it is assigned in this tariff. Then another section shows the rate applicable between all stations covered by P. & D. service for each of these columns. The areas covered include the more thickly settled parts of Canada such as Southern Ontario and Quebec, most of the Maritimes and the Prairies, and part of British Columbia. The P. & D. tariff is the simplest of all to use but it is inapplicable if the shipment is for a carload, for long distances such as from one region of Canada to another, or for low-valued goods.

If the P. & D. tariff does not apply, the shipper must consult the Index of Freight Tariffs. This publication lists numerous articles alphabetically. The name of each article is followed by the number[2] of an especial tariff or tariffs under which the article may move. Any rate quoted in the tariffs referred to in the Index will be lower than the rate under the (standard) mileage freight tariff, which is the maximum tariff of tolls which may be charged by any railway in Canada. As most of the freight transported by Canadian railways moves under special tariffs of one sort or another, many shippers and purchasers will find in these tariffs most of the rates which they need to know. Yet every shipper is likely sooner or later to have to send or receive a small quantity of more or less valuable goods which are not covered by special tariffs or even by the P. & D. tariff. Hence shippers should be familiar with the more complicated procedures as well as the simple ones.

Some of the tariffs enumerated in the Index are called "Special and Competitive" or (sometimes) "Special." They have been introduced by railways to meet competition from trucks and water-lines. There is an alphabetical list of an assortment of individual articles, each article being followed by an item number. On referring to the numerical listing of items in the latter half of the tariff, the shipper will find a description of each article listed and perhaps some relevant shipping instructions. Immediately beneath or to the right of the description, the tariff gives the rates from one station or group of stations to other centres.

If the tariff so states on its face or cover page, the rates contained therein do not constitute maxima to intermediate points. A shipper may find that some of the rates in these tariffs apply to the commodity in which he is interested but not between the particular points with which he is, at the moment, concerned. In this case he should take the matter up with the railway. If he is being denied rates which are published for another shipper in the same position as he is, he may be suffering from unjust discrimination. If circumstances justify it, he may apply to the Board of Transport Commissioners for the removal of the alleged injustice. Commonly he will find that between the two points named in the tariff competition exists and lower rates are, therefore, justified, whereas between the places of origin and destination of his particular shipment competition is non-existent or weak. In the latter instance the special tariff listed in the Index is inapplicable, and he must pay the rates calculated on some other basis.

Many of the rates in the Special and Competitive tariffs are published to expire on a certain specified date unless sooner cancelled, changed, or extended. Hence the shipper or consignee must be careful to see, either by consulting the cover page of the tariff or the freight agent of a railway, that the rate published is still in effect. This comment is pertinent to all publications relating to freight ratings and rates. It is especially important for competitive tariffs where changes are relatively frequent. Every supplement to an existing tariff must be filed with the tariff without delay. Every tariff which has become obsolete through being replaced by a new one[3] must either be destroyed or be filed clearly marked as out of date, in some place where it will not be consulted for current shipments.

Besides Special and Competitive tariffs, the Index of Freight Tariffs will list a number of "Commodity" tariffs. Technically these tariffs include: (a) "mileage scales" or "distance rates" for the products of agriculture, mines, and forests. These scales will apply between all stations of any one carrier. Typically they cover goods produced or consumed over a wide area. (b) "Specific" tariffs which cover general movements of bulky manufactured goods such as iron and steel, newsprint, and cement. As a rule these also relate to a fairly wide area but apply only from one specified point to another and not in the reverse direction, i.e. from A to B, not B to A. Often they apply to goods produced in one centre and shipped to a limited number of stations. For example, cotton duck manufactured in Yarmouth, N.S., moves under a specific tariff to Chatham and Wallaceburg, Ont., where there are sugar refineries which use duck for bags. (c) "Special" tariffs which are substantially the same as the Special and Competitive tariffs just described. They apply only on shipments from one or more specific points to one or more destinations and ordinarily do not relate to broad regions.

Many Commodity tariffs, especially those in class (a), are prepared by calculating distances between shipping points and then computing the proper rate from a mileage scale. In principle, the method is the same as that used by a shipper working from the official distance tables to the maximum class rate scale as explained below. The chief differences are that the commodity mileage scale gives much lower tolls for equal distances than the standard mileage one, that the commodity scale is not usually published or available to the public, and that the head office of the railway, not the local agent or the shipper, goes through computations and publishes only the final result. The shipper takes the rates published between various points as the official ones without worrying about the method of computation.

Item No.	ARTICLES	RATINGS LCL	RATINGS CL	CL MIN. WT. (POUNDS)
	Churns, Hand, with or without Power attachments, and Butterworkers, Hand— continued:			
8797	Churns, Wooden:			
8798	With Frames:			
	SU, loose..	200	45	20,000R
	SU, in barrels, boxes or crates.................................	100	45	20,000R
	Bodies loose or in packages, frames taken apart, in packages..........	100	45	20,000R
8799	Without Frames:			
	Loose..	150	45	20,000R
	In barrels, boxes or crates...................................	100	45	20,000R
8800	Chutes, Coal Delivery, Basement, steel, in packages.......................	85	45	30,000
8802	Chutes, Coal Delivery, Wagon:			
	Not nested...	85	45	30,000
	Nested, in packages...	70	45	30,000
8805	Chutes, Laundry, aluminum, in boxes or crates...........................	200	200	AQ
8820	CIGARS, CIGARETTES, SNUFF OR MANUFACTURED TOBACCO:			
8825	Cigarettes, Tobacco, with Paper Wrappers, in boxes having united measurement,			
	length, width and depth added, of 30 inches or more, or in Package No. 5, (see		{ 85	12,000R
	Notes 1 and 2, Items 8830 and 8835)................................	100	{ 70	30,000R
8830	Note 1:—Wooden boxes must be so constructed, strapped or sealed as to			
	prevent opening and pilferage of contents from boxes without breaking			
	seals or mutilating container. Fibreboard boxes must be so closed and			
	secured as to prevent pilferage of contents without mutilating container.			
8835	Note 2:—Packages having a united measurement, length, width and depth			
	added, of less than 30 inches, NOT TAKEN.			
8840	Cigars, Tobacco (see Note 1, Item 8830), in boxes having united measurement, length,		{ 85	12,000R
	width and depth added, of 30 inches or more (see Note 2, Item 8835)...........	100	{ 70	30,000R
8845	Snuff:		{ 85	12,000R
	In glass in barrels, boxes or Package No. 5, ORB....................	150	{ 70	30,000R
			{ 85	12,000R
8850	In inner containers, other than glass, in barrels, boxes or Package No. 5.........	100	{ 70	30,000R
8855	Tobacco, Manufactured:			
8860	Cut or Granulated:			
	Chewing, Fine Cut:			
	In pails, two or more in crates or cleated or strapped together..............	100	45	24,000R
8865	In packages in boxes or Package No. 5............................	85	45	24,000R
	Smoking:			
	In glass in barrels, boxes or package No. 5, ORB, or in pails, two or more in crates			
	or cleated or strapped together..................................	100	45	24,000R
8870	In fibre or metal cartons or in paper packets in boxes or Package No. 5..........	85	45	24,000R
	Plug or Twist:			
	In butts or caddies, weighing not less than 10 lbs. each, loose, or in butts or caddies			
	two or more in crates or cleated or strapped together.....................	70	45	24,000R
	In packages in boxes or Package No. 5.............................	70	45	24,000R
8875	Cigar or Cigarette Holders, in boxes.................................	150	150	AQ
8880	Circus Seats and Portable Grandstands, with or without Equipment of Railings,			
	Stringers or Supports:			
8885	Circus Seats:			
8890	With backs, backs folded flat, in packages............................	85	45	36,000
8895	Without backs...	70	45	36,000
8900	Circus Seat Backs, wooden or wood and metal combined, in boxes or crates; also			
	CL, loose..	85	45	36,000
8905	Portable Grandstands:			
8910	Grandstand Chairs, folded flat, LCL in packages; CL, loose or in packages.........	100	45	30,000
8915	Grandstand Platforms, in flat sections.............................	70	45	36,000
8920	Cisterns, Tanks or Vats, wooden, NOIBN:			
	SU..	200	100	10,000R
	KD, in packages..	70	40	30,000
8925	Clamps, Column or Concrete, iron, in packages; also CL, loose	70	45	30,000
8930	Clay:			
8935	Fire:			
8940	Crude, in bags, barrels or boxes; also CL, in bulk.............................	55	27	40,000
8945	Ground, in bags, barrels or boxes; also CL, in bulk..........................	55	33	40,000
8950	Kaolin or China Clay:			
8955	Crude, in bags, barrels or boxes; also CL, in bulk............................	55	27	40,000
8960	Ground, in bags, barrels or boxes; also CL, in bulk..........................	70	45	40,000
8965	Clay, NOIBN:			
8970	Crude, in bags, barrels or boxes; also CL, in bulk............................	55	27	40,000
8975	Ground, in bags, barrels or boxes; also CL, in bulk..........................	55	33	40,000

See page 4 for explanation of abbreviations and characters; see pages 359 to 370 for explanation of Package Numbers.

Finally, the shipper may find from perusing the Index of Freight Tariffs that his goods may move under "Agreed Charges" as described later. Until 1955 distributing class rates applied across Canada but now cover only "select territory" as defined under the Maritime Freight Rates Act. They are compiled in the same general manner as class rates, i.e., by means of the classification and the distributing class rate scale.

If the shipper or consignee does not find his commodity listed in the Index of Freight Tariffs, or if he discovers after consulting the tariff referred to in the Index that it does not apply to his shipment, he must consult the Classification. He is certain to find his commodity indexed in the long alphabetical list of articles toward the front of this publication. The list will refer the shipper to page and item number. He will then turn to that item in the consecutive list of items in the second half of the publication. Opposite the item number, the shipper will find (*i*) a brief description of the article, (*ii*) in the first column to the right of the description, the rating applicable to this article if shipped in less than carload lots (L.C.L.). Sometimes he will also find (*iii*) in the column just to the right of L.C.L. rating, the rating in carloads (C.L.). If for reasons to be subsequently given, no C.L. rating is given, the L.C.L. rating applies on all shipments.

Sometimes the description contains the letters O.R.B., O.R.C., O.R.D., O.R.Det., O.R.Lkge., O.R.S., O.R.W. (Owner's Risk of Breakage, Chafing, Damage, Deterioration, Leakage, Sifting, and Weather respectively).[4] These letters show what liability the railway will assume in case of loss or damage in transit. Normally the railway is fully responsible for these risks, unless the shipment has been received "In Bad Order," the shipper has been notified of the fact, and a notation to this effect has been made on the bill of lading.

Often, beneath the description, certain shipping instructions are set forth, for example, what ratings apply when the article is shipped loose or in boxes, barrels, bags, crates, etc.[5] The minimum carload weight which is needed in order that the shipper may obtain the C.L. rating is also given.[6] In the latest Classification the **DISTINCTIVE HEADINGS** in bold-faced type no longer appear. They referred to the mixing rule which was formerly different in Eastern and Western Canada, as will be briefly explained later.[7]

Assuming now that the shipper has found out the class to which his article belongs, he next must determine the distance over which it must move. To compile this information, he consults the Official Distance Tables which for the Canadian National consist of two thick volumes, one for Eastern and one for Western Canada. They state the precise distance from every point on that railway to every other point on that system's lines in the territory concerned. The Canadian Pacific's two volumes are less bulky but more confusing to the novice. Each volume gives for the territory east and west of Lakehead the distance from every point to the nearest junction point or, in some cases, to two or three junction points. Consequently it is necessary, usually with the aid of a map, to find out what appears to be the shortest route over which freight can be moved between the places concerned. Then one must compute the mileage by working from one junction point to another. In computing distance, the shortest route listed in the Official Distance Table applies. Hence it may be necessary to calculate the distance by several routes in order to make sure of the shortest one. Where the distance by a competing road is less than by the road on which the shipment originates and terminates, the shorter distance is used for rate-making purposes.

An alphabetical list of all stations covered by the Distance Tables is printed in the front of that book along with a corresponding number. After finding the proper number, it is necessary to refer to that number where it appears in its proper numerical order in the latter part of the same volume. This second section of the book lists stations in numerical order and gives mileages to other stations and junction points. Distances are published to the nearest tenth of a mile. When two or more distances have to be taken into account, the decimal fractions must be added together. Once the final distance is known, fractions less than half a mile are ignored. Those amounting to one half mile or more are rounded off to the next highest mile, that, is, they are counted as one mile.

The compiler now knows the class or rating to which his goods belong and the official distance over which they move. He then consults the tariff of maximum standard class rates, sometimes called the Standard Freight Tariff. This is a simple table showing one after another down the page the various distances or groups of distances and, in parallel columns from left to right, the rates for the various classes. The shipper follows down the left-hand side of the standard mileage scale to the mileage group in which his haul falls, for example, 97 miles in the group under 100 and 95 or over. Then he reads horizontally towards the right until he comes to the column, say class 45, which is the rating on his freight. He then has the precise rate which applies to the freight. As a rule railways are willing to provide a shipper with tables giving the actual rates applicable on his goods between his plant and the stations where his customers are located. In other words, railways often undertake the work of compilation for their patrons. As almost all rates are quoted in cents per hundred pounds, the shipper must multiply by the appropriate weight to ascertain the total charge for the shipment.

While calculating the rates, the shipper has gathered some valuable information. He has discovered the proper description of his article for rate-making purposes.[9] This is important for it ensures that arguments will not arise regarding the proper rating. Many large shippers, especially those who ship large quantities of relatively few types of articles, have bills of lading printed or surcharged with the correct names of the articles which they ship, along with the proper rating. This procedure saves time, reduces errors due to poor writing, and makes it easier for the consignee to check the rate. In consulting the Classification the shipper has also ascertained such important matters as the liability of the carrier for damage, details regarding packing, and the minimum weight in case he wishes to ship in carloads.[10]

In order to avoid the necessity of recalculating the rate on repeat shipments of the same commodity between the same two points, most shippers and many railway agents especially in small towns compile a simple table giving the rates on all shipments which they are likely to make. Shippers sometimes have these lists checked by railway rate clerks. To ensure correctness, these rates must be rechecked periodically otherwise they may get out of date, particularly if the "key" contains competitive rates.

In brief, the publications to be consulted in determining a rate are the Index of Freight Tariffs; Special and Competitive, Commodity, Agreed Charges, or other special tariffs; the Classification; and the Standard Mileage Tariff. To compute a rate or audit one already charged quickly and accurately requires a thorough familiarity with a number of books and experience in making use of the pertinent data. Yet one must not forget that description often adds an unnecessary air of mystery to what goes on during every hour of the working day in numberless traffic departments. Just as a raw army recruit would be bewildered by the description in the *Manual of Elementary Drill* of such a simple matter as standing at attention, or a child by being told and not shown, how to lace his boots, so explanations of how to compute a rate often confuse more than they enlighten. A little study will prove that ascertaining a rate is by no means as complicated as it appears at first.

The Canadian Freight Classification, No. 21, the one presently in use, contains approximately 15,000 items. It applies to all railways in Canada except the White Pass and Yukon Railway.[11] It is under constant study by shippers and the traffic managers of every Canadian railway. Whenever any question of the proper rating, minimum C.L.

weight, method of packing, etc., arises, the matter is discussed at length by the Eastern Classification Committee in Montreal or the Western one in Winnipeg.[12] Each committee consists of three transportation experts representing the shippers and three for the railways, along with a chairman who is an officer of the Canadian Freight Association and who has no vote.

The committee canvasses the factors governing the freight classification very thoroughly. Usually the two groups are able to resolve their differences in a mutually satisfactory manner. If they fail to do so, they may appeal to the Board of Transport Commissioners for a ruling. Even when no serious complaint about the proposed change has been made, the Board must approve every alteration of wording, rating, etc. Typically it accepts what has been agreed upon by the committee on which, it is important to note, shippers and railways have equal voting power and the chairman has no casting vote.[13]

The Canadian Classification formerly had ten classes of freight called first, second, third, etc., down to tenth. In addition, it had nine multiples of first, e.g., D-1 (double first). Most multiples of first have disappeared because of truck competition, which is especially intensive on valuable high-rated articles. One byproduct of the agitation for equalization was that the nomenclature of the classes was changed. Old first class became Class 100. Second class, on which rates were 85 per cent of old first, became Class 85. The same principle was applied to all other classes. The new scheme permitted new classes to be readily introduced. This had been done for cordwood, scrap iron, potatoes, and other products which formerly moved chiefly under commodity mileage scales.

Each class includes a number of articles which have little in common except that they have the same rating for rate-making purposes. Nevertheless each class has its own peculiar but very broad characteristics, as Professor Jackman has explained.

First class [now 100] includes commodities of bulky character or high value [e.g., clothing], of which a comparatively small tonnage moves and then only in less-than-carload quantities. Second class [85] comprises those commodities which are slightly less bulky or valuable [most groceries, L.C.L.], but which move in relatively greater tonnage, although still confined to less-than-carload quantities. Third class [70] comprises the ordinary merchandise commodities [toilet soap, L.C.L.; butter, C.L.] in compact packages of comparatively great weight and small cubic measurements, moving in less than carloads. Fourth class [55] covers articles of light weight and bulky in dimension [e.g., refrigerators, C.L.] or fragile in character, of comparatively high value, moving in low minimum carloads. Fifth class [45] includes general merchandise [e.g., canned fruits and vegetables] moving in carload lots, generally speaking of the same character that would take third-class [70] rate in less than carloads. This class covers a substantial tonnage. . . . Sixth class, [40] as a rule, covers flat car merchandise traffic, like machinery, agricultural implements, boats, canoes, launches, *etc.* Seventh class [33] includes railway equipment and supplies [also chemical fertilizers]. Eighth class [30] covers cereals and cereal products, potatoes, and vegetables. Ninth class [40 for horses and mules, 33 for cattle, calves, hogs, and sheep] is livestock. Tenth class [27] covers products of the forest, the mine, and the quarry. . . . Of these classes the first six may be considered as merchandise, while the other four are regarded as commodity classes.[14]

In recent years an increasing volume of freight has been carried under Special and Competitive tariffs, Commodity tariffs, and so on, at rates which often have little relation to the rating under the classification and the rate under the mileage class scale.[15] In 1945 Canadian railways derived no more than 5 per cent of their freight revenue from classified traffic. By 1950 the proportion had risen to nearly 20 per cent because of the cancellation of some competitive tolls as the operating costs of competing agencies rose faster than railway costs. By 1957 the proportion had fallen to almost 10 per cent and in the mid-1960s to about 5 per cent. Class rates remain important chiefly because of the large number of individual shipments that move under them. An increasing volume of traffic is handled under competitive rates, including Trailer-on-flat-car (piggyback), agreed charges, and incentive rates.

While the ratings on all articles are uniform throughout Canada, except in the Yukon, the relationship between the rates published on the various classes was formerly different east and west of Fort William, Port Arthur and Armstrong. In the East the rate on first-class traffic was double the rate charged on fifth for the same distance,[16] the rates for the intermediate classes being certain percentages above fifth. The rates below fifth were scaled down without any apparent regularity until the tenth class was reached. In Western Canada, the fourth class was one-half of first and the fifth 45 per cent of first. Although the fifth-class rate was a smaller percentage of first in the West than in the East, the absolute rate (i.e., the rate in cents per hundred pounds for equal distances) on fifth class freight was usually higher in Western Canada than in the East. This was because the first class rates of Lakehead were higher than east thereof. When the West was being settled, the volume of its traffic in the first four classes was comparatively small and consisted chiefly of goods being distributed from wholesale centres. The Prairies were mainly interested in low rated classes covering settlers' effects, implements, cereals, livestock, and lumber. Western rates on these classes were more favourable to the shipper compared with the first class rates than were the rates on low valued goods in the East compared with the first class rate there. Originally all class rates in Western Canada were higher than in the East in order to compensate for the lower density of traffic per mile of line. Various orders of the Board tended to equalize the rates in the two regions, and since March 1, 1955, the mileage class rates have been uniform across Canada.

Rule of Analogy

The preceding discussion of some of the mechanics of classification and tariffs throws little light on the factors which determine in what class a particular article is to be placed. In the Board's words, the classification is "a rate making scheme, devised for the purpose of according the same rating to all articles of like character from a transportation standpoint. The transportation characteristics to be considered in classifying any article are bulk, weight, value, risk, liability to damage, cost of carriage and other considerations. In other words, articles having similar value, bulk, weight, and other similar characteristics and involving practically the same cost of handling are usually assigned to the same class."[17]

In practice, the determination of the appropriate class for a particular commodity is by no means simple and the reasons why various articles are grouped together in the same class not always easy to understand. One of the most experienced members of the Board stated that he had "devoted some time to the study of different classifications and [had] not yet been able to work out an inclusive logical principle on which they are based."[18]

On account of the small number of classes and the multiplicity of articles of commerce, each class contains a wide variety of things.

With the very limited number of classes or ratings in the classification and the thousands of articles to be classified, there will be found articles taking the same rating which are in no sense counterpart, yet the various factors considered in establishing the class rating have resulted in the rate fixed being an appropriate one. Thus taking the carload rate of fourth class [55] are such articles as hockey sticks, skates, lampblack, dyes, caraway seeds, cocoanuts, electric fans, watermelons, furniture, bread, peanut butter, candy, figs, bird cages, fresh meats, earthenware bathtubs, rubber hose, and dump wagons.[19]

The present classification is the result of many years of trial and error in arriving at ratings which are reasonably acceptable to both carriers and shippers. When new articles are brought on the market, the classification is revised. For example, when starch made from wheat came into production, the Classification was amended to include that article in the item, "Corn Syrup, Corn and Wheat Starch, Corn Oil, Corn Sugar, Dextrine and Glucose," because it was very similar to some of these articles.[20] In 1962 dehumidifiers were officially put in the same class (100 L.C.L. and 55 C.L.) as humidifiers, electric air heaters, and the like.

Although the Eastern and Western Classification Committees try to keep the classification up to date, from time to time articles are offered for shipment which are not specifically listed. Rule 17 of the Classification reads that "when articles not specifically provided for, nor embraced in the Classification as articles N.O.I.B.N. [not otherwise indexed by name][21] are offered for transportation, carriers will apply the classification provided for articles which, in their judgment are analogous." A railway considered that two steel lifeboats and one steel rudder of types not previously shipped took a second-class rating because they were analogous with display racks, animal and poultry coops or crates, and coiled wire springs (not compressed). The Board held they were fourth because, notwithstanding differences in values per pound, they more closely resembled electric cooking stoves and electric refrigerators from a transportation point of view.[22]

Sometimes shippers go through the Classification, pick out an article which seems to resemble theirs but which has a lower rating than the one they are currently being charged, and then apply to the carriers for that lower rating on the principle of the rule of analogy.[23] At one time, for instance, Kleenex was shipped under "Paper Products N.O.I.B.N." by reason of the rule of analogy. Later, in order to clarify the tariff, it was put under a separate item "Cellulose Napkins, Neck Strips, Handkerchiefs." Still later the manufacturer alleged that Kleenex was analogous with "Towels, other than cotton" and asked for the lower rating applicable to that item. Now it is a well-established principle in transportation that whenever a tariff is ambiguous it must be interpreted so as to give the benefit of the doubt to the shipper.[24] This is reasonable because the railways, which drafted the wording of the Classification, presumably looked after their own interests. At the same time neither carriers nor shippers can be permitted to urge for their own purposes a strained or unnatural construction.[25] On the face of it, if Kleenex, not being made of cotton, was used as a towel, it might be rated as a "towel other than cotton." Kleenex is used for a variety of purposes—removing cosmetics and cold creams, polishing silver, wiping razor blades, cleansing eye glasses. It may be used as a handkerchief, a lunch napkin, or an emergency blotter. Yet the shipper does not argue that Kleenex should be classified under any of these categories. Accordingly, it is illogical for him to interpret the entry "Towels, other than cotton" to include Kleenex when it is just intended to distinguish some fabric towels from towels made wholly of cotton.[26]

A popular brand of dog food consists of meat (2 per cent), tallow and blood (5 per cent), lungs and bone meal (17 per cent), soya bean meal, wheat or barley (17 per cent), fish liver oil, irradiated yeast, and vitamins (2 per cent), and added water (57 per cent). The shipper claimed that because of the low percentage of meat which was deemed fit for human consumption, the product should not be classed "Feed, Animal or Poultry, meat or fish, with or without cereal or vegetable ingredient" (L.C.L., third class) but "Feed, Animal or Poultry, Prepared, N.O.I.B.N., other than condimental or medicinal" (L.C.L., fourth class). After studying the dictionary, regulations of the Department of Agriculture, definitions under the Food and Drug Act, and rulings of the Interstate Commerce Commission, the Board confirmed existing practice and rated the product third class. [26a]

A vulcanizer is a piece of equipment in which tires are cured. In the process of curing the design is moulded or pressed into the rubber. Before vulcanizers were specifically provided for in the classification, the question arose as to whether they were analogous to rubber moulds, machine presses, or machines N.O.I.B.N. The Board, after consulting dictionaries and classification committees of railwaymen and shippers, concluded they were machines N.O.I.B.N.[27] Flint pebbles or stones, one to six inches in diameter, are picked up from beaches in parts of Europe and exported to Canada for use in milling ore. They had been classified by the carrier as "Grinding Pebbles, used in pulverizing mills" (tenth) but the consignee claimed that the lower mileage scale of rates on "Stone, Cobble, Field or Rubble" was applicable. The Board considered that the railways had properly classified the articles in question. Cobblestones are typically larger than grinding pebbles (2½ compared with 10 inches), are of any kind of stone, and commonly are not hard enough for milling purposes. They are of low value, a domestic product, and used for building and paving.[28]

The Board had, again, to decide whether streetcar tickets and transfers were analogous with "Printed Matter N.O.I.B.N." (first class) or with checks and tickets such as counter sales books for retail stores, baggage room checks, and tickets for cash registers and for admission to theatres (third class). Following the usual practice that "tariffs, when ambiguous, are to be construed in ease of the shipper when they can reasonably and properly be so read,"[29] the Board ruled that streetcar tickets were third class. Yet because streetcar and amusement tickets have apparently higher values than sales books and checks for baggage, the Board left the way open for possible reclassification at a higher rate when additional evidence was available.[30]

One other illustration may be given. Prior to 1932 there was no specific provision in the classification for heel burrs, which are the small pieces of metal used in rubber heels to prevent the nail which holds the heel to the shoe from pulling through the rubber. A shipper claimed that the burrs were analogous with rivets because they were used with rivets. This reasoning, according to the Board, was unsound. The characteristics of one commodity and the article with which it is used may be entirely dissimilar as far as transportation is concerned and may justify different ratings. Ploughshares and plough parts are used with ploughs and barrel covers with barrels, but they have not the same rating. The railways argued that heel burrs were analogous with eyelets and other shoe findings. The Board decided that the rule of analogy on which the shipper had relied did not apply at all and set up a separate item for heel burrs giving them the same rating as iron and steel washers.[31]

Cost of Service

It is obvious that though the rule of analogy may be of some assistance in deciding where articles not previously shipped are to be placed in the classification, it is not of much assistance in drawing up the classification in the first instance. Moreover, as shown by the partial list of the articles in the fourth class (55) which is given above, there is often little analogy between all of the articles in any given class, except that they are put in that class for rate-making purposes. Of necessity the classification is built up primarily on the basis of the characteristics of various articles as they affect transportation and not chiefly on the basis of analogy. Consequently we must try to relate cost of service and value of service to the practical problem of setting the rate on a particular type of traffic.

Although value of service or what the traffic will bear has in the past been more important in setting particular rates than cost of service, the latter cannot be ignored. A rate must at least cover the cost of service and make some contribution, however small, to the common costs. As the following quotations show, the Board has recognized this principle in several cases. "A rate is unreasonable where too low just as much as it is unreasonable when it is too high; rates must be reasonable, having regard to the travelling [or shipping] public."[32] "While the value of a commodity has always played some part in a rate fixing yet, . . . an important factor should be the cost to the transportation company for adequately performing the service."[33]

Another instance involved the relationship of cost and distance but the Board applied the same principle as in cases involving cost and classification.

To bring about the equalization here suggested as between highway traffic to and from Prince Edward Island and the mainland, and highway traffic carried for the same total distance between points on the mainland, it would be necessary to treat the ten mile ferry movement as part of the through highway mileage making the ferry charge 50 cents per ton for the weight of freight loaded in the truck. Apart from the anomalies which result from such a proposal, it seems obvious that any such charge for traffic on the ferry would be entirely unreasonable and much below the cost of service.[34]

In considering matters of cost and the classification, the Board has sometimes compared the proposed rate or class with the toll or classification of similar products and the financial needs of carrier. "The Board cannot order the companies to put in an unremunerative rate, nor a rate so low as to be unfairly out of line with rates which are necessary to be maintained in order to permit the continuance of satisfactory operation of railways, due regard being had to proper consideration of the value of the commodities shipped and the service performed."[35] "The Board has in no case, on any commodity, directed rates as low as applied for, and . . . [was] clearly of the opinion that they would be unremunerative to the railway."[36]

When a railway argues that cost of handling should chiefly determine the classification of an article, the Board has held that "general allegations as to the increase of the cost of service, etc., are not conclusive as to the reasonableness of the rate. . . . The railway should adduce particular costs affecting the traffic in question, if increase in cost is to have any adequate weight in justifying the reasonableness of the rate attacked."[37] As Professor Jackman explains, "if general increase of costs were permitted to be used in proof of the necessity of increases in particular rates, the door would be opened to many increases which would be derogatory to the public welfare . . . [and so] a general and gradual rise in the level of rates [would be facilitated] at the instigation of the railway companies."[38]

Conversely, if shippers base their arguments for rate reductions on questions of cost, they must bring forth some affirmative evidence of the lower cost of handling their particular types of traffic. They may not content themselves with general allegations or with comparing their rates with rates on traffic generally or on other goods which, owing to their transportation characteristics, can be handled at lower costs than the freight in which they are interested. In one case involving rates on fish oil, complainants cited the rates on linseed oil but the Board decided that a bare comparison of rates on different articles proved very little.

Beyond merely citing [these rates] . . . no further evidence was given. . . . It was not contended that the commodities mentioned in any way compete with each other and it does not follow that, merely because the rates are different, there exists either unreasonableness or unjust discrimination with respect to the rate complained of. . . . With regard to practically every article that is accorded special commodity rates, a different set of circumstances and conditions prevails; one case can seldom be an exact precedent for another; each traffic situation presents points of difference and the particular facts, circumstances, and conditions existing in each case must be considered and the rates established based thereon. No data are before us concerning the conditions with respect to the rates cited for comparison.[39]

Similarly, the Board laid down in two cases that comparison of rates on one article with the average rate on all commodities carried by a railway was inconclusive.

The fact that rates on a certain commodity yield revenue per ton-mile higher than the average on all traffic, cannot be accepted as evidence of the unreasonableness of such rates. If it were accepted, the result would be a continual reduction in rates that yield higher than average revenue until all rates were on a common level. Ton-mile statistics, reflecting as they do, neither carloading, train tonnage, nor car nor train-mileage [i.e. specific costs] are far from being reliable guides in fixing freight rates. Without any change in the charge for the service, a reduction, or an increase, in the average revenue per ton-mile will be brought about by a relative difference in the length of haul or in the volume of traffic taking different rates.[40]

The 'average' gross ton-mile figure [is] for all commodities ranging from sand to silk. Obviously, such average figure could not be used without modification, up and down, when applied to particular commodity movements.[41]

Finally, the Board has declared that data for two commodities hauled different distances had little significance. A comparison of the ton-mile rate on grain moving at a statutory rate for 1,200 miles and that on a car of sugar beets moving approximately 50 miles had little probative value.[42]

Notwithstanding the Board's declarations that if particular rates are to be attacked or upheld on the basis of cost, the latter must be shown in specific form, the Board has occasionally accepted general statements. It has done this, however, only in those cases where costs were clearly so much higher than the tolls requested that the lower tolls could not possibly be justified. This was the Board's attitude in the so-called *Prince Edward Island Ferry Case* just mentioned. For similar reasons it refused to reduce the existing charge of $3 per car which the railways levied for stopping partially filled livestock cars at stations in Western Canada for completion of loading up to their capacity. The railways showed that the service given was expensive. It was often performed by mixed trains which operate on slow schedules. The average delay to train service at stop-off points varied from thirty minutes to over an hour. The same train might have five or six stop-offs with consequent difficulty in making connections. Delays were reflected in overtime labour costs. "While the carriers presented no detail figures of costs, there is without doubt good reason to rely on oral testimony of the officials whose duties are to cope with the operating matters involved in the livestock movement."[43] In a word, the board did not require detailed statistics of costs when the general picture was so clear.

Now if it is true that, generally speaking, evidence about cost must be specific and if it be also true, as pointed out in the previous chapter, that the actual costs of handling any particular type of traffic can rarely be determined, how then can cost of service ever enter into the practical problem of setting a rate? The answer is that, although costs cannot be determined in the absolute sense of the word, the cost of hauling one commodity can be compared with the cost of transporting another which has similar transportation characteristics and on which the rates are assumed to be reasonable.[44]

The principle that where costs of transportation are similar rates should be identical may be illustrated. In one case the carriers did not and probably could not show the cost of hauling brick, but they did show that the cost of handling it was substantially the same as the expense of transporting coal and stone. From these facts they argued that the rates on all three commodities should be the same. Because the rate on brick was lower than on the other articles, the toll on brick was raised.[45] On another occasion, which involved the classification of peanuts, disputants compared the transportation factors and the existing rates on peanuts, cheese, meats, lard, rice, and sugar.[46] In still another case the Board ruled that the charge for interswitching at Saint John was justifiably higher than at Halifax because the operation was more expensive on account of a heavy grade, the use of an expensive bridge, and movement through three or four terminals.[47]

In comparing costs, various transportation characteristics have to be taken into account. Rates are invariably quoted by weight[48] whereas many of the expenses of transportation, e.g., shunting, depreciation and interest on rolling stock, and so forth, vary to a large extent with the number of cars hauled. Certainly it costs very little, if anything, more to haul a car containing forty tons than one containing only five. Therefore, railways often quote incentive rates, i.e., lower tolls per hundred pounds when a car is heavily laden than when a smaller tonnage of the same commodity is shipped in a single car. Though incentive rates are not new, they got new life in the 1950s when railways began to use them to meet truck competition and keep rates in line with costs. Moreover, in order to get reasonable revenue per car, railways have to charge a relatively higher rate per hundred pounds for light-weight goods than for heavy articles. It is not suggested that railways graduate their charges so as always to produce the same gross carload revenue but still the load is an element to be taken into account. For example, live poultry in carloads is not entitled to the same classification as livestock because of the difference in tonnage moved and the aggregate earnings per car. Revenue from the reshipment of the processed birds and animals must also be taken into account.[49]

Examples of comparing cost of transporting different commodities with rates may be multiplied. Bulky and odd-shaped articles such as furniture S.U. (set-up), empty tin cans, and baskets (not nested) take a higher rate than lumber or furniture shipped K.D. (knocked down, i.e., disassembled), cans shipped flat to be blown up at destination, or baskets (nested).[50] Some perishable items such as melons cannot be piled deeply one upon the other without crushing the lower layers. Hence they take a relatively higher rate than if it were possible to load the car more nearly to its physical capacity. Formerly a refrigerator car could not be loaded near the roof because the air there would become so warm that on long hauls perishable articles would decay. If the car were provided with sufficient ice to keep the upper layers of air cool, the lower tiers of perishables might suffer from excessive cold. After lengthy research railways have succeeded in correcting this situation to a considerable extent. None the less this factor still tends to keep rates on perishables a little higher than they would be if refrigerator cars could be loaded more heavily. Long articles such as girders, telegraph and telephone poles, and boilers sometimes need to be secured to a central car with their ends projecting over adjacent cars, called "idlers," which must be hauled empty. Alternatively each end of the long article is fastened to a car, and an idler placed between. In any event an extra charge is made for the extra space occupied, or rather for the additional car space used but not actually carrying any of the weight of the load.[51] Again, the L.C.L. rate on candy in pails each weighing less than 20 pounds is higher than on candy in pails each weighing 20 pounds or more. Additional handling and extra costs are incurred when the same total weight is sent in small rather than in large pails.[52]

A clear illustration of the principle being discussed involved express. Millinery, artificial flowers, bonnets, hats, and hat frames are light and bulky. In 1910, instead of advancing the ratings on these goods, the express companies decided to accept the articles only at certain arbitrarily assigned weights which were in excess of the actual weights. Later the companies alleged that, despite the conventional weights, the charge per shipment or package was still considerably less than for heavier goods which were charged for at their actual weights and were shipped in packages of the same dimensions. The boxes of millinery were taking up more room in express cars than they were entitled to in relation to the tolls they were paying. The space in express cars is limited. A method which permitted one section of shippers to take up more than a fair amount of space for their traffic and yet pay the same tolls as the traffic of other shippers occupying much less space might easily cause discrimination. Consequently in 1931 the Board abolished the conventional weights and rated these articles at one and one-half times first instead of first class as before. This involved an increase in rates of 50 per cent and was a clear application of the relative cost of transporting various types of goods.[53]

Value of goods being carried is also an element in the cost of transportation. A railway, unlike a carrier by water, is an insurer for the goods it transports. The insurance "premium" on the more valuable articles is naturally higher than on those of less value and so the freight toll on the former ought to be a little higher. Generally speaking, the difference in premium because of higher values is of minor importance in rate-making because railway transportation is unusually safe. In a few instances, however, the railway's responsibility for the goods it carries does affect rates. Sand and grain in bulk leak from cars, china dishes are broken, soft drinks may freeze, tobacco and liquors are sometimes stolen.[54] Commercial fertilizers and many other articles may taint other goods. In order to reduce claims for loss and damage the railways have to provide "tight" cars without leaks in roof, sides, or floors through which water or dust may enter or the contents of the car escape while being constantly jiggled about in transit. Other cars must also be perfectly clean inside and be, as the stencilled notice on some cars states, "Reserved for sugar, flour, and other high class traffic." Railways also maintain their own private police forces. Costs are increased by reason of all these factors and ratings reflect this condition. Because of susceptibility to damage, railways carry some articles at Owner's Risk.

Rating explosives is an obvious illustration of risk as applied to rates. At one time shipments of high explosives had to be accompanied by an attendant who was given free transportation by the railway. In 1925 the rates were lowered because of a distinct reduction in the hazard[55] but a request made twenty years later by the manufacturers of explosives for a further reduction in tolls was turned down by the Board. By this time dynamite was being shipped in forms less sensitive to shock than formerly and claims against carriers for damage had declined markedly. On the other hand, the railways had to select cars carefully, obtain a certificate of packing and inspection from the shipper, placard each car and maintain a daily record of its location, require train crews to handle such cars with extra care, guard the cars while they were being loaded and unloaded, and isolate them in terminals. In the Board's opinion the absence of explosions was no evidence that the inherent risk of handling this class of goods had diminished. In fact, it was more by good luck than good management that serious damage had not occurred and so it refused to reduce the rating.[56]

Risk in carriage also has an influence on the method of packing which in turn affects the rate to be charged. If goods are tendered in bad condition the railway may refuse to carry them at all or may accept them "In Bad Order" or "Received in Damaged Condition," in which case it is not responsible for damage provided it notifies the shipper before the movement begins. In accordance with a long-standing practice, the same ratings apply to a commodity in carloads whether in glass, fibre, wood, or metal containers. This practice is perhaps explained by the relatively small hazard in handling carload shipments. Less than carload shipments of commodities shipped in glass were usually rated one class higher than the same commodity when packed in wood, fibre, or metal containers.[57] This was partly because oysters, honey, meat, etc., in glass are priced higher to consumers than the same goods shipped in metal cans or in bulk, and cater to a somewhat different demand. The Board considered there was no substantial competition between oysters in glass jars and in bulk.[58] In addition, when a glass container is broken, all of the contents must usually be thrown away whereas some could have been salvaged from a metal container. Recent Classifications have tended to reduce the ratings on articles in glass relative to those in metal cans. This is the result of improvements in the design of glass jugs, bottles, carboys, etc., and in methods of packing them in boxes of wood or corrugated paper.

Manufacturers of various types of containers hotly dispute with each other regarding the effect of containers on damage claims. Producers of wire-bound boxes insist that their goods will stand from $2\frac{1}{2}$ to 5 times the strain of corrugated boxes and will stack higher in cars, thus saving space. Accordingly, they say, articles packed in wire-bound boxes should be charged lower rates than the same goods in cartons of corrugated paper or fibre. The Board has not been convinced that losses are markedly different in one type of container than in the other. But the different kinds of containers do make a difference in the weight of each shipment and hence in the amount paid by the shipper or consignee.[59] As the old-fashioned wooden boxes were heavier than either corrugated boxes or wire-bound boxes made of plywood, railways experienced a little loss in revenue with the introduction of newer types of containers. But to make allowance in the rating for these factors is to attribute to the classification an accuracy in relating transportation conditions to tolls which it could not possibly display. Thus, for example, nowithstanding changes making for increased strength of electric light bulbs and improvements in packing the Board refused to change the rating on them.[60]

Other factors in the relative cost of handling various types of traffic have also to be taken into account in rate-making. It is expensive for a railway to haul cars empty to the point of origin in order to have them filled again with freight. In the case of general merchandise this cost must be spread over the entire operations of the carrier but certain types of traffic produce so much empty car mileage that they ought to pay something extra for the additional expense for which they alone are responsible. For example, gasoline causes almost 100 per cent empty mileage because it very rarely happens that a shipment can be hauled in the tank car on the reverse movement. Livestock shipments give rise to nearly 90 per cent empty car mileage because only one car in ten can be used for hauling livestock even part way back to the point of origin and stock cars can rarely be used for other types of freight. Though no one can tell except in a very arbitrary fashion how much more, if anything, it costs to haul cattle than fence posts or railway ties, one can point to the heavy empty mileage as one factor justifying higher rates on the first than on the other two.

High empty car mileage is partly the result of the need for specialized equipment and partly of the seasonality of production. For example, the transportation of grain necessitates rapid movement to Lakehead and then prompt return to the producing area for another load to be delivered before navigation closes. Even if other freight were available, the car could not be delayed at Lakehead for a return load and then delayed again for unloading at its destination on the Prairies. Some traffic, such as newsprint from numerous mills in Northern Ontario moves regularly throughout the year and can be hauled more economically than freight which fluctuates in volume a great deal from day to day and from week to week. Hence freight which moves in regular volume is entitled to slightly more favourable rates than freight which moves in uneven quantities. Finally, some freight requires special services, such as ice for refrigerator cars, charcoal and stoves or "canned heat" for heater cars, and so on. Generally speaking, extra payment must be made for these special services. Their cost is not included in the regular freight toll.

The carriers stress the special costs for which particular commodities are responsible. Almost every kind of traffic entails some extra expense or requires facilities peculiar to itself. Coal-oil in barrels may taint other goods and so is more expensive to handle than flour. But flour needs a clean dry car and hence incurs special charges of its own. What is important in this regard is the special charges for one commodity over and above the special charges typical of all other kinds of freight.

Value of Service

For reasons which were elaborated on in the preceding chapter, cost of service is normally but a minor factor in rate-making though it cannot be ignored.[61] It is value of service upon which chief attention has been directed. In the actual practice of setting rates how may value of service be measured?

Value of the Commodity

Probably the oldest method of measuring the value of the service is by means of the value of the commodity. In its first *Annual Report* (1888) the Interstate Commerce Commission stated that "in determining what the relationship should be between the rates charged for transporting two different freight articles, value is often an important factor; but this is not alone because of the greater risk connected with the transportation of the more valuable article. Improvements made during recent years in the roadbed and equipment of the carriers have rendered the item of risk in many cases of little consequence. The value of the article is important principally because of its bearing upon the value to the shipper of the transportation service and the value of the service is, and always has been considered by the carriers, one of the important elements to be considered when fixing the rates to be charged for transportation."

Thus the value of the commodity is significant in two respects: in the cost of service, since the "insurance premium" is higher for more expensive goods than for others; and in the value of service. Generally costly articles will bear a higher freight rate and still move in large volume, than will cheaper articles. If the freight rates on milk and on shoes are both increased by 10 cents per hundred pounds, the price of milk (10 gallons to the hundredweight) will go up about one-quarter of a cent per quart and of shoes (1 pound per pair) by one-tenth of one cent per pair.

With milk at, let us say, 25 cents per quart and shoes at $10.00 per pair, the difference in price to the consumer because of the freight increase is fairly important in the one case and negligible in the other. Even if the entire increase were added to the retail price of shoes, it would have no appreciable effect on demand or on the amount of this kind of freight handled by rail. On the other hand the rise in the price of milk is much more likely to affect the demand for this product and the volume of the railway's business. Certainly a point would sooner or later be reached when the same absolute increase in the freight on the two commodities would drastically cut down the traffic in the one while scarcely affecting the movement of the other.

The principle that valuable commodities can stand higher rates than less expensive ones is widely accepted in transportation. For example, the rate on malted milk is one class higher than on condensed milk. Railways quote higher rates on hardwood flooring than on cheap lumber such as hemlock, larch, and spruce[62] and higher tolls on mahogany, rosewood, satinwood, teak, and walnut than on rough lumber, shingles, and railway ties. They recognize variations in the value of ore as a justification for differences in rates and, after complaint from a shipper, the Board extended the principle to still lower grades of ore.[63] Railways charge more for transporting fertilizers such as Vigoro which have high values per pound and which are used for lawns, gardens, and flower beds, than they charge for the same products in bags weighing each over 25 pounds, or in barrels, to be used for general farm purposes.[64] As the Board has explained, "the value of the commodity hauled is an element that may properly be considered in rate-making. In general, the greater the value of the article, the greater the rate may be. There are, of course, many other elements to be considered in deciding the reasonableness of a rate, which in some cases outweigh the element of increased value of the commodity."[65]

Though rates are often related to value, they do not vary in exact proportion thereto. To make differences in rates for slight differences in value would enormously complicate the classification of goods and leave the door open for the perpetration of all kinds of fraud on the railway. Accordingly the Board has forbidden lower rates on slack, lump, or run-of-mine coal than on higher-grade coal[66] and on cheap glassware than on the expensive deep-cut glass sold by jewellers.[67]

In numerous other cases the Board has emphasized that mere differences in value do not in themselves justify different ratings but that all relevant transportation factors need to be borne in mind. The classification cannot be brought to such a high degree of refinement that minor differences in value shall be recognized.[68]

Even on the same article there is a very wide range in values in many cases and there has never, in Canada or the United States, been that attempt at refinement that would provide for different ratings on the same article based solely on difference in value. With the very limited number of classes in the classification and the thousands of articles to be classified, the grouping of articles is necessarily more or less broad. Classification is not an exact science, nor may the ratings accorded a particular article be determined alone by the yardstick, the scales, or the dollar. From its very nature and use, classification cannot be so minute as to do mathematically exact justice to every variety of commodity that may move.[69]

The grouping of articles must of necessity be more or less broad: hence a hat is a hat, silk is silk, and tea is tea, no matter how the values may vary.[70]

The value of an article is an important, although not controlling, element in the determination of classification ratings, but very little value attaches to comparisons of the percentage proportions of freight charges to the value of the commodity.[71]

It is very easy to pick out a given article in the classification accorded a certain rating, then go through the classification and name other articles of similar value with a lower rating, arguing therefrom that there should be a reduction in rating on the article first named.[72]

The classification . . . represents the work of the joint committee of shippers and carriers and naturally contains compromises and, perhaps, some inconsistencies.[73]

The Board has also made clear that, even on the same commodity, rates are not altered when the price of a commodity changes.

Rates so fixed would have no permanency nor would they necessarily have any relation to the cost of service or other factors that are controlling in the establishment of rates. [Furthermore,] prices of commodities fluctuate daily and, sometimes, such changes are substantial. General increases and decreases in rates have been based on cost of operation. Cost of transportation does not go up and down in step with commodity price levels and fluctuation in commodity price levels does not result from rates charged for transportation. . . . Again, there is to be found a range of prices at different points which bears no relation to the difference in rates to such points. To illustrate its impracticability, . . . the Railway Act requires that, unless the Board, by order, otherwise designates in individual cases, there must be 30 days' notice of increase and three days' notice of reductions. Aside from the unfeasibility of obtaining immediate data concerning all price fluctuations in all parts of the country on a vast number of commodities and articles handled, rates based on price fluctuations could not possibly be changed to keep step therewith.[74]

The point that rates are not necessarily adjusted to changing values of the freight which is shipped, was brought out in another case before the Board.

If a reduction in the price of a commodity would automatically carry with it a reduction in the rate, it would logically follow that an increase in the price of a commodity would automatically carry with it an increase in the rate. . . . The mere ability of an article to pay, aside from the question whether the increase in revenue to be derived from the increased rate is justifiably necessary, is not a conclusive justification for an increase in rate . . . . [In the past] a considerable period of time elapsed before the rates were increased, and the justification for the increase was the increased cost to which the railways were subjected.[75]

In using value for the purpose of setting rates, carriers are not required to estimate the intrinsic value of the freight as distinguished from its commercial value. Low grade, second pressure castor oil used exclusively for belt dressing was rated as castor oil (second class now 85) because it was so described on the packages, shipping orders, and bills of lading and because the rate applied to all grades thereof. It could not be rated as belt dressing (third class now 70).[76]

Another case involved Mead's Cereal, a baby food, which railways considered was a "Food Prepared N.O.I.B.N." (second class, 85) whereas the manufacturer contended that it was a "Cereal Product or Preparation" (fourth class, 55). The Board held that merely calling an article a cereal did not necessarily make it one within the meaning of the classification. As a rule, prepared cereals are composed of grain with some salt, sweetening, and malt; they are advertised in popular magazines, sold to the public through grocery stores, and are comparatively cheap. In contrast, Mead's Cereal includes edible bone meal, alfalfa, and dried brewer's yeast as well as grain; it is advertised only to the medical profession, is marketed exclusively through drug stores, and sells at a much higher price per pound than most cereals. Consequently in the opinion of the Board, Mead's Cereal is properly rated as a prepared food.[77]

Similarly, the Board held that an article labelled, invoiced, and sold as glue, which is an animal product obtained from hides and hoofs, is to be carried at the rates applicable to "Glue" and not to "Adhesive Paste," which is a cheaper article of vegetable origin. Corn flour used for adhesive purposes as a core binder for foundries is not a "Food Product (grain flour, N.O.I.B.N.)" but an "Adhesive Compound" for rate-making purposes.

The Interstate Commerce Commission follows the same principle. "If a manufacturer finds it advantageous to describe his product in a manner calculated to give purchasers the impression that it is a different and higher grade article than it actually is, he cannot consistently complain if the carriers accept that description as the basis for the collection of freight charges."[79] Similarly it has approved the inclusion of Shell

Kleanzit, Spot Remover, and Fluid for Cigarette Lighters with "Scouring, Cleansing, and Washing Compounds." The manufacturer asserted that the above trade names applied to what was really gasoline with special "additives" and therefore should bear the rate applicable to gasoline.[80]

Containers such as barrels, kegs, drums, bottles, egg cases, carboys, banana crates, and cylinders for acid, carbide gas, and soda water, are shipped under three sets of conditions: new, filled, and returned empty. The filled containers should, and do, pay a higher rate than empties because of their greater value, liability to theft, and cost of carriage because of their heavier weight. New or unused empties are perhaps somewhat more valuable than returned or used empties but the cost of transportation as measured by weight, space occupied, terminal expenses, and so on is substantially the same. If the rate on the returned empties is set too high, it would not be worthwhile for the shipper to have them returned to his plant, certainly not after they had completed more than two or three round trips and were rather "travelworn." The value of service to the shipper is definitely less on the returned than on the new empties. Consequently they get a lower rating than applies on the same packages when shipped new, provided they have been used in transportation of regularly shipped consignments and are being returned to the consignor of the original filled packages via the same line over which they were shipped when filled.[81] The reason for the proviso is that railways cannot afford to give low rates on returned empty containers unless they have made a normal, or at all events a larger, "profit" on the filled containers. Without this proviso trucks would take business from the railways by undercutting the higher rate and leave them with the relatively unremunerative traffic on the returned empties.[82] Thus, in the relationship between the rates on new and returned empty containers and between empties and filled containers, cost of service is largely ignored, being outweighed by value of service.[83]

To sum up, the value of the article is normally an important factor in determining value of service but rates do not vary in any exact ratio to value, nor with the values of different grades of the same article at any one time, or with day-to-day changes, or even with long-run changes in prices for the same goods. The concept of value of service is limited by the fact that, if extended beyond certain limits, it may ignore out-of-pocket costs. Low priced commodities, notwithstanding their low value, ought not to be transported at non-compensatory rates, or, to use the Board's words, "Regardless of the value of the traffic, the carriers are entitled to rates which are reasonable for the services they perform."[84] In another case it declared that "rates and ratings cannot be changed to meet fluctuations in the prices of commodities . . . [such rates would not] necessarily have any relation to the cost of service or other factors that are controlling."[85]

Use of Commodity

Sometimes the same commodity is used for different purposes. Many products, when used for some purposes, will stand a much higher rate than when used in other ways. Hence on the strict application of the principle of value of service rates should vary with the use to which the goods are put. In the main, railways and regulatory authorities have rejected this theory. To vary rates with use would contravene the Railway Act which requires equal charges to all persons for the same service. The cost of hauling a commodity is clearly the same no matter to what use it is put. To consider use would lead to fraud in billing goods.

In an early case the Board forbade a railway's charging a rate of 80 cents per ton on coal for manufacturing purposes and 90 cents on coal used for domestic heating and cooking. This action was taken even though the railway stated that the factory concerned could not continue to operate successfully unless it had a low rate on coal. In essence, the railway said that the value of service to the manufacturer was 80 cents per ton but the Board rejected the idea of rates based on use.[86]

At one time the rates on bituminous coal, anthracite coal, and coke were identical but in 1918 rates on coke were increased more than those on coal. In 1920 the percentage increase on coal was less than on commodities generally, including coke. In 1922 the Board reduced the rates on bituminous coal by rescinding the increase authorized in 1920 but authorized no change on anthracite or on coal from Lakehead westward. Later the Board refused to reduce the rate on anthracite but it did not set forth its reasons fully.[87] Perhaps the Board felt that the different rates on anthracite, bituminous, and on coke were justified by differences in use or in value. Obviously, the cost of transport is the same on all three mineral fuels.

The Board has held that a system of charging a higher rate on cream for domestic use than on cream for making butter was anomalous and inexpedient, even though on hauls to butter factories the railways gained the outbound traffic on butter.[88] However, the Board does allow a lower rate on windfall or bruised apples than on better grade ones. "Windfalls" are shipped in bulk or in bushel hampers and used for canning or making cider. Higher valued apples are eaten fresh and shipped in boxes, barrels, or crates.[89] There are also low rates on apple cores, skins, waste, pomace (crushed apples used in cider-making), and chopped apples.

Fox biscuits are similar in appearance and content to dog biscuits and has always had the same classification (third, 70). In 1935 it was argued that fox-rearing was getting into the hands of farmers as a side issue like poultry-raising, and that the rating on fox biscuits should be the same as on animal and poultry feed (fourth, 55). This was an indirect way of saying that because fox biscuits were purchased by the group of persons who bought cattle feed, they should be given the same rating. The judgment even suggests that those who buy these biscuits for feeding pet dogs would be prepared to pay a higher freight rate than farmers who feed the biscuits to foxes as part of a business enterprise. In any event, the Board refused to accept the contention that use should determine the rate.[90]

In some instances the Board appears to have departed from the principle just explained. Sand for building, for moulding, and sand N.O.I.B.N. carry different rates. Building sand is run-of-pit but moulding or silica sand is typically washed, dried, cleaned, and graded for size. It is used chiefly in foundries but also in filtration plants, in the manufacture of glass, pottery, chinaware, household cleaner, and scouring soaps. As far as the trade is concerned, there are two different commodities, building and moulding sand, and because they are essentially two different products two different rates are charged. But the same rate should apply to moulding sand whether used in foundries or in soap manufacture. Enamel used for covering watch dials is rated 100 L.C.L. and 55 C.L.: for use on signs within buildings, for the numbers on the outside of houses, and for dials of clocks and gauges, it is 70 and 45.

Wood charcoal, packed in multiple-wall paper bags or in bulk in barrels, and presumably used as fuel, is rated Class 70 (less than carload) but when packed in glass and probably used in medicines it rates 85. Also petroleum preparations in metal cans represented as remedies for the human body are rated under "Medicines, N.O.I.B.N." (100), otherwise they are petroleum products (third or 70). In these instances the two grades of the same product, though made of the same raw materials, are of such radically different values that they are considered as two different articles for ratemaking purposes. Blaugas and gasoline are competitive for certain purposes but the rating is different because blaugas is a more valuable and more efficient commodity.[92] No distinction in tolls is made between new and secondhand articles.[93] An application to reduce the rate on low-priced cut glass below the rate on expensive deep-cut glass handled by jewellers was refused since the two ratings of cut glass would lead to confusion and perhaps deception.[94]

Edgings and slabs take the lumber rate when used as shooks and a lower rate when used as fuel. There is no substantial difference in the edgings when used for either purpose though the value is higher in the one case than in the other. The items have been in the tariffs for years and to readjust the rates now would open a large question.[95] Consequently the two classifications were allowed to remain though they have lead to difficulties. A lumber company received a verbal order for fuel wood from a coal-mining concern. The lumberman was paid at the price per cord applicable to fuel wood. The agent at the originating point had classified the articles as fuel wood and made out a freight bill on that basis. The mining company used the wood as pit props and not as fuel. Then the railway billed the shipper at the freight rate covering pit props. The Board held that a carrier has the undoubted right to correct a bill of lading and to determine the character of the freight. It admitted that a shipper cannot be expected to police the contents of cars from the originating station to the time of ultimate use. Still, shippers and dealers are fully aware of the different rates that apply on fuel and pit props, and in quoting prices shippers should pay attention to the railway classification. Consequently, the Board upheld the action of the railway.[96]

As explained later, where a railway carries the raw material to a plant and the finished product out, it may publish a reduced rate on the inbound traffic.[97] In other words, railways grant lower rates when a product is used in such a way as to produce an outbound shipment of a finished article.

The gist of the whole matter is contained in the Board's statement that "generally speaking, the principle of rate-making is that rates on a particular commodity may not vary according to the use to which it is put, although there are a number of exceptions to the general principle under special circumstances and conditions."[98]

Social Importance of the Goods

The principle of value of service is sometimes taken to mean that the necessaries of life which take such a large part of the income of the poor should bear a lower freight toll than luxuries which are used by the rich. Carried to its logical conclusion, this argument means that freight rates should be based on the same principle as progressive taxation, such as income tax, where the rate of tax increases with the size of the income. The argument is sometimes supported by the state-

ment that the cost of transporting a specific commodity, like the benefit derived by an individual from a particular government service, is
rarely ascertainable with any accuracy.

But the analogy is fallacious because relatively valuable articles, for
example, automobiles and washing machines, are not purchased only
by the wealthy nor are goods such as bread and milk which are commonly considered necessaries of life consumed solely by the poor.
Though each person may easily draw up a list of articles which, for
him, are luxuries, the public at large is not likely to reach agreement
regarding what specific articles are luxuries and which necessaries.
The analogy between freight rates and taxes completely overlooks the
cost of railway service which, though it cannot be determined specifically
for any one article, can be estimated for one commodity relative to
another. If the analogy were, in fact, sound, it would be possible to
carry it so far as to assert that freight rates, like taxes, should be
assessed and collected by the state and not by the carrier.

Despite the objections, the Board in at least two cases seems to have
justified higher rates on luxuries on the ground that they made possible
lower rates on necessaries. "A reduction in the rating of the dearer commodities that are able to bear higher carrying tolls must necessarily tend
to curtail the ability of a carrier to make lower tolls, without which
cheaper goods cannot move at a profit."[99] An application was rejected to
take ice cream out of first and place it in second class for purposes of
express rates because it was a food. Although ice cream possessed food
value of a very high order, the Board considered it a luxury like soda
water or candy. It said also that any reduction in the express rate would
be in no case inure to the benefit of the ultimate consumer but would
simply be an added profit to the manufacturer and middleman.[100]

Now in fact low rates are given to articles of widespread use and of
typically low price, while goods of high value and of comparatively
restricted use are charged higher tolls. In one case the Board held that
"in order that cheaper goods may be carried any distance at all, the
classification must be arranged according to the ability of the various
articles to bear their share of the cost of transportation, so that luxuries
and things which move in comparatively small quantities are rated
higher than indispensables."[101] Similarly, the Board remarked that fuel
wood "has always received special consideration in the form of very
low rates as a concession made in the public interest in order to ensure
supplies of fuel at as low a cost as possible."[102]

It must be made clear that low rates on so-called necessaries are not
given as the result of ethical considerations or the desire to introduce
sumptuary regulation. Instead they are justified by the transportation

characteristics of the goods. Necessities of life move in large volume, in fairly regular amounts, are frequently less susceptible to loss and damage, and are less valuable in proportion to their bulk than luxuries. To give low rates on necessaries is justified, for the most part, by cost of service. Such goods as a general rule will not stand higher tolls and still move in volume. It pays the carrier to publish lower rates on articles in general use and charge at a relatively higher rate for luxuries. An examination of the classification will show some rough correlation between ratings and the popular conceptions of necessaries and luxuries. This relationship arises in consequence of transportation factors and not from any ethical considerations.

Prosperity or Depression in an Industry

Obviously the more prosperous an industry becomes, the better able it is to bear high freight rates. Conversely, and this is the aspect more likely to be stressed by shippers, industries in depressed circumstances allege that they cannot stand the existing rates and plead with the carriers for reductions. Railways often have tacitly admitted the soundness, within limits, of the principle of graduating charges according to an industry's current fiscal position. For example, in 1922 before the Parliamentary Committee investigating the restoration of the Crow's Nest Pass Agreement, railways offered to reduce rates on "basic commodities" such as lumber, livestock, potatoes, hay, and grain. In this way they hoped to stimulate business recovery, encourage the movement of freight, and obtain a satisfactory revenue for themselves. No carrier can thrive unless the industries upon which it depends for traffic are prosperous. To the extent that high freight rates create or aggravate depressed conditions within an industry, the carrier in its own interest may find it worth while to lower the rates. It may do this by changing the classification of the article, by lowering the commodity rates applicable to the freight in question, by including the article in a commodity tariff so that the class rate would no longer be applicable, or by carrying the goods farther than before for the same toll.

Although from a plain transportation point of view rates may be related in some rough fashion to conditions of prosperity or depression within particular industries, such a doctrine, if strictly adhered to, is liable to abuse. If rates are reduced when an industry is depressed, they ought to be raised when it becomes prosperous. Of course such action would be objected to by the shippers concerned.[103] Dispute regarding whether or not the industry actually was prosperous or depressed would be inevitable.[104] And if freight rates fluctuate with conditions between industries, then they should be higher for an individual or firm that is making money than for one which is losing. The result would be that carriers might appropriate to themselves all the profits or economic rent of every industry in the nation.[105]

The railways cannot be expected to carry on their business at a loss in order that shippers may operate at a profit. The cost of transportation to the carrier obviously sets a lower limit to the reductions in rates which it may offer a depressed industry. Moreover, the railway must guard against reducing its rates to aid shippers who are not doing all they can to cut their own costs by greater efficiency in production, better marketing, and superior service to consumers. Any reduction in the toll which it is practicable for a railway to make on any one class of goods during a business depression would probably constitute such an inconsequential part of the total costs of shippers or of prices to consumers that it would have little real effect on stimulating recovery. If for some reason or other the lower rates did not lead to an increased volume of business either for that industry or for the economy as a whole, railway revenues would be less than they might have been had the concession in rates not been given and an extra burden would be thrown on other traffic. This would be serious, especially if other industries were no better able to stand an increase in rates than the depressed industry which had been favoured by the lower rates. Theoretically society might gain by shifting the burden of the depression from weaker to stronger shoulders but neither the Board nor the railways have been given the responsibility of deciding such important matters of economic policy. The possibility of using the rates charged by railways and other public utilities as part of the mechanism for ironing out fluctuations in the business cycle is still a matter of argument among theorists.[106] Until the soundness of this particular technique in trade-cycle economics can be demonstrated, railways may quite properly object to being "guinea pigs."

Aside altogether from theory, the railways for a very practical reason fight the contention that they should reduce their rates to help depressed industries. If they adopted the practice for one industry, they would sooner or later find that they would become eleemosynary institutions for the rest of the economy. They would have to take in every foundling left on the economic doorstep of society. As long as railways are expected to function as business enterprises, as long as they are expected to cover their expenses by revenues, they must resist the pressure to become "fairy godmothers" to other segments of the economy. Yet while all this is true, the carriers must never forget that whenever their rates are higher than their patrons can bear, their own traffic and their own revenues fall off. From that straight dollar-and-cents point of view, as a pure transportation problem, the carriers might in their own interests find it advantageous to cut their tolls to help a depressed industry but they must be careful not to exalt a concept with definite limitations into a principle to be automatically extended whenever a chill wind blows upon an industry. When an industry is dying, it is better to let it succumb than prolong its agony at the expense of other shippers. Often, however, it is hard to distinguish between secular and cyclical decline.

Whatever the attitude of the railways may be, the Board has consistently taken the position that it cannot order lower rates merely because an industry is depressed:

A railway company is not called upon so to adjust its rates that the shipper will always be able to carry on his business at a profit. The rate is only one item in the shipper's costs. The obligation of the railway company is to charge a reasonable rate. It is not called upon, through the reduction of the rate, to guarantee that the business will be carried on at a profit. In other words, the needs of the business and the way in which it is carried on are not the measure of the reasonableness of a rate. . . . the reasonableness of a rate is [not] established by shewing that a reduced rate would give the applicant a greater profit.[107]

Nevertheless, the railways may of their own volition install development tolls.

When stock raisers in Western Canada asked for lower rates because of the importance of the industry to that part of the Dominion, the Board found that a great many factors affect the industry to a much greater extent than the freight rate. Without any alteration in the rate, marked changes had taken place in the industry and violent fluctuations in price. Carriers were already encouraging livestock raising by granting half rates on all pedigreed stock, transporting animals to fairs and exhibitions free one way, assisting hog and calf clubs, publishing low rates on fodder in drought years, and so forth.[108] Hence the application was rejected.

In some instances the desire of shippers to get rates which will relieve depressed conditions in their special industry is coupled with the argument that when their industry is prosperous the entire country or a large portion of it will benefit. In order to assist in the diversification of agriculture, a sugar refiner in Alberta wanted a reduction in the rate on sugar beet pulp used as cattle feed. The Board found that because cereals were then selling at extraordinary low prices, farmers were feeding their own grain to livestock in preference to beet pulp previously used. As the existing rates on beet pulp were not the reason for the small consumption of pulp beyond a certain radius of the factory, the current scale of rates was not changed.[109]

During the depression in agriculture which followed World War I, the Board was often urged to lower the rates on dairy products from the West in order to promote diversification and assist exports. The Board decided that it had no authority to grant these requests:

While members of the Board may and do, as Canadians, sympathize with policies of economic development which may through increasing diversity lead to greater economic solidarity, it is not their general opinions but the powers conferred on them by the Railway Act which determine what they can do. Very wide powers it is true, are given under the Railway Act; but the Act is not to be construed as if it were a blank cheque to be filled in as members of the Board see fit. It is not the Board's function, as delegated by Parliament, to make rates to develop business, but to deal with the reasonableness of rates either on complaint or of its own motion.[110]

Earlier the board had explained its lack of jurisdiction at greater length:

The Board's function is concerned with complaints as to unreasonableness or as to unjust discrimination, and . . . it is not empowered to put in rates simply to develop traffic; that is to say, the Board is not empowered by Parliament to act as an arbiter of industrial policy. If it were so empowered, there would have to be explicit words; and if such powers were conferred, the Board would then be able to pass upon the question whether an industry should be allowed to develop in one section or another. No such power has been conferred. The railway, subject to the inhibitions as to unjust discriminations, may give a reduced rate basis to develop traffic. It takes the responsibility of profit or loss in connection with the transaction. The Board, under the Railway Act, has no profit or loss responsibility, and its intervention in the matter of rates must . . . be concerned with matters falling within the broad categories of reasonableness and unjust discrimination, and not with the policy of developing industries through rate adjustments.[111]

Railway practice and the Board's policy may be summed up by saying that while rates on specific commodities cannot be based on prosperity or lack of it among shippers, railways cannot entirely neglect this factor if they are to maximize their own profits. How far railways go in meeting the needs of shippers by cutting rates is largely a matter within their own managerial discretion, for the Board will not interfere provided the rates are reasonable *per se*.[112]

Competition between Commodities

Another factor affecting value of service is the competition which exists between commodities. If two articles are competitive, one cannot bear a higher rate than the other without losing sales. Besides, the value of the two articles and the cost of transporting them are likely to be the same. For these reasons peanut butter, jams, and jellies are placed in the same class.[113] It would be unjust to convey at different rates slack coal and lump coal[114] which were competitive commercially, of substantially the same description, and carried at the same cost to the railway. Asbestos cement in plastic form competes with putty used in connection with furnaces, stoves, and steam heating apparatus and is given the same rate.[115]

In a sense all articles compete with all other goods for a share in the consumers' dollar but for the purpose of setting a rate the competition must be direct. In 1925 a group of manufacturers wanted the classification of rubber flooring changed to that of linoleum with which, they claimed, it was in competition. Rubber flooring is made of reworked or scrap rubber. It is used in churches, hospitals, and schools; it is distributed through contractors, and in 1925, sold for about twice as much per square yard as linoleum. The latter product consists of a base of hempen fabric on which a mixture of pulverized cork and oil is rolled. Linoleum is used in homes and sold through furniture and department stores. The majority of the Board held that the manufacturers of rubber flooring had not proven that competition existed between their product and linoleum. One Commissioner dissented, for he believed that they did compete in rendering the same service though it was possible that selling arrangements may have lessened or even excluded the competition for the time being. In his opinion, the mere fact that the existing freight rate was higher on the one product than on the other restricted competition. Rubber flooring weighs more per square yard than linoleum and in the dissenting Commissioner's opinion this fact also entitled it to a lower rate.[116]

Even when direct competition is present, it does not justify identical ratings unless the conditions of transport are virtually the same. L.C.L. rates on spring-filled mattresses are 50 per cent higher than on high grade felt mattresses of about equal value. In 1928 an application to have the ratings equalized was rejected. Although the two articles were clearly competitive with each other, spring-filled mattresses had to be shipped flat, and were more awkward to handle than felt mattresses which could be shipped in rolls or bags.[117] In this instance cost of service was expressed by the ability of an article to stand higher freight rates in competition with another article.

Raw Materials and Finished Products

The classification of a raw material and of the finished product made from it illustrates the interaction of the two principles of cost and of value of service. Typically a finished article is more susceptible to damage, more bulky, requires cleaner cars, involves more care in handling, and generally is a little more expensive to transport than the raw goods from which it is made. It is of higher value and hence can stand a heavier toll from the point of view of cost of service.

Elements of competition between transportation agencies enter the problem too. The finished article may often be sent by either truck or rail and so these rates may be forced down. In hauling the bulky, relatively low-valued raw material the railway may have a great competitive advantage so it may keep rates just a shade higher on the raw materials than they would have been if the same degree of competition had been present as in the finished article. The tolls on the raw material cannot be disproportionately higher than those on the completed article, otherwise there will be a tendency for factories to be located close to the source of supply of the raw materials and the railway may lose what business it already has. On the other hand, in a few instances there is keen competition in transporting the raw material and very little competition in moving the finished article. Pulpwood is typically floated down rivers to mills at costs with which the railways cannot compete. For obvious reasons newsprint is sent from the mill to market by rail.

By and large, rates on raw materials per hundred pounds are less than on the finished goods. Tolls on broom corn and brooms, barley and malt, iron pipe and enamelled pipe, semi-finished (in the white) furniture and varnished, polished, completely finished furniture, raw cotton and cotton fabrics, pig iron and castings are but a few of hundreds of examples. Probably lower rates on raw materials cannot be claimed as of right[118] and the Board definitely turned down a proposal to have rates on meats bear a fixed relationship to livestock rates.[119]

Often railways grant low rates on a raw material because they can get the outward haul on the finished product.[120] For example, they quote particularly favourable rates for hauling ore to smelters and matte to refineries, logs to mills, and so on if they can be reasonably certain of getting a profitable outward movement on the processed raw materials. Yet a railway is not required, nor is it in its own interest, to cut rates on the inbound raw materials below the out-of-pocket cost of handling them for the sake of getting business on the finished goods outward from the factory. Nor may a carrier offer reduced rates on the outbound article, when the effect of the reduced toll would be to give a preference to one product over its competitor.[121]

On a fairly large number of products railways quote milling-in-transit rates, technically called stop-off in transit. These are described in the chapter on Accessorial Charges. In these instances the finished article is forwarded after manufacture at the balance of the through rate applicable to the raw material.

In some years a large amount of poor quality grain accumulates in the West, owing to weather conditions. Often there is simultaneously a shortage of feed for cattle, hogs, and poultry in British Columbia, the St. Lawrence Valley, and the Maritimes. Whenever this occurs, the railways are urged to lower their rates so that the off grade grain may find a market in mixed farming areas. Western grain growers would thus get a better price for their product and be able to purchase more merchandise which would be brought in by rail at relatively high freight rates. Farmers who finish livestock, keep dairy cattle, or raise poultry would get feed at lower prices and might expand production or at least not contract it. In consequence railways and the nation at large would be better off. These arguments are especially popular during business depressions when railways have much idle equipment.

Generally railways have rejected these arguments. Costs of transport per ton-mile are the same for low grade as for high grade grain. If low rates were quoted on poor grain, why not on good grain or second grade livestock or furniture? Soon the entire rate structure would be broken down.[122] During periods of drought the railways have hauled feed into stricken areas either free or at a nominal charge. Aside from any question of charity, the railways find it worth while to lower rates in order to prevent abandonment of the drought area and to keep farmers in a position where they can come back into production when climatic conditions improve. During and after World War II, the Government subsidized the transportation of feed grain from surplus to deficit areas but the rate published in the tariff was not altered. The Royal Commission of 1961 recommended that the government should re-examine the subsidies payable to railways under Feed Freight Assistance, i.e., on feed grain from the West to Ontario, Quebec, the Maritimes, and British Columbia.

On beets manufactured into sugar at Wallaceburg a lower toll was charged than on beets hauled the same distance but handed over at Wallaceburg for export and refining in Michigan. It was shown that the inbound rates on beets barely covered the cost of movement and that it was possible to grant these rates only because the carrier obtained higher rates on the outgoing finished product. When beets were exported to Michigan, the railway did not receive any of the latter traffic, and so it might properly charge a higher toll on the raw material inbound to Wallaceburg for export than on similar shipments for manufacture there.[123]

The policy of shifting part of the cost of carrying the raw material onto rates charged on finished goods is less practicable today than formerly. Owing to intensive competition from highway carriers, railways which publish low rates on raw materials cannot be assured that they will actually get the traffic on the outbound product. Indeed, if they make their outbound rates too high, they will almost certainly encourage trucks to compete with them. Increasingly, each rate, the inbound one on the raw materials and the outward one on the finished goods, must be dealt with on its own merits.

The preceding discussion demonstrates that many elements enter into determining the appropriate class for any particular article. The factors, whether based on cost or on value of service, are numerous, indefinite, and sometimes contradictory. In any particular decision the Board does not always indicate how much weight it attaches to the various factors. Occasionally, after quoting several previous rulings, the Board seems to arrive at its conclusion by pulling the answer out of the blue. This practice of the Board "gives a mysterious appearance to rate decisions."[124] The United States Supreme Court has explained that "it is beyond the sphere of human ingenuity to establish a rule of mathematical certainty whereby a rate may be ascertained as reasonable or unreasonable."[125] In the last analysis the determination of rates is a matter of human judgment. "The task of constructing a freight or passenger tariff is an eminently practical one. The process must be tentative and experimental. Little can be calculated in advance. Tariffs are not made out of hand: they grow. Not until a rate has been put into effect, can its results be known."[126]

Carload and Less than Carload Rates

As already pointed out, many commodities are carried at two different rates, are placed in two different classes, depending on whether they are hauled in carloads (C.L.) or less than carload lots (L.C.L.). The rating on L.C.L. is higher, and so the rate per hundred pounds is greater on L.C.L. than on C.L. shipments. With C.L. freight, the shipper loads and the consignees or their agents unload the freight either at their own industrial sidings or at team tracks.[127] The railway is thus saved the expense of warehouse accommodation, of handling, and perhaps of some shunting. As the handling of the freight is performed by financially interested parties, either owners or consignees, the loss and damage is likely to be less than if railway employees do the work. Conversely, L.C.L. shipments are loaded and unloaded from cars by employees of the carrier except that heavy or bulky freight, for example, single pieces of freight weighing 2,000 pounds or over, must be handled by the shipper or consignee.[128]

Usually carload freight can be loaded much more heavily in cars than can L.C.L. Ordinarily articles of a uniform character can be packed more closely together than goods of various shapes, sizes, and weights per cubic foot. In cars with L.C.L. freight, space must often be left so that access can be had to goods which need to be unloaded en route. Sometimes small lots must be set out of the car while other goods are being loaded or unloaded, and then they must be replaced. Commodities in a car which is only partly filled slide back and forth during shunting and are often damaged. In short, L.C.L. rates are higher than C.L. rates on the same commodity owing to the heavier costs to the carrier.[129]

All commodities have L.C.L. rates but not all have C.L. ratings. The general principle is that C.L. rates are not published if a carload moves only occasionally. They are given, however, if carloads move fairly often and if the requirements of the industry or trade can be more satisfactorily met by C.L. rates.[130]

The decision on whether or not to publish C.L. rates affects the ability of small manufacturers or distributors to compete with larger ones as far as freight rates are concerned. At times business-men with small volumes of trade object to C.L. rates because they enable large dealers to send in an odd carload of freight and undercut the prices of smaller merchants who ship L.C.L. The Board has generally refused to enter into the controversy between merchants of different size. Instead, it looks solely to the number of carloads of a particular article which railways transport.[131] Incidentally, railways make special arrangements for relatively small quantities of petroleum products, vegetable oils, acids, and compressed gases shipped in tank cars.

It often happens that orders for goods cannot be arranged to fit exactly the space of the equipment supplied by the railway. A shipper may have a quantity of freight which is left over or which is in excess of the quantity which has been loaded in one or more cars but which of itself does not constitute a carload. Each car, except the car carrying the excess, must be loaded as heavily as loading conditions will permit, to the marked capacity of the car if practicable. Each car so loaded is charged at the actual or authorized estimated weight (subject to the established minimum carload weight), and at C.L. rate. The excess or "follow-lot" is loaded in another car and is charged at actual weight and at the C.L. rate applicable on the entire shipment. Carriers may handle the excess through freight stations and may load other freight in the car carrying the follow-lot (Rule 24).

More specifically, a shipper planning to send 60,000 pounds on which the C.L. rate is $1 per hundred pounds may be assigned a car with a maximum carrying capacity of 50,000 pounds. He may send the excess of 10,000 pounds, which he is unable to put in the car, as a less than carload lot but at the C.L. rate. His total freight bill for the shipment will be $600. The arrangement is designed to make the best use of the available supply of freight cars. In the absence of this rule shippers would order the largest freight car which railways had in their inventory so as to make sure they would have plenty of room for their entire shipment. In consequence there would be a serious shortage of the larger cars. This rule does not apply on bulk freight, on freight classified sixth or lower, on lengthy articles requiring more than one car for transportation, or on freight which is so light and bulky that the normal minimum carload weight is low.

Occasionally shippers may not have enough goods to bring the actual weight up to the C.L. minimum. Sometimes the freight is so bulky that it is physically impossible to put in the car enough goods to bring the actual weight up to the minimum C.L. weight which is specified in the Classification or the commodity tariff. Under these circumstances if the freight is loaded in or on the car by the shipper, is tendered as a C.L. shipment, and is forwarded without other freight in or on it, the shipment will be charged as a carload (Rule 15). Suppose, for example, the minimum C.L. rate is 24,000 pounds but because of the bulkiness of the freight or the small size of the order from his customer, the shipper puts only 20,000 pounds in the car. If the car is tendered as a carload and sent without other freight in it, and if the C.L. rate is $1 per hundred pounds, then the shipper must pay the minimum C.L. weight (24,000 pounds) at the C.L. rate ($1 per hundred pounds) or $240. If the L.C.L. rate were $1.25 per hundred pounds, it would still pay the shipper to send this lot as a carload because the actual weight (20,000 pounds) at the L.C.L. rate ($1.25 per hundred pounds) or $250 exceeds the C.L. rate at the minimum C.L. weight ($240). A saving arises even though the shipper, in order to get the C.L. rate, has to pay for a minimum C.L. weight which is 4,000 pounds in excess of the actual weight.

Normally the car will hold a greater weight of goods than the minimum specified.[132] To meet this situation, railways often adjust the minimum C.L. weight to take account of the size of the car. When this is required, the letter "R" follows the C.L. Minimum Weight figure as given in the extreme right-hand column of the Classification, and as shown on the sample page reproduced earlier in this chapter. According to Rule 34, "when the Minimum Carload Weight provided in the Classification or applicable tariff for the Articles Shipped is . . . 20,000 lbs. [in closed cars], the Minimum weight will be 28,000 lbs. for cars over 40 ft. 7 in. and not over 50 ft. 6 in., and for cars over 50 ft. 6 in. in length it will be 40,000 lbs." Similar rules may apply to other minimum carload weights given in the Classification. Rule 34 also provides for goods shipped in open cars.

In order to encourage maximum loading Canadian railways publish incentive rates, as described above. Whatever the minimum C.L. weight, the shipper may want to put more than the minimum C.L. weight in a particular car. In this event he will pay at C.L. rates for the actual or authorized estimated weight which he sends. In the above example, if he sends 30,000 pounds, he will pay $300 (30,000 pounds at $1 per hundred pounds).

Every car has a maximum physical carrying capacity which is determined by the stresses which the various parts of the car (beam, floor, walls, and draw-bar) are built to withstand. This maximum weight is stencilled on the outside of the car. If the amount which the shipper puts in a car exceeds the maximum or marked carrying capacity, the transportation company reserves the right to unload at shippers' expense any weight in excess of the marked capacity and forward it to destination at L.C.L. rate (Rule 34, note 3). Suppose a commodity has a minimum C.L. weight of 40,000 pounds, and is loaded in a car with a stencilled capacity of 60,000 pounds. Assume further that a shipper by filling the car literally to the roof is able to get 65,000 pounds in the car. Because the actual weight exceeds the marked capacity, the railway may take out 5,000 pounds and send it at L.C.L. rates. Usually the carrier asks the shipper to remove the extra 5,000 pounds at his own expense and forward it later.

The charge for an L.C.L. shipment must not exceed the charge for a minimum carload of the same freight at the C.L. rate (Rule 15). If the L.C.L. rate is $1 per hundred pounds and the C.L. rate is 75 cents with a minimum carload weight of 14,000 pounds, the minimum charge for a carload is the minimum C.L. weight multiplied by the C.L. rate (14,000 pounds at 75 cents per hundred pounds) or $105. This charge applies even though less than the minimum C.L. weight is put in the car, provided, as explained above, that the shipper tenders the freight as a carload and the car moves without any other freight in it. Suppose the shipper puts 11,000 pounds in the car. The charge would be for the actual weight (11,000 pounds) at the L.C.L. rate ($1 per hundred pounds) or $110. In accordance with the rule just quoted, the

charge for this shipment would be $105. In short, the charge for an
L.C.L. shipment is not to exceed the charge for the same shipment on
a C.L. basis.

The charge for a car fully loaded must not exceed the charge for
the same freight if taken as an L.C.L. shipment (Rule 15). Because of
the bulkiness of the freight, it may be physically possible for the shipper
to stow only 10,000 pounds in a car. In the preceding example the
freight bill at the C.L. rate will remain at $105 but at L.C.L. rates it will
be $100 (10,000 pounds at $1 per hundred pounds). In this case the
lower charge will prevail.

Minimum Carload Weight

These illustrations show the close relationship between the C.L.
minimum weight and the C.L. rate on the one hand and the L.C.L.
rate on the other. This interrelationship has to be kept in mind in
setting any or all of the three factors: C.L. minimum weight, C.L. rate,
and L.C.L. rate. One of the purposes in setting "a minimum weight of
a C.L. is . . . to insure a reasonable return to the company . . . for
its service in moving a commodity which has the exclusive use of the
car. It should be based, of course, upon what should be a fair load for
the car, but in many instances commodities which move in carlots are
not of an aggregate weight equal to the minimum provided by the
railway companies."[133]

In 1927, in a case involving broom corn, the Board ruled that railways had the right to publish low rates per hundred pounds together
with fairly high minimum C.L. weights or vice versa so long as the cost
per car was reasonable.[134] In tariffs of tolls competitive with water and
highway carriers, railways often make the minimum carload weight
much higher than the one which applies to the same commodity under
the classification. This is done in order to get the same or a larger
revenue per car than before and so more adequately to cover costs many
of which are on a car-mile basis.

The minimum C.L. weight appropriate for particular commodities is
often under dispute. Broadly speaking, shippers in smaller communities
favour a lower minimum than those in larger cities. If the minimum
is quite high, merchants in small towns will either have to forego taking
advantage of the relatively favourable C.L. rates and bring in their
freight at the higher L.C.L. charges, or they will have to carry part of
the contents of the car over into the following season. Either of these
alternatives increases the expenses of small-town merchants and renders
them less able to meet the competition of large wholesalers and retailers

selling in the same territory. For their part, distributors in the big centres prefer fairly high minima in order to increase their competitive advantage, but they do not want the minimum weight so high that they too may be overstocked on some of the merchandise which they bring in. The railways want a minimum weight high enough to secure them a reasonable return for the use of the car.[135] The Board's task is to balance the interests of various groups of shippers, of communities, and of the railways. It must set "a fair mean between the physical carrying power of the car, and the public interest as affected thereby, and the conditions under which the business is carried on."[136]

In 1925, carriers, without changing the rating, increased the minimum carload weight on asphalt roofing from 24,000 to 30,000 pounds. The physical minimum, that is, the weight of the roofing which it was possible to load in the car, is higher than 30,000 pounds because roofing is relatively heavy per cubic foot. An application for restoring the former minimum carload weight really involved the commercial minimum which took into consideration conditions of manufacture, distribution, and consumption. The complainant admitted that larger towns and cities could easily handle the larger minimum but alleged that it would deprive him of the privilege of shipping in carloads to village communities that at the time had difficulty in handling a 24,000 pound car during the roofing season. The Board did not feel that it should set a carload minimum weight based solely on the quantity the complainant could ship at one time to the small community. It said that only one shipper had complained, and the minimum of 30,000 pounds had been agreed upon by a conference of shippers and the railroads. The average loading of complainant's shipments was 30,000 pounds which in itself was less than the physical minimum. No concrete evidence had been submitted regarding the effect of the increased minimum on prices to the consumer. Moreover, there had been a corresponding increase on other roofing materials competitive with asphalt roofing. Consequently the Board denied the application for a reduction to the old level.[137]

Less than Carload Regulations

The rules for L.C.L. shipments are simpler than those for carloads. A single shipment of less than carload freight is a lot received from one shipper, on one shipping order or bill of lading, at one station, at one time, for one consignee and one destination. Two or more single shipments shall not be combined and way-billed as one shipment. They must be carried as separate shipments and at not less than the established minimum charge for each shipment (Rule 12). The maximum charge for a single L.C.L. shipment is the charge for a minimum carload weight at the C.L. rate, as already explained. The minimum charge is the first-class rate for one hundred pounds regardless of the actual class in the Classification but in no case less than $1.50 (Rule 13).[138]

Where a single shipment consists of goods of more than one class and each class is in a separate package or packages, the charge is computed for each class at its actual weight and rate but with a minimum of ten pounds for each class of freight. In calculating the weight of a single shipment of freight of one class or of each class in a separate package, any fraction of five pounds shall be waived, and five pounds or any fraction above five and up to ten pounds shall be deemed ten pounds. The charge for a package containing freight of more than one class shall be at the L.C.L. rating provided for the highest classed freight contained in the package. All of the articles need not be specified on the bill of lading. Only the article taking the highest rating need be named provided it is followed by the note "and other articles classified the same or lower" (Rule 12). On a combination article which is not specifically classified, the rate which applies is that of the highest classed article in the combination (Rule 18). This rule would apply to a combination chair and stepladder, or to a compound used both for sweeping and as furniture polish, or to combination electric and coal stoves.[138a] Where a shipment on one bill of lading consists of parts or pieces which when assembled would constitute one or more complete articles, the rating is that provided for the complete article (Rule 20).

Mixing

The mixing rule (Rule 10) to which reference has been made is concerned with shipping two or more different articles for which C.L. ratings are provided, at one time, by one consignor, to one consignee and destination, but at the C.L. rate. In the absence of this rule, each of the commodities would have to be charged the L.C.L. rate or, if the shipment consisted largely of one article, that article might be carried at the C.L. rate and the C.L. minimum weight while the remaining articles would be handled at the correct L.C.L. rate. By taking advantage of the mixing rule, shippers can send different kinds of freight in the same car at the C.L. rate. Mixing is the basis of the freight forwarding business. Forwarding companies collect small lots of household effects, general merchandise, and manufactured articles from individuals or companies and mix the goods into carloads which they consign to their agent in a distant city who distributes the goods among the consignees. These companies charge owners of the goods a little less (usually 10 per cent) than the L.C.L. rates while paying the railway the C.L. rate. The difference between total receipts from their customers and payments to the railway is the source from which the forwarders pay their own expenses and derive their profits.

Mixing is allowed only on articles which are given C.L. ratings in the classification. As such ratings are given on almost all goods moving in volume, the privilege is important in every line of trade. Under the mixing rule, when a number of different articles of the same class are mixed in carloads, they are all taken at the C.L. rate for that class and at the highest minimum C.L. weight prescribed for any of the articles. When the articles shipped are of more than one class, the C.L. rate and the minimum C.L. weight of the article in the highest class apply to all the articles in the carload. Occasionally, the aggregate charge arrived at by applying the principle in the previous sentence can be reduced either (a) by considering the articles as if they were divided into two or more separate carloads and computing the charges for each separate carload in accordance with the general principle, or (b) by taking the C.L. rate and the minimum C.L. weight for one of the articles and taking the actual weights and the L.C.L. rates on the remaining articles in the mixed carload. The shipper needs to pay the lowest aggregate charge computed on any of these bases (Rule 10).[139]

Although the mixing rule provides an opportunity for grouping small lots, getting the C.L. rate on them, and so lowering the shippers' freight bill, it does not follow that a saving in freight charges will always result. A small quantity of first class freight mixed with a large amount of third or fourth class raises the rating on the whole carload and so may result in higher, not in lower, freight charges.[140] Mixing must be done with skill and with a thorough knowledge of rates if the shipper expects to economize on his freight bill through its use.

Before March 1, 1955, when equalization of class rates was introduced, the mixing rule throughout Western Canada (Lakehead and west thereof) and between Western and Eastern Canada was different than that between stations in Eastern Canada. In the West if a mixed C.L. was to get the benefit of a C.L. rate, it had to be composed of articles coming under one **DISTINCTIVE HEADING** or, as sometimes expressed, of articles listed under "the black-faced type" in the Classification. Examples of distinctive headings are "Agricultural Implements," "Groceries," "Cereals and Cereal Products," and "Chemical." In general, in the East, goods of various classes may be mixed, whereas in the West mixing was restricted to articles handled by people in the same line of trade such as implement dealers, hardware merchants, grocers, and druggists. The difference in treatment, which originated as early as 1904, arose because wholesalers in the West put pressure on railways to cut down on the shipments of mixed carloads from Toronto and Montreal. When business was good, commercial travellers from the East sold mixed carloads to retailers in the West and so reduced the profits of western wholesalers. When times were hard, eastern wholesalers withdrew from the market and western retailers had to use local jobbers. The latter, mostly new concerns, could not be expected to sell to a widely scattered population when business was poor if they could not share in the prosperity of the good years. Restricting the mixing privilege to lines of trade instead of leaving it "open" to any class of freight with a C.L. rating in the classification served to give the West a measure of protection.

In 1925, the Board, with one Commissioner dissenting, rejected an application for a uniform mixing rule across Canada.

When a practice which has been in existence for years and which was installed at the instance of the shipping public is attacked, a special burden of proof lies on those so attacking. . . . In so far as there was specific evidence—and it was meagre—it fell far short of being conclusive. It was not the function of the Board to tear up rates and rating adjustments regardless of the effect of such re-arrangements. It should not interfere except when unreasonableness or unjust discrimination was proven.[141]

By 1950 trade conditions differed greatly from those existing when the rule was introduced. The control of distribution in the West no longer centred in Winnipeg as it once had. Other wholesale centres had grown up closer to the consumer. Abolition of the restricted mixing rule in so far as it would encourage suppliers in small towns to buy in carload lots instead of L.C.L. lots would accord with this trend. The continual addition of articles under the distinctive headings was cited as proof that the western mixing rule was out of date. The establishment in western cities of eastern Canadian wholesale houses and the rapid development of pool car arrangements by forwarding companies lessened the force of the original argument that eastern jobbers came in only to take the most profitable part of western business. The development of highway transportation within the West has tended to break down the old concept that wholesalers in smaller distributing centres serve a more or less well-defined adjacent area and need protection against jobbers in metropolitan centres. The growth of chain stores and direct dealing between many manufacturers and retailers has tended in the same direction. A few western businessmen were opposed to any change but railways did not object to applying the eastern mixing rule to Western Canada. Finally the West demanded uniformity of railway tolls with the St. Lawrence Lowlands as a matter of principle. Hence the Royal Commission of 1951 recommended abolishing the restricted mixing rule in the West.

On one matter in connection with mixing the Board has been adamant. It has refused to permit change in the classification of an article merely to give the mixing privilege or to benefit a few shippers. It would not give a C.L. rating on gramophones for to do so would allow mixing, reduce railway revenue, and flood the Board with applications for C.L. ratings on other goods to bring them under the mixing rule.[142] A few companies make only bottle caps like those on soft drink bottles. Others make caps along with various sheet metal goods such as kitchenware, eavestroughing, milk pails, and can openers. When the latter companies asked for a C.L. rating on bottle caps, the Board refused. Granting their request would discriminate against those who manufactured only caps and would favour producers of more diversified lines of goods.[143] A manufacturer of rubber footwear wanted a C.L. rating on his product so that he could mix footwear with other rubber products. His application was rejected because it would give rubber footwear an unfair advantage over shoes made of leather or felt. These competed directly with rubber overshoes, running shoes and boots, none of which had the mixing privilege.[144] Similarly the Board has refused to allow taking rubber bands from "Rubber Goods, N.O.I.B.N.," including them under "Stationery," and giving them a C.L. rating with the mixing privilege.[145] It has turned down requests for a C.L. rating on rubber fruit jar rings[146] and the inclusion of school books in the stationery list.[147] The Board feels that a broadening of the mixing privilege would endanger the classification.

To ignore the rating properly and reasonably applicable to the article considered by itself, and to provide a lower rating than would thereby be established on its merits solely to permit the mixing privilege would do violence to one of the most important principles of classification making, always held hitherto to be proper and consistent. To lower a rating, which is reasonable *per se*, for such a reason, would inevitably lead to the requirement that all articles which the shippers' convenience would suggest be shipped together, should be given the same rating. Such a principle would be obviously unsound.[148]

Future of the Classification

In 1884 when railways in Ontario and Quebec agreed on a uniform classification, they hoped that all their traffic could be brought under class rates. Within four years, they found that they had to publish commodity rates because the class rates were higher than bulky, low-valued traffic could bear. Later, they published some water competitive rates and they reduced rates on export grain from the West and on settlers' needs inbound in accordance with the Crow's Nest Pass Agreement. One effect of these changes was that railways departed from the relationships between various kinds of traffic which prevailed under the Classification and the standard mileage class rate scale. On the other hand the Maritime Freight Rates Act, the abolition of the mountain differential, the policy of equalization adopted in 1951, and the numerous general rate cases changed the level of rates without seriously disturbing the Classification. In these instances there was no material change in the number of the "pigeon-hole" into which a particular kind of freight was pushed for rate-making purposes. All that happened was that shippers paid different rates than under the (standard) mileage class rate scale or the scale as a whole was raised or lowered.

In general the Classification held its own reasonably well until the onset of intensive highway competition. At first, truckers concentrated on carrying valuable goods where rail rates were comparatively high. To protect their net revenues, railways had to cut their tolls on such traffic and they did this, in the main, by lowering the class which applied on these goods from, say, double first (200) to first (now 100). As a consequence, most multiples of first class rates disappeared from the Classification.

Before long, motor carriers were also capturing lower valued goods from the rails. If railways had continued their policy of lowering the class which applied on such freight, they would have cut tolls on the entire traffic in question, even where competition was weak or nonexistent. Hence, in order to protect their revenue wherever possible, they published competitive tolls on hauls where competition was active while retaining the old class and the existing class rates on other hauls. This scheme had the additional advantage that whenever truck competition became less intense, the railways could cancel the competitive tariff and so bring the traffic back under the Classification with its higher rates.

In time, railways also began to meet competition by Pick Up and Delivery rates and Agreed Charges. Under the former, goods are grouped according to a simplified version of the Classification. P & D. rates are lower than the corresponding class rate and they include payment for the collection and delivery of freight from the place of business of the shipper to that of the consignee. During negotiations on Agreed Charges, railways and shippers consider mainly the cost of transport by truck and the long-run variable cost of handling the goods by rail. They may pay some regard to the appropriate charge under the Classification and the class rate scale but apparently this is not too important. At all events the shipper finds the rate by consulting the pertinent Agreed Charge. He need not refer to the Classification at all.

Piggyback rates—technically Trailer-on-Flat-Car—are another means of meeting highway competition and they represent an even greater departure from the Classification. Within limits, a railway does not adjust its piggyback rate to take account of the kind of freight that is being moved. Except that piggyback may not be used for mail, explosives, inflammable liquids, and a few other things, the railway is not concerned with the contents of the trailer on top of the flat car. Thus piggyback rates tend to ignore both the Classification and the class rate. The same thing will apply to rates on goods handled in containers, should that mode of transport become popular.

The fact that the Classification has been disintegrating under the impact of competition can be brought out in another way. In 1945 Canadian railways derived no more than 5 per cent of their freight revenue from classified traffic. By 1950 the proportion had risen to nearly 20 per cent because of the cancellation of competitive tolls wherever the operating costs and the rates of competing agencies rose faster than those of railways. By 1957 the proportion had declined to almost 10 per cent and in 1961 was roughly 5 per cent of revenue. This decline was the result of progressively more vigorous competition from truckers.

The data after 1951 include the revenue which was credited to class rates on account of the integration of a few commodity tariffs, notably scrap iron, cordwood, and potatoes, with the Classification as recommended by the Royal Commission of 1951 and as carried out by the Board. The Royal Commission hoped that this process would be extended over a wide range of traffic. It also expected that the integration would be facilitated by its recommendation that classes be numbered, e.g., 100 instead of first, 85 instead of second, and so on. Under the numbering system, new classes could be readily established. Unfortunately, the Royal Commission's hopes prove ill-founded.

Despite all the pressures, the Classification and class rates are still significant. First, when a business performs a large number of services, its price list must provide for services which are not large in terms of sales and revenues as well as those services that are. Second, although class rates make smaller contributions towards gross revenues than formerly, they still cover a large number of individual shipments. Third, the Classification gives an accurate description of various kinds of goods insofar as railways are concerned. For instance, it lists over

70 kinds of agricultural implements, 15 kinds of rings, and 18 kinds of pins. Fourth, it sets out the packing requirements of thousands of articles, the liability for damage, the minimum carload weights, and other data of vital importance to shippers and carriers alike. Finally, many truckers use a modified form of the railway classification in their operations.

The fact is that it is humanly impossible for railways to quote a separate rate on every commodity they handle. Some grouping is absolutely necessary. Classifications of one sort or another are used by telephone and telegraph companies for setting rates as well as by Public Service Commissions, the armed forces, and industry for the determination of duties and the purposes of pay. Classification is basic to the customs tariff, the census, and the provision of spare parts for machines. It is also essential in the operation of a library and in the study of botany, zoology, anatomy, and other sciences. A complex society is forced to use labels in order to bring its problems down to manageable size.

8

Adjustment of Rates to Distance

RAILWAYS are concerned with moving goods and persons from one place to another. Consequently the question of distance enters into the price of almost all transportation services. The two principles of cost of service and value of service affect the adjustment of rates to distance just as they determine the classification. Cost is the fundamental reason for mileage scales being set up and carefully adhered to. Value of service explains the rather frequent departures from strict mileage.

Uniform Scale of Mileage Class Rates

When equalization was under consideration by the Board, the various factors which go into the making of a distance scale received extended discussion. These factors include: the length of the mileage blocks (5, 10, 25, 50, or 100 miles); the amount of increment in rates (in cents) from one block to the next; the relative cost of handling traffic for various lengths of haul; competition from other carriers; the pressure of commercial interests for rates low enough to allow producers to sell in distant markets; the need for protecting the revenue to the railways; and the desirability of minimizing the amount of disturbance to business when new scales were substituted for existing ones. "Despite the statement made by the Board from time to time during the hearings that it would have to look at equalization from a broad, national point of view, in conformity with the policy laid down by Parliament, the tendency generally of the parties appearing in this case was to deal with the matter with the object of preserving their own particular position or privileges in the present rate structure. This was, perhaps, only to be expected."[1]

In the end the Board set up a "Uniform Scale of Mileage Class

Rates for application between points in Canada (Levis, Diamond, and Boundary, Que., and West thereof)" in accordance with the following scheme. The rates are those for Class 100 in effect on March 1, 1955. The same information is given later in a different form.

TABLE 5

Distance (miles)	Length of mileage block (miles)	Increment per mileage block (cents per 100 lbs.)
Minimum: 20	20	Minimum: 50
Over 20, up to 60	5	5
Over 60, up to 100	10	5
Over 100, up to 200	25	10
Over 200, up to 1500	25	9
Over 1500, up to 2700	50	16
Over 2700, up to 3300	100	14

Cost and Distance

In respect of length of haul there are two elements in cost: terminal and line-haul. The former includes billing, shunting empty cars to industrial or team tracks at origin, assembling loaded cars into trains, and sorting them onto the appropriate sidings at destination. In less than carload shipments terminal expenses normally include the additional cost of pick-up and delivery, of loading and unloading between trucks and freight warehouse and between freight shed and freight cars, and of temporary storage in freight houses.

When freight goes through an intermediate terminal, for example, a car of grain from a country point through Winnipeg to Lakehead or a less than carload lot from Kitchener through Toronto to Oshawa, heavy expenses may be incurred at the intermediate centres. Much shunting may be necessary and less than carload lots must be transferred from one car to another. But railway rates cannot possibly be brought into such accurate relation with costs that higher tolls will be charged when intermediate terminals intervene than when they do not. Accordingly, it is commonly, though perhaps improperly, assumed in rate-making that when freight moves over the lines of a single company, no more than two terminal costs are to be included in the rate.

The cost of handling freight in terminals is a fairly large proportion of the total cost. This is owing to exceptionally heavy wear and tear on equipment on account of frequent and often violent stopping and starting. Locomotives and crews in yard service are frequently idle. A number of "cuts" are needed to put cars in their proper order and shunt them to or from the correct team or industrial tracks. Cars may have to be moved as many as fifteen miles from one local or suburban yard to another within the same large terminal area such as Toronto or Montreal. In order to cut down the heavy expenses of operating terminals, railways have spent huge amounts of capital on building new automated yards and where possible, eliminating the smaller "flat" yards which have become obsolete. The Canadian National's new yard on the northwest outskirts of Toronto cost $75 million and can handle 6,000 cars a day.

Expenses for handling goods along the railway line tend to increase directly with distance but not perhaps in strict proportion to it. Diesel locomotives run over two or three divisions (200 to about 350 miles) rather than over merely one, as was the practice with steam. A freight car on a long haul may spend four days in actual movement and two days at each terminal for "spotting," loading, and unloading. Another car on a haul of one day's length will typically spend the same total time in terminals. In the first instance the car is actually earning revenue for the railway for 50 per cent and in the latter for 20 per cent of the time.[2] Still further economies arise if solid trains can be handled long distances without changing the "consist" or order of cars in the train, as in the grain movement across the Prairies into Winnipeg, or in scheduled service between Windsor and Buffalo, Toronto and Montreal. Because equipment is used more intensively, depreciation and interest charges per ton-mile are less on long-haul than on short-haul movements. Probably the economies which arise as a result of line-haul factors are much less significant in rate-making than the spreading out of terminal charges over the mileage hauled. In any event on account of terminal costs, total operating costs rise with length of haul but not in the same proportion as the increase in distance. Therefore costs per ton-mile decline as the haul increases in length. In brief, rates "taper" with longer distances.

Tapering

The tapering principle has been widely recognized by railways, the Board of Transport Commissioners, and the Interstate Commerce Commission. On the uniform mileage class rate scale on Class 100 with rates in effect on March 1, 1955, the rate of taper is shown in the accompanying table.

The rate of taper slows down with longer hauls partly because of market competition, partly because of the growing importance of the cost of handling at intermediate terminals. Studies made by the Interstate Commerce Commission have shown that when a car is hauled 700 miles, total expenses at intermediate terminals are about the same as the cost of handling the car at origin and destination.³ Moreover, if rates kept on tapering indefinitely, a point would eventually be reached where railways would derive virtually no extra revenue for hauling freight an additional distance of, say, 50 miles.

TABLE 6

Mileage	Rate in cents	Rate in mills per ton-mile
20	50	500
40	70	350
60	90	300
80	100	250
100	110	222
200	150	150
300	186	124
400	222	111
500	258	103
1750	348	93
1000	438	88
1250	528	84
1500	618	82
2000	798	80
2500	958	77
3000	1102	73

Regulatory bodies in both Canada and the United States have placed increasing emphasis on the factor of distance in transportation and have tried to eliminate or modify departures from mileage scales. Adherence to distance commends itself to the public as fair and tends to cut out the wastefulness to society of long circuitous routes when direct lines can carry the traffic more economically.

Class rates, commodity rates, etc., in all parts of Canada have always been compiled with the relationship of cost and distance in mind. Though the National Transportation Act of 1967 repealed the requirement contained in the Railway Act (sec. 332) governing class rates and distance, the change is unlikely to affect the manner in which class rates are compiled and quoted. Essentially, the legislative change put class rates in the same legal position as commodity rates as far as distance is concerned. In 1928 the Board required that the broad groups of mileages taking the same rate on lumber from British Columbia and northern Alberta be split into smaller groupings in order to give greater recognition to distance.⁴ It also put into effect a logical scale of mileage rates on sugar beets.⁵ It has set up four territories in Newfoundland for the purposes of determining class rates between the island and the mainland. The rates graded upward from Port aux Basques to St. John's and branches on the Avalon Peninsula. Although the Board based its action on the Terms of Union between Canada and Newfoundland, its ruling gave greater recognition to distance. Formerly railway rates to St. John's, where water competition was keen, were often lower than to Port aux Basques and other communities which were a shorter distance by ferry and rail from the mainland.[6]

In 1927 Commissioner Oliver suggested[7] that the Board should adopt a more logical grouping of mileages for transporting grain from Prairie territory to Lakehead. In the existing scale under the Crow's Nest Pass Agreement, the rate from Winnipeg to Fort William and Port Arthur was 14 cents per hundred pounds; rates increased along the main line of the Canadian Pacific by 1 cent for each successive distance of 63, 70, 24, 107, 59, 75, 34, 76, 84, 108, 71, and 52 miles, the distances given being those between the nearest and farthest stations in each group. The groups averaged 9 or 10 stations each but varied from 3 to 14. The Commissioner proposed to double the number of groups and to step up rates by ½ cent for each group. Though the scale on export wheat from the West is not logical, the majority of the Board did not accept the suggestion of Commissioner Oliver.

A mileage scale cannot be condemned because of lack of symmetry.[8] Anamorphosis may be due to one of a number of factors. Class scales were first published for Eastern Canada in 1884. The principles on which they were based cannot now be ascertained but whatever its original justification, the initial lack of symmetry has persisted. Sometimes in constructing commodity mileage scales two or more key points are selected. The rate between these points is set on the basis of the estimated cost of operation, in comparison with similar hauls elsewhere, or more probably in order to meet market competition. Then rates from other points are adjusted or "fitted in" to the key rate. Since the other rates are not likely to "fit in" with the key rate in strict proportion to mileages, the final scale will not be symmetrical. Finally, although in a broad sense the blanketing of rates recognizes tapering, a comparison of rates per ton-mile for two nearby points in adjacent blankets will give asymmetrical results. Even on a formal distance scale the results may not be symmetrical. This was particularly true before equalization.

Adherence to Strict Mileage

Provided conditions of transportation are similar, rates on any given commodity are normally the same for equal distances along the same line of railway. At one time rates per ton on stone for four different hauls in Western Ontario were for 115 miles 90 cents, for 54 miles 85 cents, for 159 miles $1.30, and for 98 miles (the haul in question) $1.20.

Though the different producers put out goods of slightly different quality and faced competition of varying intensity, operating conditions were practically identical for all these hauls. The Board held that the rate of 90 cents established by the railway for a haul of 115 miles should be the maximum for the haul of 98 miles about which complaint was made.[9]

In many instances the Board permits railways to stick rigidly to the straight mileage rule although on the face of it some discrimination results. St. Paul and Heinsburg, Alta., are located near the easterly end of a Canadian National Railways branch line north of the North Saskatchewan River. Heinsburg is separated from Frenchman, Sask., at the westerly end of another branch of the same railway company, by a gap of some 40 miles. On account of this gap, grain consigned to Fort William from Heinsburg, St. Paul, and nearby stations has to be hauled about 330 miles farther than would be necessary if the Canadian National were to build across the gap.

South of the North Saskatchewan River the Canadian Pacific has a line along which grain can be hauled to Lakehead without the necessity for back-haul. Accordingly rates on the Canadian Pacific are two or three cents per bushel less than those from stations on the Canadian National, a few miles to the north on the opposite side of the river. Highways are poor and it is especially difficult to cross the North Saskatchewan which has steep banks. Farmers cannot save the difference in freight rates by trucking grain from north of the river to Canadian Pacific stations south of the Saskatchewan. Grain growers in the territory near the Canadian National line from Heinsburg through St. Paul are virtually forced to pay higher freight rates on export grain than are their neighbours to the south.

The Board lacked jurisdiction to require the construction of any railway line. The Canadian National already had the legal authority to bridge the gap and was free to decide when to exercise its right. The Board was without power to compel a railway to accept a rate based on other than the actual mileage over which traffic moved. It said that any departure from the straight mileage rates would create complications and discrepancies and would undoubtedly give rise to still other complaints of discrimination.[10] In other words, the Board ruled that rates from adjacent points need not be equalized when freight moved by different actual mileages.

The Board also refused to require railways to publish a rate via a route over which it was impossible for traffic to move. Two railway lines intersected at Lucan Crossing, 18 miles north of London, Ont., but at different levels and there was no physical connection between them.[11]

Departures from Distance Rates

Despite adoption of mileage scales for numerous commodities and for classified traffic and notwithstanding rulings in individual cases, mileage is not a rigid yardstick. In the Board's words, "to those who have not had experience in rate-making the argument that distance must be the principal factor appeals with force; but the history . . . shows that, while it is, of course, to be considered, yet in many instances it is a minor matter; and I am not aware that either in England or in the United States it has been held by the rate-controlling factor."[12] The objection to mere mileage comparisons is stronger when two different commodities are involved and transportation conditions such as cost of carriage, value, and volume of traffic are different.[13] Special problems are connected with traffic moving in the reverse direction, export and import traffic, the long- and short-haul clause, market and carrier competition, multiple line-hauls, and branch versus main-line rates. Each one of these factors goes to explain why mileage is not a rigid yardstick.

Traffic in the Reverse Direction

Rates in one direction are commonly but not necessarily the same as rates on the same commodity being hauled in the reverse direction.[14] When the rates on paper from New Westminster, B.C., to Merritton, Ont., were higher than on paper from the latter to the former city, the Board pointed out that "there has never been any recognized parity of transcontinental rates under which the rate eastbound has been exactly the same as that established westbound on the same commodity, or vice versa. The individual transcontinental commodity rates are governed by numerous and varied competitive conditions."[15]

Frequently the movement of freight is heavier in one direction than in the other along the same line of railway. Many cars have to be hauled back empty to the point of origin of the predominating traffic. If these return cars were filled, the out-of-pocket expense of handling them would be very little more than when empty. Consequently the railways can afford to grant very low rates to stimulate movement of freight in the lightly loaded direction. As reverse traffic develops, unit costs may decline because overhead costs are spread over more units. Thus traffic as a whole will benefit from what in other types of public utilities is called improving the load factor. "Theoretically, there is a good reason for granting, if necessary, very low rates in general to encourage back loading for otherwise empty cars; and, in fact, this was done in earlier days to a considerable extent."[16]

Sometimes traffic in the lightly loaded direction, stimulated by low rates, grows so much that the direction of the heavy movement comes to be opposite to what it was originally. If the theory of the back-haul were logically applied, the relationship between rates in the two directions should be completely reversed. Although businesses may thrive if their traffic is favoured by low rates, whenever railways try to raise rates to what might be considered a normal level, shippers object vigorously. The Board has taken the position that "it is proper to take into consideration the period a toll has been established, the investment of capital, if any, made in the belief that such rate would continue, and the further commitments made. But there is no property in a rate. The mere continuance of the rate is only one factor. It is the general reasonableness which must be considered."[17] In view of this ruling and the natural rigidity or "stickiness" of tolls, railways have to be careful not to give low rates on the back-haul if they are not prepared to continue them almost indefinitely.

Export and Import Rates

Because conditions of traffic are different, rates published on freight for export are often lower than rates on the same goods hauled over the same railway within Canada for domestic consumption. Apparently it costs the carrier no less to haul a carload of grain from Calgary to Vancouver for spotting beside a terminal elevator for export, than it costs to haul the same freight from Calgary for spotting alongside a flour mill in Vancouver for milling and sale in Canada. Yet in a sense two rail terminal charges are involved in the second movement and only one in the first. Spotting beside a terminal elevator for subsequent export is a movement at an intermediate railway terminal. It is of the same character as the terminal expense incurred at Calgary on a car of domestic grain from, let us say, Bassano, Alta., to Kamloops, B.C. The single difference is that in the Calgary–Vancouver trip the balance of the through-haul takes place by water carrier to a point outside Canada. The Calgary–Vancouver export rate is but a proportional of the total transportation charge from Calgary via Vancouver to an overseas port. The domestic rate is a charge for a complete service from shipper to consignee.

The contention that an export rate is a proportion of a through rate may easily be exaggerated. The difference in terminal expenses on the two kinds of traffic can scarcely amount to much.[18] Yet the rate on export grain from Calgary to Vancouver in 1950 was 20 cents per hundred pounds and on grain for domestic consumption 40½ cents. Under the legislation of 1967, the Canadian Transport Commission is to study this differential and report to the Cabinet. Although export rates which are tied to rates in the United States are occasionally higher, mile for mile, than domestic rates within Canada,[19] as a rule export rates are much lower than local ones. Lower export tolls are published in order to stimulate the sale of Canadian staple commodities overseas and can be justified under the principle of value of service.[20] The export rate is the amount which is not in excess of that which the railway believes the Canadian producer selling in the export market can afford to pay and still market his goods in competition with suppliers in other countries. It is designed, as far as railway rates can be, to bring prosperity to the export trades and business to railways.

Low rates on imports are less general than those on exports. They are intended to draw freight through ports served only by Canadian railways so that Canadian roads may get revenue from the long haul from seaport to point of consumption. If such rates were not published, imports would move through ports in the United States in even greater quantity than they do at present. In consequence Canadian railways would get as a rule only that portion of the total haul and of the total rate which the distance by railway from the international border to the point of consumption or distribution within Canada bears to the total rail haul. Needless to say, import rates should not be so low as positively to discourage domestic production nor may they legally be used to offset the effects of a tariff change.[21]

The board has justified low export and import rates mainly on the ground of competition.[22] In recent years competition between ports has become keener because of highway competition. This has put Saint John and Halifax at a disadvantage relative to New York which is closer to the thickly settled areas in the St. Lawrence Lowlands. It has been within the option of the railways to decide whether they will lower their rates to Canada's coastal ports to meet highway competition to another port. But in dealing with complaints over tolls, the National Transportation Commission must consider whether tolls "create . . . (*ii*) an undue obstacle . . . to the movement of commodities through Canadian ports" (sec. 16 (3)).

Blanketing

Group or "blanket" rates represent another departure from strict mileage. Instead of quoting a rate from a given point of origin to each one of possibly ten stations in close proximity to each other, railways group these places and charge the same toll to all. This simplifies the clerical problem of publishing a large number of rates, quoting them to shippers, and auditing freight bills. The difference in the distance of various stations within 25 miles of Toronto in comparison with the total distance of any of these points from Vancouver is so small that it may be overlooked from the point of view of cost of service. For this reason blanket rates are usually confined to long-distance hauls. Group rates frequently start complaints of unjust discrimination, a topic to be considered later.

Long- and Short-Haul Clause

The long- and short-haul clause is another illustration of departure from the principle of distance. According to the Railway Act, except by permission of the Board, railways might not charge a greater toll for the like description of goods over the same line or route for a shorter than for a longer distance within which the shorter distance was included. This meant that the rate for the longer distance might be the same as, but not less than, the rate for the shorter haul, one haul being included in the other. More specifically, except with the board's permission, carriers might not charge less on traffic from A to C through B than they charged from A to B. The Board gave its permission only when competition was present at the more distant and not at the intermediate station.

The legislation of 1967 repealed the long- and short-haul clause that was contained in the Railway Act but provided that the National Transport Commission might set aside any toll that created "an unfair disadvantage beyond any disadvantage that may be deemed to be inherent in the location . . . of the traffic" (sec. 16 (3) (*a*) (*i*)). Obviously the Commission may perpetuate what amount to exceptions to the long- and short-haul rule by deciding that the higher tolls quoted to intermediate points are not an *unfair* disadvantage because of the lack of rail-water competition at the intermediate point and its existence at the distant point. It will also have to rule on whether or not the relatively higher rates on traffic to intermediate points constitute "an *undue* obstacle to the interchange of commodities between points in Canada or an *unreasonable* discouragement to the development of primary or secondary industries" (sec. 16 (3) (*a*) (*ii*), italics added).

In Canada the competitive rate published to the more distant point is often "carried back" to the place where it meets the rate which is set on a normal basis. Thus the rate published as a result of competition at the more distant point in many instances fixes the maximum for any intermediate point. For example, the rate on apples from the Okanagan Valley of British Columbia was competitive at Winnipeg with the rate on American apples from the state of Washington hauled to Winnipeg by American-owned railways. The Winnipeg rate is carried back 472 miles to Morse, Sask., where it equalled the rate built up on the normal mileage basis.[23] The rate from Montreal to Saint John, N.B., across Maine is the maximum which may be charged on the longer Canadian National lines between these points. For all practical purposes on traffic from Montreal all stations on the Canadian National in New Brunswick have the same rate as Saint John.

Rates on rice, canned fruits, vegetables, and salmon from Vancouver to Winnipeg are similarly controlled by rates published by competing American lines from Seattle to Winnipeg. The rates compelled by the competitive situation at Winnipeg are extended as maxima to intermediate points. Of course the competition present at Winnipeg is absent in the intermediate territory where American railways do not penetrate. None the less Regina and Saskatoon receive the same through or inbound rates on these articles as Winnipeg. Because distributing class rates are on the same scale throughout the West, each of these three cities is able to distribute the same distance east and west therefrom. Within its own tributary area all of the cities are on a complete equality as far as rates are concerned.[24]

Regina complained of the unfairness of this freight being carried by railways from British Columbia through Regina and 357 miles beyond to Winnipeg at exactly the same toll. Because the two cities were being charged the same rate, Regina protested that railways were denying it the benefit of being geographically nearer Vancouver than Winnipeg was. Rates on the same commodities from Eastern Canada to Winnipeg were lower than to Regina because of the shorter haul. Regina argued that it should have lower rates from Vancouver vis-à-vis Winnipeg just as Winnipeg had lower rates than Regina on westbound shipments of the same goods.

The Board ruled that Regina had no legitimate complaint. Its rates on these goods eastbound from British Columbia were lower than those built up on a normal basis. Though Canadian and American railways did not compete at Regina, it was being given the same tolls as railways were compelled to publish to a more distant point (Winnipeg) in consequence of competition there. The Board said, in effect, that on traffic from the East, Regina's rates could be reduced to the Winnipeg level only when it could show that, with respect to westbound traffic from Toronto and Montreal, similar competitive conditions existed at Regina as were already effective at Winnipeg on traffic eastbound from British Columbia.[25]

Where there is no competition at the distant point, the Board has ordered the railway concerned to cease its violation of the long- and short-haul clause or else the carrier has voluntarily corrected the situation. This principle was applied in cases involving Carleton Place near Ottawa,[26] Qualicum Beach on Vancouver Island,[27] and Mille Roches which is 64 miles west of Montreal.[28]

Notwithstanding the "carry back" and the rulings of the Board, departures from the long- and short-haul clause are common. On transcontinental traffic, along the Great Lakes, and in the Maritimes, there are literally hundreds of cases where the toll to the more distant, competitive point is lower than the toll to intermediate points. These departures often give rise to complaints of unjust discrimination and will be considered in the following chapter. Shippers and consignees who feel they have been treated unfairly by railways, often try to move their freight by truck.

Multiple Line-Hauls

Multiple line-hauls represent another modification of the straight distance principle. Both the Board and the Interstate Commerce Commission have ruled that a joint rate over two or more roads[29] may justifiably be higher than the rate for moving the same product an equal distance along the lines of one railway company. This is proper because, in addition to the usual outlays, the rate must cover the expense of shunting the car from one system to another, the clerical cost of apportioning and collecting the share of the total freight bill that goes to each railway, and the elaborate accounting arrangements which must be undertaken for the per diem and repair charges on "foreign" cars.[30] Further, a railway prefers to keep traffic on its own lines. It is particularly justified in charging a little more for inter-line movements when it originates freight which it could transport to destination over its own tracks.[31] On the other hand, in order to secure revenue a carrier may decide to quote the same rate for a two-line haul in which it participates as for the single-line haul of its competitor.[32] Sometimes traffic has to move over the lines of two or more railways because no one system serves both termini. In these cases the Board has held it to be the right of the railway which initiates the movement to carry the freight as far as possible on its own line before handing it over to the connecting road.[33] In the United States the same rule applies: a railway cannot be compelled to short-haul itself unless the public interest would otherwise suffer.

Originally every joint rate was the sum of the local rate to the junction or transfer point plus the local rate from that point along another railway line to the destination. Under the Railway Act of 1903, railways had the option of publishing joint rates. Frequently the joint rates they published were less than the sum of the locals, apparently because, while a joint rate should be more than that for equal mileage on a single line owing to factors just mentioned, it should not include four complete terminal charges, i.e., at originating and junction points of one railway and at junction and destination points on the other. Where the sum of the locals was less than the published through rate, railways usually refunded the difference to the shipper.[34] The Board ruled that charging a joint toll in excess of the sum of the locals was *prima facie* unreasonable and unjustly discriminatory.[35]

In 1919 the Railway Act was amended to make the publication of joint tariffs on all freight moving over a continuous route in Canada mandatory instead of optional as before.[36] The new legislation did not state whether the joint rates were to be higher, equal to, or less than the sum of the locals. By 1922 railways were making deductions in the mileage rates to and from connecting lines when no through rates were in effect on agricultural limestone, cordwood, fertilizer, grain and grain products, lumber, and sugar beets. They were making no deductions on a number of other commodities including scrap iron, iron ore, scrap paper, coal, clay, stone, sand, brick, livestock, and potatoes. Then railways agreed to reductions on the entire list of commodities named.[37] Where the rate to or from the junction point was over 7½ cents per hundred pounds, each railway on joint line traffic had to reduce or shrink its toll by 1 cent per hundred pounds. Where the rate was 7½ cents and in excess of 4 cents, the shrinking was ½ cent. Where the rate was 4 cents or less, no shrinking was made. On freight not specifically referred to in the Order, railways have been free to set joint rates at whatever level they wished (provided they did not exceed the sum of the locals) or to refuse joint rates if they preferred.

Railways state they publish joint tolls wherever the volume of traffic justifies it. The Royal Commission of 1951 recommended that "where the rates in the joint tariff exceed the rates in a single-line tariff for the same or similar distances in the same locality the burden of proof shall lie upon the companies to show to the satisfaction of the Board that there are greater costs involved in the joint movement, and only in such case may the rates in the joint tariff be permitted to exceed the rates in the single-line tariff."[38] It also heard shippers complain of inadequate facilities at interchange points in Western Canada. At several places the lines of two railway systems intersected but no facilities had been built for interchanging loaded cars or transferring less the car-load freight. In consequence freight had often to be hauled over a roundabout route before it reached its destination, thus slowing down delivery and raising rates above what they would have been if interchange had been practicable. Railways declared they built facilities whenever the volume of traffic was large enough to warrant the expense. The Royal Commission left the matter up to the Board which in 1952 ordered interchange tracks built where required by public convenience and necessity.[39]

Main and Branch Line Rates

In numerous cases the Board of Railway (or Transport) Commissioners has dealt with the relative rates on branch and main lines.[40] All but one of these cases arose before 1927. Since then rates have generally been equal, mile for mile, within the same broad region and since equalization was ordered in 1951 they must be uniform across Canada west of Lévis and Megantic. Hence, the problem can now be regarded as being only of historical interest.[41] Even though equalization may technically be abolished, shippers will demand the same rates per mile on all lines subject, of course, to the exigencies of competition between railways and other kinds of carriers.[42]

The Bridge Subsidy

This subsidy applied for nearly twenty years and came about as a result of a recommendation of the Royal Commission of 1951. While it lasted it was clearly a modification of the normal tolls as related to distance. The Dominion paid the two major railways a total of $7 million for the maintenance of their tracks north of Lake Superior and in return they reduced their tolls on non-competitive traffic carried over this "bridge" by the same amount. The Royal Commission of 1951 expected that the public, especially in Western Canada, would benefit from lower tolls and the regions east and west of the Great Lakes would be drawn closer together.[43]

The Board of Transport Commissioners found difficulty in applying the subsidy toward the reduction of rates. The question was whether they were to be a certain percentage of the existing tolls or whether they were to be so many cents per hundred pounds regardless of length of haul. Under the first alternative, all places would benefit proportionately to length of haul and so Winnipeg, which under equalization was due to lose its constructive mileage to and from Lakehead, would gain relatively little in terms of cents per hundred pounds. But if the reductions were a flat amount, i.e., the same number of cents regardless of distance, Winnipeg would gain relatively more percentagewise than, say, Regina or Calgary. In the end the Board ordered reductions which were a combination of the percentage and flat methods. The reductions were not to apply to grain which already benefited from the low statutory rates as far east as Lakehead and Armstrong, to traffic hauled under international, overhead, export, import, local, and competitive tariffs including agreed charges.[44]

The Royal Commission of 1961 brought forth quite an array of objections to the bridge subsidy.[45] During the previous ten years the amount of competitive traffic had increased relative to the volume of noncompetitive freight hauled over the bridge. Since the subsidy did not apply to competitive freight, it covered a decreasing quantity of freight and favoured a declining number of shippers. A further difficulty was that the Board had no way of making sure that the reductions in rates by each railway were proportionate to the amount of subsidy received. One railway might carry more freight than the other and yet the subsidy (being legally based on maintaining the track of the Canadian Pacific and one of the Canadian National's lines across Northern Ontario) was substantially the same on each railway. Besides, the subsidy tended to place inland shipping at a disadvantage. Also, though trucking between Eastern and Western Canada had advanced rapidly despite the subsidy to the railways, the Royal Commission felt that there could be little question that the subsidy had inhibited the growth of trucking. Then, somewhat inconsistently, the Commission stated that competition between trucks and railways had been more effective in reducing rates in this area than the bridge subsidy had been. It said that if aid were desirable to facilitate the movement of freight over the bridge, it should apply to all commodities and all modes of transport. In addition, the bridge subsidy put British Columbia shippers at a disadvantage in selling in the West inasmuch as the cost of bringing some goods from Eastern Canada had come down while tolls from Vancouver had remained at their old level. Finally, whatever the situation may have been in 1951, ten years later the area north of Lake Superior was no longer a sort of economic desert. Its population had grown and the value of its output of minerals, lumber, and manufactured goods, mainly newsprint, had expanded rapidly. For all these reasons, the Commission of 1961 recommended abolition of this anomalous interference with the distance principle.

The National Transportation Act (sec. 74) provided for the elimination of the bridge subsidy by early 1971. Within one year after the coming into force of the Act, the Canadian Transport Commission is to authorize such increases in rates over the bridge as will yield the Canadian National and the Canadian Pacific a combined additional total revenue of $3 million annually. Within two years rates across the bridge are to be increased to yield a further $2 million, and within three years another $2 million, thus making $7 million in all. The bridge subsidy will be reduced in proportion to the increase in tolls and will expire four years after the Act comes into force.

9

Unjust Discrimination

DISCRIMINATION arose because railways, anxious to increase their net revenues, found they could make more money by cutting rates at certain points and on certain types of traffic where competition was strong and maintaining or even increasing them on non-competitive freight than they could by charging the same prices to all shippers for equivalent hauls. The practice, soon carried to excess, gave rise to charges of prejudice, unfair advantage, and discrimination. For this reason, among others, the public control of rates was instituted. One of the earliest principles included in regulatory legislation was the prohibition of unjust discrimination.

For roughly thirty years after its establishment the Board of Railway (later Transport) Commissioners dealt with a large number of cases of unjust discrimination. Since about 1935 it has considered relatively few. This is because railways have come to know their precise legal rights and are careful not to infringe the law. Shippers and their counsel can readily find out their exact legal position and avoid the expense of going before the Board if their case is weak. If it is unimpeachable, railways make the necessary adjustment in rates of their own free will. Most of all, the opportunity of using highway transport often allows the shipper to escape from what he regards as discrimination. In view of the reduced importance of unjust discrimination, this chapter is an abbreviation of what appeared in *Economics of Canadian Transportation*.

The Royal Commission of 1961 was in favour of abolishing all the existing prohibitions of unjust discrimination. In its words: "the assumption that railways have power to establish rates which are 'just and reasonable' by the criteria of the monopolistic period is erroneous. These terms lose all meaning as the criteria are eroded away by competition.

To persist in a policy which enforces standards of behaviour on one mode but not on its competitors is to assume an Olympian position, with powers to determine the economic fate of industries and regions. This is no longer realistic. Where remnants of such powers still persist, we indicate the attitudes National Transportation Policy must adopt,"[1] i.e., control of maximum and minimum rates.

The author doubts if these controls would, in fact, prevent unjust discrimination. Railways might charge two captive shippers different rates and then defend the discrepancy on several grounds. They might assert that conditions of transport were not identical. This argument would put a shipper who was not familiar with the details of railway operation at a disadvantage. Railways could easily argue, and the Board has held in numerous cases, that railways are free to meet or ignore competition as they see fit. The main reason for this ruling is that it is the carrier, not the Board, who takes the risk of profit or loss. More especially, railways could contend that since the traffic in question was subject to market competition, complaining shippers were not truly captive.

The Government decided not to accept the suggestion of the MacPherson Commission that the concept of "just and reasonable" as applied to railway rates should be abolished. Though it repealed the sections of the Railway Act forbidding undue, unjust, or unreasonable rates,[2] it enacted what appear to be the same provisions in simplified form. Under section 16 of the National Transportation Act, any person may appeal to the Commission if he has reason to believe that any act or omission of a carrier or the effect of any rate established by a carrier may prejudicially affect the public interest in respect of tolls for or conditions of the carriage of traffic within, into or from Canada. If the Commission is satisfied that the applicant has made out a *prima facie* case, it will make such investigation as it thinks warranted.

(3) In conducting an investigation under this section, the Commission shall have regard to all considerations that appear to it to be relevant, including, without limiting the generality of the foregoing, (a) whether the tolls or conditions specified for the carriage of traffic under the rate so established are such as to create (i) an unfair disadvantage beyond any disadvantage that may be deemed to be inherent in the location and volume of the traffic, the scale of operation connected therewith or the type of traffic or service involved, or (ii) an undue obstacle to the interchange of commodities between points in Canada or an unreasonable discouragement to the development of primary or secondary industries or to export trade in or from any region of Canada or to the movement of commodities through Canadian ports; or (b) whether control by, or the interests of a carrier in, another form of transportation service . . . may be involved.

(4) If the Commission, after a hearing, finds that the act, omission or

rate in respect of which the appeal is made is prejudicial to the public interest, the Commission may, notwithstanding the . . . [provisions of the act respecting captive traffic] but having regard to . . . [the legal requirement that all rates be compensatory] make an order requiring the carrier to remove the prejudicial feature in the relevant tolls or conditions specified for the carriage of traffic or such other order as in the circumstances it may consider proper, or it may report thereon to the Governor in Council for any action that is considered appropriate.

Part of the second preceding paragraph, namely sec. 16 (3) (*i*) and (*ii*), is also included among the objectives of the National Transportation Policy, sec. 1 (*d*) (*i*) and (*ii*). Furthermore, the new legislation contains provisions designed to protect shippers of small lots who might not think it worthwhile to go through the complicated and lengthy procedures open to a captive shipper who wants to protect his interests. These procedures were outlined toward the end of the chapter on Rates on Particular Commodities and the relevant section respecting small shipments reads as follows:

317. Notwithstanding section 336 [respecting captive shippers], where in the opinion of the Commission there is, in respect of the carriage of goods in less than carload quantities under five thousand pounds to or from any point in Canada, no alternative, effective and competitive service by a common carrier other than a rail carrier or carriers or a combination of rail carriers, the Commission may investigate the tariff of tolls applying to the carriage in those quantities to or from such point in Canada and if the Commission finds that the tariff of tolls of a railway company, or any portions of the tariff, are such as to take undue advantage of a monopoly situation favouring rail carriers in respect of such goods or class of goods, the Commission may disallow such tariff of tolls or any portion thereof and may require the railway company to substitute within a specified period of time a tariff of tolls satisfactory to the Commission or it may prescribe other tolls in lieu of any tolls so disallowed.

It may take several years before the full implication of these new provisions will be known. The Canadian Transport Commission, the Supreme Court, and to some extent the Cabinet will have to interpret the law and apply it to the particular situations that will arise. During the litigation, lawyers will unquestionably argue from old decisions based on the law as it stood prior to 1967. Even when the wording is different, lawyers will contend that the authorities should take what is known as "judicial notice" of old cases. Moreover, it is possible that the highest authorities in the land will rule that expressions such as unfair disadvantage, undue obstacle, prejudicial to the public interest, and undue advantage of a monopoly situation, which are contained in the National Transportation Act have the same broad meaning as the words undue, unjust, and unreasonable preference or discrimination formerly included in the Railway Act. Should this prove to be true, the changes made in 1967 will be changes in wording rather than in essential meaning. However that may be, it is pretty certain that the same sort of problems will arise in the future as in the past. Therefore, a summary of past decisions seems to be required.

As already explained, railway rates are based on the principle of differentiation or economic discrimination. At the same time the law forbids unjust discrimination. A fundamental question is at what point a rate ceases to be economically justified and becomes legally unjust. Naturally the opinions of shippers and carriers differ widely on this matter. Therefore the Board was often called upon to adjudicate disputes. Professor Jackman set forth the situation clearly.

After a careful study of the problems which come before the Board for investigation and formal decision, one is impressed with the vast amount of consideration which that body has to give to the subject of unjust discrimination in rates. It comes to the Board's attention under many guises and is frequently concealed under a great variety of other factors which complicate the issue. It is impossible to classify the various kinds of discrimination into a few classes and have them comprehensive, because there are so many aspects under which it is presented in the range of the Board's and the railway's activities. . . . In reality, the discriminations complained of are as broad and of the same nature as the practical principles of rate making, for the very principles upon which rates are made [that is, a differentiated pricing system] are frequently the bases upon which they are attacked.[3]

General Principles

Despite its prolonged and thoughtful consideration of complaints, the Board has found that "it is practically impossible to formulate any hard and fast principle which would determine when and where discrimination ceases to be harmless and becomes undue. Each particular case must be considered on its own merits with a view of determining whether the discrimination complained of is undue, unfair, or unjust after a review of the different matters open to the Board's consideration under the statutes and authorities noted."[4]

The Board's approach to problems of discrimination is identical with the practice of regular courts in legal actions where the degree or extent of the activity complained of is what distinguishes a lawful from an illegal act. For instance, a certain amount of noise or odour is inevitable in many industrial undertakings. At some point or other the noise or odour becomes a nuisance. Courts must decide where the line between what is reasonable and unreasonable, between a mere noise and a nuisance, is to be drawn. In doing so, they decline, as far as possible, to generalize. Instead, they deal with each particular complaint by itself and formulate their judgments after careful study of all pertinent facts in each special case.

Although it is not possible, by examining the Board's decisions, to lay down rules which can be applied rigidly to future cases, two general principles can nevertheless be set forth with some confidence. First, as the following quotations show, the Board permits discrimination provided it is not unjust or unreasonable.

It is not in the nature of things possible to secure anything like absolute equality of treatment to all persons who use the railways, or even like treatment to all who are using the same railway. The general public have theoretically the right to complain if the people in one or more sections of country served by a particular railway are given a better service than the people of other sections; but with every desire on the part of the railway company to accord equally fair treatment to all patrons over its entire system, circumstances and conditions are too controlling, oftentimes, to be resisted or overcome.[5]

The Railway Act . . . authorizes and justifies discrimination. It is only undue, unfair or unjust discrimination that the law is aimed against.[6]

A difference in rates may be discrimination, but not unjust discrimination of the character forbidden by the Railway Act.[7]

Discrimination may or may not fall within the provisions of the Act.[8]

The Act, as it has always been interpreted by the Board, only forbids discrimination when it is undue or unreasonable.[9]

The second principle is that complaint of unjust discrimination is not sustained by merely quoting differences in rates. The complainant must prove to the Board that his business has actually been injured by the rate situation in question.

It has been said over and over again in the decisions of the Board as well as in the decisions of other regulative tribunals that the criteria of unjust discrimination are not to be found in abstract conditions. Unjust discrimination is not concerned with mere comparisons of mileage. It is concerned with the very tangible and concrete question, is there competition between the article which has the higher rate charge and the article which has the lower rate charge? If two articles of the same or identical nature are subjected to different rate treatment, then the rate is one factor which may render it difficult for the individual with the different rate or practice to do business in a common market; that is, the very material question is—Is there actual competition in the same market between the parties affected?"[10]

In other words, the second principle is that where there is no competition between the companies and the products concerned a mere difference in rates does not constitute an unjust discrimination or undue preference.[11] Unjust discrimination can exist only where the person, commodity, or district which is favoured has profited at the expense of the individual, article, or locality against which it is claimed the discrimination has taken place.[12]

Personal Discrimination

Granting unduly preferential rates to individuals or companies is a particularly obnoxious form of unjust discrimination. It permits a railway to favour certain shippers and ruin others who may be just as efficient and worthy of survival from an economic point of view, and it leaves the way open to nepotism and corruption.

Personal discrimination was sometimes practised before the establishment of the Board of Railway Commissioners.[13] While published rates were apparently being charged to all shippers alike, secret rebates or refunds were sometimes given.[14] The Grand Trunk gave a cartage allowance to a favoured shipper.[15] The Canadian Pacific gave preferential rates to some merchants in Winnipeg,[16] and to Winnipeg distributors as a group.[17] A cordage company in Montreal got lower rates on rope than its competitors,[18] and another concern was exempt from the extra charge for switching which was normally levied.[19] One railway even published rates discriminating against shipments to other purchasers and favouring shipments of the same commodity to itself.[20] All these arrangements were prohibited by the Board.

Personal discrimination was also practised by means of contracts between a carrier and a shipper. They were defended on the ground that such contracts took precedence over the Railway Act. The Board ruled to the contrary[21] though it is bound if the contract has been validated by Dominion legislation thus making it a "Special Act" within the meaning of the *Railway Act*.[22] This principle applied to the Crow's Nest Pass Agreement. The Maritime Freight Rates Act and the Terms of Union with Newfoundland are other instances of statutory discrimination, as explained toward the end of this chapter.

Commodity Discrimination

Commodity discrimination is one of the basic principles in railway rate-making. As already explained, railways charge quite different rates for carrying various commodities even though the differences in the cost of transporting one commodity and another may be comparatively small. In the main, rates are based on value, not on cost, of service. This discrimination is economically sound. It becomes undue or unjust only when different rates are charged on two commodities having the same transportation characteristics such as value, bulk, susceptibility to loss and damage, regularity of movement, and so on. Discrimination is also unreasonable when the rates differ for two shipments of the same article and of the same weight and moving in the same direction over the same distance.

Rates on wheat and coarse grains such as corn, oats, and rye are equal. There are some differences in value per bushel and in cost of carriage per ton-mile because more tons of wheat (60 lbs. to the bushel) can be put in a car of a given size than of oats (34). But in the opinion of both the Board and the Interstate Commerce Commission, the differences are not enough to justify different rates.[23] Some products, e.g., moulding and building sand, fire-clay and common clay, charcoal for lighting fires and for medicinal preparations, malted milk and condensed milk, differ so greatly in value and use that railways classify them as different commodities and charge different rates on them. The Board has ruled, however, that crude oil is logically one commodity for rate-making purposes and that to base rates on the specific gravity of petroleum constitutes undue and unjust discrimination.[24]

Place Discrimination

Charges of unjust discrimination which really relate to persons and commodities frequently come before the Board as complaints of localities. Protests presumably have greater weight if they are backed by a community or board of trade than if they come from an individual or single company. Regina, Winnipeg, and Vancouver, for instance, have complained of discrimination in connection with the distribution of goods by wholesalers from these cities.[25] Gimli and Riverton, Man., protested that their rates on fish to Chicago were unjustly higher than on fish from Winnipegosis to Chicago.[26] In order to substantiate a charge of injustice, a community must prove that it has been positively injured by the rates currently in effect. For example, the Board has ruled that "it is not unjust discrimination to have commutation fares in effect in one locality and not to another with similar mileage and conditions. . . . A person desiring to travel to Laurentia Beach, on Lake Manitoba, is in no way injured by reason of the lower fare published to Grand Beach on Lake Winnipeg."[27]

In two cases involving grain, the Board pointed out that the mileage from adjacent points is not always identical, owing to the circuity of railway lines. This situation was general and, so the Board said, if it were to adjust the rates to suit the residents of one town, it would merely create an anomaly somewhere else. It would then have to readjust still other rates, and ultimately the whole rate structure would be upset. Lack of strict conformity of rates with mileage is inevitable in any grouping arrangement.[28] There has to be a breaking point somewhere and if the board were to make exceptions, it would ultimately disrupt the whole basis of the rates.[29]

Differences in conditions of transport have also been taken into account. On coal to Winnipeg, the Canadian Pacific charged more from Lethbridge than the Canadian Northern charged from Drumheller to the same destination though Lethbridge is nearer Winnipeg via Canadian Pacific than Drumheller was via Canadian Northern. This did not create unjust discrimination, according to the Board, since a railway may decide for itself whether or not it will meet the competition of another carrier. The conclusion would have been different if the Canadian Pacific had been handling coal from Drumheller to Winnipeg at the rate published by the Canadian Northern and charging a higher rate on coal from Lethbridge to Winnipeg. On the latter haul the distance is less and only one company, the Canadian Pacific, was involved.[30]

Conditions of transport also figure in comparing domestic with export and import rates, local with through rates, multiple- with single-line hauls, and so on. The Board has said that an export or import rate is "in no sense a necessary measure of the reasonableness of the domestic rate [nor does it prove] that unjust discrimination exists. Such rates are but proportions of through tolls governing on the traffic from point of origin to final destination. Further, import, as well as export traffic is subject to port competition and from Canadian ports it is necessary for Canadian carriers, in order to participate in the movement of the traffic and to attract it through Canadian ports, to establish rates to meet the competition through United States ports.[31]

A local rate may not properly be compared with a proportional of a through rate because conditions of transport are different.[32] A railway may legally charge more for a multiple-line haul than for a single-line haul of the same length because, as explained earlier, the cost of transporting the goods over the two routes differs.[33] Similarly the Board has declared that comparisons of branch- and main-line rates are not valid. Moreover, it will not permit use of "paper" rates to sustain complaints of unjust discrimination.[34] A paper rate is one which is published in a tariff even though no traffic moves under it. The paper rate may be higher than the traffic will bear, may have become unnecessary because of shifts in markets and sources of supply, or may have been included in the tariff merely for the sake of completeness. Finally, the Board has repeatedly held that differences in rates between the United States and Canada do not constitute an unjust discrimination of the kind forbidden by the Railway Act.[35] In a word, not every difference in rates is proof of unjust discrimination.

Though rejecting many complaints, the Board has recognized (a) that unjust discrimination does result from differences in rates where conditions of transport are similar and (b) that unjust discrimination should be corrected if it is possible to do so without, in the long run, giving rise to additional charges of unjust discrimination. An example of a complaint that was sustained involved Midland and Penetanguishene, two ports on Georgian Bay which are almost the same distance from Buffalo and Cleveland. A rate of 19.4 cents per hundred pounds from Midland to Cleveland was ruled unjust discrimination in comparison with a rate of 16.3 cents from Penetanguishene to the same destination.[36] In another case where the board felt that some new rates unjustly discriminated against dealers taking delivery of coal at points contiguous to Toronto, it reduced the differential of the smaller centres above Toronto by varying amounts.[37]

Blanketing

A large number of cases involving discrimination and distance have resulted from the blanketing or grouping of stations for rate-making purposes. The distance between two stations adjacent to each other but in different groups may be only five or ten miles, a negligible factor in the total length of haul, but the difference in rates will be anywhere from one to five cents.[38] The point in the higher rate group nearest to the origin of the traffic feels that it is being unjustly discriminated against because the railway is charging it a cent or more for an additional haul of only a few miles beyond a neighbouring town in the next lower blanket. Again, a town at the edge of one rate group will complain of being charged the same rate as a town in the same rate group which is farther away from the point of origin. It will allege that it is not being given the advantage of its geographic position. It will ask to be placed in the adjoining group which has lower freight charges or request that the existing groups be split up into smaller parts.

The general attitude of the Board is that a certain amount of departure from the cost of service principle and a small amount of injustice is inevitable where a system of blanketing is used: "Group rates of necessity result in a certain amount of discrimination; so long as the discrimination is not undue, such rates are not unlawful."[39] Where the distance between adjoining stations is short and the additional cost of hauling the traffic to the next farther station is negligible and when the natural boundary of the group would seem to lie just beyond the station of the complainants, the Board may order the blanket extended to adjacent points.[40] Even so, it refused an extension where the discrimination complained of was not unjust, and where the addition of one point would involve an entire regrouping of the territory in question. In that event, the revenue of the carriers would be appreciably reduced: "Groups long maintained are presumably fair, and should not be disturbed unless substantial justice requires it. The present group arrangement has not been the subject of complaint from other points or territory in the province."[41] In another case the Board said that anomalies are inevitable in any grouping arrangement which had to be a compromise between distance and public convenience.[42]

In order to minimize the seriousness of complaints which almost invariably arise in connection with blanket rates, carriers commonly assign to the same group all stations with a certain community of interest, for example, all those in the same metropolitan area. They try to make the break between the groups coincide with some natural barrier such as a river or stretch of unproductive territory, or with the division between groups of shippers selling predominantly in one market and those selling mainly in another. As a rule coal mines are bunched into more or less well defined groups separated by exceptional distances or by physical barriers.[43]

Long- and Short-Haul Discrimination

Complaints of unjust discrimination are a natural consequence of violation of the long- and short-haul clause. The National Transportation Act of 1967 wiped out the long- and short-haul clause but directed the Commission, in any complaint about rates or conditions of transport, to consider "an unfair disadvantage beyond any disadvantage that may be deemed to be inherent in the location of the traffic" (sec. 16 (3) (i)). For all practical purposes such disadvantage means lack of competition between rail and water carriers at the intermediate point and its existence at the distant point. Railways cut rates between stations and the more distant point where they compete with water carriers and they maintain at their former level rates between stations and intermediate points where they have no competition. Railway traffic managers try to get all the business they can at normal rates. If they see they are losing freight to competitors, they will cut their rates so long as the reduced tolls cover their out-of-pocket expenses and make some contribution, however small, to overhead.[44] If they did not bid for this traffic, the common expenses of operating the road would go on substantially undiminished. The traffic to the intermediate points would have to bear a larger amount of overhead, owing, first, to the loss of the contribution from the traffic carried at competitive rates to the more distant point and, second, to the fact that there are now fewer units of traffic to bear the overhead. Thus the freight rates to intermediate stations would have to be higher than at present. Low rates at competitive centres keep rates at non-competitive points lower than they would be without this bidding for traffic. From this point of view the intermediate points actually gain from the low rates offered to get business at competitive centres.

What is more, even if a railway were to abolish its competitive rates, manufacturers, distributors, and consumers who are located at the city where competition exists would still retain their geographic advantage over non-competitive points. They would bring in their freight at rates which are the same, or practically the same,[45] as the competitive tolls of the railway. This point was made by the Board in a case involving a jobber in Calgary who wanted the same toll as the railways were publishing on competitive traffic to Vancouver. The Board said that "if the railway companies cancelled the competitive rate to Vancouver it would remove the . . . case [of the applicant] as it was presented on this record, but it is not shown that such action by the railway companies would be of any real benefit to the applicant, as eliminating his alleged rate discrimination, because so long as there is effective water competition from Montreal to Vancouver via the Panama Canal, the Vancouver jobber would have the rate advantage regardless of the action of the railway companies."[46]

In other words, if rates increased directly with distance and no exceptions to the long- and short-haul clause were permitted, the disabilities complained of by intermediate points would remain, while railways would be deprived of some contribution to overhead which they would otherwise have received. Without this contribution the rates to intermediate points would have to be increased. There is the same justification, in theory, for violating and long- and short-haul clause as for basing rates on what the traffic will bear.

The validity of the above argument rests on a number of assumptions. It presupposes that competitive rates do, in fact, cover the out-of-pocket expenses. Typically it assumes that the competitive business can be handled with rolling stock which would otherwise be idle and therefore that the out-of-pocket cost will be small. Actually the competitive traffic may soon become so large that additional freight cars and locomotives will have to be purchased. In that event the out-of-pocket expense is increased by the full interest and depreciation charges on the new equipment. Again, a railway may be overly anxious to build up its volume of business. Because it is difficult to determine the actual out-of-pocket expenses with any accuracy even under the best of conditions, traffic managers may offer rates which do not, in fact, cover the out-of-pocket. If this should occur, the intermediate points would be burdened instead of being benefited by the application of the value of service concept to competitive traffic. The railway would have to make up out of general revenues the difference between its revenues from the competitive traffic and the out-of-pocket expenses of this traffic.

The argument also tacitly assumes that reduced rates at competitive points will get business for the railway while equal reductions at non-competitive points will not have a similar buoyant effect on railway revenues. More specifically, it is assumed that reduced rates from Montreal to Vancouver will mean more in net railway revenues in the long run than similar reductions to Calgary or Edmonton. It is open to argument whether the industrial development of Alberta was retarded by freight rates which were high relative to those to Vancouver. Low freight rates might have helped Calgary and Edmonton just as they assisted Vancouver. But there would be one important difference: the railways must share with steamship lines the traffic to and from the industries which low rates foster at the Coast; they would have the increased business in Alberta all to themselves. The spectacular growth in the industry, trade, and population of Calgary and Edmonton since 1945 was the result of the discovery of new resources of petroleum and natural gas, and not of adjustments in freight rates. In technical language, the economic argument in favour of violating the clause assumes a high elasticity of demand at competitive points, and a relatively or even a completely inelastic demand curve at the non-competitive ones. But volume of freight taken by itself will not justify lower charges at the more distant than at an intermediate point.[47]

Violation of the long- and short-haul clause can be justified only on the further assumption that rates to the more distant competitive point are never under any circumstances lower than is absolutely necessary to get the business. Normal charges, those which fully recognize the direct relationship of cost to distance, should be charged whenever a railway finds it possible to do so and still meet the competition. Ordinarily carriers can be relied upon to realize their own financial interests and to raise rates at the competitive city to their normal level whenever they can. Thus during the World War II, water competition between Eastern Canada and the Pacific coast declined in intensity and the railways quickly raised some of their rates. Though Vancouver businessmen complained of the increase, their case was economically weak.

Owing to circumstances beyond the control of railways, Vancouver temporarily lost some of the unusual advantages of its position as a seaport.

A final assumption of the argument for violation is that competition arises from water carriers or other transportation agency and not from two or more rail lines. If two railways competing with each other cut rates, one would rob the other of business or, if both cut equally, each would handle the same share of the business as before but at lower tolls. The nation's railway system is less well off financially than it formerly was. Of course, it may be that regardless of the inter-railway competition, reduced tolls would so enlarge the traffic of the rail carriers that the rates would be justified on economic grounds. In that event there would seem to be no sound reason for not reducing the rates at all points along both lines instead of confining the reductions to the distant centre where there is inter-railway competition or at least where inter-rail competition takes the form of cutting rates rather than giving better service at existing rates. As a rule, competition between railway lines should not be used as a reason for violating the long- and short-haul clause[48] except where one route is circuitous.

However sound the theory may be, non-competitive points are likely to remain permanently dissatisfied with the violation of the clause. They feel that they are seriously handicapped because their rates are higher than those to centres where there is water competition. They see freight being hauled through their city five or six hundred miles farther on to a more distant point at rates which are lower, often a good deal lower, than they are being charged. They contend that if, as carriers claim, it pays them to handle this long-haul business at such low rates, then railways can afford to cut their rates to the intermediate point. They are not likely to appreciate the railway answer that carriers are not able to collect any more on the traffic to the distant competitive point and still get the business. They refuse to admit that if railways were to haul all freight at such low rates they would soon become bankrupt. In brief, intermediate places stress cost of service and carriers rely on the value of service principle.

The Board of Railway Commissioners consistently refused to disturb economically sound relationships which had grown up around the transcontinental rate scale.[49] But the Royal Commission of 1951 tried to set up a new principle to be applied to transcontinental rates. It said that it was the disparity in dollars and cents per hundred pounds that caused the difficulty. A difference of only a few cents would scarcely be noticed. Hence Prairie rates should be held down to a relatively small differential above coastal rates.[50]

Parliament amended the Railway Act so that, on both eastbound and westbound transcontinental traffic, rates to intermediate points might not exceed the rate to the distant point by more than 33 per cent. Railways tried to carry out this one and one-third rule but soon declared it was unworkable. If they published competitive tolls to Vancouver, they would lose revenue on traffic to Alberta wherever the rate had been more than 33 per cent in excess of the Vancouver rate. On the other hand, they could keep the current rates on Alberta traffic but raise those to the Coast. Again, they would lose revenue because their coastal rates would be so high that they would lose freight to inter-coastal water carriers. For a time the railways revoked or raised their transcontinental competitive tolls and so priced themselves out of this market. They preferred to abandon this business rather than accept the enforced reduction for the shorter haul. Then beginning in March, 1953, with rates on cast iron pipe, they left Alberta rates at their original level, cancelled almost all their ordinary transcontinental competitive rates to the Coast, and published agreed charges on the latter traffic. They contended that this procedure was legal under the Railway Act. The Board upheld the railways on this question of law.[51] Later on, it approved other agreed charges on transcontinental traffic despite objections by Alberta on various grounds.[52]

Inevitably, Alberta resented what it looked on as the underhandedness of the railways in evading the one and one-third rule by the publication of agreed charges, and the people of that province were disappointed over the failure of the rule to protect them against what they regarded as unjust discrimination. So the matter was referred in 1955 to W. F. A. Turgeon who had also been chairman of the Commission of 1951. He found that the growth of highway competition between Eastern Canada and all the Western provinces had forced railways to publish competitive tolls, e.g., on canned goods, where none had existed before.[53] Besides, equalization would effect reductions in those cases where rates to intermediate territory were higher than elsewhere. Changes which had taken place in recent years suggested that Alberta was not suffering nearly as much as she claimed from the existence of competitive transcontinental rates which were lower than the corresponding charges to points in Alberta. Her industry and trade had grown rapidly; Calgary and Edmonton had expanded enormously. In brief, Mr. Turgeon refused to recommend any change in railway practice with respect to agreed charges on transcontinental competitive traffic. Speaking before the MacPherson Commission, counsel for Alberta put the whole matter of the one and one-third rule very effectively: it was a dead duck and he hoped that no one would try to dig up the corpse, even though Alberta was still suffering from the same disability, relative to Vancouver, as before.

The Board's rulings on the long- and short-haul clause continue to apply to other than transcontinental traffic. In 1940 railways began to quote a carload rate on cheese from Chicoutimi to Montreal that was lower than on the same commodity from Dolbeau. Both towns are in the Lake St. John district and are roughly the same distance from Montreal, but water competition existed from one place and not from the other. In its judgment the Board said it sympathized with the shippers who had to pay the higher tolls but the rate from Dolbeau was reasonable if taken by itself and the rates from Chicoutimi made some contribution to overhead. If the railway were to raise the latter's rates, cheese factories at Dolbeau would be no better off since cheese from Chicoutimi would continue to move at low rates by truck. The railway would obviously be worse off without the competitive traffic. It was water competition, not the railways, that was primarily responsible for causing the difference in rates.[54]

Violation of the long- and short-haul clause may arise when a railway with a circuitous route competes with another company which has a direct or short line. Normally the circuitous railway publishes the same rate to and from the competitive point as that set by the direct line. But the company with the roundabout line is not under any legal obligation either to equal the rates of the shorter line or to carry back the competitive rate to intermediate points. In other words, a railway bases its rates on straight mileage except that between competitive points where the mileage of the two lines is unequal, the carrier with the longer mileage almost always publishes the same rate as the competing line with the shorter mileage. The rate to and from the distant point may be lower than the rates to intermediate points which are non-competitive. In this event some of the rates via the longer road violate the long- and short-haul clause. More specifically, it may cost shippers more to send freight from A to an intermediate point B on a circuitous route than it costs to ship the same freight from A to a more distant competitive point C. The Board has held that "in meeting the short line mileage no necessary obligation is created to apply the same basis on intermediate distances not subjected to the same short line mileage competition."[55]

This is another way of saying that where traffic may move by several routes between two termini, the Board will not order railways to apply the same rates to intermediate points as they publish to the more distant or competitive point, though they are free to adopt this policy if they wish.[56] For example, the rates to Vancouver are generally the same from

Calgary as from Edmonton. This means that the Canadian National charges no more on the haul of 994 miles over its lines from Calgary through Edmonton to Vancouver than the Canadian Pacific charges on its direct route, 642 miles, from Calgary to Vancouver. Similarly, the rate by the Canadian Pacific from Edmonton through Calgary to Vancouver, 836 miles over the lines of the Canadian Pacific, is the same as the Canadian National rate from Edmonton directly to Vancouver, 765 miles. Shippers at Alix, which is on the Canadian National between Calgary and Edmonton, objected to that railway charging them more than it charged shippers at Calgary which is farther away from Vancouver than Alix via Canadian National. Shippers at Red Deer, the corresponding station on the Canadian Pacific, made the same complaint with respect to that railway and Edmonton. The board held that although there was discrimination, it was not undue or unjust. The competitive position of shippers of butter from Alix and Red Deer would not be changed in the least, vis-à-vis Calgary or Edmonton, if the railways on which these shippers were located raised their rates at Calgary or Edmonton as the case might be. For if they did so, butter from the two large cities would go over the other railway by direct route at the same rates as before.[57]

Since the early 1940s the railways have tried to cut down the amount of circuitous movement between this area and the Coast. As a rule the Canadian National does not haul carload freight, which originates on its lines in Calgary and its environs, via Edmonton to Vancouver. Instead, it turns these cars over to the Canadian Pacific to haul by direct route to the Coast. In return, the Canadian Pacific turns over the same number of cars at Edmonton for movement to Vancouver by the Canadian National. While this arrangement reduced expenses and speeded delivery, it made no difference in the rates charged shippers at Calgary or Edmonton, Alix or Red Deer. Some adjustments have, however, been forced on both railways in this area because of motor competition from Red Deer and Alix to Calgary and Edmonton and even to Vancouver.

A rate published in order not to violate the long- and short-haul clause on one line of railway may not be used to determine whether the rate for a haul of the same length on another line of railway is or is not discriminatory. On coal the rate from Drumheller to Winnipeg was 23½ cents per hundred pounds for 782 miles via Canadian National, the company with the shorter route. Although the Canadian Pacific had a circuitous route of 875 miles through Carbon, it published the same rate from Drumheller as the Canadian National. Mine operators at Three Hills, on a branch of the Canadian National north of Drumheller and

875 miles from Winnipeg, asked the same rate (23½ cents) as that from Drumheller to Winnipeg via Carbon, a distance of 875 miles but over the circuitous route of another railway. This was refused.[58]

In sum, the Board is reluctant to alter rates to correct alleged discrimination between places where the rates complained of are of long-standing, are part of a broad system of rate relationships, or are forced upon the railways by competition. It will remove the discrimination whenever the complainant actually suffers by the rates, where the conditions of transport are roughly identical, and where the situation can be corrected without setting up a series of other anomalies. On the whole, charges of unjust discrimination between localities have not been easy to substantiate,[59] and it is unlikely that the legislative changes made in 1967 will alter this conclusion. This is because the railways can base their case on costs of operation and, subject to a ruling by the Commission, these costs need not be revealed to the aggrieved party. They may also argue that the rates in question do not create an *unfair* disadvantage beyond that deemed to be inherent in the location of the traffic. While lower rates to intermediate points might stimulate traffic and economic development at these places, the existing rates do not constitute an *undue* obstacle to the interchange of commodities or an *unreasonable* discouragement to development. Counsel for shippers and consignees at intermediate points will, of course, argue to the contrary.

Discrimination and Market Competition[60]

Manufacturers, farmers, fishermen, lumbermen, wholesalers, indeed all businessmen, are constantly trying to extend their markets. Frequently they claim that high freight rates are restricting the volume of their sales by making it difficult for them to sell in competition with other producers. They point out also that lower railway tolls would increase the volume of traffic for the rails.[61] Although with lower rates the railways would get a smaller contribution per unit to their common expense, they would handle a much greater number of units. As traffic grows, the cost of rail operations per ton-mile will decline. Consequently, shippers contend that lower tolls will help both themselves and the carriers.

As a rule, railways are sympathetic with this sort of argument and the board gives the carriers a free hand, subject to one limitation: reductions in rates published by carriers to expand the volume of their own business and that of their patrons must not create unjust preference or discrimination against other shippers.

The intent of the law governing rail freight rates, both in Canada and the United States, is to give the carriers some latitude in fixing rates. It is their province to take into consideration commercial competition, and any other facts or circumstances affecting their interests, and they may maintain rates less than maximum reasonable rates and rates lower than we can lawfully prescribe, so long as they do not unduly prejudice other communities or shippers, or unduly burden other traffic. It is under such circumstances and not by direction of the Board that there will be found rates to the Atlantic ports, which ignore differences in distance thereto, as well as . . . [many other types of competitive rates].[62]

The Board gives railways this leeway because they, and not the Board, take the profit or loss which might result from these rates. It assumes that carriers are better judges of their own financial interests than any administrative body.

Although in exercising their managerial discretion carriers presumably look entirely to their own gain, the low rates which they publish on account of commercial competition are of great advantage to society. The rates give consumers a chance to draw from wider sources of supply. They may iron out price fluctuations throughout the year by preventing local gluts with attendant spoilage of goods, and by forestalling local dearths with accompanying high prices and inability of some consumers to fill their normal needs. These rates help bring prosperity to all parts of Canada, especially to outlying regions relatively remote from markets. While the interests of carriers in giving low rates may be purely selfish, may be based entirely on their desire to have prosperous shippers so that their own railway may thrive, the result of their rate-making activities confers great benefits on the entire economic and political community.

In a sense the railway is a partner in developing the business of its patrons, in expanding it, and in increasing the volume of freight that will move by rail. Yet it must not be supposed that a shipper can, as a matter of right, demand lower rates from a railway. "The Board has repeatedly held that it cannot order the railway to put in unremunerative rates, nor rates so low as to be unfairly out of line with the rates which are necessary to be maintained in order to permit the continuance and satisfactory operation of the railway."[63] Again, a railway is obliged to charge a reasonable rate but it is "not called upon through the reduction of the rate to guarantee that the business will be carried on at a profit. In other words, the needs of the business and the way in which it is carried on are not the measure of the reasonableness of the rate."[64]

A carrier is free to publish a rate which will allow a shipper to compete in another market; it may also withdraw the rate when it sees fit.

A woodworking company was granted a specially low freight rate on logs coming to its factory on condition that the finished products manufactured from this raw material should be handed over to the same railway for carriage to the final destination. After several years the factory became sufficiently prosperous to pay a higher rate and the railway increased the toll. Since the increased toll was neither unjust, unreasonable, nor contrary to any provision of the Railway Act, an application to cancel the increase had to be refused.[65] The board has held further that a rate put in with a view of stimulating a comparatively new business largely irrespective of resultant profit to the railway company does not create an obligation to continue an improper rate.[66]

Rates based on market competition often cause complaints of unjust discrimination by shippers who do not get reduced rates. In order to sustain their complaint, they must prove that (a) competition really exists between the two areas, (b) they are actually being injured by the railway rates which are in effect, and (c) railways or the Board could correct the situation by a rate adjustment. For example, shippers of potatoes from Ashcroft, B.C., to Vancouver, 203 miles, got a reduction in tolls in order to meet the competition of United States potatoes being shipped into the same market. These low rates could not possibly injure potato growers at Moricetown, B.C., selling in Prince Rupert, 204 miles distant, and so the Board permitted their tolls to remain at their old level.[67] Similarly, fruit growers at Vernon, B.C., were not hurt because their rate on apples into Winnipeg, 1,177 miles, were about one-third higher than the rate on apples from Grimsby, Ont., to Winnipeg, 1,286 miles. Vernon fruit farmers sold most of their crop elsewhere than in Winnipeg and they were steadily expanding their operations.[68] When a shipper of lumber from Chisholm, Alta., to Chicago complained that his rate was 60 per cent more than that from The Pas, Man., to the same destination, the Board found that it could do nothing. The price of lumber in Chicago was set by pine from the southern states. If the Board were to increase the rates from The Pas, it would merely cut one Canadian producer out of the market without benefiting the complainant at Chisholm. It might reduce the rate from Chisholm to the international boundary but United States carriers would not agree to any reduction in their proportion of the through rate. As a result, the Chisholm lumberman could not meet southern competition on significantly better terms than he now had. He would be little better off and the Canadian railways would lose revenue. As a practical matter neither Canadian railways nor the Board had the power to rectify the situation under review.[69]

Rates on export and import traffic are another aspect of market competition. A Canadian railway refused to cut its rates to offset the effect of the removal of a customs duty. American suppliers were able to enter the Canadian market and displace the Canadian manufacturer who had formerly supplied the Dominion. The Board held that railway companies are entitled to enjoy fair and remunerative rates, but have no right to attempt any rate adjustment out of line with reasonable tolls, with a view to protecting or assisting any one industry or section of the public by preventing the importation of goods from abroad: "It does not fall within the scope of the Board's powers to reduce a rate because a removal of customs duty has created a keen competition. . . . It is to another body [Parliament] that application should be made for relief."[70]

Notwithstanding that the board will not order freight rates altered to offset the effect of a tariff or raised to unreasonable levels to keep out foreign competition, Canadian railways are constantly readjusting their rates to help Canadian manufacturers.[71] They do this partly from patriotic motives and chiefly because they want the long-haul traffic from the domestic plant for themselves. If they did not so change their rates, they would have to be content with merely the short haul from the international boundary to the point of consumption. Railways also want the freight revenue on the raw materials going into the plant and on the merchandise purchased by Canadian workmen who, in the absence of the rate, might be thrown out of employment.

As a rule Canadian shippers and consignees are pleased to take advantage of the rate adjustments made by Canadian roads. On occasion, however, they have complained that the adjustments have benefited some Canadian shippers to the detriment of others. For instance, a company alleged that railways unjustly discriminated against rice cleaned in Montreal by giving preferential rates on rice cleaned in Great Britain, carried by ocean steamship to Montreal, reshipped, and sold in competition with the rice of the complainant's mill. The railways asserted that they were trying to attract traffic to Montreal and away from American ports. The Board refused to intervene[72] apparently on the ground that here again was a field for managerial discretion by the railways.[73]

Another, more complicated case arose in 1939. Flour millers in Ontario alleged unjust discrimination because rates on grain and grain products grown in Ontario and sent to St. Lawrence and Atlantic ports for export were higher than the rates from Georgian Bay points to the same oceanic ports on ex-lake grain which originated in Western Canada and the United States. The Board said this comparison was improper. The one rate covered a complete movement from farm to ocean port; the other was a proportional of the through rate from Western plains. When the total charge for transportation was taken into account, Ontario grain growers and processors were distinctly better off than their competitors in the West. Although sales of Ontario grain and flour in overseas markets were declining, the loss of markets was not caused by freight rates within Canada. It was the result of the sterling bloc being unable to get Canadian dollars, of the British government's policy of encouraging the growth of cereals at home as a precaution in the event of war, and of the dumping of grain in Newfoundland (which was not then part of Canada) and the West Indies by various European governments. In short, the basic problem lay outside the Board's jurisdiction and so it was powerless.[74]

Frequently shippers complain that their competitors in a given market are given more favourable tolls, mile for mile, than they receive. The Board has condemned mere mileage comparisons in several cases: "[Such] comparisons do not afford criteria of discrimination, but all facts material must be given weight. In other words, under the body of regulation which is developed under the Railway Act, mileage is not a rigid yardstick of discrimination; discrimination, in the sense in which it is forbidden by the Railway Act, is a matter of fact to be determined by the Board."[75] Consequently differences in rates on the same traffic for similar distances in different parts of the country are not necessarily proof of unjust discrimination. "The Board has more than once ruled that the rate charged by one railway is not necessarily a measure of what another railway should charge."[76] These findings "apply with still greater force when the rates with which comparisons are made are located under another jurisdiction, as are the railways of the United States."[77] "No inference can be drawn from a mere comparison of distances upon different portions of railways, and it does not constitute discrimination—much less unjust discrimination—for a railway to charge higher rates for shorter distances over a line having small business or expensive in construction, maintenance and operation, than over a line having large business or comparatively inexpensive in construction, maintenance and operation."[78] Similarly the Board refused to interfere when the primary cause of the alleged discrimination was the differing strength of rail competition at two seaports,[79] the cost of raising beets needed by competing sugar refineries,[80] the rates charged by ocean-going ships,[81] or the fact that American producers dumped goods on some parts of the Canadian market and not on others.[82]

To sum up, except where the railways are clearly at fault in creating unjust discrimination between markets, the Board will not intervene: "It is in the discretion of the railway whether it shall or shall not make rates to meet the competition of markets. The same principle applies here as in the case of water competition."[83] Moreover, when the competition no longer exists, a railway has the legal right to withdraw the market competitive rate.[84]

Discrimination and Railway Competition

Before railway rates were controlled by public authority, carrier competition chiefly took the form of slashing tolls. Since the inauguration of regulation, railways have competed with each other not in rates but in service. They vie in giving shippers quicker delivery of empty cars for loading, in moving cars rapidly within terminals and between cities, in spotting cars at convenient hours for loading and unloading, in locating cars which have been delayed in transit from one cause or another, in settling loss and damage claims quickly, and so on. In the passenger service, carriers compete on the basis of the speed, cleanliness, suitability of time of arrival and departure of trains, adherence to schedules, courtesy of personnel, and so forth. Competition extends to services such as hotels, express, and telegraph; to the provision of stations and other physical facilities for the health, convenience, and safety of the travelling public; to the use of more modern rolling stock for passengers and freight, and so on. Indeed since 1900 Canadians have complained little about lack of competition; in the 1930s they were severely critical of the costliness of unwarranted competition.

However that may be, competition in cutting rates, such as occurred in rate wars of the 1880s and 1890s, has ceased. Competition in rates between railways is now confined to two sets of circumstances. A carrier with a circuitous route between two centres will normally meet the rate of the carrier with the direct mileage even though, as we have seen, this may involve violation of the long- and short-haul clause. When one carrier cuts the existing rate on a certain movement of freight in the expectation that lower tolls will mean more business for both shipper and railway, its rail competitors will immediately make a similar change.

Often changes in tariffs are introduced simultaneously by two or more carriers whose traffic departments have discussed the matter beforehand. Widespread changes in individual tariffs, such as a horizontal increase of most rates or a change in the classification of an article which is carried in volume, are cleared through the Canadian Freight Association of which all railways operating in the Dominion are members. Then, too, committees of both carriers and shippers get together to iron out differences in points of view and more or less agree on a proper rate or classification. All these arrangements are subject, of course, to subsequent complaint and appeal to the Board by any interested shipper or railway. Thus in a variety of ways competition in rates has been reduced. The predatory, ruinous, and unjustly discriminatory rate-making which years ago typified inter-railway competition has now entirely ceased.

As in other cases of competition, one railway need not meet the rates of another unless it cares to do so. The Board has upheld this principle in cases over gravel to Edmonton,[85] cross-arms for telephone and telegraph poles from Lachute, Que., and Vancouver,[86] silver-lead ore in southern British Columbia,[87] and grain shipped to Victoria for export.[88] The case for non-intervention is especially strong if the conditions of transport differ over the two hauls. This case is made even stronger by the legislation of 1967.

Discrimination and Water Competition

Where complaints of unjust discrimination result from the competition of railways and shipping lines, the Board has stated its practice quite simply: "It is axiomatic, not only in this country but in others, that rate-regulatory bodies cannot overcome by an adjustment of freight rates the natural advantage which one competing locality has over another."[89] "The Board has no power to regulate tolls for the purpose of equalizing the cost of production or geographic, climatic, or economic conditions."[90] "It has been recognized over and over again in various decisions of this Board that the extent to which water competition shall be met is in the discretion of the railway. The Board has also held that it is not the privilege of the shipper to demand less than normal tolls because of such competition, unless the railway, in its own interest, chooses to meet it."[91]

The chief justification for this practice lies in the fact that whatever injury the complainants may experience is caused basically by the water competition and not by the low rates which the railways, later on, introduced to meet competition. Even if the railways voluntarily or the Board by order were to increase the competitive railway rates, complainants would be no better off. Businesses located in the city having the natural or geographic advantage of water competition would still retain their advantage of low rates because they could ship by water rather than by rail. Therefore, abolition of the water-compelled rates on the railway would not correct the condition. This principle could be illustrated by several cases, but details seem to be uncalled for now that competition from inland and costal ships is overshadowed by competition from highway carriers.[92]

The railway may take potential water competition into account as well as actual. It is not good business practice for a concern to keep its prices high until a competitor comes in to force reductions. On the contrary, the wise business man keeps his prices as low as he can with the object of discouraging competition. It is better to choke off potential competitors before they get started than to wait until they are well established before dealing with them. The Board has recognized the economic soundness of this policy[93] but has stated that if two stations adjacent to each other are subject to the same competition the railway may not give the reduced rate to shippers at one station without giving it also to shippers at the other station in the same common district.[94] In short, "water competition is a justification for rates lower than those normally effective by rail, if there is such competition, either actual or potential."[95]

Discrimination and Highway Competition

In recent years railways have had to face bitter competition from trucks and have reduced numerous rates. Apparently no shippers have complained of unjust discrimination with respect to these competitive reductions, probably because they have been quite general. Further, any shipper who is disgruntled with the rail rate he is receiving vis-à-vis his competitor can usually make arrangements with independent truckers or put on his own truck. Motor carriers will either continue to carry his freight at the same relative rates as those charged his competitors or will force the railways to make reductions equivalent to those it has already published for other shippers. Thus a shipper can easily protect himself against unreasonable preference or discrimination by the railway.

Discrimination and Pipeline Competition

The few cases relating to railways and pipeline competition are interesting because they involve not merely competition but also place and personal discrimination. In 1915 and again in 1922 Imperial Oil contemplated building a pipeline from Petrolia and Wyoming, centres of a small petroleum-producing area twenty miles south of Lake Huron, to Regina where its chief western refinery was located. In both years railways cut their rates on crude petroleum in carloads to meet the potential competition of the pipeline.

In 1928 Imperial Oil changed the source of crude for its Regina plant from Ontario to Oklahoma. Though about 500 miles were added to the haul, railways gave the same rates as from Petrolia. In 1932 the carriers further reduced rates because of the possibility of crude oil being handled from Texas and Oklahoma by pipeline to Sarnia, by tank vessels to Lakehead, and thence by pipeline to Regina. Later the Board pointed out that railways had not taken pains to study the probable volume nor the cost of building the line from Lakehead nor of transporting the crude by this route.

In 1934 the railways proposed two columns or sets of rates for crude oil, depending on its specific gravity. The Board refused to recognize rates made on this basis.[96] Railways had suggested that in determining rates on crude petroleum the Board should take into account the large revenue the carriers received on the outbound haul of the refined products. The Board pointed out that before there was a refinery at Regina, gasoline, lubricants, and other petroleum products were distributed on the Prairies by rail from Lakehead and from near Vancouver. This traffic gave the railways a long haul on relatively valuable goods. After the refinery had been established, these articles had been distributed by comparatively short hauls from that point. The Board found it hard to appreciate why railways desired to give a concession in rates on crude oil because the net effect of such a reduction was to cut down railway revenue by displacing long hauls on refined products from Lakehead and Vancouver with short hauls from Regina.[97]

The question of potential pipeline competition came up again in 1937 when railways published low commodity rates to apply to lots of five cars or more. Later, they published still lower tolls applicable to lots of 25 cars or more shipped from one station, by one shipper, on one day, on one bill of lading, to one consignee, at one destination. Some consignees in the West alleged that these rates gave unreasonable preference to one shipper who could store large quantities of crude and discriminated against owners of small refineries who had to buy in limited quantities. Railways argued, on the other hand, that they would set rates low enough to meet what they regarded as almost certain pipeline competition or whether they would stand aside and see this pipeline constructed and their traffic of petroleum in the West irrevocably lost. The rates which they set were slightly higher than the estimated cost by pipeline. The minimum quantity which a pipeline would accept from any one shipper at one time was 10,000 barrels. The railway minimum was lower, 25 cars or about 6,000 barrels, in order to make it easier for the smaller refineries to increase their storage capacity for the rail minimum. They would need an even larger "bin" for petroleum if the pipeline had been built.

The Board ordered the withdrawal of the 25-car minimum because in its view it was not the practice of pipeline companies to set their minimum quantities as high as the railways claimed. The board felt that this minimum constituted unjust discrimination against points where small refineries were located and undue preference for Moose Jaw and Regina. The Board also felt that the proposed rates did not bear a proper relation to the anticipated cost of transport by pipeline.[98] Provided it does not create unjust discrimination or publish tolls which are non-compensatory, a railway may use agreed charges to cover the movement of more than one car of the same commodity sent by one shipper at one time to one consignee.

Discrimination and Mixing

Under certain prescribed conditions a number of different commodities may be shipped in the same car at the same rate applicable to carloads instead of at the less than carload rate. This mixing arrangement as well as the special charges made by a railway for switching, icing, etc., and accessorial charges generally[99] have from time to time been the subjects of complaint regarding unjust discrimination.[100]

Discrimination and Passenger Fares

In deciding allegations of unjust discrimination in passenger fares, the Board applies the same principles as it does in freight traffic. For instance, a citizen of Brampton, 21 miles west of Toronto, asked the Board to order a railway company to issue him a book of commutation tickets to Toronto at the same rates applicable between Toronto and Oakville, a town on Lake Ontario the same distance from Toronto as Brampton. At one time commutation fares had been available from both towns. Those from Brampton had been cancelled at the request of local merchants who believed that the fares were diverting business from them to Toronto. The Board refused to reinstate commutation fares. Any discrimination which existed between Brampton and Oakville was not unjust because there was no proof that the latter had profited at Brampton's expense.[101]

Later the Toronto Board of Trade asked for an order requiring two railways to provide commutation fares between that city and all small communities within a certain radius. It alleged unjust discrimination between Oakville and Streetsville which had commutation fares, compared with Brampton, Whitby, and Oshawa which had none. It asserted that Toronto was being discriminated against unreasonably in comparison with Ottawa and Montreal where commutation fares were more common. The Board held that Toronto had not positively shown it was injured by reason of the lack of commutation fares. Because a railway sold such tickets into and out of Montreal, it was not compelled to sell them in the Toronto area.[102]

Discrimination and Express

It is within the discretionary powers of a railway whether or not it will publish rates on magazines, etc., to meet the competition of the post office on mail[103] or on parcel post.[104] A mere comparison of express tolls is not, according to the Board, conclusive as showing the existence of unjust discrimination or undue preference: there must be evidence of the traffic moving and the effect thereon of tolls, and the discrimination must be one creating actual detriment to complainants to make it unjust.[105] The disability may involve rates or service.[106] For example, shippers along a relatively short, independent railway formerly served by both major express companies were not unjustly discriminated against when one express company withdrew following purchase of the short railway by the competing major concern.[107]

An express company may decide whether or not it will meet rate competition from another carrier. If it does so it must answer any charge of unjust discrimination brought against it. For instance, an express company cut the rates on cream at one town in order to meet the rates of another railway. The board required it to extend the same rates to a nearby town where similar competitive conditions prevailed.[108]

Statutory Discrimination

The Railway Act specifically provides that if that piece of legislation and any Special Act passed by the Parliament of Canada relate to the same subject-matter, the provisions of the Special Act shall override the Railway Act. The Manitoba Agreement, a contract between a railway and a provincial government, did not bind the Board but the Crow's Nest Pass Agreement, a federal act, did so. As we have seen, the latter Agreement was set aside under the War Measures Act, then suspended entirely by legislation, then restored and modified by additional legislation and is now incorporated in the Railway Act. The Maritime Freight Rates Act is another Special Act. The traffic covered by the Agreement, as amended, and by the Maritime Freight Rates Act is among the most important in the Dominion and the rates are clearly discriminatory. But they do not come within the classes of discrimination prohibited by the Railway Act. These statutory rates may not be used to judge the reasonableness of tolls in other parts of Canada or on other types of freight.[109]

The Terms of Union between Canada and Newfoundland "take precedence over any provisions of the Railway Act to the contrary."[110] In consequence, the Canadian National was required to remove the surcharges which it had assessed in some of its tolls to cover the expense of extra handling and of transferring traffic at Port aux Basques between the narrow-gauge cars used on the island and the standard-gauge ones of the mainland. It had to establish four territorial groupings on the island. Town tariffs and commodity rates were, as a general rule, to be determined by negotiations between railways and interested parties. If negotiations failed to resolve the problem of giving Newfoundland the statutory reductions authorized by the Maritime Freight Rates Act, the Board would give consideration to an application for dealing with any specific dispute.

10

Freight Rates and Prices

THE RELATIONSHIP between the freight paid on an article and its price is complicated. So many factors influence the price of any economic good that the effect of a change in freight rates cannot be isolated from the rest and accurately appraised. The theory is reasonably clear; in practice the waters are muddied by the daily turmoil of business.

Being unable to solve the problem by observing rates and actual prices, people have widely differing opinions. "Over a period of many years, the Board has found the relation between freight rates and prices a most difficult matter to fathom."[1] Dr. S. J. McLean was influenced in one case[2] by the fact that the products in question were sold at uniform prices across Canada regardless of local conditions, length of haul, and freight charges. He stated that the benefits of any reduction would go entirely to the industries concerned and not at all to the consumer. For this reason, among others, he refused the reductions asked for. Later he stated: "If a rate or rating is unreasonable in itself, then the question of the incidence of the reduction is not a conclusive answer. . . . Rate or classification reductions, if they are small, have great difficulty in getting down to the consumer; and even if the changes are more considerable, a good part of them is likely to stick in some portion or portions of the cogs of the distributive machinery on the way to the final consumer."[3]

Dr. McLean's views seem to have been accepted by the majority of the Board. "The relationship between freight rates and the price of oranges is not . . . of record, but it may be observed that it is a matter of knowledge that there is very little, if any, difference between the retail price of oranges in California and Ottawa."[4] "It is contended by the railways that the rating applied for would not increase the consumption of rubber bands, nor result in any reduction in the cost to the ultimate customer, and it would seem apparent from these figures that the consumer would not be in any way affected, or benefited by the granting of this application."[5]

Professor Jackman examines the official statistics of the prices of various commodities as published periodically in the Labour Gazette. He shows that canned salmon, a distinctive product of British Columbia, retailed in Vancouver at 43.4 cents per pound tin, while in Winnipeg it was selling at 39 cents, in Toronto at 35, and in Montreal at 36.6. In 1923 bread sold at 6.7 cents per pound in Vancouver and 7.4 cents in New Westminster though the freight rate on grain from the prairies was the same. It sold at 7.2 cents in Calgary and 5 cents in Lethbridge, both centres of wheat-growing and milling. After quoting many other prices, Professor Jackman writes: "What makes these differences in the prices of commodities? It is indubitable that freight rates have nothing to do with them."[6] On the other hand he points out that "when the price of wheat in the world market has been determined for a particular time . . . the farmer tends to receive the amount of that . . . price minus the expenses of transportation and handling incurred between the farm and the . . . market. It is this which makes the freight rate level a matter of vital concern to the agricultural community."[7] He also states that "freight rates are usually exaggerated in prices."[8]

Whenever higher rates are proposed, either generally or on specific commodities, at least some shippers declare that any increase will drive them out of business. They imply that they cannot pass the increases on to the consumers in the shape of higher prices. Other shippers, especially farmers, claim that they bear a double freight charge. Through higher prices they pay the freight charges on the goods which they buy and because they sell their products in world markets at prices determined by world conditions, they receive a lower net price on their farms than formerly. They get the same world price but have to pay higher freight tolls to send their goods to market.

Railways assert that an increase when applied to a single unit of the article or to a single farm or business establishment is negligible. Had the proposed increase of 30 per cent gone into effect in 1947, the freight charge on a tractor from Brantford to Winnipeg would have risen by $8.17. This increase would have been spread over the tractor's useful life of eight years or better. On a per annum basis the rise in tolls would be insignificant.

To this argument farmers reply that a general increase in tolls raises the cost of transportation not merely on the finished tractor but on the coal, steel, and various raw materials that go into its manufacture, on the fuel required to operate it, and on the repair parts needed from time to time. They claim that railways seriously understate the amount of the increase in tolls when they take into account only the weight of the finished tractor. Although farmers may purchase a tractor only once every eight years or so, they buy, or in any case want to buy, one implement or another every year. Sooner or later they pay the increase on all the machines on their farms. Farmers say too that it is unfair to take one unit of a good for the purpose of showing that the economy is not adversely affected by a rate increase. If one takes the entire railway industry on the one hand, one ought to consider the total freight bill of an industry such as agriculture or coal-mining on the other. When one does so, the burden of increased freight tolls is substantial. If, as the railways contend, the increase means little to the shipper, then it should mean no more to the carrier which, therefore, need not have applied for the increase at all.

It is not easy to get at the facts through the surfeit of arguments, some of them with no more than a show of truth or reason. Only a few statements can be made without fear of contradiction. A freight toll bears some relationship to the price of an individual commodity, although the connection is never mathematically exact.[9] The forces determining prices are too complex in their practical operation to permit of statistical proof of the influence of any one of them. Rates do not fluctuate with day-to-day changes in prices. Finally, whatever happens to prices, somebody has to pay the cost of operating railways.[10]

Various attempts have been made to measure what proportion of the price of various commodities can be attributed to transportation. One of these,[11] under the direction of the Interstate Commerce Commission, reported that for the year 1941 the freight on straw as a percentage of its average wholesale value at destination was approximately 66, on watermelons 57, bituminous coal 51, sand and gravel 50, oranges and grapefruit 40, pulpwood 35, automobiles 6, eggs 5, cotton cloth 2, leather 1.2, and manufactured tobacco 0.8. About the only conclusion to be drawn from the above statistics is that freight charges are a much higher share of the prices of bulky, low-valued products like straw, coal, and pulpwood than they are of manufactured articles.[12]

The theory of freight rates and prices can be considered in either of two situations: an increase or decrease applies in the same proportion to all supplies of a certain good coming on the market; or, a rate change pertains to certain sources of supply and not to others. For the purpose of the present analysis a very important assumption must be made. It will be assumed for the time being that freight rates are the only factor which has altered in the entire economy. On this assumption, if the change affects all supplies being sold, the increase will be borne chiefly by consumers. It may be paid initially by the shipper but will be collected eventually from the purchaser of the commodity. The price of any article must in the long run cover the costs of production of the marginal or most expensive unit which society requires to satisfy its needs at that price. Unless these costs are met, society will have to go without some of the goods that it demands at that price. Consumers will bid against each other for what is available. This bidding causes prices to rise. Suppliers will soon discover that it is now profitable for them to produce more goods. As these goods come on the market, prices may have to be cut because under competitive conditions the only way to dispose of more goods is to offer to sell them for less money. If prices again fall below the costs of production, supplies will decline. Then, if conditions of demand remain unchanged, forces will be set in motion to bring costs and selling prices back into line. Eventually the price will settle at a point where the costs of the marginal unit are just covered by the selling price per unit.[13]

The important point is that the expense of transporting goods to the place where they can be used by consumers is just as much part of the cost of production as the wages of employees or the cost of heat, light, and power. In the long run then, consumers pay any increase in freight tolls. Conversely, consumers benefit from reductions in freight tolls. If rates are cut and the selling price of the good remains unchanged, producers already in the field will make higher than average profits. This will encourage present suppliers to expand output and entice new firms to enter the business. As new suppliers come on the market, prices will sooner or later have to be cut. The process of adjustment will go on until the marginal cost of production and the selling price per unit are equal or, what is the same thing, until the quantity of goods brought on the market at the going price and the amount being sold at the same price are in equilibrium. Thus, the benefit of lower freight tolls will eventually be passed on to consumers in lower prices and a larger volume of goods consumed.

The effect of changes in freight tolls on prices is stronger in some cases than in others.[14] If the demand for an article is what the economists call highly inelastic, that is, if the public demands practically the same total quantity of a good at one price as at a little lower price, then the selling price can be raised without reducing consumption by more than a negligible amount. The use of salt for seasoning is largely a matter of habit and takes very little of one's income. Even if its price were to double, few households would consume much less than they do today. On the other hand, if the price were higher, the chemical and fishing industries would cut down their purchases. They would substitute other raw materials or preservatives and where salt was essential, they would use it sparingly. The demand for no commodity is entirely inelastic but to the extent that the demand for any good approaches this state, the burden of an increase in freight rates is thrown entirely on the consumer.

Often the demand for an article is elastic. Any increase in price will choke off a substantial volume of purchases. A rise in prices resulting from higher freight tolls will result in loss of sales to the manufacturer or other supplier. The railways will then have less traffic to haul. The decreased volume multiplied by the higher rate per unit may give carriers less gross revenue than before. Their net revenue per unit will decline because in the short run railways are industries of decreasing costs and with the decline in volume their operating costs per ton-mile may be higher. In addition, because the cost of operating the road generally had increased or because the expense of handling this particular kind of traffic had grown, higher rates may be published. What is more, the decline in volume may be so large that the product of the volume times the higher toll per ton-mile will be less than formerly. Therefore railways usually bear part of the cost of increased freight tolls at least in the short run. How large the shrinkage in railway revenue will be mainly depends on the elasticity of the demand for the products transported.[15]

In the long run railways will adjust their operations to the reduced volume. They will cut their costs by laying off men, abandoning plant, or installing more efficient machinery. Meanwhile consumers will continue to pay more per unit for the goods they purchase and they will go without the satisfactions which they would have enjoyed if they had been able to buy the same quantity of goods after the increase in rates and prices as before. With due alteration of details, the converse argument applies to reduction in rates. Consumers are the chief beneficiaries but carriers and suppliers may gain from a larger volume of business.

So far, we have dealt almost entirely with conditions of demand, with what happens when consumers buy about the same or a great deal more or less of a commodity because its price per unit declines or advances. Let us now examine some factors of supply. Some articles are produced under conditions of increasing cost. For illustration, other things being equal, an increase in the number of tons of coal produced leads to higher costs of production per unit. Mine owners must go further back into the the reserves to get out the fuel. This increases the cost per ton for lighting within the mine, ventilating, transmitting power, and hauling coal to pithead. Wage costs rise because men must be paid while travelling in the mine to the face of the coal as well as for actually extracting the mineral from the seam. These increasing unit costs may be counteracted by greater efficiency in operation, by the discovery of new and more accessible resources, and so on. But for any given set of conditions, coal is mined at increasing costs per unit. This principle applies also to other types of mining, to lumbering, and to agriculture, as any elementary textbook on economics will explain.

On the other hand some industries operate under conditions of decreasing costs per unit. A factory has a heavy investment in buildings and machinery. The interest, depreciation, and obsolescence charges on these physical assets go on at the same rate per annum whether they are fully used, partially used, or relatively idle. As the volume of production increases, the fixed charges are spread over a larger number of units and the total cost per unit declines. A larger volume of output raises total costs but at a less rapid rate than the increase in the number of units of physical output. As a result, cost per unit will decline.[16]

When the demand for a good is elastic, an increase in price will lead to a marked decline in the number of units demanded. If these units are produced under conditions of increasing costs, a decline in the number of units supplied will mean that the cost of the marginal units, excluding the addition to the freight charge, will be less than before. The increase in the freight rate per unit will be partially offset by a decline in the other costs of production. The unit price to the consumer will rise by less than the amount of the increase in the freight rate. Consumers as a group will suffer partly by the rise in prices, partly by a reduction in the quantity of the goods which they are able to buy and enjoy. Carriers will be adversely affected by a decline in the volume of their traffic but in the long run they will be able to adjust their expenses to take this fact into account.

Now let us assume that the good is supplied under conditions of decreasing unit costs and that the demand for it is highly elastic. The rise in freight rates and prices will cut down the number of units required by consumers. Then just because fewer units are manufactured, production costs will rise. Costs increase because of higher freight tolls; they rise too because declining demand and output leads to higher production costs per unit excluding the new addition to the cost of transportation. Under the conditions postulated, the freight rate increase will raise unit prices by more than the amount of the increase in the freight toll taken by itself. Consumers suffer in two ways: for each unit which they buy they pay rather more than the increase in the freight toll taken by itself, and because they use fewer units they have to forgo the satisfactions they would have received if there had been no increase in rates and prices.

Whether unit costs of production are increasing or decreasing makes no material difference when the demand for an article is strongly inelastic. The public insists on the article so much that it will buy the same volume as before even though the price is higher. The unit cost of producing the article will be unchanged except for the higher freight toll.[17] The price in the market will rise by the full amount of the freight rate increase.

For almost any commodity, the elasticity of the demand curve may change from time to time. When prices rise, some consumers, typically those in the lower income groups, will buy less, while the well-to-do will buy about the same number of units as before. A further increase in prices will cut off the purchases of even the so-called better class buyers. As prices continue to rise, demand for most articles becomes progressively more elastic. Similarly, for most commodities a modest change in the volume demanded and produced will lead to no marked alteration in the cost per unit of output. For material changes in supply, there may be quite important changes in unit cost, either increasing or decreasing depending on the industry.

In sum, the net result of a change of freight rates on prices is fairly clear under the extreme conditions which can be assumed, whatever these conditions happen to be. The result is not so apparent when the conditions are in the great middle ground of economic analysis. For any particular commodity the consequences of a freight rate change can be estimated only after determining the conditions of demand and supply, and then ascertaining which of the extremes they tend to approach. If demand is decidedly inelastic, the effect on prices of a change in freight rates is about the same regardless of conditions of supply. If demand is elastic, the effect of a rate change on prices depends on whether unit costs of production, excluding freight rates, are increasing or decreasing. As so often happens in economics, the answer to a problem is not a simple "yes" or "no" but "it depends." In the long run consumers pay for increases in rates; but they may pay more, less, or the same amount as the rate boost. And carriers as well as producers are interested in the result of the rate change because it affects the volume of their traffic and, at least in the short run, the amount of their net returns.

Consumers often claim that rate increases are pyramided, that the prices they pay rise by more than the amount of the rate increase. They argue that a middleman takes a standard markup, say 25 per cent of his cost.[18] When his cost is 80 cents a unit, his selling price is $1. If freight rates go up 10 cents, his new cost is 90 cents and his selling price $1.12½. Though his costs have increased only 10 cents, the middleman has raised his prices 12½ cents because he has taken his accustomed markup on his new, and higher, cost. Since many prices are quoted in units of five cents, the middleman may raise his price to $1.15. If the middleman in our illustration is a wholesaler, the inflated price of $1.15 serves as the base on which the retailer in his turn computes his percentage markup of, say, 30 per cent of his cost. At his old cost of $1 he sold at $1.30. Now with higher costs and the same percentage markup, he sells at $1.50. A 10 cent increase in freight rates has become a 20 cent increase in prices to the consumer.

Undoubtedly pyramiding occurs in the short run, but in a purely competitive situation it cannot last for long. Pyramiding will give distributors higher than normal profits. This will induce more people into the business. More likely, it will tempt some of the existing distributors to cut their prices a little. In this way they will enlarge their sales at the expense of their competitors without reducing their gross profits below what they had formerly been. Prices will be pushed back to the point where they barely cover transportation expenses and costs (including interest and a normal profit) of operating the retail and wholesale establishments. Theoretically under pure competition there can be no pyramiding except possibly in the short run.

Perhaps the popular argument about pyramiding rests on a failure to distinguish between percentage markups and a true increase in distribution costs. If the increase in freight rates is a general one, the distributor will have to pay more for his fuel than before. If he carries the same quantity of goods on his shelves as formerly, he has a little heavier interest and insurance expenses. The declining volume of his sales caused by higher rates and prices will tend to raise his selling costs per unit, unless of course he can shave down other costs to neutralize the influence of higher costs of freight. In strict accuracy, distributors may have to get a shade more gross revenue than previously in order to cover their higher operating costs. Applying the same percentage markup to a larger original cost takes care of higher costs of operation just as effectively as raising the percentage markup.

A sound basis for the popular argument on pyramiding applies to goods produced under conditions of decreasing unit costs. Under these conditions of supply, a decline in the volume of sales brought about by higher rates and prices results in heavier unit costs of production irrespective of the increase in freight tolls. A middleman may shove up his prices at once because he applies the same percentage. In time competition would theoretically compel him to cut his prices back to the point where he receives only a normal profit. Before this has occurred, the manufacturer may have been forced to raise prices to the retailer by a small amount. He is now producing a smaller quantity to satisfy the reduced demand at the higher price, and his costs per unit are higher. It may be significant that the pyramiding argument is almost invariably made about manufactured articles and not about agricultural goods or minerals. Factories typically operate under decreasing costs and theoretically, as we have seen, the prices of their goods rise by more than the amount of the rate increase regardless of pyramiding. In farming and mining, costs per unit tend to decline as fewer units are produced and so the increase in consumer prices is theoretically less than the amount of the freight increase. The pyramiding argument has scarcely ever been put forward in rate reduction cases. Fundamentally it rests on a misapprehension. It is an inadequate explanation of the fact that retail prices sometimes rise by more than the increase in tolls.

Many articles, such as newspapers, chocolate bars, and soft drinks, are sold at prices set by custom. An increase in the freight rate on these goods is normally absorbed by the manufacturer. The cost of transportation per unit is low but one cent, the smallest convenient absolute amount of increase in price, is a large percentage of the retail price. Consumer resistance to price change is sometimes strong. A price of six cents instead of the customary five cents for a soft drink may materially cut down the volume of sales. Hence the manufacturer cannot very well shift any increase in freight tolls directly to the consumer by raising the price of his article. Instead he varies the quality of his product, cuts down on the amount sold at the customary price, or accepts less profits. Higher freight tolls on newsprint will not always result in a rise in the price of newspapers but it will affect the number of so-called features, such as syndicated columns, pictures, and coverage of world news.

Tracing the influence of a freight rate change would be much less difficult if the analyst could prevent any other changes from occurring in the economic system until the effect of the rate change, taken alone, had a chance to work itself out. It will be recalled that in beginning this analysis we assumed that only freight rates altered and that other factors in the economy remained unchanged. Though this assumption is a useful and necessary part of economic analysis, it is unrealistic. Very often freight rates are increased at substantially the same time as wages, taxes, or raw material. Rarely are freight tolls raised when other costs are coming down. General freight rate cases receive wide publicity in the press. By the time the Board hands down its decision, the consumer is psychologically prepared for higher prices. Manufacturers and distributors may have been waiting for some time to raise prices because of higher wage costs, raw material prices, or some such factor. They hesitated to quote higher prices because they were afraid customers would refuse to buy or because competitors would fail to follow their lead. But higher freight rates can conveniently be used as an excuse for boosting prices. What is caused by many factors, is precipitated by the one which is obvious and which is least likely to give rise to adverse consumer reactions.

Then too, demand curves may shift their position. Consumers may be willing to pay more, or less, per unit for all given quantities which may be brought on the market. They might have been buying 100,000 units at $1 and would have bought 90,000 at $1.10. If the position of the demand curve were to remain completely unchanged and the freight rate were to be raised by ten cents, demand would fall off by 10,000 units. At roughly the same time as the rate increase went into effect, the article in question might attain greater popularity owing to a change in fashion or an improvement in general business. After this occurs, 110,000 units would be bought at $1 and 100,000 at $1.10. The increase of ten cents in the freight toll would appear to have no effect on demand because the number of units purchased would be unchanged. On the contrary, if the freight rate change could have been dealt with apart from other economic changes, its effect would have been obvious. The effect of a change in transportation costs on prices is powerfully influenced by the state of prosperity or depression in general business at the time the new rates are published.

All these factors—shifts in demand curves, the effect of general business conditions, the strength of competition, the presence of monopoly, and the influence of wages and other prices—do not invalidate the theory of freight rates and prices which has just been expounded. They merely emphasize that a single element, whether railway tolls, wage rates, cost of raw materials, or taxes, cannot be isolated from the rest of the elements of supply or from the factors influencing demand. No one would contend that each of the factors mentioned, if taken singly, was without effect on prices. The fact that the price of Okanagan apples in Winnipeg is sometimes less than the price of the same grade of apples in Vancouver does not prove that freight rates are without any influence on prices. It merely demonstrates that freight rates are not the only factor involved. Even when you cannot see the sun and moon, you know that they still affect the tides.

Up to this point we have assumed that whenever freight tolls are changed, the rates on all supplies of the commodity coming on the market are altered by the same amount. At this stage in the analysis it is necessary to re-emphasize the assumption that freight rates are altered but other factors in the economy remain unchanged. If freight rates are changed for some producers of a given product and not for others, the effect of any change depends on whether the producers concerned are marginal or intra-marginal. As already explained, if consumers want a given volume of goods, they must pay for every unit of the particular article a price high enough to cover the cost of production (including transportation expenses) of the dearest unit which must be brought on the market to satisfy their needs. Economists call this unit the marginal one.

Different producers have different unit costs but the cost that is important for value theory is that of the producers who are barely induced to stay in production at the going level of prices. These suppliers are more sensitive to every change in demand and supply conditions than those intra-marginal producers whose costs are far below current prices and who get a surplus which, depending on its origin, is known as pure rent or pure profit. Marginal suppliers must cover all their costs, including the expense of taking goods, raw materials and finished, from the place where they are produced to the point of consumption. If they cannot meet the transportation and other costs, they will go out of production. When this occurs, the quantity of goods coming on the market will decline. Some consumers will be short of their requirements, prices will rise, profits will become abnormally high, new supplies will be shipped to market, and prices will eventually be stabilized at a level just sufficient to cover the costs of the marginal producer at the volume which the public wants. The consumer has no way of distinguishing between what is produced at marginal and what at less than marginal costs. The low-cost supplier knows this and so he can sell all his goods for the going or marginal price. By so doing, he reaps an extraordinary gain which is called pure profit or pure rent depending on whether his low costs result from exceptionally efficient management or from favourably located land.

Let us assume now that freight rates are increased on the marginal supplies and not on the rest. If the demand for the article is very inelastic, prices may rise by the full amount of the increase in the cost of the marginal unit. If this happens, the marginal suppliers will be little or no worse off than before. Intra-marginal suppliers will gain a good deal for prices are higher and their costs are unchanged. However, if the demand for the commodity is elastic and prices rise, the volume of goods taken off the market will decline. The old marginal suppliers will be driven out of the business because their costs, including the new freight tolls, have risen higher than the new prices. Consumers prefer to go without some of the supplies which they formerly bought rather than pay enough to keep the marginal operators going. Producers with costs that were previously just a little lower than the old margin will now become the new margin. The new marginal suppliers will be worse off because their pure profit or pure rent, small as it may have been, has been squeezed out.

Producers who have been intra-marginal both before and after the rate and price change, will be benefited by the change. Prices are higher and their costs are the same as formerly.

The rate increase may apply to intra-marginal suppliers and to no one else. If the increase is substantial, the costs of producers who were barely within the margin under the old conditions may be so increased that they become ultra-marginal. If the public cuts down on the volume of goods it buys, these producers will have to go out of business. If the demand for the goods is inelastic and the public will pay more for the same quantity of goods, these suppliers may keep on. Those who were formerly at the margin will now get some pure rent or pure profit, that is, they now will be intra-marginal. But it may happen that the old intra-marginal producers who are not subjected to higher freight charges may still have total costs so low that they remain intra-marginal. In this event their profit or rent will be less, but prices to consumers will not be affected. In brief, the effect of an increase, or a decrease, which is applicable on some producers and not on others will depend on the relative cost position of the producers concerned.

The impact of rate increases on different suppliers often shows up in an acute conflict of interest between suppliers who are distant from their markets and those who are close at hand. Farmers allege that what they receive for their products is the net price less the cost of transportation and handling from their farms to the central market. If all rates are increased by the same percentage, the remote suppliers will be much more adversely affected than those nearer their markets. Consequently outlying regions of a country are likely to take strong exception to percentage rate adjustments, and to agitate for equalization, low rates on the main export of the region, or for subsidies.

At any given time the connection between prices and railway tolls may not be mathematically exact. But as a general rule it is unquestionably true that under a freely competitive situation what the farmer gets is the central market price less the cost of delivery. For wheat the central market is Liverpool. On the other hand for perishable articles like peaches, berries, fresh vegetables, and milk, the market may be a fairly local one such as Toronto or Montreal. It is obviously difficult to ship these goods long distances and still keep them in good condition. Even so, the possibility of canning, dehydrating, or evaporating these goods and then shipping them to market influences prices in various localities of production. In the main, the same principle applies to all farm products. Net farm prices are directly related to central market prices less transportation costs. "The existence of departures from the expected relationship does not prove, as is sometimes alleged, that there is no discoverable relation between the prices at country points and the freight rates to the primary markets. It merely proves that there are disturbing factors that obscure the relationships."[20] The statement that what the farmer receives is the price in the central market less the cost of transportation does not disprove the statement previously made that in the long run the consumer pays the cost of transportation. The price of all units being sold in the market must cover transportation and other costs of production in the long run. The *net* price to the producer of any one unit is the central market price less the freight toll on that unit.

What is true for farmers is equally true for manufacturers selling in a common market. The less advantageously situated supplier has to absorb the difference between the freight rate charged him and that paid by his competitor nearer the market. If his freight costs rise disproportionately to those of his competitors, he may be driven out of business. Alternatively he may be able to prune the costs of his labour or material and thus remain in operation. If he is the marginal producer and the public is very anxious to get the same quantity of goods as formerly, prices may rise sufficiently to cover his higher costs. Producers who are closer to the market will get a higher profit or, more accurately, a larger rent because of their superior location. In time, industry will relocate itself closer to market and the outlying districts will suffer by loss of trade and population.

The manufacturers in question may be operating under monopolistic competition. Producers need not agree among themselves, either openly or secretly, to maintain prices but if the number of competitors is few no one of them will make any change in his price without carefully considering what his opposition will do. Rather than provoke a price war which will cost every firm in the industry some money and perhaps leave the members of it in the same relative position as before, the favourably located supplier may raise his price so that the disadvantageously placed one may continue to share in the business. He may hold up an umbrella for producers whose costs are disproportionately higher on account of the greater relative freight tolls. The public likes to think that the "little fellow" who can barely struggle along because of his higher costs is given a fighting chance. It accuses large, well-located manufacturers who cut prices of trying to monopolize the industry, of maliciously destroying competition, and of ruining the system of free enterprise. Therefore it is not surprising that manufacturers often adopt a policy of "live and let live"; they "play ball with the boys"; they do not make the most of their relatively lower transportation costs.

What is more, a manufacturer can put a brand name on his product. By fancy packaging, extensive advertising, or allegedly special ingredients, he can differentiate his goods from what, if the truth were known, are the almost identical products of his competitors. By differentiation he can get consumers to buy his articles even at a slightly higher price than those of competitors. If his freight costs go above those of other firms in the same monopolistic-competitive industry, he can raise his prices to consumers by as much or more than the increase in freight tolls and by skilful merchandising pass the increase on to buyers without much loss in volume of sales.

On the contrary farmers have always found it hard to agree to restrict output. Schemes whereby governments or farmer-owned central selling agencies withhold supplies from market until higher prices can be obtained have either broken down entirely or have been kept going by heavy government subsidies. Besides, the products of one farmer cannot be effectively distinguished from those of other producers of the same grade. A farmer cannot differentiate his product as a manufacturer can. It is no use for one farmer to advertise because consumers would as readily buy the almost identical articles of his competitors. His expenditures on advertising—even assuming that an individual farmer or a group of them had the money and the skill to carry on a campaign—would be wasted. In any event, the success of advertising for farm goods is definitely limited because the human stomach will hold only so much. When all people have eaten what they need for health, any advertising of farm goods will merely lead consumers to use one edible product in preference to another and farmers as a group will be no farther ahead. The limit to the effectiveness of advertising for manufactured goods as a class is the size of consumers' incomes.

In general, farmers must accept going prices; manufacturers can alter consumers' demands and affect prices by advertising and product differentiation. The farmer who is remote from market can do little about it except pay the higher tolls; the manufacturer faced with a freight rate differentially higher than those of his competitors can act to offset the effect of the increase.

Of course at times a rise in freight rates or other costs of production will force producers in agriculture, as in industry, out of business. Even then, the adjustment is much slower and more painful for farmers than it is for manufacturers. Farming, it has often been said, is a way of life as well as a business. Farmers, middle-aged ones at any rate, find it hard to adjust themselves to new occupations. Their life savings are tied up in their farms. In districts adversely affected by rate increases, they cannot sell their property except at a heavy loss. For years they hang on in the hope that next fall will see a larger crop or better world prices. While some farmers, like those in Southern Ontario, can shift their efforts to some other product if the freight rates on one of their main articles of production rise disproportionately, grain growers on the prairies or potato farmers in New Brunswick can raise few alternative goods. Increases in freight tolls are more serious to regions of specialized agriculture than they are to areas of mixed farming.

An industrialist faced with oppressive freight rates discharges his workers. He lets them go on relief or get jobs wherever they can. He may, though at some expense, move his machinery elsewhere and start up business close to the market. It is not suggested that he can stand a crushing increase in transportation costs without loss. The point simply is that his chances of promptly pulling out of an economically difficult situation are better than those of the farmer. An increase in freight rates bearing more severely on remote suppliers than on nearby ones is a much more serious thing in agriculture than in manufacturing.

In periods of inflation railway costs rise in common with other expenses and railways are compelled to apply for higher tolls. After World War II any proposal for a general increase in rates at a uniform percentage all across Canada immediately touched off complaints of the uneven regional incidence of freight tolls. Similar complaints would probably have arisen regardless of the method used to apply the increase. This problem has had already been considered under horizontal increases and equalization. At this point it is needful only to add that in Canada the relationship between freight rates and prices is often both a political and an economic problem.

What has been said up to this point about the relationship of freight rates and prices is true for transport taken as a whole and for the particular mode of transport which is used for the traffic in question. Although for the sake of convenience reference was made only to railways, the same principles apply to highway, water, and air transport. Some consideration has now to be given to the demand curve for the services of each of the various modes when they compete among themselves.

On so-called captive traffic where the goods must go by rail or not at all, a railway need look only at the general effect of higher tolls on the demand for the goods and its own costs of operation. It does not have to worry about higher rates diverting traffic to a competing mode of transport. Similarly, highway transport has a virtual monopoly of the carriage of relatively small lots of goods within a metropolitan area, e.g., on deliveries from retail stores to homes. In this and similar instances the demand curve for one mode of transport is identical with the demand for transport in general.

Increasingly, however, the same kind of freight may be carried by several modes of transport. On competitive traffic a small increase in, say, railway rates will have little effect on shifting freight to trucks if operating costs of the latter are rising as fast or faster than the costs of railways. But often railway tolls rise while trucking costs are stable or even declining. This may occur because of comparatively rapid technological advances in trucking, because wage rates of truck drivers lag behind those of railway workers on account of differences in the effectiveness of union activity, or because provincial governments raise the maximum load that may legally be carried in any vehicle thus adding to the revenues of truckers without materially increasing their costs. Under these circumstances a railway which raised its rates even a small amount would find that traffic would quickly be diverted to trucks. In technical language it would discover that whatever the shape of the demand curve for the transport of any one commodity taken as a whole, the demand curve for its transport by rail vis-à-vis by truck was elastic.

Similarly, elasticity manifests itself if rates of common carriers by highway increase more than the costs of private truckers. Even before the rise in rates, many manufacturers and distributors may have felt that they might be wise to pay a little more to move freight in their own trucks rather than engage common carriers. Businesses want to keep in close touch with their customers. They can do this more effectively if delivery is made by their own employees, instead of those of an intermediary, an independent trucking company. Hence, a small increase in the rates of common carriers may cause a shift in traffic to private carriers. In this event the demand curve is elastic.

The opposite effect might come about if for some reason or other, probably increased unionization of drivers of shipper-owned vehicles, the cost of private carriage rose above that of common carriers. The merchant or manufacturer might feel that the extra cost of running his own trucks would be greater than the benefits he got from maintaining a close trading relation with his customers. In that event he would switch back to common carriers. Unconsciously, he would recognize a shift in the demand curve.

Thus with the growth of competition, traffic managers have to take account not merely of the effect of an increase in tolls on the total demand for each product carried but also its effect on competitors. Where traffic is captive, a traffic manager may safely ignore actual or potential competitors and concentrate on the demand curve for the goods in question. But officials in the traffic departments of railways have, in addition, to take into consideration the political repercussions of their rates on captive traffic. Many people believe, rightly or wrongly, that almost all captive traffic is in their part of the country and that railways have the power to discriminate against them while granting unduly favourable rates to other areas where competition is more pervasive. To guard against this possibility, the MacPherson Commission recommended that no rail rate might be higher than 150 per cent above the long-run variable costs of handling the traffic. It remains to be seen whether this scheme will prove effective. However that may be, a distinction may usefully be drawn between the demand curve for transport as a whole (which may be elastic or inelastic depending on the demand curve for the goods themselves) and the demand curve for the services of a particular mode of transport (which is elastic whenever competition is keen and is closely related to the demand curve for the goods wherever the traffic is captive).

11

Accessorial Charges

THE PRIMARY FUNCTION of railways is to transport freight and passengers. As an incidental task, railways provide shippers with other services for which they are entitled to reasonable compensation. Tolls assessed for these ancillary services are known as accessorial charges.

Demurrage

Demurrage is a charge levied against a shipper or consignee for holding a car at the time of loading or unloading beyond a specified period. Less commonly, it is charged when cars are held too long awaiting instructions for forwarding, diversion, or for any other purpose. Demurrage is not intended to be a source of revenue to carriers. It is a penalty levied against those who do not release cars promptly. It is designed to prevent a shipper or consignee using railway cars for storage when his own warehouse is filled or otherwise inadequate.[1]

The Canadian Car Service Rules[2] require a carrier to notify the consignee or shipper with all dispatch after the arrival of his car, whether for unloading or loading. Following this notification and subject to certain other rules described below, 24 hours are allowed for any or all of the following: to clear customs; to file orders for placing cars in the case of patrons who do not have private sidings or industrial interchange tracks; to reconsign or reship the same freight in the same car; to inspect, grade, and complete the loading, or partly to unload, or partly to unload and partly reload when these privileges are allowed in the tariffs. If these arrangements are not completed within the 24 hours commencing at 7 AM on the day following notice, demurrage will be charged for the excess time.[3] After this 24-hour period has elapsed, the shipper or consignee is allowed 48 hours of free time (again with some qualifications to be set forth) to load or unload the car. Beyond this 48 hours, demurrage begins to be run from 7 AM. It is sometimes popularly stated that a shipper or consignee is allowed three days' free time. A careful reading of the above sentences or of the tariffs themselves will show that this is not strictly correct.

Formerly the rules governing the 24 hours of free time and the expiration of free time were relatively simple for they merely excluded Sundays and legal holidays. Since 1960, when cars are placed for loading, time shall be computed from the first 7 AM after placement or from 7 AM of the day on which the shipper ordered the empty car "spotted," whichever is the later, until loading is completed in conformity with the railway's rules governing loading and clearance and provided proper billing instructions are furnished. When a car is "spotted" for loading prior to 11 AM, time shall be computed from 7 AM of the date, provided the car was in accessible position at that hour. If the car was not in such position at that hour or if loading was commenced at or after 11 AM, time shall be computed from 7 AM of the following day.

After the expiration of the free time allowed, a charge is made for each day or fraction thereof, including Saturdays, Sundays, and holidays, until the car is released. But such Saturdays, Sundays, or holidays are excluded where they, either singly or consecutively, immediately follow the day on which the final 24 hours of free time begins to run. For instance, if the car were placed before 7 AM on Wednesday, the free time would cover Wednesday and Thursday (assuming there was no extra free time for customs inspection, etc.). If the car were not released, demurrage would be charged for Friday and also for the following Saturday, Sunday, and Monday (if it were a legal holiday) and so on until the car was released. If, however, the car were placed before 7 AM on Thursday and the car were not released on Friday, the following Saturday, Sunday, and the holiday on Monday would be excluded. The general effect of the rule is to add to the charges for demurrage without penalizing the shipper or consignee who had used up all his free time just before the close of business on Friday and was "caught by the weekend."

The charge for demurrage has been changed from time to time, as in Table 7.

TABLE 7

Days of excess time	1906	1917	1921	1951	1960	1965
First	$1	$1	$1	$3	$4	$ 5
Second	1	2	1	3	4	5
Third	1	3	5	5	4	5
Fourth	1	5	5	7	8	10*

* $15 beginning on the ninth chargeable day.

It will be noted that the penalties have become progressively more severe. Nearly 95 per cent of cars are released within the free time. All but 1 per cent of the total are released within three days beyond the free period.

There are several important exceptions to the rules just discussed. Sometimes, because of conditions along the line, the carrier cannot move freight promptly or fill orders for empty cars regularly. This leads to the "bunching" of cars, either for loading or unloading or both. In these circumstances, the shipper or consignee is allowed such free time as he would have been entitled to had the cars been placed as ordered or picked up in accordance with the daily rate of shipment.

Under the Canada Grain Act[4] only 24 hours of free time are allowed for loading grain in the Prairie Provinces during the months of September, October, and November and 48 hours in other months. This regulation leads to a more prompt release of cars during the seasonal rush of the grain trade. For many years, railways refrained from assessing demurrage on cars containing bulk grain destined for unloading at terminal elevators in Western Canada. In 1937 the Board ruled as unjust and unreasonable a proposed tariff of demurrage on this traffic.[5] In 1956 railways renewed their application. Cars were especially scarce, and the railways wanted to increase their revenues and reduce capital expenditures by better use of facilities. Farm organizations and elevator companies objected to the imposition of demurrage. The Board found that grain was being sent to already congested grain elevators. It overflowed into box cars at Lakehead and backed up in cars stored at Ignace, Kenora, and Transcona. Hence the Board allowed only 10 days free time for unloading grain consigned to all terminal elevators west of Lake Superior but additional free time at Lakehead elevators during the period between March 15 and the opening of navigation on Lake Superior was to be allowed. This decision was confirmed by the Supreme Court of Canada but in 1959 the Board's Order was suspended by the Cabinet "pending further consideration of the matter."[6]

At deep-sea ports (except on grain at Vancouver) the amount of permissible free time varies with the origin and destination of the freight. For instance, in Eastern Canada it is 5 days on cars with freight going by water to Atlantic ports in the United States and Canada (except Newfoundland); otherwise it is 10 days. Some manufacturing, mining, lumbering, and other companies do switching with their own power over the interchange tracks between the railway proper and their plants. They are allowed up to 24 hours extra, over and above the 48 hours permitted in all cases for loading and unloading.

Whenever wet or inclement weather renders loading or unloading impracticable during business hours or exposes the goods to damage, the allowance of free time is extended. But if the cars are not released within the first 48 hours of suitable weather, demurrage starts. This regulation has to be interpreted by the local agent of the railway. A fall of rain heavy enough to prevent the unloading of sugar or cement would have no effect on stone or even on fruit and vegetables where the shipper's trucks were equipped with sides and tarpaulins, and he could have driven right up to the car door.[7] The Board refused to allow potato growers additional free time whenever temperatures fell to less than 20° F above zero. If the Board were to grant this request, it would find it hard to decline others, and soon much railway equipment would be immobilized to the detriment of the general shipping public.[8]

The weather conditions to be taken into consideration are those at the actual place of loading and unloading. No additional free time is allowed because of muddy or snowbound highways over which goods are hauled to and from railway stations or because rain and snow stop the harvesting of grain.[9] But precipitation may freeze on coal or other cargo in open cars during transit and make it impossible for the consignee to unload within the prescribed time. In this event he is allowed extra time provided he makes every reasonable effort to release the cars as quickly as possible.[10]

It will be noted that the Car Service Rules make allowance for inclement weather when the freight is in the hands of railways but not when it is in the possession of shippers or consignees, even though delay in loading and unloading is not their fault. One consignee cleared snow off a road to a siding so that he might unload a car of machinery. A severe storm filled in the roadway again. Before he could dig it out for the second time, demurrage amounting to $77 was assessed and had to be paid.[11] Another shipper had to pay demurrage on cars of asphalt because he had no storage facilities and the temperature was never high enough to allow contractors to spray the contents on an airport runway.[12] A third had to pay even though the consignee cancelled his order for coal after it had been shipped.[13]

The same principles apply on freight moved to ocean ports. For instance, cars were forwarded for loading on a vessel on December 2. As a result of a storm on the preceding day, the vessel which was to carry the goods was put in dry dock. Before the cars could be released on December 31, demurrage of $540 had piled up.[14] Because of ice, steamers were unable to move freight delivered by rail to a Canadian port for export. This did not excuse the assessment of demurrage. Both rail carriers and steamships were suffering from unusual and uncontrollable conditions brought about by the war. The Board commended the suggestion that the parties should get together and work out some reasonable and amicable adjustment, so as to avoid demurrage payments in future.[15] During World War II ship operators could not control the date of sailing because their vessels had to move in convoy. Ships might be diverted to another port without notice or they might be sunk by the enemy. For reasons of national security, naval authorities would not let shippers be advised of probable dates of arrival or departure of ships. Even so, demurrage was charged.[16] It was also assessed against a contractor who supplied gasoline to the U. S. Army and civilian contractors along the Alaska Highway during the war. Requirements of customers fluctuated widely and the washout of a bridge prevented delivery to them.[17]

The Board's approach to demurrage cases is based on law. It has no legal power to change the provisions of a tariff relating to past transactions or to order refunds on tolls legally charged. Moreover, if it were to make exceptions to the rules, it would run into administrative difficulties. As the Board has said, "to consider this case an exceptional one and ignore the legal status under the provisions of the rules, would, aside from its illegality, be an injustice to and a discrimination against many others whose applications have been declined."[18] In other words, the Board must not allow the rules to be interpreted to infringe the law or discriminate unjustly against certain shippers, for example, semi-public compared with public elevators.[19] The private owners of tank cars, chiefly oil-refining companies, used to lease them to the owner of private sidings to whom they had made shipments in these cars. As neither the cars nor the track on which they were spotted was owned by the railways, no demurrage was assessed. Nevertheless, the Board ruled that a leasing arrangement might not legally be used to avoid payment of demurrage and it ordered shippers and carriers to discontinue the existing practice.[20]

The Board has freely admitted that many delays are allegedly caused by unforeseen circumstances or uncontrollable conditions such as fires within a plant, breakdown of machinery, financial difficulties and documents astray in the mail. Formerly no allowance was made for strikes in the plant of the shipper or consignee[21] though railways did voluntarily set aside the rules during the influenza epidemic of 1918–19 and reduced the *per diem* charge during the general strike in Winnipeg in 1919. In all others cases the Board has been adamant. The rules were of general application. As applied to some individual cases they may seem to work a hardship. Yet to make exceptions would be contrary to law and would open up an infinite number of practical difficulties.[22] Demurrage must be assessed in accordance with the tariffs.[23]

In 1960 these rigid rules were amended. When a strike by employees of a shipper or consignee prevents the firm from receiving, unloading, loading, or releasing cars, demurrage will be charged at the lowest rates

($5) for each day of the strike, including Saturdays, Sundays, and legal holidays with no free time allowance. In other words, the railway will not assess the higher *per diem* ($10) normally applicable on the fifth, sixth, seventh, and eighth days, and $15 a day thereafter. On the other hand, during the strike it will charge for Saturdays, Sundays, and holidays, even though it might not do so under ordinary circumstances.

Other rules of demurrage introduced in 1960 discourage shippers and purchasers of raw materials from sending goods to a strikebound plant or one that was likely to have a strike so that they would be quickly available when the plant reopens. Similar provisions deter shippers from storing finished goods in freight cars so that they can be despatched promptly when the strike is over. In effect, the new regulations stop shippers and consignees from taking advantage of the rules on demurrage to strengthen their hands in any dispute with labour. Cars shipped, reshipped, or reconsigned to a strikebound plant after two days from the effective date of a strike at such plant, exclusive of Saturdays, Sundays, and legal holidays, will not be entitled to the provisions of the rule set forth in the preceding paragraph. In short, unless shippers and consignees take care, they may have to pay demurrage at standard rates when their plant becomes strikebound.

A demurrage charge follows the car. When the original consignee refused to pay the freight bill, the shipper was notified. Before the latter could resell the property, demurrage accumulated. The second purchaser, the subsequent consignee, paid the demurrage under protest because he said that the original consignee was solely responsible for the delay in unloading and therefore was legally liable for the amount. The Board held that the railway had been within its rights in demanding payment before releasing the goods but that the second purchaser might take action against the first consignee for the recovery of the demurrage charge.

In order to check and enforce the demurrage rules, railways have set up the Canadian Car Demurrage Bureau. It has offices in Montreal, Moncton, Toronto, Winnipeg, and Vancouver, and its travelling representatives inspect stations to see that the regulations are properly and uniformly followed. They also try to prevent shippers and consignees from becoming disgruntled or angry over the enforcement of the Rules. For this reason the number of cases on demurrage brought before the Board of Transport Commissioners has been negligible since 1945.

Average Demurrage

A scheme of average demurrage has been advocated for Canada.

Under this system, one credit is allowed for each car released within the first 24 hours of free time. After the expiration of 48 hours of free time, one debit per car per day, or fraction of a day, is charged for each of the first four days. Thereafter a charge of $5 is made for each day or fraction thereof including Sundays and holidays. At the end of each calendar month, the debits and credits are balanced in accordance with three conditions: not more than one credit is allowed on any one car; not more than four credits will be applied in cancellation of debits accruing on any one car; credits earned on cars held for unloading cannot be used in offsetting debits on cars held for loading, and vice versa. If, after these adjustments, credits equal or exceed debits, the shipper is not charged for detention of cars. The railway is never asked to pay the shipper for any excess of credits. If the sum of the debits, after the adjustments mentioned, is greater than the number of credits, shippers pay at the rate of $5 per debit. Credits earned in one month cannot be carried forward to following months. Average demurrage is optional as the arrangement does not become effective until a shipper signs a contract accepting it.

Average demurrage, so it is claimed, would lead to the speedier release of cars. It would give the transportation companies greater use of their equipment and make cars more readily available for shippers. It would remove the present friction arising over the regulations relating to inclement weather and the bunching of cars. Moreover, it has worked to the satisfaction of railways and their patrons in the United States.

The Board rejected average demurrage chiefly on the ground that it would favour large shippers.[24] For example, a large coal dealer with a trestle would be able to unload cars quickly and earn credits. He would rarely have to pay demurrage. The small dealer without such physical facilities could seldom release cars soon enough to earn credits. Other things being equal, he would be more exposed to demurrage than his larger competitor. Under the present system the Board must treat the car of coal to one dealer in the same way as a car to another. The Board also said that advocates of the plan had not affirmatively established that it would increase the available car supply. When cars were scarce, a plant might delay unloading and use up its credits, and so ensure that it would have cars for the outward movement.

Reciprocal Demurrage

Reciprocal demurrage, another scheme often advocated, penalizes a railway for being late in furnishing a car to a shipper for loading. The carrier's slowness often put patrons to heavy expense and loss. Since shippers and consignees are charged for tardiness in loading and unloading cars, they feel that railways should be brought to book for their delays. They argue that by penalizing carriers, reciprocal demurrage would encourage prompt placing of cars at destination and faster movement along the line.

Railways for their part contend that it is unreasonable to compare the delay of shippers and consignees in releasing cars with that of a railway in placing cars or moving them along the line. Typically a shipper is more or less free to decide whether or not to release cars promptly. If he is short of storage space, he has a strong motive for delaying unloading. While part of the load is being manufactured, he may profitably use the car as a temporary warehouse. But a railway is in quite a different position. It cannot deliver a car to one shipper if another shipper is holding it. Try as it will, a railway sometimes cannot deliver loaded or empty cars because of inclement weather, unavoidable congestion, or tardy connecting carriers. A railway is constantly trying to spot, pick up, and deliver cars with the absolute minimum of delay, because by prompt service it adds to its immediate revenues and satisfies its customers. Its motives for expediting delivery are therefore of the strongest. Its inability always to please shippers in the matter of car supply is due to factors beyond its control. Thus, railways assert, reciprocal demurrage would be unfair to them.

Shippers begin to advocate reciprocal demurrage whenever for any reason empty cars are not immediately made available or loaded ones are delayed in delivery. Their agitation is especially active if they have just previously had to pay heavy demurrage on cars which, it may be, they have been unable to release due to matters beyond their control. So far, shippers have not seen fit to bring reciprocal demurrage to the Board's attention officially.

Stop-off Privilege

The transit or stop-off privilege is an arrangement where railways allow a shipment to be stopped off en route to permit some process to be performed on the freight and the reshipped to its final destination at the through rate applicable from the original shipping point to destination. The transit privilege was originally granted only to grain for milling into flour. For this reason stop-off or transit is often called milling-in-transit even when neither flour nor milling is involved. In-transit privileges are regularly available for milling, storing, and cleaning grain; malting barley; producing linseed meal, oil cake, and oil cake meal; storing, inspecting, and reshipping eggs, butter, cheese, apples, and other fruit; dressing (planing, or tongue-and-grooving), kiln-drying, and sorting lumber; and completing loads of canned goods, live poultry, and livestock.

In-transit arrangements grew up in the United States. As grain-growing areas spread steadily westward, flour mills were set up nearer the source of their raw material. These mills could get wheat by wagon from nearby farms. They could ship flour to eastern markets at rates which, though high, could fairly easily be borne by a relatively valuable article such as flour. At the same time mills at consuming centres could bring in wheat on relatively low through rates and then sell flour to local bakers and householders. But owners of mills located between the source of supply of wheat and the main market for flour had to pay for two rail hauls, one inbound on grain, the other outbound on flour. The rate for each of these local hauls was high. In order to save these intermediate mills from extinction, railways permitted grain which was unloaded and milled at an intermediate point to be forwarded at the balance of the through toll. In consequence all mills wherever located got the benefit of a single through rate. From a freight standpoint it was immaterial at what point along the railway line a mill was located.[25] The public got the advantage of widespread competition among mills.

The regulations regarding the stop-off privilege are relatively simple. A miller pays the inbound charge on the grain at the normal rate. At any time within the following six months (in the United States within one year) when flour is shipped out, he surrenders for cancellation the receipted freight bill or "reference" for the wheat. On the equivalent poundage of flour he pays the balance of the through rate from the originating station of the grain to the destination of the flour. Twice a year each miller submits a statement of the quantity of grain and of unused inward transit references he had at the beginning and end of the period. He also reports his receipts and shipments by rail and other agencies of transport during the period. He submits for cancellation of transit privileges any surplus of inward expense bills in excess of stocks of grain and products on hand. Railway officials have access to the pertinent records of shippers so that by checking these records periodically they may prevent fraud.

The outbound product must be of the same nature as the inbound and must not exceed the "equivalent poundages." Specifically, on wheat references a miller may send out wheat flour; cracked, crushed or rolled wheat; bran and middlings; wheat chops, wheat dust, graham flour, wheat screenings, wheat germ, etc., but not oatmeal, or cornmeal. A milling-in-transit privilege on the by-product has never been granted apart altogether from the main product.[26] The term equivalent poundage refers to the number of pounds of the main product and of the various by-products which are typically obtained from one hundred pounds of raw material, after allowance is made for normal waste and shrinkage. The tariff sets forth the official scale of equivalent poundages.[27]

Special rules apply to what are known as on-transit products. Alfalfa meal, beans (except soya beans), and dried sugar-beet pulp are commonly handled by owners of feed mills and mixed with grain into prepared feed for animals and poultry. On-transit products are charged at the local carload rate from the place of mixing or milling, not at transit rates, but their weight may be used in making up the minimum carload weight. A similar rule applies to the non-cereal portion of other feeds (provided they are not medicated or condimental) where the grain portion (commonly fish, bone meal, blood, offal, etc., which inspectors of the federal Department of Agriculture will not certify as fit for human consumption) does not exceed 35 per cent. These feeds are given to pet cats and dogs, as well as to foxes, mink, etc., on fur farms.

As compensation for the extra terminal and clerical expenses involved in milling-in-transit, railways charge 3 cents per hundred pounds for stop-offs for milling and after July, 1965, 4½ cents per hundred pounds for stop-offs for reassembling, mixing, etc. The milling-in-transit charge is the maximum to be applied irrespective of the destination of the flour or the route which is followed.[28] A railway is permitted to charge an extra amount for a haul out-of-line, that is, for the extra mileage involved in hauling the grain off the shortest line of movement to the mill. For example, wheat may be received ex-lake at Port McNicoll on Georgian Bay, shipped to Port Colborne on Lake Erie for milling, and thence to Montreal for export. The export rate on ex-lake grain and grain products from Port McNicoll to Montreal was 15 cents per hundred pounds in 1946 and from Port McNicoll to Port Colborne was also 15 cents. The distance from the Georgian Bay port to Montreal via Port Colborne exceeds the distance to Montreal direct by 221 miles. The charge for out-of-line haul was ½ cent per ton-mile making 5½ cents per hundred pounds for 221 miles out-of-line haul. When the grain was shipped from Port McNicoll to Port Colborne the shipper or consignee had to pay the toll of 15 cents per hundred pounds. On shipping the flour from Port Colborne, the miller would pay the difference between (*a*) the through rate (15 cents) from Port Colborne to Montreal and (*b*) the inward rate on the wheat (15 cents) plus the haul out-of-line charge (5½ cents) plus the milling-in-transit charge (then 1 cent), or a total of 6½ cents per hundred pounds. A railway may have to forgo the out-of-line charge because of competition.[29] The words "haul out-of-line" mean the difference in mileage between the shortest workable route and the stop-off route.[30] This may not always be the same as the difference between the route normally taken by the freight and the route through the stop-off point.

The stop-off or milling-in-transit arrangement is a privilege which the railways may grant or refuse as they see fit. The Board will not interfere unless carriers unjustly discriminate against certain shippers or localities. Railways would not give stop-off on telephone poles for creosoting and subsequent movement to destination on the balance of the through rate. The Board believed that the use of its authority for the purpose of extending the privilege might easily lead to chaos in the freight business.[31] Again, the Board denied an application of implement dealers to have carloads of farm machinery stopped-over at small towns for partial unloading. The arrangement asked for was not permitted on any other commodity in any other part of Canada. To establish it on implements would have the effect of applying carload rates to less than carload movements and lead to requests to extend the privilege to other articles. The Board confirmed the then current method of distributing farm machinery which was to ship carloads to wholesale centres and distribute in less than carload lots to surrounding towns.[32]

In general, railways restrict the privilege to cases where the material shipped into the transit point is merely processed or reworked. They will not allow it when the material is manufactured into a basically different article. Lumber may be stopped-off for dressing and so on, but not for working into new shapes such as shingles.[33] The transit privilege on wheat applies to flour, shorts, etc., but not to biscuits.[34] Endless difficulties not to mention loss of revenue to the carriers, would result if the privilege were given to articles made of several raw materials or extended beyond the primary stage of manufacturing. Under the stress of competition from trucks, railways added to the number of stop-offs allowed for completing a carload of livestock.[35] Previously they had refused to extend the privilege as it would interfere with mixed train service.[36]

In extending these privileges railways must not create unjust discrimination. Prior to 1919 it was difficult to prove unjust discrimination involving the stop-off privilege to the satisfaction of the Board. In that year the Railway Act was amended[37] to require a railway to furnish such other service incidental to transport as is customary or usual in the business of a railway company and as may be ordered by the Board. The stop-over privilege for milling, cleaning, and hospitalizing grain comes within the meaning of this subsection.[38]

In 1932 the Board dealt with a dispute which involved the stop-off privilege, unjust discrimination, and the movement of canned goods. Consignees, especially those in smaller towns, preferred to buy a car containing several varieties of fruits and vegetables since they could not handle an entire car of one product such as peas. A single cannery, especially if it were small, might not have a supply of all the varieties of canned goods which a customer wished to purchase. Hence both parties would benefit if canning companies could partly fill a car and then have the railway stop it in transit while they completed the load with other kinds of canned goods. Railways were reluctant to go to all this trouble until vessels on the Great Lakes began to pick up shipments of canned goods at various ports. They carried them to Lakehead where they were assembled into cars by wholesalers or their agents. Each car would contain several kinds of fruits and vegetables. The goods would be sent to towns throughout the West at carload rates.

To meet this competition, railways allowed stop-offs on canned goods for completion of load in Ontario but denied the privilege to canneries in British Columbia shipping to the Prairies. When the latter complained of unjust discrimination, the Board ordered the stop-off extended to them too.[39] Even when a milling-in-transit privilege was, by error, applied to dried peas, it could not be withdrawn because it might unjustly favour those who had already taken advantage of the tariff and discriminate against those who had not known of it.[40]

Diversion and Reconsignment

In addition to the in-transit privileges for processing and the like, carloads of grain, lumber, and their products from Lakehead and west thereof may be billed to Cochrane, Cartier, Capreol, Hornepayne, and Sudbury "For Orders." Similarly, certain vegetables, grain, and grain products, in carloads, may be billed to Toronto, Montreal, and other eastern points and then stopped-off or held at these centres "For Orders." In this way goods may be on their way to market while the owner is finding a purchaser or getting the best price. The railway makes an extra charge for the service and also for track storage, if any, at the stop-off point and for demurrage under the usual conditions if the car remains on railway tracks too long.

Strictly speaking, diversion means that the shipper changes the destination of the car while it is *en route*. Reconsignment means any change in destination after the car has arrived at the destination originally specified by the shipper, or any change in the name of the consignee given in the original waybill.[41] Often the two terms are used interchangeably, though the former is more common in Canada. As a rule cars intended for reconsignment are billed to a designated intermediate terminal on "hold" orders. If this is done, the intention to reconsign is implied when the shipment was made originally.

Railways will divert or reconsign carloads of freight only after they have received a written request to do so from a shipper, consignee, owner, or his authorized agent. As it is not always possible quickly to locate a car in transit, especially if the haul is long and many railways are involved, diversion is restricted to specified points (as in the examples above) and the railway merely undertakes to make diligent efforts to effect the diversion. It is not responsible for failure to do so unless its failure is caused by the negligence of its employees. The increased use of punched cards and electronic machines allows railways to trace cars faster and more accurately than when employees had to rely on visual examination of records or telegraphic reports from conductors and local agents. In 1965 the charge for diversion or reconsignment was $7.72 per car plus haul out-of-line, if any. Special regulations are published on fruits and vegetables from the United States, bananas from Jamaica through Saint John and Vancouver, and on other perishable imports.

Diversion allows commission merchants, fruit and vegetable growers, lumbermen, and others to send goods toward destination before they have actually been sold. They can thus give more prompt delivery, have perishable freight arrive in better condition, and save storage charges in warehouses. It is not always possible for producers who are located at some distance from their markets to predict what conditions of supply and demand will be like in a particular city when the goods arrive. By using the diversion arrangement, shippers distribute goods so as to avoid the gluts and dearths which would otherwise occur in particular consuming areas. Consumers are protected against excess prices at some times and the distributor against unremunerative prices at others.

Switching

Switching charges are made when cars are moved from one private siding to another, from one team track to another, between these two kinds of track, or from one local station to another in a large terminal such as Montreal or Toronto. It will be understood that no extra charge is made for the delivery or pick-up of empty or fully loaded cars to or from any siding. This service is part of the regular movement of freight. Switching charges apply only to movements made for the convenience of the shipper such as spotting a car at one warehouse for unloading part of its freight and then placing it near another warehouse, perhaps on the other side of the city, for handling the remainder. Charges for this service are published for both class and commodity traffic.

Intra-plant switching is the movement from one track to another or from one loading platform to another within the same plant; inter-plant switching is moving traffic between two branch plants of the same firm within the same large terminal. In 1965 the charge for this service was 3 cents per hundred pounds, minimum $12.86 per car, if the railway got a road-haul on the freight. On freight hauled to destination over the lines of another carrier, the railway got, in addition, a car-hire charge of $5.15 for each 24 hours or fraction thereof, including Sundays and legal holidays, during which the car in question was on its tracks. Reconsigned switching related to carload traffic on which there has been a line-haul and which is consigned from one siding to another within the switching or yard limits of one terminal, in the same car and without breaking bulk.

A few large industrial plants have their own diesel or steam locomotives to do switching within their plant.[42] By performing this service for themselves, the companies save the intra-plant switching charges made by a standard railway and they have the advantage of being able to place cars whenever and wherever they desire. Plant locomotives can also shift movable cranes, transfer raw materials and partially processed articles from one part of the plant to another in their own cars, and permit consolidation of freight into the cars of common carriers for shipment to their customers. Railways do not make any reduction from the freight rates normally payable for the line-haul, even though shipper-owned locomotives "spot" cars on the interchange tracks between the industry concerned and the railway. Making concessions might easily amount to making rebates. Canadian railways allow extra time before demurrage charges begin in order to give the industrially owned locomotive a chance to complete its work.[43]

The desire of carriers to give shippers the best possible service usually results in their being lenient in interpreting rules and assessing special charges. Yet railways must take care not to give free service to one shipper and charge others for substantially the same service because this would constitute unjust discrimination.[44] For example, a government elevator is not entitled to special treatment[45] and a railway may not give free switching to two elevators and not to a third.[46]

Interswitching

Interswitching is a charge made either by the originating road or by some intermediary such as a terminal railway company for switching in carloads from the originating carrier to another carrier which will carry the car to its ultimate destination. It applies also to freight shipped by a railway to a seaport and delivered to dock, warehouse, or elevator by a locomotive and over tracks owned by the National Harbours Board of Canada. This service is of great value to the public as it allows shippers and consignees to send or receive freight via lines of railway other than the one on which their warehouse is located. Also they can use the most direct route between two places with gains in speed of delivery and sometimes in freight tolls. Interswitching permits carriers with circuitous routes to participate in the transportation of freight where rapid delivery is not essential. Thus more competition is introduced into railway transport.

In many cases a railway will absorb all or most of the expense of interswitching. The individual shipper will not have directly to pay anything extra for the interswitching service on his freight though in the long run his tolls may be a little higher because the total costs of operating the railway are increased by the work of interswitching. Absorption of interswitching charges is common when the railway with the circuitous route enjoys a fairly large portion of the total length of haul and so receives a sizable share of the through rate. Interswitching charges vary with the relative length of line-haul and in some instances with the class of freight.[47]

Prior to about 1918 the Board took the view that if a shipper were being well served by one carrier, interswitching facilities need not be provided. The shipper had to prove that he had positively suffered by the lack of facilities before the Board would order them. This attitude was justified because newly built roads had invaded the territories of railways which had spent years of effort in building up the traffic along their lines. Hence it seemed unfair, by means of liberal interswitching provisions, to allow newcomers to appropriate the traffic of the older line. Consequently interswitching was denied the Canadian Northern when it invaded the East.

By 1918 the various roads had more or less established themselves and the new lines had traffic which the older ones were anxious to share on a reciprocal basis. So now the Board orders interchange tracks built whenever physical conditions are favourable, prospective traffic is reasonably large, the public interest is served, length of haul is reduced, and shippers and consignees are benefited. The Board will not order interchange facilities if their purpose is only to reduce the through rate or deny the originating road the advantage of the long haul.[48] Neither are they ordered merely because some shipper or carrier offers to pay the cost of construction. Normally the Board assesses the cost of construction on the firm in question, on the carrier who wants to get interchange traffic, or on the municipality which may be a party to the

application. The use of motor trucks to haul freight between factories
and railway yards has reduced the need for interchange tracks.

Interchange of Equipment

Railways in North America agree to interchange cars. The important
point is that the arrangements permit all freight cars, and to a lesser
extent passenger-train cars, of North America to move traffic from any
point on any railway line to any other point without trans-shipping, i.e.,
without unloading from one car and loading into that of another
company at the junction point.[49] Further, the plan allows freight cars
to be moved from one part of the continent to another in order to
accommodate seasonal peaks in traffic. Some railways owning relatively
few freight cars depend on other companies to send them enough cars
on interchange to make it possible for them to conduct their business.
Rather than contribute their fair share of cars to the more or less
common pool, they find it cheaper to pay the rent *per diem*[50] and use
the cars of other roads.

Cartage Arrangements

Freight may be sent at Pick-up and Delivery rates as already
described. But with this exception, rates published in freight tariffs are
exclusive of cartage. A railway undertakes to haul freight from a warehouse, team, or industrial track at one centre to a warehouse, etc., at
another place. For most carload traffic shippers and consignees have
their own industrial sidings. However, some carloads are spotted on
team tracks, and all less than carload freight is loaded into and unloaded
from cars by employees of a railway across the platform from or to a
railway-owned freight shed. Some provision has to be made for hauling
these kinds of freight to or from the place of business of the customer
of the railway.

The old Grand Trunk, following the British custom, early began to
engage carters to haul shipments to and from the railway freight house
and to charge extra for this service. Other Canadian railways had similar
arrangements at most centres of any size. In 1912 several cartage
companies refused to renew their contracts on the former terms and the
Board intervened. It had no control over contracts between carriers
and carters[51] but it did have jurisdiction over the charges made by railways to shippers and consignees. As the charges then being made did
not cover the total payments by railways to carters even at the old rates
of pay, the Board allowed an increase in the amount railway patrons
were to pay for the service. In 1913 the railways announced that they

were discontinuing the service but new arrangements, which have been continued with modifications to this day, were made.

The cartage charges vary with the size of the city and are higher per hundred pounds for less than carload than for carload lots. There is also a minimum charge for lots of 300 pounds and under. The charges apply on the first five classes of freight except on single packages weighing over 1,000 pounds per piece or package, and on specific articles which are listed and which require special vehicles or extra help to handle.

The cartage service is of advantage to both the carrier and the user of the railway. If the vehicles of a large number of shippers and consignees had to come to the freight shed with or for shipments, congestion would be inevitable. Trucks and their drivers would be idle and the work of the freight-house gang disorganized. When a cartage company picks up or delivers goods, its trucks handle reasonably full loads; they deliver freight to consignees in the most economical order, along the shortest route, and congestion at the freight shed can be avoided. Similar savings are secured in hauling freight to the railway. No advance notice of arrival of freight covered by the cartage arrangements has to be sent to the consignee while shippers need only advise the railway agent that freight is to be picked up. Neither consignees nor shippers need inquire when the line of trucks, each picking up or leaving a few hundred pounds of freight at the railway warehouse, will be shortest. Prompt delivery and collection of freight serves the consignee or shipper more satisfactorily and saves the railway money. It reduces the need for freight-shed space, cuts down the danger of theft or damage by fire, and sometimes makes it possible to close freight stations. The charges to be paid are fixed and not subject to negotiation between cartage company and consignee. No shipper or consignee is compelled to use the services of the cartage company which is under contract with the railway. If he prefers, he may use his own trucks or those of some other drayman, in which event he pays the railway only the freight rate as such.[52] Some shippers and consignees use railway cartage at times of year when their own vehicles are busy elsewhere. When their trucks would otherwise be idle, they use them to move freight between the railway and their place of business.

Loading and Unloading

Invariably employees of a railway handle all less than carload freight between cars and freight-sheds. If cartage is included, as it usually is, they also handle the goods between the freight-house and the homes or places of business of shippers and consignees. But for carload freight, the general rule is that it is loaded and unloaded by shippers, consignees, or their representatives. The exceptions to this rule include: (*a*) export and import freight at seaports; (*b*) trans-shipment from one car to another because of breakdown of equipment; (*c*) off-loading excess freight en route when a shipper loads a car beyond 110 per cent of its marked capacity; and (*d*) when a shipper or consignee asks the railway to load or unload freight into its freight-house, over the freight-house platform, or between trucks and a team track. The costs of (*a*) and (*b*) are absorbed by the carrier, but shippers are charged for (*c*) and (*d*). In addition, shippers are liable for demurrage while the freight is in cars and for storage while it is in the freight-shed.

Storage Charges

A freight station is established to accommodate the current business of a railway and its customers, not to provide for the storage of freight. When a consignee does not pick up a less than carload lot of freight within a reasonable time (96 hours excluding Sundays and holidays beginning at 7 AM on the day after the written notice of arrival was sent him), storage charges commence. These charges are higher than would be considered fair in a commercial storage warehouse. The purpose of the charges is not to make a profit for the railway but to ensure that freight-houses are kept clear for the handling of current business. Freedom from congestion in freight-sheds is in the interest of the public as well as carriers. A railway also has the right to levy charges on luggage and express left with it beyond the free time allowed.

The railways operate grain elevators at Lakehead, on Georgian Bay, and at certain seaports. The charges for receiving, elevating, storing, weighing, and delivering are given in special tariffs. There are also extra charges for mixing, cleaning, bagging, etc., when performed. These charges are within the jurisdiction of the Board of Transport Commissioners. They are roughly the same as the charges made by non-railway elevators. The latter are subject to control by the Board of Grain Commissioners.

Weighing

Since railways calculate their charges for transportation on the weight of the goods transported, it is financially important to both shipper and carrier to find the correct weight of every shipment. Besides, under the Railway Act (sec. 438) "any person . . . who knowingly or wilfully by false billing, false classification, false weighing, false representation of the contents of the package or false report of weight, or by any other device or means, whether with or without the consent or connivance of the company . . . obtains or knowingly or wilfully attempts to obtain, transportation for such goods at less than the regular tolls then authorized and in force on the railway is, for each offence, liable to a penalty" of from $100 to $1,000.

Less than carload freight is weighed at the point of origin. Articles in packages of standard or uniform weight may have only a representative number weighed in order to arrive at the weight of the whole shipment. Whenever such packages move in quantity, a shipper is well advised to enter into an agreement with the Canadian Freight Association which acts on behalf of all railways in Canada. Thereafter, the weight of the shipment for purposes of billing is computed by counting the packages and multiplying the number by the agreed weight per package.

The tariffs of the railways forbid agreed weights on a few commodities. These fall into three classes: (a) those that are almost invariably made up into packages or bags of standard weight, such as salt, flour, and sugar; (b) goods subject to inspection and weighing by government officials, such as seed grain in bags, butter, cheese, and fruits in baskets or hampers; and (c) commodities which can scarcely be weighed without damaging the goods themselves or exasperating the gang that has to man-handle them, such as barbed wire, onions, and small lots of goods in tank cars.

Freight which moves in carload lots is weighed at railway expense at the point of origin or, if this is impracticable, at the nearest track scales. Cars must be weighed while at rest. They must be uncoupled, or coupled at only one end, provided that the rails over the scales are level and the approach rails are level for at least seventy feet. To arrive at the net weight of a shipment, the weight of the empty car must be deducted from the gross weight of the car and its contents. The actual weight of the empty car is used in preference to the marked tare, which is the weight stencilled on the outside of the car itself. The actual tare may be ascertained either before the car is loaded or after it has been unloaded.

At the option of the railway, cars are often reweighed en route either to check the accuracy of a previous weighing, where the car has met with an accident, or where there is evidence of loss or change of weight in transit. Loaded and empty cars may also be reweighed at the request of shippers and consignees provided the request is made in writing, by notation on the way-bill, or by telephone if subsequently confirmed in writing. If the reweighing reveals a material error in the original weight, the railway makes no charge for reweighing though it will, of course, have to correct the bill for the cost of transport which is sent to the shipper or consignee. If, however, the difference is comparatively insignificant, the railway will charge for reweighing in accordance with its traffic. The charge is designed to protect the carrier against frivolous requests which, if they became too numerous, would hamper the efficient operation of the railway.

What is a material or significant difference is (a) an error in the tare weight in excess of 300 pounds in the case of empty cars, and (b) more than the tolerance allowed on the freight itself. The tolerance is one per cent (1½ per cent on a few commodities specified in the tariff) of the weight of the load but not less than 500 pounds when the weight of the freight is not subject to change from its inherent nature. An obvious error relating to freight which is by its nature liable to absorb moisture or dry out in transit, is commonly dealt with on its merits rather than by the rigid application of the rules in the tariff. In weighing, allowance is made for the weight of stakes, dunnage, and any accumulation of ice or snow on the empty or loaded car. Shippers and consignees who want to have an incoming loaded or empty car reweighed should give notice before the car is placed or "spotted" on a team track or his own private siding, otherwise the charge (if any) for reweighing is virtually doubled.

Special provisions have been made for weighing trailers transported on railway flat cars (piggyback). Railways do not charge for the weight of pallets, platforms, or skids, with or without standing sides and ends but without tops. This rule is rather inconsistent with the general principle that they do charge freight on the weight of containers generally, such as boxes, bags, caddies, firkins, and a myriad of other kinds. The reason for excepting pallets, etc., is that their use facilitates the loading and unloading of freight and the faster release of cars.

Shippers may at their own expense provide and install inflatable dunnage, i.e., plastic tubes, mattresses, and wrappings filled with air. The railway will return the dunnage without charge provided it is deflated and is carried at owner's risk of loss and damage. The reason for this concession on the back-haul is that use of this kind of dunnage prevents freight from being chafed, scraped, scratched, or otherwise damaged in transit and so cuts down on the size of the damage claims made against the carrier.

Special Cars

In addition to providing various types of freight cars for the ordinary run of freight traffic, Canadian railways have special equipment for perishable freight. An extra charge is made for refrigeration because it is expensive to supply and is something separate from, and additional to, ordinary transportation. Theoretically, on carload traffic shippers must at their own expense furnish salt, ice, and the labour to place these materials in the bunkers, but usually the carrier performs these services at shipper's expense at one of its regular or emergency icing stations. Carriers must show on the shipping order whether the shipper or consignee will pay for the icing and whether standard or limited refrigeration is to be given. Icing charges for potatoes and other vegetables in classes lower than fifth are higher than for more valuable fruits and vegetables which pay a heavier transportation toll. When refrigerator cars are held in transit for orders or are not unloaded within the free time allowed under the car demurrage rules, a detention charge is payable in addition to the regular demurrage payments.

If refrigerator cars are furnished for less than carload movement of meats and other packing-house products and loaded at the shipper's private siding, the charge is for the actual weight of the contents, minimum 12,000 pounds. Shipments must be loaded so that they can be taken out of the "peddler" car in station order. Icing at point of origin must be performed by the shipper; icing in transit must be paid for by him. On peddler cars of fresh fruits or vegetables the actual weight is charged for, minimum 10,000 pounds.

In 1960 the Canadian National began operating mechanically refrigerated cars. A diesel-electric power plant mounted in the door of standard "reefers" cools air and circulates it down ducts in the side walls of the car instead of passing it through the load. This method reduces dehydration in the contents of the car and provides a more even temperature throughout the car than ice does. The power plant needs refueling only every twenty days and an oil change only once every fifty days. No expensive modifications are required in existing cars and there is no reduction in usable load space.

During very cold weather perishable products often need to be protected against damage by frost. Upon receipt of reasonable notice, the railway will try to provide a refrigerator car equipped with a heater. These heaters are taken care of by the train crew, by specially trained men at important terminals or, if the number of such cars in a train is sufficient, by an attendant travelling with the cars. The carrier makes a special charge for the use of the heater, to cover interest, repairs, fuel, care, storage during the slack season, distribution to point of origin of the perishables, clerical expense, and so forth.

There are also regulations and special charges for palace horse cars (for racehorses and breeding stock), for stock cars (commonly called cattle cars), and for poultry cars. In handling livestock Canadian railways are governed both by the Criminal Code (sec. 542) on cruelty to animals and by orders of the Board of Transport Commissioners. Under the latter it is illegal to confine livestock in railway cars for periods in excess of 36 hours. Before the end of that time they must be unloaded, fed, watered, and rested for a minimum of 5 hours before being reloaded. Stockyards along rail lines are maintained either by the railway itself or by independent businessmen.

The carriers also publish rules and mileage rate allowances applicable on privately owned tank cars when used in loaded and empty movements within Canada and between Canada and the United States. Payments by the railway for the use of these cars have to be carefully controlled otherwise they could easily become a concealed rebate on the freight rate legally payable.

General

Although the purpose of this chapter has been to explain the charges which a railway may legally make for its accessorial services, three other points must be stressed. First, accessorial charges are not to be looked on primarily as sources of revenue for the carriers. Their capacity to produce revenue is chiefly indirect, for they tend to ensure better use of railway facilities for their fundamental purpose of transporting freight. Second, accessorial charges are evidence of the wide variety of services—storage, stop-off, diversion, reconsignment, switching, and special cars—which are provided by railways and which are incidental to their main business of moving property over distance. Third, these ancillary services have unquestionably helped railways retain traffic in the face of growing competition.

12

Railway Passenger Services

ALTHOUGH passenger traffic on railways has been declining steadily, the public still looks on it as very important. Ostensibly the carriage of persons differs from the transportation of property in regard to emphasis on speed, safety, adherence to schedules, and the making of connections, but modern techniques of operating freight trains have lessened the difference.

Theory of Passenger Fares

Because passengers load and unload themselves, railways and regulatory boards have assumed that terminal costs are small, and need not be taken into account in making fares, though they are significant in determining freight rates. In fact, terminal costs in passenger service are quite high. Passengers need assistance from train crew and from guides in boarding and getting off trains. Luxurious passenger stations in downtown areas are costly to build and maintain. Empty passenger-train cars must often be shunted long distances from the coach yard to near the concourse for loading, and must be hauled back to the yard for cleaning after each trip. Congestion of traffic in large passenger terminals and on tracks leading to them adds further to terminal costs.

The handling of tickets also adds to terminal costs. Passenger tickets must be sold by men who thoroughly understand routes and connections and who are tactful, patient, and cheerful. Tickets may be misappropriated or sold for less than the proper amount. Each agent's sales and unsold supplies of tickets must therefore be periodically audited. At the end of each trip conductors must submit detailed reports of ticket stubs and passengers carried. Clerks check tickets collected against tickets sold. Inspectors or "spotters" occasionally ride trains to ensure that conductors are careful that every traveller has a ticket (except employees and others with passes), that the tickets are punched or collected or both, and that passengers do not travel longer distances than their ticket entitles them to.

Though terminal costs per passenger are not as low as was formerly believed, Canadian railways still function on the theory that terminal costs are small. This is true even though, starting in 1960, they began to make a flat charge of 25 cents per ticket in addition to the charge per mile. Thus, for all practical purposes fares per passenger-miles do not decline as the journey increases in length. Tapering is unusual in the United States except in Eastern Territory.

On some journeys American competition tends to hold down fares within Canada. Distances between Western Ontario (the area from Toronto and Niagara Falls to Sarnia and Windsor) and the Prairies and Pacific Coast are less via Chicago than across Northern Ontario. Travellers via the United States save time and might save money but are inconvenienced by having to transfer from one station to another in Chicago. The possibility of using alternative short, American routes sets a limit on railway fares across Canada. The fare from Kingston, Ont., to New York City is only a few cents more than from Montreal to New York. This is brought about by potential competition via Watertown, opposite Kingston, and American roads. In order to share in the business from Kingston and adjacent points to New York City and its environs, Canadian roads carry a passenger to Montreal (183 miles) for little more than the price of a street car ticket. Ships never bid for transcontinental passengers and they took away from railways only comparatively small numbers of potential passengers by rail in the Great Lakes area.

Blanketing is another departure from the principle that fares should increase directly with distance. Obviously it would be impracticable to calculate and publish a different fare from each point to every other station in Canada. The difference in cost to the railway of two hauls, one 2,800 and the other 2,825 miles in length, is scarcely great enough to justify setting separate tolls. For shorter journeys, say up to 300 miles, a difference in length of haul of eight miles, which is the typical distance between stations, is quite a material percentage. Hence grouping stations for fare-making purposes is done only for long journeys.

In passenger service the long- and short-haul clause can rarely be departed from. If the fare from Toronto to Vancouver were less than the fare to an intermediate station such as Kamloops, travellers for Kamloops would buy tickets to Vancouver and get off the train where they wanted to, at Kamloops. Similarly, residents of Kamloops wanting to go East would have friends in Vancouver buy tickets for them and mail them to Kamloops where the passengers would board the train. Although tickets are technically not transferable, it is not possible for railways effectively to check the practice except in flagrant cases of "scalping."[1] The fare to the distant point "carries back" to intermediate points along both direct and circuitous routes until it meets the fare built up on strict mileage.

Differentiated Fares

Railways differentiate in passenger fares just as they do in freight rates. In 1965 the maximum first-class fare which Canadian railways could legally charge was 25 cents per ticket plus 3.675 cents a mile. Odd cents are included in fares between the United States and Canada, but fares between two points in Canada are rounded off to the nearest tenth or twentieth of a dollar, i.e., Canadian domestic fares end in zero or 5 cents. Under the regulations of the Board of Transport Commissioners, return fares are twice one-way fares less 10 per cent on first class and 5 per cent on coach. But discounts for round trips are not usually allowed on fares which are below the maximum permitted by the Board. The overall difference between coach and first-class fares, formerly 15 per cent, ranged from 20 to roughly 25 per cent in the early 1960s. Comparisons are sometimes hard to make because on some trips the first-class fare is increased by an amount sufficient to cover meals and seat in the chair car.

Canadian railways publish a wide variety of fares. Indeed few passengers ever pay the maximum allowed by the Board. Weekend, mid-week, and holiday fares are one and one-third times the one-way fare for the same distance. They proved popular with both travellers and railways for about thirty years after they were introduced in 1932. Gradually, most of these fares were superseded by other kinds of reductions as described later.

Convention fares at one and one-third the one-way fare, plus a small validation charge, apply up to 30 days for duly accredited delegates attending meetings of fraternal societies, scientific and educational associations, sales organizations, and the like. Reduced fares are allowed Indians, destitute persons, ministers of religion, members of Parliament, immigrants, and commercial travellers.

Military fares are also differentiated. After 1921 fares for officers of the armed services travelling on duty as individuals were $2\frac{1}{2}$ cents per mile; for other ranks individually $1\frac{2}{3}$ cents; and for all ranks in parties in special cars $1\frac{3}{4}$ cents per mile. Since 1949 these fares have been raised. They are subject to agreement between the Department of National Defence and the railways. The Royal Commission of 1951 refused to recommend that military fares be put under the Board of Transport Commissioners. Normally members of the navy, army, and air force while not on duty pay the same fares as civilians though during World War II lower fares were granted all service personnel travelling privately.

On any given train, the accommodation available to the passenger and the cost to the railway differ a little from one class to another. First-class passengers have the right to use first-class sleepers as well as parlour and observation cars, provided they pay the additional charge for a parlour-car seat or chair, lower or upper berth, roomette, bed-room, compartment, or drawing room. Coach passengers are restricted to a seat in the coach except at meal time when they may use a cafe-teria car and, on some trains, the regular diner. On transcontinental trains Canadian railways also have intermediate or tourist fares, and tourist sleepers. Railways make no distinction according to class in fares per mile on slow passenger trains without air conditioning and on fast "expresses" with coaches that are fully air conditioned. This is undoubtedly discrimination but perhaps it is not undue or unreasonable. At all events it is disappearing with the cancellation of passenger service on branch lines.

Differentiation in passenger fares has the same broad economic justification as differentiation in freight rates. By granting low excursion fares railways feel that they get revenue that they would otherwise not secure. They handle this additional business at decreasing cost per unit. It pays them to bid for this traffic as long as it covers its out-of-pocket expenses and makes some contribution to overhead. In the interest of good relations with the public, railways continued to main-tain some passenger services long after the revenue from them failed to cover out-of-pocket cost.

Besides being important in the overall picture, cost must be con-sidered in setting fares on each class of traffic. Though railways get higher gross revenues per mile from passengers travelling in chair cars and sleepers than they do from those in day coaches, the cost per mile is also greater. Pullmans and sleepers are more expensive to purchase and maintain than coaches, the number of passengers per car is less, and porters must be trained and paid. It is doubtful whether the carrier net revenue is any larger—or losses less—with pullman than with coach passengers.

At the same time value of service is significant. Higher pullman fares would encourage more people to fly. Higher coach fares might result in potential coach passengers staying at home or going by bus or private automobile. Thus, because of value of service, raising fares would worsen rather than improve the financial position of railway passenger services.

The situation is different for members of the armed forces. As a rule, troops are relatively cheap to handle because they board and alight from trains quickly, are carried in the poorer cars, and are fed at times which do not conflict with those for ordinary revenue passengers. Although the government is financially able to pay standard fares for the carriage of troops, it argues that the cost to the railway of carrying the armed forces is relatively low. Hence in arriving at military fares, value of service is outweighed by cost of service.

The highest passenger fare—that for a drawing room for one first-class passenger—is roughly three times the lowest fare, which is that for an army private or corresponding rank in the navy or air force. Differentiation is much less than on freight traffic where the highest toll per ton-mile may be more than ten times the lowest. The relative lack of discrimination is due to the difficulty of distinguishing between passengers on the basis of their ability to pay. Shippers of high-valued goods which have a rating of first class (100) will not try to send them as sand (tenth or 27) for they know that they cannot "get away with" false billing. But a well-to-do passenger who can readily afford a compartment may decide to go "coach only" and the railway can do nothing to stop him. Although pride, indulgence in conspicuous consumption, and desire for physical comfort tend to differentiate passengers in accordance with what the traffic will bear, the ease of shifting from one class to another limits the possibility of having passenger fares which are more highly discriminatory than at present. If the range in fares were greater, the probability of shifting would increase.

General Level of Fares

Passenger fares as a group have not been altered either upward or downward in unison with freight rates. During the last quarter of the nineteenth century fares in the United States did not markedly decline as did freight tolls. Presumably this was true for Canada also. In the first decade of the twentieth century the Crow's Nest and the Manitoba agreements and the competition of water carriers on the Great Lakes cut freight tolls on some important kinds of traffic. Yet passenger fares remained at the same basic level as before, though the proportion of travellers at settlers' rates may have increased.

Between 1917 and September, 1920, that is, during World War I and the immediate postwar period, passenger tolls were raised 20 per cent though rather higher increases were allowed on lines which were primarily passenger carriers.[2] In July, 1921, the increases were eliminated and the basic fares east of the Rockies became 3.45 cents first class and 3 cents coach; in mountainous territory 4 and 3.45 cents. After 1933 fares were modified to some extent. The basic toll was unchanged, but departures from standard by means of lower fares in coaches only, weekend specials, convention fares, and cent-a-mile excursions became more common. During World War II, although prices generally were frozen to their 1941 level, excursion, convention, and weekend fares were cancelled and so in reality fares were raised. The objective was not so much to increase railway revenue as to prevent or lessen congestion in passenger trains, make space and equipment available for the carriage of members of the armed forces whether on leave or on duty, and allow employees in munitions plants and shipyards to commute to their work. In 1939 the government levied an excise tax of 15 per cent on all fares including accommodation in sleeping and parlour cars. In 1949 this tax was removed but the railways increased their fares by 15 per cent. The public paid the same fares as before, but the railways retained what they had formerly paid over to the government tax.

In 1957 fares were raised by 10 per cent, a very much smaller amount than the increase in freight rates. In August, 1960, there were minor adjustments.[7] A couple of years later the Canadian National introduced the red, white, and blue system whereby fares between Montreal and the Maritime Provinces were reduced substantially. Before long the Canadian National had extended the scheme across Canada and the Canadian Pacific followed suit, though it did not technically adopt the red, white, and blue tickets.

The general idea of these reductions was that the lowest fares (red) would apply on days of light travel when coaches normally have a good many empty seats. White fares would apply when, as a rule, coaches were only half-filled. Blue fares were in force when the number of persons who were prepared to pay regular fares was normally quite large. More specifically, between November 1 and May 31, red fares apply every day of the week except Friday and Sunday when white fares are payable. During these months blue fares are in force for approximately two weeks around Christmas, three days near Easter, and just before and after Victoria Day. In June and October, blue fares apply on Friday and Sunday with white fares in force the rest of the time. In July, August, and September white fares are charged on Monday, Tuesday, and Wednesday; blue fares on other days.

Problems of Passenger Service

Despite numerous adjustments in fares, the railway share of the Canadian travel market has declined every year since 1920 except during the war. The trend is shown in the following table.

TABLE 8

Percentage Distribution, Inter-city Passenger-miles

	1928	1951	1957	1964
Railways	38	15	8	5
Buses	2	11	5	5
Private Automobiles	60	72	83	85
Airlines	—	3	4	5

SOURCE: Dominion Bureau of Statistics.

The above data exclude traffic which is basically urban or rural, e.g., social calls within the same or contiguous communities; travel by suburbanites who commute to work by railway, bus, subway, or private automobile; drives by farmers to a nearby town to shop; travel in school buses and the like.

The total market for travel has been growing steadily over the years. This is the result of growth in population, the rise in the standard of living, the increasing propensity to travel, the urge to be "on the go", and the development or perfection of new modes of travel by highway or air. Hence, though the railway share has shrunk, they still handled (including commuter traffic) roughly 28.6 million passenger-miles in 1964 compared with about 46.2 million in 1951. This traffic was, of course, spread throughout the year, distributed over several dozen trains, and hauled over thousands of miles of track. Moreover, competition prevented railways from raising their fares to a level which would meet the out-of-pocket cost of the service.

A heavy loss is the primary problem faced by railway passenger departments. Probably few railways in Canada have ever made much money on their passenger trains. In 1925 the passenger, sleeper, diner, mail, express, baggage, and milk services of the Canadian National failed by $8 million to earn their share of the gross costs when these were divided on the basis of ton-miles.[3] In the *Twenty-one Per Cent Case* (1948) witnesses for both major railways asserted that they could not ascertain what losses, if any, were incurred. On the Canadian

National only about 38 per cent and on the Canadian Pacific only about 30 per cent of the total operating expenses could be directly separated in the Company's accounts. The balance had to be apportioned on what the railways described as an arbitrary, statistical, or theoretical basis. But the witnesses were certain that Canadian passenger fares could not be increased because of competition from private motor cars, buses, and airlines. They were of the opinion that, inasmuch as passenger service was essential to Canada's economic growth and to a reasonable standard of living in many isolated communities, freight rate would have to be raised to make up the deficiency on the passenger service. In general, the Board agreed with the railway argument.[4] It reaffirmed this view in 1958 when the loss on the Canadian Pacific's passenger service was said to approach $20 million. Then in 1960 the Canadian Pacific told the MacPherson Commission that its passenger deficit was $27,651,000 in 1958 and the Canadian National reported a loss of $40,358,000 in the same year. Both figures include depreciation of equipment but not interest on money invested in the passenger service.

The declining volume of traffic and the mounting deficits raise two sorts of questions: What have railways been doing to minimize the losses? What should government policy be?

Until 1964, when the Canadian Pacific announced that it was withdrawing all its passenger trains as quickly as practicable, executives of both major railways in Canada had always stated that their passenger business had a bright future. At one time they supported their opinion by arguing that the accounting methods of the Interstate Commerce Commission exaggerated losses on passenger service. There may be some validity to this contention but in recent years the estimated losses have reached such staggering totals that there is now no doubt that passenger trains lose a lot of money. Accordingly, some railway officials have shifted their ground to the argument that most of the losses in passenger departments are caused by mail, express, baggage, milk, and generally what is called "head-end" traffic as distinct from passengers as such.

Another contention sometimes advanced was that if no passengers were carried most of the expenses of operating a railway would continue undiminished. The passenger service with a very few exceptions is a by-product and it is utterly unrealistic to charge a by-product with a *pro rata* share of all expenses. A by-product is profitable if it earns anything whatever above the costs which would be avoided if it were eliminated and that is the way passenger service operating expenses ought in honesty to be computed. On the other hand, after the Rutland Railway, which operates over 300 miles of mainline track in Vermont and northern New York, took off all its passenger trains, it found it could save about 85 per cent of the total computed costs of the passenger service. Although abandonment of passenger trains tremendously simplified operations, it has "taken all the fun out of railroading," according to one Rutland official.[5]

Many executives of Canadian railways say that good passenger service attracts freight traffic from competing railway lines and a satisfied passenger is an enthusiastic advertiser for the freight and express departments of the company. This may have been true in the past but the tendency of top businessmen to fly, rather than go by rail, has reduced its validity. Still, it is clearly through its passenger service that a railway comes most closely in contact with the rank and file of the public. Therefore, up to a point the losses can be justified in the interests of maintaining good relations with the public generally.

By the late 1950s, however, passenger deficits had become so burdensome that many railway officials questioned whether the same intangible benefits, good public relations, could not have been achieved more cheaply in some other way. On the other hand every time an official announced cancellation of a passenger train, he brought down upon himself and his company a storm of criticism from newspaper editors, Members of Parliament, actual and potential travellers, and municipal councillors. As a result the "image" of the railway was hurt, at least for the time being. Moreover, when the Canadian Pacific announced in 1964 that it planned to withdraw all its non-paying passenger trains as soon as practicable, many people felt that it was unfairly throwing a heavy financial burden on the publicly-owned Canadian National and hence on the taxpayer. In 1966 Members of Parliament virtually forced the Canadian Pacific to operate the "Dominion," its second transcontinental train, for another two years and got the Chairman of the Company to agree to operate any passenger train as long as it covered its out-of-pocket costs or came close to doing so.

In 1965 the two major roads discontinued their pool trains between Montreal and Toronto, Toronto and Ottawa, and Montreal and Quebec. This plan had been in operation since the mid-1930s. The Canadian Pacific was blamed for leaving Ottawa without adequate service to Toronto. In the end it completely withdrew from this run which the Canadian National took over. Meanwhile, the Canadian National had tried to offset criticism by introducing the *Rapido*, a non-stop train covering the 334 miles between Toronto and Montreal in $5\frac{1}{2}$ hours in winter and 4 hours and 59 minutes in summer. Later it announced that it would run an even faster train between these termini beginning in 1968.

Over the years both major Canadian railways had tried to get passengers by providing better accommodation on the one hand and publishing lower fares on the other. Some of the methods used to attract more business were faster trains, convenient schedules, air conditioning, better lights, wider windows, doors that open easily, comfortable seats, larger lounge space, smoother-riding cars, and coaches which are more pleasing to the eye both in interior decoration and in outside design and finish. For intermediate distances railways are using more and more rail-cars, which are driven by a diesel-electric power unit and have accommodation for passengers, baggage, and express either in the car containing the power unit or in the conventional passenger cars hauled by it. These rail-cars have the important advantage that they operate with a small crew and so their cost per train-mile and per passenger-mile is relatively low. Passenger service is advertised extensively and skilfully. No efforts are spared to select and train courteous, well-informed passenger agents, porters, and conductors.

Many innovations add to costs. For numerous reasons speed and air conditioning are expensive. The better coaches are dear because of the superior quality of their upholstery, reclining seats, and all-steel construction. Air conditioning machinery must be maintained. The higher capital cost means more interest and depreciation in addition to ordinary operating expenses. Some new coaches contain fewer seats than the old models and hence have a lower potential earning power. Owing to the weight of air conditioning equipment and luxurious fittings, tare weight per passenger in a modern coach is higher than in older styles. Using aluminum and magnesium instead of ordinary steel, and welding the metal parts of cars rather than riveting them, help improve the ratio between revenue and non-revenue loads. None the less this relationship is becoming steadily less favourable to carriers.

If railways were sure that new expensive rolling stock would pay for itself during its useful life, they could with confidence embark on a programme of modernizing their passenger equipment. On the other hand if they could be certain that their passenger business or the bulk of it would be diverted to private automobiles, buses, or planes within the next decade or two, they would be financially ahead if they did not buy any new cars but ran their present stock until it was worn out. As matters stand, they have no way of telling whether or not further investment in passenger cars and stations is economically sound. If present trends continue, a time will come sooner or later when it will be inadvisable for carriers to add to their investment in passenger services. By 1964 the Canadian Pacific had apparently decided that it would not acquire any new equipment for the passenger service but the

Canadian National was buying new rolling stock and converting the old to meet the preferences of travellers, e.g., for roomettes and bedrooms rather than the traditional upper and lower berths.

For years railways have been trying to recover traffic by adjusting their fares. In the 1960s the Canadian National introduced red, white, and blue fares and the Canadian Pacific made reductions too. Meanwhile, both roads had been trying several new sales "gimmicks." When only one person goes by automobile, the cost per passenger-mile is so high that the person saves money if he travels by rail. But when two or more people ride in the same automobile, the cost per passenger-mile comes down considerably. To meet this situation railways began to publish group fares, e.g., for two persons travelling together the total fare is the normal adult fare for one person plus 40 per cent of that fare for the second person. This principle was extended to the point where any group, such as a lodge, church organization or ethnic society, may engage an entire car for its exclusive use at very low fares per person. Moreover, travel by rail is encouraged by the use of rail credit cards, go-now pay-later plans, Car-Go-Rail (a rail passenger's automobile is sent by flat-car so that he can use it at his destination), Canrailpass (good for unlimited travel by rail for thirty days anywhere in Canada but sold only in Europe to tourists coming to Canada), and all-inclusive fares (rail fare and berth, meals, hotel room, perhaps a conducted tour, and all tips). As an experiment, the Canadian National started to operate two trains, one for express only, and one for passengers only, between Toronto, Hamilton, London, and intermediate points. This arrangement makes it unnecessary to hold passenger trains at stations until mail and express can be loaded and unloaded. Faster service attracts travellers to the rails and away from automobiles, buses, and even airlines. Moreover, the time of departure and arrival of the all-express and mail train can be arranged to suit the needs of shippers, consignees, and the post office rather than those of travellers. In consequence, business can be recovered from truckers.

Outlook for Passenger Services

Broadly speaking, the MacPherson Commission in its report of March, 1961, took a far more pessimistic view of the future of railway passenger traffic than railway executives up to that time.[6] Details of its recommendations and of the legislation based on them will be dealt with under "Service" in chapter 14. Briefly, the Canadian Transport Commission is empowered to determine the actual loss on any given passenger train. It will also decide whether it is uneconomic having regard to the actual losses, the alternative transport services including any highway to the principal points served by the passenger train that are available or likely to be available, the probable effect on other passenger train service or other passenger carriers of the discontinuance of the service, and the probable future needs of the area for passenger transport.

After holding hearings, the Commission may (a) reject the application to abandon because the revenues from the service cover the cost or are likely to do so in future; (b) allow cancellation of the service; or (c) order its continuance if required in the public interest. In the latter event the Commission will reconsider the application at intervals of not longer than five years.

During the period beginning ninety days after the date of application by the railway to discontinue the service and ending on the date fixed by the Commission for discontinuance of the service of part thereof, the federal government will pay the railway an amount not exceeding 80 per cent of the loss as certified by the Commission.

In a word, under the legislation of 1967 uneconomic passenger services may be discontinued or maintained by order of the Canadian Transport Commission. If continuance is ordered by reason of the lack of highways into the principal points served by the passenger train, the government will bear 80 per cent of the losses and the railway the remainder. These losses can be eliminated only by a combination of forces: willingness of railway management actively to initiate proposals for the reduction of service even though, by so doing, they annoy some parts of the country; willingness of the public to use alternative means of transport even more fully than in the past; willingness of labour unions to realize that they have an obligation to the public not to indulge in purely make-work practices; willingness of the Commission to give railways the benefit of the doubt in abandonment cases; and willingness of provincial and municipal governments to provide good highways and keep them open all year round.

It must be emphasized that although the passenger service as a whole does not pay, a few trains are profitable and their revenues will probably continue to meet their operating expenses for several more years. These include overnight trains in thickly populated areas and day trains between large cities. People patronize these trains for several reasons. Some want to be free of care and danger which they cannot avoid if they go by highway. Others dislike going to and from airports. They may not own a car, or it may be in use by some other member of the family, or it is so old that it cannot be relied on to carry its driver and passengers on a long trip safely. People in the lower income groups want to save money by travelling by rail. Recent immigrants have become so used to rail travel in their homelands that they take the train without detailed consideration of alternative means of travel. Yet, no matter how much some individual trains can be justified economically, the fact is that the general trend of the service is downward and that, if great care is not exercised, the national exchequer will be stuck with heavy losses.

Regulation of Passenger Service

The same legal principles apply to passenger fares as to freight rates. Railways claim they are entitled to their standard passenger tolls. They assert that it is solely within their discretion whether they will establish, maintain, and alter commutation fares which are lower than the standard fares. They say that the Board's powers are confined to considering and removing any unjust discrimination or undue preference which might result from these rates. "If a railway exercises the discretion given to it [to issue mileage, excursion or commutation fares], that discretion remains uncontrolled and should not be interfered with by the Board unless there is some affirmative evidence that it results in unjust and unfair discrimination between persons and localities."[7] On the other hand, in 1950 the Board held that it had jurisdiction to prescribe the rates at which commutation tickets shall be issued.[8]

Railways require that a certain number of persons travel as a group before they will issue group tickets at reduced rates and that conventions have an attendance of at least a certain minimum before they will sell tickets at excursion rates. The Board has refused to reduce these minima.[9] It would not compel railways to grant special fares to farmers attending agricultural conventions,[10] or to students going to football games,[11] or taking part in inter-university competition.[12] It declined to direct railways to provide excursion fares from Eastern to Western Canada.[13] All these matters are left to railways to decide.

For many years railways gave low fares to members of five commercial travellers' associations. To qualify for the reduced fares, members had to solicit orders at wholesale only and by means of samples, catalogues, cards, price lists, or description, from dealers or manufacturers for goods which were subsequently to be delivered. They had to travel at least three months each year and they had to sign away the usual right of passengers for compensation for loss or damage to their baggage. The Board has ordered railways to give low fares to all members of commercial travellers' associations which are *bona fide*.[14] On the other hand it has upheld the carriers in their refusal to give concessions to organizations whose status was doubtful.[15]

The National Transportation Act of 1967 apparently widens the powers of the regulatory authority over passenger fares:

338 A. (1) Any person, if he has reason to believe that a tariff of tolls for the carriage of passengers . . . or the conditions attached to . . . [their] carriage . . . are prejudicial to the public interest, may apply to the [Canadian Transport] Commission for leave to appeal such tariff or conditions. . . . (2) In conducting an investigation under this section, the Commission shall have regard to all considerations that appear to it to be relevant including (*a*) the effect of the tariff or conditions on the financial ability of the [railway] company or of other carriers of passengers to provide passenger services; (*b*) the effect of the tariff or conditions on the variety and quality of passenger services available to the public; or (*c*) whether control by, or in the interest of a railway company in . . . [a bus company] is involved. (3) If the Commission, after a hearing, finds that the tariff or conditions . . . are prejudicial to the public interest, it may make an order requiring the company to remove the prejudicial feature . . . or such other order as in the circumstances the Commission considers proper, or it may report thereon to the Governor in Council for any action that is considered appropriate.

Though this new section is not technically restricted to commuter services, it was probably added with them in mind and is to be read in conjunction with the possibility of having the Dominion subsidize such services, as will be explained shortly.

Charges of unjust discrimination in fares must be supported by some positive proof of injury. The mere withholding of commutation fares from suburban points such as Streetsville, Brampton, Woodbridge, Agincourt, Weston, and Bolton, all in the neighbourhood of Toronto, does not prove unjust discrimination. "All that has been urged upon the Board on behalf of these places could, with equal potency—in some cases greater—be urged by every so called suburban settlement contiguous to every city or town in Canada. . . . It requires no great stretch of the imagination to see how soon the railway system of this country, already saddled with enormously increased operating expenses, could be broken down if such a system were forced upon them by this Board, in assumed exercise of statutory power."[16]

Commutation Fares

In 1920 the railways proposed to raise their commutation fares. They showed that operating costs had generally increased. In particular, commutation traffic was expensive to handle. Switching was costly;

additional coaches were needed; empty cars had to be hauled beyond the end of the commutation zone as it was not practicable to cut them out of the train earlier. It costs about the same to carry a commuter as to transport a passenger at the standard fare for the same distance. Indeed the two may share the same seat. Commuters use the same station facilities as those who travel longer distances and pay larger fares. Commutation traffic is concentrated in two peaks every working day, and stations have to be enlarged in order to accommodate the crowds. The railways felt that the cost of the extra facilities should strictly be assessed against the peak load and not against traffic generally.

When railways had introduced the low fares, they had not expected that the commutation traffic itself would pay. They had hoped that standard passenger traffic would be stimulated and the volume of freight and express to suburban areas increased, but conditions had changed in ways which they could not have foreseen. Electric tramways gave cheap, frequent service; automobiles came into common use; apartment houses were built so that more people could live comfortably within the old corporate limits. The commutation service itself was not being carried on at a profit and nothing was submitted in evidence to show any indirect gains to the railways. Consequently the Board granted application for higher fares.[17]

With the rise in wage rates and other operating costs after World War II, commuter traffic again became a problem. Although fares were increased several times, total revenues pretty consistently fell below the out-of-pocket expenses of the service.[18] Meanwhile, the five-day work-week had become so popular that books of tickets good for fifty trips within one calendar month from the date of sale became too large for the convenience of many commuters. Accordingly, a smaller book, one with forty trip tickets, was introduced.

Complaints have been registered that Greater Montreal enjoys better commuter service and lower commuter fares than Metropolitan Toronto.[19] The difference is mainly accounted for by the relatively greater operating difficulties in the vicinity of Toronto compared with Montreal. The latter has two downtown stations and a tunnel to connect with the northern half of the Island of Montreal. Toronto has only one station downtown and commutation trains must run the full-distance between Toronto and Hamilton before turn-around. The Board held that the establishment of turn-around facilities in the vicinity of Oakville would not result in economies and would complicate operations. Although a larger proportion of Montreal's population is served by commutation trains than is the case in Toronto and the fares are often lower, the difference in treatment is not unjust discrimination or undue preference. No part of the Montreal metropolitan area had profited at the expense of Oakville.

The Board went on to state that railways and commuters agreed that, as the increased commutation fares approximated the corresponding tolls by bus, they could not be further raised and, since the new rail fares barely covered operating expenses, railways should not be asked to invest new capital in this class of service. The parties felt, however, that the expenditure of a few thousand dollars on better facilities for rail travel might save millions on new throughways and parking spaces for travellers by private automobile. The Board believed that the problem of congestion at the centre of a metropolis and on the approaches to it, whether by rail or highway, ought to be considered by federal, provincial, and civic authorities in co-operation with railway companies and commuters who were directly affected.

Obviously, the Board put its finger on a matter of critical importance but the solution lies more in the field of municipal government than of transport. In 1967 Ontario began subsidizing the operation of commuter trains along Lake Ontario between Hamilton and Pickering, a station just east of Metropolitan Toronto. Government of Ontario, or *GO*, transport is run by the Canadian National. It will save the province the expense of building more expressways and relieve congestion on existing streets, highways, and parking lots.

The federal government has also let it be known that it may aid commuter services. These are not covered by the normal arrangements on uneconomic passenger-train services. But where such claims cannot be entered, the National Transportation Act provides (sec. 314 J (9)) that the "Commission shall after an investigation certify the actual loss, if any, that in its opinion is attributable to the [commuter] service and report thereon to the Governor in Council for such action as he deems necessary or desirable to provide assistance in respect of such loss."

Sleeping, Parlour, and Dining Services

Canadian railways do not segregate their expenses for parlour, sleeping, and dining cars except for such obvious matters as cost of food and linen, and wages of porters, chefs, and stewards. They record the earnings of various trains in order to tell when cars should be discontinued or added. Railways lose substantially on dining,[20] sleeping, and parlour cars. They continue the service for its advertising value and because it is needed as long as any passenger train runs a distance in excess of about 200 miles.

13

Merchandise or Express Service

RAILWAYS IN Canada and the United States have traditionally divided their carriage of property into three broad groups: carload (C.L.), less than carload (L.C.L.), and express. Rates on C.L. apply when the minimum weight as laid down in the tariff is sent in a single car by one shipper to one consignee at one time to one destination. Rates on L.C.L. freight and on express cover the movement of comparatively small lots and are distinguished from each other in three ways. First, one is carried in freight trains and the other in passenger trains. Second, a railway will not collect freight from the home or place of business of the shipper nor deliver it to the residence, store, or factory of the consignee except under special circumstances. On the other hand it will pick up and deliver express as a matter of routine. Third, shipments of express are closely accompanied by an attendant while L.C.L. freight receives only general supervision.

The differences between L.C.L. freight and express were never as clear cut as the above paragraph makes out. More important, the distinctions became blurred as time went on, especially after about 1955. Although most L.C.L. freight is still handled in freight trains, it often moves between terminals at speeds which equal those of passenger trains which carry express. With the closing of railway stations in small towns under the master agency plan which is described in a subsequent chapter, express and L.C.L. freight often have to be "fanned out." The goods are picked up in small towns by motor vehicle, hauled over the highway to a freighthouse in a large city, carried by train to a distant city, and again fanned out or delivered by truck to consignees in small towns. In many instances the same truck is used for L.C.L. lots and for express.

Diesel locomotives have made it practicable for railways to haul longer trains than with steam. Rising wage rates have compelled railways to reduce costs by cutting down on the frequency of trains whenever this can be done without unduly inconveniencing shippers and consignees. Population is concentrating in large cities and declining in small towns and villages. This has resulted in a relative decline in the volume of traffic that has to be picked up or set off at places between metropolitan centres by all modes of transport taken together. What is more, truckers have captured a large share of what traffic remains at these places.

In order to recover business and hang on to what they currently carry, railways have speeded up their handling of express and L.C.L. In many cases both these kinds of traffic were handled in the same manner. In a few instances one major railway classified the traffic as express and moved it at express rates while its competitor called it L.C.L. and charged freight rates. In both cases the rates were identical. Indeed over the entire range of L.C.L. freight the rates are often close to the rates for express, especially if one takes account of the cost of pick-up and delivery which the shipper or consignee must add to the charge for carriage as such. Carriers over the highway usually have only one set of rates for small lots and in order to meet this competition rail rates, whether quoted on express or L. C. L. freight, approximate the charge by road. The essence of the matter is that, broadly speaking, railways provide for L.C.L. substantially the same sort of service as they give on express and they quote what is basically the same rate.

Despite these changes truckers have continued to make inroads on the L.C.L. and express business of the railways. The loss of traffic has been accompanied by rising costs of operation. Besides, the use of multiple regression analysis has enabled railways to pinpoint their losses more accurately than formerly. Hence, railways began to examine the costs of handling small lots more carefully than before.

On the face of things, it seemed obvious that railways were using two kinds of machinery for performing what was basically the same service, moving small lots of goods. It followed that they ought to be able to reduce their costs by consolidating the handling of express and L.C.L. freight. Moreover, integration might improve the quality of service offered shippers and consignee, and thereby enable railways to recover traffic that had been lost to trucks.

Integration into what is called Merchandise Service, or M. S. for short, could proceed more readily in Canada than in the United States. In the first place, each major Canadian railway has its own express service, whereas in the United States the corresponding service is provided by the Railway Express Agency, which is owned by all the railroad companies in that country. Incidentally, the American Express Company, well-known throughout the world, does not handle any express within the United States, is owned by non-railway interests, and is engaged mainly in extending credit and transferring funds both in the United States and abroad. The organizational pattern in Canada allowed integration to make faster progress in this country. In the second place, ever since 1884 railways in Canada have been prepared to pick up and deliver almost all kinds of L.C.L. freight. Until the Pick Up and Delivery tariff was published in 1935, they always made a special charge for this service and have continued to do so on L.C.L. freight not covered by this tariff. Railroads in the United States have provided collection and delivery service for freight to only a limited extent. Third, since Canada has only two major railways, it was comparatively easy for them to introduce plans for integration of L.C.L. and express services at approximately the same time and publish tolls on the same basis. Finally, Canadian railways may have been more influenced than their American counterparts by British practice. Railways in the United Kingdom have never made any distinction between what North Americans call express, and L.C.L. Sir Henry Thornton, who was president of the Canadian National between 1923 and 1932 and who had railway experience in both the United States and Britain, was anxious to consolidate services for small lots. His ideas along this line, as on several others, were ahead of their time.

Beginning in 1962, both the Canadian Pacific and the Canadian National began to consolidate the handling of express and L.C.L. Four unions and about 20,000 men were directly affected by the consolidation but they co-operated in the move, notwithstanding some loss of seniority and even of jobs. Inevitably, replanning collection and delivery routes, providing for the joint use of offices and terminals, retraining staff, ironing out problems of seniority, and so forth proved to be a time-consuming and expensive job. The new arrangements had to be introduced slowly and at one big terminal after another across the country. The railways completed this task in mid-1967.

Once the physical facilities were rearranged, the railways published a revised classification and a consolidated tariff. In accordance with the National Transportation Act of 1967, the new rates had to be compensatory and might not legally be in excess of 150 per cent above the variable costs of handling the traffic in question. The new tariff consists of two sets of rates, depending on whether the shipment weighs below 300 pounds or 300 pounds and over. Thus, the new arrangements continue the broad principle of a package tariff formerly applicable to express and of a minimum charge for "smalls" in the L.C.L. tariff. Rates for M. S. start with a minimum charge for a single shipment of one piece or package weighing 25 pounds or less. Then rates rise in regular increments for every 25 pounds increase in weight until a maximum weight of just under 300 pounds is reached. Shipments of one piece weighing more than 300 pounds are charged at specified rates per hundred pounds. The charge declines as the weight per shipment rises. For instance, a shipment of 600 pounds is not charged double the rate for 300 pounds but only 188 per cent of it.

All M. S. rates vary with distance, though blanketing still applies on small shipments that are exposed to competition from the Post Office. In general, rates on short hauls are raised above their previous levels while those on long hauls are slightly lower. This plan discourages the movement by rail of goods that are expensive to handle in this manner and tends to divert business to trucks which can handle it more economically. At the same time, the relatively lower rates on long hauls may recover traffic for the railways which believe they can make money on this sort of business.

By comparison with the previous tolls on express and L.C.L., the M.S. tariff gives more recognition to cost as related to the volume of a particular shipment. Goods with density less than 10 pounds per cubic foot will be charged as though that was their density. Specifically, a shipment filling 40 cubic feet will be charged as 400 pounds although it weighs less. Moreover, the volume of a shipment will be taken as the space it occupies, not its actual volume. A box containing live chickens will be charged for the breathing space that must be left around the box. The railways hope that the new rule on density will encourage shippers to pack shipments more compactly. The new tariff also takes better account of costs through its piece charge. Shipments consisting of more than one piece or parcel pay a small extra charge for each additional piece beyond the first, because it obviously costs the carrier more to handle a given shipment of 100 pounds that is made up of four or five parcels or boxes than when the same weight is contained in a single package. Even though the new M.S. tariff introduces refinements of costing that did not exist in the older tariffs, it also pays more attention to the value of the commodity than formerly.

An effort has also been made in the new tariff to limit the liability of the carrier for loss and damage. The most important of the new provisions is that railways will not be responsible for loss and damage in excess of $50 on any one shipment unless the shipper declares a higher value when he delivers the goods to the carrier and pays an extra charge for more insurance. In the past, claims for damage on L.C.L. were often excessive because the rules governing the packaging of small lots were basically the same as for the same article shipped in C.L. lots. It is obvious that the risk of damage is less when, as happened with carloads, the goods are loaded by employees of the shipper and unloaded by employees of the consignee and when the car was solidly packed with boxes of the same shape and weight than when the goods were handled by employees of the carrier and mixed in a car with a variety of articles. As a rule the car containing L.C.L. or express was only partly filled and so special care had to be exercised during shunting and while en route. The M. S. tariff gives more detailed instructions on packing but railways must be careful to see that their regulations are not so strict that business is diverted to trucks.

In the main, the new regulations on M.S. traffic improve on the older procedures without changing their fundamental character. Rates are broadly based on those which governed express up to mid-1967 and such matters as the block system, delivery limits and unjust discrimination are left unchanged. Furthermore, M.S. will not prevent the continuance of intensive competition between railways, the Post Office, airlines, and truckers for the carriage of small lots. Accordingly, we will present details about express service in summary form, knowing that they will be modified somewhat as M.S. comes into full operation.

History of Express

Travellers on early railroads doubtless often delivered parcels in distant towns to help out their neighbours. In 1839 a former railroad conductor started the first regular parcel delivery service. He operated along the railway line from Boston to Providence, R.I., and thence by steamer to New York. Within a few years many persons, partnerships, and small companies provided similar service on all railroad lines in the United States. They spread their operations across the continent first with stage coaches, the famous pony express, and then over railways.

The number of operators in the United States, once very large, was reduced from time to time by bankruptcy and consolidation. In 1900 only four remained and in 1919 these were amalgamated into the Railway Express Agency. This is a separately incorporated company though its stock is owned by all the American railroads. It has the exclusive right to handle express over the railways of the United States and has important interests in express services by air and highway. By 1960 the Railway Express Agency had so many truck routes that the Interstate Commerce Commission considered treating it as a highway carrier.

In 1963 the Canadian National was serving 164 express routes exclusively by truck and the Canadian Pacific had 143. In addition, their trucks performed pick-up and delivery services within built-up areas.

Canadian Express Companies

In Canada the express business formally got going in 1865 along the old Grand Trunk. In 1882 the Dominion Express Company was set up as a wholly owned subsidiary of the Canadian Pacific Railway. Fifty years later its name was changed to Canadian Pacific Express Company. In 1902 the Canadian Northern Express Comapny came into being. The Canadian National in 1923 unified the express businesses of its predecessors into a separate department of the Company, the Canadian National Express. On the Northern Alberta and Algoma Central railways a separate department of the Company does the express work. United States railways running in Canada use the Railway Express Agency. Other railways in Canada use the express services of the Canadian National, Canadian Pacific, or both.

The two major companies perform identical services as far as the public is concerned but the relationship between the express business and the parent railway is quite different. Canadian National Express is a department of the railway. Its receipts are taken directly into the railway coffers and all its expenses are paid from the revenues of the Canadian National Railways. The accounting arrangements for express on the Canadian National are exactly the same as for canned goods, grain, or any kind of freight.

The Canadian Pacific Express Company has a separate legal existtence. It deducts from its receipts for the carriage of express the expenses of its own operations such as maintenance of its trucks, salaries and wages of the men it employs full time, and rentals of offices used exclusively by express. Then it transfers to the railway the balance of its gross receipts from express. This amount goes into gross railway operations revenue just as do the receipts from transporting livestock, coal, or passengers. From all its total revenues the railway has to meet its numerous expenses. Some of these are directly related to the express business such as the cost of transporting express and express attendants in passenger trains, rentals of buildings used in common by railway and express employees, cost of storage space for express in railway-owned terminals, and part of the wages of agents, mainly in small towns, who handle express, freight, and commercial telegrams. Neither the railway nor the express company has reported to the public whether the balance paid by the one to the other adequately compensates the railway for services it renders on behalf of express. But express companies also do some work for their parent railway at rates that are agreed upon and are presumably fair. In particular, along several highways which parallel branch lines, they handle less than carload freight for the parent railway.

Canadian Pacific Express Company owns over 23,000 shares of the common stock of its parent. It receives dividends on these holdings like any other shareholder. It gets rent from tenants of buildings which it owns. It even collects rent from the Canadian Pacific Railway when its parent occupies space in a building owned by the Express Company and it does this even though it is not charged rent on the space it uses in railway-owned buildings.

From its rents and net income from ancillary services as described below, Canadian Pacific Express declares dividends on its common stock. As all the shares of the Express Company are owned by the Railway, the latter gets most of the revenues from sundry sources. Any surplus which remains after payment of the dividend is retained by the Express Company for working capital or investment in fixed assets. It is obvious that the affairs of Canadian Pacific Express and its parent are somewhat mixed up. Clearly neither of the major railways makes any attempt to put its express services on a strictly cost basis.

Ancillary Services of Express Companies

Express companies get revenue from many sources besides carrying goods. They issue money orders and travellers' cheques payable in domestic and foreign currencies. They handle goods C.O.D., collecting all or part of the invoice price of the goods before delivering them to the consignee and then remitting the funds to the shipper. They accept accounts, bills, and drafts for collection from business generally. They will clear goods through customs, paying whatever duty is required and collecting later from shipper or consignee. They will handle baggage checks, pick up baggage, and forward it by express. They will bank money, record deeds, pay taxes, and collect pawn tickets for the redemption of goods to be returned by express. The companies will deliver legal documents and valuable papers either for retention by the recipient or for signature and return to sender. Finally, they will provide armed guards to accompany any shipment. Needless to say, they charge for these services.

Another sort of ancillary service is that Canadian express companies, in conjunction with their counterparts overseas, will handle express between Canada and the United Kingdom and from Canada to Continental Europe. The rate is the sum of the locals, i.e., the regular express rate from point of origin to seaport plus the usual charge on small lots across the Atlantic plus the standard rate beyond.

Express Rates

Originally express rates within Canada were two and one-half times the corresponding rate on first class freight. The higher toll was justified, so it was argued, because express moved in passenger trains and was accompanied by an attendant. In 1907 the jurisdiction of the Board of Railway Commissioners was extended to express. Three years later the Board reduced express tolls chiefly on the ground that the companies were making an excessive rate of return on their small investments in real property.[1] In 1913 the Board ruled that express companies were not bound to meet rates of the Post Office on small parcels.[2] Because of rising wages and prices during World War I, express companies found that their revenues were insufficient to cover their costs. They applied for higher rates which the Board allowed in July, 1919. The increases were substantial: on the average 40 per cent in the East, 25 per cent on the Prairies, and 26 per cent in British Columbia.[3]

By this time, 1919, a good many anomalies had crept into express rates. For instance, the rate between Windsor and Belleville, 340 miles, was 50 per cent more than that between Toronto and Montreal, 334 miles. To provide a logical basis for express rates, the Board set up three zones: *A* embraces most of Eastern Canada, namely, east and south of Sault Ste. Marie and Parent, Que., but excluding the Ontario Northland Railway;[4] *B* includes the territory west of zone *A* to Crowsnest, B.C., Canmore and Edson, Alta.; and *C* takes in Crowsnest, Canmore, Edson, and west thereof.[5]

Having established these zones, the Board considered costs. Articles must be carried along the line of railway. This transportation charge (including care in transit, and insurance) varies with zone, length of haul, and weight of the article. It is roughly one and one-half times the first-class standard freight rates at the level prevailing between 1922 and 1947, arranged in fifty-mile groups. The second part is for physical handling such as pick-up and delivery, loading, and unloading. This charge is the same regardless of the zone or the distance over which the goods are to move but varies with the weight of the article. This is not strictly logical. An express company is put to the same expense to send a truck to a business or home to pick up a shipment of 100 pounds as it incurs to collect or deliver a lot of 500 pounds. Beyond a certain point, however, weight has an important influence on cost. Further, charging precisely the same amount for a small as for a large shipment might raise the rate on the smaller lot to a level higher than it could bear. As in railway tolls generally, value of service cannot be ignored. The final part of the total expense is for clerical work such as billing and auditing. This is constant for all zones, lengths of haul, and weights of shipments.

In 1919 the first class express rate was constructed with the following detailed charges:

TABLE 9

	Zone A	Zone B	Zone C	
(a) Transportation	20	25	30	cents per 100 lbs. for each 50-mile group.
(b) Physical handling	30	30	30	cents per 100 lbs.
(c) Clerical	30	30	30	cents per shipment.
	80	85	90	cents per 100 lbs. for a 50-mile haul.

According to this formula, for each additional haul of 50 miles the first class rate per hundred pounds would advance by 20 cents in zone A, 25 cents in zone B, and 30 cents in zone C. This would produce the following rates in cents per hundred pounds:

TABLE 10

	Zone A	Zone B	Zone C
100 miles	100	110	120
150 miles	120	135	150
1000 miles	460	560	660

Because of steadily rising costs of operation in the period immediately following World War I, these charges were increased in 1921 by 35 per cent.[6]

Traffic within a particular zone is carried at the appropriate rate for that zone but traffic between one zone and another is charged under the higher scale. Specifically, express between zone A and zone B is carried at zone B rates. Express interchanged between zone C and zones A and B is charged in accordance with the zone C scale of rates.

The Board's judgment of 1919 also introduced into Canada the block system of rates already in vogue in the United States.[7] Those parts of Canada which are served by railways are divided into approximately 800 "main blocks." A main block is half a degree of longitude and of latitude each way. The length of each block from north to south is constant, approximately $34\frac{1}{2}$ miles. Its width is roughly 23 miles along the 49th Parallel but narrows a little along the parallels of latitude north of the 49th and broadens along parallels farther south, because of the sphericity of the earth and the meeting of the meridians at the poles. Each block embraces some 794 square miles.

The main blocks are numbered in series beginning at Windsor, Ont. (3102). Continuing along the 42nd Parallel, the blocks of the tier are numbered consecutively to the east as far as they lie in Canada (3105). The second tier lies along Parallel 42½ and begins with number 3302, directly north of 3102, and so forth. The numbers along the 49th Parallel start at Alberni, B.C. (5819), and continue to Cochrane, Ont., which is the most easterly railway station on the mainland of Canada on this parallel. In order to provide reasonable rates for short distances, each main block is divided into 4 sub-blocks by lines intersecting at right angles in the centre and bisecting the sides. The sub-blocks are lettered from west to east, A and B being in the upper half of the block with C and D in the lower.

All express points in Canada are listed in alphabetical order by provinces in a *Joint Directory of Express Stations*. The name of each station is followed by the number of its block and the letter of its sub-block. This forms the key to the tariff. The rates from one block to another are based on weight, mileage, and zone in the manner previously described. On long hauls, mileage is computed by taking the actual distance along the shortest railway route from the most important shipping point in one main block to the chief centre of each of the other main blocks. All shipping points within a block take the same rate, which is that of the largest or representative point of the block.[8]

For shorter hauls, rates are computed on a slightly different basis in order that they may not be higher than the traffic will bear. Rates are calculated between places within each sub-block. They are compiled from each sub-block to each of the other sub-blocks of the main block in which the place of origin is located and to the sub-blocks in each of the three adjacent main blocks in all directions. In other words, each main block is at the centre of 49 main blocks. It is like the centre square on a board for chess or checkers that lacks one row along its top and another row along one of its sides. In computing mileages for these short hauls, the line of railway between the point of origin and the place or sub-block of destination is followed. Each sub-block is counted as 15 miles north and south and 12½ miles east and west. For movements between sub-blocks, rates are computed from representative points as is the case with longer movements.

When an agent or shipper wishes to know a rate he finds the number of the main block (and the letter of the sub-block if necessary) of the place of destination from the *Joint Directory*. Then he consults the Express Tariff of the originating point. The tariff gives the rate from the block of origin to all other blocks, and from the sub-block of origin to all other sub-blocks in the three main blocks in all directions, and between places in the same sub-block. Knowing the number of the block, and the letter of the sub-block if required, the agent or shipper may easily read the proper rate from the tariff. He need not make any calculations of mileage, transportation charges, clerical costs, or zone. All these details have been worked out for him in the head office of the express company and supplied to every express office in Canada in convenient form.

The block system in the United States differs from that in effect in Canada in only one important particular. American blocks are bounded by degrees of latitude and longitude rather than by one-half degrees as in Canada. Each American block is roughly 69½ miles from north to south and varies in width from about 45 miles at the Canadian border to 62 miles in the extreme south. The blocks are numbered consecutively along the parallels, the number of each block being 100 higher than the block immediately to the south. In Canada the numbers rise by 200 from south to north along any given meridian because when blocks are only half a degree wide, there might be more than 100 within Canada from west to east along any one parallel. Each American block, being roughly four times the area of a Canadian block, is divided into 16 sub-blocks, lettered A to Q (omitting J).

Generally speaking, the rates on first class express between Canada and the United States are the total of the local rates to and from the international boundary. This is not invariably true because United States rates sometimes depart from the strict letter of the block system. The Railway Express Agency publishes a *Directory of Express Stations in the United States and Canada*. This lists stations in alphabetical order by states and provinces with the appropriate block number. Each railway provides every express agency along its line with a tariff covering international movements.

Express Classification

Unlike railways, express companies have a relatively simple classification. Everything is put in what is called merchandise, first, or ordinary class except (a) the Money Classification, (b) higher than first, and (c) second class. The articles carried under first class are not listed at all but in practice they include ready-to-wear garments, motion picture films, jewelry, sera, live animals such as domestic pets, baby chicks, poultry and bees, ice-cream, cut flowers, newspapers,[9] neon signs, and machine parts.

The Money Classification takes in bullion, coins, paper currency, bonds, share certificates, negotiable instruments, and other documents. This class differs from the others in two respects. First, articles carried under it are not picked up or delivered by the express company, although if any shipment is too large or too bulky to be handled by the shipper, an express vehicle will call. In that event, the express company will not be responsible for loss until after the valuables have been delivered to its premises. Second, the rate is calculated on value, not on weight as is true of other freight and express. Thus, charges for express under the Money Classification are related to the carrier's liability for loss and to the cost of protection which he has to assume. Often, the weight of the valuables is trivial compared with the weight of the safes in which they have to be carried in transit and stored pending the departure or after the arrival of the train.

Goods which are charged rates which are a certain percentage higher than first class include millinery,[10] vehicles, boats, etc., which by reason of their bulk, fragility, or value require extra space, demand more than ordinary care, or entail more than ordinary risk.

Then the Classification lists articles taking second class rates, viz., bread, butter, cheese, clams, cream, eggs, fish, fresh fruit, honey, lard, maple syrup, meat, milk, oysters, dressed poultry, shrimps, seed, soda biscuits, vegetables, and yeast. In general, the second class rating is restricted to perishable, edible products of farm and fisheries.[11] Second class tolls were originally about 70 per cent of the corresponding first class toll.

The second-class rates originated in the desire of the companies for a better balance of traffic. In the early days the preponderance of express was dry goods, groceries, clothing, manufactured articles, parts of machinery, and innumerable small articles. These goods moved outward from the cities to small towns. Naturally the companies were anxious to get more traffic moving in the reverse direction. They found that the existing first class tolls on farm produce, fish, fruit, etc., were higher than the traffic could afford to pay and still move in volume. Therefore, express companies began to publish lower rates on comparatively low valued goods, the products of farm and sea.

In 1919 the companies were refused leave to eliminate second class rates on less than carload lots.[12] They claimed these rates were insufficient to cover costs of handling. The Board stated that granting the application would disturb trade practices of many years' standing. It was manifestly in the public interest that these second class rates should be continued because they applied to staples required in large quantities by consumers.

The companies also wanted substantial increases in second class rates on carload express. The Board refused this request; higher rates would "vastly augment" the prices of fish, fruit and cream besides giving the applicants more money than they currently needed.[13] But in 1921 it advanced the second class express rates in carloads by 20 per cent,[14] about half what the companies were currently asking for and one-fifth or less of the increase they had requested in 1919. The general level of express rates has not been raised since 1921. Indeed, many tolls (except minimum charges) have been reduced in the face of competition.

Since these decisions, the companies have been allowed to cut down some of their expenses for second class express. On less than carload lots they give free cartage service only at destination and not at point of origin. On carload lots they perform no cartage service at all. The majority of shippers and dealers using carload express service have sidings adjoining their warehouses or can easily truck from team tracks. In 1951 the Board allowed substantial increases in express rates on fish because of higher railway costs.[15]

In addition to first and second class rates, express companies have a package tariff. Many express parcels weigh only a few pounds and the minimum charge[16] for ordinary express is higher than some traffic will bear, especially for short distances. On such small parcels it is not worth while to put the agent to the trouble of consulting the *Joint Directory* and the Tariff. In particular, the parcel post service of the Post Office competes with express for package business. The Post Office blankets its rates by provinces and the express companies must do the same. On parcels weighing up to 25 pounds, both agencies quote special rates for one pound or less, over one pound but not over two, etc. These rates are published for parcels shipped within the same province, from one province to the next adjoining one on either side, and to the second, to the third, and to the fourth province and beyond. For the purpose of these regulations Nova Scotia, New Brunswick, and Prince Edward Island are treated as a single province. Rates in the package tariff are adjusted from time to time in order to keep them in line with charges of the post office and truckers.

The package tariff contains some discriminatory features because it is on a provincial basis. Toronto merchants may express small packages to Cornwall, Ont. (266 miles), at a lower charge than can merchants in Montreal who are only 68 miles distant from Cornwall. Under this tariff it is cheaper to ship a package from Cornwall to Kenora, both in Ontario (1,275 miles) than from Cornwall to Montreal, Que. (68 miles). Similar situations arise at all points which are near the boundaries of the zone. These discriminations in express tolls can be justified, or excused, only on the ground of competition with a government agency.

Competitive Rates

In order to avail themselves of the low rates published in the small-package tariff, shippers used to split their larger orders into units which did not exceed the minimum weight limit of the small-package tariff. This practice saved shippers money but was a source of irritation both to them and to the express companies. Consequently the M.S. tariff provided for a piece charge.

Express companies also published so-called "long-distance rates" up to 100 pounds for long hauls. These rates apply to shipments over 25 pounds but not to goods rated higher than first class in the Express Classification. In order to meet the competition of freight forwarders, the "long-distance tariff" sets a maximum of $10 per hundred pounds for transcontinental hauls (except on the money classification).

In addition to the above rates, express companies have numerous low rates to meet competition from highway carriers. For several reasons trucks have great operating advantages on short hauls, with small shipments of relatively valuable goods, and where speed of delivery is important. Yet this is the very field where express finds its greatest usefulness. Beginning in 1931, railways lowered express rates but did not adopt a uniform plan across the country because competition varied in intensity from one area to another. By the late 1950s, however, the operating costs of many truckers had risen well above the level of rates quoted by the express companies in 1921. Accordingly, the latter rescinded many competitive rates and thereby reinstated rates applicable under the block system. Even so, in 1963 there were still special rates out of Toronto to 120 points for shipments of over 300 pounds. In the West there were truck competitive rates at 85, 70, and 55 per cent of first class. Express companies also have Basing Tariff rates, sometimes called the 5 series. These apply to places that are off the beaten track. The express companies carry the goods to a rail terminus and then forward them by air, water, or highway to final destination.

To sum up, in 1919 the Board introduced the block system to put express rates on a logical basis. For many years the companies had to depart from it because of competition. In the early 1950s they were able partly to return to it but at a level of tolls that was below their costs. Even at that, there are still many exceptions to the formal plan of 1919. In 1963 the Express Traffic Association, which comprises the five companies operating in Canada, had 68 tariffs, Canadian National Express had 122, and Canadian Pacific Express 204. Express companies also had a few agreed charges.

Delivery Limits

Express companies pick up and deliver first class express and deliver second class at about 1,150 places in Canada without extra charge. No free service is given in rural areas, in small villages and hamlets, or in thinly settled suburban areas near large cities. The question of free delivery limits has been a fertile field for complaint. In 1911 the Chief Commissioner proposed[17] that an extra charge be made for cartage service. This would correct the discrimination which obviously existed because shippers and consignees located where there was no such service were being charged the same rates as others who could make use of free service at origin, destination, or both. Nothing came of the suggestion and the unsatisfactory conditions persisted. Citizens of newly settled suburban areas outside Toronto who were without express delivery and collection were particularly bitter.[18] They petitioned the Prime Minister not to reappoint two members of the Commission until the alleged discrimination was removed. The free delivery limits did not follow municipal boundaries, nor were they arranged according to mileage from a central office, or density of population, or indeed any recognizable principle. They were set only to satisfy the exigencies of the moment.

In 1919 the Board laid down definite rules to govern free delivery which still apply.[19] The corporate area of every city and town was mapped into four parts by lines intersecting at right angles at a centrally located point. Then "blocks" one-quarter of a mile square were drawn in all directions from the central point. These blocks as defined by the Board had no necessary relationship with city block of normal size. Free service is provided whenever the four adjoining blocks each contain at least 100 families in cities and towns of 5,000 and over, and 50 in towns from 1,000 to 5,000 persons. In villages of 1,000 or less, cartage is at the discretion of the company. Industrial plants are reckoned as one family for each five regularly employed persons.

From the four primary blocks, successive blocks of the same size are drawn. Each of these blocks is entitled to free cartage if it conforms to the same rule regarding the number of families as the main block. Four or more contiguous blocks which conform to the family rule but are separated from a free cartage area by not more than one-quarter of a mile also get free collection and delivery. Industrial and business establishments in non-cartage blocks are to get free cartage if they are not more than one-quarter of a mile from the nearest cartage block. The area intervening between the establishment concerned and the nearest block with free cartage under the preceding rules must also be served. In all instances the boundaries of the free cartage areas were to be defined by thoroughfares or topographical features nearest or most convenient to the farthest lines produced by these rules.

The promulgation of these regulations reduced the ill feeling in communities which did not have all the cartage service to which they felt they were entitled.[20] But the rules did not remove the discrimination between places with and places without free cartage service. To correct this condition, the Board ordered a reduction of 15 cents per hundred pounds where only one cartage service was performed and 30 cents where none was rendered either at origin or destination. The companies found that this order reduced their revenues but did not benefit complainants. Distributors such as mail order houses quoted uniform prices to purchasers and paid the transportation charges themselves. These distributors kept their prices at the same level whether or not the goods were shipped to centres without free delivery service. So consumers in villages and on farms did not get any advantage. Consequently the Board soon abolished the arrangement. Apparently the Board does not consider that the discrimination which remains is unjust and unreasonable.

A merchant wanted to send fish to Montreal at carload rates, retag the boxes in Montreal, and then have the express company deliver them in relatively small lots to his customers. In this way he would save himself delivery and warehousing expenses. In dismissing the application the Board said that if it were to allow this arrangement for fish, it would have to permit it for other products. Soon the premises of railway companies would be merely clearing houses for readdressing express. As a result the costs of conducting the express business would greatly increase.[21]

Unjust Discrimination

Complaints of unjust discrimination have sometimes arisen in connection with express. For example, fruit growers in the Niagara district of Ontario could load a car with a minimum of 20,000 pounds, forward it to the Maritimes at carload express rates, open the car at any number of junction points, remove a few crates, and let the car proceed until the entire load had been removed. At one time they had the same arrangement on fruit into Manitoba but it had been withdrawn by the express companies. British Columbia orchardists could open cars only twice *en route* to destination and had to pay $5 each time. Nova Scotia growers had none of these privileges. They complained of unjust discrimination especially as Ontario fruit was being distributed in the Maritimes on better terms than locally grown products.

Niagara farmers stated they had built up a profitable business on the existing basis. They feared that removal of the privilege would prevent them from meeting American competition in the Maritimes. They were quite willing to have the same arrangement extended to Nova Scotia fruit being sold in Ontario. The carload express rate was only a little above the first class freight rate. Any modification of shipping regulations would raise the prices of fruit to consumers. If the rules applicable to shipments from British Columbia were extended to Eastern Canadian fruit, the price of an eleven quart basket of peaches would go up by 10 cents. In the end the Board ordered the British Columbia scheme applied to all of Canada.[22]

Future of Merchandise Service

Since about 1930 railway express companies have been facing increasing difficulties. Their traffic is peculiarly exposed to competition from trucks which handle small shipments with economy and dispatch. The Post Office accepts larger parcels than formerly and has low rates. Since the Post Office will not collect parcels from homes and places of business, the sender must take his parcel to a main or subsidiary post office. The Post Office delivers in cities, in some large towns, and along rural mail routes. Often its free delivery limits are wider than those of express companies though in small towns they are usually not as good. It insures parcels without extra fee up to a value of $50 but the sender must ask for a receipt. For values of $50 and over, the sender must pay an extra fee and automatically gets a receipt. Express companies have about the same charges as the Post Office and allow payment on delivery instead of only in advance. They give a receipt (bill of lading) on all shipments. They insure against damage as well as loss. Express companies will carry bulky articles whereas the Post Office will not accept single articles weighing over 25 pounds or in excess of certain lengths and girth. As it is often possible to split one lot of goods into two or more parcels so that each will come within the restrictions of weight and size, postal and express services compete for a large volume business. Although the government has to pay railways for transporting parcel post and other mail matter in postal cars, railways would much prefer to have parcels go through their own express companies or departments.

Besides, the Post Office is using more and more trucks instead of trains.

Air express is beginning to cut into railway express business. This is particularly true of valuable articles such as currency and negotiable paper, perishable or style goods, motion picture and television films, and advertising formats. Shipments of air freight, as distinct from air express, may be delayed until space is available in an aircraft, and shippers and consignees must deliver and collect the goods at the air terminal. But since rates on air freight are less than on air express, goods of lower value now go by air. This trend will be accelerated as airlines cut their rates on both kinds of air cargo.

On account of all this competition, express companies have had to cut their rates until in many cases they are as low or lower than the corresponding charge on railway freight. They have vigorously attacked their operating costs by remodelling terminals, installing endless belts, using fork-lift trucks, and generally reducing the amount of physical labour while speeding up operations. They use hampers in which at place of origin or at transfer point they place parcels for various destinations or even for various consignees. Hampers cut down the amount of rehandling and reduce the chance of mislaying small parcels in transit. Express companies plan the routes of their trucks within cities to eliminate cross-hauling and waste mileage in the pick-up and delivery of parcels. On account of the withdrawal of passenger trains, they served over 300 routes by truck alone in 1962. They are also important users of piggyback, either because no passenger trains run at convenient times over the route in question or because express can be despatched by piggyback train a couple of hours ahead of the regular passenger train and, arriving at destination sooner, can be sorted for prompt delivery. Any express which arrives after the departure of the piggyback from the station at the point of origin or which is picked up or destined for stations en route can be handled in the passenger train.

At one time the two major railways in Canada considered amalgamation of their express services into one organization following the pattern of the Railway Express Agency in the United States. In this way they would cut out much admittedly wasteful competition without perhaps sacrificing quality of service. Such a move might have aroused strong public opposition. Merchandise Service, if successful, will result in profits to the railways and better service to the public without endangering the goodwill enjoyed by the carriers.

The work done by Merchandise Service or Express is essential because modern business demands prompt collection and speedy delivery of small lots of goods. In the course of a year Canadian National Express alone handles about 20 million shipments.

14

Service

BECAUSE a railway derives its income from selling transportation, it is
to its own advantage to provide its patrons with good service. Prompt
spotting of empty cars, punctual pick-up of loaded cars, their speedy
delivery at a convenient point on a team track or on the siding of the
consignee, equipment that is clean, weatherproof, and otherwise satisfactory for the article to be carried, fair and immediate adjustment of
loss and damage claims, reasonable but firm handling of demurrage
charges, courteous employees—these are but some of the requirements
of good service. Normally a regulatory commission can rely on the self
interest of carriers and on competition from other railways and agencies
of transportation to ensure that proper service is given railway users.
Occasionally the Board has had to intervene.

Adding and Cancelling Passenger Trains

Nowadays there is little possibility that railways will add to the
number of their passenger trains. In 1952, however, an application
was made for the restoration of two trains on the former Esquimalt and
Nanaimo Railway because the population of Vancouver Island had
grown and trains were safer and more comfortable than buses.[1] In
1958 Premier Frost of Ontario told the MacPherson Commission that
the railways should add to their passenger services.

In some cases of cancellation of trains, complainants have alleged
that the railway concerned could recover its traffic if it rearranged its
schedules, put on better equipment, and generally improved service.
The Board's position is that it is not legally empowered "to require
railways to enter into costly experiments for the sole purpose of developing new business."[2] The decision of whether or not to meet competition

is one for railway management, not for the regulatory authority. Specifically, the Board has refused to order a railway to replace a losing passenger train with a rail diesel car. They cost upwards of $250,000 each and have proved economic only when operated between large cities 150 to 250 miles apart.

Up to 1967 the whole matter of passenger-train abandonment hinged on two sets of factors: on the one hand the savings to the railway from reducing or cancelling the service, on the other the inconvenience to the public arising from the withdrawal. The Board judged inconvenience by considering the economic resources and population of the area being served, the location and quality of nearby roads, the likelihood that highways would become snowbound in winter or impassable when the frost came out of the ground in the spring, the frequency of service by bus, how express and mail were to be handled, and whether train crews could be employed elsewhere. Invariably opponents of abandonment stress the great economic future of the area served by the train and the disasters which, they say, will inevitably follow its cancellation. Counsel for Quebec and Fredericton have argued that good passenger-train service is necessary to maintain the dignity of a provincial capital at an appropriate level. But when all is said and done, the important thing is the trend of patronage, for it provides a realistic measure of how many people would be seriously put out by the proposed cancellation.

The savings to the railway from the cancellation were judged from an analysis of past records and future prospects. Revenues from the carriage of passengers were specially compiled and the average number of passengers handled per trip or per month was worked out for the past two or three years. The data or trend line was then projected into the future or, more often, an estimate was made of the average number of passengers needed to make the service break even financially. Revenue from mail and express was also computed and the possibility of the railway retaining part of it by running its own trucks between the communities served by the train was taken into account. Off-line revenue and off-line expenses were excluded, largely because of the great difficulty of equitably allocating them between the service that might be abandoned and the rest of the system.

Some operating costs, such as wages of crew, cost of fuel, the expenses of maintaining, cleaning, and depreciating locomotives and cars, could be directly ascertained for the train in question. Other operating expenses such as superintendence, despatching, yard switching, road maintenance, and engine-house expenses are incurred in common for a number of trains or locomotives. These were allocated on some logical basis, often by means of regression analysis as explained toward the end of the chapter on "Rates on Particular Commodities." In this connection the Board ruled that while the cost of maintaining road does vary with use, it may take some years after a cancellation of a train before all the prospective savings are actually secured. Hence, the Board allowed the specific savings which in its view would directly follow the discontinuance of the train and struck out that part of the savings which, though revealed by regression analysis, could be effected only over a longer period of time.

A railway is also entitled to a reasonable return on its investment in equipment and other physical facilities used in providing the passenger service along the line. Railways asked for a return of 11.4 per cent before income taxes which allowed the company 6½ per cent after taxes. Following the lead of the MacPherson Commission (vol. I, p. 63), the Board allowed no more on the investment used for a particular service than what railways can earn on rail investment generally under the Board's formula set forth in the chapter on the General Rate Level. In the early 1960s this gave the cost of money at about 5 per cent after corporate income tax.

In short, the Board came up with what it considered to be a fair estimate of existing losses and a forecast of what the future held. Some opponents of cancellation of passenger service have argued that losses on passenger trains along a given line should be considered in the light of the total traffic on the line. In other words losses on passengers should be set off against profits on freight traffic. The Board felt, however, that it should not compel a railway to continue to run passenger trains at a deficit when they are not reasonably needed by the public. It should not require shippers of freight to subsidize an uneconomic passenger service that is no longer patronized:

In isolated applications, the annual loss to a railway company or the net betterment it might anticipate may not be impressive to those most affected. However, the cumulative effect of such deficits, where incurred throughout the country, can be a heavy burden to a railway company. Where such cost has to be borne by other patrons it results in an additional cost to other passengers and to shippers of express and freight.[3]

Although in most cases the Board permitted cancellation of unprofitable passenger trains after it had heard all the evidence, it has not invariably reached this conclusion. On occasion it has ordered a railway to run passenger trains even at a loss to itself or run them in winter when the nearby highways were secondary ones and buses could not give proper service in cold weather.[4]

Over the years the Board has tended to be more generous in allowing cancellation of trains. Doubtless it has been influenced by (a) improvement in the quality of roads, removal of snow and treatment of ice, more dependable motor vehicles, and the like; (b) the rapidly mounting costs of operating passenger trains after 1945 coupled with the steady decline in patronage; and (c) the replacement on the Board of elderly gentlemen who were brought up in the days when Canada's growth seemed to hinge entirely on the rate of expansion of our railway network by another group that realized we are living in the age of the internal combustion engine.

The growth of bus services has not been significant in accounting for the cancellation of passenger trains. Since 1950 most intercity bus companies have made a little money but have not greatly enlarged their volume of business nor added to the frequency of their services. Even so, the Board is careful to see that, when cancellation of a train is up for consideration, buses are available to accommodate those who do not own automobiles.

The Royal Commission of 1961 made several recommendations about unprofitable passenger service. The only one which is relevant at this point is that "to facilitate the reduction of passenger deficits . . . the pertinent statutes [should] be amended to enable the railways, upon application to the Board of Transport Commissioners, to remove any uneconomic passenger service except where the Board is satisfied that no reasonable alternative public highway exists."[5]

This proposal suggests that the Royal Commission believed that in the past the cancellation of unprofitable trains had been held up by the Board's practice of weighing public inconvenience against railway operating losses. A study of the decisions of the Board gives little support for this view. At all events, the Commission's proposal merely substituted one indefinite concept for another. Instead of having to weigh losses against public inconvenience, the Board would have to decide what constitutes a "reasonable alternative public highway."

Of course, it can be argued, and with some force, that the process of cutting down the number of passenger trains to the point where the service meets its operating expenses from its own revenues has not proceeded as rapidly as it should have. But the fault seems to lie more with public attitudes and with the railways than with the law or the Board. The carriers were reluctant to annoy the public and perhaps drive even more business to their competitors by simultaneously applying for higher freight rates and for permission to cancel passenger trains. When it became impracticable to get any higher tolls, the railways turned belatedly to the reduction of their costs by scaling down the amount of their passenger service. Moreover, the losses on the service rose to such a height that railways could no longer tolerate them on the ground of maintaining good public relations. Nor could they push them off onto users of freight inasmuch as higher freight rates would drive still more business to trucks. The speed-up in the cancellation of passenger trains in the early 1960s suggests that it was the railways, not the Board nor the provisions of the law, that stood in the way of rationalization.

However that may be, the National Transportation Act directed the Commission to ascertain the actual loss of any passenger-train service which a railway applied to abandon. Under Section 314 I (1) (a) " 'actual loss' means, in relation to a passenger-train service, (i) the excess, if any, of the costs incurred by the company in carrying passengers by the passenger-train service over (ii) the revenues of the company attributable to the carrying of passengers by the . . . service." In ascertaining these costs, the Commission is to have regard to Section 67 (13) of the National Transportation Act which was quoted in connection with compensatory rates and rates for captive shippers in chapter 6.

When a railway applies to discontinue a passenger train, it must concurrently submit to the Commission a statement of costs and revenues in each of such number of consecutive financial years as the Commission may prescribe. Then the Commission shall cause such public notice of the application to be given in the area served by the passenger train in question as it deems desirable. It will review the statistics and other relevant data and determine the actual loss, if any, in each of the prescribed accounting years. If necessary, it will hold hearings to enable all persons who wish to do so to present their views. Having regard to all matters which appear to it to be relevant, the Commission will determine whether the service is uneconomic and should be discontinued, or whether it should be continued because the company has incurred no actual loss in the operation of the train in the last year of the prescribed accounting period.

Under Section 314 I (6),

in determining whether an uneconomic passenger-train service or parts thereof should be discontinued, the Commission shall consider all matters that in its opinion are relevant to the public interest including, without limiting the generality of the foregoing, (a) the actual losses that are incurred in the operation of the passenger-train service; (b) the alternative transportation services, including any highway or highway system serving the principal points served by the passenger-train service, that are available or are likely to be available in the area served by the service; (c) the probable effect on other passenger-train service or other passenger carriers of the discontinuance of the service, or parts thereof; and (*d*) the probable future passenger tranportation needs of the area served by the service.

If the Commission decides that the service should be discontinued, it will fix a date for abandonment which shall be not earlier than thirty days from the date of the order or later than one year from its date. If it decides that the service should not be discontinued, it shall reconsider the application at intervals not exceeding five years from the date of the original application or the last consideration of it.

The National Transportation Act then provides for the payment of subsidies for the continued operation of passenger trains which are needed in the public interest.

314 J. (1) In this section, (*a*) "claim period" means, in relation to any uneconomic passenger-train service, the period (*i*) beginning ninety days after the date the application to discontinue the service has been filed with the Commission . . . and (*ii*) ending on the date fixed by the Commission, or as varied pursuant to section 53 [which provides that the Governor-in-Council may at any time vary or rescind any order of the Board and the Commission], for the discontinuance of the service or part thereof; (*b*) "fiscal period" means . . . [that of the federal government, namely, April 1 to March 31]; and (*c*) "uneconomic service" means a passenger-train service that has been determined to be uneconomic by the Commission.

A railway operating an uneconomic service within the claim period may file a claim with the Commission for the amount of any actual loss attributable to the service. Under Section 314 J. (4), "the Commission shall examine the claim and shall certify the amount of the actual loss, if any, that in its opinion was attributable to the service and the Minister of Finance, on the recommendation of the Commission, may, in respect of the loss, pay out of the Consolidated Revenue Fund an amount not exceeding eighty per cent of the loss as certified by the Commission." In order to cover the possibility that claims may not be filed and cleared within the particular fiscal year in which losses have been incurred, the Commission may take the necessary adjustments on account of underpayment or overpayment from one year to the next.

Section 314 J. (8) states that subsidies under the National Transportation Act "do not apply in respect of a passenger-train service accommodating principally persons who commute between points on the railway of the company providing the service." Nevertheless, under the following subsection "the Commission shall after an investigation certify the actual loss, if any, that in its opinion is attributable to the [commuter] service and report thereon to the Governor in Council for such action as he deems necessary or desirable to provide assistance in respect of such loss."

The intent of the legislation is obvious: it is to speed up the abandonment of uneconomic passenger trains while protecting residents in communities not served by highways from being left without passenger service. The danger in the legislation is equally obvious. The Commission, and especially the Cabinet, may be overly generous in continuing passenger trains with the result that subsidies will reach an alarming and unjustified total. The fact that 20 per cent of the actual loss is to be borne by a railway ought to insure that it tries both to minimize the losses on services which the Commission rules to be in the public interest and to make application as quickly as feasible for the abandonment of non-paying trains.

Train Schedules

Although the Railway Act required carriers to get the Board's permission for cancellation of all passenger trains along any line, it made no provision for an appeal to the regulatory authority for a mere reduction in service or a rearrangement of schedules. The legislation of 1967 did not correct this omission, presumably because of the steady decline in passenger-train services.

Despite the lack of legislative directives, the Board of Transport (or Railway) Commissioners sometimes used its good offices to protect the public interest. In one case a railway cancelled a late afternoon train and substituted a morning one in order to cut out overtime and reduce costs. When some patrons complained, the Board supported the railway by pointing out that while discontinuance of the evening train would inconvenience some patrons, a morning train would benefit others.[6] In another instance it advised a carrier to rearrange its schedules to eliminate some expenses.[7]

At times the Board has had to adjudicate between the interests of patrons along various parts of a particular line. Residents of Maniwaki protested because in order to catch the daily train for Ottawa, 82 miles to the south, they had to leave their local station at 5 AM. The train left at this early hour so that it could pick up summer cottagers and others near the southern end of the line and take them to Ottawa in time for work. On the return trip the train did not leave Ottawa until after the closing of government offices which employed most of the regular passengers from points to the south. The evening train arrived in Maniwaki so late that mail could not be distributed and attended to the same day. The agricultural and lumbering communities to the north were especially inconvenienced during the summer for Ottawa was on daylight saving time and they remained on standard. Citizens of Maniwaki asserted that in both summer and winter the line was supported mainly by the patronage of the northern sections. In warm weather the number of passengers boarding the train near the southern end was much larger than the number of through passengers but they travelled only short distances and paid low total fares. Although the Board said that the people at the northern end deserved a lot of consideration, it made no change in the schedule because it was necessary to conserve rolling stock, labour, and fuel during the war.[8]

Passengers for Fort Frances, Port Arthur, and Duluth wanted the evening train from Winnipeg to leave as late as possible for it was a short overnight trip to their homes. Travellers to towns between Winnipeg and the international boundary near Sprague wanted an earlier departure. They did not like arriving at their local stations late at night and driving over poor roads to their farms. The Board set a compromise hour for leaving Winnipeg. It suggested that the railway put on a diesel-electric train between Winnipeg and Sprague. This train could give a more convenient schedule for local patrons and speed up the long-distance train which was competitive with services by other routes.[9]

Aside from the legal principles involved, these cases show how difficult it is for a railway to schedule its trains to satisfy its patrons. In addition, it must take account of the availability of crews and rolling stock, possible congestion at large terminals, and interference with the operation of freight trains.

Train Stops

The Board has also had to rule on applications for additional stops by existing trains. In these cases it take numerous factors into account. Travellers between important terminals are delayed and annoyed by frequent stopping and starting. The cost to the railway of making the stops must be balanced against the probable revenue they will derive from so doing. Grades at some stations are less favourable for starting trains than at others. The Board also considers the distance to nearby stations on the same line and on adjacent lines, the quality of bus service and of the highways in the vicinity, and generally the inconvenience to local residents through failure of through trains to stop. In one instance the Board had to take into account whether stopping at one point would cause congestion elsewhere.[10]

Though the Board has never said so in so many words, it seems to rely on the railway company to show good sense in deciding when stops should be made.[11] After all, the company and not the Board loses money if the service is not satisfactory and it profits when it pleases its patrons. In order to guarantee that a railway does not neglect the interests of the public, actual and potential travellers have the right to appeal to the independent regulatory commission. The right of appeal and the publicity given to the hearings and findings of the Board permit the railway effectively to present its side of the case and show the public the difficulties that confront it.

Stations

Towns and cities are sometimes dissatisfied with the location or physical condition of their stations. One station was located on the edge of a swamp and near a sawmill which had been closed and was not likely to be reopened because adjacent timber limits had been exhausted. Relocation of the building would not be costly. So the Board ordered its removal to a more satisfactory site.[12]

The two railways serving the twin towns of Noranda and Rouyn in northern Quebec had stations 1.2 miles apart. They proposed to close one of them, use the other for passengers and express, and build a new joint freight shed in Noranda close to the Rouyn boundary. They would save money; through passengers would not be inconvenienced by having to transfer from one station to the other; and less than carload lots could be handled more expeditiously. But the plan gave rise to some inequality of treatment since some shippers and travellers would have to go farther to the local station than formerly. The Board approved the plan, for it favoured the avoiding of duplication wherever it could be achieved without undue hardship on the public.[13] The Board refused to order the closing of one station and the opening of another because, although some shippers would gain, many more would suffer and they were already gravely inconvenienced by the abandonment of the line on which they were located.[14]

The town of La Tuque asked the Board to order the Canadian National to construct a new station more in keeping with the town's size, needs, and importance as a producer of railway revenue. It claimed that the existing station, which had been in use for nearly twenty years, was inadequate and unsanitary. The Commission decided that it was without jurisdiction to require the railway to put up a new building. But it could and did try to ensure that the accommodation in the existing station was adequate.[15]

In dealing with the stations the Board assumes no managerial functions over railways subject to it. Railways exercise the initial discretion regarding location, size, design, etc. The Board intervenes only when there has been unreasonable exercise of this descretion,[16] unjust discrimination,[17] an agreement or bad faith on the part of the company.[18] Where the distance between stations is not unreasonable, the Board will not order that additional stations be established at intermediate points. In Western Canada it is good practice to have stations six to eight miles apart.[19] The Commission refused to order a station relocated so that various shippers would have relatively equal access to it by highway.[20] It also denied applications to build stations within two or three miles of another one, or where the grade is steep and close to a long bridge.[21] In one case, the total revenue of a station being small and the saving to the railway of placing it on a new site considerable, the Board granted an application to relocate notwithstanding the objections of local residents.[22]

Up to 1951, whenever the gross revenue from all sources—passenger, freight, and express—and from both incoming and outgoing traffic at a particular station fell below $15,000 per annum, the Board's practice was to permit a railway to remove its agent entirely or substitute a caretaker. When this practice was laid down in 1910, few telephone, bus, and trucking services had been established. By reason of increases in freight rates over the intervening forty years, it took less than half the volume of business to provide the revenue originally stipulated. Moreover wages and other costs of operation had multiplied three times. Hence the Board decided in 1951 that each agency case should be dealt with on its merits having regard to earnings, distance from the nearest agency station, roads, motor services, and the operating requirements of the carrier.[23] After 1965 questions of abandonment of stations were often dealt with as part of the Master Agency plan described in chapter 18.

A non-agency or flag station is not nearly so convenient for the public as an ordinary one. The caretaker keeps the building clean and warm. He assists the train crew in placing express and baggage in an unlocked room or shelter. But he is not competent to give accurate information on fares, schedules, or connections. Passengers cannot buy tickets in advance of boarding trains. Freight and express being sent from a non-agency station must be forwarded collect. On the other hand, incoming goods which are not prepaid are sent through to the nearest agency station and consignees must sometimes drive long distances to pick them up. Goods left at the flag station by carrier or shipper may be stolen or damaged by vandals or natural causes. Demurrage may accumulate because shippers and consignees cannot be notified promptly of the arrival of loaded or empty cars.

Despite all the disadvantages of flag stations to the public, railways cannot be expected to provide facilities if shippers, consignees, and travellers do not use them. Nevertheless the Board has sometimes dismissed applications to put a station on a non-agency basis. In one case it was the only one on a branch line 33 miles long and shippers, consignees, and passengers would have to telephone or travel 70 miles to an agency station.[24] Of two nearby stations, both with gross revenues below the minimum of an agency, the Board allowed the closing of the one which would cause the least inconvenience to the public.[25] Although two stations under consideration were only 4.9 miles apart, a railway was not allowed to close one of them when the gross revenue of both was well above the minimum.[26] Yet it could discontinue two of three flag stops which were all within a distance of 3.2 miles[27] and reduce one station to caretaker status in a village which was served by two lines of the same railway company.[28]

Years ago many municipalities subsidized construction of railway lines on condition that the company erect and always maintain a passenger and freight station within the corporate limits. On account of declining revenue, railways have closed some of these stations entirely or reduced them to non-agency status. Then municipalities have sued the railway for breach of contract or asked the Board for an injunction prohibiting the railway from breaking its contract. Courts have held that the inconvenience to certain individuals is too slight to allow for assessment of damages. In fact the alleged injury might well have arisen had an agent been in charge.[29]

The courts have also ruled that "any public detriment resulting from the [railways] . . . default is suffered by those of the public who desire to make use of the portion of the line in question and not by the municipal corporation."[30] Because few individuals are likely to have the financial resources to fight a case through the courts or before the Board, this ruling is often an effective practical bar to action. In general, courts consider it improper for them to deal with cases involving stations which have been dealt with directly by the Board.[31] The Board was asked to order an electric railway subject to its jurisdiction to re-establish and continue service in accordance with an agreement. The Board refused because the order requested was neither reasonable nor expedient.[32] On appeal, the Ontario Supreme Court said it had no power to grant the order.[33]

On the face of it, these rulings seem to leave municipalities without legal recourse to enforce agreements made when the railways were

being built. Yet operating a modern railway would be nearly impossible
if every one of the contracts made two or three generations ago had to
be rigidly adhered to. Though the Board is not legally bound by such
agreements, it will not lightly set them aside. It takes care to see that no
legitimate interest will suffer.

Freight Service

Cases before the Board about freight service has been less frequent
than those about passenger service and stations. In 1916 the Canadian
Northern was unable to supply box cars to get out the grain crop along
its Goose Lake branch in Saskatchewan[34] and later in the same year
it was short of cars to move coal from Drumheller.[35] In both cases the
Board ordered other railways to provide the necessary equipment.
Throughout World War II and in peacetime when farmers could not
get box cars to move their grain or bad congestion developed at
Lakehead, a Transport Controller, appointed by the federal government, was given authority to direct railways to use their equipment as
he ordered.

In 1917, when railways in eastern Canada were congested, the
Board ordered them to rearrange passenger schedules in order to
release men and equipment for freight. On the Board's orders, a railway has had to supply oil tank cars,[36] provide cross-pieces for hanging
meat within a refrigerator car,[37] and furnish box cars to carry ore
instead of open dump cars.[38] On the other hand, the Board has refused
to order carriers to provide heater cars,[39] or special equipment as an
experiment,[40] or box cars instead of open ones for coal,[41] or doors for
box cars carrying sand and gravel similar to doors for grain,[42] or foreign cars of larger sizes instead of those of the originating carrier,[43] or
express cars for continuing a service which was unremunerative.[44]

Over the course of the years railway freight cars have increased in
size until cars with capacities of 30 tons have almost ceased to exist.
Accordingly railways had to supply shippers who ordered 30-ton cars
with 40-ton cars and those who wanted 40-ton cars with ones of 50-ton
capacity. This arrangement was useful to many farmers and small
elevators in the West who often had more than enough wheat for a
30-ton but not enough for a 40-ton car. They needed to pay only for
the actual weight of the grain shipped and not for the minimum carload
weight of the larger car. In 1940 the carriers withdrew this plan because
the smaller cars were simply not available and they were experiencing
a "dead weight loss" because some cars were loaded far below their
physical carrying capacity and even below their minimum carload

weight. The Board held that since conditions had materially changed from those existing at the time the privilege was granted, the carriers might withdraw it.[45]

The Board's part in providing passengers and shippers with suitable services is supplementary to the legal duties and social responsibilities of railway companies. It tacitly assumes that carriers are sufficiently interested in their own profits to see that their patrons are properly looked after. It is clearly unwilling to intervene except when there is undue preference or unjust discrimination, or when the public needs to be protected against an abuse of power by railways.

Abandonment of Lines

By far the largest number of cases involving service relate to abandonment of lines. Prior to 1933, the Board's powers over facilities applied only to railways actually in operation: "unless the special act of incorporation provided that a railway shall be continuously operated, the Board had no jurisdiction to compel a railway which had discontinued the operation of its railway owing to a deficit to resume such operation, even though the public interest was seriously affected by reason of its discontinuance."[46]

For all practical purposes Canada had no legislation covering abandonments until 1933. In that year the Railway Act was amended by a straightforward statement. A railway "Company may abandon the operation of any line of railway, with the approval of the Board, and no company shall abandon . . . without such approval."[47] It can be seen that the Act "lays down no principle upon which the Board should act in granting or withholding approval in such applications."[48] As the Board was left to work out its own rules, it decided that "the mere fact that a branch line of railway has ceased to show a profit from operation does not, in every case, justify its abandonment. The issue is clearly, however, whether the loss and inconvenience to the public consequent upon the abandonment outweigh the burden that continued operation of the railway line would impose upon the railway company.[49] This principle is almost identical with that adopted by the Interstate Commerce Commission.[50]

During the years 1933-66, that is, between the passing of the first legislation on abandonments and the new policy introduced as a result of the recommendations of the MacPherson Commission, the Board considered several dozen applications for abandonment. As the more important of these cases up to 1958 were summarized in the author's *Economics of Canadian Transportation*, details will not be repeated.

Nor will any attempt be made to abridge more recent cases because the new legislation lays down another set of rules.

Abandonments authorized under the legislation of 1933 fall into six broad classes. First, some were almost *pro forma*, e.g. where the road-bed was overgrown, or where the line had had no trains for five years, or had been built to aid in the construction of a hydro-electric power plant and was not needed once the plant was finished, or where no one appeared in opposition to the application.[51]

The second group of cases was more controversial.[52] In these instances the railways presented data on operating losses, the past and prospective volume of traffic over the line, the amount of capital needed to rehabilitate it, the population and resources of the area served, the condition of nearby roads, the distance from farms and hamlets to stations on adjacent railway lines that would remain in operation, and so forth. Opponents of the abandonment sometimes disputed the data on cost supplied by the railway but in general they stressed the increase in the cost of transporting their goods caused by the cancellation of rail service, the great potentialities of the district, the loss in property values which would follow abandonment, the inadequacy of road transport especially in winter, and so on. At times they said they would have patronized the railway more if the quality of its service had been higher. To this argument the railway always made the obvious answer that it was already giving more service than was justified by the revenues it received. Extra trains would only add to its losses.

In the third group of cases the Board allowed abandonment on certain conditions. In one instance the province got the old right-of-way for a highway. In another case it postponed the date of abandonment so that a lumberman could get out his equipment. Similarly, it withheld an order for abandonment because a province waived the taxes payable by a railway which ran through a provincial park.[53]

Yet the Board's power to order a conditional abandonment was restricted. It had no legal right to order a railway to compensate parties for loss in property values resulting from abandonment nor has it any jurisdiction over the disposal of real estate.[54] Normally when a railway abandons a line, it salvages all the material it can and then transfers the land to abutting landowners for a nominal sum. Some farmers will not take the land, even as a virtual gift, because they will have to maintain fences along it. They have also complained that after abandonment the ditches along the line are not kept open and their land is flooded. If the railway is not able to give the land away, it may let it revert to the municipality for non-payment of taxes.

The Board's power to order an abandonment is not conditioned or

circumscribed by contracts between railways and municipal governments. Years ago many municipalities gave subsidies to railway companies on condition that they build a line or establish a station and keep
it open in perpetuity. The Board is not bound by these contracts since,
unlike the Crow's Nest Pass agreement, they are not "Special Acts"
within the meaning of the Railway Act. Nevertheless, the Board takes
what the lawyers call "judicial note" of municipal agreements.[55]

The fourth group of abandonment cases, roughly twenty of them,
comprise those where the Board has refused permission. This figure is
approximate because in a few instances it reversed itself when the
railway reapplied. The evidence presented in this group of cases was
substantially the same as in those cases where the Board permitted
abandonment on first application. But they can, perhaps, be distinguished by the degree of inconvenience which the public would suffer
through abandonment. Parallel roads were poorer, the communities
would be isolated from hospitals, the reduction in traffic was general
throughout Canada and not peculiar to this one branch, the chief traffic
was sugar beets which were of such low value in relation to bulk that
they could not bear the higher transportation charge occasioned by a
circuitous rail route or a long haul by truck, farmers would be put to
great expense because they would have to move their export grain long
distances by truck, and so on. In one case, strange as it may seem, the
Board refused abandonment because the line was needed to bring in
crushed stone to build roads which upon completion would further
deplete rail revenue.[56]

A fifth group of cases came under the Canadian National–Canadian
Pacific Act of 1933 which admonished both major railways to co-operate
with each other in a number of ways, including the abandonment of
unprofitable and duplicating track. In the main these cases have not
raised any unique problems for the Board. In one instance, however,
it refused its permission because neither of the lines in question was
failing to earn its out-of-pocket expenses and the effect of abandonment
of one line would merely allow the other to make more money at the
inconvenience of shippers.[57]

The final set of abandonment cases—branches in Canada of railroads owned by United States companies—was sometimes awkward
for the Board to deal with. If the Canadian segment can be dealt with
by itself, no particular difficulty arises. But once the Interstate
Commerce Commission permits abandonment of the section south of
the international boundary, the position of the Canadian Board is not
easy. It does not relish being a rubber stamp for the regulatory authority
in a foreign country; yet it might prove impracticable for the American

company to operate a dismembered limb in Canada. In general, the Board takes note of what the Interstate Commerce Commission has done but has not hesitated to refuse abandonment of the Canadian portion if, in its opinion, abandonment would leave a substantial population in a promising part of Canada without any rail service whatever.[58]

Abandonment and Royal Commissions

The problem of unprofitable branch lines has come before three Royal Commissions. The first, that of 1951, left things as they were, saying that "there is always some danger of shortsighted economies. Lines which it was once thought prudent to abandon have since been justified by increases in the volume of traffic; and the growth of population has made some measure of co-operation [between the two major railway systems] unnecessary. In such questions no judgment can be infallible and the best decision is probably that reached by experienced railway officials."[59]

In 1957 the Gordon Commission criticized railways for not abandoning more of their unprofitable mileage and for not pushing ahead with pooling arrangements under the Canadian National–Canadian Pacific Act of 1933.[60] They had abandoned only 114 miles in 1955 and after fifteen years' experience with pooling they were saving only about $1 million a year. This was far below the savings that had been anticipated. The Canadian National alone had roughly 5,000 miles which failed to contribute anything to overhead costs and another 6,000 were considered marginal. Therefore, virtually all of its overhead costs were recovered from the remaining 45 per cent of its mileage. The Canadian Pacific had approximately the same proportions of non-paying lines in its 17,000 miles.

The Royal Commission of 1961 also examined the problem. It concluded that the maintenance of track on about 8,000 miles of light density line or roughly one-fifth of all mileage in Canada resulted in a loss of approximately $13 million in 1958. On the face of it, this was a small amount compared with the deficiencies on export grain in the West ($22 million) and on the passenger service ($62 million at least). But the Commission must have found it hard to separate losses on branch lines as such from losses on grain, for there were some "solely related lines," those which handled grain exclusively or almost so. Moreover, the Commission seems to have considered only maintenance of track without anything for maintenance of stations, freight-houses, and rolling stock, for real estate taxes, or for interest and depreciation on fixed assets and rolling stock. Some of these items may properly be excluded for one reason or another but, as the Commission admitted, density of traffic (net or gross ton-miles per mile of line per annum) is not a theoretically sound method of distinguishing between profitable and unprofitable lines. A low density line may make money because it traverses fairly level terrain or carries valuable traffic which pays a good rate per ton-mile. Conversely, a line with a fairly high traffic density may prove unprofitable if the prevailing level of rates on the traffic it carries is low, if heavy snows and serious flooding are common, or if the traffic is bunched during a few weeks of the year. Later on, the MacPherson Commission used branch and main lines as a basis for judging profitability. This is also fallacious for some main lines, such as the former Newfoundland Railway, certainly do not pay.

The Commission was on more solid ground when it ascertained that lines which carried little tonnage in 1931 were for the most part carrying little in 1954. They had failed to show any improvement in earning power in nearly twenty-five years. From this the Commission concluded that in the future the transport needs of the areas served by most of these lines could be met by trucks, integrated where necessary with nearby rail lines.

Although the Royal Commission of 1961 was convinced of the need to rationalize rail plant, it felt that "an abruptly implemented pro-gramme of rail line abandonment will cause dislocations which would not be in the interests of the community as a whole. . . . In the interests of change with a minimum of dislocation, the continuation of rail services on uneconomic branch lines should be supported [i.e., subsi-dized] over a period of time sufficient to enable the adjustments to be made both by investment in rail and investment tied to rail move-ment,"[61] such as grain elevators. The Commission recommended that losses up to a maximum of $13 million a year on branch lines should be met from a fund to be administered by the Board of Transport Commissioners. The money would come from the federal government and the Board would assign priorities in a large-scale abandonment programme. As rationalization proceeded, fewer and fewer uneconomic branch lines would remain and the necessity for the public to bear the losses would diminish. The Commission estimated that this transitional period might take fifteen years. In its second volume the Commission elaborated its ideas on the administration of the Branch Line Fund and discussed the basis of aid to owners of grain elevators located on branch lines which are to be abandoned.

The section of the MacPherson Report dealing with abandonment aroused much apprehension on the Prairies, even though the chairman, another commissioner, and the secretary were all Westerners. At the request of the Diefenbaker Government, the Board and the railways deferred consideration of abandonment cases during 1962 and 1963, which were election years. Then the Pearson Government asked for an additional delay so that it could deal with the MacPherson recommendations.

Meanwhile, officials of the Board, the railways, the grain trade, and the governments of Manitoba, Saskatchewan, and Alberta had met to draw up a comprehensive plan of abandonments. In 1966 the federal government forbade the Board of Transport Commissioners to consider applications for the abandonment of 17,000 miles of line in Western Canada at any time during the next eight years. In short, it "froze" certain lines which it specified, until after 1974. This left 1,839 miles "unprotected," that is, liable to be abandoned at any time within the next few years if the railway concerned could prove its case before the newly-created Canadian Transport Commission.

The National Transportation Act laid down roughly the same principles for the abandonment or continued operation of uneconomic branch line as those already set forth for uneconomic passenger trains. "Actual loss" is the difference in any financial year between costs incurred by a railway in the operation of a branch line and its revenues from the movement of traffic originating and terminating on the line. Under Section 317 A (b), branch line "means a line of railway in Canada of a railway company that is subject to the jurisdiction of Parliament that, relative to a main line within the company's railway system in Canada of which it forms a part, is a subsidiary, secondary, local or feeder line of railway, and includes a part of any such subsidiary, secondary, local or feeder line of railway."

A railway wishing to abandon a branch must submit a statement of costs and revenues of the branch in each of such number of consecutive financial years as the Commission may prescribe. After examining these statements and other relevant documents, the Commission "shall prepare a report setting out the amounts, if any, that in its opinion constitute the actual loss of the branch in each of the prescribed accounting years, and . . . [it] shall cause such public notice of the principal conclusions of the report to be given in the area served by the branch line as . . . [it] deems reasonable." (sec. 314 D (4)).

If the Commission finds that no loss has been incurred, it will reject the application for abandonment but without prejudice to any subsequent application. On the other hand if it finds that the branch "has incurred actual loss, in one or more of the prescribed accounting years including the last year thereof, the Commission shall, after such hearings, if any, as are required in its opinion to enable all persons who wish to do so to present their views on the abandonment . . . and having regard to all matters that to it appear relevant, determine whether the branch line is uneconomic and is likely to remain so and whether the line should be abandoned." (sec. 314 C (1)).

Section 314 C (2) provides that

in carrying out the provisions of this section, the Commission (*a*) may consider together as a group, on dates fixed therefor by the Commission, all applications for abandonment of branch lines that are situated in the same area or adjoining areas as determined by the Commission; (*b*) may require any company that operates one or more branch lines in an area . . . [in which a line covered by the application is located] furnish to the Commission . . . [data on each of such branch lines for a prescribed number of years] and all such figures, with the exception of those pertaining to branch lines for which applications for abandonment . . . have been filed . . . shall be treated . . . as confidential; (*c*) may require any company . . . to specify the order in which it desires the Commission to consider such applications. . . .

In determining whether an uneconomic branch line or segment thereof should be abandoned, the Commission shall consider all matters that in its opinion are relevant to the public interest including, without limiting the generality of the foregoing, (*a*) the actual losses that are incurred in the operation of the branch line; (*b*) the alternative transportation facilities available or likely to be available to the area served by the branch line; (*c*) the period of time reasonably required for the purpose of adjusting any facilities, wholly or in part dependent on the services provided by the branch line, with the least disruption to the economy of the area served by the line; (*d*) the probable effect on other lines or other carriers of the abandonment of the operation of the branch line . . . [or any segment of it] at different dates; (*e*) the economic effects of the abandonment of the operation of the branch line on the communities and areas served by the branch line; (*f*) the feasibility of maintaining the branch line or any segment thereof as an operating line by changes in the method of operation or by interconnection with other lines of the company; (*g*) the feasibility of maintaining the branch . . . either jointly with or as part of the system of another railway by the sale or lease of the line . . . or by the exchange of operating or running rights between companies or otherwise, including, where necessary, the construction of connecting lines with the lines of other companies, and (*h*) the existing or potential resources of the area served by the branch line, seasonal restrictions on other forms of transportation therein, and the probable future transportation needs of the area.

The Commission may order abandonment not earlier than thirty days or later than five years from the date of its Order. If it rejects an application for abandonment, it shall reconsider the question at intervals not exceeding five years. It may of its own motion or upon application of any person extend the order fixing the date of abandonment for upwards of five years from the date in the original order, if it is satisfied that the public interest requires such an extension. It may also rescind any Order for abandonment either upon application by the railway or upon its own motion with the concurrence of the railway.

Under Section 314 D, the Commission is empowered to order the rationalization of plant with a view to reducing operating losses on branch lines. It may adjust subsidies to meet losses brought about through rationalization. If the existing law proves inadequate to meet a particular situation arising out of rationalization, the Commission may recommend that the Cabinet take action. It may also make recommendations "in respect of any action causing or likely to cause increased expenditures by municipal or provincial authorities or increased costs of production or sudden losses to holders of rail-tied investment." It will forward these recommendations to "the appropriate authorities or to interested parties for such action as any or all of them may be prepared to take singly or collectively."

Section 314 E provides for the payment of subsidies for the operation of uneconomic branch lines in the same manner as for uneconomic passenger-train services. But the subsidies for branches are to be for the entire actual loss incurred by the railway and not for only 80 per cent. Section 314 F allows railways to transfer applications for abandonment under the Railway Act to applications under the National Transportation Act without prejudice.

Section 314 G may eventually constitute a primary limitation on the policy of rationalization. It gives the Governor-in-Council (the Cabinet) wide powers to prohibit abandonment. Notwithstanding anything in the sections that have been quoted above, "the Governor in Council may, from time to time, by order, (a) designate branch lines that shall not be abandoned within such periods as the Governor in Council may prescribe; and (b) designate areas" to be treated in the same manner. Operating losses on branches covered by this section are to be borne by the federal treasury in the same way as losses on lines dealt with by order of the Commission.

A Typical Abandonment Case

To illustrate the sort of problems which arise in abandonment cases, let us take the request made by the Canadian Pacific in 1962 to abandon 17 miles of track between Kirkella and McAuley.[62] This line runs north and south through flat or rolling country just east of Moosomin, Sask., but a few miles within Manitoba. The termini are served by lines running east and west, and the only intermediate town is Manson. Its population had declined from 85 in 1931 to 41 thirty years later. Though without a station or agent, it had a school, two churches, community hall, curling rink, general store, garage, coal shed, and two elevators. It had only one train a week, a northbound freight, for the network of lines made it practicable to send the locomotive over a circuitous route without any back-tracking.

The primary problem related to grain. On the average the area served by this line annually raised about 85,000 bushels or 38½ cars of wheat and coarse grain. Residents thought that the volume would soon grow to 100,000 because some acreage which had been badly flooded a few years earlier was coming back into production. If the elevators at Manson were closed, farmers would have to haul their grain an average of 5½ miles farther than before. A farmer who already owned a truck capable of carrying 150 bushels or 4½ tons testified that the extra haul would have no effect on his fixed costs such as licence, depreciation, and insurance. The increased cost of tires, tubes, and maintenance was indeterminate but very small. His fuel costs would be roughly 1/16 cent per bushel per mile or 2.5 cents per ton-mile. He did not include anything for his own wages.

Another witness said that most farmers had only half-ton trucks which they could safely load with 50 bushels or 1½ tons of wheat. A farmer who did not own a truck would have to spend $2,000 to get one or engage a for-hire carrier about ¾ cent per bushel per mile or 25 cents per ton-mile.

However, the elevators at Manson could be kept open for storage after the railway had gone. In that event farmers need not be put to any extra expense to haul their grain to town but presumably the elevator company would reduce the price it paid farmers living near Manson by the cost it would have to meet in hauling grain to the nearest railhead. The elevator company could use a 500-bushel semi-trailer dump truck at a cost of ¼ cent per bushel-mile or 8.7 cents per ton-mile. The average amount which a railway gets for hauling export grain under the Crow's Nest Pass agreement, not including subsidy, is ½ cent per ton-mile.

Taking one thing with another, the Board estimated that delivering grain to railhead would cost the community an additional $2,000 to $3,000 annually after the branch was abandoned. Besides, it would have to pay something more for bringing in its coal and seed grain. All other produce and supplies already moved over the highway.

The elevators at Manson were built in 1911 and by 1962 had been largely paid for and fully depreciated. But they were still serviceable and would cost $1.20 per bushel of capacity or about $50,000 to replace. They were owned by farmers' co-operatives which over the course of thirty-three years had annually paid out an average of $2,400 in dividends to members. These would be lost unless the elevators were rebuilt at railhead, that is, at Kirkella or McAuley, which was unlikely. The existing elevators at railhead might, to be sure, become congested because of the volume formerly handled at Manson but in general it was believed they could handle all the grain, especially if they were remodelled, which might be needed regardless of any abandonment.

For its part the Canadian Pacific presented evidence on the gross revenue for traffic originating or terminating on the subdivision over the past four years. Another of its exhibits showed train expenses such as fuel, wages for crew, and maintenance of equipment, as well as maintenance and depreciation of road property, taxes, supervision, and general expenses. There were also some off-line costs, notably carload billing, yard switching, and other expenses which were allocated by car-miles, car-days, or gross ton-miles. The net salvage value of assets which could be recovered from the abandoned line was about $115,200 or a little over $6,800 a mile. This material could be used elsewhere and, with interest at 5 per cent, would save the company $5,760 annually. Finally, the Railway showed that if the subdivision remained in operation for another fifteen years, it would have to spend $249,000 for the replacement or renewal of rail, track ties, switch ties, and one bridge.

The Board concluded that the estimated annual loss to the Railway ($27,100 or over $1,600 a mile) was a continuing one. Almost all the livestock and less than carload and express traffic had been lost to trucks and the line had no future except in the carriage of grain and coal. Although the Board admitted that residents would suffer some inconvenience from abandonment, it had to take everything into account. In the end it granted the application.

In a broad sense the above case, which is typical of many others, and the MacPherson Commission's plans for rationalizing plant are part of a process that has been going on for years. Economic and social conditions are in a constant state of flux. For example, many grain elevators have to be replaced even though the railway network remains as it is. They are often fifty or even sixty years old and are too small for efficient operation now that wage rates have risen so much. It is cheaper to handle grain by horizontal endless belts, called flat handling, in relatively low buildings than to erect "sentinels of the plains", equip them with upright endless belts with buckets, operate the elevating system when necessary, provide storage bins in the high structure, and finally spout the grain by gravity into railway cars.

In addition, farms have been growing larger over the years, especially since the early 1940s. Farm labour is hard to get, besides being expensive. Modern machinery enables one man to cultivate more land, seed more acres, and harvest and thresh more grain than ever before. Farm families demand higher standards of living. Because agricultural prices have been rising far less than the cost of farm machinery, clothing, consumers' durables, taxes and the cost of living generally, the only way a farmer can improve his net earnings is to produce more goods at lower costs per unit of output. Thousands of workers have left the farm labour force while others (suitcase farmers) have moved to towns, travelling back and forth between home and work. Though not every farmer has a truck, almost all have cars which they periodically use for shopping in nearby towns. As a result of these and other factors, innumerable hamlets and villages throughout the West and in other parts of Canada have been falling behind in population and the volume of their trade. Places like Manson which are without rail service may be somewhat harder hit than towns which still have trains, but all suffer from essentially the same forces. To make matters worse for railways, these towns and nearby farmers tend to bring in their merchandise by truck.

What is more, the impact of abandonment will not be spread evenly throughout the West. A few towns and most cities will benefit since the volume of their trade will grow. On the other hand, removing the rails will be a death blow to smaller trading centres, already hit hard by rural depopulation. Some farmers, those who continue to be served by the same railways as before, will not be affected one way or another while others who are left several miles from a trackside elevator will find that their operating costs have risen and the value of their farms has shrunk. In one case the Board found that farmers' cost would go up by from $52 to $136 per annum. This may seem a small amount to a city dweller on a good salary but it means a lot to a farmer who is caught up in the "squeeze" between rising costs of living and of operating his farm on the one hand and relatively unsatisfactory prices for the goods he sells on the other. The squeeze is all the more alarming in Western Canada where yields per acre, grade of product, the price of wheat in the world market, and the possibility of selling all or most of one year's crop before the next one is harvested are all subject to unpredictable fluctuations. On the other hand the cost of unprofitable lines is a heavy burden on the railways. According to President Gordon of the Canadian National, many branch lines are 60 or 70 miles long and handle about 1,000 cars of grain during the course of a year and nothing else. Under these conditions it costs the railway twice as much to get the grain to a main line as it would cost to truck it.

The impact of abandonment on municipalities and what are called line elevators is as uneven as it is on farmers. Some local governments will lose tax revenues because the railway withdraws some of its property and either abandons the rest or sells it for non-railway and presumably less valuable purposes. The assessed value of farms, stores, and the like will also decline. At the same time municipalities may be under pressure to improve their roads in order to provide better, cheaper access to a railway which, so to speak, has run away from them. Those towns which grow as a result of abandonment will have to provide municipal services for more people than formerly. Somewhere between 520 and 850 elevators out of a total of about 5,100 will have either to be abandoned or rebuilt elsewhere. Co-operatives owning elevators, commonly known as the Pool or U.G.G. (United Grain Growers), will be hurt more than privately-owned concerns such as McCabe and Richardson because over the years the co-operatives have tended to build in the smaller places. The existence of this disparity in financial loss raises difficult political questions.

Of course, it may be that the possibility of lifting about 5,000 miles of track in the West is more frightening in prospect than it will be in reality. After all, the adjustments to new patterns of agriculture and trade has been going on for decades. Rationalization of railway plant will be spread over at least fifteen years and the blow will be softened by subsidies from the federal government. In any event, the same sort of adjustment will have to take place, though probably with less severity, in all parts of Canada.

Summary

The Board of Transport Commissioners or the new Canadian Transport Commission can normally assume that railways will provide good service to their patrons because it is in their own financial interest to do so. Nevertheless, shippers have often invoked the powers of the Commission and are likely to do so more often in future because of the proposed rationalization of plant. Appeals to the Board give everyone a chance to air their views, prove that there are at least two sides to every question, protect railways against unfair criticism, and serve as a useful check against any tendency for railway officials to look primarily at railway net revenues in disregard of public welfare. At the same time the public must realize that it cannot expect railway companies to operate branches which consistently lose large amounts of money. Neither can it expect the national exchequer indefinitely to foot the bill for non-paying lines. The fact is that transportation has been going through a technical revolution and railway plant must be rationalized to take account of this fact.

15

Railway Labour

FOR a number of reasons labour is an important subject in railway transportation. In the early 1960s total payroll constituted about 55 per cent of the operating expenses of all railways in Canada.[1] An additional but undeterminable amount is paid indirectly to other labour through the purchase of supplies. From time to time shippers, the government, and the public at large become fearful of a railway strike. Wage costs determine in considerable measure to what extent railways are able to compete with other transportation agencies. Finally, railway unions are a very important part of organized labour in Canada.[2]

For many years railway labour was almost in a class by itself. It was strongly organized, commonly received a rate of pay that was the envy of workers in other industries, and enjoyed fringe benefits such as pensions and passes for free travel. Locomotive engineers and firemen, along with conductors and trainmen, were sometimes called the aristocrats of trade unionists. Moreover, with the exception of bridge and building gangs, track workers, and crews on new construction, railwaymen had a large measure of job security.

Over the course of time, other unionists have come to share these advantages. Often they have surpassed railway workers in total annual pay per man, rate of promotion, and the like. Yet working on a railway is still unique in a few respects such as geographical dispersion of the work force, the relatively high proportion of males, and frequent contact with the federal government and its agencies.

In addition, railway employees are more exposed to technological unemployment than workers in many other industries. Although stenographers, machinists, and pipefitters can readily transfer their occupational skills to non-railway jobs, locomotive engineers, conductors, train despatchers, signal maintainers, and telegraph operators using Morse code ("Brass-pounders") find they cannot take jobs in other industries without sacrificing substantially all the technical ability and experience they have acquired. The problem is aggravated because (a) the total volume of railway freight did not expand during the 1950s and early 1960s as rapidly as the volume by other modes of transport, (b) the amount of passenger traffic has declined both absolutely and relatively to the amount of travel by private passenger automobile and airplane, (c) unprofitable branch lines and non-paying passenger trains are being abandoned, (d) stations with low annual gross revenues are being closed under the Master Agency plan, and (e) diesel locomotives, hump yards, power-driven equipment for the maintenance of track, and other technological advances make it possible for each employee to do more work per hour. The number of employees on Canadian railways declined by roughly 20 per cent between 1952 and 1959. This trend continued into the 1960s.

Unionization

The twenty labour unions[3] to which Canadian railways workers belong may be divided on the basis of skill such as the engineers, carpenters, trackmen, and so forth, or on the grounds of their affiliation with other groups. The running trades—locomotive engineers, firemen, conductors, and trainmen—have three separate organizations but they act in unison on all important questions. Although men are not debarred from employment because they are not union members, in practice everyone in these trades does belong to the union.

Generally, the running trades, or so-called operating unions, negotiate with railways independently of other unions.[4] They claim that, more than other railway workers, they are concerned with regulations of the Board of Transport Commissioners relating to standards of visual acuity, colour perception and hearing,[5] periodic inspection of watches,[6] improved headlights,[7] running boards on locomotives,[8] railway crossings and drawbridges,[9] accidents on railways,[10] displacement of men through co-operation,[11] the transportation of explosives and other dangerous articles,[12] and operating orders.[13]

All railway unions except those in the running trades are collectively called non-ops, or more properly, non-operating unions. In some disputes they have acted together, though at times the Canadian Brotherhood of Railway, Transport and General Workers has put in a separate claim. The non-ops include craftsmen such as carmen, carpenters, machinists, electricians, plumbers, and pipefitters, all of whom repair locomotives, coaches, and freight cars. Most railway shopmen belong to the same unions as the corresponding craftsmen in industry generally. As a result "except in centres where the largest shops are located, the railway members are scattered and outnumbered in the locals to which they belong. For that reason their interests are largely subordinated to those of the majority craftsmen elsewhere employed, notably in the building industry."[14] On the other hand, the machinists' and the boilermakers' unions have relied on railway shopmen for their solid core of membership, especially in depressions. In good times they draw on workers in shipbuilding, aircraft construction, and the metal trades as a whole. The only exclusively railway union in the shops is the Brotherhood of Railway Carmen consisting of carpenters, cabinet workers, painters, upholsterers and welders engaged in repairing and building cars for freight and passengers.

Since 1908 the various shop unions have co-operated in negotiating with the companies. Most of the shop unions are drawn together in a number of system and regional federations and in Division No. 4 of the Railway Employees Department of the American Federation of Labor. Through this division, which has its headquarters in Montreal, the shopmen have been able to iron out the inequalities which formerly existed between different parts of the country for the same work. They have also dealt with jurisdictional disputes between different crafts.

The Brotherhood of Maintenance of Way Employees draws its membership chiefly from sectionmen, though it also includes fluctuating numbers of temporary workers engaged in building and repairing bridges and buildings. Until 1953 it had trouble unionizing the large numbers of seasonal workers, the "extra gangs" who relay steel, reballast the roadbed, and construct new lines. Nevertheless, it has been instrumental in improving the wages and working conditions of scattered track workers.

Both the Brotherhood of Railway and Steamship Clerks, Freight-Handlers, Express and Station Employees, and the Canadian Brotherhood of Railway, Transport and General Workers, the former Canadian Brotherhood of Railway Employees, appeal to clerks, freight handlers, wipers, cranemen, and sleeping- and dining-car porters. The Brotherhood of Railway and Steamship Clerks is international, being affiliated with a corresponding body in the United States. Most of its members are employed by Canadian Pacific.

The proliferation of unions has complicated the process of collective bargaining for both union leaders and company management. To be sure, the non-ops often present a common front in negotiations and so do the running trades. Moreover, non-op leaders iron out disputes between the various unions within their control. This proved especially worthwhile when the seniority rights of four unions concerned primarily with the handling of express and less than carload freight had to be integrated upon the introduction of the Merchandise Service. On the other hand, non-op leaders have not been able to eliminate several anomalous provisions which have crept into most agreements with railways. The leaders tacitly assume that the wages of one craft bear roughly the same relationship to those of another as prevailed a few decades ago when collective bargaining became effective on railways. They further assume that, with a few exceptions, there are no regional differences in going rates of wages in the non-railway field anywhere in Canada, nor in the cost of living in, say, Topsails, Nfld., Halifax, Montreal, Toronto, and Tisdale, Sask. The fact of the matter is that the relationship between wage rates of machinists, electricians, etc., in non-railway employment varies from time to time. For example, after 1945 in most parts of Canada plumbers (except those employed by railways) were able to raise their rate of wages relatively more than carpenters. Moreover, the general level of wages rose faster in Ontario than in Nova Scotia. But union-railway agreements generally provide for uniform scales across Canada and are based on historical relationships between trades. Hence, if railway agreements are compared with those covering other lines of work, they are a bit of a hodgepodge, or so it seems to the outsider.

A further complication has arisen because (*a*) both major Canadian railways are members of the Association of American Railroads since they operate branch lines in the United States, and (*b*) most of Canada's railway workers are members of international unions, international in this connection meaning Canada and the United States. In some respects this interconnection is a source of strength to Canadian unions. They can draw on American experience in bargaining and, in the event of a long strike, upon financial resources supplied in large measure by American members of the union. Furthermore, the international unions have been active in trying to bring wage rates in Canada up to the same level as those in the United States. In this way they improve the standard of living of such Canadian workers who enjoy continuous employment. On the other hand if higher Canadian wage rates are achieved without the same rough equality of productivity per man-hour as prevails in the States, the cost of living in Canada will rise, we will be less capable of meeting outside competition in world markets and even in our own, and in the long run the number of jobs open to Canadians will decline.

It has also been alleged that at times American railroads and unions have fought their battles in Canada in order to "soften up" their opposition in the United States and simultaneously put more heart into their own members. Specifically, in 1956 the Association of American Railroads planned to take a strong stand against the unions over the issue of firemen on diesel locomotives. Then some of its members got cold feet with the result that the Canadian Pacific was left to carry the ball alone. In the end, it had to face a strike and suffer a considerable loss in revenue. But it also achieved, thanks partly to a Royal Commission and mainly to the common sense of union leaders in Canada, a settlement which proved acceptable to the men and in the long run economical to the Railway. The Canadian National and its employees soon agreed to the same proposal. The strike and its upsetting effects on industry and agriculture could have been avoided, so it has been argued[15] if American railroads had been more determined in their stand or if Canadian unions had not been put under pressure by the heads of the international unions south of the border.

Sometimes, the problem is expressed in broad terms. Unions in the United States are more opposed to any changes in work rules than their Canadian affiliates. As a result they insist on the continuance of obsolete regulations governing the assignment of work, what constitutes a day's work for purposes of pay, and so on. The effect of these attitudes is to prevent railways moving with the times, reduce their power to meet competition from truckers and inland ships, and compel them to employ more people than they would need if they had greater freedom of action in modifying the conditions under which employees carried on their jobs.

However that may be, it is indisputable that the trans-border membership of both railways and workers tends to embitter trade disputes involving Canadian transport. Someone is bound to say, and many people are bound to think, that we Canadians could handle things much more harmoniously if we had "no truck or trade with the Yankees." The gist of the matter seems to be that Canada and the United States draw substantial benefits from having each other as neighbours and they must be prepared, like all neighbours, to accept some unpleasant consequences of propinquity. Trans-border connections may simultaneously be an incentive and a brake on Canada's economic progress.

Collective Bargaining

Broadly speaking, railway unions are concerned with the same sort of problems as unions generally. They do, however, want special protection against loss of their property values when divisional points and unprofitable branches are abandoned.[16] Besides, the Hanna order[17] forbids employees of the Canadian National on pain of dismissal from being candidates for either the Dominion Parliament or the provincial legislatures. The Railway claims it is lenient in enforcing this order.

Collective bargaining has long been the rule and is now the law on Canadian railways.[18] From time to time carriers and unions draw up agreements dealing with rates of wages, working rules, and so on. These agreements are for one, two, or three years and then continue indefinitely subject to cancellation on thirty days' notice by either party. After notice has been given, negotiations are conducted between the two groups. Usually the federal government intervenes in railway labour disputes under authority of the Industrial Relations and Disputes Investigation Act.[19] This legislation provides for the appointment of a board of conciliation consisting of one member selected by the unions, one chosen by the railways, and a chairman who is agreed upon by these two members. If they cannot agree, a chairman is appointed by the Minister of Labour. A strike or lockout is forbidden while the board is being appointed, while it is collecting data and hearing testimony, and for thirty days after it has reported to the Minister.

The Act requires that a board of conciliation be appointed but leaves it up to the parties concerned to accept or reject the board's opinion.[20] The theory behind the procedure is that the facts of the case should be determined by an independent body which conducts its proceedings informally and not in strict conformity with legal practice or the technical rules on admissibility of evidence. The board by its own good offices should, if possible, get the parties to agree on a solution. If it does not succeed, the views of unbiased and intelligent men backed by the force of public opinion will be accepted by both parties either as a final solution or as a basis for further direct negotiation.

In the course of time the factors basic to the success of the legislation, namely, a fair-minded board, the need for facts, and a powerful body of public opinion, have been overlooked. Each party appoints as a representative to the board a virtual advocate of its cause, rather than an unprejudiced man from the general public. The board often starts with two members whose minds are made up before they begin to hear testimony. It is one thing for a member to be partial in the sense that he tries to see that no important fact favourable to this side of the case will be overlooked in discussions by board members among themselves. It is quite another thing for a member to feel that he is "letting his side down" if he makes any concessions whatever to the other side.

Often the two members selected by the parties fail to agree on a chairman. They have to appeal to the Minister of Labour, who has ordinarily appointed a judge. On almost every bench one or more judges will be experienced in labour law and perhaps even in collective bargaining. But judges may be inclined to look for guidance too much to past decisions rather than to present needs. They may consider that labour disputes are analogous with lawsuits in which one litigant is clearly wrong and the other certainly right. Instead, in labour disputes generally and in particular according to the theory underlying the Industrial Disputes Investigation Act, compromise and conciliation are more important than the strict interpretation of a code or the rigid application of rather antiquated rules of evidence.

Labour unions say that judges tend unconsciously to favour the roads and to visualize the whole matter as a lawsuit. In his thinking a man cannot escape his professional training. A virtually permanent appointment at a good salary and with ample retiring allowances tends to destroy sympathy with ordinary workmen in their efforts to improve their lot. From these premises unions argue that, although judges are high-minded and honest, they cannot get away from the thought patterns of the social classes to which they belong. Because the board starts with two prejudiced members, minority and majority opinions are inevitable. The task of counsel and of the two members, who are in reality advocates of the men and of the railways, is to win over the chairman. In 1958, union pressure forced the resignation of C. P. McTague, former chief justice of Ontario, as chairman of a conciliation board. He had represented employers on other boards and was currently director of a bus company. Although the government later announced that in future it would try to avoid appointing judges to conciliation boards, it found it impracticable to carry this plan into effect.

One concept behind the Industrial Relations and Disputes Investigation Act was that all the relevant facts should be brought to the attention first of members of the conciliation board and then of the public at large. Unfortunately, it would seem that in recent years railways and unions try to confuse the issues and keep the press in the dark with the object of creating an opinion among the public which is favourable to their point of view. Be that as it may, the interpretation to be put on the data is more largely a matter of basic philosophy, of one's attitude toward capital and labour, than a carefully reasoned analysis of a few facts and a judicial weighing of evidence. Bargaining and especially conciliation ought to be a process by which each party recognizes the partial soundness of the other side's position and modifies its own original and often extravagant claims so that a fair answer from all points of view may be arrived at. In practice, decisions are determined by the relative strength of the parties, by how much power each side can display before the other capitulates. The chairman of one board stated:

There was no collective bargaining in the true sense of that phrase. There was a great deal of very effective argument, thorough and careful marshalling of facts. But the parties remained protagonists and never assumed the role of negotiators. There was an obvious reluctance on both sides to concede any point for the purpose of arriving at a settlement. No middle ground was even discussed before the Board. The Board was treated as a forum and did not succeed in performing its function of conciliation.[21]

Since as a rule the opinions of boards of conciliation are not accepted by both parties, the government has to interfere to avoid interruptions of service and the paralysing effect of a railway strike on the country's prosperity and on national security.[22] Besides, a strike might have political repercussions in the next general election. Further, higher wages may increase the Canadian National deficit which the federal government has to meet. Thus the Dominion government has a direct financial interest in the result of the discussions because it owns the largest railway.[23]

At times the Cabinet has been able to work out a compromise acceptable to both parties but in 1950, 1960, and 1966 compromise proved impossible. Thereupon the government of the day legally forbade the contemplated strikes or their continuance. Beginning in 1960 the government subsidized a roll-back in freight rates, forbade any increase in tolls, and gave the railways grants in lieu of subsidies recommended by the MacPherson Commission. These arrangements may have seriously handicapped the railways in negotiating with the men, for the critical question from the carriers' point of view was not what they could afford to pay out of operating revenue but how far the government would come to their aid.

In the last analysis in all labour disputes on railways the opinion of the board of conciliation appears to be ignored because usually its opinion is rejected by one or both parties and direct negotiations between management and men are resumed, with or without government intervention.[24] Perhaps, however, its influence is felt all along. The delay brought about by the board's deliberations gives a chance for tempers to cool and wiser counsels to prevail but it tends to keep things unsettled for a long time. In a broad sense it is true that the industry settles its own problems, but the board under the Industrial Relations and Disputes Investigation Act is sometimes a useful catalyst.

History of Negotiations

After the price collapse in late 1920, wage rates were cut but as prices of goods fell faster than railway wages, the real incomes of railway workers improved. When the cost of living rose in the latter part of the decade, wage rates were raised.[25] In 1931 they were reduced 10 per cent[26] and in May, 1933, a further 10 per cent.[27] These cuts were partly restored in November, 1933, and in 1935. Then in 1937 a majority of a conciliation board recommended[28] that wages be fully restored but only as the gross revenues of the carriers justified it. As it happened, under this plan the cuts would not have been made up until 1941. When the men threatened to go on strike, the government intervened. Bit by bit wage rates were raised until by April, 1938, they were restored to their 1930 level.

In 1941 the unions agreed with the railways not to strike for the duration of the war. In the same year the government froze prices to the level prevailing in September-October 1941. It also stabilized wage rates throughout all industry but permitted increases if the cost of living rose. In 1944 the National War Labour Board allowed an increase of 6 cents an hour to railway employees. Some industrial workers at jobs of comparable difficulty to those done by railwaymen had got increases between 1938, when the last agreement had been made with the railways, and 1941 when wages were frozen. The decision of the War Labour Board was expected to correct the unfair disparities between railway and non-railway workers.

In 1946, just after the war, the Canadian National and the Ontario Northland gave their employees an increase of 10 cents an hour to offset the rising cost of living. The basic wage structure had already been adjusted to include the total of the cost of living bonuses which railway workers, like other employees had got during the war under the general regulations adopted by the government. The Canadian Pacific pleaded that the cost of the additional 10 cent increase allowed by two publicly owned roads in 1946 would gravely imperil its financial position. Nevertheless, after a short delay the Canadian Pacific and other privately owned lines began to pay the additional 10 cents an hour. These rises precipitated the application for a 30 per cent increase in freight rates (with some exceptions).

Then, effective in 1948, management and men accepted the recommendation of a board of conciliation[29] that employees with one year's service should be six days' vacation with pay; those with three years', nine days; and those with five years or over, twelve days.[30] Also in 1948, the unions asked for an increase of 35 cents an hour because the cost of living had continued to rise. The companies offered 6 cents and a majority of a board of conciliation recommended 11 cents.[31] The men rejected the board's opinion, threatening to strike. The Cabinet intervened and after strenuous negotiations the parties agreed on 17 cents. An election was in the offing and it was said the Government could not afford to offend labour. Also the strike vote was almost unanimous and this immeasurably strengthened the hand of the unions during the final negotiations.

In 1950 the non-ops asked for higher wages and a five-day forty-hour week. The majority opinion of the board of conciliation was accepted by the railways but rejected by the men who voted to strike in August. At the last moment the Cabinet appointed a special conciliator, Dr. W. A. Mackintosh, an economist who was then vice-principal of Queen's University. Unfortunately his efforts came to naught because of the short time remaining before the strike deadline, the uncompromising attitude of the companies and the men, the number and variety of the unions which were attempting to bargain as one unit, and generally the ineffectiveness of collective bargaining in the industry. The strike was ended after nine days by legislation passed at a special session of Parliament.[32] The legislation ordered the men back to work and conceded them the advances in wages (4 cents an hour) already recommended by the board of conciliation. It directed that if the two parties failed to reach agreement within a specified time, the questions at issue were to be settled by an arbitrator selected by the two parties or appointed by the government.

The arbitrator, Mr. Justice R. L. Kellock of the Supreme Court of Canada, awarded the men an increase in wages of 7 cents an hour (including the 4 cents granted by law), made the increase retroactive to the day the strike officially ended, and directed that the forty-hour five-day week begin on June 1, 1951, with the same pay as the men were receiving for forty-eight hours work. The reduction in hours with no change in take-home pay would amount to an increase of 20.38 cents an hour. The railways estimated that the annual cost of the forty-hour week and the wage increase would be over $80 million or one-fifth of their current wage bill. The unions contended that this estimate was purely hypothetical. They said that greater productivity of workers and the ingenuity of the management would overcome all the increases involved.

The arbitrator raised the question whether railways might not on their own initiative have granted some increase in wages without waiting for a complete settlement. The unions had asked for a uniform percentage increase across the board, which would have produced incongruous results. Some railway workers were paid more than men doing the same type of work in other industries, and in some parts of Canada railwaymen enjoyed higher wages than workers generally. Yet on the whole railway employees got less than men in comparable trades in outside industries.

At the time many people feared the strike would permanently destroy the cordial relations previously existing between management and men. This fear proved to be unfounded. On the other hand some businesses which were temporarily forced to use trucks learned the advantages of highway transport. For this reason the MacPherson Commission thought that the strike marked a turning point in the rise of the trucking industry and in the relative decline of railway traffic. This is debatable, but the fact is that at the time of the strike both the country and the railways congratulated themselves on escaping the disasters which had been predicted. Approximately 23,000 non-railway workers were laid off as a result of the strike. Had it lasted another ten days or occurred in winter or during the crop moving season, the consequences to the nation's economy would have been much worse.[33]

In September, 1953, fourteen non-operating unions asked the major railways for greater fringe benefits without changing the rates of pay. They wanted eight statutory holidays with pay a year, double time for work done on legal holidays, longer vacations, and up to eighteen days sick leave (cumulative indefinitely) per annum. The unions estimated the cost at $34 million annually and the railways at $60 million. The latter said they could not get this much added revenue because competition prevented them from raising freight rates and passenger fares. Mr. Justice Kellock, who was chairman of the conciliation board which was set up, and the nominee of the unions disagreed on almost every point, while the third member counselled unions not to press any of their demands at the moment. The board's report was rejected by both the unions and the carriers.[34] Further negotiations broke down, and union members voted to strike on August 11, 1954. Prime Minister St. Laurent announced that he would summon Parliament, forbid the strike, and require arbitration as he had done during the strike of 1950. Rather than be ordered to arbitrate, the parties agreed to do so voluntarily. The arbitrator, Chief Justice Sloan of British Columbia, felt that the statutory and related rates on grain under the Crow's Nest Pass Agreement prevented railways from securing enough income to pay wages and fringe benefits on scales roughly equal to those in other industries. He awarded five statutory holidays, increased the length of vacations with pay, but rejected the application for sick leave.[35]

In February, 1956, unions made further demands, chiefly for an immediate increase of 18 per cent in wage rates, a health plan, three more statutory holidays, and a one-year contract. The railways refused all these requests except the last. The conciliation board under Eric Taylor of Toronto recommended 11 per cent more wages spread over 14 months, one more statutory holiday (Thanksgiving) in 1957 and another (Victoria Day) in 1958, and a two-year contract. In May, 1956, both parties accepted this report.[36]

Earlier in 1956, the Canadian Pacific, Canadian National, and 140 railroads in the United States informed the Brotherhood of Locomotive Firemen and Enginemen that they proposed operating diesel locomotives in freight and yard service without firemen. Later, all the roads except the Canadian Pacific withdrew this notice. The problem resolved itself into the question of safety of operation. Diesel firemen were acknowledged to be necessary in passenger-train service but the Canadian Pacific argued that the presence in the cab of freight trains of a head-end brakeman gave the public all the protection it could reasonably expect. Moreover, the railway would only gradually withdraw diesel firemen from freight and yard service, would re-employ them elsewhere on the railway without loss of pay until jobs as firemen in passenger service or on steam locomotives opened up, and would grant severance pay in the event that the displaced men had to leave the employ of the Canadian Pacific. Railway workers feared technological unemployment but officials of the company felt the men were standing in the way of progress and, by preventing the introduction of operating economies, were keeping railway freight rates at a high level, thus driving business to competitors and in the long run reducing the amount of work for railwaymen. Both parties felt they were "carrying the ball" for all railways and unions in North America. Since no agreement could be arrived at, the firemen went on strike and Canadian Pacific trains did not run between January 2 and 11, 1957.

The strike was ended when the disputants agreed upon the creation of a Royal Commission to report on the problem. The company agreed in advance to be bound by the Commission's decision but the men insisted on being left free to accept or reject it as they saw fit. After a considerable delay, this Commission handed down a report[37] in which it broadly supported the company but suggested retardation of the rate at which firemen were taken off yard and freight diesels. With some reluctance the men accepted this arrangement. The Canadian National continued to keep firemen on all locomotives and to operate during the strike. Later, the union agreed to apply the same policy to it as to the Canadian Pacific. Both roads are gradually withdrawing its firemen in freight and yard service while retaining them on passenger trains.

In February, 1958, unions made new demands for higher wages and better fringe benefits. The conciliation board under Mr. Justice H. F. Thomson of Saskatchewan recommended a total wage increase of 10 cents per hour payable in three stages, the last on April 1, 1959.[38] It would allow two weeks annual vacation with pay after thirty-five years of service in addition to the two weeks allowed by agreement and by the Annual Vacations Act,[39] 1958, which applied to workers for companies which come under federal jurisdiction. The demands of the unions for greater health and welfare benefits had been withdrawn from consideration by the board because the companies had already agreed to them, effective January 1, 1957. Although unions were prepared to accept the recommendations of the board, the Canadian National and Canadian Pacific would neither accept nor reject it until they had explored possible sources of additional revenue. They applied to the Board of Transport Commissioners for a 19 per cent increase in freight rates (with the usual exceptions) and the unions, after taking a vote, threatened to go on strike on December 1, 1958. Just before that date, the Board allowed an increase of 17 per cent in tolls and this decision was confirmed by the Cabinet. Thus, a strike was again narrowly averted.

The settlement had one advantage from the railway point of view. Formerly, the increases in freight rates authorized by the Board of Transport Commissioners had lagged far behind the increase in wage rates arrived at by agreement between railways and unions. Railway net revenues had suffered until the one had caught up with the other. Now, for the first time, the two increases took place more or less simultaneously. Unfortunately, this sound principle was quickly discarded. Between mid-1959 and early 1967 the federal government subsidized railways and refused to permit them to raise their tolls to keep them more or less in line with rising rates of wages and costs of supplies. The President of the Canadian National told a Parliamentary Committee that his guess was that it would take ten years for railways to move completely away from the environment of frozen freight rates.

Early in 1959, the railways applied to the Board of Transport Commissioners for a further increase of 12 per cent in freight rates (subject to the usual exceptions). All the provinces except Ontario and Quebec appeared in opposition to this proposal and also made representations to the Cabinet. In the end the government appointed the MacPherson Royal Commission and forbade any increases in the general level of rates pending receipt of its report. It also voted a subsidy of $20 million to provide a "roll-back" in freight rates. Effective August 10, 1959, the increase of 17 per cent authorized in December, 1958, became an increase of only 10 per cent, later reduced to 8 per cent. Although the trucking industry complained of the fundamental unfairness of a subsidy to its main competitor, it was assured by the government that the aid was temporary. The government also claimed that the subsidy was needed to prevent freight rates being raised to burdensome levels in those parts of the country, namely, the Maritimes and the West, where trucking competition was allegedly not as intensive as in the St. Lawrence Lowlands.

In August, 1960, the story on the labour front was repeated, like the rerun of an old motion picture. A board of conciliation under Mr. Justice J. V. H. Milvain suggested an increase of about 14 cents an hour, part of which was retroactive to the first of the year.[40] The unions were prepared to accept this, notwithstanding that they had originally asked for 25 cents. But the railways would concede only 4 cents an hour. They said that business generally was poor, their share of inland transportation was shrinking, and the government had forbidden any increase in freight rates until the MacPherson Commission had brought down its report. After the railways announced their decision, the non-ops also rejected the Milvain recommendations and voted to go on strike for the full 25 cents.

On December 2, 1960, just before the strike deadline, the Diefenbaker Government passed legislation[41] forbidding any strike on railways until after May 15, 1961, by which time it expected to have a report from the MacPherson Commission. As a matter of principle, organized labour strongly condemns any legislative interference with its right to strike. Mr. Diefenbaker defended his legislation on the ground that Mr. St. Laurent had done the same thing in 1950 and threatened the same action in 1954. Indeed, Mr. Diefenbaker argued that the Liberal Government had gone farther than he planned, for it had required compulsory arbitration and, in effect, had forbidden any strike on the issues in question. In contrast, the Diefenbaker Government was merely deferring the right to strike from December, 1960, until after May 15, 1961. On the other hand, as Liberals quickly pointed out, the St. Laurent Government had insured that the men would immediately get the minimum increase in wages (4 cents an hour) recommended by the board of conciliation whereas the Diefenbaker Government forbade any increase whatsoever for a period of over five months. In addition, it had put the railways in an impossible position by denying them the right to ask for higher rates on freight.

In March, 1961, the MacPherson Commission submitted the first volume of its report but the government decided it could not begin to implement its recommendation until it had got the second volume as well. The men voted to strike on the earliest date that they could legally do so, that is, on May 16, 1961. About ten days before that date, President Donald Gordon of the Canadian National agreed to accept the Milvain Report. Inevitably, President N. R. Crump of the Canadian Pacific had to follow suit. Thereupon the non-ops, who had threatened to strike for 25 cents, agreed to accept 14 cents as Milvain had proposed.

The mystery of where the carriers would get the money for higher wages in view of the freeze on freight rates was settled by a Government announcement. It would subsidize the railways to the extent of $50 million a year, in addition to the "roll-back" subsidy of $20 million. At first the subsidy was expected to last no more than one fiscal year, being replaced by legislation dealing directly with the MacPherson Commission's recommendations for assistance to branch lines, passenger service, and Western grain. But the subsidy was extended as a result of two general elections, public opposition to the abandonment of branch lines and the reduction of passenger services in Western Canada, and the controversial nature of the legislation when it was introduced in the House of Commons.

The increased rate of subsidy and its continuance from 1961 to the end of 1966 triggered another series of complaints by the trucking industry over unfair competition. It also led to protests that the policy of subsidizing railway labour had dangerous implications. Besides, a general subsidy of the kind being paid was contrary to an explicit recommendation of the MacPherson Commission which said that government aid should be tied to specific objectives and that every effort should be made to eliminate the subsidy by getting rid of uneconomic services which had given rise to it. In answer to these criticisms, government spokesmen chiefly argued that the subsidy was going to shippers rather than to labour.

In September, 1961, negotiations between management and men were renewed. The previous agreements had usually covered a two-year period and it had taken nearly a year and a half to negotiate the contract which was due to expire on December 31, 1961. Now the non-ops asked for an increase of 22 cents an hour in order to bring their remuneration up to rough equality with workers in the durable goods industries. This standard is described later. The non-ops were also deeply concerned about job security. According to their figures, the railway work-force had dropped from 180,000 in 1952 to 145,000 in 1959. Further reductions were in sight on account of continued automation, especially through the construction of hump yards, and the recommendations of the MacPherson Commission on the abandonment of branch lines and passenger services.

For their part, the railways contended that they had always been considerate of their employees. For instance, when the Canadian National decided to close its shops in Stratford, Ont., it had gone to great pains to attract new industries to the city. In his way it had protected its employees who had to move elsewhere against loss in the value of their homes in Stratford. It had provided alternative jobs for those who preferred to remain in that city, and thus it insured that the municipality's tax revenues were sustained. Yet, because of competition, there was a limit to the amount of severance pay which the railways could afford to disburse to employees who had to be discharged as a result of automation and rationalization of plant.

In the previous postwar negotiations, the non-ops had usually carried the ball. Once the railways had reached agreement with them, similar increases had been arranged with the running trades. In February, 1962, the Canadian National reversed the practice by agreeing first with its firemen. The two parties made a three-year contract, an obvious advantage over the two-year limit previously in effect. Under the new agreement the firemen on passenger trains were to get an increase of 4 cents an hour. A few weeks later locomotive engineers on both the major railways announced they would strike early in April unless their demands were met. In the end the strike was averted and all the running trades got increases of roughly $8\frac{1}{2}$ per cent.[42] This was less than the increase needed to keep their wages as high as those in the durable goods industry.

In August, 1962, a report by a three-man conciliation board under Mr. Justice Munroe of British Columbia achieved three distinctions: it was unanimous, it was accepted by both the railways and the non-operating unions, and it took a long first step toward settling the ticklish problem of job security.[43] The men got an increase of 4 cents an hour. This was less than they had demanded but, as the Canadian Brotherhood of Railway, Transport and General Workers explained, the nation was facing a crisis in foreign exchange, the Canadian dollar had recently been devalued, the federal government had frozen the wages of its civil servants, and the country seemed to be facing a period of economic doubt.

In addition to paying these higher wages, the railways would contribute one cent an hour into a compensation fund. The fund would be used (a) for retraining and reallocation of employees who might have to be moved from one part of the country to another, and (*b*) for severance pay to employees who lost their jobs completely. Details of the plan were to be worked out by a joint management-union committee. What is more, the unions were prepared to accept arbitration in case the members of the committee could not agree. The arrangement was welcomed by the parties that were directly affected and by the public generally. It settled the current dispute on railways and seemed to constitute a pattern for other industries faced with similar problems arising out of automation and rationalization of plant. As it turned out, the fund merely deferred settlement of a host of minor but cantankerous problems over technological unemployment and was abandoned in 1963 when the agreement expired.

In 1964 agreement between unions and railways was achieved fairly readily but two years later, in August, 1966, a strike tied up rail transport for a week until Parliament passed legislation ordering the men back to work and giving them an increase of 18 per cent in wage rates spread over two years (4 per cent retroactive to January 1, 1966; another 4 per cent retroactive to July 1, 1966; 7 per cent prospective on January 1, 1967; and 3 per cent prospective on July 1, 1967). The same legislation provided that a mediator appointed by the government should make further recommendations on wages and the revision of work rules. The government hoped that the railways and all the unions would accept the mediator's proposals. Should they fail to do so, all matters remaining in dispute were to be settled by arbitration. After lengthy meetings with executives of the railways and of the unions, the mediator, H. Carl Goldenberg, of Montreal, proposed a further increase of 6 per cent effective January 1, 1968, thus making 24 per cent in all.

Wage Levels

From the mass of statistics, the verbiage, and the moves and countermoves in these various disputes, it is not easy to pull out the significant facts. Railway wage rates were the same in Canada as in the United States for many years before they were officially equalized in 1918. When rates in Canada were lower, workers drifted across the border, and Canadian roads had difficulty retaining qualified men. Nowadays a railway worker who shifts to the United States loses his seniority and his pension which are based on years of service. Since the early 1930s fringe benefits have been about the same in the two countries but hourly wages have been higher in the United States. Equality of wage rates remains an ideal of Canadian labour leaders, particularly of the international unions. They want equal pay for the same work done by their members in the two countries. Canadian railways operating in the United States and American lines running in Canada pay wages on the American scale. Besides, a large amount of traffic is interchanged between the two countries.

Railways emphasize that the Canadian economy must control Canadian wages. Figures show that the countries differ in per capita national income, cost of railway supplies, revenue per train-mile, density of traffic, the extent of relatively unproductive territory lying athwart transcontinental railway lines, climate, level of freight rates especially those on export grain, dependence on foreign trade, taxes per mile of line, and so on. The purchasing power of wage earners in the two countries in terms of goods and services differs, regardless of whether the two currencies are officially at par or not. Wages generally, e.g., in automobile plants in Windsor and Detroit, have not been the same. While boards of conciliation have kept the relationship in mind, they have uniformly rejected the arguments that railway wages should be identical in the two nations and that Canadian wage rates should go up because those in the United States have risen.

Unions and railways come to grips on the proper relation between wage rates and the cost of living. In the 1948 wage dispute, railways contended that in terms of real income their employees were better off than in the previous periods of peacetime prosperity (1926–9) and almost as well off as in 1939. Unions criticized the statistical soundness of the official index of the cost of living, contending that it did not accurately measure the costs of the average household. Union leaders say that because negotiations about wages are long drawn out, workers should get some protection against short-run advances in prices occurring subsequently to the opening of negotiations. From the standpoint of national social welfare, the standard of living of the working man should steadily improve. They assert that it would be a backward step if the real incomes for railway workers today were merely to be preserved at the levels prevailing ten or twenty years earlier.

Usually the parties compare wage rates on railways with those in other industries. Sampling has to be used and the results are often open to question from a statistical point of view. In industry at large, rates of pay vary from one part of the country to another while with a few exceptions they are uniform on railways. Thus comparisons of railway with non-railway pay may be favourable to the roads in some places and not in others. The risk of accident and the size of fringe benefits, such as pensions, health insurance, vacations, and free travel during vacations and after retirement, are other bones of contention that make it difficult to compare fairly railway and non-railway wages.

Most railway workers are doing jobs which differ from those in industry generally. Locomotive engineers, track workers, signal maintainers, station agents, and so on have no exact counterparts outside railways. Machinists and carpenters do work which is fairly similar but not quite identical. In the long run, wages for tasks of equal difficulty tend to be the same in all lines of endeavour. If this relation did not hold, workers would desert railways for better paying jobs elsewhere. Young men choosing their trades and their first jobs would go into other occupations. Thus over the years railways will have to pay about the same rates as other employers but in the short run they may be paying more or less than going rates. Craftsmen in the same trade like to receive the same rates of pay, whether employed by railways or in industry at large. This attitude is particularly strong if the men are members of the same union.

In almost every dispute railways complain that they are unable to bear the cost of the increase or if a decrease is being discussed they will assert that they cannot survive without still lower wage costs. Theoretically freight rates may be increased to cover the higher expenses for labour but railways know from experience how hard it is to increase rates without losing traffic to competitors. Carriers emphasize that cheap transportation is essential to the well-being of the Canadian economy. They show that the country's prosperity depends on the volume of sales abroad and that our foreign trade is uncertain in both value and volume. Gross National Product and therefore railway gross earnings are basically unstable. It would be unwise to add rigidity to railway operating costs by increasing wages. Export prices of wheat, newsprint, fish, and so on cannot be easily raised if freight rates go up, with the result that while railway workers may get more pay, farmers and other producers of raw materials will get less. Railways admit this argument should not be used unreasonably to depress railway wages but still they insist that it cannot be ignored. The validity of the argument hinges on an assumption—if one group of workers get more, others will receive less—and the meaning of the words, "unreasonably to depress wages."

Railways also stress that they must get new equipment to keep up with the needs of shippers and meet the competition of trucks, pipelines, and water carriers on more or less equal terms. Recently railways have soft-pedalled this argument because unions are sensitive on this question. New equipment often leads to technological unemployment.

Unions invariably emphasize that good labour relations are one of the carrier's most valuable assets. A contented and skilled labour force will count for more than anything else in helping the railways fight the trucks. Moreover, the productivity of labour as measured by such ratios as gross ton-miles per man-hour and train-miles per train-hour is generally increasing. What the unions overlook is that wage rates have risen faster than productivity. In 1959–9 average wages on the Canadian National annually rose by 9½ per cent simple interest, productivity by 4½ per cent a year. Also higher productivity is not solely caused by more skilled or more willing workers, important as they are. It may be the result of capital expenditures on diesel locomotives, automatic block signals, lower gradients and the like, or of prosperous business conditions with heavier carloading, more cars per train, faster schedules, and so on. Nevertheless, workers have a great influence on some of the factors accounting for higher productivity. Union leaders contend that men should not be asked to accept only the going rates of wages because the industry which employs them faces greater competition than formerly. They say too that their moral claim to better pay is especially strong in an industry which, more than factories, depends on the goodwill and co-operation of its employees.

In 1950 the railways introduced the durable goods standard. They argued that railway wages and fringe benefits should be roughly equal to those in factories making durable goods such as basic iron and steel products, agricultural implements, household appliances, heavy electrical goods, and railway rolling stock. At that time the standard showed that railway workers were relatively well off. By the end of the decade the reverse was true. In consequence, railways lost their enthusiasm for the standard while unions became its devotees. In 1962 the conciliation board under Mr. Justice Monroe said that it had taken this standard into account but had not adhered to it absolutely. In fact, the rates of pay suggested by the board and accepted by the two parties left rail wages somewhat below the durable goods standard.

Interpretation of Agreements

Long experience has enabled unions and carriers to draft agreements which cover most of the matters about which dispute is likely to arise. Even so, questions of interpretation are inevitable. Those concerning the running trades and maintenance of way employees were referred to the Canadian Railway Board of Adjustment No. 1.[44] This body consisted of six members selected by the railways and six by the men. The particular unions and companies appointing representatives varied from one case to another depending on the issues involved.

Decisions were arrived at by simple majority vote but the practice was to "talk it out" and make the decision unanimous. In case of deadlock the two groups might appoint a referee jointly or ask the federal Minister of Labour to select an independent person for the position. In the 823 cases dealt with by the adjustment board from its organization in 1918 to 1964, there was never a tie vote nor any need for a referee. The decisions of the board, while not legally binding on the parties, were always accepted. Most of the questions brought before it related to straightening out seniority rights when various roads were consolidated into the present Canadian National. Other problems concerned working rules; these will be discussed later.

While the board was extraordinarily successful, it must be remembered that it did not formulate wage agreements. It merely interpreted what had already been agreed upon after lengthy bargaining. Although the cases it handled were doubtless important to the individual worker or class of worker affected, they were not significant enough to railway labour as a whole or to the carriers to justify a long controversy, let alone a strike.

For many years the operation of the board drew admiration from many quarters. Then the interpretation of agreements made in other industries began to devolve on the labour relations boards set up under legislation of provincial and federal governments. Also, the labour contracts often provide for *ad hoc* boards to deal with matters of interpretation. As a result the Canadian Railway Board of Adjustment lost some of its uniqueness and in 1964 it was abolished, being replaced by a one-man tribunal.

Seniority

Railways follow the seniority principle except in supervisory positions, though even there it is not entirely absent. Seniority means that workers with the longest period of service are the last to be laid off (furloughed), the first to be taken on, and have the preference for promotions, transfers, and assignment of work over others of equal ability.

Seniority is acquired in a particular craft and place of work. A shopman gets seniority in his own trade and in the shop where he is employed. A track worker holds his seniority among other trackmen in a division. A locomotive engineer working out of Montreal on the Canadian Pacific has seniority in one of several runs, e.g., Montreal-Ottawa via south shore (Vankleek Hill, Ont.), Montreal-Ottawa north shore (Lachute, Que.), Montreal-Smith's Falls, and so on. On the Canadian National out of Montreal, the running trades have two seniority divisions, one east and one west of that city. In any seniority division when a man is "dropped" from the list of engineers because there is not enough work for all of them, he is automatically placed at or near the top of the fireman's "board." He may displace or "bump" a fireman who is at the bottom of the latter's seniority list. The same rule applies to conductors and trainmen but not to any other two crafts.

The seniority rule has numerous advantages. It takes account of years of faithful service. It reduces labour turnover because no man wants to sacrifice a position which he has attained only after years of work. It avoids criticism of favouritism in promotion and in the assignment of daily tasks. Perhaps older workers, the ones with more experience, are as competent as younger men in doing what is required. If this is so, they should be rewarded for their devotion to the company. Moreover, experience has shown that railway workers can be quickly trained for new jobs. Engineers on steam locomotives soon became adept at handling diesels. Track workers familiar with hand-shovel and sledgehammer readily take to using pneumatic tampers and hammers, chemical weed-killers, and power equipment for pulling spikes and cutting ties.

On the other hand, seniority tends to sap workers of their energy and initiative. A man is never promoted (except to or within the executive ranks) because he does a better-than-average job. As a result a premium is placed on ripping leaves off the calendar rather than convincing a "hard-boiled boss" of the right to promotion. For several reasons seniority atrophies the whole railway labour force. It discourages younger men from entering railway work. They think promotion in pay and responsibility is far too slow and advancement to the more desirable jobs too tedious. Consequently railways run the risk of not getting their share of bright youths. By the time a man gets to the place where he can demonstrate whatever superior ability he might have possessed originally, all the psychological "drive" has been squeezed out of him. Railway employees build up a phenomenal period of service with one company but lose the initiative which they might have shown in an environment more favourable to its growth. Seniority, technological change, and the relatively slow growth of railway traffic all make for an aging labour force. One layoff may cause many dislocations and a number of dissatisfactions through "bumping" a man of lower seniority far down the list.

Seniority also makes for immobility of labour. A qualified engineer who may be working as a fireman or may even be unemployed in one seniority division, will hesitate to transfer to another seniority division where work is available because he will have to work his way all up the firemen's "ladder" before again becoming an engineer. Seniority may conflict with any policy of "share the work" during a depression. In a word, seniority protects the worker with long service but at the expense of the younger worker and to some extent of the industry.

The shortcomings of the seniority principle, which seemed so clear in the 1930s, appear less serious thirty years later. For one thing the principle now applies, though usually in modified form, to universities, the armed forces, the civil service, and numerous large businesses of all kinds. Moreover, railway unions are sometimes prepared to modify rules on which they had formerly been adamant. Four different unions managed to agree on fitting together the seniority rights of their members when the railways integrated their express and less than carload freight into a single non-carload Merchandise Service. Unions have also agreed to some enlargement of seniority districts so that a person thrown out of work by automation or rationalization of plant in one area will not always have to leave the employ of the railway or start at the bottom of the seniority list in another seniority district.

These adjustments have to be made gradually. People are sensitive about rights they have earned over the years. They are naturally reluctant to accept changes which involve postponement of promotion or of assignment to better shifts and jobs. Modification of seniority rules may also work to the disadvantage of junior men who may be "bumped" out of railway work.

Working Rules

Railway unions are often criticized because their restrictive working rules throttle the industry and prevent it from competing effectively with other transportation media. Each of the working rules was designed to protect the worker against actual or potential abuse of his legitimate rights. A shopman may be called out to repair a locomotive on a Sunday afternoon just when he is ready to go on a picnic with his family. He may take only a few minutes or at most half an hour to do the job but his whole afternoon is ruined. It is manifestly unfair for the railway to pay him only for the few minutes which it takes him to replace a part or make an adjustment. If he had not done the work quickly an important train might have been held up for several hours. The union argues that railway management must be penalized or else the practice of calling men out at any time of the day or night for trivial jobs would grow beyond all reason. Hence the agreements provide that shopmen be paid for a minimum of five hours for any work done outside of regular hours. Railways recognize the soundness of the principle but feel they should be allowed to assign some other task to make up for the time paid for but not spent on the special job.

A great many working rules relate to what constitutes a particular kind of work. A clear distinction has to be drawn between through-freight, way-freight, and mixed train service. The rate of pay depends on the type of work which is done. Employees would quickly become disgruntled if they did not know precisely what kind of work they were doing and what their pay would be. Without the rules the railway might permanently do some craftsmen out of their jobs by having the work done by different and cheaper classes of labour. Assigning work to other trades also interferes with the seniority rights of the craft chiefly interested in the job.

The trouble is that simple rules may easily be carried to uneconomic lengths. For instance, some legislatures in the United States have "full crew" laws. Trains which have been running safely and economically with a small but adequate crew are required to stop at the state line in order to take on extra men. It would seem to an outsider that these men have very little to do until, in the interests of economy, the train stops just before leaving the state in order to let them off. In 1964 American railway executives alleged that these laws required them to maintain 18,000 unnecessary jobs and added $140 million a year to their payroll. Other "featherbedding" provisions involve the hiring of superfluous workers in shops, payment for work not actually done, and so on.

Leaders of Canadian unions say that instances of featherbedding are played up by some American magazines and newspapers. These reports come to the attention of Canadian readers who then mistakenly assume that the same rules apply in Canada. Canadian unionists also point out that they did not seriously object to the removal of telegraphers whose jobs were rendered obsolete by teletypewriters and centralized traffic control. Before long, the telegraphers union will virtually cease to exist. True enough, a Canadian union struck on the issue of diesel firemen, which is often cited as another example of featherbedding. But the unions sincerely believed that these men were essential to the safe operation of trains. When a Royal Commission decided against them, they accepted the ruling with good grace, though not legally bound to do so. Further, in order to facilitate the creation of the Merchandise Services division and an improvement in the competitive strength of railways, some union members have sacrificed part of their seniority. Finally, union leaders have expressed willingness to renegotiate contracts if railways can prove that they contain make-work provisions. What unions mean by make-work often seems to be radically different from the railway interpretation of the word. At all events, our provinces have no "full crew" laws like those in over twenty states in the union.

Railways argue that they should not be forced to pay for work done beyond regular duties and regardless of the time taken to do the extra job. They also say that under many of the agreements they are required to pay "arbitraries," that is, extra remuneration before and after the "run." In the main, these arbitraries are based on conditions that prevailed in the days of steam when the locomotives had to be checked pretty carefully before and after running over the line with freight or passenger cars behind the tender. In brief, management suggests that the unions are not as co-operative as they are trying to make the public believe.

Economists point out that high wages lead railways to use less labour and more capital. This trend toward economizing on the more expensive factor in production was especially strong from about 1945 to 1957 when a period of relatively low interest rates coincided with a series of technological changes such as diesel locomotives and centralized traffic control. Economists also assert that over the whole of industry, use of so-called labour-saving devices may not reduce employment as much as many people fear. Men have to obtain the raw materials that go into the machinery, manufacture it, keep it in repair, and provide it with power, lubricants, and other operating supplies. Contrary to popular opinion technological changes may not create unemployment in the long run, especially in a diversified economy. Sooner or later workers displaced in one trade will be employed in producing new goods and services or will produce larger quantities of the old goods, which presumably are being sold at lower prices because of the technological advances. Even so, men will be thrown out of work until the employment situation has had time to adjust itself to the new development. If these men are getting along in years or if they have had highly specialized training, they may find it hard to get other jobs.

Union leaders seize upon the point that if technological change proceeds too rapidly, some of their members will lose their jobs and their accumulated skills. When railway towns, such as Havelock and MacTier, Ont., lose population as a result of dieselization and the closing of the terminal, railwaymen suffer a further loss when they try to sell their homes to take up work elsewhere on the railway or in other industries. The MacPherson Commission recommended subsidies so that branch lines and passenger-train service would not be suddenly eliminated. Delay would give shippers, travellers, highway authorities, and communities time to adjust to new conditions of transport. The Commission even considered aid to owners of grain elevators and stated that its suggestion might be used as a model for government aid to owners of other business establishments along railway lines that would be abandoned. While any slowdown in the rate of abandonment might also prove of some benefit to railway workers, they feel they are entitled to some compensation for loss in the selling prices of their homes as much as shareholders in elevator companies, whether privately or co-operatively owned, are entitled to claim for loss of part of their capital. What is more, railway workers may experience loss of jobs and skills.

To provide this protection to workers, it would be possible to pass legislation requiring that railways not reduce their staffs except in the event of reductions in the volume of their traffic caused by a decline in general business prosperity. In the course of time, the reductions brought about by death, retirement on pension, and voluntary resignation to take another job or because of ill health would bring the size of the railway work force into line with the new requirements of the carriers. But attrition might defer economies for many years, especially if railways had to hire some new men each year in order to keep the necessary complement of skills. Moreover, this method might prove unpopular with the public because it would appear to give a lifetime job to men who had, at the date of the introduction of the scheme, only a few years of service with the railways.

A better plan is the one adopted in 1962: a compensation fund which would be as much an obligation upon the railways as the payment of wages to their employees. The fund would be used for retraining, and relocating displaced workers and for severance pay. Even with this fund, employees who are let out by the railway have no assurance that they will secure other jobs before their severance pay is exhausted. Consequently, the fund does not deal with every disability which the men may meet with. In short, the unions are not opposed to change and economic progress. They do want to make certain, however, that technological advances and the rationalization of plant and services are not achieved by throwing human beings on the scrap heap.

The unions have another point. They say that railway management is inclined to overestimate the cost of the union proposals. For example, in 1960 the Canadian National estimated that it could save between $17 and $18 million a year by the removal of firemen from diesel locomotives in yard and freight service. Under the agreement with the union and in accordance with the recommendations of the Royal Commission set up after the firemen's strike on the Canadian Pacific, these savings were deferred. Then the Canadian National forecast that they would not be fully attained until 1971 and that they would not begin to show up at all until perhaps 1965 or 1966. As things turned out, firemen became scarce, presumably because some of those on the payroll in 1960 voluntarily left for other positions rather than remain in work that was redundant and psychologically unsatisfying. Under the agreement with the union, the railway could take advantage of any attrition. Hence, the first savings showed up in 1963. By 1971 they will probably total $88 million over the previous eight years.

In 1965 the Canadian National ordered crews to "run through" some terminals in Northern Ontario and Alberta. Terminals are roughly 100 miles apart. The distance was set about 1900 because the steam engines of the time had to be serviced this frequently and it took the crews of freight trains about eight hours to complete a run of this length, with some allowance for signing on and off work, checking equipment, and the like. Diesel locomotives need not be serviced nearly as frequently as steam, and crews can often complete a run of 200 miles or so in eight hours or less. In any event, the running trades are, broadly speaking, paid by the mile so that longer runs did not result in any reduction in overall pay. On the other hand the men felt that the Canadian National's order was high-handed and reduced job opportunities. The problem was investigated by Mr. Justice Samuel Freedman of Winnipeg who recommended that the current system of permitting management to make unilateral changes in working conditions during a contract should be altered. New working conditions arising from technological change should be subject to negotiation between management and men.

To sum up, rules governing conditions of work are complicated because of the number of trades needed to run a railway, the dispersion of its operations, and the variety of services performed for shippers, consignees, and travellers. The situation is further complicated by advances in technology, improvements in operating methods, and the growth of competition. At one time it appeared that railways would be hamstrung by the rigid attitudes of unions and by their unwillingness to alter rules which were inappropriate for the new conditions. Although this danger may not have yet passed, it appears that patience, tact, and willingness to understand the point of view held by the other side will eventually solve the problem of adapting old rules to new conditions and simultaneously protecting the long-run interests of workers and carriers.

Union-Management Co-operation

Union-management co-operation may be said to have originated on the Baltimore and Ohio in 1923 and on the Canadian National in 1925. On the latter company it now covers all shops and maintenance of way operations. Committees of managers and men meet together periodically to discuss continuity of employment, better working conditions, introduction of new equipment, storing and improving tools, distributing and salvaging materials, preventing accidents and fires, rendering first aid, educating new employees, and generally increasing output and lowering costs.[45]

In the course of time the union-management idea has tended to lose some popularity. Now both major railways concentrate on getting suggestions from the men. In many firms workmen hesitate to suggest an improvement. Some foremen think they know everything about the plant and will tell the worker to mind his own business. Other foremen appropriate the idea as their own and on the strength of it get a promotion or an increase in pay for themselves. Sometimes a worker with a new idea is accused by his fellows of toadying to the boss and of trying to cut them out of jobs. Before long, workers carry out their routine tasks and cease to think of better ways of doing things. The suggestion system tries to overcome these drawbacks. Of the roughly 1,400 suggestions made each year to the Canadian National, nearly 85 per cent are put into effect and the men who made them given monetary rewards.

Methods of Wage Payment

Railway workers are paid on the basis of straight time or incentive plans. Executives, traffic solicitors, ticket sellers, clerks, stenographers, and so on are paid so much a month. Common labourers, track workers, shopmen, and many other groups are paid by the hour and a few shopmen are paid piece rates. The running trades are remunerated on a dual basis,[46] which combines both piece and time rates.

Suppose for illustrative purposes that the standard wage in freight service is $8 a day. A standard day's work consists of 100 miles or eight hours. The rate is $1 per hour and 8 cents per mile. The standard speed written into the agreements is 12½ miles per hour. When any freight train is slower than this, overtime is paid at the rate of time and a half provided more than eight hours have been spent on the run. On any trip, whether completed in less than eight hours or not, the crew receive straight mileage with a guaranteed minimum output of 100 miles for the day's work.

If a locomotive engineer completes a 100-mile run in eight hours or less, he gets one day's pay or $8. If he does 125 miles in ten hours or less, he is paid straight mileage (125 times 8 cents a mile or $10) because he has kept up the average speed of 12½ miles per hour or better. If the run took him eleven hours, he would have failed to reach the guaranteed minimum output in miles per hour. Hence he would be paid mileage ($10) plus overtime. At the standard rate of speed he should have finished the run in ten hours. So his overtime pay amounts to one hour at the rate of time and a half, or 1½ times $1. If a run of 75 miles is completed in six hours or less, the engineer gets the minimum pay for one day's work or 100 miles. If the same run took the engineer seven or eight hours, he would not get any overtime. Although he did not maintain the standard number of miles per hour, he did not spend more than eight hours on the job. If the trip took nine hours, the railwayman would have failed to produce the standard output in miles per hour and would have spent more than eight hours (one working day's time) on the run. Accordingly he would receive one day's pay (100 miles or eight hours) plus one hour's overtime.

Rates of pay vary from time to time in accordance with agreements between the management and the men. They differ with the various classes of service such as through-freight, way-freight, mixed, work train, and auxiliary (clearing wrecks.)[47] They change with the class of power in the same service. Engineers who handle heavy locomotives are paid more per mile than those on engines with smaller powers. The wage rates are different for engineers, firemen, conductors, and brakemen, yet in all cases the dual system applies.

The scheme was introduced in the United States in the 1880s to speed up trains. The objective, as in other incentive plans, was to encourage workers to get a greater output from the equipment in a given period of time by paying them on the basis of units of output or "pieces" rather than on time spent. In railway work, the output of the train crew was often held down by factors over which they had no control such as the length of trains, dispatchers' orders, poor weather, failure of other trains to make connections, or breakdowns in rolling stock. Hence railways were obliged to grant the crews a minimum wage for a day's work, which was defined at 100 miles for eight hours or less. In addition the railways had to pay for overtime.

Although the idea behind the wage scheme is fundamentally sound, in recent years it has developed one serious drawback. With modern fast locomotives a crew can do a run of 100 miles in two or three hours. This will count as a day's work for pay purposes. Then the crew can take a train back to the original terminus and get another day's pay within a total of perhaps eight hours. Alternatively they have a short working day and a great deal of free time. Senior employees who have first choice of runs receive either inordinately high wages or, by limiting their monthly wages, extraordinary amounts of leisure. But one can get a somewhat distorted view of the truth if one concentrates on "premium" runs and ignores the less spectacular performance of crews on way freights and slow passenger trains. Even so, in terms of hours worked per week the running trades are better off than industrial workers generally. In 1960 the average locomotive engineer in passenger service was on the job 33 hours a week and in freight service 37.6.

Normally locomotive engineers in passenger service must stop work when they reach between 4,500 and 4,600 miles per month. Then other engineers are transferred from freight to passenger service and some may be promoted to the freight service from the seniority list of firemen. Subject to many ifs, buts, and whereases, when passenger engineers in a seniority division run less than 4,000 miles a month, the engineer with the fewest years of service is put on a freight locomotive and takes precedence over all freight engineers. If freight engineers are not working their minimum number (2,600) of miles per month, the junior freight engineer will become a fireman. He goes to the top of the firemen's "board." If the firemen, in their turn, are not working their minimum number of miles per month, the man with the fewest years of service among the firemen, in that seniority division may lose his job with the railway. He will, however, have the first chance at any vacancy which opens up when business revives. During the depression of the 1930s the maximum and minimum mileages were lowered. In this way the senior men shared the work with the juniors to some extent. Normally the list for other than assigned crews, i.e., for all crews except those running passenger and a few freight trains which operate on fixed schedules, is unchanged so long as the crews do not run less than 2,600 or more than 3,800 miles a month. This range of mileage provides a good deal of flexibility since there can be a substantial increase or decrease in mileage run before men are added to or dropped from the "board." In consequence, there is often a long lag before qualified men get back on the "board" and are assigned to duty.

Wages of Various Classes

The dual system complicates the proper relation between the pay of the various classes of railway labour. Naturally, the order of the various groups by size of annual wage varies slightly from one year to another but as a rule road passenger engineers are followed by passenger conductors, freight engineers, firemen, freight conductors, yard engineers, and brakemen. The running trades are followed as far as annual income is concerned by signal maintainers, station employees, members of bridge and building gangs, switchmen, and track labourers. Many of the latter are employed only during the summer and do not receive the arithmetic average of their class.

In the 1930s and 1940s some people thought that the running trades were receiving unreasonably high wages relative to those of other workers on railways and in other industries.[48] But after about 1950 this criticism lost some of its original validity. Throughout our entire economy, the difference in the take-home pay of skilled artisans and the unskilled workers has narrowed. Furthermore, the greater length of freight trains because of dieselization, the decline of passenger traffic, and the gradual abolition of firemen in freight and yard service has reduced the prospect of employment in the running trades. In other words, the edge has been taken off the complaints of disproportionately high wages of locomotive engineers, etc., by the technological unemployment they have already experienced and still face. In 1966–7 railway executives reversed the old thesis that they were overpaying their skilled men when they argued that railways could not afford to pay the minimum wage of $1.25 an hour as laid down by the federal government. They also asserted that the principles of an eight-hour day and a forty-hour week with penalties for overtime would be impracticable if applied to the running trades.

Passes and Pensions

In addition to money wages, railway employees receive passes for free transportation for themselves and their dependents. Passes are of various kinds—trip or point-to-point, division, system, or valid on all lines of any railway in North America. They may be valid in coaches only, in first class, or restricted to certain trains. The kind of pass received depends on the employee's length of service with the company and to a lesser extent on his wage or salary. The freedom with which Canadian railways give passes has been officially criticized[49] but the privilege is highly prized by employees because only a small portion of them, not more than 15 per cent, ride trains regularly in the course of their duties. Free transportation helps to improve the morale of the workers and to educate them in the operations of their railway. In order to reduce losses on commuter services, railway employees using these trains are now required to pay half the commuter fare.

Employees on all important railways in the Dominion come under pension plans. All are now contributory, both company and men making regular payments into a fund. The plans are on an actuarial basis, the amount of the contributions plus interest being equal to the anticipated payments of annuities from the funds. The Grand Trunk Provident Fund started in 1874 was never actuarially sound nor was the pension scheme of the Canadian National until its large profits during World War II enabled it to bring its fund up to the proper amount.

On the Canadian Pacific, and on the Canadian National (for any employee retiring after January, 1935), the pension is calculated by taking 1 per cent of his average annual earnings during the ten consecutive years in which his earnings with the company were at their maximum. This amount is multiplied by the number of years of the employee's service. The minimum pension is $300 per annum. The employee may select a pension based on straight life, life guaranteed ten years, or joint and elder survivor. Thus the amount of the pension depends on the employee's rate of pay and length of service. For the most part the pension ultimately received, or paid to his estate in case the employee should die before retirement at age 65, represents a deferment of pay rather than a net addition to it. The retirement schemes of railways are integrated with the Canada Pension Plan which became effective on January 1, 1966. Most railway workers are required to pay into the unemployment insurance scheme which is administered by the federal government. When unemployed they may draw benefits from it on the same terms as other workers covered by the Unemployment Insurance Act.

16

The Canadian Transport Commission

OVER THE YEARS media of transport which come within the jurisdiction of the Parliament of Canada have been subject to numerous regulatory authorities—the Privy Council (Cabinet), insofar as it introduces new legislation into Parliament and, for all practical purposes, appoints men to various commissions; the Ministers of Railways and Canals, Marine and Fisheries, and Transport; the Railway Committee of the Privy Council (1888–1903); the Board of Railway Commissioners (1904–38); the Board of Transport Commissioners (1938–67); the Air Transport Board (1944–67); and the Canadian Maritime Commission (1947–67). In 1967 the last three bodies were amalgamated into the Canadian Transport Commission.

It is important to note that not all media of transport within Canada come within the jurisdiction of the government in Ottawa. The provinces control railways which Parliament has not seen fit to bring within its authority by declaring them "to be works for the public advantage of Canada" as provided for under the British North America Act. The only important railways still under the provinces are the Pacific Great Eastern and the Ontario Northland, which are owned by British Columbia and Ontario, respectively. Even though the latter road, acting under the charter of a subsidiary, crosses the Ontario boundary near Larder Lake and goes as far as Noranda in the province of Quebec, it still remains outside the ambit of federal authority. This is primarily because the federal government does not want to regulate a provincially-owned railway. The provinces also have full control over intra-provincial ferries, e.g., that between Tobermory near the tip of the Bruce Peninsula and South Baymouth on Manitoulin Island. Finally, they have control of almost all transport by highway, a point to be dealt with in a subsequent chapter.

Though the regulatory powers of the new Transport Commission are extensive, several aspects of transport come under other authorities. The National Harbours Board looks after most of the larger ports of Canada while the Department of Transport retains control of the smaller ones. The movement of natural gas, petroleum, and petroleum products is a matter for various provincial commissions or for the National Energy Board, which is a federal body. The St. Lawrence Seaway is run by two separate Authorities, one appointed by Canada and one by the United States. Subject to approval by the two governments, these Authorities set tolls for ships using the Seaway. In a word, the problem of governmental control of the various media of transport is complex.

Before considering the organization and responsibilities of the new Canadian Transport Commission in detail, we shall deal with each of the constituent bodies. The discussion will assume that these bodies still exist. It seems more appropriate to say what the previous commissions were doing at the date of amalgamation than to change the tenses of all the verbs so as to show what the new regulatory body plans to do in future. Besides, the first responsibility of the Canadian Transport Commission is obviously to carry on the work of its predecessors and then, later on, co-ordinate their operations as directed by law.

The Board of Transport Commissioners

The Board of Railway Commissioners was set up as a result of a report[1] of a Royal Commission consisting of a single member, Dr. S. J. McLean, who was later assistant chief commissioner of the Board. The Railway Committee of the Privy Council,[2] which had been functioning since 1888, had not proved satisfactory. It was political as well as administrative; it did not travel around the country to hear complaints; it had little technical training for its work; and its personnel changed frequently. Dr. McLean recommended that the regulating of railways be put on a more satisfactory footing by entrusting it to a commission composed of three men of technical training who would receive salaries adequate to attract the most efficient, and who would have a long tenure of office. He proposed that the Board consist of one lawyer, one man experienced in general business, and one having a thorough knowledge of railway affairs. The commission would carry on the duties of the Railway Committee. In addition it would have authority to regulate issues of stocks and bonds, investigate the necessity of new railway lines subject to final action by Parliament, arbitrate wages, and report upon such matters as were referred to it by Parliament and the Minister of Railways and Canals.

The *Railway Act* of 1903[3] set up the Board of Railway Commissioners for Canada, consisting of three members who were to be appointed for a period of ten years. They were eligible for reappointment, would retire at the age of 75, and were removable only by vote of both Houses of Parliament.[4] Since 1908, when the Board was enlarged to six,[5] the chief commissioner and the assistant chief commissioner must be or have been a judge of a superior court of Canada or any of its provinces, or a barrister or advocate of at least ten years' standing at the bar, or in the case of the assistant chief commissioner[6] a barrister or advocate who has held office as a commissioner of the Board for at least ten years. In 1948, the chief commissioner became a justice of the Exchequer Court who was assigned to the Board for ten years,[7] but in 1957 he ceased to be a justice on appointment to the Board. The Railway Act does not lay down any particular qualifications regarding the training and experience of other members.

Jurisdiction

Under the Act of 1903, the powers of the Railway Committee of the Privy Council were transferred to the newly created Board of Railway Commissioners. The Board is to inquire into, hear, and determine any matter arising out of the Railway Act. It has full powers of a superior court regarding attendance and examination of witnesses, production and inspection of documents, and enforcement of orders. The finding or determination of the Board upon any question of fact within its jurisdiction is final and conclusive. It has authority to issue orders which may be made a rule, order, or decree of the Exchequer Court or of any superior court of any province of Canada. In short, it has all the legal powers necessary to carry out its responsibilities.

The Board has the duty of regulating rates, fares, demurrage, and other charges made by the railway companies subject to its authority. It must approve the location of stations and branch lines. It has extensive duties regarding the crossing of a railway by public highways, by farmers' roadways, by power and telephone lines, and by other railways. It deals with fencing, fire protection, speed of trains, coupling devices for locomotives and cars, braking mechanisms, headway and side clearances of cars, the number of men to be employed on trains, operating rules, and standards of visual and auditory acuity. Generally, it lays down regulations dealing with the safety, accommodation, and comfort of employees and the general public.

The Board may initiate investigations of its own motion and must do so at the request of the Minister of Transport or of the Governor-in-

Council. It may state a case for the opinion of the Supreme Court. Appeals may be taken from the Board to the Governor-in-Council, or to the Supreme Court of Canada. Thus the Board is clothed with very broad powers, subject only to appeal to the highest authorities in the land.

The jurisdiction of the Board has several times been extended, for example, to express, telegraph, and telephone companies in 1908, the Railway Grade Crossing Fund in 1909, tolls of international bridges and tunnels in 1929, and abandonment of railway lines in 1933. It was also assigned certain duties under the Maritime Freight Rates Act, 1927.[8] Under the Transport Act, 1938,[9] the Board was given some powers over transportation by air and water and over agreed charges and, on account of its enlarged duties, its name was changed to the Board of Transport Commissioners for Canada. In 1949 the Board was charged with the responsibility of regulating interprovincial and international pipelines.[10]

From time to time Parliament has placed additional railways under the Board. The Intercolonial, Prince Edward Island, and National Transcontinental Railways which were originally excluded because they were owned by the Crown, are now under the Board.[11] The Hudson Bay and Newfoundland Railways have also been made subject to it.[12] Finally, Parliament has given the Board a greater field of discretion that it had under original act. For instance, the amendment passed in 1933[13] governing abandonment left the Board to establish its own principles. All this legislation indicates that in the past Parliament has shown increasing confidence in the work of the Board of Transport Commissioners.

On the other hand, Parliament has occasionally withdrawn from the Board powers formerly entrusted to it. The Board's control over aviation and pipelines was transferred to the Air Transport Board in 1944 and to the National Energy Board in 1959.[14] During World War I, the Board administered the government's regulations concerning minimum carloads, allocation of freight cars, and so on. In World War II this work was done by a special official.

Some matters on which the Board might be expected to have expert knowledge have not been referred to it. Instead they have been dealt with by *ad hoc* bodies. Chief Commissioner Drayton was a member of the Royal Commission of 1917 and Assistant Chief Commissioner McLean acted on the Royal Commission on Lake Grain Rates in 1923. But no member of the Board served on the Royal Commission of 1931–2, on the (Duncan) Commission on Maritime Claims, 1927, or the Royal Commissions which considered the rail outlet from Peace River or the Chignecto Canal.[15] The most conspicuous example of a government ignoring the Board on a matter patently within its jurisdiction was the establishment in 1922 of a Parliamentary Committee on the Crow's Nest Pass Agreement. The government and the public, especially in Western Canada, lacked confidence in the Board and so it was passed over. Of course, it is possible to argue that disregarding the Board was essentially a tribute to it, rather than the reverse. Western objection proved that the Board was sufficiently independent not to play politics by currying favour with sectional interests. On the other hand establishing the Parliamentary Committee showed that both the government and the West feared that Chief Commissioner Carvell, far from looking at all aspects of the problem, would not be unhappy if he could stir up trouble for the Liberal party which he had left in 1917.

Criticism of the Board

In the course of proceedings before the Royal Commission of 1951 a number of criticisms were made of the manner in which the Board exercised its powers, chiefly in regard to its rate-making functions. It had refused to put in experimental rates with a view to developing industry and had allowed railways virtually complete freedom to publish competitive tolls. The Board had not laid down rules governing uniform accounting nor established a rate base and rate of return as requested by the Canadian Pacific. Finally the Board was criticized for failing to carry out the directives of the Cabinet[16] requiring equalization of freight rates to the fullest possible extent.

Some appeals from the Board's postwar decisions in general rate cases reflected on the working of the Board. The Order-in-Council issued after the appeal to the Cabinet from the Board's decision in the *Twenty-one Per Cent Case* could be taken to mean that the Board had not properly exercised its broad discretionary powers. Later, on the appeal by the Canadian Pacific from the Board's judgment in the *Twenty Per Cent Case,* the Supreme Court of Canada declared that by granting only a temporary increase for the reasons given, the Board had failed to perform the duty imposed upon it by the Railway Act.[17]

To be fair to the Board, one should judge its work in the light of the environment in which it and the carriers it controls carry on their operations. When the Board was created, railways had a practical monopoly of overland transport of persons and property. A number of privately owned railway systems were in existence. The volume of traffic was expanding rapidly and steadily. Railway securities were profitable investments and population was growing, especially in previously undeveloped areas. Aside from the problem of getting additional railway mileage built, the burning question in transportation was unjust discrimination and undue preference between persons and classes of freight. The Railway Committee of the Privy Council was ill fitted to deal with the abuses which had arisen regarding rates. The Board was set up to correct its shortcomings and to ensure that individual rates were just and reasonable.

Following both world wars the Board had to deal with the complex interrelationship of railway tolls on the one hand, and inflation of wages and the cost of railway materials and supplies on the other. As soon as the general level of rates was raised above the customary basis, different regions of Canada began to complain of discriminatory treatment. As early as 1920, but particularly since 1930, railways had to face intensive competition from a number of directions. They must pay very much higher wage rates than before 1914. The public has no longer the same enthusiasm for investing in railways. As a result of these conditions, regulatory tribunals have to watch the net revenues of carriers very carefully, otherwise railways may be unable to provide the travelling and shipping public with the quality of service it has come to expect. The Board is forced to consider the interrelationships of railway and other transportation agencies even though not all these agencies are within the ambit of its legal authority. Whereas during the first fifteen years of its existence the Board had to deal with a number of large privately owned railways, now it has to take into account the position of only two major roads and one of these is publicly owned. This in itself is a difficult problem not contemplated when the Railway Board was originally established.

In a word, the Board's general frame of reference, which was drafted in the early part of the century, has gradually become out of date. To revise the legislation with a view to possible improvements was one of the main tasks of the Royal Commission of 1951 under its terms of reference. In fact, the Commission's report left matters largely as they were. It did not recommend that Parliament legislate on rate base and rate of return, horizontal increase, stop-off privilege, and so on. In some instances the Commission expressed its views on what the Board should do and in others it proposed changes in the law, for example, transcontinental rates, interline rates, equalization, and uniform accounting.

Yet by and large the Royal Commission confirmed what the Board had been doing and the plans which it seemed to have under way. While the Commission urged revival of the policy of integrating and harmonizing the various agencies of transportation, it made few concrete suggestions for the practical guidance of either the Board or the government in formulating such a policy. As Commissioner Angus explained, the Commission set up traffic signals but did not floodlight the road. In the main the Board was left with the terms of reference set forth in the Railway Act of 1903. Fundamentally it still had to work out its own destiny and adapt old legislation to modern economic society.

As to the constitution of the Board itself, the Royal Commission emphasized that "legislation giving powers will not cure all ills. The successful operation of the Board must depend on the ability of the men who are appointed to it and the staff which they have around them. . . . The importance of [the Board's] functions and the high standard which should be maintained in the selection of its members cannot be stressed too strongly.[18] The Commission proposed that the appointment of Board members be not restricted to ten years (subject to re-appointment). "This ten-year limitation must have a deterrent effect on qualified men who realize that in accepting appointment to the Board they run the risk of finding themselves in an undesirable position, by reason of age or of altered business conditions, when they return to private life."[19] Beyond this, the Commission of 1951 did not make any concrete proposals except for amalgamation of the three federal boards having supervision over transportation. The Royal Commission of 1961 was specifically told not to consider "the performance of functions which under the *Railway Act* are within the exclusive jurisdiction of the Board of Transport Commissioners."

Character of the Board

Earlier books by this author contained a detailed analysis of the occupational backgrounds of the members of the Board of Transport (or Railway) Commissioners since its inception, their education, term of office, contribution to the work of the Board, and so on. Since the Board is to merge with other bodies into the Canadian Transport Commission, these details will not be repeated.

The study of the membership of the Board showed that commissioners had diverse educational backgrounds—correspondence courses, pharmacy, veterinary science, military affairs, law, engineering, traffic management, and transportation economics. Barristers served roughly 60 per cent of the total time of all members, agriculturists about 20 per cent, and trade unionists approximately 12 per cent. Over two-thirds of the more than forty men who served on the Board between 1904 and 1967 had been elected to public office prior to their appointment. At least one had been a full-time organizer for his party. A few had been Cabinet ministers. The most ineffective members were those who, because of age, ingrained attitudes, or poor intellectual training, were unwilling to learn a new job or lacked a judicial temperament.

However much opinions may vary on the capacity of particular individuals, there can be no question that the appointees were far different from the original plan which was that the Board should consist of one lawyer, one businessman, and one with a thorough knowledge of railway affairs. Another thing is clear. The Board has never been stronger than its head. In this respect the Board was fortunate. Moreover, throughout most of its life it also had able Assistant Chief Commissioners in Dr. S. J. McLean and Hugh Wardrope. Taking one thing with another, the quality of the commissioners has not been outstanding. They compare unfavourably with deputy ministers of government departments, the board of directors of the Canadian Pacific, or the top executives of either major railway. The presence on the Board of elderly men and worn-out politicians may have discouraged abler people from accepting posts on the Board. The Canadian Maritime Commission and the Air Transport Board have similarly contained a small minority of active, competent members and a predominance of mediocrity. The same comment might be fairly made of most human organizations.

The Board's Staff

The permanent staff do all the routine work of the Board. If a commissioner is incompetent, they do his work for him if he will let them; if not, they try to "nurse him along" so that he will do no serious damage. Occasionally, a weak commissioner becomes a mouthpiece of one of the Board's experts and this may give rise to internal dissension.

Even when commissioners have had some experience in transport —and this has been unusual though not unknown—they have to lean heavily on the permanent staff. The Board's Administrative Branch handles the Commission's voluminous correspondence with carriers, shippers, consignees, and the public at large, promulgates orders, does translation work, looks after pay, holidays, and sick leave of the Board's staff, and generally concerns itself with the internal administration of the Board. The Traffic Department deals with rates. Even though the new legislation gives railways more freedom to set their own tolls, every rate will still have to be filed in Ottawa. The Engineering Branch is concerned with way and structures including the protection of highway crossings, signals, the maintenance of track and bridges, and the location of new lines. The Operations Branch tries to protect employees, passengers, trespassers, and goods in transit or in storage on railway property. In particular, it supervises the carriage of inflammable and dangerous articles like explosives, fireworks, and propane gas. It also investigates accidents, especially those involving loss of life. The Board's legal branch advises Commissioners on the conflict of provincial and Dominion jurisdiction, the provisions of the Railway Act as interpreted by the courts, and the Board's own precedents. On occasion the Board's counsel has qualified witnesses before they gave evidence, examined them in chief, cross-examined them, and generally assisted them in presenting their testimony effectively. Ordinarily witnesses have their own counsel, while lawyers for the opposing side and sometimes members of the Board conduct further examination. Finally, the Board has a Research Branch whose functions will be expended under the legislation of 1967.

Air Transport Board

Before 1938 there was practically no official regulation of commercial aviation except the licensing of aircraft and pilots. As the evils of unrestricted competition in transport developed among non-scheduled air carriers, the jurisdiction of the Board of Railway Commissioners was extended to airlines and its name changed to the Board of Transport Commissioners. Though several cases involving air transport were brought before it, the Board was not a success in its administration of civil aviation. It was too bound by precedent, too railway-minded, and too inclined to deal only with the controversies brought to its attention. In other words, it was incapable of planning the future development of a rapidly growing industry.

Perhaps the fundamental difficulty was that the Government was too indefinite in its proposals. It did not make the Transport Act sufficiently detailed. For example, the Act did not state whether the Board was to regard Trans-Canada Air Lines, now Air Canada, as merely another carrier or whether it was to prefer it in settling disputes. Consequently the Board may have unwittingly transgressed government plans, at least as they were conceived from time to time by Mr. C. D. Howe who was then in charge of civil aviation. Possibly, the Board regulated commercial aviation for too short a period for its members to learn their jobs. Neither the commissioners nor its staff had any experience in aviation. Although few commissioners had any intimate knowledge of rail transport before their appointment to the Board, they could rely on its permanent employees for information and advice.

At all events the government set up the Air Transport Board in 1944. Composed of three members, it had substantially the same powers over civil aviation as the Board of Transport Commissioners had had, except that it was specifically directed to give Trans-Canada Air Lines the authority to operate so as to enable it to fulfil its agreement with the government. Thus the Trans-Canada Air Lines Act would take precedence over the licensing powers of the new Board.

Throughout the Act creating the Board such expressions as the Board "may make recommendations," "may advise the government," and "may report on need" often occur. It is clear from these clauses and from debates in the House that the Air Transport Board is not semi-judicial like the Board of Transport Commissioners. On the contrary it is primarily an advisory body. After it has recommended that a licence be granted a particular carrier, its order must be approved by the Minister of Transport before it becomes valid. Purely legal questions and matters relating to the ownership of airlines by surface carriers are handled, respectively, by the Supreme Court and the Cabinet.

Since its establishment the Board has advised the minister on such matters as the priority of construction of airports, the dimensions of runways, a tariff of landing fees at government-owned airfields, and the disposition of airdromes built during the war. It surveyed the flow of passenger travel in Canada and tried to estimate the potential volume of air travel. It has also participated in the negotiations with the United States and other countries on international flights. One of the most intractable problems faced by the Board was how to deal with regional carriers. One Chairman of the Board, clearly frustrated by the course of events, publicly criticized the Diefenbaker Government for its failure to decide on its air policy. Later on, the Pearson Government put down some beacon lights on the airfield of policy.

Canadian Maritime Commission

This three-man body was created in 1947 to carry out two main tasks. First, "to administer, in accordance with regulations of the Governor-in Council, any steamship subventions voted by Parliament." Second, to "consider and recommend to the Minister [of Transport] from time to time such policies and measures as it considers necessary for the operation, maintenance, manning and development of a merchant marine and a ship-building and ship-repairing industry commensurate with Canadian maritime needs." Inasmuch as this Commission is mainly an administrative rather than a judicial body, it resembles the Air Transport Board rather more than the Board of Transport Commissioners.

Creation of a New Commission

In 1967 the Board of Transport Commissioners, the Air Transport Board, and the Canadian Maritime Commission were abolished and both their functions and their personnel were transferred to the Canadian Transport Commission. The constitution and duties of the new body are best explained by summarizing the relevant legislation.

The Canadian Transport Commission consists of not more than seventeen members appointed by the Cabinet. It is a court of record, so that, broadly speaking, its rulings on fact are taken as final. Each commissioner is appointed for ten years, is removable for cause by the Cabinet at any time, retires on the expiration of his term or at the age of 70 at the latest, and, if below the age of retirement, is eligible for reappointment for a period not exceeding ten years.

The Cabinet appoints one of the commissioners as president and two as vice-president. One of the latter must be a barrister or advocate of at least ten years' standing at the bar of any province of Canada. He is to supervise the work of the committees of the Commission. His opinion on any question of law touching the operations of the Commission shall prevail, unless the president is himself a barrister or advocate of at least ten years' standing. The other vice-president need not be a barrister and is charged with the superintendence of the programs of study and research necessary to achieve the objectives of National Transportation Policy (sec. 1 of the Act and quoted in chapter one of this book) and to enable the Commission to perform its duties. The law does not specify the qualifications of commissioners generally, except that they are prohibited from having any direct interest in the undertaking of a transport company or of a manufacturer of transport equipment, or in any device, appliance, machine, patented process or article required or used as part of the equipment of any company engaged in transport.

The National Transportation Act sets forth the powers and duties of the Commission in some detail. The exercise of these functions is subject to appeal as explained later.

14. It is the duty of the Commission to perform the functions vested in the Commission by this Act, the *Railway Act*, the *Aeronautics Act* and the *Transport Act* with the object of co-ordinating and harmonizing the operations of all carriers engaged in transport by railways, water, aircraft, extra-

provincial motor vehicle transport and commodity pipelines; and the Commission shall give to this Act . . . [and the other Acts named above] such fair interpretation as will best attain that object.

15. (1) In addition to its powers, duties and functions under the *Railway Act*, the *Aeronautics Act* and the *Transport Act*, the Commission shall (*a*) inquire into and report to the Minister [of Transport] upon measures to assist in a sound economic development of the various modes of transport over which Parliament has jurisdiction (*b*) undertake studies and research into the economic aspects of all modes of transport within, into and from Canada; (*c*) inquire into and report to the Minister on the relationship between the various modes of transport within, into and from Canada and upon the measures that should be adopted in order to achieve co-ordination in development, regulation and control of the various modes of transport; (*d*) perform, in addition to its duties under this Act, such other duties as may, from time to time, be imposed by law on the Commission in respect of any mode of transport in Canada, including the regulation and licensing of any such mode of transport, control over rates and tariffs and the administration of subsidies voted by Parliament for any such mode of transport; (*e*) inquire into and report to the Minister upon possible financial measures required for direct assistance to any mode of transport and the method of administration of any measures that may be approved; (*f*) inquire into and recommend to the Minister from time to time such economic policies and measures as it considers necessary and desirable relating to the operation of the Canadian merchant marine, commensurate with Canadian maritime needs; (*g*) establish general economic standards and criteria to be used in the determination of federal investment in equipment and facilities as between various modes of transport and within individual modes of transport and in the determination of desirable financial returns therefrom; (*h*) inquire into and advise the government on the overall balance between expenditure programs of government departments or agencies for the provision of transport facilities and equipment in various modes of transport, and on measures to develop revenue from the use of . . . [such government facilities]; and (*i*) participate in the economic aspects of the work of intergovernmental, national or international organizations dealing with any form of transport under the jurisdiction of Parliament, and investigate and report on the economic effects and requirements resulting from participation in or ratification of international agreements.

In carrying out the above duties, "the Commission may consult with persons, organizations and authorities that in the opinion of the Commission are in a position to assist the Commission in formulating and recommending policy and the Commission may appoint and consult with committees being representative of such persons, organizations and authorities" (sec. 15 (4)).

For the purposes of performing its duties . . . the Commission shall [according to sec. 17] establish the following committees consisting of not less than three commissioners, exclusive of the President who shall be *ex officio* a member of every such committee: (a) railway transport committee;

(b) air transport . . . ; (c) water . . . ; (d) motor vehicle . . . ; (e) commodity pipeline . . . ; and (f) such other committees as the Commission deems expedient. (2) In respect of each such committee the Commission shall appoint a commissioner to be chairman of the committee who shall be the chief executive officer of the committee and shall in the absence or disability of both the President and the vice-president who qualifies . . . [as a barrister] preside at all sittings of the Committee and exercise all the powers of the President. (3) . . . a committee of the Commission may, in accordance with the rules and regulations of the Commission, exercise all the powers and duties of the Commission and the orders, rules or directions made or issued by a committee of the Commission have the effect, subject to . . . [the right of appeal which is described later], as though they were made or issued directly by the Commission.

The National Transportation Act also codifies what has long been the practice. In sec. 17 (5), it provides that "at any hearing of the Commission for the purpose of making an order or giving any direction, leave, sanction or approval in respect of any matter under the jurisdiction of the Commission, . . . [it] may, notwithstanding any provision of the *Railway Act*, the *Aeronautics Act*, the *Transport Act*, the *National Energy Board Act* or this Act, permit the representative or agent of any provincial or municipal government or any association or other body representing the interests of shippers or consignees in Canada to appear and be heard before the Commission subject to such rules of procedure as the Commission may prescribe."

Comments on the New Commission

The Minister of Transport, Mr. J. W. Pickersgill, told the House of Commons on September 1, 1966, that

one of the most important things . . . is to have one unified organ of government divorced from any of these different modes of transport which would look at all of them, compare one with another and, when considering the regulation of one, would take account of what was happening in the other fields and determine whether we were getting the best value by spending public money on railways, for example, or whether it would be better to scrap a branch of a railway and concentrate on a highway or an air line. We ought to be doing a lot more of this in Canada than we are today, if we are not to be burdened with expensive services which will not support themselves and for which users cannot pay—services which therefore become an increasing burden on the treasury. . . . [The main reason for the new Commission] was not that the regulatory functions would necessarily be better done by a body with separate committees, but that . . . it was just as important to have continuous research, investigation and study, and to have it done by competent people all the time, and not just spasmodically, as it was to have good regulations and able boards to administer those regulations.

For the most part critics of the legislation paid little attention to the new arrangements except to express their fears that the Canadian Transport Commission might become a bureaucratic monster. They also pointed out that a previous effort at co-ordinating the regulation of transport had failed. In 1938 the Transport Act, sec. 3 (2) was amended to provide that "it shall be the duty of the Board [of Transport Commissioners] to perform the functions vested in the Board by the [Transport] Act and by the Railway Act with the object of co-ordinating and harmonizing the operations of all carriers engaged in transport by railways and ships and the Board shall give to this Act and to the Railway Act such fair interpretation as will best attain the object aforesaid." Before the creation of the Air Transport Board in 1944, this subsection also included airlines.

The Board took account of this directive in dealing with the competition of airlines and railways between Edmonton and Waterways (McMurray), Alta., in 1941 and between Montreal and the Lake St. John district of Quebec in 1943.[20] It also had the directive in mind when dealing with a dispute over agreed charges between railways and inland ships in 1940.[21] Thereafter, the admonition to harmonize the various media of transport was a dead letter.

The basic difficulties lie outside the control of the regulatory authority. They are (i) the divided jurisdiction of the Dominion and of the provinces over transportation; (ii) the activity of private and contract carriers by highway which are not subject to governmental control except as regards safety of operations and the licensing of vehicles and drivers; (iii) the fact that the usefulness of rates as a means of integrating transport is still further restricted by the greater freedom enjoyed by railways in setting their own rates (subject to the Commission's control over maximum rates on captive traffic and minimum rates on competitive traffic); (iv) the insistence of some provinces, notably Alberta, that they should keep rates charged by truckers at the lowest practicable level in order to force railways to publish the lowest possible rates; and (v) the feeling that officials of railways and trucking concerns are in a better position to know whether the rates they publish are compensatory than any board in Ottawa, no matter how well intentioned its members may be.

Apparently Mr. Pickersgill was aware of the shortcomings of rates as a means of harmonizing various transport media because he stressed the value of the advice of the new Commission in preventing unnecessary duplication of government investment in transport facilities. Several difficulties arise in this connection. First, the Dominion government has complete control only over roads through Dominion parks and in the Yukon and Northwest Territories. To be sure, it has given financial assistance to the provinces for the Trans-Canada Highway and under the Roads to Resources programme. But in these instances it made clear that the final responsibility for the construction and maintenance of roads rests with the provinces. In theory a good deal of money might be saved if provinces refused to spend money on roads which paralleled a branch line of railway which was barely able to make ends meet financially. In practice, it would be disastrous for any political party purposely to keep the public in a given territory from having decent highways in order, in effect, to subsidize a railway.

A second limitation is that one of the basic principles of the British or parliamentary system of government is the concentration of responsibility on one minister or another. Of course, he will receive advice from his staff and from interested members of the public. But he is not obliged to accept it. If he does so and the advice turns out to be bad, he cannot escape his personal responsibility by blaming civil servants or members of a commission. Indeed, he may decide not to let the public know what advice, if any, he has received. If it is true, as Mr. Pickersgill suggested, that the Government has been receiving inadequate and biased advice, the remedy surely lies in engaging competent men and not necessarily in rolling three boards together and then enlarging its membership. The author suggests that duplication in investment in transport is not so much the result of lack of advice but of the unwillingness of Cabinet ministers and of Members of Parliament and of provincial legislatures to resist political pressures for redundant facilities. Further, at least part of what now appears to be redundant is, in fact, a price we must pay for technological change. As new forms of transport come into being, capital must be dis-invested by the older forms. Something can be said in favour of scaling down the rate of dis-investment by "phasing out" the operation, so that the older kinds of capital will be worn out by the time they are finally discarded. But care must be taken not to overdo the process and thereby deny the shipping and travelling public the benefits of modern techniques of transport.

A third point is that the new Canadian Transport Commission seems to be a muddle of executive and judicial functions. It is to advise the government on certain matters such as investment in transport facilities, subsidies to operators of ships and owners of shipyards, and grants to railways for the continued operation of unprofitable branch lines. At the same time the Commission will have to adjudicate new questions, such as who is a captive shipper, what constitutes a compensatory rate, and when a reasonably satisfactory alternative means of transport exists so that a railway passenger train or branch line can be withdrawn. Admittedly, the line between a judicial and an administrative decision is often a narrow one. Yet the Board of Transport Commissioners in respect of civil aviation and the Air Transport Board both got into trouble when they tried to act judicially and reached conclusions which did not fit in with the Minister's predilections. The author does not advocate a rigid separation of powers like that contemplated in the Constitution of the United States. Nevertheless, it is advisable to avoid a muddling of functions wherever this can be done without marked loss in efficiency.

On the face of things, savings can be secured by having one staff to deal with problems of law, economics, the filing of tariffs, and the like for all modes of transport subject to Dominion jurisdiction. Even so, an engineer who is qualified to decide whether the crossing of a railway by a highway is properly protected or whether a locomotive can be safely operated is not likely to know much about the airworthiness of an aircraft or the seaworthiness of a ship whose owners are applying for a subsidy. It seems strange that questions of mechanical safety as regards railways should come under the new Commission while similar matters involving ships and aircraft should remain with the Department of Transport. The separation is historical—and quite illogical. In any event an economist who, over the course of years, develops the sixth sense which convinces him about the soundness of a freight rate may not be in a position fairly to judge the reasonableness of a fare by aircraft or the proper size of a subsidy requested by the owner of a coastal ship.

A previous effort to integrate the research activities of the federal government on transport broke down fairly quickly. Shortly after 1945 the government set up a Bureau of Transportation Economics. It was to conduct continuous research for the Board of Transport Commissioners, the Air Transport Board, the Department of Transport, and for any other department upon request. Its publications included studies of potential air traffic, railway operations since 1923, an analysis of railway way-bills, and a study of the merchant marine. For administrative purposes it was placed under the Board of Transport Commissioners. After a few years experience with this arrangement, it was decided to divide up the Bureau and parcel out its functions by agencies. The legislation of 1967 made no reference to the Transportation and Public Utilities section of the Bureau of Statistics which collects a great many facts of interest to the regulatory boards and, on occasion, duplicates what they do. Only time will reveal whether research on various modes of transport can be truly integrated or whether, as seems more likely to the author, various experts will merely work under the same roof on problems which remain essentially different.

The size of the new Commission is a further problem. The constituent bodies regulating railways, air, and subsidies to shipping had 6, 3, and 3 members, a total of 12. The new body is to have not more than 17. It is not clear why any increase should be necessary in view of the fact that railways have greater freedom to set their own rates than formerly and the MacPherson Commission believed that general rate cases would be things of the past. If the government expected that the Commission would start a "crash" programme for the abandonment of unprofitable branch lines and passenger trains, a bigger board might be justified. In fact, abandonments will not proceed as rapidly in the late 1960s as they did a decade or two earlier. The Government in conjunction with railways and in consultation with provincial governments, large shippers, and elevator companies in the West, seems to have pre-judged what lines may be abandoned over the next few years.

In the author's view the new Canadian Transport Commission should consist of fewer but more highly skilled members than the appointees to its constituent bodies. A large board encourages regions and interested groups such as agriculture and labour to seek "representation" on it. Having once attained its objective, each area and group wants to retain its member and other interested parties put forward plausible claims for their own representatives. As a result the board tends to become larger than it needs to be to carry out its functions. Further, the range of choice when vacancies occur is very restricted, for appointees must satisfy two and probably three sets of requirements, occupational, regional, and political. In 1952 the Government announced that it was abandoning regional representation but the larger board set up in 1967 strengthens the hand of every province and interested group to insist that "its man be taken care of." By reducing the size of the Board more emphasis would be placed on the ability and fair-mindedness of the appointees. The right of appeal to the Governor-in-Council obviously ensures that no legitimate interest will be overlooked. Should a small commission find itself unable to handle its work expeditiously owing to the illness of one or more of its members or to a temporary overload, an additional commissioner might be appointed *pro hac vice*. This is already partially provided for in the Railway Act. In any event it is easy to enlarge a board if the need arises; the difficulty of cutting down on size and improving quality seems to be insuperable.

Appeals

An order or decision of the Board of Transport Commissioners or of
the Air Transport Board was not necessarily final and the right of
appeal was carried over into the legislation of 1967. Since the work
of the Canadian Maritime Commission was primarily to advise the
Minister and to administer subsidies, the question of formal appeals
did not arise with it.

Appeals were allowed from the Air Transport Board (*a*) to the
Minister of Transport where the Board suspended, amended, or refused
to issue a licence authorizing a carrier to fly a route commercially, or
attached conditions to which the applicant objected, and (*b*) to the
Supreme Court of Canada on matters of law or jurisdiction. The Act
setting up the Board was not clear on the Minister's power to dispose
of an appeal. Apparently he had no authority to direct the Board to issue
a licence though he might veto what the Board had recommended.
In practice, any far-reaching appeal was considered by the entire
Cabinet.

The Railway Act provided that the Board of Transport Commissioners might review, rescind, change, alter or vary any order or decision
made by it or might re-hear any application. An appeal might be carried
to the Supreme Court of Canada upon (*a*) any question of jurisdiction
with the consent of a judge of the Court and (*b*) any question which,
in the opinion of the Board, was a question of law or of jurisdiction or
both, leave having been first obtained from the Board. The Governor-
in-Council might at any time in his discretion, either upon petition of
any party, person, or company interested, or of his own motion and
without petition or application, vary or rescind any order, decision,
etc., of the Board.[22]

The legislation of 1967 provided that any committee of the Canadian
Transport Commission might exercise all the powers of the Commission
itself and issue orders in its name. Though the Railway Act had included
a similar arrangement, the National Transportation Act was more
explicit on the matter of appeals. Questions of rates and licences are to
be handled in the same manner as before and as described above, but
on other subject matter "where an order, rule or direction made by a
committee of the Commission in respect of a matter related to a particular mode of transport . . . is objected to by an operator of another
mode of transport on the ground that the order . . . discriminates against
or is otherwise unfair to his operations, the Commission shall, otherwise

than by that committee of the Commission, review the order . . . in accordance with such rules of procedure as the Commission may prescribe therefore, and shall confirm, rescind, change, alter or vary the order . . . or rehear the matter thereof" (sec. 17 (4)). In practice such appeals will probably be limited to the acquisition of a trucking line by another mode of transport.

During the parliamentary debate on these provisions, objection was made that the natural inclination of the Commission or its committee on appeals would be to support the decision of the panel of its own members who had heard the case initially. The same argument might perhaps be made about any appellate body. In this connection it is easy for disgruntled men to drop suggestions of bias yet hard to get complainants to make, let alone substantiate, charges of prejudice. At all events those who have lost a case on appeal may bring the matter before the Supreme Court of Canada or the Governor-in-Council.

The best approach to the problem of appeals is obviously to see what has happened in the past. Only one appeal was made on an order of the Air Transport Board. This was in 1953 when the Cabinet over-ruled the Board and denied Canadian Pacific Air Lines the right to fly freight between Montreal, Vancouver, and intermediate points in apparent competition with Trans-Canada. Of course there is no way of knowing to what extent, if at all, the Board was influenced by the knowledge that if its decision went contrary to government policy, it would be overruled on appeal. The Board of Transport Commissioners did not suffer from this disability to the same extent as the Air Transport Board because the former was a court, the latter an advisory body.

Relatively few cases have, in fact, been appealed from the Board of Transport (or Railway) Commissioners and only a small proportion of the appeals have been successful.[23] Regarding appeals to the Governor-in-Council "a practice has grown up not to interfere with an order of the Board unless it seems manifest that the Board has pro-ceeded upon some wrong principle, or that it has been otherwise subject to error. Where the matters at issue are questions of fact depending for their solution upon a mass of conflicting testimony or are otherwise such as the Board is particularly fitted to determine, it has been cus-tomary, except as aforesaid, not to interfere with the findings of the Board."[24]

All provinces appearing before the Royal Commission of 1951 would retain the present provisions of the Railway Act with regard to the right of the Governor-in-Council to vary or rescind any order of the Board, and the power of the Governor-in-Council to refer to the Board for study and report any matter within the scope of the Railway

Act. Manitoba proposed that the Governor-in-Council should be given the further power of referring any matter to the Board with directions regarding the disposition thereof. It claimed that directives from the Governor-in-Council were necessary in order to ensure that the Board should not act inconsistently with the Dominion government's view of what is in the national interest. Directives could not be contrary to the Railway Act and should be on policy matters only.

The Canadian Pacific not only opposed the proposal of Manitoba, it wanted to abolish the power of the Governor-in-Council to vary or rescind. It alleged that appeals to a political tribunal had a stultifying effect upon the Board and tended to prevent it from exercising its powers impartially and judicially. The right of appeal was a gilt-edged invitation to the public to carry decisions of the Board to a political body and to bring *ex parte* cases before it. Members of Council lacked both the time and the technical training to deal with complicated questions of tolls and other railway matters. Abolition of appeals to the Governor-in-Council would not deny Parliament's ultimate authority to control the Board because it could amend the Railway Act whenever it cared to do so. The Minister of Transport or the Governor-in-Council might also at any time refer matters to the Board for investigation and report. Though this would not ensure that the Board would decide matters in accordance with what the Government regarded as the public interest, it would make certain that the Board would study every subject which it ought to consider. Moreover, the government of the day appoints commissioners to the Board whenever vacancies occur.

Both major railways told the Royal Commission of 1951 that Manitoba's proposal would tend to reduce the Board to a mere cog in the machinery of government. It would possibly open the way to increased political pressure and lead to the political control of rates which was in vogue before the Board of Railway Commissioners was established. If the Cabinet interfered too often, it would practically destroy the usefulness of the Board, make it subservient to every whim of the party in power at the time, and discourage competent men from accepting positions on the Board of Transport Commissioners.

The soundness of Manitoba's proposal can be fairly judged only by examining the record of the Governor-in-Council in varying or rescinding orders of the Board. He has never of his own motion and without any petition or application exercised this power. On the contrary, the Governor-in-Council has acted, generally speaking, in the same way as a court. He receives a petition and before rendering judgment hears both parties who are represented by counsel.[25]

Of the roughly 60 appeals to the Cabinet between 1904 and 1965 only

4 have been allowed, 15 have been referred back, and the remainder have been dismissed, withdrawn, or abandoned. Over one-third of the total dealt with engineering matters like crossings, grade separation, construction of spurs, and location of stations. Another third concerned details of rates, e.g., on glass jars, on lumber in British Columbia, fares on the Montreal and Southern Counties Railway, the classification of ice cream, increased tolls on cream, and freight overcharges.

In almost all these cases the Cabinet supported the Board and in recent years there have been few appeals on matters of this sort. Therefore it can be argued that no harm would be done by denying the right of appeal to the Cabinet. Litigants could still go before the Supreme Court of Canada. Furthermore, the Cabinet could see that legislation was passed to rectify any defects in the existing law and insure that it was always in accord with public policy.

On the other hand one can argue that because these cases have become less frequent as time has gone on, the Governor-in-Council will not be seriously inconvenienced by having to hear an occasional case on engineering and individual rates in future. Moreover, his right to vary or rescind constitutes a residue of power, a kind of safety valve, which it is desirable to retain. Theoretically this section of the Act is easily exposed to the criticism that it makes it possible to obtain from a political body what has been denied by the judiciary. In practice, no abuse has arisen. The Governor-in-Council, like the Board and the Supreme Court, has added to the body of precedent and so reduced the need for future appeals on the same subject matter.

The final third of the cases dealt with by the Governor-in-Council concerns much broader questions than those just mentioned. They directly involve the general level of rates in Canada and often matters of economic policy such as the encouragement of exports, the general price level, the financial stability of the privately owned railway, and deficits on the Canadian National. With very few exceptions every decision of the Board allowing a general increase in tolls or increased rates on grain has been carried to the Governor-in-Council.

On these broad questions an appeal to the Cabinet has become part of the normal process of fixing rates with the result that the prestige of the Board has been lowered and perhaps the Governor-in-Council burdened with vexations which he might prefer to avoid. Furthermore, the disposition of general rate cases by the Cabinet has often settled very little, for it has customarily sent them back to the Board. Now it is by no means unusual for an appellate body to send a case back to an inferior court for retrial, but it is exceptional, to say the least, to leave the issue as unsettled, as wide open for further argument, as the

Governor-in-Council has customarily done. It should be noted, however, that in the appeal on the question of the Tax Equalization Reserve in 1958, the Cabinet's decision was unequivocal.

The legislation of 1967 may have the effect of discouraging appeals on rates. Even though it does not specifically outlaw general rate cases, it contemplates eventual abolition of them. On the other hand the true meaning of such terms as captive shipper and compensatory rate still has to be adjudicated. In addition, the parties directly affected by a line abandonment and probably the provincial government concerned will not stop until they have exhausted every remedy to prevent what they regard as unfairness to a locality or economic region of Canada. It may be that the Governor-in-Council will take refuge in the fact that the Board is in a better position to decide such matters than Cabinet ministers who lack the technical knowledge and the time to adjudicate such questions properly. In that event they will either reject the petition outright or else send it back to the Canadian Transport Commission for re-hearing or review. By so doing the Cabinet will discourage subsequent appeals on the same subject matter.[26]

Appeals to the Cabinet will not cease until railways realize that, given the kinds of competition which they have to face, no amount of regulation will insure them a fair return on their investment and that their hope lies in greater operating efficiency; until provincial governments realize that freight rates, important as they are, will not effectively remove their geographic and economic disabilities; until communities and labour unions realize that plant must be rationalized if railways are to be economically viable and heavy government subsidies are to be avoided; and until every member of the Board is as able as the best of those in office at any one time. Furthermore, cessation of appeals to the Cabinet means a break in our tradition. As the Royal Commission of 1951 phrased it, relations between Parliament and the railway companies "have always been such that Government supervision over railway matters cannot be entirely abolished. . . . It is extremely difficult to recommend that the Government should dissociate itself entirely from the activities of the railways and the performance by the Board of Transport Commissioners of its duties."[27] This principle still applies, and is recognized by the legislation of 1967.

17

Government Ownership of Railways

CANADIAN experience regarding the virtues and disabilities of government ownership of railways is not conclusive. This is due to four factors: the conditions under which the state took over the roads; the lack of some pertinent data and the intractability of the data available; the stage of the business cycle from which the problem is viewed, whether peak, depression, or normal times; and the bias of the observer. When all is said and done, the decision regarding public ownership rests with the electorate, and voters, alas, are not always influenced by pure logic.

When the privately owned railways now forming the Canadian National were taken over by the government, few persons were in favour of public ownership as such. The country's experience with the Intercolonial was not conducive to enthusiasm. To be sure, the Intercolonial was operated under conditions least favourable to success in public enterprise. It was controlled directly by a government department under a Cabinet minister, often from the area concerned, who was inevitably preoccupied with the re-election of himself and his party. Politicians frankly admitted they interfered with the railway though parties differed on which meddled less. Freight rates on the Intercolonial were not intended to cover its operating costs and interest but to foster the economic development of a region. The line was poorly located with respect to traffic, had a circuitous route between Montreal, Halifax, and Saint John, and ran in part through relatively unproductive terrain. Its own lines did not reach the traffic centres in Ontario and the West. It competed at Montreal with the Canadian Pacific and the Grand Trunk which had their own oceanic terminals, the one at Saint John and the other at Portland, Me. Inevitably it was a financial failure.

The Canadian public slid into government ownership or let themselves be pushed into it by the exigencies of World War I. Early in the twentieth century the Grand Trunk planned to build a railway from its existing terminus at North Bay, Ont., to the Pacific coast, but the federal government withheld its financial assistance until the company accepted a government proposal for a line, the National Transcontinental, from Winnipeg to Quebec City, later to Moncton.[1] The government was to build this line and lease it to the Grand Trunk Pacific while the latter would build from Winnipeg westward to the coast. The cost of the government section was estimated at roughly $61.4 million at the time the contract was signed in 1903. By the end of 1914 when the line was alleged to be completed, the cost exceeded the estimate by $100 million without interest on capital during construction. The nearly tripled cost was due to generally rising prices and wages, to the unnecessarily high standard of construction for curves and gradients, to laxity in watching expenses, and perhaps to graft.[2]

When the government late in 1913 asked the Grand Trunk Pacific to take over the line in accordance with the contract, the latter refused. Officially it claimed that the road had not yet been completed. More probably, the Grand Trunk Pacific balked at paying the interest on a capital sum so far in excess of the original estimated cost and realized that the line could add nothing to the profits or traffic of the parent Grand Trunk. In 1915 the government again asked the Grand Trunk Pacific to assume responsibility for the line. As that road took no action, the government began to operate the National Transcontinental itself. Thus inferentially it released the Grand Trunk Pacific from its contract and acquired another railway besides the Intercolonial.

Meanwhile the Grand Trunk had been financially unable to complete the Winnipeg–Prince Rupert line on account of the stringency in the money markets of the world during World War I. The Canadian Northern was also in serious difficulty. The government announced that it was faced with three alternatives. It could withhold credit, thus forcing the Grand Trunk Pacific, the Canadian Northern, and possibly the Grand Trunk into bankruptcy. Domestic borrowing was then in its infancy, and insolvency of three large railways would harm Canadian credit abroad where the Dominion had to borrow large sums in New York and London for war purposes. The provinces would seize those parts of the two newer systems on which they had guaranteed bond interest. Dismemberment of existing roads would obviously be calamitous. Indeed, it was doubtful whether without federal assistance some of the provinces had the financial resources to pay the heavy bond interest which they had in boom times glibly guaranteed.

The second alternative was to foreclose the mortgage which the

Dominion had taken against the property as partial security for its bond guarantees. If this were done, the Dominion would operate the roads until the earning power of the companies revived so that they could pay off the government debt or until the railways could raise money elsewhere. Finally, the Dominion could extend temporary financial assistance until a Royal Commission could be appointed to investigate and report upon the problem.[3]

Royal Commission of 1917

The last alternative was selected and a Commission of three appointed. Two of the commissioners, Sir Henry Drayton and Sir William Acworth,[4] rejected a proposal that the lines be allowed to go into bankruptcy as would have happened with privately owned railways in the United States. Investors in the Canadian lines believed that their stocks and bonds were backed by the government. Default would ruin the credit of Canada abroad. Perhaps the two commissioners were also influenced by the shortage of rolling stock in 1917 and the apparent inability of private finance to supply it.

In any event a majority of the commissioners rejected the idea that the Dominion should operate the lines directly because politics would enter in. The Intercolonial was a horrible example of political interference. Then the Canadian government as a railway operator would be subject to the Interstate Commerce Commission in respect of its railway lines in the United States. Our government ought not to be under the control of a creature of a foreign government. If the Dominion operated the three roads it would be morally bound to purchase the Canadian Pacific too. A government railway might lower freight rates, make up the deficiency in net operating revenue out of general taxation, and justify itself on the ground that it was promoting the general prosperity and development of the country. Abnormally low rates on the government-operated road would virtually wreck the Canadian Pacific. Finally Canada, pledged as she was to carry on the war, could not sustain the financial burden of putting the railroads into shape.

The two commissioners believed that the Grand Trunk could not survive even if it could wash its hands of its Prairie subsidiary. Its earnings were not high enough to pay dividends; its facilities were inadequately maintained; and its rolling stock insufficient. The Canadian Northern badly needed more cars and locomotives. Its common stock represented no cash investment. On the basis of present and prospective earnings the value of the road did not exceed liabilities. Since the road had been financed chiefly by bonds and the Dominion had guaranteed most of the interest, it was logical that the federal government should take over the road when it got in trouble.

Drayton and Acworth recommended that the Dominion create a separate company to own and operate all the government lines then in existence, namely, the Intercolonial, Prince Edward Island Railway, and the National Transcontinental. This corporation would also have transferred to it the private lines which were in financial straits, i.e., the Canadian Northern, Grand Trunk, and Grand Trunk Pacific. These lines would be united into a single system for operating purposes. The corporation would be administered by five trustees, three being men of railway experience, one skilled in business and finance, and one having the confidence of railway employees. When a vacancy occurred, whether through death, voluntary retirement, or expiry of term of office, the remaining trustees were to submit the name of a replacement for the approval of the government. The Railway was not to be subject to direct parliamentary control but was to be under the Board of Railway Commissioners in the same way as any private company. Drayton and Acworth attached great importance to the co-optive trustee board and the jurisdiction of the Board of Railway Commissioners as a means of freeing the company from political pressure and local interests.

Mr. A. H. Smith, the third member of the Royal Commission of 1917 and president of the New York Central, regretted that Canada had not had a body that could have prevented needless duplication of facilities. He recommended that the Canadian Pacific be left alone for it was self-contained and self-sustaining. He felt that there was no reason why the Grand Trunk standing by itself should not be profitable since, while it needed better equipment and terminals, it had a good territory in both Canada and the United States. The Canadian Northern was well constructed and managed, earning a large part of its fixed charges even though part of the road had been in operation only a year. Though its invasion of the East had been unwise and the road was handicapped by inability to raise money and by high fixed charges, Mr. Smith thought that the affairs of the Canadian Northern would improve with a return to normal conditions.

In essence, Commissioner Smith proposed to let the Grand Trunk operate its own and the Canadian Northern's lines in Eastern Canada; let the Canadian Northern run its own and the Grand Trunk Pacific's lines in the West; and let the government operate the connecting links across Northern Ontario and Quebec. The Grand Trunk would be relieved of its obligations regarding the National Transcontinental and the Grand Trunk Pacific, but would have to pay the fixed charges on the Canadian Northern lines east of North Bay. Similarly the Canadian

Northern would lease the Grand Trunk Pacific for its annual fixed charges. The connecting links north of Lakes Superior and Huron would be leased by the government for twenty-one years to the Canadian Northern or the Grand Trunk or to any other qualified operator on terms which would give the needed service at the lowest cost to the public exchequer. The Railway Act was to be amended to give the Board of Railway Commissioners control of maximum and minimum rates, the issue of securities, and the construction of new lines.

Mr. Smith believed that his plan would provide a maximum of efficiency at a minimum outlay. It would reduce government aid to the lowest possible point and centralize it upon lines that were not self-supporting. These "bridges" were not of sufficient importance to bring about the losses inherent in government operation on a large scale nor endanger private enterprise. The government should give further financial aid to the railways only on the recommendation of a Board of Trustees. It should, however, immediately provide more rolling stock under equipment trust certificates. Mr. Smith was convinced that the railroads could work out their own salvation if they were given an even break and had the co-operation of the government.

Acquisition of Constituent Railways

After receiving the report of the Royal Commission, the government took steps to acquire the Canadian Northern at once and advanced cash to the Grand Trunk Pacific to enable it to carry on. Drayton and Acworth had stated that the owners of the common stock of the Canadian Northern had not of right any claim to compensation but as many of their lines were well located, as the Company had done much for the West, and as it was economically constructed, they should retain some of their equity.

Accordingly in taking over the Company, the government proposed to set up a Board of Arbitration to value these securities. The matter was complicated because 87 per cent of the stock was pledged as security either to the Dominion or to a Canadian chartered bank for an advance of cash. One Member of Parliament asked baldly if the object of the bill were not "to save from bankruptcy the bank which was said to be responsible for all the Canadian Northern liabilities since its very inception."[5]

The arbitrators[6] heard Sir Donald Mann, one of the two chief promoters of the Canadian Northern, testify that the Company had had three plans for getting out of trouble without government help. A loan from London was stopped by government intervention through the appointment of the Royal Commission in 1917. Sale to a financial group connected with the Canadian Pacific was blocked early in 1917 by the government which feared a monopoly would be created. Inviting the provinces to pay the interest on the bonds they had guaranteed was interrupted by the federal government's decision to buy. Sir Donald Mann claimed that Drayton and Acworth had left out of consideration money in banks and land with a total value of $52 million.

The arbitrators stated the cost of reproduction new less depreciation gave a surplus of assets over liabilities, as of October, 1917, of not less than $25 million. But, the arbitrators said, while this is "an element for consideration . . . , it is not conclusive as to the value of the stock of the company. The prospective earning power is perhaps more important than any other element in ascertaining such value. And in arriving at a conclusion we have given careful consideration to the past history of the company, the location of its lines and their construction, the rate of interest on the funded and other debts of the company, the probable future growth of the population and business of the country, and all other factors which seem to have a bearing on the question."[7] As a result of their deliberations, the arbitrators set a value of $10,800,000 on the common stock of the Canadian Northern.

Early in 1918 the government opened negotiations to acquire the Grand Trunk. In March, 1919, when the Grand Trunk Pacific paid its bond interest, it announced that it could not continue operations. Hence the government appointed the Minister of Railways and Canals receiver for the road. The parent company was thus relieved of some of its pressing financial obligations. A year later the Grand Trunk agreed to sell its property to the Dominion in return for a guarantee of interest on its bonds and the payment of a sum to be set by arbitration for its common and preference stocks.

Two arbitrators, a former minister of finance and a judge of the Exchequer Court, both Canadians, held that the stocks of the Grand Trunk had no value. The Company's accounts had been manipulated to pay dividends which it had not earned. Paying these dividends had drained away resources which should have been used to maintain and improve the property. The Company admitted that it would become insolvent if it were forced to meet all its legal obligations which included large sums advanced by the Dominion government during its receivership. The stock of the Grand Trunk had no value as the Company was not likely to have any surplus above fixed charges for many years.

On the other hand the third arbitrator, former President W. H. Taft of the United States, decided that the securities had a potential value of not less than $48 million. He said that he had every reason to expect that with the return of normal conditions the stock would again pay dividends. He did not agree with government witnesses in their enthusiastic condemnation of the physical condition of the railway nor with the other arbitrators in refusing to admit evidence as to replacement values of assets. As things turned out, Taft was probably right for the "old Grand Trunk" is the heart of the present Canadian National Railways.

The majority decision shocked English investors. They could not understand how three men experienced in finance and law could differ so widely in their valuations. They had originally offered to sell in return for annual dividends of roughly $5.2 million on the preferred and a small amount (2½ per cent after 1930) on the common. The government had offered, in essence, $3.6 million to be distributed as the Company saw fit. Now the shareholders were to get nothing. The treatment afforded the Canadian Northern, the common stock of which was owned in Canada, stood in marked and not very favourable contrast to the attitude toward shareholders in the Grand Trunk, most of whom lived in Britain. Still the Grand Trunk had accepted the arbitration proposal and the proceedings before the Board were legally correct.[8] For a time the credit standing of Canadian companies in Britain suffered. No permanent injury resulted owing to the steady growth in Canada's ability to finance herself by selling securities at home, to the shift of the world's financial centre from London to New York, and to the notoriously short memory of investors.[9]

The acrimonious controversy over finance was accompanied by a less unpleasant discussion of whether the Grand Trunk should ever have been acquired in the first place. The general consensus was that the road was necessary to round out the government system of railways which was fairly complete in the West, north of the Lakes, and in the Maritimes, but inadequate in the industrialized and populous St. Lawrence Valley. A well-established carrier was required in the St. Lawrence Lowlands to fill out the pioneer roads on the Prairies and to give the Intercolonial proper access to traffic centres in the thickly settled parts of Ontario and Quebec. It was unreasonable to relieve Grand Trunk shareholders of their financial burdens in the West without taking over the earning capacity of the road in the East. The Company might have gone into bankruptcy if left alone, because its roadbed and equipment were in poor shape, it had no lines in the growing West, and it had been consistently mismanaged by its directors who had tried to run the company from London. On the other hand, it was contended that the government was merely assuming more fiscal burdens than it need have done, that the Company would have thrived by itself if given a chance, and that the method of acquisition had created a more or less permanent grievance.

The fundamental problem facing railways from 1914 to 1920 was rising costs and relatively stationary rates. The railway history of Canada might have been quite different if during World War I, the government had had an effective system of price and wage control as it had during World War II.

Organization of the Canadian National

When the government took over the Canadian Northern in 1917, it continued to operate it under the same corporate machinery as formerly except that directors were now appointed by the government instead of elected by shareholders. The Intercolonial, the National Transcontinental, and, after March, 1919, the Grand Trunk Pacific (the Minister of Railways and Canals being receiver) were added for operating purposes but retained their separate corporate identities. This conglomeration of half-derelict lines failed to cover operating expenses and fixed charges by $48 million in 1919 and by $70 million in 1920, not counting interest on the government investment in the Intercolonial and National Transcontinental. Wages, fuel, and other operating supplies were dear. Maintenance had had to be deferred. Freight rates were not set to cover the expenses of such high cost roads.

In 1921 Lord Shaughnessy, then president of the Canadian Pacific, proposed that these lines should be combined with those of the Canadian Pacific for operating purposes but that ownership of the various properties should be kept distinct. This plan might have effected large savings in operating costs and forestalled the rapid increase in government investment in railway property. But it was unacceptable because, first, the government was to guarantee dividends on the stock of the Canadian Pacific. Second, it would create a virtual railway monopoly in Canada except in the thickly settled parts of Ontario and Quebec where the Grand Trunk would continue to operate as an independent concern. Third, the apparently improving earning power of the government-owned roads at this time gave rise to a false impression of their eventual earning power. Consequently this proposal, like a somewhat similar one of Sir Joseph Flavelle, a prominent Toronto banker, was not seriously considered.

In May, 1920, the government took over the Grand Trunk. After several changes of minor importance, the Canadian National Railways in practically its present form came into being on January 30, 1923.[10] It consisted of five major roads and 139 separate companies which had to be legally kept alive for reasons connected with the 251 different issues of securities then in existence. "Thus the administration of the Canadian

National Railways, while unified from a practical and operating point of view, remained encumbered with a mass of legal and accounting ramifications."[11]

Canadian National, 1923-33

Few companies ever began operations under greater handicaps than the Canadian National. It was a conglomeration of several lines, ill co-ordinated, often competitive with each other, poorly equipped, sometimes badly built. Except for the Grand Trunk and part of the Canadian Northern, the lines were poorly located from a traffic point of view. Much mileage was through territory still in the pioneer stage of development and some was through rough, almost barren, terrain. Most of the companies had failed to earn their fixed charges under private operation and the new system had a truly stupendous debt. Under ordinary circumstances it would have gone into bankruptcy and emerged with a lowered funded debt and reduced fixed charges. The depression immediately following World War I had undermined business confidence. Trade, industry, and especially agriculture were in the doldrums.

The infant Canadian National had to compete with the well-located, well-managed, and well-financed Canadian Pacific with its world-wide reputation for service and efficiency.[12] *Esprit de corps* among employees of the publicly owned system was lamentable. Trains were rarely on time, freight was frequently lost or stolen, operating expenses were high, and no one either among the employees or the general public seemed to care whether things got better or worse.

To deal with this accumulation of difficulties, late in 1922 the government appointed Sir Henry Thornton as president and chairman of the Board of Directors. Thornton was born and educated in the United States, gathered experience on the Pennsylvania Railroad, was general manager of an important railway company in England, and then during World War I was in charge of transport services for the British armies in France. He brought to his new task a thorough knowledge of railway matters, a tremendous capacity for work, and an exceptional ability to inspire a staff. But he also brought a penchant for constant expansion of his company's physical facilities, a tendency to overlook economies, and some personal habits which did not commend themselves to Members of Parliament from rural areas.

Mr. D. B. Hanna, formerly of the Canadian Northern who had preceded Thornton as president of the Canadian National, felt the Company would have a bright future if it confined itself mainly to freight. But Thornton wanted his road to participate in fast passenger service, hotels, and coastal steamships. Thornton's primary difficulty was in placing a limit to his ambitions for the road. He believed that to survive at all the Canadian National had to give as good service as its privately owned rival in every aspect of railroading. It will always be a question how far competition between a publicly and a privately owned company in the same field of enterprise can afford to go and still remain what might be called legitimate. At some point or other competition becomes unfair because one company can draw on the vast resources of the state for financial support while the other must always adopt the approach of the balance sheet, the careful balancing of revenues and expenditures. It must not be forgotten that during the 1920s all businesses—and governments too—had extravagant ideas of the permanence of the "new era" of prosperity. Many other firms, no less than the Canadian National, expanded far beyond what in the sombre days of 1932 and 1933 seemed expedient. Further, some of Sir Henry Thornton's ideas such as wireless-telephone communication with moving trains, diesel locomotives, and very fast passenger train service represented a healthy spirit of initiative in railway matters, a spirit which railway executives too often lacked in the 1920s but developed a decade or so later following Thornton's example.

Yet when due allowance is made for "boom psychology," a desirable degree of competition, and a laudable urge to innovate, it still remains true that Thornton went beyond proper limits. The Royal Commission of 1931-2 said that through all his administration ran "the red thread of extravagance."[13] In fact Thornton was excellent on day-to-day railway operation. But on capital extensions he was over-optimistic, finding it too easy to spend money, unpopular to refuse. Thornton is reported time and again to have said privately that public enterprise would work if the people would let it: if they interfered it would fail. Pressure for branch lines, steamship services, hotels, and so forth came from many parts of the country and probably from members of the Board of Directors. Instead of resisting this regional pressure, Thornton undertook projects about which he must have had personal misgivings but expansion was so much in line with his own predilections that he gave in. And therein lay "The Tragedy of Sir Henry Thornton."[14] He was the victim of his own virtues.

Thornton's first task was to put the System into physical condition so that it could operate efficiently. From the engineering standpoint his work was unquestionably good. Grades and curvature were reduced. Roadbeds were reballasted and tracks relaid with heavier rails. Lines which closely paralleled other lines in the System were abandoned. Larger locomotives and cars were purchased. Control of stores was centralized.

The enormous task of standardizing parts and reducing the large number of types of rolling stock which were in use on the various constituent roads was begun. Cut-offs were constructed to connect previously competing lines and reduce operating mileages. Trains were speeded up and brought into terminals on time. The slogan "courtesy and service" was not only devised but practised. Thornton made a railway out of several piles of junk. Most of all, he created an *esprit de corps*; he got whole-hearted co-operation from what had been a discouraged, disunited group of men and women.

On the financial side, Thornton's administration was less successful. When the government threw the system together it did not make a careful analysis of its actual physical condition or what money was needed to put it in proper shape. It had no long-range plan for improvement but voted money for capital improvements one year at a time. Nominally the expenditures were examined by the House of Commons Standing Committee on Railways and Steamships owned, operated, and controlled by the Government and in addition were checked by the Treasury Board and the Cabinet. In practice, up to 1930, official appraisal of capital expenditures was largely perfunctory, as a study of the reports of the Committee clearly show. The amounts voted varied with the government's own revenue position, the importunity of regional groups, and the never-satisfied demands of railway executives. Even worse, up to 1930 the Company lacked an effective system of budgetary control over its own internal current operations.

In the six years 1919–24, the Dominion's obligations on account of the publicly owned railways increased nearly $711 million, or $118 million per annum. Not all these sums were used for capital improvements, for the System was unable to meet the interest on its debt held by the public and the government. The annual deficits had to be met by the federal treasury. Advances for interest were added to the previous year's total of government advances with the result that in the following year the government debt was larger than ever. Year after year the System tended to get further and further behind. If the government had in the first place reduced the capitalization to a point where the System could fairly be expected to earn the interest on it and if it had also required the System's managers to keep costs down so they could pay interest annually, a good many subsequent difficulties might have been avoided. As it was, "the long purse of the state" was available for capital expenditures and interest charges, and the incentive toward economy was feeble.

Continuing losses on the Canadian National and fear that keen competition between the two roads for the available traffic would eventually undermine the financial stability of the Canadian Pacific led the Senate, in 1925, to appoint a Special Committee to inquire into the entire railway situation. This Committee conferred with representatives of transportation, industry, and finance though not with labour leaders. No record was made of the hearings and consequently there is no way of judging on what grounds the Committee arrived at its conclusions. The Committee discussed co-operation between the two major railways, acquisition of one by the other, and transfer of the Canadian National to a private company. It then strongly recommended that the two systems be merged for administration and operation. The Canadian Pacific was to be guaranteed a stipulated dividend on its stock. From any surplus produced by the joint management, a dividend was to be paid to the government up to the maximum of the guaranteed total paid the Canadian Pacific, after which any remaining surplus was to be divided between the two properties in proportion to their respective valuations. The Committee then went on to state that unless energetic means were adopted to reduce national debt and income tax, Canada would be unable to command the foreign capital absolutely necessary for the development of her natural resources. The railway question was one of extreme importance and the utmost urgency.[15] Despite this warning, the report did not command much popular support. It was based on private hearings, and during a period of general business prosperity the public was not receptive to radical changes.

Notwithstanding all the handicaps under which it operated, the position of the Canadian National improved steadily from 1923 to 1928. In two of these years, 1926 and 1928, its net income exceeded the amount of interest on debt in the hands of the public. Unfortunately it could make almost no contribution to the interest of roughly $30 million per annum on advances by the government nor any payment on the very large sums invested in constituent roads wholly owned by the government, namely the Intercolonial and the National Transcontinental.

In 1929 the net income of the Canadian National declined below that of the previous year. In 1931 the System failed to cover its operating expenses owing to poor crops in the West, business depression, unwillingness of management to cut service in proportion to the traffic offering, and other factors. For the years 1923–31 on the Canadian National the excess of interest due the public over net income was approximately $168 million and interest on government loans $288 million. In arriving at this amount, no account is taken of interest on the capital investment in Canadian Government Railways (i.e., the Intercolonial and National Transcontinental lines), nor were depreciation reserves set up except in the case of rolling stock owned by subsidiaries operating in the United States.

The Canadian Pacific had retained its strong financial position during the same period, 1923–31. It paid dividends on preference and common stock totalling nearly $279 million and added about $36 million to surplus. In these figures are included special or non-railway income of $65 million from steamships, land sales, and interest, dividends from the Consolidated Mining and Smelting Company which is controlled by the Railway, and from other investments.

Unfortunately net railway income of the Canadian Pacific had begun to decline after 1928. This, coupled with increased interest charges on the funded debt, began to give concern. The debt had grown because in the years 1920 to 1930 inclusive the Company had added about $130 million or nearly 15 per cent to its investment. New branches, hotels, coastal steamships, and rolling stock had been built or acquired apparently in accordance with a long-range programme laid down in 1919. Interest charges had risen over 71 per cent in the eight years after 1923. The Company had been unusually successful in controlling its operating expenses once the depression set in but the decline in traffic volume was beginning to jeopardize dividends.

Royal Commission, 1931-2

Under these circumstances the presidents of both roads requested the government to appoint a Royal Commission to investigate transportation in general and railway finance in particular. The Cabinet had regard to "the vital importance of transportation to the trade and commerce of Canada, the serious and mounting deficits of the Canadian National Railways System, and the diminished revenues of the Canadian Pacific Railways System, conditions which have been brought about in part by duplication of tracks, facilities and services of every kind and in part by competition by other modes of transportation, particularly motor vehicles operating on highways."[16]

The five-man Commission[17] reported on the fundamental unfairness of competition between the publicly owned Canadian National and the privately owned Canadian Pacific and on extravagance in the administration of the former.

The Dominion government has voted unstinted financial support to the administrators of the National System. . . . As a result the Canadian Pacific, the largest taxpayer in Canada, has been subjected to the competition of the publicly-owned and operated railway lines supported by the financial resources of the country. They had honourably discharged their original contractual obligations with Parliament, and the company's lines had played a great part in binding together the western and eastern provinces of the Dominion. By common consent, the company's administrators had brought faith, courage and invincible energy to the task of building its lines through the underdeveloped west. The Company's achievement commanded the admiration of both railway operators and the public, and has been a material factor in causing Canada to be favourably known upon three continents. Their operations brought profit to shareholders, and the enterprise became a national asset of acknowledged value and importance to the Dominion.

Confronted with the unrestrained competition of the publicly-owned railway, the Canadian Pacific claimed that to protect their business it was necessary that they should meet their competitors in the construction of branch lines in prairie sections and generally in the character of service and equipment incident to the activity of their aggressive rival. If good sense had prevailed the executive officers of the two systems would, in 1923, have planned together to meet the transportation requirements of the country, and would have refused to promote or permit irrational and wasteful competition. . . .

Following upon the consolidation of many lines into the Canadian National System, in 1923, the railway has been energetically administered, and has deservedly won approval by its success in welding together the various working forces of the separate companies in the consolidated system.

Running through its administrative practices, however, has been the red thread of extravagance. The disciplinary check upon undue expenditure, inherent in private corporations because of their limited financial resources, has not been in evidence. Requisitions of the management have been endorsed by governments, and successive parliaments have voted money freely, if not lavishly. . . . There has been . . . a great sense of expectancy that the publicly-owned enterprise should give all and sundry the railway service desired, and there is no evidence that the representatives of the people in Parliament exercised any appreciable restraint upon railway estimates placed before them.[18]

The Commission deplored duplication in railway-owned hotels, coastal steamships, and passenger services,[19] and demanded that it should cease.

Had this competition existed between private companies, each dependent upon its own resources to raise capital and pay the bill, it is likely that years of adversity would have brought wisdom. But one of these competitors was backed by the long purse of the state. . . . The evils of this unfortunate competition did not rest there. Challenged by the State-subsidized National System, the Canadian Pacific felt compelled, in defense of its own interests, to meet the challenge. Now in the interests of both railways and of the taxpayers of Canada there must be cessation of aggressive and uncontrolled competition, and while the Canadian Pacific must be afforded proper protection from the State-subsidized activities of the Canadian National, it is not possible to absorb the privately-owned company from a share in the general competitive folly.[20]

The Commission might have added that Sir Edward Beatty was not a whit less aggressive than Sir Henry Thornton.[21]

The Commission then discussed contributory causes of the railway problems. The world depression which began in 1929 had progressively increased in severity with each succeeding year. The percentage decline in the net income of railroads in the United States exceeded the reduction on the Canadian Pacific. This was no doubt owing to the drastic economies in working expenses and services undertaken at an earlier date on the Canadian Pacific than on the American roads. An increase of traffic of even 20 per cent above the figures for 1931 would result in substantial improvement in the railway position in Canada.

The Commission said that in the preceding decade highway transport had challenged the supremacy of railways in carrying both passengers and freight. In many cases traffic had been diverted because conveyance by road was intrinsically cheaper and more convenient. But insofar as diversion was due to road vehicles not bearing their fair share of the cost of highways, then diversion might well be opposed to the best interests of the country. Aviation, great in potentialities, was still in its infancy. Waterways, developed by the government at great cost, furnished shippers of long-haul bulk commodities during the season of navigation with a service at rates which railways could not meet. The Panama Canal was a means of increasing the flow of export trade through Vancouver and providing an alternative route for trans-Canada traffic.[22]

The Commission recognized the general level of freight rates as a problem but refrained from making any specific recommendation about it beyond stating that in determining what is fair and reasonable to the railways regard should be had among other things to the cost of providing these services, including remuneration on the capital invested. In respect of contractual relations with labour, the Commission considered that, with the continuance of good relations between management and employees and a frank recognition of the serious financial situation, much could be done to ease the position of the railways, without imposing any undue hardship on the men. The Commission called attention to the excessive capitalization and overhead charges on the Canadian National as well as to duplicate mileage and lines of light traffic density. In the main, the Commission considered all the factors just mentioned as contributory. It clearly believed that wasteful competition between the two roads was at the heart of the Canadian railway problem.

The Royal Commission discussed the administration of the Canadian National Railways in some detail. The government, instead of accepting the recommendation by Drayton and Acworth of the Royal Commission of 1917 that the Board of Trustees be a self-perpetuating body, had

created a board of no more than 17 directors appointed by the government and holding office from year to year. Their functions had been in
practice nothing more than advisory. When occasionally directors did
act, it was, apparently, always in the direction of spending more money.
Usually they gave formal approval to programmes of expenditures
which they regarded as the main concern of the president and the
government. This left the railway open to political influence and to
public pressure by communities, business, and labour. Of direct political
interference by ministers and Members of Parliament in the detail
operations of the railway, there was little or none. It was in the larger
sphere of policy that political considerations led to unwise and unnecessary capital expenditures, the result of which was to create an atmosphere in which the ordinary principles of commercial operation of the
railway were lost sight of.[23] Although the Commission did not explain
what it meant by ordinary commercial principles, presumably it believed
that expenditures by the Canadian National should be judged by the
same criteria as those of the Canadian Pacific.

On the matter of operating efficiency, the Commission said "the
immense expenditures of the Canadian National for the improvement
of its property, the larger additions to its rolling stock, the advantages of
increased tractive power, and the more generous expenditure upon the
upkeep of its property, should have made possible a great improvement in operating performance. Whether the improvement actually
secured has been commensurate with the expenditure involved is a moot
question."[24] In seeking a "yardstick" by which to measure the operating
results of the Canadian National it was customary to take Canadian
Pacific Railway performance but this could not be regarded as an absolute criterion—operating costs were bound to be affected by differences
in size of properties, type of construction, general physical condition,
differences in character and volume of traffic, average length of haul,
and train and car loadings. However, the information placed before the
Commission by the experts indicated that the operating costs of the
Canadian National were in some respects, notably supervisory, station
and yard expenses, much higher than they should have been.[25] It would
appear that the Commission repudiated taking the Canadian Pacific as a
yardstick for the Canadian National and then proceeded to use it.

The Commission laid down certain principles in the light of which
specific proposals were to be judged. The identity of the two systems
should be maintained. The management of the Canadian National
should be emancipated from political interference and community pressure. The two railways should co-operate to eliminate duplicate services
and facilities and avoid extravagance. The burdens of the National

System should be brought within reasonable dimensions and extravagant operation checked. The privately-owned road should be reasonably protected against arbitrary acts by the publicly owned system.

The Commission proposed abolishing the existing Board of Directors of the Canadian National and replacing it by three trustees appointed by the government. All trustees were to be men of proved business skill and capacity and the chairman in particular was to have financial, administrative, and executive ability of a high order. Eventually appointments were to be for seven years. Vacancies among the trustees were to be filled by the government from a panel of eight named by the remaining trustees. While the responsibility for the direction and control of the System was to be laid upon the trustees, a chief operating officer with the titular rank of president was to be put in charge of the entire working of the railway in detail. Special provisions were to be made for the budget of the System, for its annual report to Parliament, and for a continuous audit.[26]

The Commission recommended that a statutory duty be imposed on the trustees as well as on the directors of the Canadian Pacific to adopt as soon as practicable such co-operative measures, plans, and arrangements as should, consistent with the proper handling of traffic, be best adapted to removing unnecessary or wasteful services or practices, avoiding unwarranted duplication in services, and using property jointly. The trustees of the Canadian National and the directors of the Canadian Pacific were to set up joint committees to carry out the exhortation to co-operate. In the event of failure to agree, an immediate reference could be made to an Arbitral Tribunal consisting of one representative from each railway and the Chief Commissioner of the Board of Railway Commissioners. The powers of the Tribunal could be invoked by either railway or by the Dominion or any provincial government. In case of conflict between the Tribunal and the Board, the decision of the former was to prevail. There was to be no appeal from the Tribunal's rulings except on a question of law.

All the members of the Royal Commission concurred in these recommendations, but some members would have preferred a plan which would have established a complete dissociation of the government from the responsibilities of competitive railway management. The Commission concluded its report with a serious note of warning. Failing the adoption of the plan proposed or some equally effective measure to cut costs, reduce the burden on the federal treasury, and improve the financial position of the privately owned railway, the very stability of the nation's finances and the credit of the Canadian Pacific would be threatened.

The recommendations of the Royal Commission were speedily embodied without substantial change in the Canadian National–Canadian Pacific Act of 1933.[27] As it happened, the conversion of the large Board of Directors of the Canadian National into a three-man Board of Trustees did not work out satisfactorily. The authority of the trustees and of the ordinary officials of the road was not clearly marked out. Some officers especially in the financial and law departments seem to have reported directly to the chairman of the Board. The two other trustees divided between them the responsibility for more or less supervising the other departments of the road. Confusion was inevitable; the president tended to become a figure-head; and orders from operating officials and from the trustees must often have conflicted. The *esprit de corps* within the Company soon showed signs of weakening.

The upshot was that in 1936 the Board of Trustees was abolished and a board of seven directors appointed in its stead.[28] The new Board was sufficiently small to avoid the tendency, when the Board had been large, for every regional and almost every occupational group to demand, and often receive, a member on the directorate. Of course, these pressures cannot be entirely avoided even when the board is small (7 members to 1961, 12 since then). Each of the provinces and large economic interests such as agriculture and banking want a representative. Since 1936 the directors have dealt only with broad policies. The actual operation is carried out by the president and other company officials.

Co-operation under the Canadian National–Canadian Pacific Act

Though the Commission of 1931–2 believed that co-operation would in a relatively short time lead to annual savings of $35 million, after a five years' trial the actual joint net economies were only $1,772,000 per annum. What is more, the Canadian National continued to lose money at an alarming rate. Through the 1930s its deficits ran from $35 to $61 million a year and substantially all the revenue which the Dominion collected from taxes on corporate and personal incomes went to cover the losses. In 1932 the Canadian Pacific had to forgo dividend payments on its common stock and in 1933 dividends on its preference stock as well.[29] In sum, the co-operative plan failed to get anything like the savings expected.

As a result of these conditions, the Senate early in 1938 appointed a Special Committee to "enquire into and report upon the best means of relieving the country from its extremely serious railway condition and financial burden consequent thereto." Though the persistence of depression may have been partly responsible, according to witnesses before the Senate Committee voluntary co-operation failed because of defects in the organization set up by the railways to carry out the plan, and chiefly because of the difficulty of balancing gain and disadvantage as required by the Act. A large number of schemes for pooling passenger trains and for line abandonments were considered. Some of these were put into effect, for example, on passenger service between Montreal and Quebec, and between Montreal and Ottawa and Toronto. Others failed for a variety of reasons. The Canadian Pacific was reluctant to pool its trains with the Canadian National between Windsor, Ont., and Toronto because it would have to give up its long-standing but not legally irrevocable agreement with the New York Central (Michigan Central) for the exchange of traffic to and from Chicago. It feared that service via the Canadian National would deteriorate below Canadian Pacific standards and that if the New York Central lost its passenger connection with the Canadian Paciffic, it would refuse to interchange freight as freely as it had before.

Competition existed between terminals such as Vancouver and Winnipeg but two through services were needed in order to serve all intermediate points such as Edmonton and Saskatoon, Calgary and Regina. Co-operative train services between Winnipeg and Montreal were held up by the Canadian Pacific's unwillingness to have its passengers enter or leave Montreal by the obsolete Bonaventure station of the Canadian National. If the Canadian Pacific's Windsor station were used, the Canadian National stated it could not expeditiously deliver fresh halibut, a very profitable kind of traffic, from Prince Rupert to New York and Boston.

Abandonment of duplicating railway mileage was tied up by the difficulty of "pairing." Was the abandonment of the Canadian Pacific Lake Shore line through Belleville to Toronto compensated for by the abandonment of the Canadian National line from Bala to Wanup, the upper half of the Toronto-Sudbury line? Or was the abandonment of the Canadian Pacific Woodstock–Windsor, Ont., line a proper balance for Bala-Wanup?[30] The Canadian Pacific believed that this "swapping" was impracticable and had slowed down progress. The Canadian National felt that if one took a sufficiently large number of pairs one would not be far out. In any event why hold up benefits to the country while fighting over a few dollars? In some instances the railways agreed between themselves on abandoning certain lines but the Board of Railway Commissioners refused consent. The essential difficulty was in valuing gain and loss, and then balancing them. "If one railway is giving up some line and all its potentialities it naturally desires to make sure that it is getting reasonable compensation for it."[31]

Although there were numerous stalemates and the savings from co-operation were small, the powers of the Arbitral Tribunal were not invoked. Neither road wished to incur the odium which might result.[32] Though the two railways were frequently admonished to apply the Canadian National–Canadian Pacific Act more aggressively, they never got beyond the pooling or joint operation of passenger trains between Toronto and Montreal, Toronto and Ottawa, and Montreal and Quebec City. By 1960 the Canadian Pacific was anxious to eliminate as many non-paying passenger services as it could. The MacPherson Commission recommended that the Act be repealed which was done in 1967.

Unification

By far the most controversial topic in the 1930s was the proposal of Sir Edward Beatty to unify the two major railways. This plan was first advanced before the Commission of 1931–2 and later presented before the Senate Committee.

Under unification the two roads would retain separate ownership of their existing properties but would be operated as one railway by one management. The facilities currently being used by the Canadian Pacific or the New York Central are technically owned by a great many constituent companies but operated as one unit by one company. In the same way, the two Canadian railways would continue to hold legal title to their properties but would be operated as an entity by one management in the most economical way without regard to which company owned the particular facilities in actual use.

Unification differed from co-operation and from amalgamation. Co-operation contemplated that the two railways would continue to be separately owned and operated except that common action would be taken to eliminate unnecessary wastes of competition. Unification and co-operation were similar in that each railway would have title to its property; they differed in the amount of inter-railway competition that would be allowed. Unification would entirely eliminate competition between the two systems, whereas co-operation would attempt to cut out only those aspects which were socially undesirable while preserving what was reasonable. Amalgamation or consolidation would mean a merging of properties, including assets and liabilities, making them belong to one company. Under unification, ownership would be separate. In both unification and amalgamation operation would be under one management. Whether or not the distinction between unification and amalgamation was of any practical importance was hotly disputed.

The main advantage of unification was asserted to be a great saving in railway operating costs. These savings would be divided between the Canadian Pacific and the government in some agreed proportion. Sir Edward Beatty claimed that after a readjustment period of five years, they would amount to at least $75 million a year based on the traffic volume of 1930. The savings would be greater in years of heavier traffic. Mr. S. W. Fairweather, then director of the Bureau of Economics of the Canadian National, forecast savings in the neighbourhood of $50.3 million annually on the traffic of 1930 and $56.4 million in a normal year. He assumed a docile or practically helpless public, and an equally helpless staff of employees. Consequently, he said, his estimate was theoretical, not realizable in practice, because the public would object to too great a reduction in services.

The anticipated savings would come from many sources: reduction in overhead; rerouting freight to secure a longer haul over the unified system's lines and thus a larger share of the two-line revenue; consolidating less than carload traffic and express, commercial telegraph, and passenger services; increased locomotive loading; joint use of terminals; eliminating unnecessary locomotive and car shops, and so on. About one-third of Sir Edward's estimated savings would be derived from applying to the locomotive, car, and track mileages of the unified system the unit costs of the Canadian Pacific for 1930. The estimates contemplated abandoning about 5,000 miles of duplicate or uneconomic trackage.

All the estimates of savings were sharply criticized. The Board of Transport Commissioners has been careful to protect the interests of communities in the continuance of rail services even when the line in question does not cover its operating expenses. Unless it could be assumed that the Board would break away from precedent, the legislation governing abandonments would have to be changed.

Yet even if the statute were altered, a fundamental economic difficulty would remain. It would be far from easy to decide which lines should be abandoned. From Kamloops, B.C., to near Vancouver the lines of the two railways parallel each other for 242 miles. For the most of this distance they run through mountainous territory where operating costs are high. After abandoning one line, it might be difficult expeditiously to handle all the traffic over the remaining facilities, especially during a heavy crop year in the West. Floods, washouts, and landslides interrupt service on either or both lines almost every year. Other abandonment proposals included one of the lines from Winnipeg to Lakehead, between Lakehead, North Bay, and Sudbury, and in the Maritimes. Opponents of unification said these lines were needed in big crop years, gave service to local communities, or were essential in national defence.

Savings of nearly $15 million in maintenance of way could be secured, so it was argued, from applying Canadian Pacific unit costs of 1930 on a track mileage basis to the mileage of the unified system. Officials of the Canadian National declared that their road had a relatively large mileage of light traffic lines compared with their competitor, that there was a minimum below which costs could not possibly be cut, and that their expenses had already been pared to the bone consistent with a proper standard of service. Compared with the privately owned system, the Canadian National had many more wooden trestles and bridges, more untreated ties, etc., on which maintenance charges were necessarily heavy. In consequence their costs per mile were higher than on the Canadian Pacific. Hence it was unlikely that managers of the unified system would be able to cut unit maintenance charges on the unified system to those current on the Canadian Pacific.

Though they placed their chief emphasis on savings, advocates of unification called attention to other possible advantages. It "would take the Canadian National out of politics and political control and place it and the Canadian Pacific under one management. The logical course would be to make the Canadian Pacific the basis of management since this company has shown distinctly successful results in promoting Canadian interests. By this means the entire organization would be removed from the political arena. Neither the Royal Commission of 1916–17 nor that of 1931–32 even hinted at any possibility of the Canadian Pacific being influenced by, or subject to, political motives."[33] Furthermore, it would be easier for the Board to deal with one system than with two, particularly because it would eliminate the strong–weak road problem in setting the general level in rates. The shipper might save something in freight rates through abolition of two-line hauls and switching charges. Service might be improved because traffic would go by the most direct route. Freight trains could depart more frequently and operate on faster schedules since on the unified road there would be enough freight to justify such services whereas there was an insufficient amount on either of the two roads. A unified system might be financially better able to keep up with the rapid technological changes in railway operating methods. It might be able to raise money more cheaply than either of the existing companies. The scheme for voluntary co-operation had failed miserably and a new policy was imperative to relieve the country from the heavy burden of Canadian National deficits and the Canadian Pacific from inadequate dividends. Sir Edward Beatty was sure that, even without unification, his road had a great future, for it was well located, well managed and well maintained. But it was the largest single taxpayer in Canada and was anxious to get relief from the crushing burden of taxation and the threat to the financial stability of the country due to losses on the Canadian National.

In all discussions of unification, fear of monopoly occupied a prominent position. This was especially so in the West which must sell its staples of production in distant markets at world prices and bring in most of its needs—farm machinery, hardware, clothing, fruits, consumers' durable goods, and so on—long distances by rail. It has not the benefit of water competition as have the Maritimes, the St. Lawrence Valley, and the Pacific coast. Its highway system was not well developed. Moreover, the furious struggles in the last fifteen years of the nineteenth century against the monopoly of the Canadian Pacific had not been entirely forgotten.

Outside the West, the complaint against monopoly, when analysed, seems to have been based on the apprehension that a unified road would be less efficient than the two existing ones because it would lack the spur of competition. A distinction might usefully be drawn between monopoly in the sense of open defiance or insolent nonchalance, and monopoly in the sense of inefficiency, the "dry rot" in a firm which does not have perpetually to face active competition. As to monopoly in its first connotation, the danger did not appear to be too great. Public opinion is a great regulator of all public-service activities. Railway officers have a finer sense of responsibility than they formerly had.[34] Like businessmen generally, they realize that the true interest of their roads lies in maintaining and strengthening the goodwill of shippers and the general public.

It is the second aspect of monopoly, the insidious blight of inefficiency, that is more dangerous and about which opinions differed keenly. Advocates of unification asserted that in the past railways might have been able to ignore shippers' needs because they had a virtual monopoly over land transportation beyond a few miles' distance. Today they must meet competition in a number of forms: trucks, buses, and inland steamships; airlines and pipelines; railways in the United States; the struggles of various producers for markets, or what is called commercial competition. Opponents of unification pointed out that while commercial competition is unquestionably a factor in rate-making and railway operation, rate cases before the Board have clearly shown that it is within the discretion of a railway whether or not it will meet market competition. If a unified system chose to ignore this type of competition it would be perfectly within its legal rights as the law and the practice of the Board now stand. Railways object to any change in the law forcing them to sacrifice their managerial discretion in regard to market competition.

Competition from American railway lines and from inland and coastal steamships was strong at many places but the unified railway could legally ignore this competition. Though some shippers could use transportation services other than those of the unified railway, they could do so only at some additional expense and inconvenience. Some shippers, notably grain-growers of the West and newsprint manufacturers of the Shield, would find it impossible to use alternatives.

The management of the unified road might be so desirous of impressing the public with the fact that it was not a monopoly that it would fight the trucks to the bitter end. Even as it is, the railways are sometimes accused of trying to drive the trucks out of business. Intensification of inter-agency competition which might come about by unification might well interfere with the co-ordination of various transportation agencies into a well integrated system to provide for all the country's needs.

Whether unification would result in isolating railways from political influence was also a moot question. Of the need for eliminating politics, there could be no doubt. The report of the Royal Commission, 1931–2, made this abundantly clear. At the same time the management of a privately owned railway should not be credited with powers which it does not as a rule possess. Private roads cannot ignore public opinion in abandoning lines, as the experience of both the Canadian Pacific and United States lines has shown.[35] The Canadian Pacific was not able to prevent restoration of a modified Crow's Nest Pass agreement, rate adjustments to get traffic moving through Canadian ports, the use of Canadian coal on railways or the provision of railway facilities far in excess of the ability of the country to support. In fact, there are two questions which are complementary to each other. Could a unified road resist politics? Would such a system influence politics? In other words, it is just as important to keep politics out of railways as it is to keep railways out of politics. Transportation has so long been used as an instrument of national policy in Canada that it is claiming too much to say, as protagonists of unification often did, that their plan would be a sovereign remedy for one of the admitted ills on the Canadian National in the 1920s.

In the 1930s organized labour was unanimous in its opposition to unification. Labour leaders asserted that the savings would come almost entirely from wages. Though this is an exaggeration, it is still true that the estimated wages bill on the unified system was far below the combined wages of the two companies. Advocates of unification did not admit any losses to labour in the long run. The normal turnover on Canadian railways from voluntary change of occupation, retirement, death, and physical injury is 5 or 6 per cent per annum. This rate of attrition would soon allow the re-employment of men who might have been thrown out of work by unification schemes. If necessary, the rate at which facilities were rearranged under unification could be slowed down sufficiently so that no one would lose his job. Alternatively men displaced by unification could be pensioned along the lines of the scheme applicable to voluntary co-operation.[36] In short, the interests of labour could be protected at the expense of some of the expected savings in the first few years. Thereafter only normal expenditures for pensions would be required. Gains from unification would be reduced for a time but as the labour force was readjusted they would increase.

After examining arguments of this sort, the Royal Commission of 1931–2 dismissed Sir Edward Beatty's unification plan rather curtly: "The time is not opportune for giving serious consideration to this particular remedy; neither complete public nor complete private ownership is possible. To establish a monopoly of such magnitude and importance would place in the hands of those responsible for the administration of the system powers that would, if not properly exercised, prejudice the interests of the Dominion as a whole. . . . Should the population of Canada greatly increase, the volume of freight traffic would grow, and the railway mileage be materially enlarged, with the result that the management of so great a system might well become unwieldy and necessitate segregation. . . . [The Commission had] a natural and justifiable hesitation to commit, finally, future generations, and even the present one, to a policy adopted under the stress of difficult circumstances, which may not be best adapted to a new set of conditions difficult to forecast."[37]

The Senate, after its study in 1938 and 1939, placed its reliance on voluntary co-operation.[38] During World War II Sir Edward Beatty's successor in the presidency of the Canadian Pacific announced that the road had dropped its campaign for unification. The Royal Commission of 1951 made some suggestions for improving the functioning of the Canadian National–Canadian Pacific Act.[39] Most witnesses favoured the continuance of the system of two large railway organizations, with the necessary corollary that the Canadian Pacific must be allowed to live as a privately owned railway. The Commission had no reason whatever to recommend either unification, amalgamation or public ownership of all railways in Canada.[40]

The Royal Commission of 1931–2, the Senate committee, and the advocates of unification largely overlooked two critical items: the world's worst depression and a devastating drought in the West. True enough, the President of the Canadian National stated that his road should not be judged solely from the standpoint of interest on invested capital. His Company was building up the country and had large potential earning capacity. What it needed was more business plus all the economies that could be brought into effect.[41] In 1932 the Canadian Pacific stated that "with the decline in the basic industry [grain growing] of the country disappeared also the hope which has been entertained of an increase in general traffic. Your Directors can only continue to exhort patience until the turn of the tide."[42] Yet for all this, the problem was looked at as if the depressed conditions of the thirties would continue indefinitely.

Unification appears to be a dead issue, a subject only of historical interest. In fact, it may be merely quiescent. American plans to amalgamate some of their big railroads, e.g., the New York Central and the Pennsylvania, will unquestionably influence public opinion in Canada. The Canadian socialist party (N.D.P.) would obviously like to nationalize our railways and the fact that its platform is made after extended discussions with trade unions suggest that one of the old stumbling blocks, opposition from organized labour, is not insuperable. Finally, huge and persistent deficits on the Canadian National, inability of the Canadian Pacific to pay dividends, or public unwillingness to subsidize non-paying branch lines or consent to their abandonment, might force a government to adopt the more drastic remedy, or palliative, of unification.

Recapitalization

A more or less persistent problem in public ownership of the Canadian National has been its capital structure. In 1937 this was revised by eliminating capital stocks and old debentures which boards of arbitration stated had no real value, by striking out loans made by the government after 1923 to cover deficits, and by getting rid of the accrued interest on these loans.[43] These reductions totalled $1,167 million. Simultaneously a securities trust was set up to hold all the stocks of the Canadian National which were owned by the government and to keep a record of the investment of the Dominion in the Canadian Government Railways (the former Intercolonial and the National Transcontinental). This Capital Revision Act did not in any way affect the net debt of the federal government. The capital stocks which were eliminated had been acquired without cash payment by the Dominion. The old debentures, the deficits, the interest upon the deficits, and appropriations for capital expenditures in Canadian Government Railways had already been embodied in the net debt of Canada.

During World War II the Government of the United Kingdom purchased $391 million of the interest-bearing securities of the Canadian National which were owned by residents of Britain. Then the United Kingdom sold these securities to the Canadian government, thus acquiring Canadian dollars to pay for essential war supplies. In 1949 the federal government held $743 million of interest-bearing obligations of the Canadian National while the general public owned $629 million.

The Canadian National asked the Royal Commission of 1951 to recommend a recapitalization so that some of its bonds bearing a fixed rate of interest would be replaced by securities (common stock and income bonds) on which a return would be payable only if earned. The same principle would apply to capital that might be needed in the future to finance extensions of lines. Officials of the Canadian National said it had an excessive capital burden of $1,533 million. This sum included interest-bearing obligations assumed with the acquisition of insolvent railways, the run-down and semi-finished condition of properties taken over, the cost of co-ordination, expenditures on Canadian Government Railways, the acquisition of unremunerative lines in the national interest, and losses on development lines. The Company's proposal would reduce the interest charges in 1948 from nearly $45 million to $14.2 million. According to the Company these proposals, if put into effect, should enable it on the average to meet its fixed charges including rent for leased roads and equipment, and interest on its unfunded and long-term debt in the hands of the public.

The Company argued that nothing short of these measures could be deemed adequate treatment of its capital structure. Its plan constituted a settlement of past sins and mistakes. Its fixed charges were about twice as large a percentage of gross revenue as those of the Canadian Pacific or large American roads. Its average annual earnings per mile had been about 9 per cent less than those of its major competitor and 51 per cent less than in the United States. Traffic density was respectively 7 and 50 per cent lower. Management was being blamed by uninformed opinion for large deficits which were inescapable under existing circumstances, and the view was widely held that the Company could not be operated at a profit. These factors injured the morale of officers and employees. The adjustment asked for would not cost the government any money and might save some because from a psychological point of view relief from heavy losses would stimulate the management to greater efforts.

The Canadian Pacific alleged that these proposals threatened its existence as a private enterprise. It was apprehensive lest recapitalization of the Canadian National would give rise to demands for lower freight rates regardless of a fair return on investment in railway property of the Canadian Pacific. The Royal Commission concluded that "it was undesirable for the Canadian National Railways to have recurring deficits in the face of what has been found by the Board of Transport Commissioners to be efficient management. On the other hand, it must be borne in mind that if fixed charges were reduced to a point where substantial surpluses are shown, the shipper and his representatives might not look with favour on the payment of dividends on shares held by the Government."[44] The problem resolved itself into a search for a capital structure which would not impose too heavy a burden of fixed charges in bad years but would ensure that a reasonable portion of surplus earnings would be paid to the owners, the public of Canada, as a return on invested capital in good years.

In 1952 Parliament adopted a simpler capital structure than the Royal Commission had recommended.[45] One-half of the long-term debt was changed into 4 per cent preferred stock to be held by the government, on which payments by the System were contingent on earnings after interest and income tax. Interest on the remaining half of the long-term debt must be paid regularly. In addition $100 million was interest-free until 1962. From 1952 on, the government was to buy more preferred stock from the Canadian National in amounts equal to a small fraction of its total net revenue for each year. Until 1960, this fraction was set at 3 per cent. The first effect of the recapitalization plan was to raise the proportion of equity capital from 34.5 per cent on December 31, 1951, to 67.5 per cent on January 1 of the following year. The ratio of borrowed money to total capitalization was correspondingly reduced. These ratios were roughly in line with those on most privately-owned public utilities in Canada.

As things turned out, this plan of recapitalization was only a partial success. Because of rising wage rates and prices, the cost of modernizing plant, including diesels, automated yards, centralized traffic control, and new freight cars, proved much more expensive than anticipated. New lines also had to be built into mining areas in northern Quebec, Ontario, and Manitoba. Besides, a line was constructed by the Canadian National acting as agent for the Dominion between Grimshaw, Alta., and Hay River, N.W.T., on Great Slave Lake. Moreover, after 1957 the prevailing rate of interest rose from about 3 to 5 per cent. Yet modernization and extensions are essential if the Canadian National is to hold its own in the face of intensive competition from other media of transport and if it is to develop the economic resources which are naturally tributary to its lines.

By 1961 the funded debt of the Canadian National was $1,675 million, or two and three-quarters what it was after the recapitalization of 1952. The ratio of debt to equity had become roughly equal. The annual fixed charges had risen from $25.4 million to $72.3 million or 2.9 times over the same period. Although the Railway had cash surpluses in 1952,

1953, 1955, and 1956, its net cash deficit over the ten years 1952–61 came to just over $251 million. Clearly the Railway was slipping back into the same unfortunate position that it had occupied throughout all of its history except for a few years during World War II and the 1950s. Accordingly, in 1963 the President of the Company proposed another recapitalization. In 1966 the railway was obliged to pay out $64.7 million for interest, or twice what it owed ten years earlier. Its net deficits over the years 1962–6 exceeded $186 million. The chief encouraging factor was that the deficit for 1966 ($24.6 million) was much below the peak ($67.3 million) recorded in 1961.

General Conclusions

The Canadian National began under severe handicaps—poor physical condition of buildings, track, and rolling stock, a hodgepodge of lines which were close to bankruptcy under private ownership or which had never paid their way under government operation, heavy bonded indebtedness, almost complete lack of *esprit de corps*, and so on. Nevertheless by 1923 the organization had been at least partly "shaken down."

The Company was favoured by a dynamic president who inspired the staff with new confidence, fused the various constituent parts together, and rehabilitated the system from the engineering standpoint, but whose ambition overreached sound economic limits. The System was undoubtedly subjected to reprehensible political pressures from various sections of the country. And it suffered, like all other businesses, by being carried away by the "new era" prosperity of the late 1920s and the devastating depression and drought of the next decade.

From the standpoint of income and expense statements, the System looks like an unqualified failure. Prior to 1923 the constituent parts of the Canadian National had huge losses and the government had advanced substantial sums for capital purposes. All this was to be expected in a period of postwar inflation, depression, and corporate organization. But subsequent to 1923, better things were expected. Yet over the years 1923–51 the Company met its operating expenses, taxes, and all fixed charges in only seven years, five of them during the war. In the 1960s it experienced further deficits, despite the recapitalization of 1952. Some of its losses must be attributed to embalming in the capital structure and physical assets of the Canadian National all the mistakes of the past on both private and publicly owned roads. Some are due to business depression and a downward secular trend in rail transportation. Some have been caused by regional pressures which the management of the Canadian National should and could have resisted but failed to do so. Some may be the result of the perfectly legitimate desire of a country of magnificent distances to use railways as bands to make the nation one. Some of the losses may be due to downright inefficiency, or to lack of capacity of directors or staff or, more probably, to the attitude that a few hundred thousand dollars more on the staggering deficit is neither here nor there. The problem of how much weight is to be given to each of these factors makes an accurate appraisal of public ownership of railways in Canada difficult if not impossible. One study[46] of the statistical measures of efficiency was highly critical of the Canadian National but such analyses are subject to so many qualifications that no answer can be taken as final.

The experience of the Canadian National does show that a publicly owned railway can be operated without political interference in appointments, promotions, and discharges. A more insidious danger is regional pressure for new lines and services. Politics enter at the level of general policy rather than detailed operation. Despite assertions that public ownership is responsible for keeping in operation branches which are not economically justified, our discussion of line abandonment has indicated that, while there may be a grain of truth in what is alleged, the wholesale condemnation of public ownership on this ground is not fair. Certainly before the Board of Transport Commissioners, counsel for the Canadian National fight no less hard to win their case than lawyers of the Canadian Pacific.

Employees of the Canadian National are not without their influence[47] but generally in their lobbying they combine with Canadian Pacific employees and with labour generally. In labour disputes on railways the Canadian Government may have been embarrassed by its ownership of the largest railway in the Dominion. Railways are so vital to the economic and social welfare of a country that no government can allow strikes to drag on and must do all in its power to prevent them from starting. There is no evidence that the federal government has readily acquiesced in the demands of unions but the secrecy which surrounds negotiations between management and men and the subsequent conciliation by the government makes it difficult to appraise this matter. None the less, it is clear that railway labour does not "shop around" threatening to switch votes from one political party to another in accordance with pre-election promises.

On the matter of rates, when restoration of the Crow's Nest Pass Agreement was before a Special Parliamentary Committee in 1922, the then Canadian National seems to have accommodated itself to the political exigencies of the time. Later officials of the present Canadian National frequently warned of the danger of freight rates being at uneconomically low levels. In the rate cases after World War II the Canadian National supported the applications for higher tolls except in the Canadian Pacific's appeal to the Supreme Court on a matter of law and on the Crow's Nest Pass rates before the Royal Commission of 1951. Superficially, the Canadian Pacific bore the brunt of the attacks by provincial governments on the applications for increases but this was primarily because the Board took the privately owned system as the yardstick.

It is sometimes alleged that being able to borrow on more favourable terms than private companies in the same line of business is an advantage of public ownership. While this may be true, it is likely that during the depression heavy deficits on the Canadian National weakened the fiscal position of Canada and raised the cost of all public borrowings. In comparison with the Canadian Pacific, the government railway was less prompt and less aggressive in cutting its staff and its services in the depression beginning in late 1929. The management claimed to have foreseen the downturn but decided not to add to unemployment by discharging men and reducing purchasing power.[48] If the Canadian National had discharged men as did the Canadian Pacific, the men would probably have had to go on relief and be supported by taxpayers. There is something to be said in favour of keeping men at work on a government-owned railway, if the government has to keep them in any event. On the other hand this policy is costly to taxpayers and tends to make executives of the national system indifferent to costs of operation, or overly concerned with practices which will not embarrass the government of the day.

Contrary to the usual criticism of public enterprise, the Canadian National was a conspicuous innovator. Under Sir Henry Thornton it operated the first diesel-powered railway train in North America, experimented with vehicles which would run on both rails and highway surfaces, started the use of radio-telephonic communication from a moving train, began a radio broadcasting network, and so forth. Given proper leadership, there seems no reason why a publicly owned company need be hidebound and bureaucratic. In 1962–4 the President of the Canadian National was strongly attacked for his alleged failure to hire enough executives who were bilingual or whose mother tongue was French.

Any government-owned company is in a difficult position. It cannot ignore the wishes of its owners any more than a privately owned concern can flout the desires of its shareholders. Those who put up the money have theoretically the right to call the tune. At the same time, a company cannot overlook the rights of employees, patrons, suppliers of equipment, and the public at large. It is more difficult to hold the various conflicting interest in proper balance in a state-owned institution than in a privately owned one. The operation of a government-owned corporation is a test of public morality, a measure of how competently a democracy can manage its own business affairs. It would be untrue to suggest that the Canadian National or the public of Canada have solved all the problems of running such an enterprise. It would be idle to assert they have made no progress. In essence, public ownership is a question of economic and political philosophy.

18

Highway Freight Transport

THE earliest settlers in Eastern Canada depended primarily, and at first exclusively, on water transport. Before long, roads were needed to provide communication inland from the sea coast, the banks of navigable streams, and the shores of the Great Lakes. These roads were built and maintained by adjacent landowners. During part of the French régime a royal official, *le Grand Voyer*, attempted, for the most part without success, to get farmers and parishes to keep roads in decent repair.[1] Under early British rule colonial governments constructed several through or trunk roads in the St. Lawrence Valley and the present Maritime Provinces. These were built chiefly for defence and the administration of justice but of course were used by settlers. During the nineteenth century, the mileage of roads increased steadily because of the growth of population and the spread of agricultural settlement.

History of Road Transport

All these roads were unbelievably bad. In rainy weather they were quagmires; in winter they were impassable owing to snow and pitch-holes; in summer they were dusty, rutted, veritable bone-shakers. Fortunately few people needed to travel along them for any distance. Travellers and immigrants used the rivers and lakes. Farmers lived a comparatively self-sufficient life or sold their produce in nearby towns or military camps. The poorness of the roads was due to ignorance of engineering principles, lack of machinery to reduce the back-breaking labour involved, inability to finance new construction, and most of all, apparent absence of a strong demand for anything better. The few turnpikes built from time to time were only a little superior to the public roads. The volume of traffic and hence the amount of revenue was low and highway users objected to having to pay tolls—as they still do. All in all, up to 1900, probably even up to 1920, roads were in execrable condition judged even by the lowest of present-day standards for rural roads.

In the 1890s the bicycle craze led to some effort at improvement near the cities. In 1894 the Ontario Good Roads Association, the first propaganda or pressure group for highways, came into being. Ontario also led the way with provincial government assistance to highways. In 1901 it granted $1 million for building roads for experimental and demonstration purposes. It wanted to show communities in various parts of the province what a good road looked like according to the standards of the time and to prove that good, or at least better roads, could be cheaply built from local raw materials. Though they received some advice and financial aid from the province, cities, towns, villages, and townships remained basically responsible for all roads. Traffic was still small in amount and local in character.

The introduction of the private automobile completely changed this picture. In 1901 Mr. T. A. Russell built a few cars in his bicycle plant near Toronto. Then in 1904 the Ford Company of Canada, followed four years later by McLaughlin Brothers (now General Motors of Canada), set up plants in Windsor and Oshawa, respectively. From that time on, the increase in the registration of motor vehicles was amazing.[2]

The early automobiles were heavy, clumsy, and undependable. They cost a lot to begin with and were expensive to operate. "Motoring was still [1915] a series of adventures in which the driver pitted his skill and his luck against mechanical imperfections and the hazards of the road."[3] Conditions changed rapidly. By 1920, certainly by 1925, cars were cheap and reliable. They were relatively free from mechanical breakdowns and were easy to steer and repair. Women and men who lacked mechanical aptitudes were able to drive. Trained repairmen and well-equipped garages were widely distributed. The initial cost of an automobile came down steadily. Cars could be bought on the instalment plan. People wanted to "keep up with the Joneses"; in technical terms, the motive of conspicuous consumption was strong. All these factors made the private passenger car popular. And with more cars on the roads, the demand for better highways became irresistible.

In all provinces of Canada the history of highway construction and finance followed a broadly similar course. The Ontario government established a Department of Highways in 1913 and gave more money to counties for road work. In 1917 it started to assume sole responsibility for building and maintaining important or trunk roads. Since then it has steadily extended the system of provincial highways.[4]

The provinces had to take an active part in highway construction for several reasons. The cost of building the roads required by fast cars and heavy trucks rose rapidly. Road surfaces had to be wider and thicker; bridges had to be stronger; curves and gradients had to be more gentle than for horse-drawn vehicles. Wages and prices of materials went up sharply from 1913 to 1929, except for a brief recession beginning late in 1920. Local government units were unable to finance such heavy capital expenditures especially when they could see no way of recovering their costs from the traffic using the new roads. Suburban and rural municipalities were unwilling to build roads that they felt would be used more by tourists and city residents than by local taxpayers. Some stingy municipalities inadequately maintained their roads and so made a lengthy journey unpleasant. When municipalities did spend money, they often wasted it for they lacked competent engineering advice and experience. Further, provincial governments may have been influenced by lobbying of organized motorists, truck operators, or local interests, and may have seen some political value in using highway moneys for party patronage. Finally, the provinces took the view that improved trunk roads and scenic highways would attract touring motorists and add to provincial prosperity.

Whatever the reasons, provincial governments began to relieve municipalities, especially rural ones, of the burden of building and maintaining roads used largely by through, as distinct from local, traffic.[5] The provinces widened and straightened existing roads, resurfaced them, cut down grades, built bridges, erected traffic signs, cleared highways of snow, policed them, and so on. Simultaneously counties[6] took over and improved more of the secondary main roads. In turn, municipalities were able to bring up the quality of the roads remaining under their jurisdiction. Improvement in secondary roads was called for by the widespread ownership of autos and trucks by farmers.

For many years the federal government played a minor role in highway affairs. In 1911 the Conservatives introduced a bill to permit the Dominion to build roads. This legislation was defeated in the Senate which then had a strong Liberal majority. In 1919 Ottawa gave the provinces some grants-in-aid, i.e., financial assistance provided the provinces would spend equal amounts. These grants were abandoned because of constitutional difficulties. For many years the Dominion Department of Railways and Canals employed a highways commissioner who gave leadership to the provinces in their efforts to improve roads. Through the Railway Grade Crossing Fund which is administered by the Board of Transport Commissioners, the Dominion materially assists in reducing or eliminating hazards where railways and highways intersect.

In 1931 the Dominion made grants for completing the Trans-Canada Highway. The money was voted chiefly to relieve unemployment. Without federal aid, the provinces might not see fit to build a good road through the difficult terrain and sparsely settled districts which in some places separate the densely populated parts of different provinces. By 1940 it was possible for motorists to drive across the Dominion without entering United States territory but long stretches of the highway particularly across Northern Ontario, the Prairies, and British Columbia were not hard surfaced. In 1948 the Dominion conferred with the provinces about the route of the Trans-Canada Highway. It also agreed to spend $150 million on the project though it stressed that the primary responsibility for roads lay with the provinces.

In 1962 the Trans-Canada Highway was completed across mainland Canada and three years later across Newfoundland. The required standard was a hard-surfaced, two-lane roadway at least 22 feet wide, with ample shoulders and bridge clearances, good sighting distances, low gradients, gentle curvature, a maximum carrying capacity of nine tons for any axle, and the elimination of most railway crossings. When finished, the Highway cost nearly $700 million and the Dominion's contribution had reached $400 million.

The federal government through the Department of Northern Affairs maintains the Canadian section of the Alaska Highway which it purchased from the United States in 1946. This Highway, 1,600 miles long, from Fort St. John, B.C., to Fairbanks, Alaska, was constructed for military purposes during World War II at the expense of the American government. The area traversed does not seem to possess large or easily exploitable resources. The route is much too far from thickly settled communities to attract more than a trickle of tourists. Continued operation of the Highway can be justified not on economic but on military grounds.

In 1958 the Dominion started the "Roads to Resources" programme for the development of mines, forests, commercial shipping, and the tourist trade. It aided about 100 projects ranging in length from one 15 miles long in Prince Edward Island to 320 for the Stewart-Cassair road in British Columbia and 505 for a road into Uranium City in Northern Saskatchewan. On projects within a province, the Dominion paid one-half the cost with a maximum contribution of $7.5 million to each province. Most provinces carried out work in excess of the amount covered by the dollar-for-dollar grant from the Dominion. Hence, total expenditure exceeded $177 million and was spread over eight years. Roads in Western Canada will eventually be linked with 600 miles of roads in the Yukon and 1,300 in the Northwest Territories. Territorial roads are built solely by the Dominion. The Roads to Resources programme was renewed in 1966.

Starting in 1962 the federal government pays two-thirds of the cost of any access road constructed by two or more mining companies. It also makes grants to each territorial government for building tote-trails. Finally, the Dominion builds all roads in national parks. Altogether in 1959 the federal exchequer met about 10.5 per cent of the total expenditures of $1,021 million made by all levels of government on highways, rural roads, and urban streets. The provincial governments provided about two-thirds of the total (including assistance to municipalities), and municipal governments the remaining 22 per cent.

Technological Change

Motor vehicles and the highways over which they operate have undergone rapid and continuous technological change. Greater durability, the self-starter, balloon or low pressure tires, easier and safer steering mechanisms, the closed car, shatterproof glass, better springs, lower gasoline consumption per mile, the use of higher octane gasolines to improve performance and reduce consumption, seasonal grades of oil, better repair facilities, reduction in road shocks by smoother road surfaces, automatic gear shifts, power brakes, long-lasting and eye-catching exterior finishes, attractive decor inside–these are but a few of the better known improvements. These changes made driving and riding easier, safer, faster, and more comfortable. Wear and tear on vehicles and roads was lessened. Year-round driving was possible wherever snow was removed from road surfaces, and in the years 1926–39 operating costs per vehicle-mile were cut in half.[7]

Buses have also been vastly improved. Placing engines in the rear and side minimizes skidding, improves road traction, facilitates steering, and besides giving better insulation reduces engine noise and fumes within the bus. It cuts down tire wear because more of the weight of the vehicle is placed on the dual tires at the rear. Side or rear engines improve the appearance of the bus and increase passenger capacity without lengthening the wheel base. This is important in parking and in manœuvring through traffic. Buses have also been improved by better heating and lighting systems. They are built to give passengers more leg- and headroom. Seats are better upholstered. Discomfort from swaying, rocking, and rough riding has been cut down. Up-to-date buses are much safer than the older models on account of safety glass, ability to "hug the road," wider visibility for the driver, faster acceleration, and quicker acting brakes.

Although these trends are likely to continue, it remains to be seen whether future progress will be rapid enough to counterbalance higher wage rates for drivers and maintenance men, higher prices for gasoline and diesel fuel, increased taxation, and the expense and inconvenience of traffic congestion. In the past any tendency toward growing costs per bus-mile could be offset by building buses with more seats. In this way cost per passenger-mile, the important factor in getting business and making money, could be kept down. At present buses seem to have approached their maximum size. They are difficult to manœuvre in traffic, notwithstanding the astonishing skill of the drivers. Private car owners object to "big buses that take up three-quarters of the road." To prevent destruction of highway surfaces, governments limit the weight to be carried on each axle. For these reasons the trend toward larger buses is likely to stop except insofar as small buses are replaced by ones of the largest size now in service. With the comparative closing of the old means of economizing, buses are in danger of failing to retain some of the competitive advantages they had had up to the present. Of course, it may be that technology will turn in other and equally profitable directions.

In trucks the general advances in the automotive industry have quickly been absorbed. Indeed all the early trucks and many of those currently used in local delivery service are essentially converted passenger cars. Trucks of from one to five ton capacity resemble passenger automobiles in a general way but have more powerful and more durable engines. Their chassis is more heavily built, and typically they will stand more abuse. The largest trucks are quite different from other motor vehicles. To an increasing extent commercial transports are equipped with diesel engines. At first diesel trucks had high obsolescence charges per annum because technological improvements were rapidly introduced. As soon as the rate of change slowed down, depreciation charges per annum or per ton-mile were reduced. Diesel engines are heavier than gasoline engines of equal power but their fuel costs are from 40 to 60 per cent lower. They consume less fuel per horsepower of output and they use a relatively low priced product instead of valuable high grade gasoline. Diesel-powered trucks do not accelerate as quickly as those with gasoline engines.

The largest commercial vehicles are either tractor-trailers or tractor-semi-trailers. The former consists of a power unit moving on its own wheels and pulling a box-like, two-axled carrying unit. The semi-trailer or "semi" has a similar power unit to that of the tractor-trailer except that it has a steel plate over its rear axle to carry the fore part of the trailer. The trailer has a rear axle of its own and auxiliary wheels near its forward end. The latter may be lowered to support the semi-trailer when the tractor unit is disconnected.

Both trailer arrangements permit either a larger load to be hauled or a smaller power plant to be used than in a truck of the conventional type. Also, while the trailer or semi-trailer is being loaded or unloaded, the power unit may be released for other work. Conversely the carrying unit need not be idle while the tractor is undergoing repairs. This economizes drivers' time, reduces capital expenditures, and gives shippers better service. After drivers got experience in handling the units and a mechanism was perfected for braking all the wheels simultaneously, tractor-trailers proved easier to manœuvre than trucks of equal capacity on single chassis.

All the heavier types of trucks are now designed with a view to distributing the weight of the loaded vehicles over as large a number of square inches of road surface as possible. This is necessary to forestall the criticisms frequently made that heavy trucks break down existing road surfaces and necessitate thicker, more expensive pavements than would be required for pleasure vehicles alone. Unless these criticisms are disposed of, taxes on trucks will rise. To keep down contact weight, truck manufacturers and operators put on large pneumatic tires and take care to inflate them properly. Manufacturers have increased the number of axles per vehicle and the number of tires per axle to four and even eight. Operators try to distribute the revenue load evenly within the truck or trailer. The significant point is that the taxing system has directed technology along certain lines.

Advances in metallurgy such as stainless steel, aluminum, and shot welding have permitted either a reduction of gross weight on the surface of the highway or an increase in payload relative to tare. Clutches and transmissions are more durable and efficient than before. Engines weigh less per horsepower. By better design and construction the weight of the chassis can be reduced without sacrifice of strength. There are "trombone" trailers which expand for extra long articles, high-cube trailers for especially bulky articles, and trailers which can be split in two and superimposed one on the other when being hauled back empty to the home garage or base. There are special vehicles for local parcel delivery, milk, household effects, petroleum products, lumber, bulk cement, heavy machinery, automobiles in transit to dealers, garbage, fire protection, street flushing, and so on. The multiplicity of models tends to raise the costs of manufacture and repair, but this is more than offset by improved serviceability for the user. All these advances, it must be emphasized, are additional to those which trucks have borrowed from passenger cars.

Future technological change in trucks will probably be toward fewer models, more diesel engines, superchargers for gasoline engines, fore-wheel drive to meet temporary power demands, faster highway operation, and greater use of light-weight metals and plastics. Any tendency toward large sizes will depend on whether provincial governments amend their current restrictions on width, height, length, and axle load. The present regulations are determined by clearances in underpasses and by the prevailing concepts of what the dimensions of trucks should be to make the roads tolerably usable by motorists. Restrictions are also set by the maximum weights which highway surfaces and bridges can reasonably be called upon to withstand.

Over the years provincial governments have permitted bigger and heavier vehicles to use their highways. Whenever a province increases permissible truck lengths, heights, and widths, or raises the legally allowable weight by a ton or so, it improves the competitive position of the trucking industry. As a rule the cost per vehicle-mile is not raised by a slightly bigger load. Therefore, heavier loading and larger cubic capacity have reduced cost per ton-mile and, other things remaining unchanged, have either added to the truckers' profits or permitted them to cut rates.

The industry has also benefited from the efforts of all provincial governments to agree on maximum gross loads, maximum weight on any axle, and dimensions of truck bodies. Uniformity makes it simpler for trucks to operate between different provinces. Starting in 1960 some of the provinces agreed on reciprocal licensing. Formerly, the owner of a truck had to pay the full licence fee in each province in which he operated. Now he is charged full fees in his home province plus $10 per ton of capacity in the other provinces coming under the agreement. This arrangement facilitates the growth of inter-provincial trucking besides slightly lowering costs of operation. It is also in effect between some Canadian provinces and American states.

Any discussion of technological change in highway transportation is incomplete without referring to highways themselves. By 1920 roads and streets suitable for horse-drawn vehicles were being improved by surfacing with gravel, asphalt, or concrete, by reducing grades and curvature, and so on. These developments have continued because of the growth of engineering knowledge, the demands of highway users and chiefly perhaps, because of the increasing ability and willingness of the public to finance new construction through the gasoline tax.

Technical changes in highways also include very great advances in methods of construction. Bulldozers, mechanical ditchers, concrete mixers, trucks to move gravel for surfaces and earth for shoulders, and other machines take much of the human labour out of road building and help offset rising wage rates and cost of materials. Without gasoline-powered construction equipment, it would be virtually impossible to build roads for gasoline-propelled vehicles. Research in civil engineering is continuous, especially on quick-setting cements, frost damage, stabilization in soils, and treating ice and snow-covered surfaces.

Express Highways

The growth of interurban traffic by passenger car, bus, and truck has created new difficulties. Typically the same highway handles local and through vehicles; the pleasure seeker and the commercial operator; taxi-cabs; buses; a chauffeur-driven limousine; a furniture van; a Rolls Royce; a Model T Ford; and a modern ten-ton truck. Highways become congested because of the number of vehicles and their varying speeds. Congestion slows down all traffic, raises the cost of operating cars and trucks, and leads to general dissatisfaction. Congested roads are usually more hazardous than other highways because of the close contact of vehicles with each other, poor visibility, and chiefly the impatience of drivers who speed up, "cut in," and try to "beat the light" in order to make up for time lost.

Hence the demand has grown for express highways to be used solely by fast vehicles. Local traffic is excluded from these highways by regulation, by the admonitions of police constables, or by the natural caution of poky highway users. Expressways are built for speed. They have gentle gradients, wide surfaces, broad shoulders, and well-banked (super-elevated) curves. Intersecting roads are carried over or under the expressway by bridges or underpasses. "Clover leafs" are built wherever access to the main road is permitted. On these highways traffic moving in opposite directions is separated by a boulevard or grassy median. Vehicles going in the same direction are channelled into well-marked lanes. In short, expressways permit traffic to move continuously, with greater safety, and without being delayed by traffic lights and slow vehicles.

Express highways have other advantages. They allow country roads and city streets to be used for their original purposes unhindered access to abutting land. They make it possible to restrict heavy traffic to surfaces especially designed and maintained to carry it. Thus they help eliminate the adverse effects of heavy traffic on ordinary pavements and gravel roads. By concentrating heavy, 24-hour a day traffic in definite channels, they minimize the bad effects of noise on workers and sleepers. They save the time of private motorists and commercial truck operators although at the price of using more gasoline per mile on account of higher average speed. On the other hand they cut down the waste of gasoline because of delays. They reduce wear and tear on brakes, clutches, and tires which is heavy on congested roads resulting from frequent, sudden stops and starts. Express highways attract tourists and stimulate intercity movement of passengers and freight. The add to social amenities by encouraging people to live away from the heart of cities. More highway travel increases provincial revenues from gasoline taxes.

Unfortunately express highways are very expensive to build. Right of way through farm lands or built-up areas is dear. The expense of grading, drainage, bridging, surfacing, and landscaping is heavy. Revenue from gasoline taxes, though higher than before, may not be enough higher to cover the interest, depreciation, and maintenance charges on the expensive highway. Motorists who do not use the high-class facilities may object. They may assert that they are subsidizing trucks and extra-provincial tourists while their local roads are being neglected. High-speed highways take business away from diesel and street railways which may have to be abandoned or operate at heavy losses. Owners of service stations, tourist camps, and hotels along a parallel but older road occasionally complain of losing business. Any redirection of the flow of traffic has an effect on adjacent businesses and property values. However, it would appear that cities were not seriously hurt when they were bypassed by Ontario's Highway 401, now called the Macdonald-Cartier Freeway. This was because of two factors: the quick recovery of local business which had been scared away from some service stations by the speed and congestion of through traffic; and the strong upward secular trend of local traffic. The expansion of through traffic along expressways accounts for the establishment and growth of service centres to sell gasoline and refreshments to travellers. But regardless of whether or not super-highways are economically justified, the public demands them whenever the volume of inter-city or metropolitan traffic leads to chronic daily congestion.

Toll roads are essentially express highways reserved for drivers who are prepared to pay a toll (usually about 2 cents a mile) for their use, in addition to the normal fuel tax. These roads are built by a provincial or state government or even by a privately owned corporation. Construction is financed by means of bonds. These have a first claim on the receipts of the toll-road authority and may, in addition, be guaranteed by the provincial government. When all the bonds have been paid off, the highway is turned back to the government free of charge. A main argument in favour of toll roads is that they provide the public with first class highways more quickly than if it depended on the exigencies of the provincial budget. Moreover, people who use the roads, including commercial truckers and American tourists, pay for them in direct proportion to use.

Sometimes highway users object to duplication in payment for the highway, once through the toll per mile and again through the gasoline tax which goes to the province even though the toll taken by itself is expected to cover the cost of the toll road. As a rule, however, motorists are willing to pay these charges in order to have the advantages of speed, direct route, and gentle grades which the up-to-date toll road provides. Some people fear that the presence of toll roads may discourage construction of high class ordinary highways connecting the same termini. If this happens, motorists who are reluctant to pay for the use of the toll road find themselves discriminated against. Toll roads are practicable only where the volume of through traffic is large and fairly regular throughout the year. At off-peak periods, when nearby free roads are not congested, motorists will use them in preference to paying tolls. In metropolitan areas, toll roads are impracticable except for bypass or other through travel. The owners of the toll road will find that the toll they get for a few miles travel is less than the cost of collection while motorists discover that time wasted at toll gates exceeds time saved on the super-highway and so they will use ordinary streets.[8] Canada's first toll highway, the Montreal-Laurentien Autoroute, was opened in 1959. Several toll bridges, most of them between the United States and Canada, have been in operation for years.

Because highway accidents are so common and so destructive of property values and human life, safety engineering is a study in itself. (Reductions of grades and curves, traffic signals, signs which warn of curves, crossroads and schools, markings on pavements, stop-streets, better visibility along highways, speed limits, police patrols, grade separations, traffic lanes, one-way streets, licensing all drivers, training professional truck drivers, parking restrictions, appeals to local pride, carefully inspected brakes and lights—these are some of the methods used to combat the appalling toll of life and property on highways. (Road transport has many accomplishments to its credit but safety is not one of them.)

Working Conditions

Besides the general or social desirability of limiting hours throughout all sections of industry, a tired or incompetent driver of a motor vehicle is a menace to himself, to other highway users, and to pedestrians. In 1939 a Royal Commission in Ontario stated that in a substantial number of cases men were reported as working from 67½ to as many as 115 hours a week for wages ranging from $9 to $12.[9] A wage of $15 for a working week of 60 to 84 hours was found to be very common. By 1949 most provinces had a maximum of 10 hours work in any 24-hour period, except in an emergency. Saskatchewan and British Columbia had an 8-hour day, 44 hour week for truck drivers, emergencies excepted. As a rule, unions are in favour of some flexibility in hours of work, otherwise drivers would be forced to be away from home, to lay over at a distant or "foreign" terminal, perhaps for a weekend. Companies operating common carrier trucks between two provinces or between Canada and the United States come under the labour code of the government in Ottawa. In 1967 this provided for a minimum wage of $1.25 an hour, an 8-hour day, and a 40-hour week. Long-haul trucks frequently carry two drivers: one drives while the other sleeps in a bunk in the cab. As a rule wages constitute half the cost of running a trucking company.

Employees of trucking concerns belong to one of a number of unions. The two largest are the International Brotherhood of Teamsters, Chauffeurs, Warehousemen and Helpers of America, and the Canadian Brotherhood of Railway, Transport and General Workers. Many truck drivers, for instance, those working for breweries and dairies, belong to their appropriate industrial union. This makes it hard for union leaders to secure uniformity of wages and working conditions throughout the trucking industry. If unions push the wage rates of drivers employed by commercial truckers beyond a certain limit, some shippers will buy or lease trucks, and have them driven by their own employees. They will pay their truck drivers either at non-union rates or at a scale which approximates the remuneration of unionized workers in their own plant. The latter scale may be below that deemed reasonable by the Teamsters and other unions which appeal to all drivers irrespective of the character of their employer's business. In 1962 during a strike by members of the Teamsters Union, violence erupted in both Montreal and Toronto when owners of trucks engaged non-union men to drive vehicles through the picket lines.[10] In 1966 a strike in Ontario lasted 14 weeks and involved 8,500 truck-drivers and maintenance men and 55 truck-lines. The walkout came to an end when the men accepted an offer of a reduction in the length of the work-week from 48 to 44 hours at once, to 40 hours starting in 1968, and increases in wages of roughly 42 per cent for skilled workers spread over the next two and one-half years. The control of wages and hours, whether by legislation or by agreement between unions and management, has the effect of strengthening the hand of owner-operators of trucks who are, of course, exempt from these kinds of control.

Workers in the terminals and warehouses of truckers are paid by the hour, and drivers either by the hour or the trip. The latter method speeds up delivery, reduces loafing at "coffee stops" and prevents "manufacturing" mechanical break-downs to add to the hours on the job. Payment by the trip does not, so it is claimed, result in dangerously fast driving because usually a return load is not available until the following night. More especially, a sealed device in the vehicle makes a record on a tape of rates of speed and time spent in travel and at rest stops. In other words, the truck contains a sort of mechanical policeman which enables the employer to improve efficiency, cut costs, and up to a point protect the public against reckless driving. Driver-salesmen on trucks of bread, dairy, soft drink, and similar companies are paid by commission on their sales. Different companies have their own schemes of supplementary bonuses for safe driving, penalties for accidents, and so on. Seniority is not as important in the trucking industry as in railways, probably because labour turnover is relatively high, especially among handlers of freight in terminals. Drivers with the longest service have the choice of runs, get preference when despatchers' jobs are open, and are the last to be laid off.

Classes of Operators

Truck operations may be classified in various ways: urban, suburban, and inter-city; local and long distance; for-hire and shipper-owned; private, common, and contract carriers. Private carriers include trucks owned by plumbers, radio, television and telephone repairmen, and the like. In these instances the basic object of the truck owner is to sell a service and not to provide transportation. Other private carriers are primarily concerned with the sale of goods. Since they own both the truck and the goods it carries, their vehicles are called shipper-owned.

By law the term common carrier applies to those vehicles whose owners hold themselves out to carry freight for all members of the public up to the limit of the capacity of their vehicles, provided the freight toll is paid in legal tender. The third class, contract carriers, comprises vehicles whose owners have special and individual contracts with shippers. As a rule they agree to carry all or most of a shipper's freight during a given twelve months. Of course, even common carriers have contracts with shippers for carrying goods but these are entered into with members of the public generally, if and when they desire to ship. A contract carrier has a relatively continuous contract with one or two, or at most four or five, shippers. Contract carriers are not nearly as numerous as other classes. Often their vehicles are used for special reasons, such as the collection and distribution of mail, and the pick-up and delivery of less than carload freight. Sometimes they are used when the fleet of a private carrier is too small for the work at hand because of a seasonal peak in business, the need for speedy completion of a construction job, or an abnormal number of break-downs in the regular fleet.

Sometimes shippers want to minimize their investment or escape the worries of managing and repairing a fleet of trucks of their own and perhaps incurring losses on it. In these cases, they will use contract carriers all the time or else lease vehicles more or less continuously. A contract carrier provides both vehicle and driver: with leasing, the lessor will hire the truck and provide his own driver. For most purposes in economics, shipper-leased trucks are treated in the same way as shipper-owned.

The distinctions between the above classes are frequently blurred. For example, a person obtained orders for coal at a single sum delivered in the purchaser's bin, and then bought the coal at the mine. He delivered it as agreed and took the difference between the cost of the coal and its sales price as his compensation for performing the service of transport and as his profit. Although he argued that he was legally the owner of the goods transported and therefore a private carrier, the Interstate Commerce Commission ruled that he was primarily engaged in the business of transport and so had become a common carrier.[11] In practice, he is called a "grey" operator. It is hard to tell except by going to court whether he is a *bona fide* common carrier, and therefore subject to government control over his rates and entry into the business, or whether he is in essence a shipper-owner, and consequently free of such regulations.

In the early 1960s roughly 33 per cent of the trucks registered in Canada were owned by farmers, 40 per cent were shipper-owned and engaged in intra-urban transport, over 20 per cent were shipper-owned and used in inter-city transport, and the remaining 6 per cent were classed as for-hire. But according to the Dominion Bureau of Statistics, the proportion of ton-miles handled by these four groups was, respectively, 4, 14, 34, and 48 per cent of the total. Because of their heavier average load per vehicle (10.8 tons compared with 5.2 tons for all trucks), and their more intensive use (about 18,600 miles per annum), the for-hire vehicles are far more important in serving the transport needs of Canadians than their numbers suggest.)

Regulation of Safety in Trucking

Government regulation of motor carriers relates to safety, wages, admission to the industry, and rates. It is agreed that trucks should be mechanically safe and have proper brakes, lights, tires, and so forth. Drivers should be well trained, sober, and physically fit. Although the safety standards of the organized trucking industry have been consistently improving, the physical condition of a few trucks still leaves much to be desired. The appalling toll of deaths and injuries on highways indicates that a good deal still remains to be done to make transportation by rubber-tired vehicles reasonably safe.

Trucks are also regulated in order to make the highways usable for other vehicles. Semi-trailer trucks tend to jack-knife when slowing down if their brakes are not applied on all wheels at a uniform rate and pressure. Buckling is particularly likely when roads are slippery with rain, sleet, snow, or fallen leaves. It is being overcome by improvements in brakes and by careful maintenance from day to day. During buckling, oncoming traffic is endangered by being forced off the road, or by crashing into other moving vehicles or into the side of the truck which is at fault.

Heavily laden trucks with inadequate tractive power can travel up long grades or short steep ones only at a snail's pace. As a result they hold up vehicles coming behind them. Horse-drawn vehicles or semi-obsolete models of passenger cars have the same effect. Very long highway transports, especially "carryalls" or "caravan" automobile carriers, may obstruct other traffic because cars are unable to pass in the face of oncoming traffic. Drivers are put under added strain while passing long vehicles moving in the same direction. They become excited and prone to accident. Their nervousness rises if the transport is travelling beyond or close to the legal limit of speed or if two long trucks are moving at average speeds with no more than the legal distance (usually 100 feet) between them. A truck with a very wide body, a projecting load, or loose tarpaulins flapping in the wind may make the highway unserviceable for other drivers. These difficulties are being overcome by better police work, self-discipline on the part of the industry, wider road surfaces, extra lanes for heavy vehicles going uphill, expressways, and signs directing the drivers of all trucks to keep to the curb lane.

Regulation of Admission

Regulation of admission to the industry, rates, and routes of motor carriers typically excludes vehicles owned by farmers and farmers' co-operatives and used solely in transporting agricultural products and supplies; trucks for carrying goods solely within the corporate limits of a city, town, or village; mail trucks; school buses; military and police vehicles; hearses; taxicabs; self-drive, rented passenger cars; and so forth.[12] Provincial regulation over admission and rates also excludes private and contract carriers. Owners of all the above types of carriers (except taxicabs) are free to enter the transportation business as they see fit and to charge whatever rates they like. Regulating these carriers except as regards taxation and safety would unnecessarily interfere with private enterprise and be of little value to the public at large.

In 1963 all provinces of Canada except two—Alberta and Newfoundland–required that "for-hire" carriers get certificates of public convenience and necessity before starting business. Certificates,[13] sometimes called franchises, are grants, revocable for cause, of the privilege of using the highways and conducting business thereon. They place definite responsibilities upon the holder and protect him against unwarranted encroachment by other common carriers. They are issued only after the applicant has given proof of financial responsibility. As a rule he must show that he has the capital to acquire the necessary vehicles, to maintain them properly, to pay for loss and damage to property of shippers and of other highway users, and so forth. He must establish that he has had some experience in highway operations and usually that he is prepared to adhere, so far as physically possible, to a definite schedule of services.[14]

In particular the applicant must demonstrate that there is a real demand for his services. This does not just involve having a few shippers state they would use his vehicles if they could or that they are dissatisfied with existing trucking or railway arrangements. He must show that the volume of business in prospect is large enough to cover all his operating costs including fair wages, proper maintenance of his vehicles, and taxes. In short, he must prove that the proposed enterprise has a reasonable chance of success.

At one time certificates were never granted if another common carrier by road was already providing for the needs of the shipping public. Later some jurisdictions, especially Ontario, allowed competition on high density routes. For a time Quebec forbade the expansion and in a few instances even the operation of trucks owned directly by a railway or indirectly through a railway-owned trucking line operating as a separate corporation. In a few early cases railways successfully objected to the award of certificates because they claimed they were already supplying shippers and consignees with safe, rapid transportation at fair rates. Then provincial regulatory bodies began to allow motor carriers to enter the field in competition with the railways on the ground that the kind of service provided by one agency differed from that of the other. When regulation of admission to the industry was relatively new, most certificates were awarded under the provisions of the "grandfather clause," that is, upon proof that the applicant was *bona fide* engaged in highway transport along the routes in question prior to the date of the legislation and therefore had a pre-emptive right to the certificate.

Certification forestalls "wild catting" and ensures a reasonably high standard of service along the route concerned. Prior to regulation new truckers entered the business at will, slashed tolls to get freight, paid inadequate wages, worked themselves and their men inordinately long hours, and maintained their trucks so badly that they endangered other highway users. Some truckers gave service only when they felt like it, took only the business that paid them best, and could not make good in case of accident, or loss or damage to property.

Admission to the industry is controlled to prevent the wastes of unrestrained competition, and to ensure adequate service, fair wages, and responsible management. Having fewer competitors leads to greater stability in rates, even in the absence of any formal control over them. Official regulation of admission permits individuals and companies to buy up the franchises of small operators. They can consolidate services into larger, more efficient units without fear that new common carriers will enter the field and undermine the large organization by slashing rates and paying sub-normal wages. Thus certificates of public convenience and necessity are useful in giving the public some of the benefits of large-scale production and specialized management. At the same time the large organization has not an air-tight monopoly on the various routes assigned to it. The regulatory board may cancel its certificate if it does not live up to the terms of its franchise, and shippers are always free to engage contract carriers or put their own trucks on the road.

Long-haul trucking raises special problems of finance, risk, and managerial ability which tend to keep down the number of operators. For local operations, however, there is never any shortage of applicants for certificates because of the comparative ease of buying or leasing a vehicle. Of course, certification of itself cannot guarantee high standards of either business management or business ethics, and there are still a few irresponsible operators. But the effect of regulation, the expansion of reputable trucking companies in influence as well as in size, and the growth of provincial associations of truckers have collectively lifted the industry to a generally high level.

Regulation of Trucking Rates

It is universally recognized that governmental regulation of the rates charged by private and contract carriers is impracticable. On the wisdom of regulating the rates of for-hire carriers, opinions differ widely. For instance, in 1961 the MacPherson Commission advised against such control. A few months later a Royal Commission in Newfoundland reached the opposite conclusion. Within another two years Ontario began to require that rates be filed, which is a halfway measure to full control.

For many years railways were enthusiastic supporters of rigid control over truckers. They assumed that truckers were taking business away from them primarily because they under-maintained their vehicles, overworked their drivers, paid subnormal wages, discontinued service when they felt like it, made inadequate provision for loss and damage to goods or vehicles belonging to third parties, left poorly paying traffic to the rails, and did not pay their proper share of the cost of roads. In short, railways felt that truckers competed unfairly and so trucking rates should be controlled by governments in order to ensure a reasonable equality of competition between the two agencies.

As time went on, conditions changed. The trucking industry raised its standards of performance and got rid of most of the fly-by-night operators. Highways were cleared of snow so that truckers could give regular year-round delivery. The provinces increased taxes on motor fuel and vehicles. Labour unions, already powerful on railways, began to organize truck drivers and force increases in wage rates. Gradually railways came to understand that they had overlooked some of the causes behind the growth of the trucking industry. Instead of having advantages over railways only in cost, truckers could often give quicker delivery, more personalized service, and more frequent departures than railways. Therefore, measures to equalize costs would not necessarily restore traffic and prosperity to the rails.

What is more, the public would not tolerate regulating trucking to death in order to keep railways alive. Nor would they tolerate being called upon to sacrifice the superior services which trucks give in some respects, just to help the older mode of transport. Moreover, if regulation resulted in raising rates considerably above the cost of handling the traffic by truck, shippers would put their own vehicles on the road, and thereby nullify some of the benefits which the railways hoped to get from the strict regulation of their competitors.

Excessive regulation of trucking rates brings up the problem of enforcement. It is one thing to oblige railways to adhere to their published tolls, for there are only about twenty such companies in Canada and two of them do over 90 per cent of the business. It is quite another thing to enforce rates on thousands of truckers, particularly when the majority of them own no more than one or two vehicles. Furthermore, even if provincial governments were convinced that they should rigidly control trucking so as to help railways, even if they believed that comprehensive regulation of rates could be enforced, they are unlikely to keep in step with each other. Any marked discrepancy in the extent of regulation from one province to another leads to confusion and perhaps ill-feeling whenever inter-provincial traffic is involved.

Thus, in the course of time and for a variety of reasons, railways lost confidence in the regulation of trucking rates as a means of protecting their traffic and their revenue. Therefore, they have developed other means of meeting highway competition. These include faster service, agreed charges, incentive rates, and piggyback. They have also used technological improvements to cut their costs and offset rising wage rates and increasing costs of supplies. Finally, they have got greater freedom to quote rates on short notice. This has come about through the leniency of the Board of Transport Commissioners in enforcing the letter of the law regarding advances in rates, by changing the law in 1967, and by liberalizing the legislation on agreed charges.[15] In short, as railways sharpened their competitive tools, they came to place less reliance on the need for making the regulation of rates charged by for-hire carriers as strict as those which currently applied to railway rates. While railways are still pleased with any tightening of regulations over trucking, they do not place their main reliance on this line of defence. Indeed, the fact that they now have great freedom to quote rates as they see fit (subject to maximum tolls on captive traffic and minimum ones on competitive traffic) means that they have weakened the strength of their arguments in favour of strict governmental controls over the rates of carriers by highway.

For the most part, the discussion of regulation of truck rates has shifted away from road-rail competition to the effect of such a move on the trucking industry itself and on the economy at large. For example, it has been argued that fixing prices (rates) would remove the most effective means known for the sound development of a new industry, for lower costs, and for better service. The price charged by transportation agencies is the most satisfactory method of determining which mode can most effectively serve society as a whole and shippers in particular. Regulating price may distort the forces of competition and interfere with the effective working out of the system of private enterprise. The rate cutter is useful for he drives out the inefficient and points the way to progress.

The main objection to this argument is that unrestrained competition often has anti-social results such as low wages, long hours, unsafe vehicles, and under-the-counter deals. Moreover, government regulation of rates would not prevent a carrier from reducing rates whenever he wished, provided he filed all changes with the proper authority and did not create unjust discrimination. The government would have the power to investigate the general rate level and reduce it if necessary. The regulatory authority would see that rate reductions and increases did not take the form of unjust preferences and discriminations. The likelihood of high or unduly discriminatory rates persisting for any length of time is reduced and perhaps eliminated by the fact that an aggrieved shipper can put his own vehicles on the road. If necessary, he will lease trucks until rates quoted him by common carriers have been reduced. Despite these qualifications, if public regulation is too rigid, it may stifle initiative and retard development.

Truckers differ in their views about regulating rates. In a study prepared for the MacPherson Commission in 1960–1, Dr. D. W. Carr found that some of the larger and longer established truckers supported public enforcement of rates for the increasing volume of their traffic, mainly less than truckload lots of merchandise, that fell into uniform classes and required standard techniques in handling. "On the other hand, for traffic subject to improved efficiency, or for firms that were more efficient or progressive than most, rigid adherence to a system of established rates was looked upon as a handicap. . . . The more efficient firms . . . appeared anxious to reserve a measure of freedom in rate setting so that they might use their competitive advantages where necessary to attract profitable traffic."[16]

The smaller operators are as divided in their opinion as the larger ones. Some want freedom to cut rates and pick up or deliver traffic in new areas whenever they think they can do so profitably. Often the owners of one or two trucks are prepared to work more energetically, for longer hours, and at lower incomes than unionized drivers. Many do their own repairs and have their wives look after the office work. They find regulation more burdensome and the submission of reports to the government more irksome than bigger operators with larger, more specialized staffs. Commonly, they have strong emotional feelings about the sanctity of free enterprise.

By contrast, other small operators think that control of rates and entry is worth the bother. They want to be protected against irresponsible, fly-by-night interlopers. They want some assurance of a tolerable income for their hard work and a fair return on their investment. Because they typically do business on a narrow margin of profit, they do not see how they can make ends meet if they are intermittently exposed to losses of traffic and revenue. In general, they sincerely believe that in the long run they can give better service to their customers under a system of control than under a philosophy of dog-eat-dog.

Officials who are responsible for the control of truckers must take care to favour neither the large nor the small operators. For in applying for certificates covering new routes or in opposing applications from other truckers who might take business away from them, large companies have several advantages. They have better equipment, larger financial resources, more competent legal advice, and a wide reputation. The big firms are in more or less continuous contact with the regulatory body and they become skilled in presenting their side of any case. Their arguments are often viewed more sympathetically than those of actual or prospective operators who are less well-known. It is equally possible that a board, or some members of it, may feel that the little fellow is entitled to take a chance on operating his own business, even though every independent or outside observer is certain he can never meet his costs. A board member may even start with the conviction that the little fellow should always be preferred to the "big shot" just because he is small. A conscientious board is on its guard against both these dangers.

The attitude of shippers towards rate control has not been consistent. For example, in 1948 shippers' organizations in Ontario asked the provincial government to proclaim the provision in the Motor Carriers' Act which authorized rate control. In 1963 they took exactly the opposite position. Among shippers, the main opposition to rate control comes from those who fear increases in tolls and a decline in quality of service. The chief argument of those who favour regulation is that in periods of depression lack of control has resulted in rickety vehicles, poor service, and heavy mortality of operators. Besides, an air of suspicion pervaded the industry because truckers were alleged to have favoured certain shippers and granted secret rebates. Shippers played off one operator against another and "chiselled" rates below their proper economic level. Shippers objected because on occasion truckers increased rates without notice. This was especially serious when shippers had made firm contracts to sell goods at prices predicated on the continuance of the former tolls. Even in 1960-1, when the volume of traffic was fairly high, Dr. Carr found that "there were frequent complaints of detrimental price cutting and much emphasis on the need for establishing uniform rates at a satisfactory level."[17]

As a sort of halfway measure between full control of rates and no control at all, some shippers and truckers favour the filing of rates, either with a provincial board or with a privately operated rate bureau. As a rule, filing does not necessitate approval of the rates by either bureau or province, but bureaux are helpful to small operators who may lack experience and ability to compute their own costs and are financially unable to hire experts to do the job for them. Although any carrier is technically free to change tolls whenever he wishes (subject to giving notice of advances or reductions), filing almost invariably lends greater stability to rates. It also tends to prevent favouritism in the charges actually paid by shippers. At the same time, so it is alleged, filing avoids the expense and rigidities that are often associated with outright control of rates by a regulatory authority.

When rates are filed with a traffic bureau, no sanctions can be imposed on highway carriers who refuse to file their tolls, other than criticism by other truckers. Managers and members of rate bureaus must take care that they do not infringe Dominion legislation forbidding combines in undue restraint of trade. Under the Combines Investigation Act, "every one who conspires, combines, agrees, or arranges with another person to limit *unduly* the facilities for transporting . . . any article . . . [or] to prevent, or lessen, *unduly*, competition in the . . . transportation or supply of an article . . . is guilty of an indictable offence and is liable to imprisonment for two years" (R.S.C., 1952, c. 314, sec. 32 (1). Italics added). Note that no offence is committed unless the effect of filing is detrimental to the public. Rates filed with any governmental regulatory agency are, of course, exempt from these provisions, partly because it can be assumed they are not detrimental to the public, partly because, being filed in accordance with the provisions of another statute, there is no question of conspiracy, combination, or agreement among the parties concerned.

When filing is required by law, the government can enforce its rules in the courts of the land. In Ontario, which began to require filing on May 1, 1963, no licensed trucker may change his rates for a period of 30 days after they are filed with the Highway Transport Board. It is illegal to charge any rate other than that filed in the tariff. These regulations do not apply to operators of fleets of four vehicles or less, to carriers of livestock and farm supplies, to most dump trucks, and construction vehicles.

Some provincial governments oppose regulation of rates because they consider that unrestricted trucking will keep down transportation tolls of both rail and highway carriers. Other governments object on general principles to interference with private industry or claim that enforcing the regulations would cost too much money. In fact the industry tends to police itself. If a trucker loses business to a competitor, he can usually find out from the shipper or consignee whether the rates have been cut. If they have, he will either lay charges or, more probably, have the industry bring pressure on the rate cutter to keep his prices in line.

The gist of the matter is that governments can control rates cheaply and efficiently if the industry is prepared to co-operate. If the industry as a whole or an obstreperous minority within it refuses to support control, the cost of administration may exceed the benefits received by shippers, consignees, truckers, and the general public. Commissioner J. B. Eastman has stated that control "is a cumbersome and time-consuming process, often exasperating in its delays, expensive, but better than rate wars."[18] Public regulation is sound only to the extent that it is sensibly applied. It should not be utterly condemned because it will not be perfect. One of the virtues of regulation by commission is that the hearings are public. All the parties who have an interest in any particular case are free to appear and present their views. The commission presumably bases its decision on the facts placed before it plus those which its own research and technical staffs supply.

In 1965 there was no regulation whatever of rates charged by truckers in Newfoundland, Nova Scotia, Prince Edward Island, and Alberta.[19] Rate tariffs must be filed with the governments of Ontario and New Brunswick but otherwise there is no control. In Quebec rates must be filed with the provincial Transport Board which may amend any rates to make them fair and reasonable, and must approve changes proposed by truckers. Only British Columbia, Saskatchewan, and Manitoba carefully control rates for intra-provincial movements of freight.

Jurisdiction over Trucking

For many years the concensus[20] was that the Dominion had jurisdiction over interprovincial and international traffic by highway. This view was finally confirmed in 1954.[21] Meanwhile in 1937 and again in 1940 bills were introduced into Parliament for the federal control of trucks engaged in this traffic but were withdrawn in the face of strong opposition from truckers and some shippers. They alleged that the volume of such traffic amounted to no more than from 3 to 5 per cent of the total business of intercity highway carriers. Consequently, any benefits brought about by regulation would not be large enough to justify the expense. Furthermore, the Dominion, being the owner of a transcontinental railway which often ran at a deficit, could not be expected to deal equitably with an industry with which it was in keen competition. On the other hand, the Dominion was urged to regulate interprovincial and international carriage by highway because in so doing it would give a lead to the various provinces and encourage them to exercise similar control over traffic which was entirely within their borders. With the increasing amount of regulation by the provinces, this argument lost much of its strength. The fact that the Dominion satisfactorily regulates other agencies of transportation, including civil aviation, pipelines, and inland ships, which are competitive with railways seems to have been overlooked.

The Royal Commission of 1951 said that the time had come "when Parliament might well reconsider this question of control,"[22] especially since two agencies of transport, railways and interprovincial trucking, both subject to Dominion jurisdiction, were competing with each other. The Government rejected this recommendation for two reasons: it felt that it should not complicate the problem of controlling an industry which mainly came within the ambit of provincial authority; and the trucking industry was strongly opposed to intervention by Ottawa, since it would be superimposed on provincial regulation and the Dominion owned the biggest railway in the country.

Despite its reluctance to regulate interprovincial and international motor traffic, the Dominion could not legally divest itself of its jurisdiction except by amendment to the British North America Act. But it found a way out of its difficulty by turning the administration of this part of its jurisdiction over to the provincially appointed boards which supervised intra-provincial trucking. As things turned out, the provinces were at first unwilling to assume any additional administrative functions. Still, by 1960, six years after the Dominion passed the enabling legislation,[23] Quebec, Saskatchewan, and Alberta (though it abstained from regulating almost all intra-provincial trucking rates) were controlling most of the economic aspects of interprovincial and even international trucking. Other provinces merely required the filing of rates on such traffic.

The National Transportation Act of 1967 contained lengthy provisions (sec. 29 to sec. 31) for the regulation of extra-provincial motor vehicle transport by the Canadian Transport Commission in the event that the federal government should decide to take back the regulation of these carriers. The Minister of Transport made it clear that the Dominion would repossess this field of administration only if the provinces were to consent that it should do so. On the basis of past experience, it is fair to say that provinces will expect to receive concessions of some sort or other before they give up any of the administrative powers they possess, either of their own right or by virtue of administration delegated by the Dominion.

All the interprovincial and many of the intra-provincial operators deal with matters of mutual interest through the Canadian Trucking Associations, Inc., in Ottawa and its affiliates in the provinces. These groups supplement and in a way are substitutes for control by governments. The entry of railways into the trucking business through the operation of their own vehicles or by the purchase of independent trucking lines has complicated the work of these associations but apparently has not significantly altered their approach to problems of transport.

Taxation of Motor Carriers

(Taxation is more important to highway carriers than to any other transportation agency. The public provides the right of way for highway users and seeks to recover its expenses by means of taxes of various sorts. The costs of maintaining way and structures appear among the expenses of railways. The corresponding costs appear as taxes in the financial accounts of commercial highway operators and private motorists.)

Originally the cost of constructing and maintaining highways and bridges was included in the ordinary tax levy and was paid in the main by owners of property in proportion to their assessment. Looking backward, we can see the theoretical soundness of this arrangement. Roads and streets met a social necessity. They provided access to schools, churches, doctors, post offices, and the law courts; they permitted neighbours to keep in touch with each other; they allowed farmers to market their produce and get the supplies they needed; roadside ditches helped drain adjacent lands; and the right of way accommodated telephone and hydro-electric power lines, gas and water mains, sewers, and fire alarm systems. The benefits of having reasonably passable roads were shared by each and every member of the community. As most highway users were owners or renters of real estate, it was fair that they should pay for the roads in proportion to the values of their real property.

With the advent of automobiles, highways had to be built to a standard far beyond what was needed in the "horse and buggy days." The new roads were costly to construct, especially with the cyclical rise in prices during and after World War I. They required careful maintenance, regular policing, and an elaborate system of traffic control. Commercial truck and bus operators were using the highways as places of business in a sense and to an extent that never applied to draymen moving freight to and from railway stations, to farmers hauling a few hundred bushels of grain to market, or to retailers delivering to nearby customers. Many highway users came from relatively distant points. As they did not ordinarily own property in more than one municipality, they paid nothing for the upkeep of many roads which they used. Yet they complained loudly if local roads were poor.[24]

Some car and truck owners used the highways a great deal; others did so only occasionally. Still other users had not much realty but kept their wealth in stocks, bonds, or merchandise which, in the absence of a general property tax in Canada, was not directly assessed for tax purposes. Landowners began to feel the pinch of heavy taxes for roads at the very time when the cost of education, public health, and social security was also growing apace. Naturally they were anxious to get relief from taxes wherever they could. Though it received little attention in popular debate, the great merit of determining highway expenditures on a commercial basis is the superior economy of the normal utility-cost relationships. Instead of applying a vague concept of social values, expenditures on highways as a whole and on individual roads could be related as closely as may be to the gross revenues received from users of the facilities. Thus for various reasons the demand arose that those who actually used the roads should pay for them.

This demand was more easily expressed in editorial columns and on the hustings than in fair and just legislation. Highways continued to meet numerous social needs such as education, recreation, health, police and postal service. If the concept of "social-necessity use" or "community benefit" was accepted in the early period, it should have been equally sound of the motor age.[25] The problem was how to bring the concept down to practical terms. Although attempts to apply the theory, were made in Ontario, Britain, and the United States,[26] in the end this problem like many another, was settled by the course of events.

The volume of traffic on trunk highways and the main thoroughfares of big cities has grown much more rapidly than the volume on rural roads and on streets in the purely residential parts of towns and cities. By the early 1960s, probably 90 per cent of the vehicle miles in Ontario were run on 10 per cent of its road mileage. While every road is used

CANADIAN TRANSPORTATION ECONOMICS

for a variety of purposes, it is clear that heavily travelled routes are mainly used by through vehicles. On local roads, the reverse is true. The busiest roads, the provincial highways, are paid for from taxes levied against highway users. Country roads and ordinary city streets are built and maintained by cities, towns, townships, counties, and other authorities deriving their legal powers from the provincial government and their funds chiefly from taxes on real property.

Obviously the distinction between a local and a through road, or between a highway used for social necessity and for business purposes, is not clear-cut. Moreover, the matter is complicated by the involved methods adopted by some provinces for arriving at how much assistance they will give to counties and municipalities for the construction and maintenance of the more important roads, streets, and bridges within their boundaries. The provinces also make grants to cities, towns, villages, and townships for schools and public health. These grants release revenue from municipal taxes for spending on roads. Yet despite all these complications the distinction between roads for community benefit and for through traffic is useful in settling the problem of who should pay for roads. By and large, practice confirms the theory that road users should pay for heavily travelled highways used largely for commercial purposes, while owners of adjoining property should pay for local roads which are needed mainly for their social or community value.

The cost of expressways and other heavily used roads relative to the cost of local ones has gone so far in some American states that it has been argued that the cost of the latter can be ignored without seriously damaging the principle of justice. On this premise, one can conclude that road users should pay the entire cost of the road system. Up to a point this is what is happening in Ontario and Quebec. Municipalities have for years been pleading their inability to finance such ever-more-costly services as education, public health, welfare, and roads, including snow clearance. By means of grants of one sort or another, provincial governments have relieved municipalities of more and more of their costs, thereby releasing taxing power for roads.

Inter-urban roads, which are the responsibility of provincial governments, have been modernized at a more rapid rate than either ordinary rural roads or streets in metropolitan areas. For a time it appeared that spending on roads by provincial governments was approaching an upper limit or ceiling. Then the problems of urban sprawl, ribbon development, and downtown strangulation became acute. Eventually the need for expressways, circular or bypass roads, and subways became so great that provincial governments were forced to enlarge their financial assistance to intra-urban transport and, in the case of Nova Scotia, to the Dartmouth-Halifax bridge. Meanwhile, the number of automobiles had risen faster than anticipated and so more costly inter-city roads were needed. In short, provincial expenditures on roads broke through the ceiling previously envisaged.

Insofar as (the provinces get revenue from taxes on motor fuel, drivers, and vehicles, these increased expenditures will be met from road users. It should be noted that, given certain rates of taxes,(total receipts from road users will rise rather steadily because more and more people own cars and drive more miles per vehicle per annum. Any increase in provincial revenues and expenditures on roads will tend to relieve or at least lessen the increase of taxes on real property. The relief will be particularly welcome in large cities where the cost of building a mile of expressway or subway runs into millions of dollars.)

Road Funds

One proposal for dealing with highway finance is to set up a road fund as has been done in California, Ghana, and elsewhere. The fund is credited with all taxes collected from highway users and charged with interest on highway debt plus the cost of maintenance and depreciation of roads. In the past, depreciation charges have often been underestimated and even ignored. Public officials miscalculated the increasing weight and speed of motor vehicles, the growth in their numbers, and the life of road surfaces. It is assumed that officials of the road fund will not fall into this error which has resulted in present-day motorists being called upon to pay costs which under a policy of accurate amortization should have been covered by motorists in previous years. In short, the road fund would be run along more business-like lines than a government department.

The road fund would have the further advantage of assuring the motorist and trucker that the taxes he pays on vehicles and fuel will be used solely for his benefit. They will not be diverted to other purposes such as social security or education. The general taxpayer is also pleased, for he knows that he will pay for roads only in proportion to use. If for reasons of health or preference, he does not drive a car or if, because of his location, he does not have access to a high-class road, then he is not forced to pay for what he does not use. It is further argued that under the fund highways will be built only where needed and not partly to win votes. Besides, the public will not be burdened with a huge debt contracted because roads are built far in advance of need. In a broad sense the roads of the state or province will be run like a gigantic toll road or toll bridge, rather than on a quasi-political basis as at present.

In Canada the concept of a road fund has often been used for purposes of accounting or determining public policy but no funds as such have been set up. For one thing, the fund principle assumes that roads are to be judged almost entirely on the basis of their earning power, that is, of their ability to produce revenue from users. In consequence, the fund tends to neglect the need for roads which have a high community value. In theory this problem could be overcome by segregating the two kinds of roads. The problem is to secure a proper balance between roads and revenue. The probability is that the fund would start by having no more roads than it could properly finance from its revenues. Later it would succumb to constant pressure to take on more mileage. Eventually it would run short of the money to carry out its functions effectively.

Rigidly applied, the fund would remove both spending on public works and the raising of money for public purposes from control by the legislature. Less rigidly applied, officials of the fund might be allowed to use their discretion only on the side the spending while the legislature reserved the right to tax. Both arrangements are unsound because the elected representatives of the people should always have the power to hold one cabinet minister or another responsible for every detail of what goes on in the government. Officials of a Road Fund could cover up their mistakes in the same way as any private business. On the contrary the operations of provincial departments of highways come under regular scrutiny by opposition members in the House, newspaper editors, and the general public. Officers in the department can be called before a committee of the legislature to explain their actions and in the legislature itself the Minister of Highways must either defend them or resign. In a word, road funds run counter to two important principles of the British or parliamentary system of government: ministerial responsibility, and the legislature's power of the purse.

Although road funds as used in some American states are out of place in the system of government followed in Canada, the idea is valuable for testing the relation between expenditures on highways and the revenue collected from road users. This relationship has frequently changed. During most of the war gasoline was rationed, trucks could not operate beyond a radius of fifty miles from their base or home garage, and the construction of highways had to be deferred. By means of subsidies the Dominion protected the provincial governments against loss of revenue which resulted from reduced sales of motor fuel.

Removal of rationing and prosperity after the war caused a rapid increase in gasoline sales. Moreover, the provinces absorbed most or all of the special war tax of 3 cents a gallon which the federal government had imposed in 1941 and removed six years later. Relatively low expenditures on construction coupled with buoyant receipts from taxes on highway users permitted most provinces fully to cover their highway costs including interest and probably depreciation. In 1948 in Ontario and perhaps in some other jurisdictions highway users were contributing funds which were used for general purposes. In other provinces such as the Maritimes, with smaller, more scattered populations and fewer vehicles per mile of road, highway receipts did not equal expenditures even in the postwar period and by the early 1950s expenditures on roads and streets were out-running receipts in every province.

In the mid-fifties three bodies—the Royal Commission on Canada's Economic Prospects (the Gordon Commission), a Select Committee of the Ontario Legislature, and the Canadian Tax Foundation—examined the financing of roads. All agreed that expenditures had increased very rapidly and that rates of taxation had not risen proportionately.[27] For example, in 1955 the Tax Foundation reported:

One of the most important inferences that can be drawn from available information, however, is that the present level of user charges in most provinces is inadequate. In 1953 the ratio of user revenues to total road, street and highway expenditures for all Canada was 59 per cent. The motorist in 1953 was paying about three-quarters of the proportion of total costs allocated to him under most formulæ, and it is hardly likely that this ratio has increased in the meantime. While there is a good deal of variation among provinces it is apparent that if recent experience is indicative of the long range position some increase in user charges is due in every province.[28]

Later the Tax Foundation brought the statistics up to date and concluded that in 1961 the provinces of Ontario and Quebec collected about the same amount from taxes on gasoline and diesel fuel[29] and from the sale of licences for vehicles, drivers and chauffeurs, as the province and the Dominion spent in that year on the construction, maintenance, and administration of highways, rural roads, bridges, and ferries within the province. In most other provinces, revenues from highway users were less than 50 per cent of the expenditures, while in Newfoundland they were only one-third.

These data must be used with caution. They include capital expenditures on new roads and improvements on old ones but nothing for obsolescence of roads and for interest on highway debt. As far as possible they exclude spending by municipalities. On the other hand, they take in what the Dominion spent on the Trans-Canada Highway and the Roads to Resources programme. The Dominion levies no specific taxes on the use of highways as such. The sales taxes which the federal and some provincial governments collect on motor vehicles and spare parts, being included in a general levy on most goods, should not be allocated directly to roads.

The low rate of taxes on road users relative to total spending on roads by Newfoundland and other provinces may, perhaps, be justified on the ground that once good roads are provided, the volume of traffic will grow rapidly and soon taxes on highway users will cover all or a much larger part of the costs involved. Also, some provincial governments may prefer to collect less from users than they spend on roads in order to reduce trucking rates and force railways to cut tolls. In this event shippers within the province benefit, while the losses experienced by railways are borne by taxpayers across the Dominion, either by direct subsidy to cover deficits on the Canadian National, or by collecting less income tax from the Canadian Pacific, or both. The inadequacy of provincial rates of taxation on highway users and the consequent lowering of railway rates also adds to the mileage of non-paying rail lines. When these are abandoned, shippers may suffer and the provinces concerned will have to build new roads or improve old ones.

The best policy is to make highway users pay all highway costs. This point was stressed by the Royal Commissions of both 1951 and 1961. However, neither body discussed whether the federal government should try to recover its share of the cost of the Trans-Canada Highway from users. Though the earlier Commission might be excused because at the time it brought down its report the Highway was just getting under way, the MacPherson Commission was clearly negligent in not referring to this matter. It may have believed that it would be unfair for the Dominion to tax the gasoline and diesel fuel used throughout the country in order to recover the cost of the transcontinental highway used by a relatively small number of motorists and truckers. The same objection might be made, though not with quite the same cogency, to intra-provincial highways.

Taxation of Classes of Vehicles

The relation of total expenditures to total receipts is only part of the problem. An equally complex question is whether different classes of motor vehicles are paying their proper share of the total revenues and whether expenditures are made over the network of roads within a province in ways that will bring the greatest good to the greatest number. The provinces secure revenue from highway users by means of taxes on gasoline and diesel fuel, registration fees on vehicles, licensing of drivers and chauffeurs, a tax on bus-seats per vehicle-mile, and fines. Fines go directly into the general coffers, as do other penalties collected by law enforcement officers. The sales taxes levied by the Dominion and some of the provinces on new vehicles and parts also go into the general revenue of the government concerned.

The licence for vehicles has several purposes. It helps compensate the state for the expense of tracing stolen cars. It may possibly constitute a tax on general property or on the business carried on by means of motor vehicles. The most important feature of this tax, however, is that licence fees can be set in order to take account of the expense of wear and tear on the highways caused by vehicles of different gross weights. The fuel tax imposes a lesser burden per ton-mile on the heavier vehicles than on the lighter ones because fuel consumption does not increase directly with the size and weight of the vehicle and its load. Licence fees graduated upward for heavier vehicles tend to equalize taxation on a ton-mile basis over all vehicles. A tax of so much per ton-mile on trucks and their cargoes has much to commend it on the ground of equity but is hard to police.

Licence fees may also measure readiness to serve. They may justifiably be imposed to make certain that every vehicle owner contributes something to the maintenance of highways even though he may use them only occasionally. Although many farmers rarely go farther than the nearest town, the facilities of the whole provincial highway system are there for the farmer whenever he cares to use them. Because he never or rarely drives along a provincial highway is no reason for exempting him from all payments for its upkeep.

The fuel tax is by far the largest source of revenue for highway purposes. It has many of the features of a rental fee or toll. "The essence of a tax, as distinguished from other charges by government, is the absence of a direct *quid pro quo* between the tax-payer and the public authority. . . . It . . . is exacted from all alike and without any regard to the individual's use of the services supplied."[30] The tax on petrol is like the sale of postage stamps. It is of direct and measurable benefit to the individual who pays it and he pays in proportion to his use of the service. The licence fee, which is largely a tax in the true sense of the word, is paid only once per annum.

In discussions of highway finance, controversy centres on the proportion of the total cost to be borne by owners of trucks, buses, passenger cars, and motorcycles. It is claimed that trucks require wider and thicker road surfaces than any other motor vehicles and therefore that the taxes paid by their owners should be higher than those paid by other motorists. It is admitted that some elements in the cost of road construction such as right of way, fencing, and drainage structures, are not appreciably higher on a highway used by motor vehicles generally than they would be for private passenger cars alone. It is asserted, however, that the paved surface and bridges must be wider and heavier and grades gentler on account of trucks and that due to their weight trucks are more destructive of road surfaces and bridges than other vehicles. Because buses and trucks require facilities in excess of the requirements of ordinary passenger traffic, they should pay for this excess in addition to their share of the ordinary requirements.

Though this principle of payment is generally accepted, its application to practical affairs is complex. The action of the elements may be more important in destroying road surfaces than the weight of vehicles passing over them. In comparison with passenger automobiles, trucks have more axles, and more and larger tires. The weight of the vehicle is spread over the number of square inches of contact between the tire and the road. The number of pounds per square inch is greater for a loaded truck than for a private automobile but the difference is not in strict proportion to the gross weight of the two vehicles. Owing to alternate freezing and thawing of surface and sub-surface structures every spring and fall, road pavements, like ordinary sidewalks, must be thicker than actually needed by the weight of the load supported. This is particularly important in Canada with its severe frosts. The thickness of the pavement varies with the nature of the subsoil, the quality of the drainage, and so forth, as well as with the weight of the vehicles. On city streets, the periodic tearing up for gas and water seems to be especially hard on pavements.

Private passenger automobiles, no less than trucks, require expensive highways. When they travel at speeds of sixty miles an hour or more, they need gentle curves and gradients for economy and speed, long sighting distances for protection against on-coming traffic, and wide shoulders for safety's sake. Pleasure-seeking motorists, not commerical traffic, are responsible for landscaping and general beautification of highways. Much of the investment in highways is undertaken to accommodate daily, weekly, and holiday peaks of traffic. Private passenger cars are chiefly responsible for the congested roads. Broadly speaking, trucks use roads at off-peak periods. Hence, truck owners say, they should not be accused of adding disproportionately to the cost of highway construction.

Recent studies have indicated that trucks are more destructive of road surfaces than was previously believed. One overloaded truck may partially wreck a highway and other heavy trucks will complete the breakdown of the surface. The destruction caused by overloading may not show up for days or even months. Police have difficulty checking overloading because trucks which are breaking the law sometimes take detours around weighing stations. Truck operators find overloading adds so much to their profits that they take a chance on being caught. Engineers seem to agree that trucks increase highway costs above what they would be for private passenger cars alone but they cannot say with certainty how much the increase amounts to.

The licence fees for trucks and buses differ considerably from one province to another and it is hard to detect any underlying principle. The economic soundness of licence fees for trucks may be judged on the basis of either incremental costs or ton-miles. The former was the method used by the Ontario Royal Commission of 1933, but the Gordon Commission of 1955 said it required much engineering data which was not available. Therefore, following the ton-mile method, the Commission took

seven classes of vehicles, by weight groups, ranging from 3,500 pounds up to the maximum allowed for each province. . . . To these were applied an average annual mileage to derive the annual gross ton-miles performed. The annual taxes (gas and fees) paid by each class of vehicle were then divided by ton-miles to obtain the ton-mile contribution for each class of vehicle. . . . On a ton-mile basis, passenger cars pay from a low of 3.2 times as much as do heavy gasoline powered vehicles in Saskatchewan to a high of 4.8 times as much in British Columbia. Light commercial vehicles [panel delivery trucks] pay from 3.3 to 5.3 times as much as heavy gasoline powered commercial vehicles in Manitoba and Quebec respectively. A similar comparison with heavy diesel powered commercial vehicles is even more revealing, reflecting greater fuel economy. Passenger cars pay from 3.7 times as much in Manitoba to a high of 6.3 times as much in British Columbia, while light commercial vehicles pay from . . . 4.0 times as much in Manitoba to . . . 6.9 times as much in Quebec. It is debatable, of course, whether or not the weight and mileage relationship between a private passenger car and a transport truck is an equitable basis for tax computation, but certainly the data points to the need for sound research on the problem in the interests of equity in highway finance and in the conditions of competition in the transportation industry.[31]

It would be unrealistic to complete the discussion of the gasoline tax without the statement that commercial truckers have a well-organized lobby which can make its influence felt in government decisions. Though private motorists are not brought together into a strong organization, they all have votes. In more technical language, cost of service is not the only element in gasoline taxation. Value of service, what the traffic will bear, cannot be entirely neglected.

Parking

However much opinions may differ on how the costs of highways are to be distributed among the various classes of users, there is no question that, theoretically at least, part of the cost of building and maintaining highways ought to be borne directly by the owners of parked vehicles. For all practical purposes cars and trucks pay for highways only when they are moving. When they are parked, they pay nothing in gasoline tax. What is perhaps more serious, they prevent other vehicles from using the roads. A parking space slightly exceeds the width of a car and is at least one and one-half times its length. Traffic is slowed down when it has to travel around even a single parked vehicle and it is often interfered with when drivers try to squeeze into or get out of cramped quarters. In order to make streets useful for moving vehicles, in order to permit them to fulfil the purpose for which they were built, parking may be forbidden at the busy times of day, or may be limited to one or two hours' duration. Motorists complain because they are inconvenienced by having to go farther afield to find parking space on a quiet street or have to pay for storage in a downtown garage or parking lot, or are fined if they break the law. Other drivers grouch because "parked cars take up all the street." Parking meters were originally designed to reduce disputes with policemen regarding fines for overparking. Provided the rates are fairly high, meters can be used to equalize costs among highway users and they economize on policemen and police time for it takes less time to check meters than to chalk and check tires.

The Highway Network

Another problem in highway finance is the apportionment of total provincial revenue among various roads. A study made in Iowa indicated that the average cost of operating a passenger car per mile was eight cents on earth roads, five cents on gravel, and three and one-half cents on pavement.[32] On gravel roads expenses for gasoline were 10 per cent higher than on pavement, for oil 40 per cent, for tires 100 per cent, and for car repairs 150 per cent more. In a sense, the motorist pays for good roads whether he has them or not. As the motorist has smaller bills for gasoline, tires, and repairs when he has good roads than when he has to use poor ones, he can afford to pay a higher gross price for gasoline (including tax) without raising his total costs. Because of advances in refining methods and the great economy of sending petroleum by pipeline rather than by rail, the cost of gasoline excluding tax has generally declined over the years. Governments have taken advantage of technological developments in highways and motor vehicles and in the processing and distribution of gasoline. They have been able to collect higher and higher taxes on motor fuel without arousing the antagonism of highway users on whom they are levied.

Superficially it is unfair to collect gasoline taxes from motorists in small, out-of-the-way communities for constructing highways in thickly settled areas and at the same time require them to pay for their lack of good roads through higher operating costs per vehicle-mile.[33] Although it would be impracticable to require motorists and truckers to pay for each individual road in proportion to their use of it, the volume of traffic using individual roads should be at least one of the factors determining where the province should spend highway revenues. Periodic surveys of the number and kind of vehicles passing a given point are useful aids in deciding what roads are to be improved but statistics cannot supplant sound judgment and a sense of fairness.

19

Road-Rail Competition

IT IS OFTEN SAID that railways once had a virtual monopoly of inland transport and that the internal combustion engine forced them into a competitive world for the first time. Such statements contain a large measure of truth but they are not correct in detail.

Early Competition

The first Canadian railways faced competition from coachmen and teamsters as well as from schooners and steamships. They easily disposed of long-haul road transporters. Indeed, during the last quarter of the nineteenth century railways sometimes advocated better roads so that shippers and consignees could haul goods to and from stations cheaply and regularly.

Carriers on inland waters were persistent competitors of the rails. Owners had little chance of taking their vessels elsewhere when they lost even part of their traffic to the rails. If they tied up their vessels, they would lose their entire investment. A small contribution to interest and depreciation was better than none. So they kept on operating as long as they covered their out-of-pocket expenses and a little more. Schooners and even small steamers could be run with skeleton crews, helped by poorly paid casual labour. Ships plied not only the Great Lakes and the St. Lawrence River, as they still do, but the Richelieu and Ottawa Rivers, the Rideau Canal, the Grand River, and the Thames below Chatham. They called at numerous places where today commercial shipping is non-existent or negligible.

By the early twentieth century schooners and small steamers were becoming obsolete. Larger steamships were cheaper to operate per ton of cargo but could not run up shallow rivers or into minor ports.) Moreover, they tended to concentrate on moving grain, iron ore, and lumber at rates below what railways could afford to charge. At the same time, they carried merchandise of all sorts, commonly called package freight. By about 1908 they stabilized their rates on package freight at certain differentials below the corresponding rate by rail. The differentials took account of slower delivery, the cost of hauling to and from docks, and the seasonality of the movement. In effect, the railways gave up competing for some kinds of freight while on other kinds, railways and ships competed on quality of service but not by cutting rates below an accepted floor.)

Meanwhile, the railway industry had been engaged in civil war. For nearly 40 years after 1860 the Grand Trunk and American railways fought intermittently over the traffic between Chicago and the Atlantic coast ports of New York and Boston. This competition was largely on the basis of rates. After i's completion in 1885, the Canadian Pacific in co-operation with steamships along the Pacific coast followed the same guerilla tactics on freight between New York and California. In the 1890s the Canadian Pacific and the Grand Trunk fought each other in Ontario and Quebec by cutting freight rates and passenger fares.[1])

(These rate wars resulted in the bankruptcy of many railways and in undue preference and unjust discrimination.) Railways cut rates at places where they faced competition from water carriers and other railways. Then, in order to retain as much revenue as they could, they kept the old rates at stations where competition was weak or absent. The public objected to the inequity of such rate-making practices. They looked at the high rates and condemned the railways for having a monopoly. They took this attitude because the economic philosophy of the time was almost unanimous in favour of free competition. Under other circumstances the public might have looked mainly at the rates at competitive points. Had it done so, it would have condemned the evils of excessive competition such as undue preference to certain localities and shippers, poorly maintained equipment, losses to investors in railway shares and bonds, and the impossibility of attracting enough new capital into railways to meet the needs of shippers for adequate transport.

In either case the public would have called for government intervention. Effective control began in Canada in 1904 and in the United States two years later. The nominal controls, which had existed for many years in both countries, had broken down because of shortcomings in the laws and their administration and because of the opposition of railway executives.) A railwayman would act on the principle that sooner or later all his competitors were certain to break the poorly framed laws or the numerous agreements made by railways among themselves. Hence, he should "get the jump" on the others by cutting rates, surreptitiously if he could get away with it, openly if he had to. In the early nineteenth century, however, the executives came to see that they gained little by such tactics. Rate wars merely resulted in each road carrying about the same amount of freight as before but at lower rates. Therefore, each railway would be wise to adhere to the old rates, to live and let live, to "play ball with the boys."(Thus, in order to maximize and especially to stabilize its income, a railway would maintain rates and hope its rail competitor would do the same. In economic theory this is called duopoly or, if several railways are involved, monopolistic competition.)

There was another reason for stability of rates. After about 1875 traffic in the United States was being carried at progressively lower costs per ton-mile. The decline in operating costs was brought about by the steel rail, bigger locomotives, larger cars, and generally more efficient management. As a result, efficiently operated railways could afford to slash their tolls on competitive traffic and still make money. These reductions in rates forced other companies either into bankruptcy or into the adoption of the latest equipment and operating methods. But after about 1900 the rate of technological advance slowed down and railway operating costs began to rise because of higher wage rates. So the dangers of cutting rates became more serious and, conversely, the advantages of stable rates more self-evident. In a word, government regulation was a useful buttress to stabilized rates; the basic support was provided by the railways themselves.

Once rates were stabilized, economists began to advance arguments in favour of maintaining the status quo. They said that railways were natural monopolies: unnecessary duplication of properties was wasteful and contrary to the best interests of economic society. In addition, American lawyers talked about railways being strongly affected with a public interest and fit subjects for extensive control by legislatures and regulatory commissions or boards. The fact is that it was to the self-interest of railways to keep rates as stable as they could without invoking a harmful amount of public criticism and animosity.

The Emergence of New Competition

(Stability of rates and relatively strict adherence to the Classification lasted from roughly 1904 to about 1950, due allowance being made for the changes in the general level of rates brought about by changing wage rates and material prices. It was only during this period—indeed perhaps for only part of this period—that railways could be said to have had a virtual monopoly of inland transport and this statement is true only if monopoly is measured by stability of tolls. It is not true if the criterion of monopoly is the popular one of excessive or monopolistic profits.

In the 1930s truckers forced railways to cut many of their tolls. By comparison with what came later, these reductions were not insufferable from the railway point of view. In the 1940s the expansion of the trucking industry was retarded by wartime restrictions and postwar shortages. Consequently, it was not until approximately 1950 that highway carriers began again to tense their muscles.

It is a mistake, moreover, to look upon trucks as the only competitors of railways. Private passenger cars, buses, and airplanes hurt railway passenger revenues. The growing use of electricity, fuel oil, and natural gas have ruined much of the carriage of coal by rail. In effect, pipelines and electric wires are competitors of railways. Finally, the St. Lawrence Seaway plus the use of trucks to connect lake and river ports with shippers throughout the St. Lawrence Lowlands revitalized competition from inland waterways.

What is more, the total bill for transport by various modes has not risen as fast as total spending on goods and services of all kinds. This is the result of two sets of factors. First, factory managers have found methods of reducing waste in production and so have cut down the quantity of raw materials that must be transported. They have also developed new methods of packaging and therefore reduced the tare weight that must be carried. Besides, they have located their factories and assembly plants so as to minimize their total transportation costs on incoming raw materials and outgoing finished products. Second, society is spending relatively more of its income on personal services such as entertainment, meals in restaurants, dry-cleaning, and health services, and comparatively less on bulky foodstuffs, heavy clothing, and massive furniture. Excluding private automobiles, the transportation component was a much smaller part of the expenditure of a typical Canadian family in 1960 than in 1920. In short, the railway problem is a complex of competition from other media of transport, the discovery of new resources, new techniques of production in all industries and in methods of operating railways, new spending habits, and so on.

Competition between railways and motor carriers has had three main effects: it has deprived the rails of traffic, it has reduced rates and fares by rail, and it has introduced or at least re-emphasized certain

hitherto neglected aspects of what constitutes good transportation service.) Trucks have simultaneously upset the railway rate structure and
put competition on numerous other bases besides rates./ Road-rail competition is a fight for traffic. It also means that railways must re-adjust
both their prices and the kind of service which they offer for sale.)

The Growth of Trucking

Although the economic significance of trucking is far broader than
can be measured by figures of ton-miles and number of vehicles registered, it is wise to begin with some statistics.

TABLE 11
Inter-city Ton-Miles Performed in Canada by Type of Carrier

Year	Total (billions)	Rail %	Road %	Water %	Air %	Oil Pipeline %	Gas Pipeline %
1938	53	51	3	46	*	†	†
1946	77	72	5	24	*	†	†
1951	105	61	8	30	*	1	†
1956	145	54	7	27	*	11	†
1961	152	43	11	26	*	14	6
1965	201	42	9	27	*	14	8

SOURCE: Dominion Bureau of Statistics
* Less than one-tenth of one per cent
† Negligible or non-existent.

The above data are for intercity traffic only. They do not include
rural, intra-urban, and suburban carriage such as local delivery of
farm produce, fuel oil, bread, and merchandise of all sorts. e.g.,
deliveries by department and other stores. Note also that the data
relate to physical volume and not to revenue. Much of the traffic
carried by rail, inland ships, and pipelines is handled at low rates per
ton-mile. By contrast, much traffic by truck pays comparatively high
rates per ton-mile. The number of truckers is large and not all of them
keep accurate records of ton-miles performed. Consequently, the data
for road transport are based on a sample and on an estimate worked
out by methods developed in the United States. Possibly some allowance should be made for the fact that as time goes on the Bureau
of Statistics gets a more complete coverage of motor carriers. Finally,
the data take no account of the occurrence of strikes which may affect
the percentages slightly.

A few calculations made from the above data will show that, although
the rail proportion of all traffic has generally declined, the number of
ton-miles performed by railways more than doubled between 1938 and

1946, rose to 65 billion in 1951 and a peak of nearly 79 billion in 1956. By 1961 it had slipped back to about the level of ten years earlier and then, helped by a truckers' strike in 1963, it spurted ahead again to nearly 87.2 billion in 1965. It should also be noted that neither railways nor inland ships ever carried natural gas. Therefore one can argue that pipelines for natural gas do not compete with the older agencies. They have, however, reduced the carriage of coal by railways.

Another index of the growth of highway traffic of property is the number of registrations of trucks, trailers, road tractors (power units), and other commercial freight vehicles. In 1938 the total was 221,000; in 1946 roughly 366,000; in 1951 over 720,000 and in 1965 approximately 1,500,000. These figures include trucks of all sizes and those engaged in local as well as inter-city transport. Unlike the data on intercity ton-miles, these figures are accurate in the sense that they count every vehicle licensed during the years in question. But this does not mean that all these trucks were in use, or capable of being in use, throughout the year. Some were wrecked in accidents or torn apart by dealers in scrap metal. Others were purchased brand-new during the late summer and autumn. A few were registered in more than one province. Inasmuch as these discrepancies amount to about the same percentage (perhaps 5) from one year to another, the over-statement is not serious if one only wants to show the trend of growth in the industry. A more serious matter is that the figures give no indication of the relative carrying capacity of the vehicles. In 1960 one big truck loaded to capacity could carry as much as ten or fifteen trucks of the largest size available in 1920 and twice as much as a typical truck offered for sale in 1938.

Reasons for the Growth of Trucking

Obviously the primary cause of the growth of the trucking industry is technological. Some of the improvements in roads and vehicles were set forth in the preceding chapter. In technology railways have been handicapped because all their cars must be interchangeable with those of other roads in regard to coupling, clearances, etc. Each railway has its own minor peculiarities of design which limit the savings from mass production of a strictly uniform product and of its repair parts. Because of the short working life of highway equipment, it is relatively easy to scrap obsolete models and use only the latest and best. The longevity of railway rolling stock means relying on old equipment and slowing down the rate at which better facilities can be made use of by carriers and shippers. However, the speedy adoption of diesel locomotives suggests that railways are quick to take advantage of technological changes if the prospective gains are considerable.

Trucks have a further advantage over railways in being able to give complete or door-to-door service. Although railroads with their cartage arrangements and Pick-up and Delivery rates try to equal this service, they are handicapped by the extra cost of transferring freight between trucks, railway warehouses, and freight cars at both origin and destination. For short distances trucks avoid these expenses of handling. What is loaded on the truck at the plant of the shipper is unloaded from the same truck at the factory, store, or home of the consignee. But the small one- or two-ton truck suited for local delivery is ill fitted for economical transport for longer distances. Conversely the ten- or fifteen-ton heavy duty truck which can haul freight for long distances along trunk highways at low cost per ton-mile is not well adapted for delivering a hundred pounds or less to plant, store, or home. For this reason trucking firms operating between large cities have had to purchase terminal warehouses and transfer freight from one type of vehicle to another. Even so, their terminal operations are less elaborate than those of railways. The larger truckers have retained some of their advantage over railways in the cost of door-to-door service while the smaller truckers operating from towns and villages into nearby cities have very considerable economies in this regard, particularly because as a rule they pay lower rates of wages.

With door-to-door services, shipper and consignees do not need to haul freight to and from the carrier's freight shed. This saves them time, trouble and expense. Goods are transferred between vehicles and warehouses fewer times in highway than in rail transport; in consequence the chance of damage is less. Then too, a truck is a relatively small unit of transportation so that trucking companies can usually give more frequent service. Because of this, trucks may arrive and depart at more convenient hours than trains. The "unit of sale" is smaller and conforms more closely with the hand-to-mouth buying of modern trade.

Because they save the time needed to transfer goods across warehouse platforms and from one type of vehicle to another, trucks are faster than trains for short distances. However, they tend to lose out to railways on longer hauls because of their generally slower speed *en route*. For overnight deliveries, say 250 to 350 miles, the time is about the same by road and by rail. This is partly because few shippers want to despatch goods after the day's work is normally over, and few consignees want to receive them before their normal hour of opening in the morning. This gives a space of about 15 hours for delivery. There is no special point in rushing delivery if the truck or railway car has to sit beside the consignee's warehouse until the doors are opened.

On longer hauls, trains are faster except that on so-called transcontinental runs, e.g., Toronto-Vancouver, fully loaded trucks can equal or better railway time. They do not stop to pick up or set off any freight *en route*. In many instances they leave immediately after the trailer is loaded, whereas a carload of freight may have to be held until the next train is scheduled to depart.

At one time trucks were more likely than trains to be held up by snow, sleet, and ice. This drawback has been overcome, largely at public expense, by better snow clearance plus use of sand and calcium chloride. Large trucks, like locomotives, are now equipped with devices for spreading a little sand in front of the driving wheels. This gives the tires a better grip on slippery spots and steep grades, and also prevents skidding, slewing, and crashing into the rear of vehicles which suddenly stop or slow down.

Of course trucks may be delayed on congested city streets or even on through highways by slow-moving traffic or by accidents. Part of this trouble can be offset by the proper location of warehouses and garages, and by rescheduling the time of departure and arrival of trucks. The case for rescheduling is particularly strong if the truck can depart at the time when it is most convenient for the shipper to despatch goods and arrive when the consignee prefers to receive them.

Railways have had to speed up their services in order to compete with trucks more effectively. At one time all less than carload lots moving by rail to and from smaller communities were delivered and picked up by way-freight. They had to be unloaded and loaded by train crews, a slow and expensive operation. Another trouble was that way-freights must not interfere with the operation of fast freight and passenger trains. Frequently they wasted valuable time sitting on sidings. But diesel locomotives are able to haul longer trains and railway passenger traffic is declining. Accordingly, the number of through trains is smaller, interference by way-freights is less, and so the movement of both carload and less than carload freight is speeded up. Besides, and even more important, collection and delivery of small lots to intermediate points is now often made by railway-owned trucks. Under their master agency plans, Canadian railways propose closing numerous small stations and serving the communities by truck from a large terminal or rail-head.

Generally, all carload freight has to go through one or more terminals. In the past these were often congested and were operated by slow, inefficient methods. With the construction of automated hump yards near Moncton, Montreal, Toronto, and Winnipeg, the movement of freight through terminals is accelerated. Moreover, diesel locomotives have reduced the running time between terminals, thus further shortening the time of delivery.

Compared with railways, trucks have the great advantage that their service is more personalized. This applies particularly to shipper-owned and shipper-leased trucks but it often accounts for common and contract carriers getting business away from the rails. Especially during the late 1950s and early 1960s shippers came to see that they could increase their sales by having courteous delivery men, scheduling deliveries to meet the convenience of customers, handling rush orders or delivering perishable merchandise in a hurry, settling loss and damage claims more promptly than was possible when a commercial carrier was used and, better still, eliminating damage to goods through care in stowing the goods in the vehicle and moving them over the highway. A driver could also make certain that the merchandise of his employer was attractively displayed in the shop of every customer and that stale goods were either removed or shifted to the front of the shelf or bin so that they would be sold first. In brief, shippers trained their drivers to act as salesmen as well as mere handlers of merchandise.

In addition, the shipper's truck becomes a kind of travelling billboard and advertises the product as it goes along the highway. Shippers who want this advantage must be prepared to spend money on their trucks by frequently painting, washing, and polishing them. Sometimes they have to provide neat, clean uniforms for their men. The driver can also build up goodwill for his employer by being obliging to other highway users and aiding stranded motorists. Obviously, the manufacturer of soft drinks, confectionery and other consumer goods is likely to gain more from using his own vehicles in this way than the manufacturer of heavy machinery.

There is a danger, of course, that an inconsiderate driver may scare away customers. A firm may spend a hundred thousand dollars on advertising in the press and over the air, and then throw most of it by hiring a few stupid truck drivers. Companies may train and exhort their men to drive carefully, indicate to a motorist who wants to pass when the road is clear, and be friendly with consignees, but it is hard to control drivers once they leave the home garage. Moreover, truck operators complain that union leaders make it hard for them to discipline a driver who is not co-operative. Although they can, as a rule, get rid of drivers who injure third parties or get a lot of tickets for traffic violations, trucking companies complain that the agreements with the unions prevent them from discharging drivers for aggressive ill-humour or for minor accidents such as scratches on fenders or careless unloading of freight. In the course of time, the cost of appeasing irate customers may reach sizable figures.

After taking everything into account, many shippers conclude that the advantages of operating their own trucks are important enough to justify paying a little more per ton-mile than if they used common carriers by road or rail. Even so, they hope that by running their own trucks they can reduce their costs below the rates charged by for-hire carriers. In many instances they have succeeded in giving better delivery to their customers and also in cutting costs.

Not every shipper finds it worth his while to put his own trucks on the road. Often he gets what he regards as satisfactory rates and service from railways and commercial truckers. Sometimes his customers are too scattered, they buy in too small lots, they require too frequent deliveries, or their purchases are too seasonal to justify the use of shipper-owned trucks. The lack of back-haul traffic is another handicap, though occasionally shipments of finished goods outbound may be integrated with the haul of raw material inbound, or else the routes taken by the trucks can be arranged in circular fashion in order to minimize empty mileage.

In some cases, manufacturers and their traffic departments think they have enough to worry about without entering the shipping business. Other executives, after studying the matter, decide that the profits from running their own trucks are too uncertain to justify taking the risk. Costs may exceed estimates, or railways and for-hire truckers may cut rates once they are faced with do-it-yourself competition. Some shippers try to protect themselves against capital losses by leasing all or some of their trucks, either throughout the year or during the seasonal peak of business. They may even buy or lease a few vehicles with the object of forcing reductions in rates by common carriers and not with the intention of remaining permanently in the business of transport.

Despite numerous problems, the number of shipper-owned and shipper-leased trucks has been growing rapidly. This development has caused concern to all for-hire carriers, whether by rail or highway. Indeed, some students of transport are of the opinion that eventually railways and for-hire truckers will have to co-operate to meet a common threat from shipper-operated vehicles. Meanwhile, the existence of the latter complicates the task of regulating motor transport since all private carriers are exempt from provincial requirements regarding rates and admission to the industry.

The simplest method open to railways to meet competition from trucks is for them to give personalized service too. This is easier said than done. By comparison with trucking firms, railways are huge organizations, their operations are widely dispersed geographically, they deal with large numbers of customers, and in general their employees are older than those in trucking. Railway workers tend to work to rule, not to the extent that the railway is practically immobilized (as might happen during a wage dispute), but in the sense that the rate of innovation is slowed down and railway workers are less prepared than employees of trucking concerns to go to a little extra trouble to please a customer.

Unquestionably, there are many exceptions to this general attitude. When a railway worker does something beyond the call of duty, he will be praised by his superiors and perhaps commended in the staff magazine. All the same, it is not easy to reward him, since promotion is mainly by seniority and under the agreements with the unions rates of pay are standardized. On the whole, Canadian railways have a good *esprit de corps*. The top executives do all they can to promote a good relationship between the rank and file of their employees and their customers. Heretofore, they have been handicapped by their remoteness in a distant head office. This is one reason why railways are beginning to decentralize their operations.

Relative Costs by Road and Rail

(The numerous difference between road and rail services—rate of technological change, door-to-door delivery, elimination of transfer between one vehicle and another, frequency of departure, dependability, speed of delivery, and personalized service—all show up in cost and in rates) For many years, railway executives underestimated the importance of all the factors except rates. Therefore, they concentrated on rates as a method of recovering traffic from their competitors.

The railway approach was apparently substantiated by analyses of the relative costs of moving goods by road and by rail. One such analysis was prepared by experts employed by the Royal Commission on Canada's Economic Prospects (the Gordon Commission). While admitting that few truckers knew their costs except in a general way, these experts estimated that for intercity traffic in 1954 costs per vehicle-mile were 50 cents for trucks up to 2½ tons capacity, 36 cents for trucks between 10 and 15 tons, and 41 cents for over 15 tons.[2] They believed that in Canada to move a ton of freight one mile, cost from 0.2 to 0.5 cents on the Great Lakes, 0.3 cents in pipelines, 1.5 cents by rail, 49 cents by air, and 5 or 6 cents by motor vehicles.[3] The arithmetic average has limited value for comparative purposes because costs on railways and by truck vary a good deal depending on length of haul, size of load, and so on. For instance, on a small or medium sized shipment for short distances, trucks will certainly have lower costs than railways while the reverse is generally true for bulky articles moved over long distances.

Furthermore, it sometimes happens that a truck operator, having a reasonably full load in one direction, is prepared to cut rates drastically in order to attract business on the return trip. He does this because the costs of driving his truck back home are substantially the same whether it is empty or filled. The back-haul rate which he quotes need be high enough only to cover his relatively low out-of-pocket costs. In this event the rate will be below his average or all-inclusive costs, i.e., costs which include interest, depreciation, and wages. Second, the statisticians assumed that shippers were concerned only with getting their freight from one point to another. As shown in preceding paragraphs, the cost per ton-mile may be the same by road as by rail and yet the value which shippers get for their money in terms of speed, convenience, and frequency of service may be quite different. In brief, the statistics did not compare like with like. Third, truckers can reduce their costs below the arithmetic average for the industry by specializing their operations, particularly by using bulk carriers, for cement, sugar, and flour, thus eliminating the cost of packaging, or by getting maximum loads in their vehicles in both directions on every trip.

An important economic difference is that although motor carriers have lower terminal costs than railways, they have higher line-haul expenses per ton-mile. A truck with a load of 10 tons or, more commonly, 3 or 4 tons, requires a single employee. A train with 15,000 tons has a crew of four. Even after allowing for differences in wage rates on the two agencies and for varying proportions of men employed in maintaining roadway and equipment, trucks are at a disadvantage in line-haul costs per ton-mile. Due chiefly to the great size of the transportation unit, line-haul costs by rail are low while for all movements by rail, terminal expenses are high. As terminal charges are fairly constant for all distances, terminal cost per ton-mile declines as length of haul increases. The combined terminal and line-haul costs on a ton-mile basis are lower for highway carriers than for rail up to the point where the cheaper terminal expenses of trucks spread over ton-miles are more than offset by the more favourable line-haul costs of rail carriers. (The use of piggyback rail service, which is described in some detail later, combines the most favourable features of trucks in short-haul and of railways in long-haul operations. As already explained, by specializing their operations, some truckers have been able to reduce their costs and offset the advantages of railways in the long-haul.)

Relative Rates by Road and Rail

Difficult as it is to make a fair comparison of the relative costs of handling traffic by road and rail, it is even more difficult to reach a satisfactory answer on their relative rates. This is mainly because both modes of transport, especially railways, differentiate in their tolls in accordance with what the traffic will bear and still move in volume.

The trucking industry got its start by under-quoting railway rates on valuable goods, especially those in Class 100 (formerly first). The differentiated railway rate structure provided them with a great opportunity to build up their business by cutting prices. In the course of time, railways lowered tolls in order to recover some of their lost traffic. Eventually the rates by truck came, in many instances, to determine rates by rail. On the other hand, many truckers use the railway Classification, or a simplified version of it, in quoting rates.

It is often stated that the rates charged by the trucking industry are identical with its costs. This is true in the long run and for the entire range of traffic. For if rates as a whole were far below costs, operators who were losing money or at least some of them, would withdraw from the business and the remainder would then be able to raise their prices. Conversely, if rates got far above costs, including a reasonable profit, more truckers would come in and rates would decline. Though investment in trucking is not nearly as fluid as some analysts assume, if one considers the industry as a whole, the long-run trend is toward equating costs and rates.

Whether rates for hauling any particular kind of goods for a certain distance are identical with costs of handling them plus a fair profit depends on the circumstances. When a trucker carries only one kind of freight over the same haul throughout the year, he will know his average costs and will quote rates which are close to them. If he did not do so, his customer would purchase or lease vehicles and do his own transport. But some shippers may find it impracticable to put their own vehicles on the road for reasons just given. Besides, commercial truckers cannot readily find their costs of handling any particular shipment when volume is variable, lengths of haul differ, and a number of different kinds of freight go in the same vehicle. Under these circumstances truckers, like railways, run into problems of joint or common costs and, like railways, they resort to what the traffic will bear.

Moreover, the trucking industry has no aversion to following the theory of monopolistic competition. A trucker may calculate that he can make more money by quoting the going level of rates and letting his competitors by rail and road have some of the business than he can by reducing the rate and getting more of the traffic for himself, at least temporarily. If all truckers adhere to this principle, a differentiated rated structure may persist. Truckers in a certain area may also undertake to file their rates with a bureau, or else filing may be required by the provincial government. Filing permits any trucker to learn what his competitors are prepared to charge and often facilitates charging what the traffic will bear.

For a number of reasons, the trucking industry gives the impression of being more competitive than it actually is, though a prolonged period of business depression may restore the dog-eat-dog practices of the 1930s. First, most truckers share the popular view that prices should be closely related to costs. Since costs are frequently difficult to obtain with any accuracy and since even the most careful cost accounting includes a large amount of judgment, the trucker may sincerely believe that his costs and rates are closely related, though a different method of accounting would show considerable discrepancy between the two. Moreover, the general public is not always convinced of the economic soundness of a differentiated rate structure. To the extent that truckers can justify their rates on the basis of cost rather than on value of service, they are able to improve the public "image" of the industry. This is especially true if they can simultaneously leave the impression that railways are following an unfair or unreasonable theory of rate-making.

Despite what has been said, truckers do face price competition from time to time, or at least they have done so in the past. Inevitably, they pay more attention to those factors which cause them to lose money than to other elements, stable rates, which support a regular return on their investment. Thus, the second reason for overemphasizing price-cutting in the trucking industry is the harmful effect it frequently has on net income.

Third, instability in rates may result from the activities of trucking brokers. These men search out traffic to be moved and then, having got the business, lease vehicles and hire drivers to handle it. They invest little of their own capital, have low operating expenses (little more than the costs of an office, a desk, and a telephone), and enter transportation only when they are fairly certain of making a profit or at least breaking even. They use human and physical resources which might otherwise be idle and commonly undercut the rates of what may be called conventional truckers.

Fourth, trucking is a relatively new industry. Hence, it is possible that like railways in their youth, there are considerable differences in the costs and efficiency of different operators. As time goes on, all truckers tend to adopt the same methods of operation and the range in efficiency is reduced. When this occurs, shippers will have less opportunity to play one operator off against another in order to get lower rates. Similarly, truckers will be less disposed to offer to carry traffic for less than the going rates.

Finally, most operators sooner or later reach the stage, that of monopolistic competition, where they take the position that rate-cutting is shortsighted. As a result rates will be stable, except insofar as changes in the price of fuel, the cost of licences, or the rate of wages will raise or lower substantially all prices in the industry.

The strongest pressure for stable rates often comes from the larger operators who have big capital investments and sizable office staffs. In consequence, they cannot afford to put their future in jeopardy by cutting rates. But a small trucker who has less to lose may be prepared to take a chance. Moreover, should a rate war break out, the public will blame the big companies for trying to drive the little ones out of business. The truth often is that the small operators start the rate-cutting, give rebates, pay low wages, and are generally a more disturbing element than the big "outfits." In trucking, as in most industries where monopolistic competition predominates, the big firms hold an umbrella over the smaller ones. In the past the railways said they performed this service for the trucking industry; now the big trucking lines tend to protect the owners of one or two trucks.

In other words, rates on truckload lots moving for either short or long distances are likely to be more closely related to average cost than rates for less than truckload lots. Expressed in different terms, rates on valuable articles moving for relatively short distances are often differentiated whereas on truckload lots, rates are pretty close to average or long-run costs. But a trucker may quote rates on back-haul movements that approach his out-of-pocket costs if he has to do so in order to get the business. Any revenue he gets in this way is welcome, because he has to get his vehicle back to its home garage in any event.

The author's thesis is this: the differentiated rate structure lasted for roughly the first half of this century on railways because they were prepared to adhere to it in the hope of maximizing their profits. A differentiated rate structure is developing in part of the trucking industry for the same reason. Cost of service is rather more important in highway transport than in rail because of the comparative ease with which a shipper may put his own vehicles on the road if he has reason to believe that the rates he is being charged are getting too far out of line with the cost of handling his business. But in many instances it is economically impracticable for him to engage in do-it-yourself transport. In these cases, mainly in the carriage of less than truckload lots, he will be charged differentiated rates whether he ships by truck or by rail. Thus value of service has a part to play in road transport as well as cost of service.

At the same time, in the railway industry where value of service was at centre stage for so long, cost of service is getting more and more of important the spotlight. A differentiated rate structure will develop in the one industry and persist in the other because operators think it will bring them higher profits than rates based strictly on cost (assuming costs can be correctly ascertained) and because shippers are willing to pay and still send their goods in volume. But in neither industry will value of service exhibit the same strength as it once showed on railways. This is because the opportunity open to the shipper of putting his own trucks on the road has narrowed the range of differentiated rates that may be charged by both railways and for-hire truckers.

Length of Haul by Road and Rail

Having started by taking much short-haul business away from the rails, truckers have steadily increased both their average and their maximum economic range of operation. In 1926 there was "coming to be a fairly well defined body of opinion that in general, the economical range of motor truck operation does not exceed 50 or 60 miles. Some who, for various reasons, are advocating the use of motor trucks, place their limit considerably higher than this figure, even specifying 125 or 150 miles as economically possible. On the contrary, railway officials and many others who are conservative in their statements would place the limit of this short-haul movement at 25 miles."[4] In 1932 the Interstate Commerce Commission said that "the area in which the truck has most effectively supplanted rail traffic is that which can be served one or more times during the day; the area within which overnight delivery can be made is a fertile field for the truck; to points more distant, the service advantages of the truck are lessened until a zone of indifference or disadvantage is reached."[5] By 1940 the average haul of trucks which operated for hire and which were under the jurisdiction of the Interstate Commerce Commission was 150 miles. As many intra-state or short-haul movements were not controlled by that body, the typical length of haul, excluding intra-city deliveries, was less than 150 miles. Meanwhile, a few trucks were travelling up to 1,000 miles with loads of household goods, perishables, or other articles when assured of an adequate back-haul.[6] In 1950 the Vice-President (Traffic) of the Canadian Pacific stated that very, very little freight moved by rail for less than 50 miles and not a large amount for less than 100 miles.[7]

A study for the Gordon Commission in 1956 stated that "the greatest concentration of intercity motor truck activity is on routes between 20 and 600 miles in length. A great volume of motor carrier traffic also moves on routes up to 1,500 miles in length. But beyond that point there is considerable doubt as to whether or not line-haul motor carrier operations are profitable or practical."[8] Certainly the transcontinental services by truck, which started during the railway strike of 1950, got into financial difficulty before long. Executives found it difficult to control operations effectively over such attenuated routes, especially if breakdowns occurred between terminals. Long distance trucking was also hurt by the cost of duplicate licence fees and by regulations regarding axle load and dimensions of truck bodies which varied from one province to another.

In addition, railways took measures to recover their traffic. They could run faster trains because of dieselization. They cut rates by means of agreed charges and they modified the mixing rule. Formerly if a shipper in Western Canada wanted to send different kinds of goods in the same car and at the carload rate, he could include only commodities sold by the same group of traders such as implement dealers, hardware merchants, and grocers. In Eastern Canada he could mix various classes, e.g., 100, 85, and 50, and still get the carload rate. In short, the Western rule on mixing was more restrictive than the one in the East. In 1952, following the recommendation of the first Royal Commission under Hon. W. F. A. Turgeon favouring uniformity or equalization of rate-making practices across Canada, the Western rule was made as liberal as that in the East. In 1955, the procedure for introducing agreed charges was simplified and accelerated, in accordance with the proposals of another Royal Commission under Mr. Turgeon. So, having reference to conditions in the mid-1950's, the Gordon Commission was right in declaring that transcontinental trucking was so specialized and profits so marginal that a single change in tariffs by a competitive transportation agency could be sufficient to mean business disaster for a motor carrier.

By 1960 transcontinental trucking had recuperated. Several weak firms had been forced to the wall but the survivors got new equipment by leasing and by integrated ownership. In the main, chartered banks and investment dealers refuse to handle the financial paper of truckers because their operations are too risky. In some instances transcontinental haulers borrowed from friends and other individual capitalists or from automobile finance companies. But even by paying high rates of interest, they could not get enough funds from these sources. Some firms then hired drivers who owned or had leased tractors or power units and, to a less extent, trailers. This arrangement solved three problems: it provided equipment; it got a supply of responsible drivers; and it allowed the trucker to use whatever money he had for paying traffic solicitors and workers in terminals and repair shops. As soon as business began to pick up, many operators re-invested most of their profits in still more equipment and in working capital. Leasing is especially important in transcontinental operations because of the size and cost of the individual units and the number of sets of equipment that are needed. It is also used in short-haul trucking but to a smaller extent.

Meanwhile, outside capital was being invested in long distance trucking.[9] In the early 1940s the DuPont interests bought control of a warehouse in Toronto and through it, purchased the Direct Winter line. Roy Thomson, the newspaper magnate, Canadian Motorways and Canada Steamship Lines bought up several firms and expanded their operations. Finally, both the Canadian Pacific and the Canadian National acquired trucking concerns. Because of the prevalence of competition, the five largest trucking companies handled less than 3 per cent of the intercity ton-miles in 1960. Even so, long-distance trucking could not have reached this size without the investment of so-called responsible capital.

Long-distance truckers have also been assisted by changes made by provincial governments in regulations such as reciprocal licensing, greater uniformity in truck dimensions and axle loads, and increases in permissible length and weight. In addition, they have gained from the Trans-Canada Highway, the construction of stronger road surfaces and bridges, and the clearing of snow. Diesel engines are better than gasoline ones in the movement of heavy loads for long distances.

Long-haul truckers have also worked hard to improve their own operations and reduce expenses. They have cut their costs per ton-mile by careful loading thus utilizing all possible space and attaining the maximum axle-load allowed by the governments of each state or province which the vehicle will run through. Besides getting full loads in both directions, long-distance operators have simplified and mechanized the work of loading and unloading trucks and the movement of freight through their terminals. Furthermore, they have concentrated on service including closer supervision of refrigeration for perishables, and scheduling departures and arrivals to meet the convenience of shippers and consignees. They have perfected cattle-liners to haul livestock from Alberta to Central Canada with only one stop for feed and water as compared with two for the railways. When furniture moves by truck it is packed with blankets. When it moves by rail, it must usually be crated at considerable expense for labour and crating material. Freight has to be paid on the weight of the slats and boxes. Because trade associations of movers co-ordinate all inter-urban movements as much as possible, vans are likely to obtain a return load for all or a large part of the distance back to the point of origin. Hence for this kind of traffic trucks are superior to trains even for long hauls.

Sometimes a change in technology benefits railways. Dieselization is a clear example, though it also helped truckers. At one time almost all new automobiles were delivered from the factory to the local dealer by motorized "carryalls." Then the makers of railway rolling stock devised a special freight car for passenger automobiles. As a result railways recaptured most of the traffic except for short hauls. Other technological changes that have helped railways recover traffic are improved methods of refrigeration, box cars with cushioned underframes (to reduce the effect of impact in switching and in transit), D. F., or damage free, cars (equipped with movable bulkheads to minimize the shifting of freight within the car), and covered hopper cars (some with pneumatic means for unloading free-flowing bulk cargoes like sugar and cement).

In brief, the relationship between typical lengths of haul by rail and by highway is constantly changing. In the early 1960s trucks had an undisputed advantage in picking up and delivering less than carload lots of freight within the same working day. Highway and railway carriers competed intensively in making overnight deliveries, i.e., over distances of from 150 to 350 miles. For longer hauls, railways had some advantages in speed and, broadly speaking, considerable advantage in cost per ton-mile. But by specializing their operations, truckers were continually challenging the railways on long-hauls as well as on shorter ones.

Whatever the future holds regarding the average or maximum economic length of haul of trucks, one thing is certain. Truckers have ceased to be just feeders to railways and inland ships. Nor do they confine their operations to intra-urban, suburban, and other short-haul movements. Instead, they now constitute an independent transportation agency in the same sense as do railways and ships, and they carry freight within steadily expanding areas.

Cost Reductions of Railways

As soon as railways began to realize that the trucking industry was not a dependent child but a lusty young adult, they changed their competitive tactics. At one time they had the idea that governments should use legislation to put "the upstart in its place." When the approach failed, they turned to more aggressive measures of their own devising. These included reductions in operating costs, the rail-head principle or master agency plan, piggyback, containerization, railway-owned trucks, agreed charges, and incentive rates.

Not much need be said at this point on reductions in operating costs. Mention has already been made of dieselization, larger cars, longer trains, automated hump yards, mechanized accounting, elimination of non-paying passenger trains, abandonment of unprofitable branch lines, and the like. Unfortunately for the railways, the benefits of these technological advances have often been eaten up by higher wage scales and interest rates. All the same, railways would be much worse off if they had not been alert to the latest changes in technology and the need to rationalize plant.

Railways have to keep their costs well under control in order to prevent or minimize increases in rates and the diversion of traffic elsewhere. Equally important, they need to preserve or widen the differential between their rates and those of their competitors in order to offset the fact that their competitors can often give faster, more personalized service than they can. Frequently, the shipper is as much interested in the quality of the service he gets as in the fact that some agency lugs his goods from one place to another. In other words, the shipper is concerned not simply with what he has to pay but with what he gets for his money. From some points of view, railways cannot hope to provide all the services of highway carriers. Hence to offset their disabilities in some respects, notably in personalized services, they must quote low rates. This does not mean that railways purposely disregard the needs of shippers. On the contrary they are very aware of the importance of satisfied customers. It does mean that they are not technically fitted to do all of the things that are suited to the trucking industry. A simple way for railways to hang on to traffic is to keep their own rates low and thereby show the shipper that the extra services which he may get from truckers are not worth the price he has to pay for them. At the same time railways need to keep costs down so that they can take full advantage of their superiority over trucks, e.g., in the movement of bulky freight long distances.

Rail-head Principle or Master Agency Plan

Another approach open to railways in meeting highway competition is for them to integrate their operations more closely with road transport and with the needs of shippers. This is done by means of a master agency plan or rail-head principle. Railway companies will use their own trucks or those of their subsidiaries to fan out from a rail terminal such as Moncton, Saint John, Quebec City, and Montreal. Freight will be picked up by trucks operating over the relatively short distance between the shipper and rail-head. Then it will be moved over fairly long distances between rail-heads by train. Finally, it will, if necessary, be carried by trucks which radiate from the rail-head nearest the destination of the goods. Basically, all that happens is that highway vehicles will be used for pick-up and delivery within a radius of, say, 75 miles of each rail-head. In essence, the principle is only an extension of a time-tested practice of Canadian railways. For decades they have been delivering less than carload lots within the boundaries of cities and larger towns by means of horse-drawn vehicles and then trucks. Now they are extending this service to wider areas.

The rail-head approach is tied in with changes in organization. The despatching and arrival of trucks has to be integrated with the arrival and departure of through trains. If this is not carefully done, a shipment may be delayed for 24 hours until the next train is scheduled to depart. If such delays occur too often, the shipper may decide to use trucks for the through haul, since a fully laden truck may be sent forward without regard to movements of other truck loads or carloads of freight. Because the overall time of delivery via rail-head ought to equal or better the elapsed time of movement by highway, through trains have to be speeded up. With dieselization, more fast freight trains, often called "manifests" or "highballs", have been scheduled by both major Canadian railways. Then too, techniques have to be perfected for accelerating and mechanizing the handling of freight between highway and rail carriers. Terminals may have to be relocated, redesigned, and rebuilt. If costly mistakes are to be avoided, detailed study and planning is essential. Less than carload freight and express services are being integrated with each other and the creation of the Merchandise Service is in itself a complicated job.

What is more, if railways are effectively to meet the competition of truckers, they must be more alert to the needs of shippers and consignees than was sometimes the case when they were in a more or less monopolistic position. Decisions will have to be made more promptly and operations will have to become more flexible. This, in turn, means an increasing decentralization of management, accounting, and rate-making. All in all, experimentation is necessary to set up rail-heads serving areas of appropriate size, to realign the railways' traditional lines of authority, and develop new techniques as well as standards of service. "In a transformation of this magnitude, which the railways have apparently concluded is essential to meet the new competition . . . progress must of necessity be slow."[10] Pilot or experimental rail-heads were started by each major railway in the late 1950s, but it may take a decade before they are in general use across Canada.

The rail-head principle is tied in with the master agency plan. Stations in villages and small towns are closed and the work formerly done by local agents is to be concentrated at rail-heads and larger towns. Shippers and consignees who formerly did business at local stations may telephone officials at the master agency without charge. In this way they can get information on rates, schedules, anticipated time of arrival of cars and of less than carload freight coming by truck, etc. They will also be able to order empty cars "spotted" at their station or private siding. Although the rail-head principle and master agency plan were primarily designed to retain merchandise traffic and reduce costs, the railways hope that it will not involve the sacrifice of carload freight.

Piggyback

Often looked on as something modern, piggyback is as old as rail transport itself. When steam railways were just starting, land-owners in England and even in Nova Scotia had their carriages loaded on flat cars, hauled to destination by a steam locomotive, unloaded, and then pulled along the highways by their own horses. A similar arrangement was made later on by companies operating travelling circuses. For a few years after 1926, railroads chiefly along the Chicago-Buffalo-New York City route, experimented with containers, a special sort of piggy-back, to be described later. Then in 1952, following new American experiments, the Canadian National and Canadian Pacific began to offer their patrons in Toronto and Montreal the opportunity of loading their freight in railway-owned highway trailers, which were then hauled to specially constructed loading ramps. The automotive power unit was disconnected from the trailer and the latter was pulled on to a flat car, anchored there, hauled over the rails to destination, unloaded from the flat car, connected with another automotive power unit, and delivered to the consignee. Essentially, a tractor-trailer was used for pick-up and local delivery but a railway flat car carried the trailer between the two cities. The tractor part of the tractor-trailer was released for continued service within a single city. The loaded part moved over the streets within metropolitan areas and over rails between cities.

As the service demonstrated its worth, it was extended. By 1965 it was available at over 100 terminals across Canada. Although the amount of capital needed to build ramps for loading and unloading trailers and space to park them is not very large, railways have not found it advisable to provide facilities for piggyback at smaller cities and towns. Stopping at intermediate stations would delay delivery of freight between large metropolitan areas which are the chief source of traffic and revenue. In time the prospective volume of piggyback at smaller centres may become large enough to justify the investment in piggyback marshalling yards and the operation of special trains to serve them, something like way-freights only faster. Meanwhile, railways can use the master agency plan to serve many of the less populous, intermediate communities.

The advantages of piggyback service are numerous. Loss and damage to freight is reduced because of fewer handlings than in shipping by truck-rail-truck. Besides, the flat car runs on smooth rails and the trailer rests on rubber tires during the entire movement. The serviceable life of the trailer is lengthened and the number of tractor or power units needed to handle a given volume of business is reduced. Railways are less hampered by weather than highways; as a rule they have wider clearances through bridges and subways; and they are not legally prevented from operating on Sunday as are trucks (except in the carriage of milk). Piggyback gives a complete door-to-door service to shipper and consignee. This is of growing importance because many businesses prefer to avoid the congestion and the high cost of land in downtown areas by locating in suburbs, preferably near an express highway. The charge made by railways for hauling a trailer on a flat car is a little less per mile than the cost of moving the trailer over a highway. The rate saves the trucker money and is profitable to the railway. The private motorist is happy that some of "those huge monsters" are taken off the roads.

Some objection to piggybacks has been made by the Teamsters Union, which is active among truck drivers, but the service was naturally welcomed by railway unions. Driving an intercity transport is strenuous work. The pay is good, but a man's working life is short, ulcers and accidents being the chief occupational hazards.

The growth of piggyback may be slowed down by further improvements in highways and by the reduction in operating costs of trucks relative to rail transport. In the early 1960s, at least some of the piggyback traffic between Montreal and Toronto was the result of the poor condition of the roads near the Quebec-Ontario border and the incomplete state of Ontario's Highway 401. In Northern Ontario the absence over long distances of skilled men and of repair depots encouraged movement of piggyback or the diversion of trucks away from the all-Canadian route to south of the Great Lakes. Some shippers hesitate to commit too much of their traffic to piggyback because of fears that a strike on railways would leave them with an inadequate number of power units to move all their trailers over the highways between cities. If this occurred, they would either have to cut back their operations or try to lease trucks and hire drivers wherever they could. But if they steered clear of piggyback and used over-the-highway transport exclusively, they would be exposing themselves to the possibility of a strike by truckdrivers. They would face the same danger if the men who drove their trucks to and from the marshalling or piggyback yards of the railway belonged to the same union as the inter-city truckers who had gone on strike. In a word, the risk of loss by strikes of workers is inescapable in modern business.

Piggyback traffic should preferably be in balance, otherwise the expense of hauling numerous empties adds to overall costs. Because of lack of standardization in the design of "hold-downs" or "hitches" or stanchions which secure the trailer to the flat car, piggyback freight is not being interchanged between railways. The new service has apparently not adversely affected the amount of freight moving by boxcar, though it may do so eventually.

"One Canadian railway is experimenting with a rail-water-highway co-ordinated service for the handling of bulk liquids. Specially designed aluminum containers, each having a capacity of 12,000 pounds and set in its own steel cradle, will be moved close to a thousand miles by rail, transferred by swivel cranes to ship, from ship to flat cars, and finally from flat car to truck by special hydraulic lift. If successful, this technique would open up many avenues for movement of liquid products, as it will make possible more expeditious service and improve the condition of the product on arrival."[11] Canada Steamship Lines is also in a position to institute "fishy-back" services for it owns Kingsway, one of the largest transport companies in southern Ontario and Quebec, as well as Gosset & Sons Transport which connects Lakehead with Calgary, Edmonton, and Whitehorse. In December, 1958, Kingsway bought Arrow Transport, which has a licence to operate from Quebec City to Winnipeg.

Piggyback, fishy-back, and eventually birdy-back (the movement of laden truck bodies or containers by airplane) will secure to shippers and consignees the advantages of trucks in short-haul operations, where their superiority is greatest, and at the same time retain the benefits of railways, inland ships, and airplanes in the long haul. From many points of view, it would be highly desirable if, after years of animosity, some large trucking companies and the railways could co-operate with each other in the movement of freight. The purchase by railways of trucking lines facilitated this co-operation but some independent truck operators are afraid that railway ownership of trucking companies and the extension of piggyback to non-railway trucks will eventually force their entire industry to be dependent on railways. They say that piggyback is one of the weapons which railways are using to restore their monopoly of inland transport.

In view of the relative ease of entering many parts of the trucking business, these fears are unquestionably exaggerated. Nevertheless, as long as they exist, they prevent the use of piggyback by independent truckers. If this attitude were to change, there is no technical reason why the trailers of common carriers by highway could not move by rail between big terminals, regardless of ownership. Indeed it is conceivable that independent trucking firms and possibly even shippers might purchase their own flat cars and pay railways to haul them, with laden trailers, to destination. This arrangement would be similar to that made by the Pullman Company, meat packers, and a few petroleum and chemical companies in the United States. The National Transportation Act of 1967 (sec. 16) insures that each carrier, i.e., any person engaged for hire or reward in transport, treat every other carrier in equitable fashion. This should prevent railways from giving preferential treatment to their own trucks in the event that independent truckers decide to send trailers by piggyback.

Containers

The use of containers is another means used by both truckers and railways to compete more effectively with each other. They may also be used to speed up the loading and off-loading of ships and, in conjunction with either trucks or railways, will accelerate the movement of freight through oceanic and inland ports.

In a broad sense a container is anything from a coffin to a ship, a teacup or a jug, which is capable of holding a solid, liquid, or gas. In a technical sense it is a box-like package which can be filled with freight and moved by means of a crane or by being pushed along skids from one mode of transport to another, or between the warehouse of shipper or consignee and a mode of transport. The modes of transport may be truck-rail, truck-rail-truck, truck-ship, and truck-plane. Containers, called tippers which are open at the top, have long been used for moving coal in Britain. Experiments are being undertaken to devise a container like the rear part of a tractor-trailer or tractor-semi-trailer from which the wheel assembly can be detached when not needed for over-the-highway transport.

The advantages of containers are speed of delivery, reduction of loss and damage, and virtual elimination of pilferage which is a serious matter when shipping by sea. In 1966 Canadian Pacific launched the *Beaveroak*, a ship that was specially equipped for handling containers. The chief drawbacks of containers are the cost of the crane or hoisting machinery of some sort to load and unload the containers, the weight of the container, the cost of returning empties, and the difficulty of getting freight which is balanced in direction and volume. Efforts are being made to manufacture a light-weight, collapsible container and to set up a national and even an international organization to handle this sort of business. In the meantime the use of pallets and of lift-trucks has resulted in marked economies in moving goods within the warehouses of shippers and consignees, in shifting freight in the sheds of railway, ships, and trucking companies, and in transferring goods into freight cars, trucks, and planes.

Railway-Owned Trucks

In a way railway ownership of trucks and trucking companies seems to be an attempt of railways to compete on precisely the same basis as trucks. In fact, it is the natural outcome of a long-run trend. In the early 1920s, railways began to acquire trucks and buses for the short-haul movement of express, less than carload lots, and passengers. At an even earlier period they had owned drays and cartage companies. All these vehicles were used as feeders to the railway. It was not until the late 1930s that railways began to make much of an effort to run intercity services by bus and truck.

By 1949 the Canadian Pacific Railway Company owned Canadian Pacific Transport, Dench of Canada, and O.K. Freight Lines which gave it trucking franchises between Winnipeg and Vancouver with two relatively short gaps which have since been closed. These subsidiaries also had franchises for service off the main or through route into Weyburn, Coutts, Red Deer, Edmonton, and Vernon for a total of 3,800 miles. In the same year Canadian Pacific Express operated over 2,600 route miles in seven provinces. Vancouver Island Coach Lines, 534 miles, and Quebec Central Transportation (buses), 804 miles, completed its network. Then in 1958 the Railway purchased Smith Transport, one of the largest trucking firms in Canada. By 1960 it was able to provide a fairly comprehensive national trucking service. It reached communities between Halifax and Vancouver Island. Some of its routes, e.g., into eastern Nova Scotia, entered areas which had not previously been served by the parent Company. As a result, the two major railways were competing over a more extensive geographic area than formerly.

The Canadian National was a little slower than its rival in entering highway transport on a big scale. Presumably this was because of the difficulty of persuading the Dominion government to advance the necessary capital. Some truckers said that while they did not greatly mind having to face competition from road vehicles run by the privately owned Canadian Pacific, they thought that public funds should not be provided the Canadian National to buy trucking companies that would compete with private enterprise. However, in 1960 the Canadian National purchased Midland Superior Express of Calgary and East-West Transport, both long-distance haulers. Later it secured Husband, Hoar, and Toronto-Peterborough, all major firms serving the area between Windsor, North Bay, and Montreal.

As a rule, railway-owned truck lines have continued to operate as separate for-hire carriers. In other words, there have been few modifications of the franchises held by each subsidiary. All the same, each railway company is trying to integrate its truck lines with each other and, where possible, with purely rail operations.

Integration of highway and rail carriers is sometimes difficult, even when both are controlled by the same holding company. The first difficulty is that it is expensive to transfer freight from truck to railway car at point of origin, and from car to truck to destination. When this is done, railway-owned trucks often cannot compete on the basis of either cost or speed with independent truckers. The second problem is that railways have hitherto been highly centralized in their organization. As a rule railway employees are less prepared to meet the needs of customers than truck drivers who are in business for themselves, or else subject to close supervision by the owner of a small trucking line.

The first of these difficulties, the expense of transfer between railway and truck, is dealt with in three ways. In many instances, the railway frankly recognizes that railway-owned trucks must provide a direct, over-the-highway service between shipper and consignee. In other instances the cost of transfer is being overcome by use of piggy-back and containers. Finally, railways use trucks fanning out from rail-heads. Although this arrangement will not eliminate all transfers between truck and railway car, it may reduce other costs of operation.

The second problem, over-centralization of administration, is solved either by leaving the newly purchased companies in the hands of their existing management, or by decentralization of the railway's operations, or both. If railways carry out their present plans, their head office will be relatively small, concerned only with general policies. Rail-heads will be the real nerve centres for the operations of both trains and railway-owned truck lines.

Reductions in Rates

Cutting rates is a quick and in the short run an effective way of meeting competition. However, this policy will not permanently recover much traffic if the competitor progressively lowers his costs, has the advantage of more rapid technological change, and can provide better service than the price-cutter. Under these circumstances the reductions in rates will merely slow down the rate of loss of traffic to other carriers. A price cut may act as a dyke which temporarily stops the onrushing tide. Sooner or later, the competitors breach the dyke again. Then the first carrier will erect a new barrier in the shape of lower rates, but this will be broken in its turn.

Eventually, competition between railways and trucks will reach some sort of stability where each carrier is unable to cut rates any further without impinging on its costs of operation or where each believes that it is better to leave rates as they are, take a fair share of the business, and let his competitor live too. In technical language, the competition will either go on until rates get as low as long-run costs, or operators in both modes of transport decide to follow a policy of monopolistic competition. This is what has happened among different railways and between railways and inland ships with regard to package freight. Until this day arrives for road and rail transport, there will be numerous rate adjustments, a series of measures to rationalize plant by elimi-nating unprofitable segments and expanding those that pay, not to men-tion loud and continuous cries of imminent disaster and unfair tactics. The MacPherson Commission proposed that the federal regulatory authority should be given the power to set the minimum rates which a railway might legally charge. The scheme, embodied in legislation in 1967, is clearly a device to protect the net revenues of both railways and truckers and to stabilize the rate structure for the benefit of shippers.

Not all reductions in rates are shortsighted and ineffectual. Many of them are economically sound because they are based on the costs of handling the traffic. Far from being foolish or vindictive attempts to recover traffic one formerly carried or steal what rightfully belongs to another kind of carrier, these reductions are wisely designed to make the most of some technical advantage in the movement of freight that is possessed by one mode of transport and not by another.

Agreed Charges

When railways began to reduce rates in order to meet competition from o'her carriers they frequently found that shippers used steamships or trucks during the summer and then in bad weather, when operating costs were high, sent their freight by rail. Railways felt they could give lower tolls if they were assured of all or most of the business of certain shippers throughout the year than they could if, because of competition, they received only the less profitable portion left by trucks. Consequently, in 1938 the law was amended to allow one or more shippers in a certain trade to enter into a contract with a railway to ship all or a large proportion of their traffic by rail. In return the railway would give slightly lower rates than those otherwise in effect. Basically an agreed charge is a quantity discount which railways can afford to give because they get most of the transportation business of shippers who come under the agreement.

Under the law, when traffic goes by rail from or to a competitive point or between competitive points on the line of two or more carriers by rail, the various railways must join in making the agreed charge. Unjust discrimination and undue preference are specifically forbidden. In order to insure that every shipper likely to be affected by an agreed charge learns of it without delay, the Board notifies all shippers in the same line of business and boards of trade in centres of the industry concerned.

The primary object of agreed charges is to enable rail carriers to meet actual and potential competition from motor trucks, whether for-hire or shipper-owned. On occasion railways have also published agreed charges to meet competition from foreign manufacturers.[12] In doing so they are not concerned with appeasing protectionist sentiment but with building up a paying volume of traffic for themselves. On imports from overseas or from the United States, Canadian railways often have only the relatively short haul from the seaport or the international boundary to the consumer. Import rates are normally lower than domestic rates over the same haul. If the same goods were produced within Canada, our railways might have a longer haul at better rates on the finished goods, plus the revenue on the movement of the raw material, plus the traffic on goods purchased by Canadian workmen who might otherwise be out of employment. Agreed charges can be used to meet this situation without extending the benefit of the low rates to overseas or American suppliers.

Agreed charges can also be used to permit what amount to multiple-car rates. Heretofore Canadian railways never allowed any lower rates to a shipper who sent four, five, or a dozen cars or even a trainload at the same time than to the shipper of only one car. They felt that such rates would unjustly favour large shippers to the detriment of small ones. With the growth of big business and the tendency of all media of transport, especially pipelines and inland ships, to quote what amounts to quantity discounts, this argument has lost some of its strength. Moreover, railways feel that they should pass on to their patrons some of the economies of multiple-car shipping. These economies arise because a railway saves in making out way-bills and freight-bills, in spotting a "cut" of several cars rather than one, in picking up the cut and marshalling it in the train, and so on. Despite objections by truckers, the use of agreed charges covering multi-car movements has been approved by both the Board and the Cabinet.[13] A shipper of captive traffic who wishes to take advantage of the provisions of the National Transportation Act that are designed to protect him, must sign what amounts to an agreed charge.

Objections to agreed charges have come chiefly from shippers who allege unjust discrimination and from competing agencies of transport who fear loss of business. When the legislation was introduced, shippers asserted that the arrangement went back to the days before the establishment of the Board. They said that carriers would again be able to make special contracts with favoured shippers and vary tolls from person to person. They stated that agreed charges derogated from the system of regulation under the Railway Act and did not give adequate protection to the small shipper.

Now it is true that shippers have occasionally complained that agreed charges were unjustly discriminatory,[14] but in general Canadian experience has shown the early fears of the evils of agreed charges to have been exaggerated. Once an agreed charge is made with some members of a trade, the Board extends its coverage to all other shippers in substantially the same position who make the necessary application. In this way the Board removes any unjust discrimination between those who have had the benefit of the agreed charge and those who have not. Rates arrived at by broadening agreed charges are called fixed charges.

The chief controversies have been over the legal rights of water carriers and truckers, liberalizing the rules governing agreed charges, and the relationship between these rates and the business of road transport. As for the first controversy, under the original legislation as interpreted by the Judicial Committee of the Privy Council,[15] then the highest court of appeal for Canadians, if an inland shipping line objected to an agreed charge and if its traffic were adversely affected even to a small extent, it could prevent the Board from approving an agreed charge on railways. This ruling could have had the effect of precluding railways from making agreed charges on a huge quantity of freight moving in the most thickly populated parts of Canada. During the season of navigation several ships operate on fixed schedules between Montreal, Kingston, Toronto, Port Colborne, and ports on the upper lakes as well as intermittently from a number of other places. Especially since 1945, they have arranged with truck lines to haul freight between ports and interior points such as Peterborough, Kitchener, and London. As things turned out, inland shipping companies were soon co-operating in publishing several agreed charges.[16] Then in 1955 the Transport Act was amended to make such arrangements obligatory. In 1956, the Board ordered railways to permit Canada Steamship Lines to take part in an agreed charge on corn starch, corn syrup, glucose, etc., from Cardinal (near Prescott) and Port Credit, Ont., to the Pacific coast.[17]

Like inland shipping, the trucking industry is also affected by agreed charges published by railways. Truckers (except those engaged in inter-provincial and international trade) do not come under Dominion jurisdiction. Therefore, under the original legislation they were not legally entitled to object to an agreed charge made by railways. As the Board declared in 1958, truckers are not "entitled to complain under the Railway Act that railway rates are unjust, unreasonable, non-compensatory or lower than necessary to meet competition. . . . The party by whom or on whose behalf such a complaint is made must have a more direct interest than that of a competing carrier. . . . That is not to say, however, that a person or company engaged in the trucking business might not have a status as a 'party interested' in a complaint alleging unjust discrimination in railway facilities, rates or services."[18]

The Board then decided on its own motion to investigate the compensatory character of the rates that had been brought to its attention by the Trucking Association. What is more, it heard witnesses present testimony on behalf of the truckers. In 1967 the trucking industry was given wider powers to complain about agreed charges. Truckers could appeal any competitive rate which they considered below the minimum allowed by the legislation, i.e., below the variable cost to the railway of handling the traffic in question.

Altogether aside from their status in law, truckers object to agreed charges on the ground that they give railways an unfair competitive advantage. On the other hand railways have protested that the law governing agreed charges should allow them greater freedom in quoting rates to meet competition from truckers. Although the legislation authorizing agreed charges was passed in 1938, at the end of 1950 only 23 such charges were in effect, all of them in the Prairie Provinces, Ontario, and Quebec. They applied to roughly 125 shippers, covered only seven commodities (chiefly petroleum products), and accounted for a total revenue of only about $10 million. Because of these disappointing results the Canadian National, with some support from the Canadian Pacific, asked the Royal Commission of 1951 to recommend greater flexibility in publishing agreed charges. The Company argued that an agreed charge was essentially a special form of competitive rate. Since the Board was not required to approve competitive tariffs before they took effect, its prior approval of agreed charges should not be necessary either. The Railway also favoured doing away with the necessity of getting the consent of a rival rail carrier. It wanted authority to publish lower tolls for a number of cars than for one. Shippers could still legally lodge a complaint about unjust discrimination but could not object to the agreed charge as such. In brief, the Canadian National claimed that the current practice was cumbersome and slow. Under its proposal, the Board need not approve an agreed charge before it became legally effective but it might disallow an agreed charge if the rates charged under it were not compensatory.

The Royal Commission of 1951 rejected the Canadian National's plan. Its scheme placed on the complainant the burden of proving that a railway rate was non-compensatory, thus practically putting him out of court. The Commission felt that the existing procedure for filing and approval was entirely satisfactory and warranted no criticism. Moreover, agreed charges tied all or most of a shipper's traffic to the rails for a year, and gave lower rates than those published under other provisions of the Railway Act. Hence, some safeguards were required, notably approval by the Board. Finally, the legislation of 1938 had not had a fair trial because of the war and the postwar boom.[19]

These recommendations were not favourably received either by railways or the government. So in 1955 the question was reexamined by Mr. W. F. A. Turgeon who had been chairman of the Royal Commission of 1951. Although by 1954 the estimated revenue from agreed charges was over $20.6 million or 6.2 per cent of the total rail revenue compared with 2.4 per cent in 1949, railways still complained of the slow or "shackling" procedure of getting the Board's approval of new agreed charges. The long delay had the effect of discouraging shippers from entering negotiations for agreed charges and of contributing to the steady deterioration in the net earnings of rail carriers. Mr. Turgeon said the paralysing results of the railway strike of 1950 bore witness to the importance of rail services and to the railways' need for adequate revenues.

Since 1938, when agreed charges were first permitted, and since 1951, when the Royal Commission had submitted its report, the trucking industry had attained great vigour. On account of better roads, the completion of the Trans-Canada Highway, the strengthening of the industry through the formation of larger companies, and so on, trucking was bound to make further progress. These facts did not support the truckers' oft-repeated allegations that agreed charges were unfairly hurting their business. Mr. Turgeon thought that since 1951 public feeling had become more favourable towards this kind of toll. Hence, he proposed[20] that the approval of the Board be no longer necessary before an agreed charge became operative and that it might become effective 20 days after filing, instead of 30 as currently required.

These statutory changes left railways relatively free to introduce agreed charges whenever they decided it was necessary and profitable to do so. Between 1952 and 1962 the number that were issued each year rose from 3 to 201; the total number in effect was 25 at the end of 1952 and 1290 on December 31, 1962; and the share of railway revenue from such charges expanded from less than 3 to roughly 20 per cent of all rail revenue. Even so, agreed charges are not effective in keeping traffic from truckers where shippers consider that the quality of the service rendered by truckers is worth the difference in rates between road and rail. In 1961, for example, dressed meat was often hauled eastward from Alberta because truck drivers supervised the refrigeration equipment more carefully than railway employees. Presumably railways believed that if they widened the differential by cutting their rates, they would fail to cover their out-of-pocket costs.

Representatives of the trucking industry told the Royal Commission of 1961 that they did not object to agreed charges when they were used to translate the benefits of competition into lower rates to the consumer. But they were also "potent monopolistic weapons to eliminate or weaken competitors." They tied shippers to the rails and so withdrew freight from competition. Truckers also alleged that at least some of the rates were below rail costs. In some instances, so they said, railways handled, say, 60 per cent of a shipper's traffic at rates below those of truckers and competed with highway carriers for the remainder. Then they offered the shipper an agreed charge and lower rates provided he sent 90 per cent of his traffic by rail. If the shipper agreed to this, the trucking industry lost traffic and revenue. In the opinion of many truckers, railways were using their superior bargaining power to take unfair advantage of their competitors by road. Moreover, the fear that railways would use this power in the future sometimes prevented truckers from acquiring new, specialized equipment for the bulk handling of freight. Thus agreed charges were retarding the sound economic growth of highway transport. On the other hand some truckers suggested that if the shipper was a large one and the agreed charge covered no more than 75 or even 90 per cent of his traffic, enough business was exempt from the agreed charge to allow one or two truckers to operate profitably.

Although truckers are right in stating that every agreed charge ties traffic to the rails, the alleged monopoly is only for one year. At the end of that time, the shipper is free to decide whether to continue with the existing arrangement, hire common or contract carriers by road, or put his own vehicles on the highway. However, during the currency of the agreed charge, the operator who formerly did the shipper's trucking may have sold his equipment and be unwilling to buy a new fleet unless reasonably assured of having the traffic for a long time in the future. For their part shippers are reluctant to enter into contacts lasting several years because a better offer might come along in the meantime. The net result, so truckers contend, is that the railway knows that the shipper will be in a weak bargaining position at the end of the year. Hence it is in a good position to raise the agreed charge at the end of the year when the agreement comes up for renegotiation.

Railways have sometimes been attacked on the very opposite grounds. During the general rate cases in the 1950s, counsel for those provinces which opposed the increases criticized railways for not raising agreed charges as much as rates generally. Indeed, they often did not raise them at all. The railways answered that competition often prevented increases when the agreed charge expired at the end of a year and few agreements contained an acceleration clause which would have permitted the railway to raise the rate during the year in the event that its operating costs rose or it got permission from the Board of Transport Commissioners to raise the general level of rates.

It will be noted that although traffic is withdrawn from competition between rail and road during the currency of the contract (one year), railways still compete with each other in the quality of their service. Sometimes they also compete with inland ships which come under the charge and always there is the prospect of highway competition at the end of 12 months, subject to the limitations given above. Railways also point out that the average revenue per ton-mile from agreed charges exceeds average ton-mile revenue on all traffic, excluding the abnormally low statutory rates on grain. This argument glosses over the fact that each kind of traffic involves some special expenses and that the cost of handling freight covered by agreed charges may be higher than the cost of hauling freight generally. Besides, the average ton-mile revenue produced by agreed charges has been declining steadily.

There is no question that agreed charges have proved to be a potent competitive weapon in the hands of the railways. Yet the trucking industry's arguments against them are often exaggerated. This is evidenced by the rapid growth in highway transport notwithstanding agreed charges by rail. Moreover, contract carriers do business under what amounts to an agreed charge, and in Quebec the Highway Transport Commission has authorized a number of these charges for the truckers under its control. Finally, by giving personalized service, shipper-owned and for-hire truckers have neutralized the lower tolls which railways may have offered under agreed charges. At all events, under the legislation of 1967 truckers can take action before the Canadian Transport Commission if they have reason to believe that any competitive rate is unremunerative to the railway.

Incentive Rates

For decades railways have published lower rates per ton-mile when a car is heavily laden than when it contains only a few tons of the same kind of freight. Some expenses of handling a carload are the same regardless of the weight of the load. These include preparing waybills and freight-bills, marshalling cars into trains, spotting a car in front of a door in the consignee's warehouse or on a team track, calculating the interest and depreciation on the car, etc. Other expenses, such as fuel for the locomotive, and wear and tear on the track, increase only slightly with heavier loads. Consequently, on the basis of cost, a railway can afford to reduce its rates per hundred pounds with every increase in load per car.

This principle is valid only within limits, however. First, it should not be carried beyond the point where it is physically impossible to put that many tons in the car. Second, the rate per ton-mile must always be enough to cover the railway's out-of-pocket costs and preferably something more. Third, the railway must take care not to give undue preference to large shippers and large cities, and unjustly discriminate against small ones. Finally, it must not unfairly compete with truckers by reducing rates below cost.

This last point was seized upon by the trucking industry in 1958 when it complained that railways were quoting unremunerative tolls for the carriage of several commodities in Western Canada. At the time truckers had no legal right to complain to the Board. However, as we have seen, the Board raised the question on its own motion and allowed witnesses to present testimony on behalf of truckers. In the end their contentions were set aside. In the Board's words, "there is nothing inherently sacred or stable in the freight-rate structure. . . . The Board has concluded on the evidence that the rates are no lower than necessary to meet the competition and, as far as the incentive rates at higher minima [carload weights] are concerned, the railways have justified them on the basis of lower unit costs when cars are loaded to greater weights."[21] The legislation of 1967 requires that minimum rates be compensatory to the railways. Moreover, it permits truckers to protest that any railway rate which affects them is below the compensatory level.

These provisions will have to be administered cautiously. If truckers protest an excessive number of rates, they may be able to keep the rate structure of the railways in a chaotic state. If the Commission exercises its power to postpone the effective date of rate reductions until after it has had an opportunity to investigate them, it may be denying shippers the benefits of lower rates to which they are entitled. On the other hand, if it allows such rates to go into effect and then, later on, finds they are non-compensatory and illegal, it may temporarily have given low rates to some shippers who were not entitled to them.

Perhaps the Commission will be able to develop rough and ready guidelines so that it can dispose almost automatically of rates that are clearly above or below the minimum allowed by law and withhold for detailed consideration only those reduced rates which are close to the minimum. It is also possible that railways will exercise restraint in quoting competitive rates which are dangerously close to the minimum and that truckers will not challenge rates unless they are confident of winning their case. In brief, the legislation will have to be carefully administered if it is simultaneously to protect the net incomes of railways and truckers, and still allow railways a tolerable amount of freedom of action.

Co-ordination

While carriers by road and rail are obviously competing in numerous ways, many people argue that what is needed is more co-ordination between the various modes of transport. In 1938 Parliament provided that the Board of Transport Commissioners should co-ordinate and harmonize the operations of all carriers engaged in transport by railways and ships. Prior to the establishment of the Air Transport Board in 1944, the same principle covered airlines. Although the Board made two or three attempts to carry out this directive, it soon gave up the effort.[22]

Nevertheless, the Royal Commission of 1951 urged that the policy be revived.[23] The Royal Commission on Canada's Economic Prospects (1955) was favourably disposed toward co-ordination of rail and highway services in the interests of efficiency, economy, and the utilization of each carrier to its best advantage.[24] The MacPherson Commission (1961) did not refer specifically to the old policy of co-ordination but its emphasis on competition as the major factor in rate-making suggests that it assumed that the free play of competitive forces would bring about all the harmonization that was economically and socially desirable. Even so, the legislation of 1967 (sec. 15 (1) (c)) directed the Canadian Transport Commission to "inquire into and report to the Minister on the relationship between the various modes of transport within, into and from Canada and upon the measures that should be adopted in order to achieve co-ordination in development, regulation and control of the various modes of transport." The harmonization was apparently to be directed more toward investment than toward regulation. Subsection (h) states that the Commission shall "inquire into and advise the government on the overall balance between expenditure programs of government departments or agencies for the provision of transport facilities and equipment in various modes of transport, and on measures to develop revenue from the use of transport facilities provided or operated by any government department or agency."

The theory behind the doctrine of co-ordination has much to commend it. Each agency of transportation has a sphere of usefulness in which it has a virtual monopoly: each competes with the other in a broad area where elements of cost have to be weighed along with speed of delivery, courtesy of employees, and other intangible elements. Economic loss arises when either trucks or railways reach out into the field which naturally belongs to the other, when they fritter away the profits they make from carrying on their proper functions and conduct an exhausting war for traffic which from the social point of view ought to be going to the other agency. Similarly, private passenger automobiles, buses, railways, and airplanes have fields of virtual monopoly the boundaries of which are determined by considerations of speed, level of fares, safety, convenience, and so on. Between these fields there are zones of competition where the public ought to have the right to choose the kind of carrier it prefers. It is obviously as wasteful for an airplane to fly passengers overland for distances as short as 25 miles as it is for a railway to run trains over tracks paralleling a good highway for the sake of a half dozen passengers.

Many years ago, railways reached a tacit understanding with ships along the St. Lawrence and the Great Lakes. Both agencies still compete with each other but they do not reach out for non-paying business nor do they waste resources of capital and men in an uneconomic battle with one another. Eventually the same degree of harmony and co-ordination will prevail between all transportation agencies as now subsists between rail and water-lines along the Great Lakes–St. Lawrence system. The real question is how this integration can be brought about.

Co-ordination, harmonization, or integration could be provided for in a number of ways. Transportation companies would own and operate various media and integrate their services in such a way that shippers would receive the best service at the lowest possible cost. Presumably the corporation would be a railway, because it possesses the financial power to bring about the integration. After a shipper had called up a railway office (or more accurately the transportation company's office) and stated what goods he wanted to send, what quantity, and to what destination, the transportation company would decide whether it would be more economical to send them by rail, truck, water, or air.

All these alternatives would rarely be present in any one case. In some instances, for example, grain from a Prairie elevator to Lakehead, only one means would be practicable. In cases of doubt, the transportation company would decide the best means of transport. It would do this with all the facts relative to cost, speed, safety, dependability, and so on before it. Its careful judgment would replace decisions of shippers who are sometimes poorly informed, prejudiced, and influenced by the uneconomic rates occasionally published by various carriers at present. The shipper would be protected against the abuses of monopoly since presumably the two major railway systems, now transformed into two transportation companies, would continue to compete with each other with this difference: their competition would extend throughout the whole range of transportation media.

In some respects Canadian railways have already become transportation companies. To be sure, they rejected proposals to build pipelines for moving petroleum and natural gas from Western Canada because, so they said, they lacked experience in that business and should use all the capital at their command to modernize their rail services. On the other hand the Canadian Pacific through a subsidiary owns substantial blocks of shares in Trans-Canada Pipe Lines and Union Gas. Each major road owns an airline and coastal ships, and one has package freighters on the Great Lakes. Each has a few bus lines and each uses trucks for local collection and delivery as well as for line-haul service. The latter expansion has given rise to bitter opposition. Truckers say that railways are trying to re-establish their monopoly of inland transport. On the other hand railway-owned trucks carry but a small percentage of intercity traffic by road, and the comparative ease of entering the business is an effective barrier to monopoly. Besides, truckers have their trade associations and rate bureaus which can be regarded as semblances of monopoly. Nevertheless, the trucking industry is adamant in its opposition to railway ownership of intercity trucks as a means of co-ordination. In their view such ownership is essentially a method of unfair competition.

The National Transportation Act (sec. 16) is designed to give truckers some protection:

In this section (a) the expression "carrier" means any person engaged for hire or reward in transport, to which the legislative authority of the Parliament of Canada extends, by railway, water, aircraft, motor vehicle undertaking or commodity pipeline; and (b) the expression "public interest" includes, without limiting the generality thereof, the public interest as described . . . [in the National Transportation Policy, sec. 1 of the Act, and toward the end of chapter I of this book].

(2) Where a person has reason to believe (a) that any act or omission of a carrier or of any two or more carriers, or (b) that the effect of any rate established by a carrier or carriers . . . may prejudically affect the public interest in respect of tolls for or conditions of the carriage of traffic within, into or from Canada, such person may apply to the [Canadian Transport] Commission for leave to appeal the act, omission or rate, and the Commission shall, if it is satisfied that a *prima facie* case has been made, make such investigation . . . as in its opinion is warranted.

(3) In conducting an investigation under this section, the Commission shall have regard to all considerations that appear to it to be relevant, includ-

ing, without limiting the generality of the foregoing, (*a*) whether the tolls or conditions specified for the carriage of traffic under the rate so established are such as to create (*i*) an unfair disadvantage beyond any disadvantage that may be deemed to be inherent in the location or volume of the traffic, the scale of operation connected therewith or the type of traffic or service involved, or (*ii*) an undue obstacle to the interchange of commodities between points in Canada or an unreasonable discouragement to the development of primary or secondary industries or to export trade in or from any region of Canada or to the movement of commodities through Canadian ports; or (*b*) whether control by, or in the interests of a carrier in, another form of transportation service, or control of a carrier by, or the interest in the carrier of, a company engaged in another form of transportation services may be involved.

(4) If the Commission, after a hearing, finds that the act, omission or rate in respect of which the appeal is made is prejudicial to the public interest, the Commission may . . . make an ordering requiring a carrier to remove such prejudicial feature in the relevant tolls or conditions specified for the carriage of traffic or such other order as in the circumstances it may consider proper, or it may report to the Governor in Council for any action that is considered appropriate.

These sections mean that truckers may challenge rates published by railways on the ground that they are contrary to the public interest, create an unfair disadvantage to shippers, or constitute an undue obstacle to trade. On the face of things, the law will prevent railways taking undue advantage of any monopolistic power they possess by quoting rates which are unduly high or which are unjustly discriminatory as regards certain kinds of trade and certain classes of shippers. But the law will also protect truckers if they are able to convince the Commission that the tolls of the railway prejudicially affect the public interest in general and the trucking industry in particular. Moreover, in ruling on such rates, the Commission is to pay especial attention to the effect of railway ownership of trucking lines.

Even if truckers are unsuccessful in challenging rates, they may protest any proposed acquisition by a railway of a trucking line. Indeed, this principle is applied to the entire range of modes of transport. Section 20 of the National Transportation Act reads as follows:

(1) A railway company, commodity pipeline company, company engaged in water transportation, or person operating a motor vehicle undertaking or an air carrier . . . that proposes to acquire, directly or indirectly, an interest, by purchase, lease, merger, consolidation or otherwise, in the business or undertaking of any person whose principal business is transportation, whether or not such business or undertaking is subject to the jurisdiction of Parliament, shall give notice of the proposed acquisition to the Commission.

(2) The Commission shall give . . . such public or other notice of any

proposed acquisition . . . as to it appears reasonable in the circumstances, including notice to the Director of Investigation and Research under the *Combines Investigation Act.*

(3) Any person affected by a proposed acquisition . . . or any association . . . representing carriers or transportation undertakings affected by the acquisition may, within such time as may be prescribed by the Commission, object to the Commission against such acquisition on the grounds that it will unduly restrict or otherwise be prejudicial to the public interest.

(4) Where objection is made . . . the Commission (*a*) shall make such investigation, including the holding of public hearings, as in its opinion is necessary or desirable in the public interest; (*b*) may disallow such acquisition if in the opinion of Commission such acquisition will unduly restrict competition or otherwise be prejudicial to the public interest; and any such acquisition . . . within the time limited therefor by the Commission . . . is void.

In a word, the Board will have to rule whether any future acquisitions of trucking lines by railways, inland ships, etc., are in the public interest. Its rulings will, of course, be subject to appeal to the Supreme Court of Canada and to the Cabinet. The new legislation will not prevent co-ordination of modes of transport but will tend to ensure that such co-ordination, if achieved through the acquisition of a carrier in mode of transport by a carrier in another mode, will conform with the public interest. In addition, the law will provide the trucking industry with an opportunity to voice its complaints before the Commission that has wide responsibilities for the maintenance of a sound transport system within Canada and, if need be, before the Cabinet and the highest court of law in the land. It may be, however, that railways and inland ships have already gone as far in acquiring truck lines and bus companies as they think economically desirable. In that event, the new legislation which has just been quoted will become a dead letter.

Courts have yet to rule on whether, under the British North America Act, a trucking company owned by a railway is in pith and substance a railway operation, in which case it comes under Dominion jurisdiction, or whether in essence it is trucking, that is, the exercise of a property or civil right, in which event it comes under provincial control. But under Quebec law, transfer of control of any trucking firm operating within the province must be approved by the provincial Transport Board. This body authorized the transfer of Smith Transport to the Canadian Pacific on condition that the Railway should admit the jurisdiction of the Board over the operations of Smith within Quebec. Later on Quebec imposed a somewhat similar "deal" on the Canadian National. Nova Scotia has also frowned upon extension of railway-owned trucking within the province. It is clear that the entrance of railways into highway operations is not constitutionally smooth.

Joint arrangements might be made between the different kinds of carriers regarding through routes, joint tariffs, the proper interlacing of times of arrival and departure, abandonment of unprofitable branch railway lines and their replacement by independently owned truck services, joint use of terminals, and so on. This sort of integration has been started but on a very restricted basis. The main difficulty is that neither railways nor trucks are prepared to give up their separate ambitions. Each agency feels that it should retain all the business it now has and reach out for more. Each feels that if it gives up traffic—even traffic which it itself may find unprofitable—the other agency will strengthen its financial position and strike out for more business in some other direction.

Piggy-back and containers are two of the most promising methods of co-ordinating road and rail transport. Another means is rigid control of transport so that, for example, truckers might be forbidden to operate beyond their economic range. Aside from the problem of deciding precisely what this range is, the scheme soon runs into problems of enforcement. Truck drivers may take a chance on not being caught or they may switch trailers and even cargoes in order to escape the regulations. It is not too difficult to make certain that large carriers by road obey the law for their books may be audited by the regulatory authority. Many small truckers keep inadequate records and they are so numerous that auditing becomes expensive. Besides, shippers might resent being ordered to ship their goods by a certain kind of carrier. Rigid control designed to enforce co-ordination and give financial protection to railways has been tried in several countries. Indeed, at one time Canadian railways proposed this sort of super-regulation but in recent years they have recognized its shortcomings and placed their hopes in piggyback, decentralization, railway-owned trucks, etc.

Co-ordination can also be achieved or at least approached by a better control of public investment. Some of the present difficulties in transport have indubitably arisen because governments have spent vast sums on improving highways, airports, and inland waterways, thereby taking traffic away from the hard-pressed railways. The author does not suggest that in order to preserve the existing railway network, the public should be asked to forgo the benefits of the lower costs and the better service which the new modes of transport can often provide. What he wants is, first, to make certain that the users of the new facilities supplied at public expense pay for them through taxes on fuel, tolls, and landing fees if this is at all possible and, second, that railways be given an opportunity to scale down or "phase back" their investment with a minimum of loss. The trouble is that governments have often gone ahead with large investments in some directions without being sufficiently careful of whether users of the new facilities are able to pay for them and without considering what is to be done with existing investments which the new projects have made redundant.

More specifically, the federal government has financially aided the building of the Trans-Canada Highway without making any specific charge upon its users. The Highway parallels the Canadian Pacific throughout practically its entire length from Vancouver to Saint John, N.B. and thence to Moncton. The Canadian Pacific has no lines in Prince Edward Island or Newfoundland, and very few in Nova Scotia. Similarly, the Dominion built the St. Lawrence Seaway which, contrary to government assurances made before it was started, is not able to pay its way. As a consequence, tolls will probably be insufficient to pay operating costs and amortize the investment over fifty years, which was the original plan.

Similarly, provincial governments spend large sums on trunk roads between metropolitan centres while tending to neglect those in outlying areas. This policy can be justified on the ground that revenues collected from users of busy roads are more likely to meet the costs of construction and maintenance than revenues from lightly travelled highways. Yet railways also have relatively low costs where traffic is heavy and many of their branch lines do not pay. Sound economic planning would balance these and other factors with the object of minimizing the overall cost of transport to the economy. Better roads in some rural areas would allow the railway to abandon its line without inconveniencing the public too seriously. Then, too, municipalities spend fortunes on expressways and street widening in order to get automobiles downtown. When parking near the city centre becomes nearly unobtainable or intolerably expensive, city councils call upon railways to provide commuter service. With more intelligent planning, commuter trains would have been subsidized earlier and the waste of capital on expressways reduced.

Careful supervision of investment in the interests of proper co-ordination and the elimination of waste is particularly important when one of the major railways is publicly and the other is privately owned. The danger is that the government will invest on a lavish scale in its own system while the private enterprise is starving for funds because it cannot cheaply raise capital in the open market in competition with other users of capital, including the government. The unfairness of one concern being backed by "the long purse of the state" was stressed by the Royal Commission of 1931–2. Before the Royal Commission of 1951, the Canadian Pacific was apprehensive that the situation would recur. Fears that private investors in railways would be unfairly treated were expressed by Conservative backbenchers in 1962. They also criticized public ownership as such. It can be argued, however, that by deferring Canadian National requests for capital to purchase trucking lines until after the Canadian Pacific had acquired a fair-sized network, the government had handicapped its own railway. Also it unnecessarily added to the costs of the Canadian National because as time went on the trucking lines demanded, and got, higher prices for their physical assets and goodwill. Yet in general since the mid-1930s the Dominion has met the legitimate needs of the Canadian National for capital without endangering the financial stability of the privately-owned system. Nonetheless, the danger remains.

In a democracy it is, perhaps, too much to expect that economic planning will work out to perfection. All the same, the Canadian economy would benefit and the overall cost of transportation could be reduced if public bodies could co-ordinate their investments with each other and with the railways more effectively than they have done in the past. The integrated plan of line abandonments which grew out of the report of the MacPherson Commission is clearly a step in the right direction. Knowledge of what railways plan to do over the next few years should make it possible for provincial governments and for elevator companies and other concerns which are dependent on the rails effectively to carry out sound policies of investment and disinvestment. The chief danger to the plan is that disinvestment, or what the MacPherson Commission called rationalization of plant, will not progress fast enough. In its legislation of 1967 the federal government clearly expected that greater co-ordination of investment could be achieved. It directed the Canadian Transport Commission to make intensive studies of this matter. In the author's view the primary difficulty to be overcome is not lack of knowledge but pressure from the public which simultaneously demands the construction of new highways, and refuses to consent to the abandonment of redundant branches of railways. Research on investment is needed to enlighten the public even more than to show public officials what has been going on. Planning will have to be done on the basis of regions.

Co-ordination cannot be achieved easily. Jurisdiction over transport is divided between the Dominion and the provinces. Truckers are numerous and many of them have only one or two vehicles. Shippers can often evade burdensome restrictions by putting their own vehicles on the road. It will take time for truckers and railways to bury their grudges, especially since new subjects of controversy are almost constantly arising. Moreover, it is not easy to preserve all the virtues of competition and simultaneously get integration of services. In short, it is hard to decide in many instances whether the public interest is better served by co-ordination than by competition.

Summary

Road-rail competition is constantly widening into new geographic areas and different kinds of traffic. It takes the form of improved service and the publication of new rates. Fundamentally, it is a conflict between various sorts of technological change. Until the late 1950s, it was usually a struggle between organized and unorganized labour. Within the trucking industry there is ~~frequently~~ conflict ~~of interest~~ between the big operators and the smaller ones, as well as between for-hire and shipper-owned transport. These difficulties are complicated by the differing policies of investment and control exercised by federal and provincial governments. In part, these difficulties go back to the division of legislative powers under the British North America Act and in part they are the result of differences in the financial resources of the ten provinces. Added to all this, there are strongly-held emotional attitudes by truckers, railways, and some provincial governments. These prejudices are the inevitable outcome of prolonged and often bitter competition and the frustrations of trying to settle problems in the face of so many institutional and personal obstacles.

The objective of public policy should be to reduce the painfulness of readjustment for railways and to ensure that the growth of other agencies is economically sound. No detailed policy can be formulated in advance though certain principles can be laid down. So far as possible, each agency should pay its costs from its own revenues. Subsidies, whether direct or indirect, should be avoided if not entirely ruled out. Rates should be fair and reasonable, neither unduly preferential nor unjustly discriminatory. Regulation should not be introduced except where necessary to protect the public interest. In every instance welfare to the public, not benefits to a selfish group, should be paramount.

Stability will eventually be achieved. In the meantime interested parties will abuse each other, newspaper editors will "view with alarm," and politicians will lay down any number of smoke screens. Transportation is going slowly through a technological and economic revolution associated with the internal combustion engine just as it experienced sweeping changes following the introduction of steamships and steam railways.

20

Highway Passenger Traffic

A PRECEDING CHAPTER has sketched the history of highway transportation, outlined some of the technological changes, and discussed highway finance. It made incidental reference to buses and private passenger automobiles but passenger traffic on highways is so important that more detailed consideration is called for. Carriage of persons over, and under, the roads is the primary task of private passenger cars, taxicabs, urban and interurban buses, street cars, and subways.

Private Passenger Automobiles

Motorists agree that driving a private automobile is much more expensive than using common carriers. Studies prepared for the Gordon Commission[1] estimated that the cost of owning and operating an automobile in Canada in 1954 was $1,278 in the first year of its life, $982 in the second, $830 in the fifth, and $567 in the tenth, or a total of $8,362 over the car's service life of ten years. On the assumption that it was driven 8,000 miles a year, the cost per vehicle-mile was nearly 16 cents in the first year, 12.3, 10.4, 7.1 cents in the second, fifth, and tenth years, and 10.45 cents over the car's life.

Some expenses of operating a car such as gasoline, oil, grease, washing, tires, and repairs vary rather closely with mileage run. Others are functions of time such as licence for driver and vehicle, insurance for public liability, fire, and theft, interest on the investment in car and garage, and depreciation. The more miles run, the lower the cost per car-mile because expenses which vary with time are spread over more car-miles. Reducing the unit cost of service can be accomplished by increasing those expenses which vary directly with mileage. Thus, by increasing his total expenses per annum, a motorist can cut down his costs per mile. Whatever his annual mileage, a motorist may reduce his passenger-mile costs by always driving with a full load. Indeed, if four or five persons drive together for long mileages each year, they may get costs per passenger-mile lower than on public-service vehicles. In short, many factors determine the cost of running a car.[3] Further, driving, already dangerous, is not becoming safer.

Despite all these disadvantages, motorists continue to drive. They enjoy the privacy of their own means of transportation, the freedom to come and go whenever they like, the ease of reaching places not accessible by public carriers. They enjoy the thrill of "sitting behind the wheel," of handling a powerful machine on a good highway, of always passing the car ahead, or even of "hogging the road." Of course they complain at times of constant expense, danger, delays in traffic, trouble in finding parking space, and the mental strain of driving. Yet few persons who have once owned a car give it up except in case of great necessity. The psychological satisfactions of car ownership seem to outweigh the financial drawbacks. In short, value of service is more important than cost of service.

Taxicabs

Taxicabs are highway vehicles which economically are intermediate between private automobiles and public buses.[4] They are expensive compared with either of the alternatives mentioned but are fast, relatively private, and go by direct route. The passenger is driven by a competent chauffeur and ordinarily has complete coverage by insurance. Also he ought to pay something for "readiness to serve," for the privilege of getting a cab at his door promptly at any time of the day or night in all kinds of weather and for the idle time while driver and car are waiting for his call. Although shortwave radios cut down by 40 per cent the empty mileage which develops when the cab goes to pick up a passenger, he must still pay for some dead mileage. In 1954 the estimated cost[5] per vehicle-mile was 8.484 cents. This assumed that a taxi lasted three years, went 50,000 miles a year, and got 12 miles to the gallon. The annual salary, including tips, of a taximan averaged $2,600.

Buses

Buses are passenger-carrying motor vehicles available to all members of the public who tender their fare and are not drunk or otherwise obnoxious. In other words, except for school buses, they are common carriers.) For sightseeing or chartered service their advantages are obvious. (They operate in inter-urban service. They connect two or more large cities and join towns and villages with the city to which they are economically and socially tributary.) In this work (buses have several advantages over railway trains. They may pick up and set off (embus and debus) passengers at any point en route.) Most inter-urban bus companies discourage stopping anywhere except at designated places. Even so, (bus stops are always more frequent than railway stops. As a general rule buses are faster than railway trains for short distances[6] but tend to lose this advantage after 150 to 200 miles, except where they operate expresses, i.e., buses which do not stop at intermediate points.)

(Buses are better than trains on light traffic routes. Because they have smaller seating capacities, they can run more frequently. Therefore, their schedules are likely to be more convenient for travellers.) In theory, a rail-liner (a single car with diesel power plant and space for passengers, mail, luggage, and express or such a car with one or two conventional railway coaches attached) offers somewhat similar advantages, but the trend of traffic away from the rails had gone so far before rail-liners were introduced in any significant numbers that they proved relatively ineffectual in recovering business lost to automobiles. In general, bus fares are slightly lower than rail.

(Inter-urban buses are sometimes slowed down by congestion on the roads, by bad weather, and by mechanical breakdowns,) though the latter drawback has now been largely overcome. On long trips their patronage is cut because they cannot provide sleeping and dining facilities, except at rest stops. Until recently they did not have lavatories aboard. Since buses typically avoid factory districts and slum areas, they can usually offer the traveller more interesting views than trains. On the other hand some passengers dislike being immersed in fast highway traffic.

Though (buses ~~often~~ compete with trains, their main rival is the private automobile. As a result fewer buses ran between cities and between rural areas and nearby towns in 1966 than in 1946. Their share of this travel market fell from 12 to 4 per cent but, unlike passenger trains, they made modest profits. Meanwhile, they were carrying more people within larger cities and metropolitan areas.

In urban and suburban transport, buses are used in somewhat different ways depending on the size of the city. In metropolitan communities, motor buses have their greatest usefulness in congregating and dispersing passenger to and from junction points with street car lines and subways. One trouble with buses is that, being operated by one man, passengers must pass the fare box in single file in order to ensure that each passenger pays his fare. Where five or six passengers are picked up at every stop, some travellers must wait outside, perhaps in snow and rain, while others enter in single file, deposit fares, or get change and tickets. This slows down service. But when a large number of passengers is loaded or unloaded at one point, the operator can throw the bus out of gear, collect fares and transfers, make change, and give directions to strangers. If the bus enters a subway station for loading or unloading, the problem is further simplified. In light traffic areas such as newly opened subdivisions or areas with single-family dwellings on fairly spacious lots, buses give good service because, as a rule, only one or two patrons board or get off the bus at any stop.

In smaller cities buses can satisfactorily handle all persons travelling by public means except those who hire cabs. They can do this because the number of passengers getting on and off buses at various points conforms to the principles just mentioned. In a sense subways and street cars are wholesale handlers of passengers while buses are retailers.

Street Railways, Buses, and Trackless Trolleys

Horse-drawn street cars were introduced in Canada in the 1840s. A short electric line was one of the attractions at the Canadian National Exhibition in Toronto in 1885. In June, 1886, the first commercial electric railway in Canada and probably the first in North America ran between Windsor and Walkerville, Ont.[7] This was followed by one in Vancouver in 1890 and many other cities quickly thereafter. By 1905 a few inter-urban and rural lines or radials had been built and many more were planned. The increasing use of passenger cars and of trucks choked off this development.

Within cities and their suburbs vigorous competition between street cars and motor vehicles began about 1920. Veterans bought Model T Fords, and cruised the streets of our larger cities for passengers. They charged 5 cents, the traditional fare of urban transit, and concentrated on the shortest routes where they could be reasonably sure of getting a full load. Even so, many owners of jitneys went bankrupt or left for better-paying jobs. Passengers who were injured through fault of the driver often found it impossible to collect damages. Public transit companies naturally objected to unregulated competition and persuaded city councils to legislate against jitneys. So, if the jitneys did not die a natural death, they were outlawed.

Competition between vehicles propelled by electricity and by gasoline or diesel fuel did not cease with the collapse of the jitney business. In a sense the competition extends even to vehicles which are owned by the same transit company. In 1925 the mileage of electric railways (including radials or inter-urban lines) reached a peak of 1,738 and thereafter began to decline. Abandonment of track was especially common during the 1930s so that by 1940 the total mileage was 1040, or 700 below the peak year. No track was lifted during the war because buses and automobiles were hard to get and, as a result of the rationing of gasoline, many motorists had to leave their cars at home. By 1955 the mileage had declined to barely 500. Nine years later, the mileage was 72 and Toronto was the only Canadian city with street cars.

(The relative advantages of tramways and buses, once a matter for argument, is now largely of academic interest. Street cars were superior for handling large numbers of people at low fares and with extraordinary safety. They were economical users of street space, an important point in congested traffic. The overload capacity, or the ratio of possible standing passengers to the number of seats, is lower on buses than in street cars.) People who do have to stand are less comfortable in rubber-tired vehicles than in cars running on rails.

On the other hand(rubber-tired vehicles involve lower investment costs than steel-wheeled ones. They can provide more frequent service because of their smaller seating capacity. They pick up and let off patrons at the curb)—an advantage in slushy or rainy weather or where private automobile traffic is heavy(They can manoeuvre through street traffic more easily.) Though much depends on the relative age of the vehicle, the carefulness of the driver, and the smoothness of the roadway, buses are usually less noisy than street cars. These features attract some patrons away from automobiles, whereas street cars might not do so. Further, buses are operated by one man: an important economy especially when wage rates are rising. Unlike trams, an out-of-order or "crippled" bus can easily be pushed to the side of the road in order that other traffic, including buses, may get round it. Buses have shorter lives than trams and, in spite of a lower initial cost, higher depreciation charges per annum. They are also more expensive to maintain per vehicle-mile. Still, for the same seating capacity the investment in buses is less than in street cars. In general, technological advances, such as dieselization and increased size, which have been made since 1945, have tended to give buses a competitive advantage over street cars and thus to reverse the situation which prevailed just after the introduction of P.C.C.[8] cars in the late 1920s.

In several cities street cars were continued primarily because urban transit companies had large amounts of capital in their power plants, transmission systems, street cars, and track. They would lose substantially all this investment if they replaced their street cars with buses.

It was far more economical to keep the street cars in operation until the assets had become worn out. In other words(continued operation of some street cars was explained chiefly by the financial inability of the bus service to bear the full costs of its own operations plus interest and amortization charges on the investment which would have to be abandoned.)

(A trackless trolley or coach is another means of conserving investment. Basically, the vehicle consists of the chassis of a bus with the power unit of a street car. It draws energy from two parallel wires and trolleys a foot or so apart. It runs on rubber tires rather than rails and so must be steered.) Its lateral range of movement is twenty to twenty-five feet on either side of the trolley wires. It can reach or place passengers at or near the curb and can weave through other vehicular traffic.(Its capital cost is rather more than that of a gasoline- or diesel-powered bus, but its life is longer.) It is more dependable than a vehicle with an internal combustion engine though less so than a conventional street car.(It equals a street car in cleanliness and freedom from fumes and is less noisy. In short, it has the seating capacity and rate of acceleration of the better street cars without the capital cost and restrictions of track.)

Trackless trolleys were very popular with the public because of their intrinsic advantages and the feeling that their introduction showed a commendable spirit of progress on the part of the management of the urban transit company and the community at large. As time went on, trackless coaches lost their novelty, the overhead trolley system had to be replaced, and the electricity from the central power station could be sold elsewhere. Hence, since 1957 trolley coaches have slowly declined in terms of passengers carried, miles run, and number of vehicles in use. Gasoline and diesel buses are winning out over all types of electrically-driven vehicles except subway trains.)

Subways

Neither buses, street cars, nor trackless trolleys can do their jobs effectively if street congestion prevents them from moving except at a snail's pace.) Consequently, urban transit is being forced underground.) In 1954 Canada's first subway was opened in Toronto. It ran from Union Station to the corner of Yonge and Eglinton, a distance of 4.5 miles and cost $52 million. Within the next ten years it stimulated the investment of about $10 billion in apartment and office buildings along its route. In 1963 a more or less parallel route was opened from Union Station under University Avenue and Queen's Park to Bloor Street.)

Part of an east-west route along Bloor and Danforth was completed in 1966 and the remainder a year later. The scheduled time taken to travel along these two streets during the rush hour was about 55 minutes in 1952, 63 minutes in 1960, and will be 29 minutes when the subway is finished. By 1970 the Yonge Street subway will be extended another 2.5 miles to Sheppard Avenue. In 1966 Montreal opened an attractive subway too.

The Rush-hour Problem

The primary operating problem of transit companies is the rush-hour business. There are, in fact, a number of peaks—in winter, at any season of the year when inclement weather makes driving or walking unpleasant, before and just after athletic meets and the openings and closings of theatres, and around church time. Each of these minor peaks can be handled without embarrassment. It is the morning rush to work and especially the evening return from factory, office, and retail store that causes the most trouble.

Rush-hour business is expensive to handle because it requires extra rolling stock, more employees, and larger car barns or parking lots. Consumption of electricity, gasoline, or diesel fuel is excessive. Vehicles start more frequently, move slowly, and waste power in braking. All the mechanism is put under severe strain. Breakdowns and collisions are more common. A crippled vehicle holds up traffic coming behind it and, on narrow streets, delays traffic in both directions. Crews get paid for a six- or eight-hour day. By overlapping the shifts it is practicable to reduce the number of partial days worked but never to eliminate them. Some crews who are hired for the morning or evening rush get a full day's pay for three or four hours' work. Others are delayed in getting back to garage or barn and may draw overtime. Slow service and crowded cars during rush hours force patrons to other means of transport. Although gross revenue increases at the daily peaks of traffic, expenses rise still more. With the possible exception of the extraordinarily light traffic hours of midnight to 5:00 A.M. (Sundays 2 A.M. to 8:00 A.M.), the rush-hour business is the least profitable for transit companies.

To cope with daily peaks in traffic, managers of street railways have exercised much ingenuity. On the physical side they have cut down the number of stops, lowered the height of entrance and exit steps above the pavement, and installed rear exit doors with treadles. They train motormen and drivers to take advantage of every moment, though too sudden stops and starts bother passengers. Vehicles are designed for rapid acceleration and quick braking. One-man street cars have two doors for boarding, and a vestibule near the driver with a single lane past the fare box into the seating area. Two-man cars have longer rear-end platforms or the fare box in the centre of the car. These measures are taken so that patrons may get aboard and then have time, particularly in cold weather, to dig change or tickets out of their purse or pocket while the car is already in motion.

(Street car companies or city councils have built loading platforms on the street. These protect patrons from being run into by automobiles. Passengers can easily and quickly step up into or down from a car.) They may cross from the curb to a position near the tracks at safe and convenient times. Where there is no loading platform, passengers have either to dash through traffic and endanger their lives while they stand near the tracks, or wait nervously on the curb until the tram has drawn up at the corner. Then the motorman opens the car doors to hold up automobiles and waits until passengers walk from the sidewalk into the car(Safety platforms help automobile drivers, street car patrons, and the company itself.) Safety zones painted, usually in yellow, on the pavement, and broad white bands to make pedestrian lanes from curb to track have some of the advantages of platforms. They are cheaper and do not obstruct automobiles as much as islands but are declining in popularity since they give tramway patrons less protection than platforms, traffic lights, or zebra crosswalks. One advantage of buses is that they can draw in to the curb to load and discharge passengers.

On the psychological side companies have tried to get passengers to co-operate in reducing delays and cutting down peaks. They continually admonish patrons to move well back in the car, leave by the doors marked "exit only," have exact change ready, buy tickets in strips, not wait until the last moment to push buzzer if they wish to alight, go early to avoid the rush, shop in the middle of the day. Transit companies encourage queues. They put up signs saying that the car or bus is full. They have engaged guides who are stationed at busy intersections during rush hours to sell tickets, give directions to strangers, and assist the infirm. The guides, like despatchers in subway stations, see that too many people do not try to board an already overcrowded vehicle. Finally, by getting the doors closed promptly, guides enable the car to get moving.

Companies have attempted to get passengers and their employers to accept staggered hours. They have tried to persuade stores, factories, and offices to have different times for beginning and quitting work) During the war when patriotic motives were strong and overcrowding on street cars even worse than in normal times, staggering was intro-

duced on a limited scale in a number of cities. With the cessation of
open warfare the scheme quickly broke down. Relatives or neighbours
who had been accustomed to ride together to their various places of work
often found it inconvenient or impossible to do so because their hours
were different. Some people who got out of work early stayed downtown to shop, came home in the rush anyway, and defeated the purpose
of the plan. Businesses on one schedule were unable to telephone or to
deliver or pick up goods during the early morning or late afternoon to
firms which were on different hours. Housewives, especially in homes
with small children or several adult workers, disliked getting bread-
winners off to work at different times and preparing meals at all hours.
Adam Smith's dictum that "of all pieces of baggage, the most difficult
to transport is a man" seems to apply with peculiar force to patrons of
urban transit.

Finally, transit companies have tried financial methods to even out
the peak. A few have sold weekly passes. These are not to be confused with free passes issued to employees. The conductor can tell at a
glance that the passenger is entitled to ride. He makes one sale a week
instead of several. The pass is less expensive to print than the equivalent value in tickets and no transfers are needed. Pass-holders use street
cars more frequently, particularly in non-rush periods during the day
and evening. Sometimes the pass-owner, knowing that he can travel
himself without paying anything extra, will take along a friend who
pays a regular fare.

Although passes speed up operation and may stimulate business, if
their price is too high, people will be deterred from buying. Purchasers
run the risk of losing the pass before it expires and of not getting full
value from it on account of illness or "free lifts" in automobiles. If the
pass is priced too low, the company may receive less revenue than
what it would have got under regular fares. At any price whatever, the
company loses some revenue since the pass, while not transferable
according to the conditions printed on its face, is often lent by the pass-
holder to his friends who would otherwise have paid the regular charge
per trip. Accordingly the weekly pass has lost favour with transit companies.

Another financial scheme is the use of discriminatory fares. The
company may charge less from 9:30 A.M. to 4:00 P.M. so that shoppers
and others will travel after the morning rush is over and before the
evening one begins. It may charge more after midnight and before
5:00 A.M. when traffic is light and expenses per passenger-mile high.
Such discrimination is not unjust or unreasonable for the fares charged
recognize cost of operation as a factor in rate-making.[10] Expenses are

heavy during the rush hours and the middle of the night.) They are a little lower in the evenings when the number of passengers approximates the capacity of vehicles then in operation, when street congestion is not serious, and when some buses are needed to take home crowds of moderate size after the places of entertainment close. Expenses are slightly lower in the middle hours of the day than at times of peak traffic, because vehicles may be operated by crews working out the remainder of their shift, patronage is good but not excessive, and congestion created by private automobiles is not intolerable.

The chief drawback of discriminatory fares is that the difference in passenger-mile cost at various times of the day and night is not large enough to justify marked variation in tolls. And when the difference in fares is small, not enough passengers will travel during the slack day-time hours to make the scheme worth while. Because costs of operation are steadily rising, transit companies feel that they need all the revenue they can get. Consequently they must raise fares during the slack-time hours of the day by cutting out the rate concessions formerly made. Urban transit fares in Canada are generally lower than in cities of the same size in the United States.

In many cities children going to and from school are allowed lower fares than children travelling for other purposes. These discriminatory fares are sometimes criticized because they tend to favour pupils attending private and parochial schools compared with those within easy walking distance of public schools. There seems no sound reason why public transit should be required to subsidize any kind of education.

(The rush-hour problem is much worse in some places than in others. Urban transportation is more difficult in semi-circular cities like Toronto and Hamilton than in communities such as London, Ont., or Regina which are spread out more or less equally in all directions. Cities like Halifax, with their chief shopping, factory, and residential districts on a peninsula are hard on a transit company, but the pressure has been eased by the Macdonald Bridge to Dartmouth. In Vancouver the important shops, office buildings, theatres, docks, and railway stations are on a peninsula and the largest residential areas are spread out on the mainland. This situation is relieved by fairly wide streets, the relative cheapness of bridging False Creek, and a short broad isthmus. Ottawa has the problem that most of its buses are brought through a single bottle-neck, Confederation Square. In Montreal traffic has to be routed round the mountain[11] which occupies the centre of the metropolitan area.) Traffic is badly congested on Ste. Catherine Street where the largest department stores and the main motor bus lines near the foot of the mountain are located. To relieve the congestion, Sherbrooke

Street, a parallel thoroughfare, has been widened for the primary use of fast motor vehicles, and a subway has been built.

Almost every city in Eastern Canada suffers from narrow streets especially in their older sections. Many have steep hills, notably Halifax, Saint John, and Quebec. These add to the expense of tractive power in one direction and to the risk of accident, and wear and tear on the brake system in the other direction. Toronto has numerous ravines and Edmonton a deeply entrenched river. The location of street car routes, the level of fares, and the speed of travel by public means have influenced the growth of cities and the distribution of commercial, manufacturing, and residential sections. In short, any large city has transportation problems peculiar to itself.

Operating problems of transit companies are also affected by the so-called "riding habit." This is the outgrowth of custom, the location of industrial plants and shopping districts, and the availability of parking space. In Ottawa the patronage of buses at noon-hour is slightly higher than in most cities, because civil servants, who comprise the bulk of wage earners, have one and a half hours for lunch and some of them go home. Hamilton is heavily industrialized but as it happens, some plants are within walking distance of residential areas. So the morning and afternoon rush-hour peaks are lower than would normally be expected in a city of its size. Cornwall, though not large (15,000), supported a street railway for many years after equally populous cities had gone over to buses because the two largest industrial plants were on the outskirts and at opposite ends of the city. In many places most of the theatres and stores, except corner groceries and drug stores, are down town. Housewives and entertainment seekers must travel considerable distances to have their wants satisfied and so patronize the transit system. Since World War II there has been a trend towards having subordinate shopping districts or supermarkets. Thus relatively more people can avoid using public transit though in some places, such as Kingston, where the new shopping centre is on the edge of the city, the bus company has been helped.

To sum up, the rush-hour problem varies in intensity from one city to another but everywhere it remains the chief difficulty in the day-to-day functioning of rapid transit. Every company is continually trying to cope with it. Several plans have alleviated but none has solved the problem.

Past Economic Difficulties

In the 1930s rapid transit companies were hard hit by the depression.

During the war they were hurt by heavy taxes on excess profits and by slow delivery of equipment they badly needed to cope with the sudden increase in traffic. Companies in a secularly declining industry find it hard to attract new capital even when their business is temporarily growing. Some companies were hurt when labour unions or city councils with an eye toward the votes of working men refused to allow them to reduce costs by introducing one-man cars.

After 1945 urban transit companies were faced with rising wage rates, material prices, and interest rates. At the same time they suffered from the "stickiness" of their fares. Often they had to carry on protracted negotiations with city councils or appear before a provincial regulatory authority before they could raise fares at all. When they did so, patrons objected. They had grown accustomed to the old rate which they had been paying for years. For a time, higher fares induced people to drive their own automobiles or cancel trips for shopping, visiting, and entertainment which they might otherwise have made. The effect on the riding habit of an increase in fares normally wears off within a few months. In general, patronage is hurt more by a series of small increases in fares spread over two or three years than by larger increases at less frequent intervals. Another trouble is that transit companies cannot raise fares by small amounts because of the awkwardness of making change or selling tickets for odd sums. Wider use of metal tokens would speed up service. Often a company refrains from raising fares as long as it can in the hope that an increase will not be necessary. In the meantime it may have to let its equipment deteriorate badly. The public becomes critical and the increase when it does come will seriously reduce patronage.

Urban transit companies, like other highway users, suffer from traffic congestion. Being tied to rails, trams were unable to weave through traffic to the extent of moving as much as an inch or two sideways. Much of the congestion on streets is caused by moving or parked motor cars. The vehicles which have taken business away from the public transportation agency make it more difficult for the agency to run its own buses and street cars.

Transit companies have not benefited from the steady growth of urban populations as much as one might expect. In smaller cities the possible gains to street railways have been offset by more intensive competition from private cars. In places with fewer than fifty or sixty thousand persons, automobiles can be operated fairly easily on account of shorter distances, less congested streets, and more convenient parking facilities. In larger communities a growing population aggravates congestion and adds greatly to the expenses of operating a transit company. Toward the periphery of a city, buses may run with only a few passengers. Half-way to the shopping or factory centre, they may become so crowded that people are left standing on street corners. This results in ill will, loss of business, high operating costs per passenger-mile in outlying areas, and slow progress in downtown sections. Turning buses and street cars round before the end of the line obviates these difficulties but interferes with all vehicular traffic, may require expensive land, and reduces frequency of service along some parts of the route. In Canada fares are typically uniform within city limits. As the city spreads out, the company must haul a passenger a longer distance for a given fare. The extra cost of carrying some passengers an extra mile or so is not as important to the transit companies as heavy overcrowding on lines downtown. Extra fares charged by the Toronto Transit Commission to fringe communities have led to bitter criticism and to lawsuits.

High profits obtained by transit companies in the early years of the century often led municipal councils to impose obligations on the local street railway for the cost of paving, bridging, street cleaning, and snow removal. These costs became burdensome and unfair when revenues began to decline. For example, when the Ottawa Electric Railway was privately owned, it had promptly and at its own expense to remove all snow from curb to curb along some streets on which its cars operated. This cost money and helped free-wheeling competitors.

Current Problems

It is obvious that the biggest current problem of urban transit companies is competition with private passenger automobiles. Many car owners prefer to drive to work, to shop, and to places of entertainment but are deterred from doing so by traffic congestion and scarcity of parking space. On the other hand the increasing cost of operating urban transit systems has resulted in higher fares which discourage travel by common carrier. Street railways, buses, and subways are undoubtedly the most economical agencies of passenger transport, but the psychological satisfaction of driving one's own car typically more than offsets the higher cost of travelling by automobile. Broadly speaking, higher fares are more likely to discourage patronage from urban transit companies in smaller cities than in larger ones because the parking problem is more easily solved in smaller places.

Associated with competition between owner-driven and public transport are the problems arising out of the growing industrialization and urbanization of Canada. This has resulted in congestion that threatens to overwhelm private motorists, common carriers, and metropolitan areas taken as a whole.

As more and more people purchase private cars and patronage of public transportation falls off, fares are increased and this brings about a further shift to automobiles adding still further to congestion. The result of all this —quite apart from the misfortunes of public transit—is that most city streets designed for an earlier day and age are hopelessly inadequate to cope with the present-day volume of traffic. Cities are turning to expressways as a means of speeding up vehicle movement. . . . The U.S. experience with expressways, however, has been that while more vehicles can be accommodated, there is little relief from congestion as the growth of private cars soon catches up with the additional capacity provided. Expressways, moreover, are very costly, some two-and-one-half to four times as much as subways to handle the same number of passengers [and] . . . they are no solution to the . . . movement of people by public transportation. . . . City streets are just not spacious enough to be shared by public transit vehicles, passenger cars and commercial vehicles. The cost of widening, improving and building new city streets . . . is almost prohibitive at today's prices. . . . Subways are an ideal solution, but a costly one. Few Canadian cities can afford a subway sufficiently extensive to provide real relief.[13]

In 1941 a Canadian expert on urban transit stated that "essentially the problem before all street railways is one of gradual change-over to other types of operations."[14] By 1960 the change-over was reasonably complete but the problem of finance had become acute. Construction costs, wage rates, and interest charges had sky-rocketed while patronage of public transit was generally declining, especially if measured in relation to the population of the area served. Any higher fares would merely have the effect of encouraging more people to drive their own cars. In some instances the revenues of rapid transit authorities were inadequate to cover operating expenses plus interest on the existing investment let alone provide funds for expansion and further modernization.

Accordingly, transit commissions were forced to turn for aid to the municipal government. But municipalities, in addition to financing education, police and fire protection, and a host of other activities had to find capital for expressways, street-widening, and downtown parking space. In order to deal with the broad problem of urban transport, especially in metropolitan communities, several proposals have been made: monorails, no fares on public transit or at least no further increase in fares in order to encourage its use and keep some automobiles off the streets; very heavy parking fees or possibly the prohibition of parking in some areas downtown; peripheral parking so that one may leave his car at or near the terminus of the subway and continue his journey to his downtown office by public transport; a surtax of two or three mills on all real estate in the metropolitan area to meet deficits on the existing system and the interest charges on costly extensions; a special levy on downtown offices and stores on the theory that they stand to gain more than uptown or suburban shopping centres by a transit system which brings customers quickly and cheaply to their doors; a municipal or provincial subsidy to inter-urban railways to provide more commuter services and thus relieve congestion on streets; city planning which will at least avoid compounding existing mistakes; special or exclusive traffic lanes for buses which will allow them to move faster; a direct grant from the province to transit companies on the ground that a government which has assumed the responsibility for trunk roads between cities should also contribute to intra-urban travel; and so on. It is obvious that the problem is too complicated for an easy or inexpensive solution.

21

Civil Aviation

ACCORDING to an American transportation economist, Canada has every requisite for a great future in air power except a large population and certain important raw materials.[1] Canadian progress in aviation is the result of several factors: geographic and economic conditions within the Dominion, a strategic position on the air map of the world, the relative ease of purchasing suitable equipment and borrowing operational techniques from the United States and Britain, the energy and ability of her own people, and the lively interest which Canadians have always taken in every form of transportation.

History to 1936

During World War I Canadians actively participated in air warfare. Afterwards veterans flew the old "crates" at air "circuses" and engaged in stunt flying, sightseeing, and mercy flights. Later they used planes in timber cruising, ærial photography, spotting forest fires, and detecting rum runners. In 1921 two Junkers flew down the Mackenzie River Valley with men and supplies for the oil fields at Norman. Three years later daily flights with passengers and mail were made from railhead at Haileybury, Ont., to Rouyn, a mining field 325 air-miles due north of Toronto and 25 miles east of the Ontario-Quebec boundary.

Late in 1926 Mr. James A. Richardson, a prominent grain merchant of Winnipeg, started an airline into northern Manitoba. He provided the first responsible money in Canadian civil aviation. By the end of the decade prospectors and surveyors had been flown into Churchill, Coppermine, Aklavik, and many other isolated points. The stock-market crash in 1929 choked off the boom and Richardson may have lost from one to two million dollars on his ventures.

Fortunately the revival of non-scheduled or "bush flying" was not long delayed. The American revaluation of gold in 1933 greatly stimulated mining and prospecting in the Canadian North. By 1937 this second boom began to level off. All through the twenties and thirties bush fliers performed a service of real value to Northern Canada. It was claimed that "Canadian bush services use more up-to-date equipment, better flying aids, and more thoroughly trained pilots than many European main lines."[2]

Meanwhile, the Dominion government was not entirely losing sight of its responsibility for controlling and promoting civil aviation.[3] In 1919 Parliament set up an Air Board to study æronautical developments, undertake research, prescribe air routes, license aircraft and pilots, provide for safety and proper navigation of planes and so on. In 1922 these responsibilities were taken over by the Department of National Defence and in 1936 by the Department of Transport. The latter was given the added duty of airport traffic control. The regulations on safety, certification of pilots and aircraft, the operation of airports, etc., have been changed from time to time to take account of larger, faster planes, increased demands on the skill of pilots, blind flying, and our agreements with other countries. The primary difficulty is to frame rules which will provide adequate protection to pilots, passengers, and innocent third parties without limiting the healthy progress of civil aviation.

Ground Facilities

Fortunately Canadian aviation was able to get soundly started without heavy capital investment in ground facilities. Bush flyers used pontoons in summer and skis in winter. They landed their planes on the innumerable lakes scattered throughout the Laurentian Shield. They could construct a wharf and simple hangar from their own resources. In bad weather, flights could readily be delayed. Pilots and passengers were content with poor accommodation in planes and at terminals. Even in isolated areas, they could subsist in case of a forced landing. Beam flying was not yet perfected. Bush flyers could manage without much government assistance and even yet they have received much less than main-line services.

During the air boom of the late twenties, dozens of municipalities in the more thickly settled parts of Canada built small airports. Although getting some federal aid in money and advice, in the main they sank their own funds in the facilities.) The cities concerned were motivated by civic pride and the desire not to be left off any projected air routes. This municipal activity practically ceased in the early thirties because of the depression and the increased cost of airfields occasioned by the new, larger planes. Even so, a number of civic airports, particularly those near larger cities, proved valuable assets later.

In 1927 the federal government began an airway for the eventual use of transcontinental mail and passenger services. Planes would follow a series of illuminated beacons. By the end of 1930 the Dominion had completed over 1,300 miles, chiefly on the Prairies and from Toronto to Windsor. Then because of the depression, construction of airports and airways ceased until after 1935. As planes became larger, faster, and more numerous, landing strips had to be lengthened and measures to control aircraft as they were landing and taking off had to be introduced. Hence, the Dominion was forced to abandon its policy of relying on municipalities to build fields. Early in 1940, Canada finished a transcontinental airway with radio beams to mark the path of flight. After the war a few military airfields were taken over for civilian uses.

Generally speaking, the Dominion has concentrated its expenditures on airfields in the thickly settled parts of Canada and paid relatively less attention to the needs of the north-south routes. This policy can be justified because of the uncertain life of many northern mining camps and the enormous capital needs of inter-urban traffic.) On the other hand the policy raises the cost of transport and may slow down the rate of economic development in the North because it is cheaper to operate aircraft with retractable wheel undercarriages than with pontoons or skis. Non-retractable landing gear reduces the ærodynamic lift of the aircraft.

Unlike the United States the Canadian government did not at first assume responsibility for building numerous small landing fields for light, private planes. It believed that such facilities could be more cheaply constructed and administered by local government units. It was not prepared to gamble money on these fields until flying for pleasure by individuals in their own planes had proved successful. A number of flying clubs across the country had kept up enthusiasm for private flying. Business flying, or the use of private planes by newspapers, oil companies, chain department stores, meat packers, and so on, has grown very rapidly since 1950. The high cost per plane-mile is offset by flexibility in scheduling compared with public transport, the possibility of executives holding private discussions of business problems en route, and the advantage of making on-the-spot investigations. Business and personal flying would unquestionably increase if there were more landing fields across the country and if, in landing and taking off, such aircraft were not inconvenienced by the needs of big commercial airliners using the same facilities. In 1965 the Department of Transport announced that, in future, it hoped to spend more money on the needs of private flyers.

Even though the Dominion has cut down its spending on fields in Northern Canada and on assisting private and business flying, it is still faced with heavy and growing expenditures for civil aviation. An airport for so-called main-line services requires a great deal of land, and land near metropolitan centres is expensive. So are waiting rooms for passengers and their friends, aprons where planes can stand to be loaded and unloaded, facilities for parking cars and for handling luggage, runways, control towers, floodlights, boundary and runway beacons, and the like. It is also expensive to maintain and operate all these facilities, to remove snow, and to control aircraft as they land and take off.

Some modern planes, though economical of fuel at high altitudes and fast cruising speeds, are extravagant users of gasoline while coming down or circling an airport preparatory to landing. Hence, they must be "talked down" fairly quickly before they run out of fuel or "burn up all the profits." The old method was to stack aircraft at busy airports. As each plane arrived above the airfield, it was ordered to circle 500 feet above the next lower aircraft, which was the one that had arrived just before it had. When the lowest plane in the stack had landed, the traffic controller allowed each aircraft to drop 500 feet in altitude, just as every playing card in the deck or stack of cards comes down one space when the bottom card is pulled out. Though stacking is still the basic principle, planes which are big consumers of fuel while circling at relatively low speeds preparatory to landing and others which, during a long hop, have used up most of their fuel, must often be run through the stacks. This is a ticklish operation, expensive in the amount of fuel used by all other aircraft in the stack, and likely to become more common with supersonic aircraft.

Another problem is emergency landing fields. In the original plan for Canada's transcontinental air service, emergency fields or landing strips were to be located every 30 miles. This soon became unnecessary because of multi-engined aircraft, high-altitude flying, more accurate information on weather and flying conditions, better contact between pilots in the air and controllers on the ground, and the increased ability of planes to carry enough fuel for long flights. Big intermediate fields, e.g., at Gander and Goose Bay, were once regularly used for servicing trans-Atlantic aircraft. Now jet planes are able as a rule to fly directly overseas without touching down at intermediate points. But on occasion they land for more fuel when likely to face, or having recently faced, heavy head winds or other adverse flying conditions. At times also fog and sleet cause a plane to be rerouted to an airport which was not its original destination. Thus some fields are used for emergency purposes, though hardly to be classed as emergency fields in the original or basic sense of the term. In any event, they have to be maintained by governments.

Of course, it is possible that some technological breakthrough will permit a large reduction in the cost of airfields and simplify the problem of traffic control. Helicopters, UTOL and STOL (Vertical and Short Take Off and Landing) aircraft are obvious possibilities. But the general trend of the costs of constructing and operating airports and aids to navigation has been sharply upwards. This has raised three serious problems aside from how the Dominion will get all the money needed to carry out the work.

First, the facilities at most airports are used by a number of commercial airlines, by non-scheduled operators, by private flyers, and sometimes by military planes. Some airports were built as relief projects during the depression. Others, though originally built for military purposes, are now used by civilian planes. Thus the problem of allocating capital costs to types of traffic virtually cannot be resolved.

Second, weather reports are useful to farmers, fishermen, truckers, merchants, and citizens generally as well as to air carriers. Though the latter require more detailed, up-to-date, accurate, and expensive data than other users of the service, the public at large has clearly benefited from the improvements in the meteorological service which commercial aviation demanded. Again the difficulty of allocating joint costs is almost insurmountable.

Third, as a practical matter airlines are financially incapable of reimbursing the government for more than a negligible proportion of expenditures made on their behalf. All governments hope that eventually the revenues they collect at airports from landing fees, rentals on ticket offices, newstands and restaurants, and from parking will cover their costs. This objective has been reached at Montreal and a few of the world's busiest air terminals but speaking generally governments must provide physical assets and intangible services for the use of commercial aviation on a generous scale and without expectation of more than a nominal return for many years to come.

The enormously increased cost of new airports with wide, long, thick runways, complicated traffic control systems, better accommodation for passengers and so on is borne by the taxpayer. The benefits from using larger planes accrue to commercial airlines and to the relatively limited number of persons and companies who use their services. To be sure, the public derives some indirect gain from progress in civil aviation. But lack of balance between the needs of airlines and the cost of airports and thus a mal-distribution of advantages and expenses is essentially an unhealthy situation.[4]

Air Travel

Important though the problem of airport finance may be to the tax-payer, it is not a major issue for commercial airlines. Instead they are more concerned with the kinds of traffic they handle, and having enough revenue to meet their expenses.

Until airlines can greatly reduce their operating costs, their chief revenue will come from the carriage of passengers, except in areas, such as Northern Canada, where surface transportation is slow and costly. For distances of over about 300 miles, travel by air is faster, and more comfortable than travel by surface carriers. Trips by plane take less time than by surface carrier because planes fly so fast and usually go by more direct routes. By comparison, railways and highways must go through passes in the mountains and they must avoid swamps, inlets of the sea, and rough terrain generally. Inland ships must follow the meanderings of rivers: ocean-going vessels must go round islands and headlands. Savings in time are largest where the alternative surface carriers go by water (Halifax-St. John's, Nfld., and Vancouver-Victoria) or follow circuitous routes (Halifax-Montreal and Toronto-New York) or go over rough terrain (Calgary-Vancouver).

Early commercial aircraft had cruising speeds of 100 miles per hour or a little better. In 1939 the average cruising speed was 200, in 1962 roughly 550, and by the early 1970s will probably be 1,100 miles per hour. Early aircraft had to touch down frequently to refuel and to pick up passengers. Because of technical advances, modern aircraft can fly long hops and with the growth of traffic it is economical to schedule increasing numbers of non-stop or direct flights. Thus there are fewer touch-downs, or more over-flights. Travellers between distant points benefit from the faster overall speed and greater comfort of direct flights. Passengers to and from intermediate points also gain, for they are more likely to get a seat and they usually find the times of departure and arrival more convenient than formerly. Under the old scheme of operations the interests of potential and actual travellers at the smaller, inter-mediate stops were often partly sacrificed to meet the requirements of people in the bigger termini who provided most of the traffic and revenue. The increasing use of planes with higher seating capacity than before tends to keep down the number of direct flights. This is offset, however, by the rapid expansion in the volume of traffic which is caused, at least in some measure, by the attractiveness of direct flights to travellers.

On short flights airlines are handicapped by the very heavy expenses of the take-off and landing of a conventional aircraft and by the time a traveller must spend in going between the centre of a large city and its airport. Because of the cost of land, the prevalence of noise, the risk of accident, the need to keep surrounding buildings low, and the increasing length of runways, airports can hardly be located near city centres. The air terminal at Gatwick, south of London, is unique because it has frequent service by electric trains past its very door. Everywhere else, taxicabs, limousines, or private automobiles must be used to connect with the airport. As these vehicles are comparatively slow on congested city streets, airlines try to overcome the waste of time on the ground by spending less time in the air and by using endless belts for quickly handling luggage. Eventually they may use helicopters between city centre and airport. At present, on short trips, such as between Montreal and Ottawa or Toronto and London, Ont., it is almost as fast to go by train as by air, if elapsed time is reckoned from city centre to city centre. Even so, many travellers feel that the novelty and prestige of flying, convenience of times of departure and arrival, and the more personalized service by air are worth the difference of a few dollars in fare. The busiest air route in Canada is between Vancouver and Victoria but it is an unprofitable one for the airline because of the dis-economies or high operating cost per passenger-mile and per plane-mile on such a short flight (less than 80 miles).

The relative safety of air and surface transport is prominent in the minds of those who have never flown and commonly ignored by those who have. In the early days of civil aviation, an air crash caused a drop in patronage for several days. Over the years the effect of an air disaster on patronage has become much less. Air travel has become safer because of multi-engined aircraft which eliminate the chance of a complete failure in the power plant, altimeters which work on the same principle as radar instead of on differences in air pressure as one ascends or descends, automatic pilots which are more accurate than humans, the use of radio beams to show the correct path of flight and of radar to spot flying aircraft, bigger planes which can fly above and around storms, etc. In addition, the careful investigation of accidents by regulatory authorities in every country, by the airlines, and sometimes by manufacturers of aircraft and engines has greatly contributed to air safety. Airlines have been doubtful about the value of advertising to counteract the fear of flying. For one thing the appearance of the advertisement may happen to coincide with a bad accident. In the main, airlines have had to rely on the assurances of satisfied customers that travel by airplane is safer than by automobile, as in fact it is.

Air sickness or *mal d'air* is another handicap that has been largely overcome. At first airlines tried to divert the passengers' attention by attractive stewardesses and free reading matter. These have been continued but airlines no longer find it necessary to engage only trained nurses. On some flights about half the attendants in the cabin are men. Pressurized cabins, better lighting in the aircraft, more comfortable seats, the lessened fear of accident, marked reduction in noise and vibration within the aircraft while taking off, in flight, and while landing, and flights high enough to get above the turbulent air along the earth's surface, all these have served practically to eliminate air sickness.

As for relative cost of air and surface travel, one must take account of meals, berth, tips, the comparative cost of a cab or limousine to the airport and a taxi to the railway station, and the cost of the tickets themselves. When this is done, the cost of going first-class by air is about the same as the most expensive method of travel by rail, that is, in a first-class compartment. Relative cost is probably not too significant in either promoting or discouraging first class travel. As a rule such passengers travel on expense accounts. A business or government foots the bill and costliness merely adds to the prestige enjoyed by the traveller. Thus, first class fares make for what economists call a reverse demand curve. Instead of higher prices reducing demand, as is usually the case, they increase use. On the other hand, fares for cheaper accommodation such as economy class and charter flights have a noticeable effect in attracting traffic. In the main these fares are higher than fares for tourist or coach accommodation by rail. Costs per automobile-mile are high, but the expense per passenger-mile can be reduced if several persons travel together.

Actual and potential travellers by air consider many other factors. Young people who contemplate a longish overland journey probably think first of driving a car and then of flying. Going by bus or train does not cross their minds unless they are particularly hard up. Older people may prefer trains because they like freedom from care, leisurely meals, and even the clickety-clack of the wheels riding over the joints of the rails. Some enjoy the scenery, which is not visible in high-level flying. Others hate the ride to the airport or else think they sleep better in a lower berth than in a strange hotel room.

At first, airlines tried to treat every passenger as a guest but this is not easy when 100 or more passengers board an aircraft at the same time.

Another recognition that airlines are now agencies of mass transport is the so-called air bus service. For example, on flights of Pacific Western Airlines between Edmonton and Calgary reservations for seats have been abolished, passengers are accommodated on a first-come, first-served basis, and they handle their own luggage. Clearly airlines are losing one of their original advantages, personalized service, except perhaps for passengers travelling on first class fares.

(From the standpoint of patrons, air travel raises questions of speed, safety, air sickness, fares, and personal preference. But for airlines by far the most critical thing is cost of operation. Now air service is expensive on account of the costliness of the aircraft, its fuel, and its maintenance; the heavy interest, depreciation, and insurance charges on the aircraft; the relatively small number of seats per plane compared with a train, the seasonality of traffic, and the provision of personal services such as reservations for passengers, free reading matter and free meals aloft, free accommodation and meals if the plane is grounded while a trip is in progress, and the attention of stewardesses.)

Whenever a new kind of aircraft is introduced, costs temporarily bounce above their old level because air and ground crew must be retrained, new spare parts and repair shops must be acquired, and planes must be flown on familiarization flights before going into regular service. The higher costs brought about by the replacement of turbo-prop planes (propellors driven by jet turbine engines) by jet aircraft (straight jets without conventional propellors) mainly accounted for the heavy losses of airlines in the early 1960s.

The cost of air travel per passenger-mile is strongly affected by the load factor, which is the ratio of seats occupied to total seating capacity. Obviously it costs little more to fly a plane with a passenger in every seat than with half the seats empty, and the net revenue in the one case is much higher than in the other. An airline can achieve a high load factor by providing little more accommodation than enough for the minimum number of passengers asking for seats on any flight. In this event, when the number applying for airline reservations exceeds the number of available seats, the airline will lose business to competitors and it will lose goodwill with the travelling public. Alternatively, an aviation company can have ample capacity at all times so that every traveller can get a seat without delay. Under these circumstances the airline's costs per passenger-mile will obviously be high. An empty seat represents an economic waste. Of course, every agency for the carriage of passengers—railways, ships, urban transit systems, or intercity buses—faces the same problem of congestion at certain times of day and at certain seasons of the year. In deciding when to acquire additional equipment, each has to take into consideration convenience to the public, maximization of its net revenue, and the likelihood of driving business to its competitors if the purchase of new facilities is delayed too long. On airlines, the problem is aggravated by the high cost of interest, depreciation, and insurance on idle aircraft and by the exceptionally rapid rate of obsolescence.

Moreover, competition between airlines is intense and the public is quickly attracted to the company with the most modern planes. New kinds of aircraft often develop unexpected weaknesses or "bugs" when first used commercially. Because of the cost of grounded planes and the creation of a certain amount of fear in the public mind, an innovator may have to pay a heavy price for his initiative. On the other hand, an airline management which invariably follows someone else's lead will gain a reputation for technological backwardness which is bad for business. The problem is complicated by the lengthy time lag between the date of ordering planes and their ultimate delivery. In many ways air travel is still a luxury whether it is sold to individuals going on a holiday or to business men. Consequently, a relatively minor decline in general business prosperity will have very serious repercussions on airline revenues, as is evidenced by the recurrent financial crises in the industry.

Fares by Air

Despite the rapid rise in wage rates and in material prices which occurred after the end of World War II, the revenue per passenger-mile of Air Canada which carried from 80 to 90 per cent of all air traffic in Canada, declined from 6.77 cents in 1949 to 5.82 cents in 1966. Besides, air travellers got faster, more comfortable service for their money. The decline in average revenue per passenger-mile was made possible by greater operating efficiency as measured by productivity per man-hour, and was started by the introduction of family and tourist fares. Family fares were published originally because it was believed that many wives, thinking that flying was dangerous, discouraged their husbands from going by air. Hence, when business was slack and seats would otherwise be empty, wives who accompanied their husbands were allowed to fly without extra charge. Canadian airlines publish off-season and charter fares to Europe and the Caribbean, and they stimulate sales by advertising, credit cards, and plans to fly now, pay later.

As soon as civil aviation reached a respectable size, proposals were made for differentiated fares similar to pullman and coach fares on railways. The introduction of such fares was delayed by the shortage of aircraft during and immediately after the war. There was little point in cutting fares when every seat could be filled with passengers paying standard fares. Later, airline officials thought it was better to build up volume at slack times during the winter rather than to encourage traffic throughout the year by cutting fares at all seasons. By 1948 a few companies in the United States began to put additional seats in semi-obsolete aircraft, eliminated free meals while in flight, and cut out reservations. By reducing costs per seat-mile, they were able to operate at a profit even at low fares. The Civil Aeronautics Board, which regulates commercial airlines in the United States, was anxious to protect the revenues of operators flying up-to-date planes on regular schedules. Accordingly, it restricted companies which provided only tourist services to what it called irregular and intermittent flights. It required their planes to leave at inconvenient hours, and would not permit these companies to give notice of time of departure of aircraft except a few hours in advance of take-off. Some non-scheduled operators, or "non-skeds," used travel agents to evade these regulations and there was danger that they would seriously cut into the revenues of "full-service" companies. Therefore, non-skeds have had to confine their operations to charter services where the entire plane is engaged for a conducted tour or for some ethnic, religious, or other group or, in Northern Canada, for prospectors and mining companies.

Meanwhile, the standard airlines had been experimenting with tourist services of their own. They soon came to realize that tourist fares would tap a large and profitable market without impinging too disastrously on the revenues to be secured from first class traffic. On most domestic routes in both Canada and the United States there are now two classes of service. But regional carriers—Quebecair, Eastern Provincial, Trans-Air, NorCan and Pacific Western—and some local services of Canadian Pacific Air Lines use a single class, having found that the expense of maintaining two classes in the aircraft was in excess of the increased revenue received from the first class. Often airlines have to turn down economy passengers while their first class section is half empty. Yet these airlines say they have a duty to the public to provide a choice of comfort and price as long as the public demands it. In 1963 a first class passenger via Canadian Pacific Air Lines from Toronto to Vancouver paid $47 more than the economy fare and got a little more leg room, a little wider seat, and a better steak. Obviously, while some air fares are based primarily on cost of service, others have a large element of value of service.

As a rule, tourist fares are about 20 per cent below first class fares. Although planes carrying only tourist passengers are flown on regular schedules, tourist and first class passengers are often carried in the same aircraft. In the trans-Atlantic service there were four classes: deluxe, first, tourist, and economy. They were differentiated from each other by the amount of noise and vibration which the passenger was likely to experience, the quality of the meals, the amount of leg-room, the number of seats per row (2 + 2, or 2 + 3 abreast with the aisle between), and upwards of $100 difference in fare. Companies with heavy traffic found it possible to fly different aircraft for the different classes, but Air Canada handled all four classes in the same ship. In 1960 all the trans-Atlantic airlines agreed to have only two classes, first and economy.

Air Cargo

Air cargo includes air express and air freight. These differ from each other in a number of particulars. Air express has a high priority. Space is specifically allotted for it on all flights where there is a regular movement, whereas air freight may either be delayed in departure or taken off the plane at an intermediate stop if space is not available because of the volume of mail or express that has to be carried or because one or more flights have had to be cancelled. On transcontinental routes, air express normally goes in the nose, tail, or belly of a modern passenger plane, while air freight is typically sent in an older aircraft which is too slow or uncomfortable to be competitive with the equipment of other airlines in passenger service. Specially constructed cargo aircraft are coming into use as volume grows. Since May, 1955, Air Canada flies all-cargo planes five days a week between Vancouver, Montreal, and intermediate points. Like airlines in the United States, it gives first-day delivery up to 1,500 miles from point of origin, and second-day delivery beyond. On most north-south routes in Canada, freight is carried in the same planes as passengers, mail, and express, but where the volume of traffic is large enough, a plane will be flown with a payload of cargo alone.

A further difference between air express and air freight is that the airline through the Merchandise Service of its parent railway carries out surface transport for express but not for freight. Thus the air carrier arranges for the pick-up and delivery of express, providing complete door-to-door service. As a rule air freight must be delivered to the airport by the shipper and collected at the terminating airport by the consignee.

From the standpoint of shippers, the basic disadvantage of air cargo is its relatively high cost. In 1951 Air Canada got about 53 cents per ton-mile from freight, express, and excess baggage. By 1966 it had cut this average to 23.88 cents but air cargo was still restricted to articles of high value or great perishability or to situations where speed is much more important than cost. Goods moved fairly regularly by air over main line routes include motion picture films, dresses, furs, costume jewelry, and sera, in addition to the largely seasonal items of cut flowers, baby chicks, and turkey poults. A manufacturer who needs a replacement part in a machine or a component for a product which is otherwise ready for delivery will have it sent by air, regardless of cost. In Northern Canada, where surface transport is slow and expensive, the cost disadvantage of airlines is comparatively less than in thickly settled areas. Accordingly, planes handle mining equipment, foodstuffs, furs, fish, and a wide range of other goods between relatively isolated points and railhead. Construction of the Distant Early Warning (or DEW) and the Mid-Canada Lines of radar stations in the mid 1950s gave rise to a large and profitable, but temporary, volume of business to several carriers by air.

From the operating standpoint, air cargo has created numerous problems. With present wage rates and traffic congestion, it is expensive to handle air express between the centre of a town and its airport which may be twenty miles away. Many shipments originate or terminate at places which have no airports of their own. Shipments by air must then be interchanged with commercial carriers on the ground. This is sometimes slow and awkward, and is always expensive. Frequently, stowage of property in the aircraft is difficult and, if improperly done, results in heavy claims for loss and damage. Air traffic is often unbalanced in direction. For example, despite a lot of hard work by Air Canada, the movement of air cargo from the St. Lawrence Lowlands to Western Canada is much heavier than in the reverse direction.

For years cargo capacity was far in excess of demand. Up to a point this was inevitable because it took time to build up a paying volume of traffic. Moreover, the chief selling point of air cargo is speed in delivery. This advantage is partly nullified if flights depart every second or third day. Airlines used advertising, salesmen, and reductions in rates to fill space that would otherwise be empty. Frequently, these efforts eased but did not solve the problem. Completion of the DEW line left many companies with surplus equipment which was either scrapped—for many old aircraft had been hastily rounded up to get a defence job done in a hurry—or sold abroad, sometimes for more than the undepreciated value of the aircraft, to countries whose travellers are less concerned with comfort than Canadians. The possibility of making sales outside Canada at a good price is rapidly disappearing, for the introduction of jet aircraft has thrown large numbers of semi-obsolete piston-driven planes on the market. Yet, taking one thing with another, the problem of excess capacity is becoming less serious. By the early 1960s the volume of cargo was increasing at roughly 16 per cent annually, i.e., doubling every five years, which compared with an average rate of about 10 per cent annually, or doubling every seven years, in the 1950s.

Air Mail

In the development of civil aviation the Post Office has played an important role. The benefits of speedy communication are obvious to everyone. Hence nearly every country at one time or another has used compensation to airlines for carrying mail as a means of subsidizing commercial aviation. Especially in aviation's infancy, air mail pay was a large proportion of the industry's gross revenue. Postal needs, real or alleged, have sometimes been connected with military activity.

In Canada the Post Office had authorized some experimental flights with air mail in the early 1920s and planned extensions as conditions warranted. In 1927 it inaugurated a regular service from Montreal to Rimouski, Que., where planes contacted trans-Atlantic steamships picking up and delivery overseas mail and saving from 24 to 48 hours time. It also arranged to have mail flown into isolated communities such as the Magdalen Islands, Sept Iles, and Red Lake. Later in the decade air mail was carried into other centres not conveniently reached by surface transport and also between urban communities such as Toronto and Montreal, Vancouver, Victoria and Seattle, and so on. Many of these services were curtailed during the depression but after 1935 they expanded again owing to the mining boom in the North and the establishment of Trans-Canada Air Lines.

On some of the early routes air mail was paid for by the sale of special stickers for the envelope. The entire revenue from these stickers went to the airline operator with the Post Office getting the regular surface rate for sorting, pick-up and delivery at origin and destination. Soon the Post Office began to sell air mail stamps, retain the revenue from their sale, and remunerate the airline operators on a poundage or plane-mile basis. In 1930 it paid $12.61 per pound of mail for the approximately 300 air-miles between Toronto and Montreal and $2.47 for the 100 miles from Montreal to Ottawa. The Post Office believed that on practically every route cost of operation exceeded revenue.

In the course of time air mail grew in popularity, at first slowly and then very rapidly when Trans-Canada gave regular inter-urban and transcontinental service. The Post Office benefited more than carriers from this growth in volume because under many contracts it paid the same rate for any weight up to one or two hundred pounds. An increase in the number of letters raised Post Office revenue without a proportionate increase in mail compensation paid to airlines.

In the late 1930s keen competition between small operators slashed air mail payments. In 1939 the "bush" air mail rate varied from 2.5 to 13.8 cents per plane-mile. In the same year Trans-Canada got 60 cents per mile and Prairie Airways 40 cents. The Post Office was accused of discriminating against northern operators and favouring the government-owned company. In 1940 the government was criticized for arbitrarily cutting Trans-Canada's compensation because it forecast a surplus on operations in the next year. There were also suggestions that the government should use the Post Office to assist northern development, particularly since many small companies were in financial difficulties.

Beginning in April, 1946, Trans-Canada's compensation was changed from a plane-mile to a pound-mile basis. After the war the Company's passenger business expanded rapidly and it was anxious to increase the number of its flights. The Post Office was against this expansion since it would be called upon to make additional payments for transporting substantially the same quantity of mail. As the Postmaster-General would not approve additional flights if the Post Office were thereby put to additional expense, Trans-Canada claimed that payment per plane-mile was inhibiting it from developing its passenger traffic. Conpensation by pound-miles got round this difficulty. The new rates compared favourably with those paid transcontinental air lines by the United States.

Contracts of the Post Office with Trans-Canada differ from those with pioneer operators. Up to July 1, 1948, all mail carried by Trans-Canada was surcharged. The sender paid 3 cents per ounce above the regular postal rate for surface mail. In some "bush" services air mail had to be surcharged and mail with only regular postage affixed was sent by railway, dog team, or steamship along inland or coastal waters. In other cases all first class mail went by air whether surcharged or not, while the lower classes went by surface carrier. In a few instances all mail including letters, newspapers, and parcel post was flown in without extra charge. This was done when the compensation paid airlines was less than what would have been charged by surface agencies owing to the difficult terrain and circuitous routes over which they would have to operate. Since July, 1948, all first class mail posted in Canada for another place in Canada is sent by air whenever the airlines have space to accommodate it and time is saved. In order to ensure that letters will actually go by air senders may affix air mail stamps. With the inauguration of the all-up service, the basis of compensation was changed, first, to a lump sum per month ($450,000 monthly in 1950), and then to a progressively descending scale of rates per ton-mile as the volume of air mail traffic increased. This arrangement covered air parcel post as well as air mail, that is, letters sent by air. Air Canada's average receipts per ton-mile from the air service declined from $2.03 per ton-mile in 1948 to 86 cents in 1960. Although these returns are higher than on air express and air freight, the conditions of transport are not identical. A few feeder services are still paid by the plane-mile but most are on a pound-mile or ton-mile rate.

These contracts are negotiated between the Post Office and the carrier concerned. Some of the factors considered are the potential postal revenue of the route, speed and frequency of service, the amount of the airline's non-mail revenue, profits of the carrier, and rate of remuneration on comparable routes elsewhere in Canada. Unlike the Civil Aeronautics Board in the United States, the Canadian Transport Commission has no jurisdiction over these matters.

Arriving at a correct figure for air mail compensation is intrinsically difficult. Mail is carried under conditions of joint cost. There is no practicable method of breaking down the total costs of operating an airline between passengers, express, and mail. Mail occupies relatively little space per pound. Usually it can be stowed in out of the way places, inconvenient for passengers. It does not require luxurious accommodation, pressurized cabins, or terminal space at airports. Aside entirely from cost of service, one must consider the effect of tolls on the volume of mail traffic.

The whole matter may be considered from the standpoint of postal receipts and expenditures. Here again, joint cost and value of service enter in. Some expenses are incurred in common for air mail, ordinary first class mail, newspapers, and parcel post. These expenses include picking up mail from street boxes or suburban post offices, sorting it in originating and terminal offices, delivering it to homes and offices, and perhaps carrying it for part of its journey by surface agency. Office expenses, like handling money orders and operating the postal savings bank, are often inextricably intertwined with those of handling mail as such. Because few letters weigh exactly one ounce each and the postal rate is a flat one for letters up to this weight, Post Office revenue per pound of air mail ranged from less than $3 to over $4 (at the air mail rate of 7 cents per letter). When compensation to airlines is by plane-mile, more letters bring the Postal Office more revenue but may not involve it in any extra expense except for services on the ground.

The Post Office charges the public the same rate regardless of distance,[5] while its payments to carriers often include a mileage element. As a result, movements of air mail for distances up to possibly 300 miles may be profitable but long hauls, especially when mail goes without surcharge, may lose heavily. Further, the element of public welfare cannot be overlooked. It is universally recognized that all parts of a country are entitled to good mail service even if it has to be conducted at a substantial loss. For this reason the Post Office cannot run on strictly business principles. It does not pay interest, depreciation, and maintenance on the buildings which it uses. These are provided for it without charge by the Department of Public Works. On the other hand, until 1949 it kept no record of the enormous quantity of mail which it received and delivered for other departments of government. In short, it is impossible accurately to determine by how much, if at all, what the Post Office pays the airlines for carrying mail exceeds what it receives from the public, net after covering various expenses on the ground.

The complex problems of air mail pay have tended to recede as the non-mail revenues of the carriers have grown. In the twenties and thirties carriers depended so heavily on air mail compensation) for their bread and butter that the cost to them of handling this traffic or, alternatively, what the Post Office could afford to pay them for services rendered, was vital. With the rapid growth of their passenger and express business, mail revenue has become a small part of total receipts.§ At times, when planes were smaller than they are today, the volume of mail was so large that passengers, a better paying type of traffic, had to be displaced and operators complained, as did the disappointed passengers. Airlines may have to schedule flights to meet the requirements of the postal service, even though a different hour of departure or arrival might be more convenient for passengers or for shippers and consignees of air cargo. In other words, the carriage of mail may reduce revenue from other sources and so it should bear a higher rate per ton-mile than property other than mail. On many flights, the Post Office reserves so much space in the aircraft even though it may not use all this space every day. Though the rate is quoted in terms of ton-miles, the actual tonnage of mail carried and hence the ton-miles actually performed, may differ from the ton-miles which are reserved and paid for. There are, in brief, several differences in the conditions of the transportation of air mail and air express. Even so, the establishment of air express services, for which the airlines themselves set the tolls, subject to filing with the Air Transport Board, has given the Post Office a chance to judge the reasonableness of air mail compensation by reference to kinds of traffic with somewhat similar costs. The use of the ton-mile basis has simplified comparisons between the various Canadian and United States lines. The cost of airports and navigational aids has increased relatively to that of actually operating airlines and so the direct subsidy for ground facilities far outweighs the concealed subsidy, if any, in mail pay. Though still important, air mail compensation has ceased to be the burning question it was in the early 1940s.

Future of Air Services

The outlook for Canada's airlines depends on the rate of growth in traffic, the speed and costliness of technological change, and government policy. A comparison of passenger-miles in Canada and the United States shows that the average Canadian travels only about half as many miles per annum as the average American.[7] The difference is accounted for largely by the greater use of the private passenger car in the United States and thus is a reflection of better driving conditions throughout the year, lower initial cost of automobiles, and the somewhat lower price of gasoline. Other factors affecting the amount of travel include Gross National Product per capita, the amount of consumer disposable income and its distribution among various classes, and the distance between large urban centres. The chief explanation, however, lies in the propensity to travel, the urge to be "on the go," which varies from one country to the other, and even within the same country, for reasons which are hard to find.

Aside from these general considerations which influence travel by all media, the volume of air travel in Canada is held down by the distribution of population. About 60 per cent of all Canadians live in the area between Quebec City and Windsor, which is an airline distance of about 600 miles. This is long enough for flying to be economical both for travellers in terms of time saved and for an airline in terms of economy of operation. Unfortunately, the community of interest between Quebec and Windsor is not nearly as great as between many other cities in the St. Lawrence Lowlands. The number of commercial and social contacts increases as the distance shortens, but expenses increase on short flights, as pointed out earlier. By comparison, the United States has many large nodes of population—in New York, southern New England, and Pennsylvania, and at Detroit, Chicago, New Orleans, Seattle, San Francisco, Los Angeles, and so on. The size and prosperity of these cities and the distances between them favour air travel. Canadian cities outside the St. Lawrence Lowlands are advantageously located as far as transportation by air is concerned but are much smaller than their counterparts in the United States. Also, there are language and cultural hurdles to travel in Canada which do not exist south of the border. The attractions of winter resorts in California and Florida are clearly significant.

Despite these limitations, (the volume of travel by air in Canada is growing at about the same rate (roughly 15 per cent per annum) as in the United States and forms about the same proportion of the total passenger-miles by all modes of transport. The annual rate of increase means doubling every five years and obviously cannot be sustained indefinitely. If it were, the day would come when everyone would spend all his time flying. Even so, there is still a large market to be tapped, especially if fares can be reduced.

Similarly, the potentialities of air cargo are huge, provided rates are cut. In its early years the traffic was confined to valuable or perishable articles, to emergency shipments of repair parts, and to movements where surface transport was slow and even more expensive than air. In the late 1950s traffic solicitors (salesmen) began to stress how a firm could save money by establishing a central warehouse for repair parts and finished articles, use airplanes to deliver these goods to almost any place in Canada overnight or within a day or two, and thereby reduce charges for storage and interest. Total investment is cut down because new machines or parts may be readily delivered anywhere in Canada.

(The key to the expansion of air cargo is lower rates brought about by technological change.) Some of these changes are individually small, e.g., the use of pallets and fork-lift trucks for loading and unloading. Others are more spectacular like Canadair's CL-44, an all-cargo aircraft with a swing-tail. This allows cargo to be handled through a wide doorway about the same elevation above the ground as the floor of a truck. In older planes, loading had to be done through a narrow entrance in the side of the fuselage and well above the ground. The door sill often sloped downward, and long articles had to be twisted round to get them inside the plane.

(The other important source of revenue, air mail, has only modest possibilities. This is because so much mail consists of newspapers, advertisements, mail order catalogues, and magazines which are charged such low rates per pound that the Post Office cannot afford to send them by air, though it may do so as a public service to very remote offices. (First class letters, which pay better from the postal point of view, have to meet competition from long distance telephone calls, teletypewriters, and telex. At all events, air mail compensation is now a small part of the total revenues of most airlines.)

On the side of supply, commercial aviation is being revolutionized by the "jet age." In the first place, capital investment must be enormously increased. Broadly speaking, a North Star ($700,000), which Trans-Canada Air Lines adopted after World War II, cost about six times as much as a DC-3, which the Company used when it began operations in 1939. A Super-Constellation (1954) cost three times as much as a North Star, and a jet-propelled DC-8 (used on flights of over 500 miles by 1961) cost nearly $6 million (including sales tax but not spare parts) or three times as much as a Super-Constellation. In 1958 the Company began construction at Montreal of a large maintenance base for the new planes which, together with additional hangar facilities at other stations, cost about $25 million. All in all, Air Canada's total investment in property and equipment, which was $30.4 million in 1948, rose to about $100 million in 1957, and exceeded $300 million in 1964. Moreover, the Company expects that it will have sooner or later to invest upwards of $1 billion in supersonic aircraft. Whenever radically new aircraft are acquired, large sums have to be spent on training men to service the "ships" and on familiarizing air crew with their operation.

On account of their larger size and greater speed, the new jet-turbined fleet had a carrying capacity far in excess of piston-engined aircraft formerly in service. A Lockheed or DC-3 could cruise at roughly 200 miles per hour, a North Star at 225, a Super-Constellation at 310, while a DC-8 cruises at 550. Air Canada, which flew about one billion available seat-miles in 1953 and 1.96 billion in 1957, provided roughly 6.6 billion in 1966. In brief, in the early 1960s civil aviation entered a new world of technology and economics. The next series of revolutionary changes will be associated with supersonic aircraft which fly 750 miles per hour or better.

Air Canada

Whatever the future may hold for airlines in general, each company will have to work out its own destiny. For Canadians this means consideration, first, of the history and prospects of Air Canada (called Trans-Canada Air Lines before 1964), Canadian Pacific Air Lines, and the regional carriers, and second, of government policy on competition.

After 1935 Canadians, while taking pride in their accomplishments in bush flying, became concerned over the lack of a transcontinental or main-line service within Canada. Scheduled air operations in the United States and Europe were proceeding apace. It was relatively easy for Canadians to go by rail, by motor car, and even by air from Montreal, Toronto, Winnipeg, and Vancouver to the United States. Thence they could fly to parts of Canada, the United States, and overseas via American carriers. Many Canadians feared that unless the

Dominion acted quickly, the channels of travel would become set in favour of American companies and Canada would be precluded from ever having its own transcontinental and international airline.

Furthermore, American interests were already offering to operate a trans-Canada service. This was objectionable on nationalistic grounds. The American lobby in Ottawa was so aggressive that the government was reluctant to deal with it. In 1938 Canada agreed with the United Kingdom and Eire (now the Republic of Ireland) to establish a trans-Atlantic air transport company as part of an all-British route around the world. Canada obligated herself to participate in the trans-oceanic service and to operate across her own territory. The government was vitally interested in civil aviation because of its obvious influence on national defence, the carriage of mails, and Canadian progress generally.

Early in 1936 the government urged private airline operators in Canada to organize a transcontinental service. Apparently these firms could not see how they could raise the necessary capital without direct government assistance. Then the government approached the two major railways and Canadian Airways, the strongest of the air transport companies. The Dominion undertook to build the necessary airports and communication system. The aviation company was to be run on a non-profit basis but the government would guarantee it against loss. Each of the three component companies was to name two directors on the Board. The government was to appoint three directors because it would underwrite the losses.

Both the Canadian Pacific and Canadian Airways rejected the government's proposal.[8] They could see no essential difference between directors representing the government and those nominated by the government-owned railway. In effect, five of the nine directors would be government appointees although the Canadian National and the government together contributed only one-third of the money. Canadian Airways may have foreseen difficulties in raising its share of the funds.

In the end the government set up Trans-Canada Air Lines as a subsidiary of Canadian National Railways. In the course of time the Air Line has become a separate entity for all practical purposes. It submits annual reports to Parliament and its executives are examined by the House of Commons Committee on Railways, Airlines and Shipping. Its policies are also reviewed in the House itself, in the Cabinet, and in the Department of Transport. Thus, its performance and plans are gone over in a far more thorough manner than is ever done by shareholders in a privately-owned company.

Trans-Canada Air Lines officially came into being in May, 1937.[9]

Men thoroughly experienced in commercial aviation in the United States were placed in charge of operations and technical services but Canadians took over these responsibilities a year or so later. The new company made use of the accounting, advertising, legal, purchasing, secretary's, and treasury departments of its parent, the Canadian National, and then gradually cut free. Training flights began in 1938 but in April, 1939, regular passenger service from Vancouver and Edmonton via Lethbridge to Toronto and Montreal was inaugurated. By mid-1940 the company had, roughly speaking, completed its original programme. Its planes flew daily from Vancouver to Moncton, N.B., and several times a day between Toronto, Ottawa, and Montreal, as well as regularly between Toronto, London, and Windsor, Ont.

After only three years of operations, Trans-Canada earned a surplus. This was due to the steady extension of its routes, the boom in passenger traffic during the war, and the spectacular growth in domestic and overseas mail. Some criticism was made that the surpluses were derived from excessive payments by the Post Office for carrying air mail. Furthermore, Trans-Canada did not pay more than a pittance for the use it made of airports, aids to navigation, and public weather information. In this respect it was in the same position as other companies engaged in commercial aviation throughout the world at that time.

In the immediate postwar period, Trans-Canada ran deficits because of rising wages and material prices, shortage of some equipment, and the establishment of new routes and additional flights in anticipation of increased business which did not develop as quickly as hoped for. Later the company obtained new aircraft, the North Stars, which could be operated more economically and had larger seating capacities than the original fleet of Lockheeds.[10] Soon the company was again on its way to profitable operation of domestic services. In the 1950s Trans-Canada had surpluses which, however, did not aggregate much more than the cost of a single jet-propelled aircraft. In judging this company's profitability, one should bear in mind that a much larger proportion of its total capitalization is represented by bonds than is the case with privately-owned concerns. In the early 1960s the company failed to earn all its interest charges because of the costliness of jet aircraft and competition with Canadian Pacific Air Lines. Fortunately, by 1964 Air Canada had recovered to such an extent that it was able not only to earn all its operating expenses and interest on bonded debt but to declare a dividend of 3 per cent on its shares which are held by Canadian National Railways on behalf of the government.

Air Canada has the Canadian share of trans-border flights (between Canada and the United States) except the one between Vancouver and San Francisco. It also flies the most important route across the North Atlantic (Canada to London), and has several flights in what it calls Southern Service (to Florida, Bermuda, and the British West Indies). In 1966 it became the first carrier in North America to schedule direct flights between this continent and Soviet Russia. Although Canadian Pacific Air Lines serves the Orient, Australia, Mexico, San Francisco, Amsterdam, etc., it is fair to say that Air Canada has the primary responsibility for external services in Canada's name.

The problems of Air Canada are both numerous and complex. They include working out a fairly equitable arrangement between publicly and privately owned companies, the uncertainty that often overhangs all airline operations, technical difficulties still to be overcome, heavy seasonal fluctuations in traffic, and other aspects of the industrial environment in which civil aviation functions. In a rapidly changing, highly competitive *milieu*, a company can expect continuously to be presented with difficulties and uncertainties. On the whole Canadians are satisfied with their publicly owned airline. The company is efficiently operated, though in 1958 in the emotional atmosphere surrounding the application for a competitive air service, Canadian Pacific Air Lines made sweeping criticisms of Trans-Canada's operating costs. A British expert engaged by the Department of Transport concluded that the mistakes made by Trans-Canada's employees were no more numerous or more serious than errors made on airlines in the United States and Europe. Though faced with many problems, Air Canada has been a success.

Canadian Pacific Air Lines

Canadian civil aviation has also been developing rapidly in Northern Canada. Having survived the boom of the late twenties, the depression of the early thirties, and the second boom which occurred from 1933 to 1937, bush flyers entered the war period in a muddled condition of affairs. They had hoped that the liberal provision of the government toward physical facilities, meteorological services, and air mail compensation on the transcontinental route would presage more assistance to non-scheduled operators. When the expected aid was not forthcoming, they blamed the government. They considered that they could handle some governmental air activities, notably forest fire patrols and aerial photography, more cheaply than the Air Force. They were discontented over the government's tardiness in regulating air routes and fares. Later they complained of long delays in applying the regulations to particular companies and areas. Until the regulative machinery was working smoothly, companies could not get protection against competitors invading their territory. Until their earnings became larger and more stable, they could not raise capital.

Fundamentally bush flyers were suffering from declining business. A new mining field being opened up in an isolated area creates paying traffic by air both of men and equipment. The majority of the "strikes" do not amount to anything. The "prospects" which do produce gold use surface transport as quickly as they can. Thus, northern flying, like the mining industry on which it so largely depends, is a "boom-and-bust" economy. An aviation company can hope for fairly steady prosperity only if it is able to shift equipment and personnel from declining to expanding mining fields. But just prior to 1939 the number of air transport companies was large while the mining industry as a whole was ceasing rapidly to expand its operations. Hence no company could save itself by going elsewhere. Bush flying was characterized by bitter competition and rate cutting. In an effort to stabilize the industry, the various firms formed a separate jointly owned company to divide up the business. This arrangement was only moderately successful and may have contravened the anti-trust laws.

During 1940 traffic declined even more than in the previous two years. Prospecting and gold mining shrank owing to the shortage of labour and the impossibility of raising venture capital. Gold mines which were large producers kept operating during the war because Canada was in urgent need of United States dollars and exporting gold was an easy way of obtaining them. Producing gold mines were generally able to use surface transport whereas "prospects" were dependent on air. Flying and ground personnel were attracted to the Air Force or to war industry. Later carriers were unable to get priorities on aircraft repair parts so that planes were often in danger of being grounded. Neither the government, which was preoccupied with the war, nor the numerous independent operators seemed competent to handle the difficulties confronting the industry. At the same time everyone realized that these operators had made a significant contribution to Canada's development in the past and their potential value in the post-war economy was tremendous.

The opportunity of performing a national service and sharing in what in the long run promised to become a profitable enterprise was seized by the Canadian Pacific Railway. For over ten years it had been financially interested in Canadian Airways, the largest privately owned airline in Canada, and in three other operators. Thus it was relatively easy for the Railway to buy up most of the bush flyers.[11] In 1942 it amalgamated all its aviation interests into a single subsidiary, Canadian

Pacific Air Lines (C.P.A.L.).

The Railway expected that the new concern could operate at lower costs than its predecessors. It would eliminate duplicate service, get better facilities for repairing aircraft, standardize equipment, reduce the number of planes needed in reserve, and use the skill and experience of certain departments of the Railway. It also hoped to obtain higher rates and fares. With its large financial resources, the Canadian Pacific could provide better equipment as soon as it was available after the war. In particular, it could afford to wait for profits until the anticipated post-war boom in mining materialized.

Moreover, the Railway seemed to feel that the airplane might eventually replace ships and pullmans. It intimated that it might substitute aircraft for the ocean-going steamships which the enemy had sunk. It probably felt too that it must take part in civil aviation in order to meet the competition of the Canadian National and its airline affiliate effectively.

The timing of the purchase was excellent. Canadian Pacific fell heir to some war contracts of its member companies. It ran schools of instruction and did overhaul work for the British Commonwealth Air Training Plan. Owing to high business activity, its planes were fully loaded with passengers and express at most seasons of the year. Extra flights were added as soon as equipment and personnel were available. The work of building aluminum and hydro-electric plants on the Saguenay River and the rapid growth of the port of Chicoutimi called for daily service from Montreal and Quebec City to the Lake St. John district. The task of constructing the Alaska Highway and the pipeline from Norman Wells to Whitehorse and of exploiting the petroleum and uranium resources in the Mackenzie basin, in addition to the purely military activity in Alaska and the Canadian North, enormously increased the company's northern business.

Canadian Pacific Air Lines was able to secure some craft by reducing or eliminating services to some mining centres and by acquiring planes on top priority from the United States. It watched operating expenses closely and increased or stabilized rates and fares. By 1944 it was so thriving that it planned twenty new routes within Canada besides international and trans-oceanic services. The internal routes which it was already flying or had in mind were so arranged that when the time was opportune the airline would need to fill in but a few gaps to have a transcontinental service. Further, it had obtained through the United States Army for use along the route of the Alaska Highway, planes which no other commercial airline could get. This equipment, or the older planes which it would release, might be used elsewhere. In a word, Canadian Pacific Air Lines was challenging Trans-Canada.

In order to deal with these new problems the government decided first, that surface carriers should divest themselves of their air affiliates within one year of the end of the war in Europe and second, that a new body should be set up to carry out the government's air policy. Hence in 1944 the Transport Act was amended to cancel the jurisdiction of the Board of Transport Commissioners over civil aviation,[12] and the Aeronautics Act was changed to include the divestment order and to set up an Air Transport Board.[13]

Under the new policy Canadian Pacific Air Lines concentrated on building up its existing services in the hope of getting a good price for them in what amounted to a forced sale. After the government lifted the divestment order insofar as it applied to the two railways, Canadian Pacific Air Lines expanded cautiously, especially on trans-Pacific routes. In 1955, however, it proposed operating an air freight service between Vancouver, Edmonton, The Pas, Toronto, and Montreal. This scheme was approved by the Air Transport Board and then came before the Cabinet which alone had the power to permit an airline, which was owned by a railway, to violate the divestment order any further. After hearing argument by counsel of both Trans-Canada and Canadian Pacific Air Lines, the Cabinet refused the latter's application because it believed that the prospective volume of traffic was not sufficiently large to justify the virtual duplication of air services over the route. Later on, in 1958, C.P.A.L. got the right to fly once daily each way across Canada, as will be described shortly.

For many years Canadian Pacific Air Lines operated at heavy losses, in one year over $4 million, which the parent Railway had to assume. The head office and base for major repairs are in Vancouver, rather remote from the main centres of North American commerce. The company disposed of some routes, e.g., in Quebec and out of Winnipeg and Kenora, which had good potentials as regional carriers and it voluntarily took on overseas routes which have low traffic densities. The author's own view is that this Air Line turned down its greatest opportunity to contribute to Canadian progress when it withdrew from most of its north-south routes, but executives of the Canadian Pacific Railway and Air Lines were not content to serve as feeders to Trans-Canada Air Lines or to Air Canada. Hence, Canadian Pacific Air Lines has steadily pressed for what it claims would be a fair share in the big market between Canada's major cities. In 1958 it got the right to make one flight daily each way between Vancouver, Toronto, and Montreal. In 1967 the government announced that Canadian Pacific Air Lines could expand its services over the transcontinental route provided that by 1970 it did not take more than 25 per cent of the traffic. Meanwhile, starting in 1964, the Air Line was making money.

Regional Carriers

Besides the two major airlines under the Canadian flag, there are (a) five so-called regional or independent air carriers licensed to operate scheduled commercial air services within Canada, and (b) several other companies performing a variety of jobs, none of them on regular schedule.

One regional airline, Eastern Provincial (called Maritime Central up to 1963) serves the four Atlantic Provinces, the Magdalen Islands, St. Pierre et Miquelon, Sept Iles, Labrador, and the Eastern Arctic. Quebecair with headquarters at Rimouski operates along the St. Lawrence River between Sept Iles and Montreal and northward to Wabush and Schefferville (Knob Lake). TransAir flies from its bases at Winnipeg and Churchill into adjacent parts of Ontario, Minnesota, and the Northwest Territories as well as throughout northern Manitoba. Between 1947 and 1965 the Saskatchewan government ran its own airline, Saskair, into the northern part of the province. Then it sold its assets to a group of businessmen in Prince Albert and La Ronge, who organized North Canada Air, Ltd., popularly known as NorCan. Finally, Pacific Western Airlines, Limited, provides local services within British Columbia, the Yukon, and parts of Alberta, Saskatchewan, and the Northwest Territories.

These independent airlines have frequently experienced financial losses for they are obviously dependent on the rate of development in Northern Canada, including the construction and servicing of defence installations. But even in more thickly settled regions they have had losses. For instance, when Air Canada converted to jets, it was anxious to get rid of its route, commonly called the milk run, which provided local service between Winnipeg, Saskatoon, North Battleford, Edmonton, Regina, Swift Current, Medicine Hat, and Calgary. The flights or "hops" along this route are too short for the economical operations of jets or even turbo-prop planes. Experience proves that a company can operate a repair base more cheaply if it concentrates on one type of aircraft rather than keep machinery, spare parts, and skilled men for repairing several kinds. Then too, a locally based airline is usually able to keep more closely in touch with the needs of its market than one whose main energies are directed toward its transcontinental and international routes. Therefore, in 1963 Air Canada sold its planes and other assets used in servicing the milk run to TransAir for $500,000.

Although at the time Air Canada was accused of disposing of assets belonging to the people of Canada for perhaps half their true value, events proved the reverse. Prior to the takeover of the route, traffic had started to fall off to a degree not realized by either Air Canada or TransAir. The basic trouble was that in October, 1963, the railways reduced some of their fares by more than half. They were offering transportation at fares between 1.7 and 2.5 cents per passenger-mile, or less than one-third the amount at which an airline with a reasonable load factor could operate profitably. TransAir presented exhaustive evidence to the Air Transport Board showing how, on the one hand, it had tried to stimulate traffic by lowering fares, changing schedules, and advertising, and how, on the other, it had pared its costs. When it applied in 1964 to abandon the southern leg of its route west of Regina, no one seriously questioned that TransAir had done its best to make the route a success. The only counter-arguments were, first, that the trial period had been too short to constitute a fair test of the route, and second, that the under-valuation of $500,000 on assets sold by Air Canada to TransAir constituted a sort of subsidy that would offset operating losses until the line could be put on a paying basis. The Air Transport Board ruled that it had no legal authority to investigate the adequacy or otherwise of the consideration made under a contract freely entered into by two airlines and that, even if the facts were as alleged, it could not justifiably order a company to continue operating services which were losing $150,000 a year. The Board added that other Prairie services were also losing money though not to the same extent. Indeed, in 1962 Pacific Western had been allowed to discontinue its service between Saskatoon, North Battleford, and Prince Albert.

The difficulties of supplying local air services have not been confined to the Prairies. Kingston, Peterborough, Hamilton, Kitchener, Sarnia, and probably other places in Southern Ontario would like to "get themselves on the air map." For two or three years in the early 1960s Nordair flew a scheduled service between these places. It gave up after losing a lot of money. Operating costs over short hops were heavy and the volume of traffic was small and erratic. In addition, the authorities had to take care that Nordair did not handle passengers in direct competition with Trans-Canada, e.g., between Montreal and Toronto via Kingston, or Toronto and London, which was a point of call for aircraft of Nordair to and from Sarnia.

The Dominion government has the legal power to subsidize local air services but is unwilling to be drawn into spending a lot of money for the benefit of relatively few travellers. It has designed a formula which provides an incentive to the carrier to develop more traffic and become more efficient. Subsidies are paid only on services to remote areas where surface transport is inadequate, where air services are essential to promote development, where regular operations by air appear to have good chances of future success, and where the government can avoid higher expenditures on alternative transport. Regional carriers may not become directly competitive with either Air Canada or Canadian Pacific Air Lines but some incidental competition may be allowed. Although some mainline routes may, in time, be transferred to regional carriers, the government does not envisage any wholesale transfers. In 1967 the government authorized regional carriers to make chartered flights along some of the routes normally reserved to Air Canada. The Minister of Transport emphasized that regional airlines were expected to operate without subsidies, that the two major airlines had an obligation to assist the regional operators by supplying them with technical advice and publishing joint fares, and that, in general, regional and main line operators should co-operate in providing every section of the Dominion with air services which can be justified economically. As a result, government subsidies will be minimized and regional airlines will have a good chance to be commercially viable.

Non-scheduled Operators

In addition to scheduled flights for passengers, mail, and express, the regional airlines are prepared to carry freight between any two points within their region whenever a profitable volume is offered and it is safe to take off and land a plane. For this sort of traffic they have to compete with what the Department of Transport calls (*a*) regular specific point air services—operated by air carriers who offer public transportation of persons, mail, or goods by aircraft serving designated points on a route pattern and with some degree of regularity, at a toll per unit, (*b*) irregular specific point air services—similar to the above, except that the service is to either a defined area or a specific point or points and is not on regular schedule, (*c*) charter air services, which briefly means that the entire aircraft is engaged by one shipper or by a party of persons travelling as a group, and (*d*) contract air services, which differ from all the above in that the air carriers do not offer transportation to the public at large but carry persons or property or both in accordance with one or more specific contracts. In order to prevent unfair competition between scheduled and non-scheduled operations, the Air Transport Board controls the rates of charter air services but not of the other services listed. Several companies, notably Wheeler, do the sort of work described in this paragraph. More specifically, they carry freight, fly sportsmen to and from places suitable for fishing, hunting, and skiing, do aerial photography and surveying, and dust crops with insecticides, fungicides, and weed-killers.

Divestment

Government activity in civil aviation takes numerous forms: certification of pilots, licensing aircraft, building and operating airports, providing weather information, and most important of all deciding how much competition will be allowed. When the government set up Trans-Canada Air Lines, it assumed that the supplementary or feeder services would be operated by a number of independent companies. When Canadian Pacific Air Lines came into existence, the government apparently thought it would never be more than the strongest of the regional carriers. One reason for this view was that the parent Railway had turned down the government's offer to participate in the new main line or trunk service. Consequently, the government was surprised and perhaps annoyed when it became clear that Canadian Pacific Air Lines was about to challenge the publicly owned company along the transcontinental route.

As explained, the divestment order of 1944 required that surface carriers get rid of their air affiliates within one year after the end of the war in Europe. One effect of this policy would have been to deprive Canadian Pacific Air Lines of the financial support of its parent and necessitate sale of the airline. The government hoped that it would go to small operators, preferably to war veterans. Above all, the government wanted to avoid the evils of excessive competition which had been so evident between railways in the 1930s. It believed that Canada's population and the volume of traffic likely to go by air were both far too small to justify creating more than one main-line service across the country or along external routes.

The divestment order was sharply criticized.[14] Because it applied to all surface carriers, it would prevent Gray Coach Lines, a well-financed, efficiently operated bus company, from carrying out its intention of operating helicopters over short distances. Divestment was contrary to the government's policy included in the Transport Act of 1938 directing the Board of Transport Commissioners to co-ordinate various transport agencies so far as it was possible to do so. The divorce of air and surface carriers would add to the costs of the former—an increase in expenses which they could not stand—by forcing them to set up their own legal, advertising, and other departments instead of using those of their parent railways as before. It would deny them the benefit of the long experience of surface carriers in traffic solicitation. While the policy in the United States was completely to separate air and surface carriers, in 1944 that policy was under attack. Most of all, the divestment order was alleged to be a device to throttle the legitimate ambitions of the Canadian Pacific, give unfair advantage to Trans-Canada, and deal an indirect blow to private enterprise. Finally, it was unreasonable to expect returning veterans to have sufficient money to start an airline or keep it in operation long enough to build up a profitable business.

In 1946, the government postponed the effective date of the divestment order for an additional year and later cancelled it as far as the Canadian Pacific and the Canadian National were concerned. The government explained that at the time the order was made the public was not getting the service it deserved.[15] Relations between the government and Canadian Pacific Air Lines were far from satisfactory. The non-competitive position of Trans-Canada was being challenged. The government thought it would be easy to divide up Canadian Pacific Air Lines and return it to small operators. The great expansion of air activity in the North which was anticipated after the war would require additional services. Whereas formerly Canadian Pacific Air Lines was ambitious to extend its operations to other parts of Canada, it now found that it had ample work in developing the regions in which it was already operating. The management of the company had changed and its new officials were co-operating closely with the Air Transport Board. Other airlines which cared to enter the business and were able to raise capital could find scope for their activities in parts of the Dominion not then served. In short, the divestment policy was abandoned because of changed conditions.

Airline Competition

Prior to 1958 Trans-Canada Air Lines was often accused of having a monopoly. This was a half-truth because it competed with Québecair for traffic between Montreal and Sept Iles, with American air carriers on the two most important trans-border routes (Montreal–New York, and Toronto–New York), with Canadian Pacific Air Lines (later with Pacific Western) in parts of the West, and indirectly with numerous companies flying out of New York on the trans-Atlantic route. All the same, Trans-Canada had the only service connecting the country's major cities. It is fair to say that some of the changes of monopoly emanated from those who had an ingrained prejudice against public ownership and whose theories were upset by Trans-Canada's annual profits. Yet it should also be stressed that many Canadians sincerely believed that competition would improve the quality of air service without adding, and perhaps even reducing, the overall cost to the economy.

By the early 1950s both major political parties said they favoured airline competition. In 1952 a Liberal Minister of Transport said the government was considering allowing competition along a few routes. His Conservative successor stated in 1958 that it was time to introduce some measure of competition on transcontinental routes. The rapid growth of airline traffic seemed to indicate that competition could be introduced gradually, without major detrimental effects to existing operations. Accordingly, he engaged Stephen F. Wheatcroft, an English aviation economist, to report upon the desirability of such competition.

In his report Mr. Wheatcroft dealt with the efficiency of Trans-Canada Air Lines, airline competition in the United States, and the probable effect of the gradual introduction of competition on the net revenues of the existing transcontinental carrier. On the first point, he criticized the company for not providing sufficient capacity in the past to meet traffic demand on many major routes. But in the future it planned to reduce its average load factor so that its capacity ought to be adequate at all times except for the highest peak of demand. It had delayed ordering new aircraft in the early 1950s because its executives rightly thought that more efficient planes would be available in two or three years. The public may have benefited in the long run from this delay but meanwhile it had been deprived of some air service and some tourist fares which it had a right to expect. Mr. Wheatcroft gave the company almost full marks for scheduling, that is, for planning times of departure and arrival to meet the convenience of travellers, shippers of air express, and the Post Office. As soon as justified by the volume of traffic, it had introduced direct flights, e.g., one between Toronto and Edmonton without an intermediate stop at Winnipeg as before.

Trans-Canada had been subjected to a vast amount of criticism for alleged inefficiencies in making reservations and in handling baggage. Mr. Wheatcroft recognized that some of these complaints were justified. All airlines made mistakes. There was no evidence that Trans-Canada made more mistakes than other airlines. In Wheatcroft's view, there could "be little doubt that a major reason for the undue degree of public criticism to which TCA has been subjected is that passengers with small grievances have magnified these into major complaints because they do not have the normal redress of taking their custom elsewhere. . . . Competitive operations, in other words, might well make the public more appreciative of the service provided by TCA."[16]

Trans-Canada's efficiency was the result of an internal tradition that it had a special responsibility as the national airline. It faced both direct and indirect competition. Indeed, approximately 85 per cent of its route mileage in 1957 was exposed to competition, and almost 50 per cent of its revenue was earned on these competitive routes. It knew that its reputation as a carrier in the highly competitive international network was influenced by the standards of its domestic service. Finally, "any airline enjoying an exclusive franchise on any routes knows that it is particularly vulnerable to public criticism if it allows its standards to fall: particularly when there are potential competitors anxious for the exclusive franchise to be abolished."[17]

Mr. Wheatcroft was rather critical of the company's tardiness in introducing tourist fares, of the use of profits from routes with high traffic density to subsidize those where traffic was thin, of the quality of the North Stars which it had purchased, and so forth. Yet on the whole he was very favourably disposed towards Trans-Canada. He was also concerned with the impact of the jet age.

The airline industry faces . . . a revolutionary change in the size as well as the technical nature of its mainline equipment. Beyond 1961 it is to be anticipated (and sincerely hoped) that there will be a period of stabilization in the aircraft used. The major problem of introducing airline competition in Canada therefore appears to be that this change of policy is being contemplated at a time when it is very difficult for the industry to cope with this extra complication. In the mid 1960's, however, it ought to be possible to extend competition with less concern about its adverse economic consequences.[18]

Briefly examining civil aviation in the United States, Mr. Wheatcroft quoted the Civil Aeronautics Board's so-called "presumption doctrine" which holds that "since competition in itself presents an incentive to improved service and technological development, there would be a strong, although not conclusive, presumption in favour of competition on any route which offered sufficient traffic to support competing services without unreasonable increase of total operating cost."[19] Mr. Wheatcroft went on to say that the government had come very close to accepting the same policy for Canada. On the other hand many observers had concluded that excessive competition was the basic cause of the financial difficulties faced by the airlines of the United States in the mid 1950s. In Wheatcroft's opinion, these troubles did not invalidate the presumption doctrine; they did make clear the possible dangers of such a scheme. There could be little doubt that

the effect of unregulated airline competition in Europe has been an uneconomic expansion of the route network and the introduction of many direct flights which are not justified by the traffic offering between the cities concerned. The result of this is . . . a very low average frequency, . . . a very low density of traffic per route . . . [and] the relatively high level of operating cost. . . . The effect of competition, certainly on international services, has been to put pressure on the carriers to make the quality of service the main competitive feature and, in consequence, to provide a standard of service which is more expensive than the fare level permits. . . . Choice of service may sometimes increase the overall costs of operations. . . . Competition may indeed have a beneficial effect [in more adequate service, greater efficiency, more rapid technological progress, and so on] but, on the other hand, there are serious dangers that unrestricted competition may lead to adverse results. It should be the duty of the regulatory agency to avoid these adverse results.[20]

Mr. Wheatcroft approached the problem of the financial impact of competition on Trans-Canada Air Lines by pointing out that its routes could be divided into four groups: (a) those which operated at a profit ($9.4 million in 1957), namely trans-Atlantic, Caribbean, and transcontinental; (b) those which lost $2.6 million in 1957 but are expected to be profitable in the next few years, i.e., Quebec and Sept Iles, Newfoundland, and transborder or going to and from the United States; (c) those in the Maritimes and on the Pacific Coast losing $3 million in 1957 but which may become profitable in the longer term; (d) those on the Prairies and in Northern Ontario and Quebec which lost $2.7 million in 1957 and are operated primarily as a "social obligation" showing little prospect of becoming profitable. It was abundantly clear that the profit which Trans-Canada makes on its trans-continental services is a vital factor in the over-all self-sufficiency of the airline. Its operating margin was so low, as was the case with most other major airlines, that the introduction of competition on the transcontinental routes would likely create an over-all deficit.

Mr. Wheatcroft preferred direct government subsidies to operators of unprofitable but socially necessary routes rather than internal cross-subsidization—the use of profits on some routes to make up for losses on other routes operated by the same carrier. He thought that small airline companies could perform local and regional operations at lower cost than a trunk-route airline. Most of the small airlines were in financial trouble and would probably need government aid to survive. Until the government relieved Trans-Canada of some of its unprofitable routes, the introduction of main-line competition would lead to a deficit unless, of course, traffic grew at a very rapid rate. In Mr. Wheatcroft's view, the maximum capacity which could be allowed a new competitive carrier would be two or three daily services. Even then, Trans-Canada would have the problem of disposing of some of the new aircraft which it had on order and this would involve various additional costs, including capital losses.

Meanwhile, Canadian Pacific and Pacific Western Air Lines had applied to the Air Transport Board for the right to fly between Vancouver, Edmonton, Regina, Winnipeg, Toronto, Ottawa, and Montreal. Pacific Western, which had got its start flying men and equipment for the Distant Early Warning or DEW Line, withdrew its application. Hearings before the Board developed into a legal brawl in which no stone was left unthrown. While professing support for the Wheatcroft report, both Canadian Pacific and Trans-Canada attacked it indirectly. The former company said the growth of Canadian air travel would soon eliminate the short-run loss, if any, of Trans-Canada which, in its turn, asserted that losses would be heavier and more persistent than Wheatcroft had suggested. Canadian Pacific witnesses made sweeping charges of inefficiency on Trans-Canada which the Board rejected.

Although the Air Transport Board said that Canadian Pacific Air Lines had not proven its case, it recommended that the government grant it the right to fly once daily between Vancouver, Edmonton, Winnipeg, Toronto, and Montreal. It could carry domestic passengers on this flight but the scheduled times of arrival and departure must be integrated, as far as possible, with the company's overseas services. It would appear that the recommendation was chiefly designed to provide Canadian Pacific Air Lines with a more economical and satisfactory route between its overhaul base in Vancouver and its existing services connecting Montreal with Amsterdam and Lisbon.

In 1958, shortly after Canada's two major airlines began to compete with each other on the transcontinental route, albeit on a limited scale, both started to lose money heavily. Though undoubtedly competition was a factor in the loss, the expense of converting from piston and turbo-propellor engines to straight jets was a big factor. Many Canadians, including some airline officials, urged more co-operation between the two companies with the object of cutting costs without any sacrifice in the quality of service. Although nothing was done about these matters, both companies were back on a paying basis by 1964.

In 1966-7 Mr. Wheatcroft was engaged to study commercial aviation in Canada for the second time. He found that competition had neither produced any new traffic nor improved efficiency. He also suggested that Canadian Pacific could expand its operations on the so-called transcontinental route (Vancouver-Toronto-Montreal) without serious effects on Air Canada. In other words, traffic was expanding at such a rate that two companies could operate at a profit provided they shared the business in an equitable manner. In the end the government was prepared to allow Canadian Pacific Air Lines to have no more than 25 per cent of the transcontinental business within Canada by 1970. Moreover, Canadian Pacific would be allowed to handle passengers at Edmonton, Calgary, and Ottawa in addition to its original stops at Vancouver, Winnipeg, Toronto, and Montreal. However, it would not be permitted to make non-stop flights between two cities when another of its regular stops intervened. Thus, it might not schedule a non-stop service between Vancouver and Winnipeg, thus over-flying its normal stop at Calgary or Edmonton. The general principle was to allow more competition along Canada's cross-country air route without endangering the financial prospects of Air Canada.

International Civil Aviation

Canada's aspirations to fly its own international services are inevitable in a world like ours. By 1958, her airlines connected her with every continent except Africa. Like every other country except the United States, Canada's policy is to have only one airline under her flag flying to a given destination abroad. This does not necessarily mean a monopoly for a Canadian airline because there is always indirect and often direct competition with aircraft registered in other countries. For example, instead of flying direct to London by Air Canada, a Torontonian may fly to New York and thence by one of several airlines across the Atlantic. Alternatively, he may fly direct by British Overseas Airways Corporation (BOAC) whose schedules are integrated with those of Air Canada. If he wants to take the time and trouble, he can fly Canadian Pacific Air Lines to Amsterdam and thence back to London. If he goes to Montreal, he has a choice of KLM (Royal Dutch Airlines) to Amsterdam, Air France to Paris, Lufthansa to Hamburg, Sabena to Brussels, Scandinavian Air Services to Copenhagen, and Alitalia to Rome, and thence from any of these cities to London. Alternative routings are available from almost every other large city in Canada to most parts of the world. In consequence, both Air Canada and Canadian Pacific Air Lines have competition with other companies between their various termini. But the two Canadian carriers do not compete with each other in international services except in an indirect fashion, including the relative attractiveness of the West Indies and Mexico, and of Britain and Portugal or Italy as centres of the tourist industry.

Flights between Canada and the United States raise problems too. Since the first bilateral agreement was made in 1938, the objective has been to equalize the number of transborder flights, the number of passengers, and the prospective profits between the two countries. The volume of traffic alters over time and so do the centres of economic interest. For example, the growth of business following the discovery of natural gas in Canada led to the establishment of air services between Montana and Alberta. Consequently, these bilateral agreements have to be renegotiated from time to time.

Canada's "chosen instrument" in transborder flights is Air Canada, though TransAir does land regularly at International Falls, Minn., which is just across the border from Fort Frances, Ont., and Canadian Pacific Air Lines flies between Vancouver and San Francisco. Several companies fly the routes or schedules reserved for planes of United States registry. Air Canada competes directly with American Airlines between Toronto and New York, and with Eastern Air Lines between Montreal and New York. Elsewhere, e.g., Toronto-Buffalo and Duluth-Fort William, the route is reserved to the aircraft of one country or the other.

The principle that each country has jurisdiction over the air above its territory (including territorial waters) is thoroughly established.[21] But trade, especially by air, cannot always confine itself within national boundaries. The essential problem is how far a country is prepared to accept the Five Freedoms: (1) the right to fly over the territory of a foreign country without landing; (2) the right to land on the territory of a foreign country for non-traffic purposes, e.g., take refuge from inclement weather, refuel, or do emergency repairs; (3) the right to put down in a foreign country passengers, mail, and cargo taken on in the state whose nationality the aircraft possesses; (4) the right to take on passengers, etc., for the state whose nationality . . .; and (5) the right to take on (or put down) in a foreign country passengers, etc., for (or from) the territory of any other foreign state. Almost every country accepts the first two Freedoms (subject to the right to designate air corridors or, what is the same thing, the prohibition of flying over areas of strategic importance). But many countries, including Canada, dislike accepting the Fifth Freedom because it might mean its own airlines would be displaced by foreigners. For instance, Air Canada has objected to Air France having the right to carry local passengers between Montreal and Chicago on its through flights between Paris, Montreal, and Chicago. Finally, most countries accept Freedoms three and four only after making bilateral agreements with other countries whereby each retains a fair share of the international traffic or at least is able to attract passengers on the same terms, as far as number and convenience of flights is concerned, as the other party to the agreement. By 1965 Canada had signed over twenty such agreements, the most important being with the United States and Britain.

Problems of air navigation, landing procedures, safety, and so on are dealt with through the International Civil Aviation Organization, which has its headquarters in Montreal and is an agency of the United Nations. Matters of frequency of flights, fares, and quality of service on the North Atlantic and other routes are agreed upon by the operators concerned through the International Air Transport Association, which also has its head office in Montreal.

22

Inland Shipping

SHIPPING along the inland waters of Canada is nowadays practically confined to the St. Lawrence River and the Great Lakes with a small but growing volume along the Mackenzie. In pioneer times, waterways constituted almost the sole right of way for transportation. The Indian birch bark canoe was readily adopted by white men and proved ideal in the fur trade. It was made of local raw materials, could be readily repaired, was easy to portage around rapids and between the headwaters of streams, and for its size carried a fair load. Unfortunately the canoe was poorly suited for grain and other bulk produce. Hence, long, relatively narrow bateaux made of pine or cedar with carrying capacities of upwards of five tons gradually came into use as the volume of freight grew. After about 1810 bateaux were replaced by other vessels, called Durham boats, of the same general type but with seven times the maximum load. Both kinds of boats were rowed or poled whereas canoes are paddled.

Sailing vessels were used along the St. Lawrence from the earliest days of the French régime and were introduced in the fur trade on the Great Lakes in 1679. About 100 years later, when farming communities were being established along the shores of Lake Ontario and the eastern end of Lake Erie, sailing vessels brought in settlers and their effects, carried their exports of potash, farm produce, and lumber on the first lap of their journey overseas, and maintained communications between one little settlement and another. Lacking cheap and efficient transportation, settlers were typically forced into self-sufficiency or became dependent on local markets such as military posts. The traffic, though vital to the community, was not large in amount.

Steamships began to operate between Montreal and Quebec in 1809 and to ply Lake Ontario in 1816. Though much superior to sailing vessels in speed and dependability, their use on the St. Lawrence-Great Lakes was hampered by ice, by the falls of Niagara, and by numerous rapids along the St. Lawrence between Prescott and Montreal, 120 miles downstream. Ice could not be avoided but by 1848 canals had been built so that boats drawing not more than eight feet of water could travel from the head of Lake Huron to Montreal, and from Kingston to Montreal by an all-Canadian route via the Rideau Canal and the Ottawa River. After 1855 an American canal at Sault Ste. Marie permitted ships to circumnavigate falls in the river connecting Lakes Huron and Superior.

While the elaborate and expensive canal system helped open new areas to settlement, it failed to live up to the hopes of the politicians and businessmen who promoted it or of the British and Canadian governments which supplied the capital. The water route via Montreal was unable to overcome the strong economic pull of the Erie Canal and New York City. The growing use of steamships with deeper draughts reduced the value of the shallow canals and necessitated trans-shipping cargo at Buffalo and Kingston from the relatively large lake steamers to small canal vessels or barges. Finally steam railways, of which a considerable mileage was built in the ten years immediately following completion of the canals, took business away from the inland waterways.

Though steamships and a decreasing number of sailing vessels continued to ply the Lakes and the navigable rivers of Ontario and Quebec, interest in canal construction did not revive until toward the end of the century. Then the objective was to provide cheap transportation for the export grain of the rapidly expanding area west of the Great Lakes. The Welland Canal was deepened to 14 feet in 1887 and a canal with a depth of 18 feet completed on the Canadian side of the St. Mary's River in 1895. The shallow sections in the St. Clair River and the canals along the St. Lawrence were dredged or rebuilt to depths of 4 feet.

At first, the tonnage moving along the improved route was disappointing owing mainly to the slow progress of settlement in the Canadian West. Fortunately, after about 1896, this settlement expanded prodigiously. The volume of freight being offered for transportation from Lakehead to Montreal soon became too large to be handled expeditiously by the artificially constructed parts of the channel. Steamships with still deeper draughts were coming into favour because of their low operating costs per ton-mile. The United States deepened its canal between the two upper lakes from 14 to 25 feet and in 1913 Canada began to construct a new Welland Canal to 30 feet. In the new Welland, eight locks replaced twenty-six and since they were electrically operated, vessels could clear from one lake to the other much more rapidly.

A proposal to construct a canal from Georgian Bay via the French and Ottawa rivers to Montreal was rejected. It would be very expensive to build and would have a constricted right of way throughout its length thus adding to the hazard of ice and shortening the season of navigation. The government was obligated elsewhere to build artificial channels capable of performing substantially the same functions. A plan for a water route from the foot of Georgian Bay by the Severn River, Lake Simcoe, and the Trent Valley to near the outlet of Lake Ontario was partially completed but never attained any importance for commercial traffic, though used by tourists and summer cottagers with motor boats and yachts. The roughly 100 locks along the Rideau and Trent systems have clearances of from 6.5 to 9 feet. Those along the Richelieu are 6.5 feet deep. From time to time it is proposed that the latter be vastly improved in order to provide a channel for ships between New York City and Montreal via Lake Champlain, but the scheme would be uneconomic. The canals along the St. Lawrence were not deepened or substantially improved in the fifty or sixty years preceding the opening of the St. Lawrence Seaway in 1959.

Economics of Canal Construction

The economic soundness of public expenditures on canals is hard to appraise correctly. No tolls were charged for the use of Canadian canals from 1903 to 1959. Though there was a small service charge for wharfing, the vessel might free itself of this charge if it supplied its own men. The federal government bore the entire cost of canal construction and operation but the public accounts, especially as regards interest and depreciation, were not set up to show accurate costs. The public got the benefit of some lower freight tolls by both water carriers and railways. The latter reduced their rates on some commodities to meet water competition but may have had to raise tolls on other goods to cover their total expenses.

The costs of canals are presumably borne by all parts of the country but the gains go chiefly to the two areas which use the facilities, namely, the Prairies and the St. Lawrence Lowlands. Canals permit Canadian grain to be sold in the markets of the world in competition with other countries and have allowed manufacturing and trade in the St. Lawrence

Lowlands to expand and thrive beyond what would otherwise have been possible. Yet it must always be remembered that charges for interest, depreciation, repairs, and the operation of canals are not eliminated when they are borne by the public through taxes rather than paid by shippers and consignees through canal tolls and freight rates. It is theoretically possible for shippers and taxpayers to be identical persons, who individually pay taxes in precise proportion to their use of the canals. In this event, whether the cost of the canals is collected by way of taxes or of tolls is immaterial. On the face of it, exact coincidence of taxpayers and canal users would be impossible and a residuum of costs will have to be borne by the general taxpayer.

The Season of Navigation

Aside from the natural obstructions of falls, rapids, and shallow water, the chief limitation on the St. Lawrence-Great Lakes system is the short season of navigation. The minimum is seven months, roughly from the first of May to the beginning of December. As a rule the season is eight months, early or mid-April to early or mid-December. The channels connecting the Lakes with each other and Lake Ontario with Montreal are comparatively narrow. Ice forms in these bottlenecks while the Lakes themselves are still suitable for navigation. More especially, ice accumulates in the constricted channel in St. Mary's Bay at the mouth of Lake Superior above Sault Ste. Marie. If ships could penetrate this barrier, they would have little difficulty on the lower Lakes and their interconnections. Most important of all, freshwater spray freezes on a vessel making it hard to operate and eventually capsizing it. Icebreakers could keep channels open, but nothing so far devised will prevent fresh water freezing on the bows and decks of ships. Insurance rates on hulls and cargoes increase toward the close of navigation.

Another trouble is that the St. Lawrence flows northeasterly from Lake Ontario. In both spring and fall, ice typically is present below Montreal, or fog and floating ice exists in the Gulf, while navigation is still open on the Lakes. In the spring icebreakers are used below Montreal to fracture the sheets of ice into pieces which the swift current sweeps out to sea. In the autumn most ships will not venture upriver to Montreal toward the close of navigation for fear they will be frozen in and thus prevented from earning revenue on the high seas during the winter. Nevertheless, since 1961 ships of Danish, German, or Russian registry, which have been specially reinforced against the pressure of ice, have been serving Quebec City and Montreal every month of the year.

An idle season four months long has numerous economic effects. Interest, depreciation, and obsolescence of canals, ships, and terminal facilities go on whether or not they are in use. Money has to be spent in preparing the physical assets for the winter lay-over and in making good the ravages of ice and frost before navigation reopens. Buoys must be collected in the fall, stored ashore, and replaced in the spring. Men are idle for a good part of the year. Shipping companies must either employ casual labour with attendant costs for hiring, training, and supervising, or they must pay sufficiently high wages during navigation to be reasonably assured of getting the same men back in the following spring. Grain is stored in expensive elevators at Lakehead throughout the winter in order to be available for the first ships to haul out in the spring. The investment in ships and grain handling facilities is very much higher than it would need to be if navigation could be carried on throughout the year.

As much of the total crop as possible must be moved down the lakes between the time, about September 1, when the first Western grain reaches Fort William and the close of navigation. Facilities which are entirely idle in winter and used far below capacity in the middle of the summer, work day and night in the late fall. The rush along the lakes is reflected backward on railways serving the West. Rail carriers, like water-lines, have unused resources at certain times of the year and overworked equipment and men for a few weeks. Though idleness and operating either far below or to the very limit of capacity are all expensive, the alternative—not to have enough physical assets and trained men to handle the seasonal peak of business—is even more expensive. The only offset to these costs is an insignificant one: ships docked at Lower Lake ports can be used as storage warehouses for grain and flour during the winter.

For various reasons, the rush to get grain down the Lakes before freeze-up is not as great as it used to be. Combines and swathers have speeded up the work of harvesting on the Plains compared with binders and threshing machines. Trucks have replaced teams and wagons for delivering wheat to country elevators, freight cars are larger, and trains are both faster and longer, especially since diesels came into use. Higher speed equipment is used for handling grain between trucks, bins in country elevators, freight cars, terminal elevators, and ships on the high seas or on inland waterways. These factors allow us to get grain from the field to salt water more expeditiously than ever before. In addition, our capacity for storing grain in both rural and terminal elevators has risen. Western wheat is now sold by a government board which has authority to control delivery by farmers to country elevators. Year-round deliveries to ocean-going ships can be made through Vancouver. In short, except in years when unusually large sales have been made late in the season, e.g., to Communist China and Russia, the autumn rush to move the grain crop has lessened. In consequence, the pressure on railways in Western Canada and on shipping on the Great Lakes is not nearly as heavy as it used to be. Even so, the enormous benefits which Canada derives from using the Great Lakes and the St. Lawrence River as a channel for transport would be increased still further if the season of navigation lasted all-year round.

Kinds of Traffic

When Canadians discuss navigation along the St. Lawrence and the Great Lakes, they tend to assume that only wheat is transported. In fact, during the 1920s the tonnage of all grain through the Sault Ste. Marie canals was typically about half that of bituminous coal and from 7 to 30 per cent of the tonnage of iron ore) On the other hand the value of wheat was generally greater than that of the iron ore traffic and in the big crop year, 1928, was 40 per cent of the value of all traffic. Other grains—oats, barley, and corn—were about a quarter of the wheat tonnage and a smaller ratio of the value.)

Bituminous coal was mainly handled in American bottoms. Generally it was carried by vessels returning to Lake Superior for another cargo of ore. At one time Canadian grain boats back-hauled Pennsylvania anthracite and West Virginia bituminous to Sault Ste. Marie, Fort William, and Port Arthur for consumption as far west as Winnipeg. Beginning about 1920 this tonnage declined because coal mines in Alberta could supply the Prairies and much of Ontario west of Lake Superior. A minor source of tonnage for American ships was limestone from the upper peninsula of Michigan for use as a flux in blast furnaces.

By the early 1960s the amount of coal moved along the Lakes had materially declined because of the discovery of huge reserves of petroleum and natural gas in Alberta. Nevertheless, a few million tons were still carried for use in the steel mill at Sault Ste. Marie and in Minnesota. It also moved across Lake Ontario for use by the steel complex in Hamilton and by the thermal-electric plants of the Ontario Hydro-Electric Power Commission near Toronto. All in all, coal remained second in volume to iron ore except in a few years when ore was displaced by wheat. Other grains, such as oats, barley, flaxseed and corn, total between 40 and 60 per cent of the wheat tonnage.

Prior to World War II almost all the iron ore was carried by ships of

United States registry from the mines of Minnesota to Gary, Ind., and to Cleveland, Ashtabula, and other Lake Erie ports. With the impending exhaustion of the high grade ores of Minnesota and the opening of a mine at Steep Rock 140 miles west of Port Arthur during the war, Canadian vessels began to participate in this traffic. Later on, some traffic developed in beneficiated iron ore from sources in Northern Ontario. After the opening of the St. Lawrence Seaway in 1959, steel mills in the Cleveland-Youngstown-Pittsburgh area began to get ferrous raw material from the enormous reserve near the Labrador-Quebec boundary. Large American steel producers, such as the United States Steel Corporation, have their own specialized ore carriers.

Grain

For Canadian ships, grain comprises the bulk of the tonnage, though package freight provides an important source of revenue particularly on the Lower Lakes. The receipt of grain at Fort William followed closely the government's construction of a railway, later given to the Canadian Pacific, from Lakehead to Selkirk, near Winnipeg. At first, grain was shipped in sacks because early attempts to transfer it by pipes and spouts from railway cars to ships were unsuccessful. Then two-wheeled carts were used to move grain over runways from one kind of carrier to the other. In 1886 an elevator was built at Fort William. Grain was shovelled from railway cars into pits, then raised by constantly moving belts with buckets attached to them, spilled into bins well up in a high building (the elevator itself), and thence allowed to flow by gravity down pipes, through spouts and hatches, into ships. The design of elevators was steadily improved. They were made fireproof by using concrete and tile instead of lumber and the elevating mechanism was perfected. A machine was devised for mechanically staving in grain doors, grasping the freight car firmly in strong arms, and turning it endwise and sideways so that all the grain flowed out of the car without any hand labour.

Improvements in elevator construction and operation at country shipping points, at Lakehead, and at Lower Lake ports and Montreal were of vital importance to western farmers. Grain growers are concerned with the over-all cost of moving grain from their farms to the world market because the net amount which they get for a bushel of grain, obviously significant in their prosperity, is the world price in Liverpool less the cost of transport, insurance, and so on. To Western farmers any savings in the physical handling of grain are important, whether they come from technological changes in terminal facilities, railway operation, ship construction, or from some other source. The grain movement down the Lakes cannot properly be viewed solely as a matter of ships and their operation but as part of a long haul in which many transportation agencies and grain handling facilities participate.

Fort William and Port Arthur have large storage elevators and a well-designed yard for classifying or sorting out freight cars to the various elevators at which they are to be unloaded. With the hump or gravity yard the railways can handle in ten or twelve hours all the cars which the elevators can unload in twenty-four. Prior to 1909 a shipper with grain in ten elevators would have to ask the vessel he engaged to call at all these ten elevators and load a few thousands of bushels at each. When a number of ships had to call at several elevators, congestion was inevitable. Time was lost in coming alongside and in adjusting and disengaging loading equipment. While ships waited until berthing space was empty, interest, insurance, and many operating expenses continued just as if the vessel were earning money actually moving freight.

In 1909 the Lake Shippers' Clearance Association[1] was formed to reduce the expense, and speed up the "turn around" of ships in port. Each elevator gives each shipper or consignee a receipt for the number of bushels it has received on his account. These receipts are taken immediately to the office of the Association which gives the holder credit for so many bushels on its books. When the shipper or consignee wants to send grain down the Lakes, he advises the manager of the Association of the name of the ship, its capacity, and probable date of arrival. The manager assigns the ship to a single elevator which has at least enough grain in storage to fill the ship and which will not, at the time the ship concerned arrives, be loading another vessel. The ship will take full cargo at the elevator to which it was assigned. After it has cleared, the Association will debit the account of the individuals concerned with the total number of bushels shipped.

The Clearance Association can function effectively only because Dominion government officials carefully grade all grain. A shipper with documents for 10,000 bushels of Number 2 does not normally care whether the grain he gets in Montreal is the same grain he shipped in Port Arthur provided it is grain of the same grade. In fact his chances of actually receiving that lot are exceedingly remote, for grain of a certain grade is inextricably mixed together during the process of elevation and spouting and while being dumped into the holds of ships and the bins of elevators.

Up to 1943, that is, before farmers were required to sell through the Canadian Wheat Board, dealers commonly purchased space in advance of purchasing the grain. They signed contracts with operators of vessels before they actually bought the cargo to fill the vessel. Since 1943 when the Wheat Board assumed full control of the marketing of Canadian wheat in foreign markets and began to supervise the export of oats and barley, exporters sell the grain before engaging space and approaching the Wheat Board for the release of the necessary grain. In addition, the Board often disposes of wheat in its own name without the intervention of a middleman.

Compared with dealers, millers need more regular supplies of grain. So they often hired a vessel for the entire season except the last trip. In the rush to get grain down the Lakes before navigation closed, rates on the last voyage typically reached high levels and ship operators wanted a chance to profit from the extraordinary charges. Milling companies sometimes contracted to ship all their grain via the ships of a certain line or to supply them with cargoes regularly for most of the season. Since ship operators were thus assured of a fairly regular volume of traffic, they charged milling companies a differential of one-quarter to one-half a cent below the "going" rate at the time the vessel sailed. When the going rates throughout the season were likely to be unduly depressed, the contract usually provided for a minimum rate under which no differential or discount would be allowed. In short, most ships operated on open contracts, taking their chances of getting freight to fill their holds, but some vessels had season contracts with a single shipper.

Rates for grain fluctuate throughout the shipping season. As explained, just before navigation closes when the amount of grain seeking transportation is large relative to the nearby tonnage, rates may rise abruptly. The opening of navigation in the spring normally finds the elevators at Fort William and Port Arthur filled to capacity, especially if the harvest on the Plains during the previous crop year was late and navigation on the Lakes closed earlier than usual. The Liverpool price may be good, owing perhaps to a poor crop in the Argentine whose wheat normally arrives in volume in England during April and May. When this condition prevails, shippers want to get their wheat down the Lakes with the least delay and so the shipping rate may be fairly high. It will not, however, reach the same level as for the last trip of the season because some shippers can hold their grain a little longer until rates come down.

Prior to compulsory marketing through the Wheat Board and the more regular flow of wheat through export channels, shipping was slack during July and August and as a rule rates were relatively low at that time. Then in early September rates began to rise, typically reaching

their annual peak immediately before navigation closed. Thus throughout any given season of navigation, lake rates will fluctuate almost
daily. The same vessel may carry grain for several shippers at slightly
different rates, and ships sailing at substantially the same time may
charge different amounts. In this respect lake shipping charges resemble
those made by ocean-going bulk cargo vessels.

Though the establishment of compulsory marketing has tended to
even out the flow of grain throughout the season of navigation, it has
not prevented the variation in rates which takes place from one season
to another.[2] These annual changes are the result of several factors. The
amount of Western grain to be shipped varies markedly from one
year to another depending on weather conditions, acreage sown, the
ability of the Canadian Wheat Board to dispose of all its stock, and
the encroachment of the port of Vancouver which pulls grain from
areas otherwise exporting through Lakehead. The season of navigation
down the Lakes may be longer or shorter than average, thus depressing
or raising the level of rates for that season and perhaps for the next one.
The level of wages and cost of ship supplies, including fuel, obviously
influence the rate level. The size and number of ships in service is
another factor. Also in years of high water a vessel can carry several
thousand more bushels of grain that it can when water levels are low.
This factor is particularly important because for safety's sake vessels
should clear the sills of canal locks by at least one foot.[3] Finally technological change is as important in transportation by inland water
carrier as by any other medium.

The Great Lakes Fleet

The early steamships on the Lakes were apparently of the same
general type as steamers used elsewhere in the world. By 1900 the
famous whalebacks had come into common use for grain. They were
whale-shaped with pointed ends and rounded sides. Their machinery
was located aft and the bridge right up forward; the cargo hold was
long and clear of obstructions. When travelling light, the weight of the
machinery and fuel might lift the prow out of the water. While loaded
and in a heavy sea, the long midship section might be awash. These
ships have now been entirely displaced by steel bulk freighters. "As a
result of special attention to design, English builders began to turn out
in 1923 and 1924 a highly economical, lower lake steamer capable of
carrying fifteen to thirty per cent more wheat at the same daily operating
costs. The capital cost was low, about $100 per gross ton, a figure at
which some shipping companies were showing the depreciated value of

their whole fleets, then having an average age of fourteen or fifteen years. [These developments] meant that a considerable part of the fleet became definitely and finally obsolete."[4] The new ships had somewhat the same appearance as the whalebacks but were slightly narrower of beam and deeper of draught. Their holds were divided into compartments so that on any one trip they could carry different kinds of grain or different grades of the same grain.

Because the same vessel can handle more freight per annum if it is loaded and unloaded promptly than if it has to spend a good deal of time in port, technological changes in equipment for handling cargo have added to the effective carrying capacity of the fleet. The average time spent in port per vessel was nearly 30 hours in 1922 but only a little over 17 in 1931 even though the average size of the vessels had materially increased between the two dates. The record for loading seems to be 555,000 bushels of wheat in 5½ hours or about 52 tons per minute. Of course, it takes longer to unload a vessel since gravity cannot be used to the same extent. In 1959 the National Harbours Board built two special plants at Montreal and two at Quebec City. They incorporate a belt-and-bucket elevator, which dredges grain out of the hold, and pneumatic equipment for sucking up the grain. Each plant has a rated capacity of 13.5 tons a minute or roughly 50 per cent more than the mechanical unloaders previously in use.

Large vessels are considerably cheaper to build and operate, per ton of capacity, than are small ones, at least up to the point where they are unable regularly to get a full load. But size is definitely limited by the dimensions of the locks and by the depth of water over the sills of locks and, to a lesser extent, in shallow channels. Still, reductions in cost brought about by larger vessels and faster handling have virtually destroyed the all-rail movement of grain from Lakehead to Montreal which had been important up to 1914. In 1946-7, when the average freight rate on grain between these two points was 10 cents a bushel, the all-rail rate was 15 cents. At one time a good deal of grain was brought down the Lakes by ship to ports on Georgian Bay and then moved by rail to Montreal. After the opening of the St. Lawrence Seaway in 1959, the volume of ex-lake grain declined, even though the Board of Transport Commissioners ordered rates to be maintained at a relatively low level. At about the same time ships began moving grain for feed or export from Montreal to Baie Comeau, Saint John, or Halifax, thus further cutting into railway traffic.

New lake vessels built in the 1920s rendered many older ships obsolete and raised financial difficulties for many companies. In 1929 the investment in shipping companies operating along the Great Lakes was somewhere between $50 and $60 million of which more than half consisted of mortgages of one kind or another and the rest of preferred and common stock. After 1930 net earnings of shipping companies fell disastrously and interest on their bonds was either in default or in jeopardy. Financial troubles were caused by technological change, drought and a succession of poor crops in the West, and the shipment of grain through Vancouver. The new Welland Canal allowed vessels with capacities of 450,000 bushels or more to take their cargoes another 200 to 250 miles farther down the Lakes, that is, from Port Colborne to Kingston or Prescott before having to transfer them to smaller vessels, canallers, which handled at most 100,000 bushels. These ships were small enough to operate through the old-fashioned canals to Montreal,[5] and had engines of comparatively high power, sufficient to bring them up some stretches of swift water in the open river. Because some canallers were displaced from their former trade, they added to the surplus tonnage already existing and further depressed rates. From 1920 to 1926 "a few really efficient operators were able to pay for new ships with a life of over thirty years in from three to five years from earnings."[6] In consequence of high profits made by a few operators, especially during the record crop years of 1928 and 1929, new ship-owners eagerly entered the business. Whereas in 1921 the Canadian Great Lakes fleet numbered 100 ships with 240,000 gross tons capacity, ten years later it consisted of 230 ships and 575,000 gross tons.

During the depression the companies agreed not to commission one-third of their tonnage. Some companies including Canada Steamship Lines, the largest Canadian ship operator, went into bankruptcy. By 1938 bonded indebtedness had been written off. The excessive valuation of tonnage which had been acquired when construction costs were so high immediately after World War I or which had become obsolete through technological improvements, had been recognized and reduced. Vessels which were overly expensive to operate had been sold for scrap. In 1950 Great Lakes carriers were in a stronger financial position than at any time in the preceding twenty-five years. Moreover, the fleet was steadily being converted from steam to diesel power.

Within a few years after (the St. Lawrence Seaway was opened, Canada's inland fleet had again changed. Big ships or upper lakers were able to go between Lakehead and Montreal, Quebec City, and Baie Comeau. Provided water levels are high enough, some of these vessels can transport 800,000 bushels of wheat and they draw upwards of 26.5 feet of water. They have displaced the old canallers, the small vessels (100,000 bushels) with shallow draughts (less than 14 feet) which were capable of going through the antiquated and now abandoned locks along the St. Lawrence. Also, after the opening of the Seaway, the number of specialized ore carriers, mainly of American registry, increased. These changes were financed with relative ease, either by Canadian companies which received a federal subsidy for the construction of new ships or by American steel mills.

Regulation of Lake Shipping

Ships engaged in carrying bulk cargo along the St. Lawrence—Great Lakes system do not need to obtain licences from any official body beyond the usual certificates of seaworthiness, boiler inspection, etc., which are required by the Department of Transport for the protection of life and property. Rates are not subject to official regulation except that, on grain, vessel owners operating between Port Arthur, Fort William, and any other port in Canada or the United States must file their contract of carriage with the Board of Grain Commissioners immediately after the contract is entered into and before the grain is laden. If this Board is of the opinion that any rate is unreasonable, excessive, or unjustly discriminatory, it may prescribe reasonable maximum tolls.[7]

The Board has seldom found it necessary to exercise these powers. Normally, there is an abundance of tonnage seeking cargo and competition keeps rates in check. The Board of Grain Commissioners interferes only when rates appear to be unreasonably high, in one instance when it thought a monopoly was functioning. In setting maximum rates the Grain Commission does not attempt to give a fair return, carefully ascertain costs of operation, or prevent unjust discrimination though it does not ignore these factors. Its chief consideration is the need to attract sufficient American bottoms into the trade to empty Canadian elevators at Lakehead, as far as it is possible to do so, before the close of navigation.

Package Freight

Besides bulk cargoes, inland shipping handles package freight which consists of relatively small lots of fairly valuable commodities such as farm implements, canned goods, automobiles, hardware, and general merchandise in bundles, boxes, barrels, kegs, and hampers. Package freighters ply between numerous ports on the St. Lawrence River and the Great Lakes usually on regular schedules. Some of them carry passengers as well as freight. Vessels handling package freight exclusively either have their power plants amidships or resemble small bulk carriers. All package freighters are equipped with booms and winches but frequently use fork lift-trucks for loading and unloading cargo through the side. They have carrying capacities of 2,000 gross tons and upwards, with an average of perhaps 5,000 tons.

(The Canadian Transport Commission) has had jurisdiction over this trade since 1939.[8] It issues licences on the grounds of public convenience and necessity after considering whether suitable facilities are already provided either by rail or water along the routes or between the places in question; whether, if the licence were issued, facilities would be in excess of requirements; whether or not the issue of the licence would tend to develop complementary rather than competitive functions of transport; and the quality and permanence of the service offered.[9] Licences are for periods of one year. Upon recommendation of the Commission, the Governor-in-Council may exempt vessels from the licensing provisions.[10]

Package freighters use the same freight classification as railways. Tolls approved by the Board are at a differential below the corresponding charge all-rail. The differentials vary from class to class and are changed from time to time. In 1955 the Board of Transport Commissioners laid down that on traffic between the area west of the Detroit River and places west of Lakehead, the differential of water-rail (i.e., ship to Lakehead and rail beyond, or vice versa) below all-rail should be 34, 29, 24, 19, 15, 14, 11, 10, and 9 cents per hundred pounds on classes 100, 85, 70, 55, 45, 40, 33, 30, and 27 (the old classes 1 to 10, omitting 9). On traffic hauled rail-lake-rail between these two areas (e.g., Peterborough to Toronto by rail, Toronto to Fort William by water, beyond Fort William by rail), the corresponding differentials below all-rail are 25, 21, 18, 14, 11, 10, 8, 8, and 7 cents. On traffic between Windsor, Sarnia, Goderich, and ports on Georgian Bay (i.e., between places which are closer to the West than ports on Lakes Erie, Ontario, and the St. Lawrence) and stations west of Lakehead, the differentials are greater. For example, water-rail below all-rail has a differential of 44 cents per hundred pounds on class 100, and 12 cents on class 27.

In 1958 the Winnipeg Chamber of Commerce objected to the Board's raising the water carriers' portion of the joint through rates whenever railways got authority to raise their tolls. Representatives of the Chamber claimed that water carriers should prove they were in financial need of higher tolls and should, in any event, make application for higher rates. The Board disagreed with this argument and conformed with traditional practice. Inland shipping companies may publish agreed charges in the same manner as railways and must not contravene the sections of the Transport Act prohibiting unjust discrimination and undue preference.)[11]

International Problems

Until 1964 ships registered in any part of the Commonwealth were free to engage in the carriage of goods and passengers from one port in Canada to another port in Canada, commonly known as the coasting trade. But in practice almost all traffic between Montreal and any Canadian port to the westward was carried in ships of Canadian registry. This was because only a few ocean-going ships could get through the shallow locks of the St. Lawrence. With the opening of the Seaway, more ships were able to share in this part of our coasting trade. So in 1964 the law was changed to restore the *status quo* as it existed before the advent of the Seaway.[12] Traffic between any two Canadian ports on the Great Lakes and the St. Lawrence west of Havre St. Pierre is now reserved to ships registered in Canada. Commonwealth ships continue to enjoy equal privileges with Canadian ships between any two ports elsewhere in Canada, e.g., between St. John's and Halifax, or Montreal and Vancouver via the Panama Canal.

The United States prohibits Canadian ships from carrying goods and passengers directly between any two ports on the Great Lakes and the upper St. Lawrence in the United States. Canada had a similar rule until 1923 when as a result of the recommendation of a Royal Commission the trade between Canadian ports on the Great Lakes was thrown open to vessels of United States registry.[13] At the time there was a shortage of Canadian tonnage, freight rates were relatively high, and it was hoped that American ships could be induced to use the St. Lawrence River route between the Great Lakes and the high seas instead of trans-shipping their freight at Buffalo for forwarding to New York by rail or via the Barge Canal. This hope came to naught and the surplus of Canadian tonnage seeking cargoes after about 1930 led the government in 1934 to apply again the restricted rule against United States shipping. The regulation does not prevent American vessels from handling freight between a Canadian and an American port (e.g., Toronto and Rochester) or even between two Canadian ports provided a call is made en route at a port in the United States (e.g. Toronto, Rochester, Kingston). It does, however, prevent them from participating directly between two ports in Canada, e.g., Montreal and Toronto, or Sarnia and Fort William.

The Governor-in-Council has authority to suspend this coasting law[14]

and on the advice of the Board of Grain Commissioners has sometimes allowed ships of United States registry into the grain trade between
Port Arthur, Fort William, and other Canadian inland ports. This has
been done if, just before the close of navigation, it appears that the
available tonnage of Canadian registry will not be adequate to clear
Lakehead elevators of their grain. In 1967 complaint was made that
ships which were American for all practical purposes were being registered in Canada through Canadian subsidiaries in order to participate
in the coasting trade involving Canadian ports on the Great Lakes.

Shipping in the Mackenzie Basin

Along the Mackenzie and its tributaries as well as on the Yukon,
ships handle ore, petroleum, mining supplies, foodstuffs, and general
merchandise. The ships are propelled by diesel engines and paddle-
wheels because in places, especially at the delta of the Athabasca River,
the rivers are too shallow for relatively deep draught vessels equipped
with propellers. A good deal of freight is loaded on barges which are
pushed along by tugs, some of them with paddle-wheels coming up
underneath the centre and thereby protected from sand bars and rocks.
From Waterways near the junction of the Clearwater and Athabasca
rivers and the head of steel from Edmonton, vessels can go 1,600 miles
north to Aklavik and Inuvik, near the mouth of the Mackenzie, except
for a portage of sixteen miles around rapids between Fitzgerald and
Fort Smith on the Slave River. Freight can also be brought by road
and soon by rail from Grimshaw to Hay River and then delivered or
received from vessels operating along the Mackenzie above the restrictions of shallow water in parts of Lake Athabasca. Prior to the Hay
River Highway, ships ran on the Peace River as they still do on Great
Bear River and Lake. It would be unrealistic to suggest that navigation in these Northern waters is easy or large compared with the
Mississippi or St. Lawrence although it is very important to the areas
concerned.

By virtue of the Transport Act, 1938, the Board of Transport
Commissioners (since 1967 the Canadian Transport Commission)
licenses vessels exceeding ten tons gross and plying the Mackenzie, the
Yukon, and their tributaries, and sets rates on both bulk and package
freight. Control has protected carriers against ruinous competition
among themselves, guarded shippers against exorbitant rates, and
facilitated determining the proper rate to be charged by a government-
owned concern, Northern Transportation, Ltd., for hauling mining supplies and pitchblende for its parent, Eldorado Mining and Refining,
Ltd., which is also government owned.

Licences were issued under the "grandfather" clause to vessels of four large companies (Hudson's Bay, McInnes Products, which is primarily a fishing concern, Northern Transportation, and Yellowknife Transportation) and a few individuals with one or two ships each. In 1965 the government purchased Yellowknife and consolidated its operations with those of Crown-owned Northern Transportation. In this way it hoped to offset higher costs of labour and a threatened increase in freight rates.

At first, classification and rates varied from one licensee to another. Carriers published different rates over different routes of substantially the same length. Counsel for independent companies claimed that Northern Transportation was making 60 per cent on its invested capital, though he questioned whether a Crown corporation was entitled to any profit. He said that the government was charging so much that gold mining was being retarded by high tolls on fuel oil. Mining companies and local residents contended that shipping rates should be cut with a view to encouraging expansion in the Mackenzie district which had great potential wealth and was important for defence.

In reply, Northern Transportation called attention to the short season of navigation, tortuous channels, shifting shoals and bars, fast passages of rock-strewn shallow water, and large bodies of deep water. These created serious problems in designing and operating vessels. Lack of drydocks necessitated beaching vessels for repairs and during the winter months. Only eighteen miles of channel were marked. The Fitzgerald-Smith portage added to operating costs and lengthened transit time by about five days. Six handlings were needed to move freight from the Mackenzie River to vessels plying Great Bear Lake. Traffic volume had always been irregular from year to year and the ratio of north to southbound tonnage was about nine to one at Waterways in 1950. The amount of freight was expected to decline when the current mining boom collapsed.

After examining the financial statements of the water-lines the Board laid down a uniform classification, standard mileage class rates, and official distances.[15] All goods are fifth class unless otherwise provided for. Classes higher than fifth apply to articles of light density, greater value, and high susceptibility to damage. Batteries with acid, buildings (set-up), canoes, skiffs, livestock, and poultry are first; acids, agricultural implements, airplanes in sections, automobiles, batteries in crates, beer, firearms, fine furs (other than beaver, muskrat, wolf, and bear), furniture, household goods, groceries, outboard motors, personal effects, and so on are third; articles weighing 2,000 to 10,000 pounds per piece or package are 110 per cent of the rate normally applicable and those weighing over 10,000 pounds are 120 per cent of the rate otherwise applying.

Labour on Great Lakes Steamships

The labour force on steamships operating on the Great Lakes is strongly organized. Attempts at unionization made during the 1920s proved abortive but poor conditions prevailing in the next decade played into the hands of union organizers. Wages for wheelsmen, excluding means and berth which were provided by the operators, were cut from about $70 to $45 a month and for deckhands from $45 to $30. Since the season of navigation did not exceed eight months and some ships laid up during the slack season in July and early August, the total annual income of workers was deplorable. Ships ran with skeleton crews; men had to work harder because of the "stretch-out"; and they were discharged if their ship stopped off in port for more than a few hours. By tradition and by law the master of the vessel could, if he were so inclined, domineer over his crew.[16]

In 1935 the Marine Workers Union set itself up in Toronto and at about the same time the National Seamen's Union was organized in Montreal. Though neither group had any money for hiring professional organizers, both grew rapidly, later amalgamating into the Seamen's International Union. After striking in 1938, they were able to start the industry out of its characteristic state of low pay, long hours, and poor living conditions. During the war the men accepted this situation but in 1948 they claimed they worked a twelve-hour day at two-thirds the wages paid by American Lake carriers for an eight-hour day. The Dominion Marine Association, the ship-owners, said that a shorter watch was economically unsound. If it were adopted, the Lake boats could not compete with railways. The men had plenty of spare time in their twelve-hour shift and as a rule their work was not strenuous.

Trouble flared up in Montreal when a ship captain refused to let a union shore-delegation board ship, discharged crew members who left ship to meet the delegation ashore, and then replaced them with non-union workers. Men on strike were imprisoned under the Canada Shipping Act which made any seaman who left ship without seven days' notice liable to arrest without warrant and to three months' imprisonment. After government intervention, management and men agreed to a 20 per cent increase in wages, the eight-hour day, and preference to union members in hiring. The Canada Shipping Act has been amended to hold ship captains more accountable for their treatment of men.[17] The system of four-hour watches has been introduced while the quality of the food and the ventilation of sleeping quarters have been improved.

In the 1950s crews and stevedores were often restless but serious trouble did not erupt until the early 1960s. In 1963 longshoremen at Quebec, Trois Rivières, Sorel, and Montreal went on strike. Because the West feared that the strike would disrupt delivery of wheat overseas and perhaps result in the cancellation of a contract of sale to China, the government was urged to pass a law to end the stoppage and require that the points at issue be settled by arbitration. Instead, it appointed a Royal Commission under Judge Lippé and the men voluntarily returned to work after six days. In the end they got an increase of 30 cents an hour spread over three years.

Another big dispute arose out of the fact that the Seamen's International Union (S.I.U.), the largest on the Lakes, had been expelled from the Canadian Labour Congress (C.L.C.) for raiding another Congress affiliate in order to recruit members for itself. Nevertheless, the S.I.U. had retained its membership in the American Federation of Labour-Congress of Industrial Organizations (A.F.L.-C.I.O) in the United States. This body, like the C.L.C., is composed largely of members of international unions, i.e., those which operate in both countries. As a rule, the two central organizations see eye to eye on most matters but in this instance the C.L.C. organized the Canadian Maritime Union (C.M.U.) to replace the S.I.U. which it had outlawed. These conflicts within organized labour led to further trouble. At times affiliates of the A.F.L.-C.I.O. in the United States refused to handle the cargoes of ships manned by members of the C.M.U. Besides, the conflict led to some nasty remarks being made about Canada by a few Americans, including the U.S. Secretary of Labour.

But Canadians were also unhappy about the S.I.U. and especially about its leader, Hal Banks, an American who had come to Canada and been allowed to stay so long that he could not legally be deported on the ground that he was an undesirable alien. In 1962, Mr. Justice T. G. Norris, whom the government had appointed a Royal Commissioner to study the matter, reported that Banks was a "bully, cruel, dishonest, greedy, power-hungry, contemptuous of the law" and recommended that he be prosecuted for criminal conspiracy by preventing men from working, interfering with trade, and committing violence. Brought before the court, Banks skipped bail and fled to the United States. Though castigating Banks in stronger language than that customarily used by a Royal Commissioner, Mr. Justice Norris also accused Canada Steamship Lines, the biggest operator on the Lakes, of co-operation with Banks. It had encouraged him to come to Canada because it believed that the old Canadian Maritime Union was led by Communists.

As a solution to the problem, the Royal Commissioner proposed that the government appoint three trustees for the S.I.U. They would control the union funds, supervise the negotiation and administration of collective agreements, and oversee the operation of so-called hiring halls which decide which members of the union will be engaged to man the docks and ships. As set up in 1964, the trustee board consisted of a judge and two men experienced in union matters.[18] The board faced great difficulties, for leaders of unions like to run their own affairs. Nevertheless, it has preserved peace and had its jurisdiction extended through 1968.

Each ship's crew is divided between those who must hold licences issued by the Department of Transport (captains, mates, and engineers, and those who need not hold certificates or pass examinations. Unlicensed crew members include: (*a*) deck or the forward crew who assist in docking the vessel, do painting, attend to hatches, etc., and who are paid as wheelsmen, watchmen, and deckhands; (*b*) the engine-room crew who are on and off duty every alternate six hours; and (*c*) stewards who work from 5 a.m. to 8 p.m. preparing meals and cleaning the officers' quarters.[19]

St. Lawrence Waterway

The prospect of materially improving the physical facilities for shipping along inland waters has long attracted attention. What was then called the St. Lawrence-Deep Sea Waterway was examined in 1920-1 by the International Joint Commission. This is a permanent body consisting of three commissioners from Canada and three from the United States whose function it is to investigate and report upon outstanding questions regarding the boundary, and in particular the boundary waters, between the two countries. This Commission stated that the scheme was justified but advised further study by qualified engineers. In 1924 President Coolidge appointed a Commission to study the project. Its report which was presented to Congress in 1927 dealt mainly with the relative merits of (*a*) an enlarged canal following roughly the route of the Erie or, as it is technically called, the New York State Barge Canal, (*b*) a new all-American route from Lake Ontario at Oswego to the Hudson River at Albany, and (*c*) the St. Lawrence route which the Commission favoured.[20]

Almost simultaneously Canada appointed a National Advisory

Committee. Its report, dated 1928, pointed out that the capacity of Canada's railways was already in excess of the transportation needs of the country. Since our railway tolls were lower than those in the United States, the benefits of the seaway would be relatively less. On the whole the Committee thought the project was premature whether for navigation or for power. It recommended that Canada co-operate in any further studies which the two countries might undertake jointly provided the Dominion did not bind herself to assume excessive financial burdens.

The Joint Board of Engineers appointed by Canada and the United States on recommendation of the International Joint Commission reported in 1926. It estimated the cost of a channel 25 feet deep between Kingston and Montreal and full development of power resources at from $394 to $424 million. The Board thought that deepening the river channels connecting some of the Great Lakes to the same depth would cost $41 million. No large additional expenditures would be required on the new Welland Canal which was shortly to be completed. The Americans on the Board favoured a channel of 25 feet while Canadians recommended one of 27 feet. The latter would cost more but would accommodate larger ships and permit freight to be hauled for less per ton-mile.

The project was strongly supported by President F. D. Roosevelt who felt it would produce hydro-electric power cheaply and hold in check electric rates charged by privately owned utilities in the United States. It would also add to the war potential of both countries and be important in lowering costs of transportation between the most highly industrialized section of North America and the markets of the world. During and immediately after World War II an acute shortage of power in Ontario and impending shortages in Quebec and New York State revived interest in the scheme. The high grade ferrous ores of Minnesota were approaching exhaustion. Steel mills in Cleveland, Youngstown, and Pittsburgh were planning to bring in ore from the newly discovered resource along the Labrador-Quebec boundary. Big business in these areas felt that the St. Lawrence Waterway was essential to cheapening the cost of transporting one of their primary raw materials and to preserving their prosperity.

In 1932 Canada ratified a treaty with the United States but it was rejected by the American Senate. In 1941 a modified treaty was dealt with in the same manner. Opposition came from railways, the ports of New York and Boston, coal miners who feared that additional low cost hydro-electric power would displace more coal, and various parts of the country which would not directly benefit from expenditures in north-eastern United States.

Generally speaking, up to the outbreak of World War II, Canada was less enthusiastic than the United States in promoting the Seaway. After the war, the positions were reversed. Canada was short of hydro-electric power and wanted to sell iron ore, while President Truman was less vigorous in supporting the scheme than Roosevelt had been. When the United States held back, Prime Minister St. Laurent announced that Canada would apply to the International Joint Commission, which has detailed control of boundary waters, for per-mission to erect the necessary facilities at its own expense. An all-Canadian project would cost only $30 million more than a joint venture because the configuration of the land and the nature of the subsurface in Canada was not much less favourable for construction than the sites in the United States where some of the structures were to be erected under the original plans. Mr. St. Laurent's announcement had the effect of swinging the balance of opinion in Congress in favour of joint construction. The Seaway was officially opened by Queen Elizabeth II and President Eisenhower on June 26, 1959, though it had already been used commercially for about two months.

The Seaway cost $470 million of which Canada's share was $330 million or 70 per cent. These sums did not include anything for the improvement of inland ports, for ships, nor for the Welland Canal. Construction took 5 years and provided work at one time or another for over 60,000 people. About 6,500 residents of towns that were flooded had to be relocated in two new communities at a cost of roughly $30 million.

In order to make the project more acceptable to Americans and avoid the allegation that traffic through it would be subsidized to the detriment of railroads and ports in the United States, each of the countries agreed to set up government-owned corporations to operate the facilities.[21] The St. Lawrence Seaway Authority of Canada and the St. Lawrence Seaway Development Corporation of the United States are required to charge tolls on ships and their cargoes. Tolls are to be high enough to cover the costs of operation, maintenance, interest, and of amortization of the cost within 50 years. The scale or tariff of tolls is subject to approval by the governments concerned. From 1959 to 1966 the fees were payable 71 per cent in Canadian funds and 29 per cent in American, with the proceeds going to the respective Authorities in the same ratio. In 1967 the ratio changed to 73 to 27 in order to take better account of the relative cost of interest on the investment and operating expenditures incurred in the two countries.)

The fees for use of the Seaway between Montreal and Lake Ontario are 4 cents per gross registered ton (laden or in ballast) plus 40 per cent per short ton of bulk cargo and 90 cents per ton of general cargo. (The total charge per loaded vessel ranges between $9,000 and $13,000 per trip. Bulk cargo means all goods loose or in mass. It includes grain, flour, cement, ore, coke, coal, pulpwood, raw sugar, and scrap iron as well as domestic package freight. General cargo is everything else (exclusive of ships' fuel and stores, and the personal effects of crews). Most general cargo consists of automobiles, electrical goods, glass, and general merchandise to and from overseas ports. In addition, hides, lard, beans, paper, and chemicals are exported while oranges, wine and coffee are brought in through the Seaway.)

Obviously, an accurate forecast of the volume of traffic was essential if the obligation to amortize the investment within 50 years was to be met. As things turned out, the original forecast was not reached as quickly as anticipated while operating costs were a good deal higher than expected. The Seaway has carried few products of the forest and almost no petroleum products. Pipelines for liquid fuels have displaced tankers while the use of natural gas, fuel oil, and diesel fuel has cut into the market for coal. Even so, the movement of coal has slightly exceeded expectations, largely on account of the decision of the Hydro-Electric Power Commission of Ontario to erect thermal-electric plants near Toronto and to buy coal from Nova Scotia as well as from American mines. The movement of grain has lived up to expectations, though it has been somewhat unstable from year to year because of uncertainty of our finding markets abroad.

One disappointment was that the trade in iron ore fell below the forecast. This was not caused by any decline in the demands of steel mills in Ohio but rather because cheap methods were devised for pelletizing and sintering Minnesota and Ontario ores, thus improving their quality. Indeed, Quebec ores, though comparatively rich in their natural state, had to be reduced to pellets to make them more competitive with ores from Lake Superior. One result of pelletizing is to reduce by as much as 30 per cent the weight of the ore that has to be transported to supply a given quantity of iron. Therefore, the revenue of the Seaway Authority is cut down. Exploitation of some of the ferrous deposits south of Lake Superior had been stopped because the ores were too hard for mining cheaply by conventional means. The difficulty was overcome by flame-cutters using cheap natural gas. Finally, in November, 1964, Minnesota made tax concessions to mining companies to better their competitive position relative to Labrador-Quebec.

Producers in the latter area still have advantages, including highly efficient transport along railways to the ports of Sept Iles, Port Cartier, and Havre St. Pierre. Nevertheless, their outlook is not quite as rosy as it appeared just before the Seaway was opened. The expected famine in iron ore has not materialized even though by 1966 the tonnage of ore moved along the Seaway exceeded that of the next largest item, wheat.

(Officials of the Canadian Authority have several other explanations of why the Seaway has been running at a loss.) It suffered from "teething troubles" such as shortage of skilled pilots, inexperience of masters and crew, inadequate equipment for loading and unloading, and lengthy delays to ships using the Welland Canal. In the early 1960s the Seaway was hurt by low water levels in the Great Lakes. Officials also pointed out that it takes time for trade to adjust to a new channel of transport.

(The volume of traffic through the Seaway lagged about two years behind the forecast until 1966 when it caught up. By the end of that year Canada's share of the Seaway debt was roughly $353 million including $35 million in deferred interest which was met out of the general revenues of Canada. It is expected that the debt will continue to rise to a peak of $366 million at the close of 1971, then level off, and finally be reduced as traffic and revenues from users exceed operating expenses and annual interest charges.) Even so, it is problematical if the Seaway will be free of debt by the year 2009, as originally planned.

The Welland Canal is in a rather special position. It is technically not part of the Seaway at all, having been constructed entirely at Canada's expense and being opened thirty-two years earlier. From time to time, groups of Americans agitate for an all-American route, virtually a revival of the Erie Canal, which would compete with the Seaway. The Welland Canal also gets congested. Three of its locks are already twinned, thus allowing traffic to move both ways at the same time. One lock is a large low-lift structure which handles several ships at a time and causes few delays. In 1964 the Canadian government announced that all the locks would be twinned, at an estimated cost of $150 million, which is 10 per cent more than the entire canal cost in the 1920s.

Tolls on the old Welland were removed in 1903 and the new Welland was free of tolls until 1959 when the Seaway was opened. Then tolls were set at 2 cents per registered ton, 2 cents per ton of bulk cargo, and 5 cents per ton of general cargo. Where applicable, the tolls on cargo but not on registered tons were added to the tolls along the Seaway. Hence a vessel using both the Seaway and the Welland, i.e., going between Lake Erie and Montreal, paid 4, 42, and 45 cents per registered ton, ton of bulk cargo, and ton of general cargo, respectively.

Grain growers in Western Canada, the Steel Company in Hamilton, and shippers and consignees in Toronto object to tolls on the Welland on three grounds: they add to the cost of doing business, the canal was toll-free for roughly six decades before 1959, and its capital cost has already been absorbed in the public debt. At the same time manufacturers in Toronto and Hamilton are not averse to the continuance of tolls between Montreal and Lake Ontario because they provide a sort of protective tariff to industry in the Toronto-Hamilton area.

During the election campaign of 1962, Prime Minister Diefenbaker announced that tolls would be suspended forthwith. His policy ran directly counter to a major recommendation of the MacPherson Commission that the costs of each mode of transport should be paid directly by the people who used it. When the Liberals came to power in 1963, they considered reinstating tolls on the Welland but took no action until 1967. In that year the United States government vetoed a proposal to raise tolls along the Seaway proper, i.e., between Montreal and Lake Ontario, by 10 per cent in order to increase the probability that the Seaway would be paid for out of revenues within 50 years, as originally planned. Although the Americans allowed Canada to take 73 per cent of the receipts from fees for using the Seaway as such, instead of 71 per cent as in the past, the Canadian government felt that it should not continue to let shippers use the Welland without charge. Accordingly, it assessed a lockage fee of $160 a trip ($20 for each of 8 locks) on vessels with cargo, and half this amount on vessels in ballast. These fees are to be increased in regular steps to a maximum of $800 per trip in 1971.

During the long years when construction of the Seaway was being debated, its protagonists declared that it was justified by the substantial reductions it would permit in the cost of moving grain overseas from Western Canada. The estimates ranged as high as 8 or 10 cents a bushel, though as time went on they were cut to 5 and even to 2 cents.[22] In 1966 the Canadian Seaway Authority estimated the saving at 4.2 cents a bushel. It suggested that all the savings, a total of $13.5 million in 1965, went to Western farmers, though in fact some of them may have been shared with consumers overseas. This point was discussed in the chapter on Freight Rates and Prices.

The effect of the Seaway on railways is indeterminate. Some American lines decided to fight it by slashing tolls on traffic between inland cities and Atlantic ports. In general Canadian carriers by rail maintained their existing rates, except on sugar where there was a scramble for business. Because it is now more economical for so-called lakers (vessels plying Lakes Superior and Huron) to proceed as far down as Montreal rather than unload at ports on Georgian Bay or at Port Colborne, Kingston, etc., railways have lost most of their traffic in ex-lake grain. Yet taking one thing with another, they seem to have come out even on the Seaway.

Before the Seaway was started, many of its advocates had enthusiastically prophesied that any number of ocean-going ships would ply the Great Lakes and upper St. Lawrence regularly during the season of navigation. Up to a point their predictions have been fulfilled. But then a few such vessels went into the Great Lakes long before the Seaway was opened. Although the number of ocean-going ships in the Lakes increased greatly after 1959, they remain a small proportion of the total number plying these waters and they carry perhaps no more than 10 or 15 per cent of the total tonnage.

This situation is the result of several factors. A channel with a minimum depth of 27 feet (less one foot or a foot and a half to ensure that the vessel will clear the sills of the locks) excludes the world's largest and fastest vessels. Owing to the differing specific gravities of salt and fresh water, the same vessel rides lower in the latter than in the former. This means that an ocean-going ship is able to carry less cargo on the inland waterway than it can on the high seas; otherwise it has difficulty clearing the sills of canals. It costs next to nothing more to operate a ship that is "full and down" (every cubic foot space filled and the total weight of the cargo brings the vessel down to her Plimsoll or maximum load line) than to run it when it is only partly filled. Hence, when an ocean-going ship has to unload 5 or 10 per cent of the weight of her cargo at Montreal in order to clear the channels farther up, her costs per day are undiminished while her costs per ton rise. Her daily net revenues on inland waters will be less than on the high seas unless, of course, rates on the Lakes are high enough to compensate for the higher ton-mile operating costs. This is unlikely because the lakers operate at a high level of efficiency. On the other hand, when ocean-going ships deliver cargo to ports on the Great Lakes, they save the cost of trans-shipping at Montreal.

Lake ships cannot safely be operated in salt water. They settle too high in the water and according to salt-water standards their length is out of proportion to their draught and beam. They roll excessively in a rough sea and without expensive structural changes are in the danger of capsizing. The dimensions of a laker are determined mainly by the size of the locks through which it has to pass. It is fairly cheap to make locks long but expensive to make them wide and, most of all, to make them deep. Generally speaking, the larger a vessel is, the lower its costs of operation per ton-mile. So long as the ship is seaworthy, it is immaterial whether size is attained by increasing length, draught, beam, or a combination of two or three of these factors. Naturally the canals along the Great Lakes and St. Lawrence are designed for economy and so inland ships have to be relatively long and narrow too. Their maximum dimensions are draught 25 feet 6 inches, beam less than 75 feet, and length 750 feet. Any vessel with a length ten times its beam is considered unfit for travel across the high seas.

Ocean vessels or "salties" typically have high superstructures whereas lakers are cut low toward the water. Salties are more easily shifted by a high wind than their counterparts on inland waters. This is of no great significance on the high seas or even on an open lake but it does mean that in canals and other constricted channels, ocean-going ships have to advance slowly. In particular, they tend to warp or bind against one side of the lock during transit. Furthermore, because salties are usually general purpose carriers, they take a little longer to load and unload than specialized carriers of ore and grain, or even the general cargo vessels on our inland waters.

In the mid-1960s a Canadian yard built two tankers with thicker and stronger steel than conventional vessels and with bulbous bows which are expected to help break choppy water and lessen wave resistance. In summer these vessels will ply the Seaway and Great Lakes while in winter they will operate along the Atlantic seaboard. American shipbuilders are also experimenting with ocean-going lakers which might, for example, carry iron ore from Sept Iles to Lake Erie ports or from Venezuela to Sparrow's Point, Md., depending on the season.

Owners of ocean-going vessels are presumably not specially concerned because their ships may slow down the movement of other carriers using the Seaway, the Welland, and the Lakes, but they are aware of the fact that their ships can produce fewer ton-miles per day on inland waters than on the high seas. This is important because it costs somewhere between $5,000 and $15,000 every day a ship is idle. Slower rate of travel is equivalent to idle time. Besides, a ship that fails to get out of the Seaway before the freeze-up—and this has happened to as many as four ships in some years—will be idle all winter. For all these reasons, the Seaway has been less successful in attracting ocean-going vessels than many people expected. What has happened is that lakers now go down to Montreal where their cargoes are trans-shipped into deepsea vessels. Conversely, Montreal has become the point of trans-shipment from oceanic to inland ships. In brief, the Seaway has failed to convert the Great Lakes into a sort of Mediterranean used mainly by sea-going vessels. Instead it has served to extend the route of the big upper lakers closer toward salt water.

The failure of more than a small but growing number of salties to penetrate into the Great Lakes basin has resulted in a substantial growth of business at Montreal which had originally feared that the Seaway would ruin it. The Seaway also made possible the port of Baie Comeau, 250 statute miles by air below Quebec City. Vessels come down this far with grain which is transferred to ocean-going vessels and then go in ballast to Sept Iles for a back-haul of iron ore. Toronto, Hamilton, and the bigger ports on the American side of the Lakes have gained but the smaller ones—Prescott, Kingston, Port Colborne, Midland, and Port McNicoll—have gone behind or advanced but slightly. Midland has, however, found that its shipyard is busier than before because of government subsidies and the need to replace the carrying capacity of perhaps 120 obsolete lakers and canallers.

Technological change, such as hovercraft, conventional barges, or tugs pulling partly submerged plastic containers, may influence the future of the Seaway. Its usefulness in national defence, another motive behind its construction, has fortunately not been tested. The hydro-electric power which was developed simultaneously with the works of navigation is all being used. Neither the fears that it would allow overseas manufacturers to flood the market in the basin of the Great Lakes and destroy its industry, nor the hopes that it would allow producers there enormously to expand their sales abroad have materialized. Broadly speaking, the Seaway seems to have accelerated economic development along the previously existing pattern rather than brought about radical changes. Even the mining in Labrador-Quebec, which was the direct result of the Seaway, has had to compete with the older source south of Lake Superior rather than supplant it. In brief, the Seaway has provided an important route for transport, but its revenues after operating expenses may not be large enough to amortize its capital cost over 50 years as originally expected.

23

Ocean Shipping

CANADA is not herself an important operator of merchant ships although in some post-war years she has been the world's third largest trader. Although most of our external trade goes by rail across the U.S. boundary, in the early 1960s ocean-going ships handled 27 per cent of our imports and 40 per cent of our exports. Hence, Canadians should have some understanding of the kinds of services offered, ocean rates, and marine insurance. The experience of the Canadian government with a state-owned merchant marine is both interesting and salutary.

Classes of Vessels

Although vessels may be classified by motive power, tonnage, or both, the significant division for trade is by the services they render shippers. Tramp vessels are not limited in their operations to a particular route but shuttle along the trade routes of the entire world wherever cargo is available. As a rule tramps handle shipload lots of bulky commodities such as grain, coal, lumber, ore, sugar, heavy steel, or general cargo. If they cannot obtain a full load from one shipper, they may be put "on berth," that is, they will accept cargo from other shippers bound for the same or a near-by destination.

Tramps are typically chartered, the contract between the vessel owner and the shipper of the goods being known as a charter party. Principally chartering is by trip where the owner furnishes vessel, crew, and fuel. In effect the owner rents the boat and its facilities for a particular voyage. The rate may be gross: a single payment covers insurance, loading, and unloading and the charterer has merely to deliver the freight f.a.s. (free alongside ship). Sometimes the rate is net: the owner of the vessel assumes responsibility only for transportation as such and the charterer delivers the goods aboard ship, stows them away, removes them at destination, and provides for his own insurance. When operators of liners want to supplement their own services during the peak season or put a vessel on a run preliminary to establishing a line service, they may charter a vessel on a time basis, that is, so much per deadweight ton per day or month. Less frequently they charter bare-boat, the owner renting the vessel to an operator who supplies his own crew and fuel.

Typically tramps are built for economy of operation and not for speed. The better modern tramps have capacities of 12,000 to 15,000 net tons and speeds of 20 knots, or roughly 23 statute miles per hour. Tramps use public port facilities rather than privately owned docks. They serve the ports of the world that do not have a sufficient tonnage to justify operating vessels on regular schedules and they handle the seasonal peaks in the traffic of grain and the like.

Liners operate over definite routes between fixed points and on previously announced schedules of departures and approximate dates of arrivals. Some carry freight exclusively; most have accommodation for freight and a few passengers; a few liners are chiefly in the passenger business, the freight which they carry being enough to give proper trim to the vessel or to use space not suitable for passengers. In size and speed some of the better tramps differ but little from the liners in use on all except the world's busiest water routes. Of course some liners are truly "monarchs of the sea"; as Kipling writes, "The Liner she's a lady." In general, express liners are faster, larger, and more elegantly equipped than their slower sisters but the word "liner" takes in the luxurious "Queens" of the North Atlantic as well as prosaic vessels going back and forth on regular schedules between the more important ports of the world. Liners carry most of the world's water-borne general cargo, passengers, mail and express. They compete with tramps for bulky commodities which they commonly need to fill up their holds and they face intense competition from airlines for passengers.

The final group of vessels is the industrial carriers. These are owned by the shipper whose goods they transport, such as Imperial Oil, United States Steel Corporation, and United Fruit Company. Often they carry freight for other shippers too, particularly if the owner-operator's freight traffic is unbalanced in volume and direction. Their chief business is to handle one type of freight such as petroleum, coal, ore, and fruit.

Industrial carriers typically have low operating costs per ton-mile. They have special facilities for transferring their cargo between wharf and vessel, and are designed to allow the maximum space for a particular product. Owners of industrial carriers are able to control delivery of their raw materials more closely than if they had to rely on common carriers. Hence they are better able to avoid inadequate reserves on the one hand or redundancy of stock on the other. At times industrial carriers may operate in one direction in ballast. Their special construction may preclude handling any other product or the need of the owner for prompt delivery of his own goods may be so great that it would not be worth while to delay the vessel until other articles could be sought and stowed away.

From time to time vessels shift from one service to another. As a general rule the volume of tramp tonnage declines in boom times and increases in slack ones, since ships tend to be put on scheduled or liner services whenever the volume of traffic between two ports grows to a point where such a service will pay. Conversely liners are withdrawn when business falls off and the vessels, now acting as tramps, search the world for paying traffic. For the same reasons vessels move in and out of the industrial carrier class. For example, in the late 1950s the new oil tankers coming from shipyards in large numbers were much bigger and faster than their predecessors. Hence, oil-carrying capacity increased more rapidly than demand and rates fell. After the rise of Castro, the United States banned imports of sugar from Cuba and in 1961–2 started to draw on more distant sources. At the same time Communist China and the U.S.S.R., wanting to help the Cubans, worked out big deals for exchanging sugar for petroleum products. These shifts in trade caused an increase in the rates on dry cargo relative to those on petroleum. As a result some tankers were adapted to the carriage of free-flowing solids, such as sugar and grain. The change-over checked a rise in dry-cargo rates and caused chagrin among owners of tramp vessels who had been having some lean years. Ocean "freights" or charges are in a constant state of flux because of the impact on ocean shipping of changing economic and political conditions throughout the world.

Notwithstanding many examples to the contrary, the trend toward specialized or industrial carriers is gaining strength. The cost of operating vessels at higher rates of speed has become more favourable relative to the cost of moving the same cargo more slowly. Usually countries subsidize liner service but not tramps. Ocean freight now consists of more manufactured and processed goods than formerly; the kinds of freight which typically move by liner have increased more rapidly than bulky freight which ordinarily goes by tramp. The movement of bulk cargoes seems to be less seasonal than it once was on account of larger storage facilities near the sources of supply. Modern business demands greater speed and regularity in transport than before World War I. This trend favours liner service and discourages tramps.

Ocean Rates

Ocean shipping rates differ in many ways from railway freight rates. Vessels operate on high seas which are free, in peacetime at least, to all the nations of the world. In theory anything that will float may be used in ocean shipping. Vessels may be taken out of storage or purchased second-hand whenever the volume of trade grows. Government regulation of rates and of entrance to the industry is impossible since only international action would be effective. On the sea uncontrolled competition is the rule except in so far as it is restricted by the companies themselves. Generally on bulk cargo the forces of supply and demand function without let or hindrance.

In ocean shipping (except charter parties) rates are quoted for specific commodities, not by classes as on railways. Ship operators quote rates in cents per ton but a ton is either by weight or by space, whichever will give more revenue to the carrier. A weight ton is 2,240 pounds though occasionally a short ton of 2,000 pounds is used. For package freight and other relatively light cargo, rates are quoted in space or measurement tons of 40 cubic feet. Weight tons are used when 2,240 pounds of the freight involved occupy less than 40 cubic feet. Measurement tons are used when 2,240 pounds of the commodity require more than 40 cubic feet of space. The units for measuring the size of vessels, e.g., deadweight and displacement tons, are quite different from those used in computing tolls. On shipments to and from Continental Europe metric tons (2204.6 lbs. avoirdupois) or cubic metre tons (35.314 cubic feet) are commonly used.

Rates vary with the quality of service offered by different vessels and are typically unstable. A fast ship may charge higher rates than a slow one even when both ships are owned by the same company. Ocean rates on goods shipped in bulk fluctuate constantly with the supply of shipping space and the amount of freight seeking transportation. The costs of operating a ship are relatively fixed. Interest, depreciation, and obsolescence go on whether the ship is operating or idle. Once the vessel is put into service the wages of captain and crew, insurance on hull, and the cost of fuel and ship supplies are substantially the same whether the vessel is fully or only partially laden. Consequently if a ship cannot get a full cargo, or something approaching a full cargo at going rates, it can afford to slash rates if it is necessary to do so in order to get additional freight. It is more profitable for the vessel's operator to accept some traffic at rates barely high enough to cover his very low out-of-pocket expenses than it is for the ship to sail without that business and that revenue at all. Hence in the absence of agreement among operators, rates especially on bulky shipments change without notice. They may vary from day to day and even from hour to hour. Rates are not uniform from one shipper to another even on the same commodity and on the same vessel. Secret rebates are occasionally given, and ship operators do not publish rates though some conferences do so on general merchandise. As a rule the rates on bulk cargo are allowed to move freely in accord with the cliché, the laws of supply and demand.

Intense competition is no more pleasant to ship operators than it is to businessmen generally. It exaggerates both the profits and the losses from ship operation. Owing to the unwillingness of operators to withdraw their vessels promptly from service when business drops off and their inability to construct new ships without delay when business picks up, intensive competition introduces an element of quasi-rent which may be at times positive (a profit) and on other occasions decidedly negative (a loss). A company which has suffered losses for many years may find that as soon as it begins to make a small profit, its trade is invaded by tramps and all chance of recouping the deficits of the past disappear. The shipper may seem to gain from periodically depressed rates but he suffers when rates rise to abnormally high levels. Low rates may drive liners off a particular route and the tramps which replace them will typically give less frequent, less dependable, and slower service.

Conferences

In order to protect their own profits and safeguard the long-run interests of shippers, ship operators try to avoid the effects of intensive competition whenever they can. Small companies often amalgamate voluntarily or are bought out by a single big concern. This trend, which can be traced back at least to 1900, has been facilitated by two factors: the rising cost of vessels has served to keep down the number of tramps; and the declining importance of the smaller ports combined with concentration of shipping at the larger ones has made it easier for a single enterprise to exercise control. The difficulty is that amalgamation is expensive to create and to maintain against the inroads of small and sometimes irresponsible carriers.

Ship-owners may come together to develop traffic, get favourable harbour regulations, formulate plans for meeting the demands of labour, and consider the interests of the trade generally. Sometimes ship-owners form conferences or shipping rings which may have permanent officials and elaborate rules and penalties. At other times they have a single "gentlemen's agreement," a series of understandings arrived at after an informal luncheon, or some such social function. The conference may fix actual rates which must be charged by all members except bulky commodities on which rates are "wild," that is, allowed to seek their own economic level. More commonly the conference sets minimum rates and lets members get higher rates whenever they can on account of faster service, relative shortage of shipping space, or any other reason. Still more often, conferences agree that lines with circuitous routes or slower vessels will be allowed to charge a certain differential, 5 or 10 per cent, below the going charges. Typically the conference either restricts the total number of sailings, "staggers" the dates so that two or more vessels are not competing for business between two ports at the same time, or skips some small ports so that delivery to a big terminus will be speeded up from all of them. For example, a ship on its way to London from West Africa may call at ports A, C, and E while a week or so later another ship will connect B, D, and F with London. This plan avoids the delay and expense of calling at every minor port. It works well as long as there is little local traffic between, say, A and B. Finally, the conference may set quotas for its various members. Any participant who exceeds his annual quota has to pay so much per ton into the funds of the conference. At the end of the year these funds are divided among members who have fallen below their quotas or percentage of the total business of the conference that has been assigned to them.

Agreements made by conferences cannot be enforced in the courts because no international authority has jurisdiction over such schemes. So, a conference has to provide its own remedies for non-adherence to agreements. In the main it relies on the good sense and integrity of its members. It may try moral suasion, attempting to make the recalcitrants see the errors of their ways and the shortsightedness of not living up to an understanding which is for the benefit of the dissenter as much as for other conference members. The conference may have a system of heavy fines or may declare forfeit the bonds which the members have deposited with the conference executive as evidence of good faith. The most effective means of dealing with interloping tramps or other ships of non-conference members is the deferred rebate. Shippers are promised a rebate of 5 to 10 per cent of their freight payments at the end of a designated period (three, six, or twelve months) provided they have meanwhile shipped their freight destined for ports served by the conference exclusively by way of conference lines. This scheme tends to keep all the trade within the conference. Interlopers have difficulty in getting any business, while conference members have little incentive to go after business by recklessly cutting rates. Conference contracts typically carry what is known as the Fall Clause whereby, if conference lines for any reason reduce a rate, all shippers who sign the conference contract automatically become entitled to the lower rate.

On other occasions conferences make contracts with important shippers giving them rates lower than those charged generally, provided they promise to dispatch via the conference lines their entire shipments to certain ports during stipulated periods. This arrangement differs from the deferred rebate only in that one is made before and the other after shipment.

The operation of conferences may be abused. Certain shippers may be favoured to the detriment of others. Small shippers may be ruthlessly destroyed. Improvement in services due to better vessels may be indefinitely postponed. Conference members may agree to share losses on a "fighting ship" which will operate for a few months at very low rates, drive legitimate competitors of the conference out of business, and thus permit the conference to raise its rates to higher levels than ever to recompense it for its temporary losses.

Despite all their potential shortcomings, a properly managed conference may benefit both ship owners and shippers. It may stabilize rates and eliminate the fluctuating charges which seriously interfere with trade. It may distribute sailings more regularly throughout the year and thus tend to ensure full loads. By protecting the revenues of carriers the conference may ultimately lead to the construction of better equipped and faster vessels. In brief, a conference may overcome the disadvantages of unbridled competition in a socially desirable way or it may abuse its more or less monopolistic power to the detriment of society.

In 1925 the Canadian government proposed putting its own vessels on the high seas in order to break the alleged monopoly of the North Atlantic Shipping Ring.[1] After the death of the gentleman who was to promote and operate the venture, the whole scheme fell through. The Coastwise Operators' Association of British Columbia and the Associated Newfoundland Lines on the east coast consist mainly of the larger operators. Both organizations agree on rates for small lots and publish a consolidated tariff. Rates for full shiploads are not dealt with. Though not technically members of the conference, small operators and Canadian National Steamships on the Atlantic coast and Canadian Pacific Steamships in British Columbia waters adhere quite closely to the agreed-on rates. Both conferences are voluntary, relying on the good faith of their members rather than a system of fines, bonds, or formal contracts. Neither conference grants rebates or makes contracts with shippers debarring them from using non-conference ships. On its transoceanic services Canadian Pacific refuses to pay deferred rebates but sometimes gives more favourable rates to regular customers.

The Transport Act, 1938, gave the Board of Transport Commissioners authority to license ships operating between one port and another in Canada but the Governor-in-Council might exempt any ship or class of ship from the operation of the Act. The provisions were not to apply to the transportation of goods in bulk nor to ships engaged in the transportation of goods or passengers between any ports: (1) in British Columbia, (2) on Hudson Bay, in the Maritime Provinces, or on the Gulf and River St. Lawrence east of the western tip of the Island of Orleans, (3) outside Canada, (4) between ports in British Columbia, and the Maritimes and the Great Lakes. In affirmative terms, the Act was to apply between ports on the St. Lawrence River, the Great Lakes, and interconnecting rivers. The basic purpose of the Act was to restrict admission to the industry unless conditions of public convenience and necessity were satisfied. Control of rates was indirect: by preventing too many ships from entering the business, the Act would lessen the probability of ruthless competition and of drastic rate cutting. As the sections of the Transport Act relating to ocean shipping have not yet been proclaimed or brought into effect for all practical purposes Canada, like Britain, does not regulate deepsea carriers except as regards safety. Commonwealth and foreign ships are excluded from handling traffic between two Canadian ports on the Great Lakes and the St. Lawrence River above Havre St. Pierre, as explained in the previous chapter.

In the United States measures of control over conferences are reasonably complete. In 1916 Congress forbade the use of deferred rebates, fighting ships, and retaliation or unfair practices against any shipper. The legislation applied to all carriers touching United States ports whether operating between states of the Union or with foreign countries. All conference and pooling arrangements were made subject to review by the Maritime Commission which must be satisfied that the agreements are not discriminatory or unfair as between carriers, shippers, exporters, importers, or parts of the United States, and not detrimental to the commerce of the country as a whole. Conferences must admit new lines as members whenever the applicant is a *bona fide* common carrier in the trade route involved. Common carriers by water in United States foreign commerce are required to file export rates on all commodities (except those carried in bulk) within a period of 30 days after they have become effective. A similar requirement applies to imports but only from the east coast of South America to Pacific coast ports. The Maritime Commission has jurisdiction over these rates to the extent they are discriminatory or detrimental to the commerce of the United States. In a word, conferences are subject to some official control in the United States but not in Britain.

In 1964 Canadian shippers got up in arms over rates charged by the Trans-Atlantic Conference. In consequence, our government referred the matter to the Restrictive Trade Practices Commission. After lengthy hearings the Commission found that fifteen firms engaged in carrying freight both ways between Canada and Britain operated in a combination to fix rates and inhibit competition from tramps. It thought that shippers and ocean carriers should be able to bargain fairly over rates. But the Commission said, excessive rate competition and instability in shipping schedules would harm Anglo-Canadian trade. Hence, shipping companies should be able to arrange guarantees with shippers for the handling of certain quantities of cargo over a period of time. This was necessary in view of the high capital investment required for up-to-date ocean-liner services. Nevertheless, all shipping companies should make their tariffs available to any interested member of the public, and contracts between shippers and shipping lines should (a) include provisions for termination on 90 days notice, and (b) be limited to 85 per cent of a shipper's consignments.

Marine Insurance

Marine insurance is so involved that no more than the barest outline can be given here. In general, railways are liable for loss and damage to the goods they accept as freight, but the liability of steamship companies is limited to negligence in loading or in stowage or in the proper delivery of cargo. The company must provide a seaworthy boat and choose its officers and men with reasonable care. Beyond this it is not legally required to make good any claim for loss or damage which may be laid against it. Specifically ship operators are not liable for theft, embezzlement, latent defect of vessel, Act of God or the Queen's enemies, insurrection and civil strife, barratry (any wrongful act wilfully committed by master or crew; Fr. *barat*, fraud), and so forth. The shipper of goods by sea assumes considerable risk, whereas one by land has relatively little. Almost invariably owners of goods being transported by vessel shift the risk of loss and damage to marine insurance companies because their rates are low and an insurance policy facilitates finance, as explained later.

Hull insurance, which is taken against destruction or damage to the vessel itself, is arranged by the ship's owners, usually through the famous medium, Lloyd's of London. Cargo insurance is obtained by the owners of each lot of goods and is sold in Canada by branches of British and American concerns. It is customary to insure for the full value of each shipment plus 10 per cent to cover freight, consular fees, forwarding charges, other incidental expenses connected with the shipment, and even anticipated profit. In insuring ordinary property, the face amount of the policy must be no more than the fair market value of the goods, otherwise the owner might prefer to destroy the property and collect the insurance money. To deter him from doing this, insurance companies will pay claims only up to a certain proportion of the market price of the assets insured. In ocean shipping owners are not in possession of the goods at any time while the insurance is in force and so could not destroy them even if they liked. Hence they may insure up to the full value.

The hazards covered by marine insurance are of different types. If the entire cargo and probably the ship too are destroyed, losses are borne by the particular parties whose property has been lost or they are shifted to their insurance companies. Sometimes the loss is partial, that is, all or part (say 60 per cent) of A's goods are destroyed, the property of other shippers remaining intact. Partial losses are known as "average," a word of obscure origin but apparently associated with the Old French *avarie* (damage) or the Teutonic *halverage* (partnership). It is possible to get a policy "with average," one to cover all damages whatever, one which will give full protection against partial loss. Except on very valuable articles, this kind of insurance policy is unusual because it is too expensive. Commonly, the policy is F.P.A. (free of particular average) 3 or 5 per cent. In this case the company will pay claims only if they exceed 3 or 5 per cent or whatever the figure F.P.A. may be. If the loss is less than the percentage stated in the contract, no claim is allowed; if it exceeds the percentage, full claim is payable by the marine insurance company. F.P.A. policies protect the companies against trivial claims, guard against the minor losses which frequently occur when goods are being stowed or loaded and unloaded, and save the owners the higher premiums of policies "with average."

Another kind of partial loss is called "general average." This arises from any sacrifice or extraordinary expense purposely made or incurred for the preservation of the ship or its contents from danger. General average arises from throwing overboard (jettisoning) in a storm to lighten the vessel, burning cargo when the fuel supply is exhausted, cutting away the superstructure to save the vessel, flooding a hold to put out a fire, hiring tugs to tow a vessel to port from an imperilled position, and unloading cargo to release a stranded vessel. These expenses or sacrifices are made for the general good. They are incurred for the benefit of all shippers and therefore all should contribute *pro rata* for the loss of the goods of a particular shipper or of part of the ship.

To recapitulate, general average is a sacrifice or expense that is voluntarily made, that is designed to protect the interests of the enterprise as a whole, and that has been in some degree successful. If the effort is unsuccessful, losses must be borne individually. Finally the event which led to the expense must have been fortuitous. Obviously great difficulties arise in deciding what has been purposely sacrificed and what has been destroyed as a direct result of purely natural causes. It may take months, even years, to complete the adjustment. If a shipper is not adequately insured with a reputable company, his goods may be held until he puts up a sufficient guarantee to protect other shippers. Eventually the general average loss is assessed against all the owners of cargo and ship or, in practice, against the companies with which they have insured.

In marine insurance policies certain hazards are normally excluded such as war, riots, strikes and lockouts, clandestine theft, theft committed by passengers or members of the ship's company, inherent vice (natural deterioration), inadequate packing, seaworthiness but not leaks which are from peril of the sea, that is, leaks against which a reasonably prudent ship-owner could, by taking thought, have guarded. All these risks, except poor packing and inherent vice, may be insured against by adding clauses to the standard policy and paying additional premiums. A shipper must take extreme care to see that he is insured for every eventuality against which he desires to be protected.

The rates of marine insurance vary with the ship, destination, commodity, length of voyage, the amount F. P. A., and so on. In time of war insurance against loss by enemy action, i.e., war risk insurance, varies with the voyage, whether the ship is convoyed or not, the probability of damage by subsurface raiders, enemy airplanes, saboteurs, etc. Many insurance companies periodically reduce rates to any of their clients who have had few claims for loss or damage during the preceding few months. This arrangement encourages shippers to pack and handle their goods carefully.

Obviously it would be inconvenient to both parties if a large shipper had to take out separate policies for each one of his numerous shipments. In such cases open policies are used. The insurer or shipper contracts with the marine insurance company to report to it daily all shipments it has made during that day. At the end of each month the insurance company computes the amount of premiums payable, bills the shipper, and is remunerated by a single cheque. The method saves both parties time and expense.

Documentation of Overseas Shipments

A number of documents are necessary when goods are sent overseas. If port facilities are being used nearly to capacity, the shipper may need a shipping permit from the harbour authorities so that he may deliver his goods on a specified wharf on a particular day.[2] Once he delivers the goods, he will get a dock receipt. From the nearest Canada Customs House, he will secure a manifest, a document which provides the data for Canadian export statistics and helps to ensure that contraband material is not sent abroad. From the nearest British or foreign consul of the country to which the goods are destined, the shipper must obtain a consular invoice. The number of copies required and the fees payable vary with the country of destination. The purpose of the consular invoice is to prevent understatement of price with a view to avoiding payment of import duties abroad. When goods are brought into Canada, the consular invoice must state that no other invoice has been or will be sent.

If goods are being sent between Canada and any other part of the British Commonwealth and Empire or between Canada and any foreign country to which the "intermediate tariff" applies,[3] a certificate of origin is required in order that the goods may qualify for the lower rates of customs duty payable on Canadian goods upon importation into the other country and vice versa. Without this certificate goods of countries which have not the same tariff arrangements with other countries as Canada has, might be sent to the Dominion and then forwarded abroad as goods of Canadian origin. If this were to occur, the foreign country or other part of the Commonwealth would be unjustly deprived of revenue while Canadian producers of the same article would be discriminated against. Usually the certificate of origin is included in the consular invoice. Finally, the shipper will get a policy of marine insurance and a bill of lading.

Financing Overseas Shipments

Ordinarily when a merchant sells overseas, he does not care to wait for payment until the goods are delivered and the proceeds of their sale remitted through normal banking channels. Indeed, for all he knows, the purchaser abroad may receive the goods and never remit the money. To avoid this difficulty the vendor will take all the documents mentioned above to his bank where he will prepare a draft on the buyer. A draft is an unconditional order in writing drawn by one person (the Canadian vendor) on another (the purchaser abroad) ordering him to pay on demand or at a fixed or determinable future time a sum certain in money. Usually the draft is payable so many days after the date of the draft or after sight, i.e., after the draft has been presented to the purchaser for acceptance. Because these arrangements were worked out when transportation was less dependable than it is today, it became customary to draw up drafts in duplicate or even in triplicate and to forward them by different vessels. If one vessel were lost, the duplicate draft would be presented to the purchaser and paid. Normally the purchaser would honour "this first bill of exchange, the second [bill of exchange] remaining unpaid."

The bank will take possession of all these documents and will immediately pay the vendor the face of the draft less interest at the going rate for the length of time between the day the documents are presented and the date of maturity of the draft. Then the bank will forward the draft and all the accompanying documents to its branch or corresponding agent, another bank, abroad. This other bank will present the draft to the purchaser for acceptance, that is, for acknowledgment by him that he owes money which the draft represents. The purchaser expresses his acceptance of the obligation by writing across the face of the draft the word "accepted" followed by his name. On the day the draft matures (so many days after date or after sight) the agent of the Canadian bank abroad will present the draft for payment. If the purchaser abroad pays the draft at maturity, the Canadian bank gets its money back and has made a profit on the transaction. If he refuses to accept the draft when it is first presented to him, i.e., if he dishonours it by non-acceptance, or if later he dishonours it by non-payment, the bank may sue the drawee (the vendor) for the amount of its loan.

The bill of lading which is included among the other documents is both a receipt for the goods and a contract between the transportation company and the shipper for the carriage of the goods under the terms and conditions set forth on the document. The bill may be negotiable; the right to receive the goods from the transport company at destination may be transferred by endorsement which merely means signing the bill in much the same manner as a cheque. Some bills of lading are non-negotiable; in this event the transportation company will deliver the goods only to the consignee named on the document. As the Canadian bank or its agent overseas keeps possession of all the documents until the draft has been paid, or at least until the importer has made arrangements for paying, the bill of lading used in overseas trade is almost invariably negotiable. If the buyer refuses to pay, the bank will endorse the bill of lading in its own name, obtain the goods, sell them to someone else in the same line of business in the overseas port, and then bill the drawee for any difference between what it receives and the amount of its loan.

If the goods are lost at sea, the bank will collect on the marine insurance policy and so recover its money. As explained, the face of the policy is for the full value of the goods and so is adequate to cover the bank's loan to the vendor. In London and to some extent in New York and other exporting centres, men specialize in knowing the credit standing of international traders in particular lines of business or in certain areas. For a relatively small fee these men will themselves accept bills of exchange in the possession of banks, will pay the bank off entirely, and assume all the risks in case the vendor dishonours the draft. Thus from the bank's point of view this method of finance is unusually safe. Consequently its charges are low. Exporters may send goods abroad even though they are not intimately acquainted with the credit standing of the purchasers. The financial machinery is closely related to the shipping arrangements.

As can be seen, the business arrangements for the shipment of freight overseas are complex. Typically they are performed by several distinct agencies. Steamship companies employ traffic solicitors in coastal and inland cities wherever the volume of business warrants. These men try to obtain traffic for the shipping company which employs them and will help exporters with their shipping problems. Freight forwarders will take freight destined overseas from industries and merchants in seaports and in inland cities. They will see that the freight is delivered in good order, first to the vessel at the port of departure and then to the consignee abroad whether he lives in a seaport or interior city. If the exporter has a full shipload of freight to send, a ship broker will arrange for him to charter a vessel. By telegraph, cable, or wireless, ship brokers exchange a vast amount of information about the availability of cargoes and of empty shipping space. They perform "the complicated task of bringing together the vessels and the freight so that one may be profitably employed and the other economically carried."[4]

Another class of specialists in international trade are the customs house brokers. They clear imported goods through customs and complete the necessary documents for the export of commodities. Still other business men concentrate on placing marine insurance on cargoes and hulls. The principal business of some commission houses and manufacturers' agents at seaports is to arrange for the purchase and sale of goods in foreign markets. A few large firms have a number of departments each of which specializes in a particular activity. In this way a single firm can provide the exporter or importer with a complete service. A businessman who wants to sell or buy abroad need not be dismayed by the apparent perplexities of the paper work. He will find plenty of specialists to undertake the technical problems for him at a reasonable fee.

If the shipper prefers, he may have a Canadian railway issue him a through bill of lading to cover moving the freight from a shipping point in the interior of this country to the destination abroad. The export toll by rail to the seaport is filed with the Canadian Transport Commission. Local agents quote the rate for the ocean part of the trip after consulting one of their superior officers in a large city. Because the Canadian Pacific owns and operates its own vessels in trans-Atlantic and trans-Pacific services, quoting through rates is often relatively easy. Even so, many shippers find it profitable to engage an agent at seaboard who will shop around and frequently get a lower rate for the ocean service than the railway has quoted. A railway must protect itself against possible increases in the rate between the time it quotes the through rate at the interior point and the time when the goods arrive at seaport or when it makes a firm contract with a ship operator for their carriage by sea. Consequently the rates it quotes may be a little higher than those the agent of the shipper in close contact with conditions at the seaport may be able to obtain. Shippers typically use agents when the volume of their overseas trade is large and ocean rates are fluctuating. They use through bills of lading when they ship only small quantities and conferences have stabilized rates.

Coastal Shipping

Canada's oceanic shipping falls into three classes: coastal, intercoastal, and overseas. The number of calls made at Canadian ports by vessels in the coasting service exceeded 125,000 a year in the early 1960s or not quite four times as many calls as sea-going and inland international ships (e.g., Toronto-Rochester, N.Y.) at Canadian ports. But their net registered tonnage totalled less than 20 per cent more. Ships in coasting service are small as a rule, though the Canadian overall average is pulled up by the big carriers for handling grain and ore. More typical of coasting services are ships of between 500 and 2000 gross tons. Along the British Columbia coast, sheltered from oceanic storms by Vancouver Island, the Queen Charlotte's, and numerous other partly-submerged mountain peaks, a good deal of traffic moves by scow and barge of roughly 300 tons each. The Canadian National also runs an "aquatrain," or ferry with accommodation for 24 standard-gauge freight cars, between Prince Rupert and the Alaska Railway at Whittier, a distance of 810 miles.

Coastal shipping is subsidized in a number of different ways. Buoys, lighthouses, foghorns, weather information, and other aids to navigation are supplied without direct charge to shippers. Facilities at harbours are either entirely free or can be used on payment of a small sum which is not intended fully to remunerate the government for the expense it has incurred. The Post Office pays vessel owners when they carry mail. Formerly mail compensation was often in excess of what would have been charged for commercial freight of the same total weight and value, and so constituted an indirect subsidy. In recent years Canadian subsidization through mail payments has been cut down if not entirely eliminated. Instead, direct subsidies are made on the recommendation of the Canadian Maritime Commission. This three-man body was set up in 1947 to "be responsible to and be subject to the direction of the Minister" of Transport and "to administer, in accordance with regulations of the Governor-in-Council, any steamship subventions voted by Parliament."[5] The Commission assumed duties formerly exercised by officials of the Department of Trade and Commerce. In the 1950s about $2 million was paid annually in subsidy for services along the British Columbia Coast, the north shore of the Gulf of St. Lawrence, to the Magdalen Islands and to Grand Mannan, between Owen Sound and Manitoulin Island, between Prince Edward Island and Nova Scotia, and especially between St. John's and the outports of Newfoundland. By 1964 the subsidies had risen to about $9.4 million because more services were added and operating costs had gone up without commensurate growth in revenue.

Before deciding whether or not to recommend that the government grant a subsidy, the Maritime Commission examines the present and prospective volume of business of the applicant, the reasonableness of his operating costs, probable ancillary expenses by the government on harbour works and navigation aids, the extent of competition, and similar factors. It also takes into account broad questions of public convenience and necessity. In a sense it considers the moral obligation of the federal government to provide a minimum of service to communities which would otherwise be completely isolated.

In recommending a subsidy, the Commission negotiates with the applicant and finally draws up a formal contract. The applicant undertakes to keep his boat seaworthy, provide sailings at stipulated intervals and oftener if required, call at certain ports, and charge certain tolls for passengers and the various kinds of freight which he typically moves. The Maritime Commission does not set tolls in the same way as the Board of Transport Commissioners. It has no authority to police the water-lines to see whether ship-owners adhere to the tolls agreed upon. But its power to refuse to renew the contract and the subsidy unless the ship operator adheres to his agreement gives it practical control of rates.

In most instances contracts are renegotiated annually but a few are for terms of three, four, and seven years. One contract was for fifteen years because the operator had to purchase a new vessel and wanted some permanency of his subsidy. Renegotiation permits periodic reassessment of the advisability of continuing the subsidy. It tends to ensure that the line is efficiently operated and that tolls charged on commercial business are as large a proportion of the expenses of operating the service as feasible. The Commission's general policy is that subsidized services provide "for the regular transportation of passengers, freight and mails to outlying and isolated districts and for the carriage of their products to domestic markets or to ocean ports for export, all of which are essential to the communities served and to the public need."[6]

Subsidization is theoretically endangered by the possibility of competition. Schooners and small steamships might quickly come into any trade as soon as the volume of traffic grew, deprive subsidized carriers of some revenue, and force the government to increase the subsidy. In order to ensure proper use of public funds, it may be necessary to authorize the Maritime Commission to license all the operators in a particular service. In 1967 all the functions of the Maritime Commission were taken over by the Canadian Transport Commission.

Inter-carrier competition (water and rail) is not important in the broad picture of coastal shipping but it is significant in a few instances, e.g., along the south and east coasts of Nova Scotia. On the whole railways haul freight to and from the larger seaports while coastal vessels distribute and collect persons and property from the small outports which are scattered along the shore and which are not reached by rail. Since the admission of Newfoundland to Confederation on March 31, 1949, the more important steamship services around the island and along the coast of Labrador have been operated by the Canadian National Railways.

Intercoastal Shipping

Intercoastal shipping relates to traffic by vessel between ports on the Great Lakes, St. Lawrence, and Atlantic coast on the one hand and the Pacific coast on the other. The scheduled service between Montreal in summer, Halifax in winter, and Vancouver, was discontinued during the war but has since been revived. It carries a variety of goods at rates which are substantially lower than the normal tolls by rail. These rates could be cut even more if the volume of return traffic from Vancouver to Montreal were to grow or if wayward business, e.g., at San Francisco, could be built up. This inter-coastal service, though at times confined to one ship, forces down the tolls on transcontinental traffic by rail and causes violations of the long- and short-haul clause.

Railway tolls need not be as low as water rates for the railway to get the business. Shippers by water have to pay for marine insurance, often for cartage or for rail haul at local rates to and from docks, and they incur more interest due to longer time in transit. Goods are less certain to arrive on a specified date when they move by water than when they go by rail. This adds to the risks of marketing. Perishable articles cannot advantageously be sent by the circuitous route through the Panama Canal. Intercoastal shipping is not controlled by public authority except as regards safety. Shippers using coastal or inter-coastal services need not get manifests, consular invoices, and the like which are needed in trade with countries outside Canada but should take out marine inshrance. Coastal and intercoastal trade is financed in exactly the same manner as domestic business.

Merchant Navy up to 1914

Canada's overseas merchant marine has had a long and troubled history.[7] In pioneer days lumber was plentiful and labour was skilled enough for constructing the simpler types of sailing vessels. Almost every port in New Brunswick, Nova Scotia, Newfoundland, and along the lower St. Lawrence River and the Lower Great Lakes had its shipyard. The ships which were built were used in fishing and in the local carrying trade. From the Atlantic ports and Quebec City they were often laden with lumber and sailed to Britain where both ship and cargo would be sold. At first the ships were so poorly constructed that Lloyd's refused to give them a good rating but by 1850 the quality had improved. Eventually ships built in the Maritimes achieved such a high reputation for speed and general performance that they literally sailed the seven seas and were known the world over.

From 1850 to abott 1865 the industry enjoyed a tremendous boom owing to the California and Australia gold rushes and the expansion of Maritime trade with the United States under the Reciprocity Treaty of 1854–66. After 1875 Canadian shipbuilding declined steadily owing to the re-entry of United States–built ships into the world's carrying trade after the American Civil War, and especially because of the competition of the much more efficient iron and later steel steamship. By 1885, Maritime shipbuilding was a pitiful shell of its former greatness.

In the nineteenth century steamships as well as sailing vessels were built in Canada. A Canadian ship, the *Royal William*, manned by Canadians, has the distinction of being the first vessel (1833) to use steam all the way across the North Atlantic though she also hoisted sail when the wind was favourable. In 1840 Samuel Cunard of Halifax established a trans-oceanic steamship service that made his name famous. In 1878 the Canadian merchant marine, sail and steam, numbered 7,196 vessels totalling one and a third million tons; Canada was fourth among the shipowning nations of the world.

As ships built of steel began to supplant iron steamships as well as wooden sailing vessels, Canada fell behind. She lacked a local iron and steel industry, the technical skills of a highly developed engineering industry, and a powerful domestic demand for ships such as had existed fifty years earlier. She could not compete with Britain in either the construction or the operation of steel vessels. Within twenty-two years, 1878–1900, the tonnage of ocean shipping registered in Canada decreased by almost 50 per cent. In 1914 only two Canadian firms were engaged in overseas shipping, William Thomson of Saint John, N.B., with nine ships in the Caribbean trade and the Canadian Northern Railway with fortnightly sailings to Bristol. Canadian Pacific Steamships, though owned by a Canadian railway, was incorporated in Britain and its ships sailed under the flag of the Mother Country.

Merchant Navy, 1914–39

During World War I, yards at New Glasgow, Quebec, Montreal, Toronto, Collingwood, Port Arthur, Vancouver, and Victoria built about 40 steel cargo vessels ranging from 1,800 to 8,800 tons deadweight capacity and 40 wooden vessels which were used for mine sweeping. All these ships were designed and paid for by Britain. Late in 1917 the Dominion proposed to build its own ships and operate them under a government proprietary corporation known as the Canadian Government Merchant Marine. The programme was undertaken because of the imperative need for providing ships to make up for the immense losses due to Germany's submarine warfare. Huge amounts of foodstuffs and war materials had to be carried overseas. British shipyards, previously the world's main source of ocean-going vessels, were working at capacity. Britain had to requisition certain ships registered in that country but engaged in trade with Canada. The Canadian government was coming into the ownership of a large system of railways. It believed it should have ships to carry the cargoes that would be transported over these rail lines. The Canadian Pacific had its own shipping services and the Canadian National should be put in a position to compete. A merchant marine was necessary if Canada were to expand her export trade and especially to develop new trade routes which apparently would open up after World War I. Each ship would bear the name "Canadian" in addition to some other designation and therefore would advertise the country. Later the government added the reason that shipbuilding should be continued in order to give employment during the immediate post-war depression. Perhaps too, it was influenced by the shipbuilding programme of the United States.

The first ship was completed in the month of the armistice and by December, 1919, 19 cargo vessels had been delivered. Altogether the government ordered 63 vessels, the last being delivered in 1924. The fleet comprised 2 ships of 10,500 tons each, 25 of 8,300 tons, and the rest ranged downward to 2,800 tons. The total deadweight tonnage was a little less than 375,000. Included in the fleet were 7 oil burners, 13 vessels with refrigerator space and 2 vessels with good passenger accommodation for the Canada–British West Indies run. Canadian Government steamships plied to Liverpool, London, Glasgow, the Mediterranean, Newfoundland, the West Indies, Australia, and New Zealand.

In each of the years 1919 and 1920 the Canadian Government Merchant Marine reported a profit of rather more than $1,000,000 after providing for organization costs, operation expenses, and hull insurance but not depreciation and interest. As only part of the fleet had been delivered, the government was encouraged to continue building. In 1921 the profits of the previous two years were more than wiped out. Costs of construction rose far beyond expectations thus adding to the annual burden of interest and depreciation charges. Freight rates in the trans-Atlantic service fell by 65 per cent and to South America by from 17 to 50 per cent. Little cargo was offered for transportation owing to the brief but severe depression of 1921. Some Canadians argued that the Marine was building up new trade routes and could not be expected to make money in its early years. Others asserted that Canadian manufacturers and exporters failed to use the publicly owned service. Instead they shipped by vessels of other countries whenever they could save even a small amount in rates or get a little better service.

By 1922 the world's shipping space greatly exceeded demand. Expenses of operating Canadian vessels were high due to heavy interest, depreciation, and wages. Incidentally only about 60 per cent of the crew was Canadian born. There was no evidence that British or foreign ships had ever discriminated against Canadian merchants. Finally, the Canadian protective tariff tended to keep out imports and discourage traffic in the ships on which the government was lavishing money. Despite all these objections, the government kept on building ships long after it was obvious to almost everyone that the relative shortage of space which had existed when the programme was inaugurated had been more than corrected.

After 1921 operating losses piled up year after year. Gradually the number of vessels in the fleet declined as a result of sale to other interests, scrapping, or marine disaster. In 1926 there were 46 ships, in 1931 23, and in 1936 only 6. Although a few enthusiasts urged that modern, faster ships should replace those in operation, the government decided that the disastrous experiment in ocean shipping did not warrant further expenditures on new vessels. In 1936 the last ships were sold to a company which undertook to provide service between Canada and Australia—New

Zealand for at least five years without government subsidy. When the books of the Canadian Government Merchant Marine were finally balanced they showed an original investment of about $80 million and a recovery of capital of roughly $5,400,000. The latter was made up of the sale of six vessels to the Canadian National Steamships (West Indies) for roughly $900,000 and of 56 vessels to other buyers for $2,400,000, and insurance on four ships lost at sea of $2,100,000. The net cash deficit on operations to 1936 was nearly $14,000,000 to which must be added over $8,400,000 for interest due and unpaid. The total losses, capital and current, came to nearly $95 million.

Some of the reasons for this wholly calamitous experience have already been given. Contracts for construction were let at abnormally high prices, an average per ton of $191.50 for the entire programme compared with the 1913 price of no more than $60. With interest at 5 per cent, depreciation 5 per cent, and hull insurance 3 per cent, the annual fixed charges on a Canadian-built vessel would be $253,500 compared with $78,000 on a pre-war ship built on the Clyde. The SS. *Canadian Miner* of 2,778 tons deadweight cost $583,467 and had accumulated $77,627 in depreciation before it was sold for $96,000 in 1926. At that date the same vessel could have been built in Canada for $277,800 and in Great Britain for $184,000. Often the vessels were inefficiently operated. One ship paid its full complement of men their usual wages while it spent five months in dry dock. In Halifax at one time no less than 15 ships of the Canadian government were tied up supposedly awaiting repairs. In fact they were being kept in commission although no freight was likely to be offered for transportation owing to the business depression. The Canadian Government Merchant Marine associated itself with the North Atlantic Shipping Ring. Because the government company had obligated itself not to cut rates, Canadian apples were sent to Britain in Norwegian vessels while publicly owned Canadian ships were idle. Many of the ships were too small and slow for economical peacetime operation and the architect was charged with sacrificing utility for beauty. Probably the primary cause of the enormous deficits was the government's decision to complete its original programme even though after 1921 the world's ship capacity was far in excess of probable requirements.

Despite the liquidation of the Canadian Government Merchant Marine, Canadian ports have never lacked the service of shipping companies. In 1939 there were direct services to 26 countries from ports in Eastern Canada and to 25 from the West coast. Canadian National Railways operated luxurious passenger ships to the West Indies and the Canadian Pacific had its famous *Empresses* on the trans-Atlantic and Oriental routes. Both companies had ships operating along the Pacific coast to numerous points in Canada and to Skagway and Ketchikan, Alaska. What amounted to a ferry service was provided by the Canadian Pacific from Saint John to Digby, N.S., and by the Canadian National between Borden, P.E.I., and Tormentine, N.B. Its service across the Straits of Canso has been replaced by a causeway. Along both coasts small ships served outports and the Imperial Oil Company had 10 deep-sea tankers carrying crude oil mainly from the Caribbean to eastern Canadian refineries.

Following completion of the post-war shipbuilding programme of the government, not a single ocean-going steamship was built in Canada until after the outbreak of war in 1939. In fact, from 1930 to 1939 Canadian shipyards built only 14 vessels exceeding 150 feet in length and 3 of these were for government use. The comatose condition of the Dominion's 14 fairly large shipbuilding plants was relieved during the depression of the thirties only by a small amount of repair work.

Merchant Navy since 1939

The strident demands of war completely changed this situation. By the end of hostilities Canada had 21 large yards, 4 major outfitting establishments, and 65 smaller plants. Employing at their peak about 100,000 persons, the yards built over 1,000 vessels including the famous corvettes as well as frigates and naval supply vessels. Over 398 merchant vessels of various types were built at an average cost per deadweight ton of $181. Of the 363 dry cargo ships constructed, 90 were sold to the United States for lend-lease to the United Kingdom, 2 were bought by the United Kingdom, and 13 were lost by marine disaster or enemy action. The remaining 258 dry cargo vessels were owned by the Canadian government. At the end of hostilities, 150 of these were operated by the government's wholly owned subsidiary, Park Steamships, 16 were on loan to the United Kingdom, 1 was on loan to Australia, and 91 were on charter to the British Ministry of Transport.

These vessels typically had a deadweight capacity of 10,000 tons, draught of 27 feet, speed of 11 knots, and carried a crew of about 50. Their cost ranged from about $1,400,000 to $2,000,000 depending on the yard, the current cost of materials and wages, and the extra features which were incorporated in many of the vessels. It is difficult to compare costs from one country to another on account of variations in the design of vessels, differences of costs among yards even within the same country, and the secrecy which even yet surrounds some of the cost data. Generally Canadian costs were higher than in Great Britain while for some types and in the better yards, they were lower than in the United States.

Park Steamships operated at a profit during the war but the government announced in November, 1945, that it planned to sell all the vessels it could, preferably to Canadian buyers, and to tie up the surplus, if any. By March, 1949, Park Steamships acting for the Canadian government in co-operation with War Assets Corporation and the Maritime Commission had sold 31 vessels to foreign interests and 139 to Canadians. All these ships were sold at heavy capital losses. For example, the 3,600 ton tankers costing about $1 million each were disposed of for something over one-third this amount. Seventy-one of the 10,000 ton Victory type vessels which cost about $1,658,000 each were sold at an average price of $461,034. The government took the view that capital values would decline rapidly as they did in 1919 in the face of competition from newer, faster, more economical ships. If one takes into account the operating profits of Park Steamships and receipts from the sale or anticipated sale of vessels to private owners but does not consider interest on investment, the government will recover approximately $200 million out of a total expenditure of a little over $270 million. This is a very creditable showing, especially since the vessels were built primarily for the purpose of waging war. The loss was about three-quarters of the deficit on the smaller fleet built during and after World War I.

In designing the wartime fleet the government tried to get vessels suitable for profitable operation under peacetime conditions. The ships were larger and faster than the types built twenty-five years before. Immediately after World War II it was believed that the 15 knot diesels of 7,500 tons deadweight with refrigeration equipment and accommodation for twelve passengers would compare favourably with the better types of tramps and liners on the secondary trade routes of the world. It was soon realized that these vessels are somewhat too slow for commercial business, particularly if the volume of oceanic trade should decline to the levels of the thirties or even of the twenties. Whereas the 4,700 ton wartime vessel had a daily consumption of 20 or 22 tons of coal, post-war vessels of approximately the same size and speed consume about 16½ tons of fuel. Burning 10 or 12 tons of diesel fuel a day, a post-war ship can average 12 to 20 knots while the wartime vessel of the same class would burn 15 to 17 tons and do only 9 to 10 knots. When it comes to loading and unloading cargo, wartime vessels with steam winches are slow and costly compared with modern vessels with better arranged hatches and with electric winches. A coal-burning vessel of the 4,700 ton class needs a crew of 41, one using petroleum for steam-raising, a crew of 36, and a diesel vessel of the same size only 28 men. In many trades, such as along both Canada's coasts and in the British West Indies, the 4,700 ton vessel is as large as can be accommodated in most harbours and is easily manoeuvred in narrow channels. On the other hand the 10,000 ton ship is rather too small for trans-oceanic services.[8] In short, the size of war-built vessels is not particularly suited to Canada's peacetime requirements.

Although withdrawing from actually operating ships, the government made it clear that it did not propose to stand idly by and see the Canadian merchant fleet disintegrate. Vessels registered in Canada carried about 11 per cent of Canada's overseas trade in 1910, 35 per cent in 1925 when the Canadian Government Merchant Marine was at the peak of its operations, about 11.5 per cent in 1940, and 23 per cent in 1947. Canada's overseas trade had grown over the years. While the relative proportion carried under the Canadian flag has fluctuated and on the whole declined, the physical tonnage moved in ships of Canadian registry had slightly increased. Briefly the government's policy was to retain a merchant navy adequate to our needs, to have it operated under private not public auspices, to make it pay its way if at all possible, to regard it as a vital part of the nation's defensive armoury, to consider that shipbuilding and repair are inseparably related to the merchant navy, and to appoint a Maritime Commission to administer subventions and advise the government on policy. In 1967 the Canadian Transport Commission took over these duties.

Shipping on the high seas is notoriously unstable. In 1946-7 Canadian ship-owners found remunerative work for their vessels in carrying food, clothing, farm machinery, and factory equipment for the relief of war-stricken Europe and they started cargo-line services to Africa, the Mediterranean, India, and Australia. During 1948 competition became keener. Construction of new ships began to catch up with wartime losses. Some countries diverted freight to ships under other flags because they were short of Canadian dollars. The United States decided that most goods which it sent under programmes of foreign aid would have to be carried in American bottoms. In 1950-1 Canadian shipping was revived by the Korean War. Unfortunately, prosperity proved to be short-lived and thereafter rates proved unsatisfactory to high-cost operators like Canada, the United States, and even Britain.

The problem of our comparatively high costs could have been met either by subsidies, or by modernizing our fleet and reducing its size. A subsidy adequate to bring our costs down to about the level of most countries would cost Canada more than $20 million a year, with prices and wage rates at the level of the late 1940s. It would provoke some other nations to follow suit and a few, notably the United States, to increase the subsidies which they were already paying. Canada did not want to start a war, even on subsidies.

The other alternative, having fewer but more efficient ships, seemed a sounder approach. About 80 per cent of the vessels which had been operated by Park Steamships during the war had been sold to Canadians on condition that they would not be transferred to non-Canadian registry without the consent of the government. In 1948 it empowered the Maritime Commission to authorize the sale of these ships to non-Canadians. The Commission was to take into account the owners' plans for replacement, the effect of the sale upon existing trade routes, and other relevant factors. Permission was to be denied if the vessel might still be usefully and profitably employed for the time being in the bulk-carrying trades.

In consideration of permission to sell, the owner agreed with the government to use the proceeds of sale to acquire a modern vessel within five years. The Commission might extend the time limit if it saw fit. In the meantime it held the funds in escrow or essentially in a compulsory building reserve. The plans for ships built with funds from the reserve had to be approved by the Commission. Every effort would be made to ensure that the new vessels were modern, had low operating costs, and generally were in a position to compete with non-Canadian carriers without the assistance of large subsidies from the Dominion. Proceeds from the sale of two or three old vessels might be devoted to buying a single modern ship. The new ocean-going fleet which was in contemplation was to be roughly 750,000 deadweight tons compared with 980,000 such tons as of March, 1949, rather more than 1,000,000 tons in 1945, 242,000 tons in 1939, nearly 425,000 tons in 1925, and about 335,000 tons in 1920. Although the Commission found it difficult to forecast our shipping needs, it considered that a fleet of 750,000 tons, provided it contained "a proportion of modern and efficient vessels, should be able to secure profitable employment under normal conditions in time of peace, and still be adequate for the purpose of carrying our essential imports in time of war."[9] By the end of 1953 it had become clear that this hope was unfounded, that Canadian vessels could not compete with ships of other nations having lower wages and tolerating poorer working conditions, and that the amount of subsidy needed to keep a Canadian merchant navy of 750,000 tons in operation in the face of competition would reach millions of dollars per annum. Under these circumstances the government permitted Canadian ship owners temporarily to transfer their vessels to British registry and so take advantage of the lower wage rates prevailing on British ships. Canadian seamen who were thrown out of work were to get jobs on Canada's inland ships or be retrained for other occupations.

In 1955 the eight cargo-passenger vessels in the Canadian National's West Indies Service, which was the last large fleet in Canada's merchant navy, were tied up in Halifax because the Railway and the union could not agree on wage rates. After the strike had lasted several weeks, the ships were transferred to Cuban registry, but before delivery was made the place of registration was changed to Trinidad for political reasons associated with the rise of Castro to power. Some Conservatives, who were then in opposition, were outspoken in criticizing what they called the loss of these ships, but when they came into office in 1957 they made no changes.

The West Indies Service had cost the federal treasury $13 million since its creation in 1892. If the demands of the labour union had been met in 1955, the annual deficit would have totalled an estimated $400,000. According to the Minister of Transport, it cost 50 per cent more to operate a ship under Canadian registry than under the registry of most other countries. Officers aboard the ships would continue to be Canadians but the crews would be recruited in Trinidad. In 1959 Canada presented two ships to the newly formed but impermanent Federation of the West Indies for service between the islands.

The transfer of the Crown-owned fleet reduced the number of deep-sea cargo ships under the Canadian flag to 10 and simultaneously raised the number of Canadian ships registered outside Canada to 78. The practice of reregistering in countries with lower levels of wage rates, fringe benefits, hours of labour, etc., is not confined to Canada. It has been widely practised by Americans and others, and accounts for the technical expansion of the merchant marine of Panama and Liberia.

Need for a Merchant Navy

Back of these details lies a basic question of whether Canada ought to have a large merchant marine at all. The arguments for and against have been worn threadbare by several decades of discussion in the United States. Protagonists include the ultra-nationalists and those who would personally profit from a large merchant navy, such as shipyard owners, steel manufacturers, workers employed by the groups just named, civic authorities in seaports and shipbuilding centres, and members of the Royal Canadian Navy. They contend that a large merchant navy is essential to maintaining and developing Canada's foreign trade. It is necessary to protect Canadian shippers against high ocean rates, to allow the raw materials and manufactured products of Canada to be sold in the markets of the world in competition with those of foreign countries, and to prevent foreign carriers from discriminating against Canada exporters and importers. A Canadian merchant navy would save the ocean freight bill and ensure that the money is spent in Canada rather than abroad. Other governments are subsidizing their shipping. Canada must do the same if she is to maintain her present position in world affairs. Advocates of a big merchant marine have contended that a commercial fleet is essential to Canada's defence, that it constitutes an auxiliary fighting navy, and that, even in these days of push-button warfare, we must take care to make sure that we can get indispensable raw materials and can supply our allies with foodstuffs and weapons which are basic to our mutual protection.

Opponents of this policy concern themselves chiefly with economic factors. They assert that there is no evidence of any real connection between the size of a country's merchant navy and the volume of its foreign trade. Canada's commercial shipping consistently declined in importance from 1885 to 1920 and again from 1925 to 1940. In the last half of the first period the Dominion enjoyed prosperity and a remarkable expansion in her foreign and domestic commerce while in the latter part of the second period of time she experienced her worst business depression. A Canadian merchant marine is not needed as protection against high shipping charges because the sea is a highly competitive avenue of transport. In order to get business foreign ships give the lowest rates they can. They dare not discriminate against Canadian shippers. If one ship operator were to do so, carriers of other countries would quickly enter Canadian ports and take advantage of the ill will which had been stirred up. Canadian ships are expensive to build and operate and hence their owners favour higher rates and strict enforcement of the restrictive practices of conferences rather than the reverse. A Canadian merchant fleet would displace the shipping services of Great Britain and other countries and so deprive them of dollars they already sorely need to buy Canadian goods. Payments for ocean transportation if made to Canadians rather than to the British would merely destroy part of the market for Canadian wheat, metals, and other goods. The nation as a whole might not be any better off than before. Canada cannot hope to compete with other countries in subsidizing shipping and should not provoke or encourage wars of subsidization which in the long run are a foolish "beggar my neighbor" policy. The needs of national defence can be better served by whole-hearted co-operation in agencies promoting peace or by a well-equipped fighting navy, army, and air force than by the indirect and extravagant methods of a merchant fleet. In peacetime Canada would gain because, when other countries heavily subsidize their merchant fleets, ocean freight rates are kept artificially low.

The gist of the matter is that on purely economic grounds a merchant marine for Canada is hard to justify. The daily operating costs for a standard wartime vessel of 10,000 tons deadweight, not including fuel oil, interest, and depreciation, were said in 1948 to be $972 for United States vessels, $810 for Canadian, $525 for British, and $422 for Italian. The master of a ship under the American flag got about $688 a month, under the Canadian $475, under the Italian only $71. The basic monthly wage for an able seaman under the flags of the United States, Canada, Britain, and Italy was $266, $170, $81, and $31 respectively.[10] To the nationals of some countries the rates of pay and a seafaring life are attractive. To most Canadians the pay aboard ship will not compensate for the loneliness and unpleasantness that often accompany life at sea. After the initial thrill has worn off, most Canadians prefer to remain ashore. Vessels flying the Canadian flag are often largely manned by nationals of other countries.

Labour-management relations aboard Canadian ships have often been unsatisfactory. Work stoppages, numerous breaches of discipline, and the general lack of co-operation have materially increased the day-to-day costs of running Canadian ships. Shippers sometimes have not used Canadian vessels when alternatives were available because owing to labour troubles our ships were less likely to arrive on time. On the surface these difficulties are the outgrowth of the "Captain Bligh" tradition, the relative inexperience of Canadian ship-owners and seamen, the comparative lack of educational facilities for the training of crew, the struggles between two unions to control the men, and so on. Perhaps the fundamental difficulty is that broadly speaking operating vessels is attractive only to the capital and labour of economically poor countries. In a nation with a relatively new and expanding economy and a high standard of living, money and men can be more profitably employed in many other directions than in ocean shipping where competition is keen and earnings typically both low and fluctuating.

From whatever angle one views the world's shipping, one comes back sooner or later to the spirit of nationalism in one of its most vicious forms short of war. A large merchant navy for Canada or for any other country which like the Dominion is at a decided economic disadvantage in ocean transportation is a matter of national prestige and national defence. As to nationalism, one can only quote Adam Smith's dictum that "defence is better than opulence." If that be true and if, to the profound regret of all, world peace cannot be attained in our time, then professional economists have really no right to interject their logic into an insane world.

Shipbuilding

Some of the ships on the ways when hostilities formally ceased in 1945 were completed though most of the orders were cancelled. Some naval vessels still had to be repaired and others were converted to commercial use. To help replenish wartime losses, in 1946 Canadian shipyards delivered 60 merchant ships totalling 50,000 deadweight tons, a figure exceeded in that year by only the United Kingdom, the United States, and Sweden. In the following three years deliveries of merchant vessels were 42, 87, and 20 with tonnages of 82,000, 154,000, and 75,000 respectively. Average monthly employment in the shipyards was 15,000. Ships were delivered to France, the Netherlands, Portugal, Brazil, Argentina, and China. As other countries had expanded their output, Canada ranked about eighth among shipbuilding nations. At the beginning of 1950 Canadian yards had orders for only three ocean-going vessels. Approximately 40 berths could build dry cargo ships up to 10,000 tons deadweight. At least 12 of these slips could be extended to handle dry cargo ships up to 18,000 tons deadweight and tankers to about 20,000 tons. These berths have a total potential annual output of roughly 500,000 gross tons of ocean shipping. In addition, five berths at Canadian Great Lakes ports have a potential capacity of 100,000 gross tons per annum. They have built vessels up to 650 feet long for lake service but until the completion of the St. Lawrence Seaway no ocean-going ship constructed could exceed 260 feet, the maximum length of the old locks.

Opinions vary on the exact difference in the cost of building ships in Canadian and foreign yards. Within any one country costs differ from yard to yard. Sometimes the industry will not quote a firm price for the vessel but only state a fixed price for overhead and profit and have the purchaser pay the actual cost of materials and labour. Shipbuilders are reluctant to give details of their costs or make estimates on fictitious vessels. The Canadian Maritime Commission believes that Canadian prices are higher than those of our principal European competitors but generally lower than in the United States. The total number of direct man-hours required to build a vessel is about the same in Canada as in Britain, but in 1962 the average hourly rates of pay were $1.85 in Quebec and the Maritimes and $2.45 in British Columbia. These compared with 95 cents in Britain, 40 cents in Japan, and $2.95 in the United States. This difference is important because about 50 per cent of the selling price of a ship is direct labour. Materials are somewhat more costly in Canada owing in part to differences in the standard of living but the government remits 98 per cent of the customs duty and all of the federal sales tax on materials brought into Canada for use in building a ship.

Up to 1961 the Maritime Commission was not able to do much to help Canadian shipbuilding beyond allocating orders from the Navy, Department of Transport, and Canadian National Railways to the yards most in need of economic sustenance. Then the Diefenbaker Government announced a capital subsidy of 40 per cent (35 per cent after March 31, 1963) of the costs of construction in Canada of ships (other than fishing vessels) of Canadian registry. On fishing trawlers the subsidy is 50 per cent provided the new trawler replaces an old vessel withdrawn from service. On wooden fishing vessels the capital subsidy was increased from $165 to $250 per gross ton.

These subsidies, which reached a peak of $40 million in 1963–4, unquestionably helped shipbuilding. By the end of 1966, some 530 vessels had been built and another 67 were under construction. The subsidies might have proven of greater long-run benefit if they had been concentrated on the most efficient yards rather than being spread rather widely, presumably for political reasons. They have tended to perpetuate the over-capacity which has plagued Canadian shipbuilding for decades, except during times of war. Moreover, a company in Nova Scotia built a three-storey plant for processing fish on an 160-foot barge and qualified for a shipbuilding subsidy of $190,000. The "ship" is moored permanently alongside a public wharf and presumably will never go to sea. Financial aid to fishing may be justified but hardly under the guise of subsidies to shipbuilding. A basic difficulty is that Canadians are unwilling to invest in commercial shipping where the rate of return has traditionally been low and erratic.

In 1965 the Pearson Government called a temporary halt to the subsidies. Later it decided to continue the subsidy but at the rate of 25 per cent of the cost of a vessel until the end of 1968. This is to be reduced by 2 per cent per annum until it reaches 17 per cent in 1972 and thereafter. The government also plans to spend $390 million on its own vessels between 1965 and 1970. This outlay will average nearly 50 per cent more than the programme which was adopted for reasons of defence following the crisis in Korea. About 40 per cent of the money will go on ships for the Royal Canadian Navy with the balance for the Departments of Transport, Northern Affairs, and Justice (the Royal Canadian Mounted Police).

In 1962 Canada set up a Coast Guard to take over 241 vessels that were used as icebreakers, floating weather stations, servicing buoys and lighthouses, and supplying police posts in the Arctic as well as for search and rescue, surveying, and research. Canada now has the world's second largest fleet of icebreakers.

Regulation of Overseas Shipping

Prior to 1934 Canada's merchant marine was controlled mainly by the laws of Great Britain though as early as 1869 the Dominion Parliament decided what vessels might be admitted to our coasting trade. The Canada Shipping Act, 1934, provides for clearance papers for ships, the duties of harbour masters, inspection for seaworthiness, health, safety devices, the signing on of crew, offences under the Act such as insolence, swearing, smoking below decks, not being clean, washed, and shaved on Sunday, interrupting divine service by indecorous conduct, and so forth. The Act reserved inter-coastal and coastal shipping to vessels of British ownership except with permission of the Governor-in-Council. After a prolonged inquiry, a Royal Commission on Coastal Shipping reported in 1957 that the above provisions should not be changed.[11] The possible gains to Canadian ship-builders and operators through reserving this traffic to vessels of Canadian registry were not considered adequate to out-weigh the possible disadvantages to shippers and consignees from the reduction of competition. The legislation regarding admission to Canada's coasting trade must be distinguished from the rules governing shipping on the Great Lakes and the St. Lawrence River west of Havre St. Pierre, which were discussed in the preceding chapter. The customs tariff provides that the British preferential rates, those granted to other members of the British Commonwealth and Empire, shall apply only when the goods are imported through Canadian ports and have been sent from a British port abroad or through the usual centre of export.

Administration of Harbours

Ten of the principal harbours of Canada—Halifax, Saint John, Chicoutimi, Quebec, Trois Rivières, Montreal, Churchill, Vancouver, St. John's and Baie d'Espoir (since 1949 when Newfoundland entered Confederation) are administered by the National Harbours Board. This organization was set up in 1936 as the result of a report by Sir Alexander Gibb,[12] a British authority on harbours and port development. The Board is responsible for the operation of port and other facilities which had a book value of about $350 million in 1960. The facilities include piers, wharves, jetties, transit sheds, grain elevators (including the government-owned elevators at Prescott and Port Colborne, Ont.), cold storage warehouses, cattle sheds, terminal railways, travelling overhead and floating cranes and from 1925 to 1963 the Jacques Cartier bridge in Montreal. Capital expenditures are financed by advances made to the Board by the government on deposit of certificates of indebtedness which totalled just over $200 million in 1965. The National Harbours Board loses money every year ($3.4 million in 1964), but its costs are relatively much less than they were when each of the harbours now under its control was administered by its own local board.

Local harbour commissions of municipal and federal appointees still administer the affairs of the ports of Belleville, Toronto, Hamilton, Windsor, Winnipeg, New Westminster, North Fraser, and Port Alberni, under the general supervision of the Department of Transport. The Department has complete authority over about three hundred other public harbours. In addition to these publicly owned facilities, there are docks and freight-handling equipment owned by private interests such as railways, pulp and paper companies, sugar and oil refineries, and grain companies.

Harbour commissions get revenue from a variety of sources, chiefly top wharfage which is a charge for providing accommodation for cargo on the docks or in storage warehouses before it is loaded and after it has been unloaded. Over the years much of the work of loading and unloading cargo has been mechanized and, in particular, much cargo is handled in bulk. To load a 10,000-ton ship by hand-labour and slings takes 100 men a minimum of 5½ days. Bulk-loading a vessel that is twice as large can be done by 12 men in 4½ days. The relations between ship-owners and dock labour are often strained and strikes are not uncommon.

24

Pipelines

TO MOST PEOPLE pipelines are a new development. In fact, they have been used for centuries to carry water and since 1875 to move petroleum and natural gas in Western Ontario, where one of the world's first oil wells was drilled about 1860. Gathering lines brought petroleum from scattered wells to central storage tanks for use in nearby refineries or for transmission to a distant refinery by wooden or steel barrels, railway tank cars or, later on, trunk pipelines. By 1913 an oil refinery at Sarnia, Ont., was connected with the pipeline network of the United States at Cygnet, Ohio, by a line 6 inches in diameter, 150 miles long, and with a daily capacity of 6,000 barrels. In 1926 gathering lines were built to connect oilfields in the Turner Valley with Calgary.

In 1941 a trunk pipeline 236 miles long between Portland, Me., and Montreal eliminated a voyage of 1,181 miles by water. Its purposes were to shorten the water route from ports along the Gulf of Mexico and the Caribbean, to cut down the risk of loss by enemy submarines, and to enable Montreal to obtain crude throughout the year, thus eliminating the need to provide extra storage capacity to meet the expanded demand due to the war. Except for the refinery at Sarnia and two or three in the Montreal area, Canadian plants continued to rely for their crude on tankers (at Vancouver and Halifax), on tank cars (on the Prairies), or on the American pipeline system plus tankers (on the Great Lakes).

This picture was entirely changed by the discovery of a fabulous reserve of petroleum near Leduc, Alta., in 1947 and by subsequent discoveries of natural gas elsewhere. Trunk or long distance pipelines were laid down rapidly. In 1950, the first year for which complete statistics are available, there were 1,400 miles of trunk pipeline in operation in Canada. Six years later the total was 5,807 miles plus about 1,500 miles in the United States which is used exclusively to transport Canadian crude. By 1962 the Canadian network consisted of roughly 9,500 miles of gathering and trunkline pipe for oil and 5,000 miles for natural gas. The number of barrel-miles of petroleum and its products sent through trunk lines rose from 32 billion in 1952 to roughly five times as much ten years later. The average daily sendout of natural gas increased nearly three times between 1959 and 1960, being over 1.6 billion Mcf. (i.e., thousand cubic feet) in the latter year. In the 1950s over $1.3 billion was invested in pipelines in Canada.

Even if space were available, it would be unwise to attempt a description of the location of these lines because it would get out of date quickly. Besides, that invaluable compendium, the *Canada Year Book*, gives current details. Broadly, the Canadian system falls into six divisions (*a*) lines for natural gas and crude petroleum from Alberta to Vancouver; (*b*) similar lines to the important cities of the West; (*c*) a pipeline for petroleum from the West to the international boundary roughly south of Winnipeg, then to Duluth, Minn., and via the Straits of Mackinac to Sarnia; (*d*) a pipeline for natural gas from the West, north of Lake Superior via Kapuskasing, to Toronto, Ottawa, and Montreal; (*e*) lines in the area between Sarnia and Montreal for petroleum products such as aviation and automotive gasoline, lubricating oils, oil for domestic heating, and fuel oil; and (*f*) the relatively old Montreal-Portland line.

Pipelines are one of the most economical transportation agencies, having costs per ton-mile in 1956 of 0.3 cents, which compares with 1.5 cents by rail, 5 or 6 cents by highway, and from 0.2 to 0.5 cents in inland ships. Since then, the average rate per ton-mile by road and rail has risen by about 10 per cent while that by pipeline has generally declined. For instance, when the Interprovincial Pipe Line Company completed its line between Edmonton and Sarnia (1,743) miles in 1953, it charged 64 cents a barrel (35 Imperial gallons) which compared with $4 all-rail. By 1960 it had reduced its rate to 50 cents a barrel.

Pipelines enjoy low costs for several reasons. They are in continuous operation, are never interrupted by bad weather, and have no problems of the return of empty containers or freight cars, trucks, or ships. A pipeline uses a narrow right of way and it can keep its costs down by avoiding urban centres. It does not disfigure the landscape nor interfere with the movement of persons or other kinds of freight. Though leakage is not unknown, a properly-built pipeline requires less maintenance than any other kind of transport. This is an important consideration when wage rates are rising. Salaries and wages are rarely more than 10 per cent of operating revenues; interest charges are fixed for the life of the bonds; and royalty payments to owners of subsurface gas and petroleum are set for several years in advance. Therefore, pipeline companies can make long-term contracts with little likelihood of having to escalate prices to users of the products they transport and sell. This is an obvious advantage to domestic users and especially to industries which carefully weigh the relative advantages of coal, hydro-electricity, petroleum products, and natural gas as sources of heat and motive power over the next decade or more.

Pipelines benefited enormously from four kinds of technological change which have occurred since about 1940. First, methods were devised for economically fabricating large diameter steel pipe capable of withstanding fairly high pressures per square inch and therefore of carrying large quantities of petroleum, petroleum products, or natural gas in a given period of time. Second, by means of aerial surveying, the route could be determined far more quickly and economically than by the traditional means of level, chain, and rod. Third, machinery was devised or improved for quickly welding lengths of pipe together, for digging ditches, wrapping pipe to prevent corrosion while in the soil, for letting the pipe into position, and finally for back-filling the trench. Fourth, a market was found for some constituents of natural gas, notably propane and butane, which had formerly proved dangerous if carried in the same pipeline as natural gas. These constituents are collectively called liquified petroleum gases (L. p. g.'s) because they are readily liquified if brought under pressure. Once the pressure is reduced below a certain level, they turn to gas and become highly inflammable. Formerly they had to be "flared off" (burnt in the open air) or returned underground at well-head. Now they can be bottled in cylinders for use in domestic heating or in the production of various petrochemicals. In consequence, the movement of natural gas is safer than formerly and its price is lowered. The same principles apply to casing-head gasoline which is another common constituent of natural gas as it comes from the ground.

The carrying capacity of a given pipeline varies with a number of factors—its size, the character of the terrain which it traverses, the viscosity of the crude petroleum, the frequency and power of the pumping stations, and of course, the demand of consumers. Of these factors, the diameter of the pipeline has the greatest economic significance. The cost of building a 20-inch line is only 60 per cent more than the cost of a 10-inch line but, other things being equal, its capacity ($2 \pi r^2$) is four times as great. Hence, if both lines are used to capacity, the investment per barrel is only 40 per cent as much for the larger as for the smaller line. Expressed algebraically, if the cost per mile is x for the smaller line and its throughput is y barrels per day, the cost per barrel is $(x \div y)$. On the larger line the cost per barrel is $(1.6x \div 4y)$.

Pipelines are used for petroleum products as well as for crude petroleum and natural gas. Quantities or "blocks" of aviation gasoline, high-octane gasoline for automobiles, regular-grade gasoline, diesel fuel, and fuel oil are sent through the same line, one after the other. The quantities can be measured so accurately that there is little chance of mixing. If any admixture should occur, there will be a slight up-grading of, say, the medium grade of gasoline for automobiles with the top grade. At the end of a "run" or series of blocks of different products, the pipeline can be cleared out by means of a "plug" of water containing a detergent.

The primary limitation on pipelines is obvious. Their economic value depends on how long the reserves of petroleum and natural gas will last and this fact has an important effect on financing its construction. Gathering lines and pipelines for petroleum products are financed by refineries from their own budgets but trunk lines for natural gas and crude oil are financed by large bond issues and by common stock. The bonds are amply secured because they will mature long before the reserve will be used up and reasonably firm contracts are made with customers for the purchase of large volumes of gas or petroleum over a period of years. The common stock is much more risky. Its owners have the right to get dividends only after all operating expenses and bond interest have been paid. The value of the stock depends primarily on the discovery of new reserves and on the development of new markets. Eventually, when the reserves are exhausted, the common stock will be worthless, since pipe and pumping stations have almost no scrap value. As far as Canada is concerned, depletion of Western resources of liquid and gaseous fuels is not of immediate concern. New reserves are still being discovered and the chief problem for perhaps the next twenty-five years is one of markets. This involves the substitution of Canadian for foreign crude, which comes into Halifax and Montreal from Venezuela and the Middle East, and the sale of Canadian gas and petroleum in the United States. Once the marketing problem is solved, new pipelines will be necessary.

Pipelines are unique among Canadian transportation media in that for all practical purposes they have never received any subsidies whatever from Dominion, provincial, or municipal governments. To be sure, the federal and Ontario governments lent Trans-Canada Pipe Lines a substantial sum to allow it to complete its pipeline for natural gas north of Lake Superior quickly. This loan was soon repaid in full for the company was able to complete arrangements with private investors.

Control of Pipelines

In 1949 Parliament required that the route to be followed by international and interprovincial pipelines be approved by the Board of Transport Commissioners before construction began.[1] Regulation was necessary in order to give the public reasonable protection against the hazards inevitably involved in the movement of inflammable liquids and gas. The Board had to satisfy itself that the applicant for leave to construct a pipeline was financially responsible.

In 1958 a Royal Commission under the chairmanship of Mr. Henry Borden recommended the creation of a National Energy Board. It would set prices of gas and if necessary require pipeline companies to renegotiate the terms of any existing contract either for the sale or delivery of gas to companies which in turn sell to the consuming public. As matters stood, provincial governments set rates charged by a gas distributing company, such as the Consumers Gas Company of Toronto, operating wholly within a province, but they had no jurisdiction over interprovincial and international concerns, the "wholesalers" who sell gas to "retailers," such as Consumers Gas, who sell in turn to householders and industrial users. The Commission felt that without public control of both wholesale and retail operations, companies might make exorbitant profits. Besides, complaint had been made that prices charged by a company were unjustly discriminatory against people in Saskatchewan as compared with those in Ontario. Only a regulatory board which drew its authority from Dominion legislation could deal effectively with such situations. The Borden Commission also recommended that the prospective National Energy Board should control charges for the transmission of petroleum, bearing in mind the need to protect Canadian producers of crude oil, Canadian consumers of refined products, and the competitive position of Canada in world markets.

The Commission discussed the rate base-rate of return method for arriving at the financial needs of pipelines. As a rule, under this scheme the total value of assets is taken, and the same return on this rate base is allowed for all concerns in the industry. This allows a company with a high bonded debt to pay a larger rate of return to its shareholders in good years than a company which keeps its debt low. Suppose two companies have assets of $1 million each, and are allowed a return of 8 per cent on this base; but Company A has $800,000 in 5 per cent bonds and $200,000 in common stock, while Company B has $200,000 in 5 per cent bonds and $800,000 in stock. On these suppositions, Company A has net operating income (8 per cent of $1 million or $80,000) less bond interest (5 per cent of $800,000 or $40,000) or $40,000 available for stock which has a par value of $200,000. This is a return of 20 per cent. The stock of Company B will receive $80,000 (8 per cent of $1 million) less

$10,000 (5 per cent of $200,000) or $70,000 on a total par value of $800,000, giving a return of 8.75 per cent. This example shows the principle of "leverage" in the issuance of bonds, though it is somewhat exaggerated and over-simplified. For instance, any company, even in the field of public utilities where income is considered to be more stable than in other industries, would hesitate to have a ratio of debt to equity of 80 to 20, because a relatively small decline in net earnings would wipe out what was normally available for common stock dividends. If earnings declined still further, the company might be unable to pay interest on its bonds and if it failed to do so, the bondholders could legally force the company into bankruptcy. Though there are practical limitations to leverage, its advantages to owners of common shares are beyond doubt.

The Borden Commission was not concerned with the possible decline in earning power, which is so prominent in discussion of the rate base-rate of return method for railways, but rather with the fact that different pipeline companies have different proportions of bonds. Therefore, to set the same rate of return for all of them on a rate base of original cost of assets would give an inordinate return in terms of per cent on the stock of companies with high leverage and give a much lower percentage on the common stock of companies with comparatively few bonds. Hence, the Commission proposed to have the Board set the rate level for each company to cover its operating expenses plus interest actually paid on bonds plus a return on the equity. Their plan would thus eliminate the effect of leverage.

According to the Borden Commission, the amount of the equity, which was to be the rate base for pipeline companies, was to be the original cost of assets (less depreciation) which remained after the par value of the bonds had been deducted. Every company would get the same rate of return on its base. The Board tentatively set the rate at 8 per cent per annum. As a result, the proposal was strongly criticized, chiefly on the grounds that the suggested rate was too low for such a speculative industry and would discourage investment in all Canadian industries, especially by American capitalists. These criticisms proved unfounded for, as we have seen, Canada's pipeline network grew rapidly.

The National Energy Board was set up in 1959 for the broad purpose of assuring the best uses of energy resources in Canada.[2] It is responsible for the regulation in the public interest of the construction and operation of oil and gas pipelines that are subject to the jurisdiction of the Parliament of Canada, the tolls charged for transmission by such pipelines, the export and import of gas, the export of electric power, and the construction of lines over which such power is exported. The Board is also required to study all matters related to the generation and use of energy in Canada and to recommend such measures as it thinks advisable in the public interest. The Board consists of a chairman, a vice-chairman, and three other members.

It will be observed that the Board has a wide range of responsibilities over energy of which regulation of pipelines, a phase of transport, is only one. In practice, it has been more concerned with the export of natural gas[3] and with the constuction of pipelines than with setting rates that may be charged by common carrier pipelines, i.e., those which serve all refineries and retailers of natural gas who wish to use the line. The Board may also set rates for private carriers, e.g., through the pipeline for petroleum products between Sarnia and Toronto, which is used solely by Imperial Oil. But such regulation would be superfluous since it would be equivalent to requiring Imperial Oil to take something out of its vest pocket and put it in its trouser pocket.

Commodity Pipelines

Though up to 1967 all pipelines in current use had been confined to handling gases and liquids, they may eventually be practicable for solids. In Ohio, coal has been pulverized and mixed with an equal quantity of water. After being pumped through a pipeline, the slurry or slushy mixture was treated to separate the solid matter from the liquid. Wood chips for use in manufacturing newsprint have been sent by pipeline. Experiments have been conducted in the use of capsules suspended in a liquid or gas and moved through a pipeline. The capsules could contain grain, concentrates of mineral or metallic ores, or liquid chemicals. The theoretical possibilities of commodity pipelines are exciting.

In order to be prepared for future developments, the National Transportation Act of 1967 (sec. 22 to sec. 28) empowers the Canadian Transport Commission to issue certificates of public convenience and necessity for commodity lines. Before doing so, it must have regard to "(a) the economic feasibility of the pipeline; (b) the financial responsibility and financial structure of the applicant, the methods of financing the pipeline, and the extent to which Canadians will have an opportunity of participating in the financing, engineering and construction of the pipeline; and (c) any public interest that in the opinion of the Commission may be affected by the granting or refusing of the application." The Commission is to set rates charged by commodity pipelines. The Cabinet is to decide whether the Canadian Transport Commission or the National Energy Board is to regulate a combined pipeline, which is a commodity pipeline through which a solid plus oil or gas or both can be moved.

Under sec. 3 (b) commodity pipeline "means a pipeline for the transmission of commodities and includes all branches, extensions, pumps, racks compressors, loading facilities, storage facilities, reservoirs, tanks, interstation system of communication by telephone, telegraph or radio and real and personal, movable or immovable property and works connected therewith, but does not include a pipeline for the transmission solely of oil and gas, or either.'"

NOTES AND INDEX

Notes

ABBREVIATIONS have been used throughout the Notes. Ann. Rpt., Comm., Proc., Rpt., Ry., Ryl. Comm. need no explanation. Others are listed below:

A.C.	Appeal Cases (decided by the Judicial Committee of the Privy Council, sitting in London)
A.C. & H.B. Ry.	Algoma Central and Hudson Bay Railway
B.R.C.	Board of Railway Commissioners, Annual Report
B.T.C.	Board of Transport Commissioners, Judgments, Orders, Regulations and Rulings (volumes numbered consecutively after J.O.R.R.)
C.F.A.	Canadian Freight Association
Can. Mfrs.' Ass'n.	Canadian Manufacturers' Association
Can. Nor. Ry.	Canadian Northern Railway
Can. Pass. Ass'n.	Canadian Passenger Association
C.R.C.	Canadian Railway Cases
C.R.T.C.	Canadian Railway and Transport Cases (volumes numbered consecutively after C.R.C.)
Dom. Atl. Ry.	Dominion Atlantic Railway
D.L.R.	Dominion Law Reports
E.C.R.	Exchequer Court of Canada, Reports
E. & N. Ry.	Esquimalt and Nanaimo Railway
G.T.P.	Grand Trunk Pacific Railway
G.T.R.	Grand Trunk Railway
Grt. Nor. Ry.	Great Northern Railway
I.C.C.	Interstate Commerce Commission
Jackman, *Economic Principles*	W. T. Jackman, *Economic Principles of Transportation* (Toronto: University of Toronto Press, 1935)

J.O.R.R.	Judgements, Orders, Regulations, and Rulings of the Board of Transport (or Railway) Commissioners for Canada
M.C.R.	Michigan Central Railroad
N.Y.C.	New York Central Railroad
Nor. Alta. Ry.	Northern Alberta Railway
Nor. Pac. Rld.	Northern Pacific Railroad
P.C.	Privy Council (Cabinet), Orders-in-Council
Ry. Ass'n. of Can.	Railway Association of Canada
R.S.C.	Revised Statutes of Canada
Ryl. Comm.	Royal Commission
S.C.R.	Supreme Court of Canada Reports

Chapter 1: Transportation in the Canadian Economy (pp. 3–27)

1. See especially G. P. de T. Glazebrook, *A History of Transportation in Canada* (Toronto: Ryerson, 1938); H. A. Innis, "Memorandum on Transportation," Ryl. Comm., 1951, *Rpt.* pp. 282–93.

2. Ryl. Comm., 1917, *Rpt.*, *Sessional Paper* no. 20g, p. xx.

3. Ryl. Comm., 1931–2, *Rpt.*, p. 85.

4. Ryl. Comm., 1951, *Rpt.*, p. 187.

5. *Ibid.*, p. 249.

6. *Ibid.*, p. 148.

7. In 1944 Parliament withdrew the jurisdiction over civil aviation from the Board of Transport Commissioners.

8. Ryl. Comm., 1951, *Rpt.*, p. 70.

9. *Ibid.*, p. 131.

10. *Ibid.*, p. 135.

11. *Ibid.*, pp. 282–93.

12. Ryl. Comm., 1961, *Rpt.*, vol. I, pp. 67–8.

13. C. L. Dearing and W. Owen, *National Transportation Policy* (Washington: The Brookings Institution, 1949), p. 15.

Chapter 2: The Rate Structure Surveyed (pp. 28–47)

1. Technically a rate covers the transport of freight or express, a fare the carriage of passengers, and a charge the payment for icing, demurrage, storage, excess baggage, and so on. In practice the terms are sometimes used interchangeably. The Railway Act uses the all-inclusive term, tolls.

2. *International Rates Case* (1907) reprinted in (1914) 17 C.R.C. 123, 138–40; and in (1917) 7 J.O.R.R. 346. See also *Simcoe Bd. of Trade* v. *G.T.R.*, (1920) 10 J.O.R.R. 500: *Sault Ste. Marie* v. *C.P.R.*, (1922) 27 C.R.C. 153, 168; 12 J.O.R.R. 61, 70.

3. For 400 miles and for classes 1 to 10 (omitting ninth, livestock, on which commodity rates applied up to 1950) distributing class rates are below standard mileage class rates by the following percentages: 25, 24, 26, 25, 25, 28, 16, 20, 22.

4. Including Winnipeg, Portage la Prairie, Brandon, Regina, Moose Jaw, Saskatoon, Calgary, Edmonton, Lethbridge, Medicine Hat, Fernie, Kamloops, Nelson, and Vancouver.

5. The terminal rate on first class traffic between Fort William and Winnipeg was 21 per cent less than the standard mileage rate; at Regina it was 13 per cent less; at Calgary 7 per cent less; and at Vancouver 2 per cent less. Ryl. Comm., 1951, *Rpt.*, p. 96. The Royal Commission left the Board to deal with this matter but stated that the elimination of terminal class rates in Western Canada would tend towards the attainment of the goal of equalization.

6. R. A. C. Henry and Associates, *Railway Freight Rates in Canada*, a study prepared for the Royal Commission on Dominion-Provincial Relations (Ottawa: King's Printer, 1939), pp. 122–61, gives the history of the commodity rates on grain, cement, coal, pulpwood, lumber, and newsprint paper.

7. *Equalization Case*, (1955) 72 C.R.T.C. 1; 44 J.O.R.R. no. 24A, 1; *ibid.*, (1957) 75 C.R.T.C. 119; 47 J.O.R.R. no. 13A.

8. For a complete discussion, see Ryl. Comm., 1951, *Rpt.*, pp. 149–51.

9. *Ibid.*, pp. 100–1.

10. *Ibid.*, pp. 102–5.

11. *Re Freight Rates between Canada and the United States*, (1958) 48 J.O.R.R. 337; *Increased Export and Import Rates on Grain*, (1958) 48 J.O.R.R. 373. See also *West Lorne Co.* v. *Chesapeake & Ohio Ry.*, (1953) 70 C.R.T.C. 25; 43 J.O.R.R. 25. For the special arrangements which are necessary when the currency of one country is at a premium in terms of the other, see *Can. Fruit Wholesalers' Assoc.* v. *C.F.A.*, (1958) 76 C.R.T.C. 302; 43 J.O.R.R. 25.

12. Ryl. Comm., 1951, *Rpt.*, pp. 105–6.

Chapter 3: The General Level of Rates (pp. 48–83)

1. Ryl. Comm., 1931–2, *Rpt.*, p. 13.

2. It was probably for this reason that the directors of the Canadian Pacific continued paying dividends on preference and ordinary stock in the 1920s and early 1930s even though the dividends were fully covered by earnings only in 1926 and 1928.

3. Dividends are technically declared by the shareholders at the annual meeting of the railway, but no dividend may exceed the amount recommended by the Board of Directors. As a practical matter the directors declare dividends.

4. The Temiscouata Railway was bought for the scrap value of its assets but estimated operating losses on the road capitalized at 4 per cent amount to $6 million. In 1951 the Canadian National undertook to absorb the poorly maintained line of the Quebec Railway, Light and Power Company from near Quebec City to Murray Bay.

5. P.C. 2434, (1920) 26 C.R.C. 148, 151: P.C. 886, (1925) 33 C.R.C. 131–2; 17 J.O.R.R. 132–3: *Twenty-one Per cent Case*, (1948) 62 C.R.T.C. 1, 56—7; 38 J.O.R.R. 1, 35—6: *Eight Per Cent Interim Case*, (1949) 64 C.R.T.C. 1; 30 J.O.R.R. no. 13A, 1: Ryl. Comm., 1951, *Rpt.*, pp. 69–70.

6. *Eight Per Cent Interim Case*, (1949) C.R.T.C. at p. 4; J.O.R.R. at p. 3.

7. *Twenty-one Per Cent Case*, (1948) C.R.T.C. at pp. 43–8; J.O.R.R. at pp. 28–31: *Seventeen Per Cent Case*, (1952) 77 C.R.T.C. 113, 277–80; 48 J.O.R.R., no. 16A, 1, 3–5: *Seven Per Cent Case.*, (1953) 70 C.R.T.C. 1, 8–9; 42 J.O.R.R. no. 24A, 1, 4–6: *Eleven Per Cent Case*, (1957) 74 C.R.T.C. 209, 216–17; 46 J.O.R.R. no. 19A, 1, 9.

8. *Seventeen Per Cent Case*, C.R.T.C. at p. 278, J.O.R.R. at p 4.

9. *Uniform Classification of Accounts for Class I Common Carriers by Railway* (Ottawa: Queen's Printer, 1955).

10. Ryl. Comm., 1961, *Rpt.*, vol. II, p. 78.

11. *Fifteen Per Cent Case*, (1958) 76 C.R.T.C. 53, 76–7; 47 J.O.R.R. no. 19A, 1, 19.

12. *Twenty-one Per Cent Case*, (1948) C.R.T.C. at pp. 48–54; J.O.R.R. at pp. 28–34. See also A. W. Currie, "Depreciation Policies of Canadian Railways," *Canadian Chartered Accountant*, Feb., 1949, pp. 59–68.

13. *Ry. Ass'n. of Canada* v. *Can. Mfrs.' Ass'n.*, (1920) 26 C.R.C. 130;

140; 10 J.O.R.R. 429, 436: *Bell Telephone Co.* v. *Montreal & Toronto*, (1927) 34 C.R.C. 1, 3; 16 J.O.R.R. 229, 231: *Ottawa* v. *Ottawa Electric Ry.*, (1946) 59 C.R.T.C. 136, 156, 161, 162; 36 J.O.R.R. 533, 536, 541. The Railway Act, s. 2, s.s. 37 (*e*), defines "working expenditure" as including "all rates, taxes. . . ."

14. P.C. 1958–601, reprinted in 48 J.O.R.R. 95.

15. *Twenty-one Per Cent Case*, (1948) C.R.T.C. at p. 29; J.O.R.R. at p. 19. It might be added that it would also be unfair to the Canadian National which had outside income of only $4 million in 1946 compared with the Canadian Pacific's nearly $23 million.

16. *Western Rates Case*, (1914) 17 C.R.C. 123, 193: *Re Eastern Tolls*, (1916) 22 C.R.C. 4, 26, 32, 33, 34; 6 J.O.R.R. 133, 146, 150, 151: *Re Freight Tolls*, 1922, 27 C.R.C. 153, 169; 12 J.O.R.R. 6, 71.

17. *Twenty-one Per Cent Case*, (1948) C.R.T.C. at pp. 35–6; J.O.R.R. at p. 23.

18. *Eight Per Cent Additional Case*, (1950) 64 C.R.T.C. 139, 152; 39 J.O.R.R. no. 23A, 1, 9.

19. *Twenty-one Per Cent Case*, (1948) C.R.T.C. at pp. 42, 43; J.O.R.R. at p. 27. The Board allowed a surplus of 2 per cent of capital investment or of par value of capital stock in *Western Rates Case*, (1914) C.R.C. at p. 194: *Bell Telephone Co.* v. *Toronto*, (1921) 27 C.R.C. 231, 244: *B.C. Telephone Co.* v. *Vancouver*, (1921), 27 C.R.C. 259, 265; 11 J.O.R.R. 216, 220: *Bell Telephone Co.* v. *Montreal & Toronto*, (1927) C.R.C. at pp. 3, 34; J.O.R.R. at pp. 231, 252: *Ottawa Electric Ry.* v. *Ottawa*, (1928) 34 C.R.C. 316, 323, 337; 18 J.O.R.R. 176, 180, 190.

20. *Seventeen Per Cent Case*, (1952) C.R.T.C. at pp. 285–6; J.O.R.R. at pp. 7–9.

21. *Eleven Per Cent Case*, (1957) C.R.T.C. at p. 226; J.O.R.R. at p. 16: *Fifteen Per Cent Case*, (1958) C.R.T.C. at pp. 60–1; J.O.R.R. at p. 7.

22. *Twenty-one Per Cent Case*, (1948) C.R.T.C. at p. 37; J.O.R.R. at p. 24.

23. Ryl. Comm., 1951, *Rpt.*, p. 63.

24. Cases referred to were: *Dawson Bd. of Trade* v. *White Pass & Yukon Ry.*, (1911) 11 C.R.C. 402: *Western Rates Case*, (1914) C.R.C. at p. 123: *Edmonton, Dunvegan & British Columbia Ry.* v. *Central Rys.* (1920) 26 C.R.C. 153: *Manitoba & Saskatchewan* v. *Ry. Ass'n. of Canada*, (1920) 26 C.R.C. 298; 10 J.O.R.R. 429: *General Investigation*, 1925–7, 33 C.R.C. 127; 17 J.O.R.R. 133: *Twenty-one Per Cent Case*, (1948) 62 C.R.T.C. 1; 38 J.O.R.R. 1.

25. *Rate Base-Rate of Return Case*, (1954) 76 C.R.T.C. 186; 43 J.O.R.R. no. 23A, 1. The Supreme Court refused leave to appeal. *Ibid.*, (1954) 76 C.R.T.C. 12.

26. *Federal Power Comm.* v. *National Gas Pipeline Co.*, (1942) 315 U.S. 575: *Federal Power Comm.* v. *Hope Natural Gas Co.*, (1944) 320 U.S. 591, 603. Confirmed in *Colorado Interstate Gas Co.* v. *Federal Power Comm.*, (1945) 324 U.S. 581: *Panhandle Eastern Pipe Line Co.* v. *Federal Power Comm.*, (1945) 324 U.S. 635, 649. See also M. G. Glaeser, *Public Utilities in American Capitalism* (New York: Macmillan, 1957), pp. 334–44: P. J. Garfield and W. F. Lovejoy, *Public Utility Economics* (Englewood Heights, N.J.: Prentice-Hall, 1964), pp. 69–70.

27. Decisions of the Board and of the Interstate Commerce Commission illustrating alternatives to horizontal increases are set forth in Ry. Comm., 1951, *Rpt.*, pp. 52–61.

28. *Ibid.*, pp. 61–2.

29. *Seventeen Per Cent Case*, (1952) C.R.T.C. at p. 291; J.O.R.R. at p. 12.

30. *Ibid.*, C.R.T.C. at p. 289; J.O.R.R at p 10: *Eleven Per Cent Case*, (1957) C.R.T.C. at p. 235; J.O.R.R. at p. 21: *Seventeen Per Cent Case*, (1958) 77 C.R.T.C. 113, 132–5; 48 J.O.R.R. no. 16A, 1, 20–3.

31. Ryl. Comm, 1951, *Rpt.*, pp. 124–7: An Act to Amend the Railway Act (1951) 2nd sess., 15–16 Geo. VI, c. 22, s. 332 A: R.S.C., 1952, c. 234, s. 336.

32. *Circular no. 272*, (1952) 42 J.O.R.R. 232: *Order no. 82339 (Equalization Case)*, (1953) 43 J.O.R.R. 232: *Equalization Case*, (1954) 71 C.R.T.C. 22; 43 J.O.R.R. no. 23A, 1: *ibid.*, (1955) 72 C.R.T.C. 1; 44 J.O.R.R. no. 24A, 1: *ibid.*, (1960) 80 C.R.T.C. 324; 50 J.O.R.R. 39.

33. *Ibid.*, (1957) 75 C.R.T.C. 119; 47 J.O.R.R. no. 13A, 1.

34. *Ibid.*, (1960) 80 C.R.T.C. 241, 324; 50 J.O.R.R. 39.

35. *Domestic Grain in Western Canada*, (1955) 72 C.R.T.C. 257; 45 J.O.R.R. 339: *ibid.*, (1956) 74 C.R.T.C. 113; 45 J.O.R.R. 441: *ibid.*, (1957) 47 J.O.R.R. 321. In Jan., 1959, the Supreme Court rejected an appeal in this case.

36. Ryl. Comm., 1961, *Rpt.*, vol. II, p. 530.

Chapter 4: Crow's Nest Pass Rates (pp. 84–112)

1. 60–61 Vict., c. 5. For details on the history of the agreement, see A. W. Currie, *Economics of Canadian Transportation* (Toronto: University of Toronto Press, 1959), *passim*.

2. *Statutes of Manitoba*, 1901, 1 Edw. VII, c. 38.

3. *Ibid.*, c. 39. When the tariffs were being prepared it was discovered that 85 per cent of the existing toll to Winnipeg (420 miles from Port Arthur) less the Winnipeg cartage charge of 3 cents per hundred pounds was equal to the existing rate for 290 miles. Hence, for the purpose of constructing tariffs, the actual distance of 420 miles was assumed to be 290 miles. This was the origin of the "constructive mileage" to and from Lakehead.

4. *Western Rates Case*, (1914) 17 C.R.C. 123.

5. W. A. Mackintosh, *Economic Problems of the Prairie Provinces* (Toronto: Macmillan, 1935), pp. 284–5.

6. *Fifteen Per Cent Case*, (1917), 22 C.R.C. 49, 69; 7 J.O.R.R. 411, 434.

7. *Twenty-five Per Cent Case*, (1918) 8 J.O.R.R. 277: *Ry. Ass'n. of Canada* v. *Can. Mfrs.' Ass'n.*, (1920) 26 C.R.C. 130; 10 J.O.R.R. 283.

8. (1922) 12–13 Geo. V, c. 41. Actually Parliament suspended the agreement for one year and gave the Cabinet authority to extend the suspension by Order-in-Council for a further period of one year.

9. *Re Freight Tolls*, 1922, 27 C.R.C. 153; 12 J.O.R.R. 61.

10. P.C. 2007, dated Oct. 2, 1923, reprinted in (1925) 30 C.R.C. 393, 397–8; (1923) 13 J.O.R.R. 173.

11. *British Columbia* v. *C.F.A.*, (1923) 13 J.O.R.R. 173.

12. *Re Crow's Nest Pass Rates*, (1924) 29 C.R.C. 238; 14 J.O.R.R. 147.

13. *Ibid.*, [1925] S.C.R. 155; 2 D.L.R. 755; (1925) 30 C.R.C. 32.

14. An Act to Amend the Railway Act (1925), 15–16 Geo. V, c. 52. The pertinent sections are now contained in the Railway Act, R.S.C., 1952, c. 234, s. 328, s.s. 6.

15. *British Columbia* v. *C.F.A.*, (1925) 30 C.R.C. 393, 408; 15 J.O.R.R. 272, 288.

16. P.C. 308, dated Feb. 23, 1927, reprinted in (1927) 17 J.O.R.R. 132-3.

17. In 1897 the Crow's Nest Pass rates applied to grain, flour, oatmeal, and millstuffs. In 1952 they covered: barley, buckwheat, corn (except corn for popping), oats, rye, spelts, wheat, alfalfa meal, barley cleanings, breakfast foods or cereals (uncooked in bags, barrels, or cases), bran, buckwheat flour, chopped feed, corn flour, cornmeal, crushed oats, feed grain in sacks, flour made from grain only, grits, groats, malt, middlings, millfeed, oat hulls, oatmeal, pearl or pot barley in bags or barrels, rolled oats, rolled wheat, rye flour or meal, sweepings and screenings, shorts, barley sprouts, wheat meal, flaxseed, and rapeseed. Charges for stop-off and out-of-line hauls may be increased notwithstanding the Agreement. *Robin Hood Mills* v. *C.N.R. & C.P.R.*, (1952) 42 J.O.R.R. 163.

18. J. L. McDougall, "The Relative Level of Crow's Nest Grain Rates in 1897 and 1965," *Can. Journal of Eco. & Pol. Science*, Feb. 1966, pp. 46-54.

19. Ryl. Comm., 1951, *Transcript of Evidence*, p. 15619.

20. *Submission of C.N.R. to Ryl. Comm.*, 1951, p. 191.

21. Ryl. Comm., 1951, *Transcript of Evidence*, p. 19241.

22. *Ibid., Rpt.*, p. 250.

23. *Labour Gazette*, Jan., 1955, pp. 53–4.

24. *Seventeen Per Cent Case*, (1958) 77 C.R.T.C. 113, 141; 48 J.O.R.R. no. 16A, 1, 32.

25. *Ibid.*, C.R.T.C. at p. 135; J.O.R.R. at p. 23.

26. Ryl. Comm., 1961, *Rpt.*, vol. I, pp. 65–6.

27. *Ibid.*, p. 65.

28. The Interstate Commerce Commission believed that multiple-car rates on grain would be 20 per cent lower than single-car rates on long hauls and had "no hesitancy in finding . . . that the Big John [an aluminum, covered hopper car capable of handling a revenue load in excess of 100 tons] represents a major breakthrough in the control of cost and a notable advance in the art of railroading." *Grain in Multiple-Car Shipments*, (1963) 321 I.C.C. 582, 587.

29. *Fraser Valley-Surrey Farmers' Co-op.* v. *C.N.R.*, (1935) 43 C.R.C. 97; 24 J.O.R.R. 344. In the first postwar general rates case, *Twenty-one Per Cent Case*, (1948) 62 C.R.T.C. 1; 38 J.O.R.R. 1, the Board refused to increase the rate on domestic grain because it felt that it would widen the difference between export and domestic rates. It abandoned this position on most subsequent general rate cases. See also *Domestic Grain in Western Canada*, (1955) 72 C.R.T.C. 257; 45 J.O.R.R. 339: *ibid.*, (1956) 74 C.R.T.C. 113; 45 J.O.R.R. 441: *ibid.*, (1957) 47 J.O.R.R. 321. In Jan. 1959, the Supreme Court rejected an appeal in this case.

30. *At and East Grain Rates*, (1961) 82 C.R.T.C. 87; 51 J.O.R.R. 99, with renewals every year to 1967.

Chapter 5: The Maritime Freight Rates Act (pp. 113–21)

1. The amount of circuity has been exaggerated. On the assumption that any line between the Maritimes and Montreal, which was built on a purely commercial basis, would follow the route of the Canadian Pacific across the state of Maine, the distances from Montreal to Moncton are: by direct route via Saint John 577 miles; by former Intercolonial 648 or 71 miles farther; and by former National Transcontinental 613 miles or 36 miles farther. From Montreal to Saint John via direct line (Canadian Pacific) is 488 miles; via Intercolonial through Moncton 737 miles or 249 more; via National Transcontinental through Moncton 703 miles or 215 more. Thus an excess of 250 miles over the most direct route can be arrived at by taking the most circuitous route to Moncton and thence to Saint John. The Duncan Commission seems to have accepted the word of Sir Sandford Fleming, the chief engineer of the Intercolonial, who wrote that strategic reasons made the line 250 miles longer than would have been necessary on commercial principles.

2. Ryl. Comm. on Maritime Claims, *Rpt.*, p. 21.

3. (1927) 17 Geo. V, c. 44; now R.S.C. 1952, c. 174.

4. It appears that some Maritime interests wanted the reduction extended to Montreal which was the western terminus of the Intercolonial after 1898 and the gateway to Central Canada in a more real sense than Diamond Junction and Lévis. The chief objection seems to have been that this proposal would expose the Maritimes to competition from Montreal wholesalers. Canada, House of Commons, Committee on Railways, 1929, *Proc.*, pp. 67–9.

5. Re Maritime Freight Rates Act, 1927, [1933] S.C.R. 423; (1933) 41 C.R.C. 56.

6. Nova Scotia, Ryl. Comm., Provincial Economic Inquiry, *Rpt.* (Halifax: King's Printer, 1934), p. 65.

7. *Transportation Commission of Maritimes Bd. of Trade v. C.N.R.*, (1936) 44 C.R.C. 289; 25 J.O.R.R. 437.

8. *Nova Scotia v. C.N.R.* [1937] S.C.R. 271, 274, (1937) 46 J.O.R.R. 161, 164.

9. Nova Scotia, Ryl. Comm., Prov. Economic Inquiry, *Rpt.*, p. 66.

10. Ryl. Comm. on Dominion-Prov. Relations, 1937–40, *Rpt.*, vol. II, p. 193.

11. Ryl. Comm., 1951, *Rpt.*, pp. 228–37.

12. *Ibid.*, 1961, *Rpt.*, vol. II, pp. 203–19.

13. Canada, House of Commons, *Debates* (unrevised ed.), Sept. 6, 1966, pp. 8107–8.

14. *Ibid.*, pp. 8101–4, 8106–8; Dec. 21, 1966, pp. 11471–5; Jan. 9, 1967, pp. 11539–42; Jan. 18, 1967, pp. 11963–74; Jan. 23, 1967, pp. 12103–17; Jan. 27, 1967, pp. 12358–9.

Chapter 6: Rates on Particular Commodities (pp. 123–61)

1. For the Board's conclusions on the older methods of computing cost see *Re Inquiry into Costs of Transportation of Coal*, (1927) 17 J.O.R.R. 439.

2. *Ibid.*, p. 442.

3. This statement assumes that a railway spends the same total amount of money on maintaining the plant in good as in bad years. Actually the railway may vary its expenses in strict proportion to total traffic or wage rates may be cut in depression and raised in good times so that cost of maintenance per unit of traffic is constant. But interest, property taxes, and many other expenses cannot be varied with the trade cycle.

4. Jackman, *Economic Principles*, pp. 94–102, 143–4; W. Z. Ripley, *Railroads: Rates and Regulations* (New York: Longmans Green, 1912), pp. 44–70; Douglas Knoop, *Outlines of Railway Economics* (London: Macmillan, 1913), pp. 67–97.

5. Jackman, *Economic Principles*, p. 101.

6. It will be noted that as soon as the traffic volume and gross revenue change, the proportion of the various divisions of expenses to total expenses necessarily changes too. Interest, etc., was 15 per cent of total expenses when revenue was $100 but is only 13.6 per cent when revenues grow to $110.

7. It is sometimes said that value of service is the difference in the price of an article in two places. Yet the difference in price may be wholly accounted for by the transportation charge so that, by this reasoning, the value of service is whatever the rate happens to be. However where an article being sold in B can be produced cheaply at A and at a higher cost at B, the difference in the cost of production may measure the value of service. Where an article can be produced at A and at C for shipment into a common market at B, the rate from A cannot exceed the difference between (*a*) the cost of production at C plus the freight from C to B and (*b*) the cost of production at A. In this instance the possible freight rate from A is determined by the actual rate from C and the relative costs of production at C and A. Difference in prices in two areas often determine value of service but more frequently this explanation is superficial for it fits some important situations but not all.

8. *Chouinard* v. *C.N.R.*, (1937) 46 C.R.C. 218; 26 J.O.R.R. 471. Cases where the transportation charge approximates, or exceeds, the value of the commodity at point of shipment are not unusual. *Eustis Mining Co.* v. *B. & M.*, (1925) 30 C.R.C. 388; 15 J.O.R.R. 15: *Can. Sugar Factories Ltd.* v. *C.P.R.*, (1932) 40 C.R.C. 299; 22 J.O.R.R. 163: *Canada Wood Products Co.* v. *C.F.A.*, (1933) 41 C.R.C. 324; 23 J.O.R.R. 281

9. *Imperial Coal Co.* v. *P. & L.E.*, (1888) 2 I.C.C. 436.

10. *Sand, Gravel, Crushed Stones and Shells within the Southwest*, (1929) 155 I.C.C. 247, 277. In 1951 after the Board had not increased commutation fares in the Toronto and Montreal areas as much as the railways had applied for, the carriers asked the Board's leave to appeal to the Supreme Court on the question of whether the Board had the power to require railways to publish tariffs that fell short of meeting out-of-pocket expenses. The railways defined out-of-pocket as the amount which would be saved if the commutation services were discontinued. The Board was not prepared to find that the commutation fares failed to meet out-of-pocket and refused leave. *Can. Pass. Ass'n.* v. *Lakeshore Municipalities*, (1951) 66 C.R.T.C. 145; 40 J.O.R.R. 373.

11. *Associated Growers of B.C. Ltd.*, (1927) 17 J.O.R.R. 303, 363. The Board refused the request of a mining company for particulars of the cost of operating a branch line carrying its ore to the smelter. The company wanted

a breakdown of wages, fuel, track and trestle repairs, maintenance of equipment, administrative expense, depreciation, and so on. "The Board . . . has never found it possible to lay down a precise formula whereby the reasonableness of a rate could be accurately determined. In all its experience it has found that many and varying factors enter into each case. The Board has, however, never adopted the cost of providing service as the sole indicator of the reasonableness of any rate. In a general way it may be stated that the cost of service factor is more particularly valuable in determining whether any particular rate is reasonably compensatory to the carrier in cases where there may be reason to believe that a rate is at the borderline of cost. In this event the principal consideration would be whether such rate was so low as to cast an added burden upon other traffic." *Granby Consolidated Mining, Smelting and Power Co.* v. *C.P.R.*, (1950) 64 C.R.T.C. 243; 39 J.O.R.R. 298, 299.

12. Because their first tariffs were not published, the early history of railway rates is obscure. Canals were differentiating their tolls long before railways began. See W. M. Acworth, *Elements of Railway Economics* (Oxford: University Press, 1905), pp. 103–8; W. T. Jackman, *Development of Transportation in Modern England* (Cambridge: University Press, 1916), vol. II, pp. 728 ff.

13. The revenues from the transportation of watermelons and of coal in the Pocohontas region were 1.32 cents and 0.54 cents per ton-mile in 1939 and the contributions above out-of-pocket costs were 0.51 and 0.25 cents per ton-mile, respectively. Based on the volume of watermelon and of coal traffic, the contribution to fixed costs and profits made by watermelons approximated $53,000 compared with approximately $75,000,000 for bituminous coal. *Class Rate Investigation, 1939,* (1945) 262 I.C.C. 447, 588.

14. This is also the chief reason why suburban theatres have no afternoon shows except on Saturdays when children are free to attend. For the same reason downtown moving picture houses have morning showings on Saturdays and not on other days.

15. *Rail Freight Service Costs in the Various Rate Territories of the United States,* 78th Congress, 1st sess. (1943), Senate Document no. 63, p. 75. See also M. O. Lorenz, "Cost and Value of Service in Railway Rate-Making," *Quarterly Journal of Economics,* vol. XXX, no. 2, Feb., 1916, pp. 205–32.

16. K. T. Healy, *The Economics of Transportation* (New York: Ronald Press, 1940), p. 197. It is possible that older transportation economists were deceived by cost reductions brought about by increasing volume (true decreasing costs) and cost reductions resulting from improved technology in a rapidly expanding industry. In theory economists made a clear distinction between true decreasing costs arising from conditions when volume increased and other things remained unchanged, and decreasing costs due to changes in technology. In practice they seem to have confused the two factors. Moreover the period 1873–96, when the older theory of railway rates was being formulated, was one of declining material prices and wage rates which made for lower costs per ton-mile. Then, too, the theory assumed that the existing volume of traffic remained unchanged and that the new or additional business attracted by the lower tolls merely filled up unused capacity and so could be carried at low rates. In time the older or previously existing volume grew

until the railway plant or some parts of it were operating at capacity. Then the traffic which was originally additional became expensive to handle because it was superimposed on a high peak load. Eventually the additional business, instead of incurring low costs, actually was being handled at average or higher-than-average costs.

17. *Pick-Up and Delivery in Official Territory*, (1936) 218 I.C.C. 441, 491.

18. *Ibid.*, pp. 491, 492, 493. Possibly objections similar to those of Commissioner Eastman were in the back of the mind of Assistant Chief Commissioner McLean when he said: "If rates are fixed on an out-of-pocket costs basis, other charges appertaining to railway operation must be borne by other commodities. There may be conditions under which a railway exercising its discretion carries goods that pay only out-of-pocket costs. It does this subject to such attack, if any, as may arise. It may do this with a view to develop business or on account of meeting competition; but for whatever reason it may so act it does so subject to such complaint as may arise under the Railway Act. The Board, in the absence of specific sanction or direction as embodied in law, is not empowered to make rates on the basis of out-of-pocket costs." *General Investigation*, 1925-7, 33 C.R.C. 127, 199; 17 J.O.R.R. 131, 180.

19. J. A. McDonald, "Some Notes on the Economics of Transportation," *Can. Journal of Eco. & Pol. Science*, Nov., 1951, p. 521.

20. *Rail Freight Costs, supra.*

21. Ryl. Comm., 1961, *Rpt.*, vol. III, pp. 288–303.

22. *Akron, Canton & Youngstown Rld. Co. v. A. T. & S. F.* (1963) 321 I.C.C. 17, 39.

23. Ryl. Comm., 1961, *Rpt.*, vol. II, pp. 203–5.

24. *Ibid.*, vol. II, p. 65.

25. *Ibid.*, p. 63.

26. His criticisms, modified, are now contained in A. C. Pigou, *The Economics of Welfare* (4th ed.; London: Macmillan, 1948), pp. 274–317. See also A. C. Pigou, "A Contribution to the Theory of Railway Rates," *Quarterly Journal of Economics*, Aug., 1891, pp. 438–65: *ibid.*, Feb., 1913, pp. 378–84: *ibid.*, May, 1913, pp. 535–8: D. P. Locklin, "A Review of the Literature on Railway Rate Theory," *ibid.*, Feb., 1933, pp. 167–230: F. W. Taussig, "The Theory of Railway Rates Once More," *ibid.*, pp. 337–42: Nancy Ruggles, "Recent Developments in the Theory of Marginal Cost Pricing," *Review of Economic Studies*, 1950.

Chapter 7: The Classification (pp. 162–210)

1. The reader who is not interested in the mechanics of traffic may wish to turn directly to page 168.

2. Each tariff bears two sets of numbers on the upper right-hand corner of its cover page. One number gives the abbreviation of the name of the railway followed usually by the letter E or W (East or West), according to the area in which it is effective, and (invariably) by figures. The tariff also has a C.T.C. (Canadian Transport Commission) number. A few tariffs, especially those governing movements over more than one line of railway, bear the name of an agent, the number of the agent's tariff, and the letters C.T.C.

followed by a number. Every agent must have the carrier's authority to file new tariffs but is not himself in the direct employ of a railway.

3. When the number of supplements to a tariff becomes too voluminous for convenience, the supplements are consolidated to contain all changes in the original tariff that are effective up to the date of the consolidated supplement. Periodically the entire tariff is reprinted to incorporate all changes to date.

4. While the term "Owner's Risk" may seem to place the risk entirely on the owner, the rule is "intended to cover risks necessarily incidental to transportation, but no such limitation, expressed or otherwise, shall relieve the carrier from liability for any loss or damage which may result from any negligence or omission of the company, its agents or employees." By paying rates 25 per cent over and above the rates otherwise payable, the shipper may have "Owners Risk" conditions removed and the goods transported at "Carrier's Risk" (Rule 25 of the Classification). Provided in all the following cases the shipper signs the necessary release forms, livestock carried at lower rates than the railway may legally charge is handled with liability limited to stipulated amounts (e.g., horses not exceeding $200 each); the railway's liability for injury to or loss of household goods, furniture and settlers' effects and on clothing, wearing apparel and personal effects (all second-hand) in trunks which are securely corded is restricted to 10 cents per pound; railways are not responsible for loss or damage to freight after it has been unloaded at flag stations; and attendants in charge of livestock who travel free or at reduced fares by freight train must release the railway from some of the liabilities which it normally assumes toward passengers. In 1963 (53 J.O.R.R. 367) the Board allowed the Canadian National to limit its liability under its Car-Go-Rail plan to $500 on any automobile. Under the plan a passenger by train has his automobile hauled by rail to some station where it is unloaded for his use there.

5. The Classification contains Rules (5, 7, 18, 19, 21, 40, 41) for the construction of fibreboard containers and of wooden boxes, crates, firkins, barrels, kegs, carboys, and paper bags; the conditions of acceptance and the basis of charges if the container is not up to standard; the meaning of such terms as "nested," "in the rough"; and the marking of packages or articles offered for transportation. Shippers should pay careful attention to these rules.

6. See pp. 202–3.

7. See pp. 205–7.

8. Or he follows immediately to the right of the dividing line running down the middle of every page, except the cover page, in the tariff.

9. For the most part brand names are excluded from the list of articles (e.g., Kleenex is indexed under "Cellulose Napkins"), but a few of them have crept in. Typically adjectives follow nouns rather than preceding them as in colloquial English.

10. For other rules in the Classification see below.

11. The White Pass and Yukon Route has its own classification with four broad classes.

12. To make sure that no interest anywhere in the Dominion is overlooked, information is constantly being interchanged between the two committees. Also, before application is made to the Board for any change, copies

of the proof-sheets incorporating the proposed change are circulated among all shippers and shippers' organizations such as the Canadian Industrial Traffic League and the Transportation Department of the Canadian Manufacturers' Association.

13. For the general attitude of the Board, see note 73 *infra*. In the United States it is often alleged that rate-making committees of the carriers have acted as monopolistic organizations and to the detriment of the public. No similar complaints have even been made in Canada, apparently because of the way in which the committees are constituted.

14. Jackman, *Economic Principles*, p. 158.

15. A few commodity rates are more or less closely related to the corresponding class rate, for example, the specific rate on petroleum in the West is 40 per cent of fifth, newsprint paper is generally 75 per cent of fifth, and woodpulp 85 per cent of tenth. But most commodity rates are not directly based on the class rate and articles in the same class are not necessarily on the same commodity mileage scale. "While the articles may all take the same classification rating [and hence the same standard maximum class rates], the commodity rates thereon may have a range of 60 to 90 per cent of the class rate, and yet the situation does not result in discrimination of the character prohibited by the Railway Act." *Fraser Valley–Surrey Farmers' Co-op.* v. *C.N.R.*, (1935) 43 C.R.C. 97; 24 J.O.R.R. 344, and the cases therein cited. One of the objectives of Equalization was to bring commodity mileage scales more in line with Mileage Class rates.

16. The percentage relationships did not hold exactly. Numerous percentage increases and decreases in all rates were made as a result of the Board's decisions in the general rate cases. Rounding out the absolute increases to the nearest cent slightly distorted the original basis. Prior to 1884 the Classification had four numbered classes for valuable goods and four special classes for more bulky articles. The latter bore no particular relationship to first class but were calculated on a ton-mile basis. In 1884 all these classes were incorporated in the now familiar ten classes and the lack of exact relationship between them continued. The relationship of the classes (omitting ninth, livestock, for which a commodity rate was published) in 1950 for hauls of 400 miles was 100, 88, 75, 63, 50, 46, 39, 39, 34 in Eastern Canada and 100, 85, 67, 50, 45, 38, 27, 27, 22, in the West. For this distance the first class rate in the West was 48 cents per hundred pounds higher than in the East but the tenth class rate was 3 cents per hundred pounds less. In 1955 the Board changed the relationship to 100, 85, 70, 55, 45, 40, 32½, 30, 40 (on horses, mules, and ponies, and 32½ on cattle, calves, sheep, and hogs), and 27½, all across the country. *Equalization Case*, (1952) 69 C.R.T.C. 306 324.

17. *General Steel Wares* v. *C.F.A.*, (1938) 48 C.R.C. 89, 92; 28 J.O.R.R. 143, 144.

18. Dr. S. J. McLean in *Berliner Gramophone Co.* v. *C.F.A.*, (1912) 3 D.L.R. 496, 500; 14 C.R.C. 175, 179. Confirmed in *Stokeley-Van Camp* v. *C.F.A.*, (1944) 57 C.R.T.C. 15, 21; 33 J.O.R.R. 330, 333.

19. *C.N.R.* v. *Northern Transportation Co.*, (1941) 53 C.R.T.C. 148, 157; 31 J.O.R.R. 165, 170.

20. *Order 69652*, (1947) 37 J.O.R.R. 127. Similarly, the Board has ruled that "Link Instrument Trainers" are analogous with "Airplanes, with power,

taken apart" (double first) rather than with "Machines, N.O.I.B.N. set-up, in boxes or crates" (first class): *Re U.S. General Accounting Office* (1957) 75 C.R.T.C. 19; 47 J.O.R.R. 4. Following this case, they were classified as "Aircraft trainers, instructional, non-flying."

21. Rule 46 provides that descriptions in the Classification are to be read in connection with context and headings. A heading includes the sub-species, so to speak, of a commodity; for example, "roots, not ground nor powdered," are divided into cassava, chicory, ginseng, laurel, ginger, licorice, soap weed, tumeric, yucca, and N.O.I.B.N.

22. *C.N.R.* v. *Northern Transportation, supra.*

23. "In view of the powerful commercial incentives to obtain favourable rate adjustments, it is not strange that incongruities in relationships, real or apparent, should be seized upon as ground for complaint." I. L. Sharfman, *The Interstate Commerce Commission* (Washington: The Commonwealth Fund, 1933), vol. IIIB, p. 497.

24. "Tariffs are not to be construed by intention. They are to be construed according to their language. Where a tariff prescribing certain tolls is headed 'machinery' although the articles contained in the item are those used in connection with tanning, the same tolls are available for machinery of other types such as for a pulp mill." *Spanish River Pulp & Paper* v. *C.P.R.*, (1915) 19 C.R.C. 381, headnote. See also *Robin Hood Mills* v. *C.P.R.*, (1922) 28 C.R.C. 50; 11 J.O.R.R. 469: *Dominion Traffic Ass'n.* v. *C.N.R.*, (1933) 41 C.R.C. 206; 23 J.O.R.R. 63: *Meigs Pulpwood Co.* v. *C.N.R.*, (1924) 30 C.R.C. 18; 14 J.O.R.R. 100.

25. *Dome Mines* v. *C.N.R.* (1933) 41 C.R.C. 42; 23 J.O.R.R. 53: *Guy Tombs Ltd.* v. *C.N.R.*, (1935) 44 C.R.C. 216; 25 J.O.R.R. 322.

26. *Kotex Co. of Canada Ltd.* v. *C.F.A.*, (1933) 41 C.R.T.C. 158, 164; 23 J.O.R.R. 191, 194.

26a. *Swift Canadian* v. *C.F.A.*, (1955) 72 C.R.T.C. 273; 45 J.O.R.R. 243. An application for leave to appeal to the Supreme Court of Canada was dismissed. *Ibid.*, (1955) 72 C.R.T.C. 279.

27. *Dunlop Tire & Rubber Co.* v. *C.F.A.*, (1926) 16 J.O.R.R. 128.

28. *Dome Mines, supra.*

29. *United Grain Growers* v. *C.F.A.*, (1918) 24 C.R.C. 138, 140; 8 J.O.R.R. 153, 154.

30. *Edmonton* v. *C.F.A.*, (1943) 56 C.R.T.C. 114; 33 J.O.R.R. 182.

31. *Dominion Traffic Ass'n.* v. *C.F.A.*, (1932) 40 C.R.C. 213; 22 J.O.R.R. 218. Shippers described two carloads of rubber belting used in conveying ore and grain respectively as a rubber stationary conveyor (fifth) and as a grain conveyor (sixth). Because the merchandise shipped was only a portion of a conveyor, which when complete consisted of belt, angle irons, braces, idlers, and various other things, the Board held that the proper classification of the goods was "Belting" (fourth). *Gutta Percha & Rubber* v. *C.N.R.*, (1932) 44 C.R.C. 388; 22 J.O.R.R. 1.

32. *Burlington Beach Commissioners* v. *Hamilton Radial Electric Ry.*, (1918) 24 C.R.C. 39, 41.

33. *National Dairy Council* v. *Express Traffic Ass'n.*, (1921) 27 C.R.C. 207, 214; 12 J.O.R.R. 204, 210.

34. *Summerside Bd. of Trade* v. *C.N.R.* (*Prince Edward Island Ferry Case*), (1947) 60 C.R.T.C. 274, 289; 36 J.O.R.R. 379, 387. This case relates

to distance rather than to the classification as such but it illustrates, nonetheless, the influence of cost. Upon evidence of the cost of service, the Board fixed the proper toll for handling carload freight between a car barge and team tracks or private sidings ashore. *Kelowna Bd. of Trade* v. *C.P.R.* (1915) 19 C.R.C. 414.

35. *Western Ontario Municipalities* v. *G.T.R.*, (1915) 18 C.R.C. 329, 335; 5 J.O.R.R. 116.

36. *Canadian Sugar Factories* v. *C.P.R.*, (1932) 40 C.R.C. 299, 312; 22 J.O.R.R. 163, 171.

37. Dissenting opinion of Commissioner McLean in *International Paper Co.* v. *G.T.R.*, (1913) 15 C.R.C. 111, 117–18; but confirmed by the Board in *National Dairy Council* v. *G.T.R.*, (1919) 26 C.R.C. 113, 117–18; 9 J.O.R.R. 443, 454.

38. Jackman, *Economic Principles*, p. 221. The railways might be restrained from increasing all their low rates by the fact that any higher rates would choke off the flow of some commodities of low value. Nevertheless the danger which Jackman mentions is always present once the theory being discussed is accepted.

39. *Gainers Ltd.* v. *C.F.A.*, (1935) 43 C.R.C. 309, 315; 25 J.O.R.R. 2, 5. An interesting but inconclusive case on the relationship between the rate on a particular commodity and the financial needs of the carrier is *N.S. Shippers' Ass'n.* v. *D.A.R.*, (1924) 28 C.R.C. 95; 14 J.O.R.R. 117, 271.

40. *Sask. Co-op. Creameries* v. *C.N.R.*, (1933) 41 C.R.C. 131, 134–5; 23 J.O.R.R. 55, 57. Where the applicant used the operating cost per gross ton-mile of all revenue freight to arrive at the estimated cost of handling certain log traffic, the United States Supreme Court said: "In using the above composite figure in the determination of this issue, . . . [the complainant] necessarily ignored, in the first place, the differences in average unit cost on the several [railroad] systems; and then the differences of each in the cost incident to the different classes of traffic and articles of merchandise, and to the widely varying conditions under which the transportation is conducted. In this unit cost figure no account is taken of the differences in unit cost dependent, among other things, upon differences in the length of haul; in the character of the commodity; in the configuration of the country; in the density of the traffic; in the daily loaded car movement; in the extent of the empty car movement; in the nature of the equipment employed; in the extent to which the equipment is used; in the expenditures required for its maintenance. Main line and branch line freight, interstate and intrastate, carload and less than carload, are counted alike." *Nor. Pac.* v. *Dept. of Public Works*, (1925) 268 U.S. 39, 44.

41. *Re National Dairy Council*, (1927) 17 J.O.R.R. 303, 401.

42. *Canadian Sugar Factories*, C.R.C. at p. 307; J.O.R.R. at p. 168.

43. *Western Livestock Shippers' Ass'n.* v. *C.P.R.*, (1940) 51 C.R.T.C. 321, 326; 30 J.O.R.R. 340, 343. Value of service was also involved in this case for the Board went on to say that "any reduction in the stop-off charge would tend to increase the number of stop-offs and hence the number of delays which are already burdensome." On account of the slow schedules and the long delays at stop-off points, it was hard to avoid complaints from passengers on mixed trains.

44. "Where a rate which has been for some time in force was increased,

the burden of proving that such increase was reasonable was on the railway: ... a rate established in the first instance by a railway of its own volition was presumptively reasonable; ... it was incumbent on the railway, if such initial rate were unreasonable, to shew with reasonable conclusiveness what changed conditions or increase in cost of operation justified the advance of the rate." *C.F.A.* v. *Cadwell Sand & Gravel Co.*, (1913) 15 C.R.C. 156, 157. Yet "the whole question is one of reasonableness, and while the continuance of the practice affords evidence of its reasonableness, it is not conclusive." *Can. Mfrs. Ass'n. Interswitching Case*, (1907) 7 C.R.C. 302, 308: *Davy* v. *Niagara, St. Catharines & Toronto Ry.*, (1909) 9 C.R.C. 493: *Dominion Sugar Co.* v. *C.F.A.*, (1912) 14 C.R.C. 188: *International Paper Co.* v. *G.T.R.*, (1913) 15 C.R.C. 111: *National Dairy Council* v. *G.T.R.*, (1919) 26 C.R.C. 113; 9 J.O.R.R. 443: *Moose Jaw Bd. of Trade* v. *C.F.A.*, (1928) 34 C.R.C. 362; 18 J.O.R.R. 331: *Increased Rates on Agricultural Implements*, (1950) 65 C.R.T.C. 351; 40 J.O.R.R. 174.

45. *C.F.A.* v. *Cadwell Sand*, at pp. 164–5.

46. *Planters Nut & Chocolate Co.* v. *C.F.A.*, (1933) 41 C.R.C. 339, 344–5; 33 J.O.R.R. 284, 286–9.

47. *Queen's Central Agric. Society* v. *C.N.R.*, (1927) 34 C.R.C. 100; 17 J.O.R.R. 541. Though this case does not relate directly to distance, it does show the importance of relative cost.

48. Rates are usually expressed in cents per hundred pounds, but with very low rates, such as those on coal and scrap metal, the toll is published per long or short ton. This system of quoting rates is fairer than any other because the charge is made proportionate to the service rendered. It is the only system whereby inequalities amongst shippers resulting from differences in the size of the cars can be obviated. An application to place the charge for mill refuse on a per car basis was refused. *Chouinard* v. *C.N.R.*, (1937) 46 C.R.C. 218, 221; 26 J.O.R.R. 471, 475 confirming *Waterloo* v. *G.T.R.*, (1918) 24 C.R.C. 143. The Board would not require seasoned and unseasoned wood to be carried at the same carload toll irrespective of weight. Shippers without capital for drying kilns and open air storage facilities claimed they were at a disadvantage compared with lumber dealers who had the money to invest in kilns, yards, and in wood being stored during the drying process. *Roberts* v. *C.P.R.*, (1915) 18 C.R.C. 350.

49. *Warrington* v. *C.F.A.*, (1919) 24 C.R.C. 155; 8 J.O.R.R. 521.

50. "Nested" (Rule 21) means three or more different sizes enclosed each within the next larger, or three or more of the articles placed one within the other so that the upper article will not project above the next lower article more than one-third of its height. "Knocked down" involves taking the article apart in such a manner as to reduce materially the space occupied (Rule 19). Although the rule does not provide a fixed amount of reduction in size of the article shipped, the word "materially" in practice means that the shipment K.D. occupies no more than two-thirds of the cubical contents of the article S.U.

51. Rule 29. See also *Rideau Lumber Co.* v. *G.T.R.*, (1908) 8 C.R.C. 339, 344–5; 4 B.R.C. 260, 262–3.

52. *Re Classification No. 18*, (1932) 22 J.O.R.R. 92, 98. The effective date of this change in rates was postponed for about six months so that manufacturers could work off their current stock of smaller pails.

53. *Express Traffic Ass'n.* v. *Montreal, Toronto, & Vancouver Bds. of Trade,* (1931) 39 C.R.C. 88; 21 J.O.R.R. 29.

54. Even when it was proven that loss by pilferage had materially decreased, the Board refused to reduce rates. The immunity from theft was, it said, the result of the very large outlay on railway police services made to secure safety for this class of freight. *Man. Liquor Comm.* v. *C.F.A.,* (1924) 14 J.O.R.R. 258.

55. *Re Canadian Explosives Ltd.,* (1925) 15 J.O.R.R. 307. See also Classification (Rule 6) re marking shipments of explosives and other dangerous articles.

56. *Ontario Mining Ass'n.* v. *C.N.R.,* (1945) 58 C.R.T.C. 17; 34 J.O.R.R. 265.

57. *Re Proposed Classification No. 17,* (1925) 15 J.O.R.R. 177, 216. In *Re Classification No. 18,* (1932) 22 J.O.R.R. 92, 96 the Board stated there was no uniformity in the classification on L.C.L. shipments when packed in cans or cartons in boxes and barrels, and when shipped in bulk in barrels or boxes.

58. *Connecticut Oyster Co. Ltd.,* (1922) 12 J.O.R.R. 169, 171.

59. In some carload traffic such as very heavy machinery and lumber, the shipper must provide his own planks and other materials for preventing the freight from shifting in the box car or coming loose on a flat car. The weight of the dunnage, unless otherwise provided for in the classification, is charged at the rate applicable on the freight it accompanies. Since flat cars have increased in size, the dunnage allowance for stakes and tie boards used in carload shipments of lumber has been increased from 500 pounds per car to 200 pounds per set of stakes. *Seguin* v. *C.N.R.,* (1952) 69 C.R.T.C. 265; 42 J.O.R.R. 217.

60. *Dalyte Electric Ltd.* v. *C.F.A.,* (1925) 30 C.R.C. 382; 15 J.O.R.R. 257. Because they are competitive with each other, fibreboard and wooden cheese boxes were given the same rating. *Canada Cheese Box Co.* v. *C.F.A.,* (1917) 22 C.R.C. 347; 7 J.O.R.R. 263. No change was made in the classification of nailed wooden boxes set up (seventh) competing with wire-bound wooden boxes knocked down (tenth). *Wilson Bros.* v. *C.F.A.,* (1929) 19 J.O.R.R. 284.

61. Few students of transportation would agree with Chief Commissioner Carvell that "the cost to a company carrying the goods is the true criterion, and not the selling price." *Consumers' Metal Co.* v. *G.T.R.,* (1921) 27 C.R.C. 127, 128; 11 J.O.R.R. 229.

62. *Seaman, Kent & Co.* v. *C.P.R.,* (1912) 13 C.R.C. 420.

63. *Hudson Bay Mining Co.* v. *Grt. Nor. Ry.,* (1913) 16 C.R.C. 254.

64. *Re Classification No. 18,* (1932) 22 J.O.R.R. 92, 94. See also note 58 *supra.*

65. *Can. Lumbermen's Ass'n.* v. *G.T.R.,* (1910) 10 C.R.C. 306, 313.

66. *Twin City Coal Co.* v. *C.P.R.,* (1918) 23 C.R.C. 181; 9 J.O.R.R. 287.

67. *Wallaceburg Cut Glass* v. *C.F.A.,* (1918) 22 C.R.C. 408; 8 J.O.R.R. 6. Costume, Imitation, or Novelty Jewelry, not silver or gold, nor mounted nor set with precious stones, is rated 200 (L.C.L.) if released to value not exceeding $1.00 per pound: otherwise these goods are not carried by freight at all, presumably because of the possibility of theft in transit or of fraud in

making claims for loss or damage. They may, however, be sent by express.

68. *Shanahan's Ltd.* v. *C.F.A.* (1939) 50 C.R.T.C. 388; 29 J.O.R.R. 451.

69. *Planters Nut & Chocolate Co.* v. *C.F.A.*, (1933) 41 C.R.C. 339, 346; 23 J.O.R.R. 284, 288.

70. *Horne Co.* v. *C.F.A.*, (1916) 22 C.R.C. 344, 347; 6 J.O.R.R. 443, 444. Confirmed in *C.N.R.* v. *Northern Transportation Co.*, (1940) 30 J.O.R.R. 23, 25.

71. *Thermos Bottle Co.* v. *C.F.A.*, (1929) 36 C.R.C. 115, 118; 19 J.O.R.R. 302, 305. See also note 119 *infra*.

72. *Victory Mills* v. *C.F.A.*, (1946) 59 C.R.T.C. 225, 230, 36 J.O.R.R. 61, 64.

73. *Re Proposed Classification No. 17*, (1925) 15 J.O.R.R. 177, 181.

74. *Saanich Fruit Growers' Ass'n.* v. *Express Traffic Ass'n.*, (1935) 43 C.R.C. 362, 366–7; 25 J.O.R.R. 109, 111–12.

75. *National Dairy Council* v. *G.T.R.*, (1921) 27 C.R.C. 209, 214; 12 J.O.R.R. 144, 146. Confirmed in *ibid.*, (1927) 17 J.O.R.R. 391, 399–400. See also *Canadian Sugar Factories*, C.R.C. at p. 305; J.O.R.R. at p. 167.

76. File 33365.85, not reported but referred to in *Meredith Simmons & Co.*, v. *C.F.A.*, (1942) 55 C.R.T.C. 239, 242; 32 J.O.R.R. 385, 387.

77. *Mead, Johnson & Co.* v. *C.F.A.*, (1933) 41 C.R.C. 377; 23 J.O.R.R. 253.

78. *Meredith, supra.*

79. *Mead, Johnson & Co.* v. *Atlantic Coast Line Ry.*, (1930) 168 I.C.C. 157.

80. *Shell Petroleum Corp.* v. *Abilene & Southern Ry. Co.*, (1933) 191 I.C.C. 147.

81. *Re proposed Classification No. 17*, (1925) 15 J.O.R.R. 177, 203; *Ashdown Hardware Co.* v. *C.P.R.*, (1931) 38 C.R.C. 217; 21 J.O.R.R. 195. New and second-hand milk and beverage bottles have the same rating (fifth) but the carload minimum weight is 30,000 pounds for the new and 18,000 pounds for the used containers. At these weights, the carload earning to the carrier is considerably less on second-hand than on new bottles though the expense of transportation is about the same in both cases. Beverage companies have a large investment tied up in bottles all over the country and a reduced carload minimum weight for the return movement enables them to get a quicker return than if the bottles had to be held until a larger minimum weight of empties had been accumulated. Thus while value of service does not affect the classification of bottles, it does influence the minimum carload weight. *Consumers Glass Co.* v. *C.F.A.*, (1931) 38 C.R.C. 77, 85–8; 21 J.O.R.R. 1, 5–6. On the relative rates on new bags and on cleaned and reconditioned bags, see *Can. Used Textile Bag Dealers' Ass'n.* v. *C.N.R.*, (1952) 69 C.R.T.C. 260; 42 J.O.R.R. 213.

82. In Saskatchewan the trucker must satisfy himself that the empties are returned to the consignor of the filled containers via the same transporter by which they were originally shipped; otherwise the trucker must assess charges at the regular rates for new containers. "Rules and Regulations under the Vehicles Act," *Saskatchewan Gazette*, April 1, 1946, 23, 32.

83. If used containers could not be cheaply returned to the shipper, they would have to be scrapped after being used only once. Prices of goods to the consumer might have to be increased and the railway's traffic volume would

be adversely affected. In many instances, the cost of the container is nearly equal to the commodity placed in it and in one instance it was six times as valuable. *Blaugas Co.* v. *C.F.A.*, (1910) 12 C.R.C. 303, 314.

84. *Sand, Gravel, Crushed Stones and Shells within the Southwest*, (1929) 155 I.C.C. 247, 277.

85. *Planters Nut*, C.R.C. at p. 342; J.O.R.R. at p. 285.

86. *Manufacturers' Coal Case*, (1904) 3 C.R.C. 438; 1 B.R.C. 70.

87. *Re Canadian Retail Coal Ass'n.*, (1927) 17 J.O.R.R. 303, 379–81.

88. *Riley* v. *Dominion Express Co.*, (1913) 17 C.R.C. 112. This case confirmed *Manitoba Dairymen's Ass'n.* v. *Dominion Express*, (1912) 14 C.R.C. 142, 143, 149; 7 D.L.R. 868, 869, 874. The principle that rates might not vary with use was followed in regard to other products in *Western Retail Lumbermen's Ass'n.* v. *C.P.R.*, (1916) 20 C.R.C. 155, 157; *Hay & Still* v. *G.T.R.*, (1917) 21 C.R.C. 43; 6 J.O.R.R. 474.

89. *Dominion Canners Co.* v. *C.N.R.*, (1924) 13 J.O.R.R. 296.

90. *Ross Miller Biscuit Co.* v. *C.F.A.*, (1933) 40 C.R.C. 387; 23 J.O.R.R. 5. The Board pointed out the higher value per ton of dog and fox biscuits as compared with prepared poultry and cattle feed.

91. *Traffic Adjustment Bureau* v. *C.P.R.*, (1932) 40 C.R.C. 272; 22 J.O.R.R. 216. Actually in this case the shipment was billed as silica sand and charged at the N.O.I.B.N. rate but the Board stated that had the shipper questioned the reasonableness of the rate for future shipments, it would unquestionably have found that the rate charged was unreasonable. The Board had no power to make a retroactive change in the tariff or order a refund in the charge which was paid. Hence the rate assessed by the railway stood with respect to a shipment already made. The descriptions of the various types of sand were clarified in *Pettinos* v. *New York Central*, (1945) 35 J.O.R.R. 1.

92. *Blaugas Co.* v. *C.F.A.*, (1910) 12 C.R.C. 303. Followed in *Roberts* v. *C.P.R.*, (1915) 18 C.R.C. 350; *Waterloo* v. *G.T.R.*, (1918) 24 C.R.C. 143.

93. For the special case of used containers being returned empty see above.

94. *Wallaceburg Cut Glass* v. *C.F.A.*, (1918) 22 C.R.C. 408; 8 J.O.R.R. 6.

95. *Canada Wood Products Co.* v. *C.F.A.*, (1933) 41 C.R.C. 324; 23 J.O.R.R. 281. Almost the same facts were similarly dealt with in *Firstbrook Boxes Ltd.* v. *C.P.R.*, *ibid.*, C.R.C. at p. 243; J.O.R.R. at p. 241.

96. *Becker Lumber Co.* v. *C.P.R.*, (1935) 43 C.R.C. 386; 25 J.O.R.R. 103.

97. See *infra*.

98. *Becker Lumber*, C.R.C. at p. 389; J.O.R.R. at p. 104.

99. *Montreal Bd. of Trade* v. *C.F.A.*, (1903) 15 C.R.C. 429. See also note 130 *infra*.

100. *National Dairy Council* v. *G.T.R.*, (1921) 27 C.R.C. 209, 223; 12 J.O.R.R. 144, 149–50.

101. *Horne Co.* v. *C.F.A.*, (1916) 22 C.R.C. 344, 347; 6 J.O.R.R. 443, 444.

102. *Becker Lumber*, C.R.C. at p. 390; J.O.R.R at p 105.

103. For example, the railways voluntarily reduced the rate on wool from Kamloops, B.C., to Weston, Ont., as a measure of relief to the western

rancher. Later they restored the original rate. The Board refused to order republication of the old toll because there was no evidence that the new or restored rate was *per se* unreasonable and because it thought the railways were within their rights in adjusting rates to meet the needs of the shipper. *Kamloops Bd. of Trade*, (1927) 17 J.O.R.R. 408.

104. In the *Twenty-one Per Cent Case*, several industries in the Maritimes claimed that they could not bear any increase in rates. If an increase were allowed they would have to close down or move to Central Canada. In order to test the validity of this testimony, the railways asked for, and the Board approved, the production of financial statements. In rendering its decision the Board faced two difficulties. On the one hand the hard-luck stories of shippers might not be based on fact and if this were the case carriers might be imposed upon. On the other hand, the practice of producing statements might permit a carrier to take unfair advantage of a shipper's ability to pay. Also it might lead to revealing to competitors, details of his operations which a shipper might prefer to keep secret.

105. "The result [of Central Pacific Railroad policies] was that from the middle 'seventies to 1910 the major share of the profit of virtually every business and industry on the Coast was diverted from its normal channel into the hands of the railroad and its controlling group. The merchant who brought in stock from the East paid freight bills so high that to sell his goods at all he had to cut his profit almost to the vanishing point. The degree of prosperity of every business and industry was directly dependent upon the officials . . . who fixed the railroad's freight rates." Oscar Lewis, *The Big Four* (New York: Knopf, 1938), pp. 365–6.

106. B. W. Lewis, "Public Pricing of Electric Power," in Temporary National Economic Committee, *Economic Standards of Government Price Control* (Washington, 1941), pp. 1–54; D. H. Wallace, "A Critical Review of Some Instances of Government Price Control," *ibid.*, pp. 397–431.

107. *Perrin* v. *Express Traffic Ass'n.*, (1923) 28 C.R.C. 389, 392; 13 J.O.R.R. 156, 159.

108. *Sask. Stock Growers Ass'n.*, (1927) 17 J.O.R.R. 303, 305–15. See also *Sask. Dairy Ass'n.*, (1925) 15 J.O.R.R. 202.

109. *Canadian Sugar Factories*, C.R.C. at p. 311; J.O.R.R. at p. 171.

110. *Sask. Co-op. Creameries* v. *C.N.R.*, (1933) 41 C.R.C. 131, 132; 23 J.O.R.R. 55, 56.

111. *Coalhurst, Alta., Bd. of Trade* v. *C.P.R.*, (1923) 31 C.R.C. 396, 399; 13 J.O.R.R. 259, 260–1.

112. *National Dairy Council* v. *C.P.R.*, (1922) 28 C.R.C. 75, 83; 12 J.O.R.R. 144, 149–50: *B.C. News Co.* v. *Express Traffic Ass'n.*, (1912) 13 C.R.C. 176: *Massiah* v. *C.P.R.*, (1914) 17 C.R.C. 88, 90: *Crushed Stone, Ltd.* v. *G.T.R.*, (1918) 23 C.R.C. 132; 8 J.O.R.R 199, 200: *Ross Leaf Tobacco Co.* v. *Pere Marquette Ry.*, (1927) 32 C.R.C. 320, 321; 27 J.O.R.R. 27, 28: *Halifax Harbour Com'rs.* v. *C.N.R.*, (1930) 37 C.R.C. 247, 252; 20 J.O.R.R. 221, 236: *Saanich Fruit Growers Ass'n.* v. *Express Traffic Ass'n.*, (1935) 43 C.R.C. 362, 364–7; 34 J.O.R.R. 345, 356–9: *Surrey Co-op Ass'n.* v. *C.N.R.*, (1941) 43 C.R.T.C. 62, 72–5; 31 J.O.R.R. 446, 451–5.

113. *Toronto Bd. of Trade* v. *C.F.A.*, (1913) 16 C.R.C. 442.

114. *Twin City Coal Co.* v. *C.P.R.*, (1918) 23 C.R.C. 181; 8 J.O.R.R. 256.

115. *Sterne & Sons* v. *C.F.A.,* (1918) 23 C.R.C. 171; 8 J.O.R.R. 164.

116. *Re Proposed Classification No. 17,* (1925) 15 J.O.R.R. 177, 232, 244.

117. *Marshall Ventilated Mattress Co.,* (1928) 18 J.O.R.R. 474. It developed that the patents on the spring-filled mattresses had recently expired and the patentee was experiencing more competition from new producers of the spring-filled product than from existing suppliers of felt mattresses.

118. In 1916 the rate on wire from Hamilton, Ont., to a number of destinations in Ontario was higher than that on wire fencing and netting. *Re Eastern Tolls,* (1916) 6 J.O.R.R. 133, 239. But in *Kemp Mfg. & Metal Co.* v. *C.P.R.,* (1909) 10 C.R.C. 161, rates on a manufactured product were reduced to those of the raw material in order to remove unjust discrimination between one area of the country and another.

119. *Prov. of Alta. & Gainers Ltd.* v. *C.P.R.,* (1928) 35 C.R.C. 37; 18 J.O.R.R. 406. Western packers wanted rates on fresh meats to be 142 per cent and on packing house products like lard to be 117½ per cent of the livestock rate from Winnipeg eastbound. The weight of hogs when slaughtered and dressed runs from 75 to 80 per cent of the weight of the live animals. The applicants said the revenue per car on dressed meat should be the same as on livestock after taking into account the heavier loading per car in the case of products. The Board pointed out that a carload of fresh meats, all moving at the same rate, may contain beef, pork, mutton, veal, and lamb cut from animals which, when living, moved at different rates. It said too that existing rates on meats were not shown to be unreasonable or unjustly discriminatory. In *Adolph Lumber Co.* v. *Grt. Nor. Ry.,* (1919) 24 C.R.C. 173; 9 J.O.R.R. 55, the Board ruled that it was impracticable to compare tolls on a product and on the quantity of material required to produce it.

120. *Plaunt* v. *A.C. & H.B. Ry.,* (1928) 35 C.R.C. 73; 18 J.O.R.R. 441, which confirmed *International Paper Co.* v. *G.T.R.,* (1913) 15 C.R.C. 111, 115: *Farquharson* v. *Grt. Nor. Ry.,* (1923) 28 C.R.C. 410, 411; 13 J.O.R.R. 189, 190: *Queen's University* v. *C.P.R.,* (1923) 31 C.R.C. 315; 13 J.O.R.R. 191.

121. *Nukol Fuel Co.* v. *G.T.R.,* (1921) 27 C.R.C. 123; 11 J.O.R.R. 215.

122. *Jackman, Economic Principles,* pp. 188–9. Somewhat the same arguments were advanced in favour of lower rates on stocker and feeder cattle when shipped from a central market to country points for finishing. The Board denied the application. *Eastern Canadian Live Stock Union,* (1927) 17 J.O.R.R. 303, 321-6.

123. *Michigan Sugar Co.* v. *Chatham, Wallaceburg & Lake Erie Ry.,* (1910) 11 C.R.C. 353. To anticipate a later discussion, charging different rates for transporting the same commodity over the same distance could not be unjustly discriminatory in this case, because there was no competition between the two refineries. The one could not be injured on account of lower rates granted the other.

124. D. P. Locklin, *Economics of Transportation* (Chicago: R. D. Irwin, 1947), p. 464.

125. *Hudson & Manhattan R.R. Co.* v. *United States,* (1940) 35 F. Supp. 495, 496.

126. W. Z. Ripley, *Railroads: Rates and Regulation* (New York: Longmans Green, 1913), p. 101.

127. A team track is a siding in a railway yard, convenient of access and egress, where shippers who do not have sidings of their own to their plants or warehouses may drive teams or motor trucks for the purpose of loading or unloading cars.

128. This is Rule 27 in the present classification. The Board upheld the original of this rule in *Vancouver Machinery Depot* v. *C.P.R.*, (1924) 29 C.R.C. 315; 14 J.O.R.R. 227.

129. In *Berliner Gramaphone Co.* v. *C.F.A.*, (1912) 14 C.R.C. 175, carriers argued among other things that granting the application of the company for C.L. rates would reduce railway revenue. The Board said it was questionable whether the railway actually did receive less revenue from C.L. freight than from L.C.L. even though the rate per hundred pounds was lower. See also *Southern Class Rate Investigation*, (1925) 100 I.C.C. 513, 635.

130. A carload rating on cigars was refused because such cars rarely moved and only one shipper would be affected. *Ledoux* v. *C.F.A.*, (1911) 12 C.R.C. 3. But a C.L. rate on cut glass was allowed even though only one shipper was likely to benefit because much of his output actually did move in carloads. *Wallaceburg Cut Glass* v. *C.F.A.*, (1918) 22 C.R.C. 408; 8 J.O.R.R. 6. The Board dismissed an application for a carload rating on blankets, knitted underwear, batting, comforters, and wool socks stating that "dry goods, as a whole, might bear higher rates than charged, without necessarily increasing their cost to the consumer; but by assessing rates according to the value of the service, the movement of low grade commodities is made possible, which could not always be the case were the cost of service alone considered, and any needless reductions on the more valuable descriptions of traffic, which are not commonly shipped in carload lots, must necessarily tend to an increase in the rates on the cheaper commodities which cannot be moved long distance at higher rates than are now charged." *Brock (Western) Ltd.* v. *C.F.A.*, (1931) 38 C.R.C. 326, 328; 21 J.O.R.R. 277, 278.

131. *Zwicker* v. *C.N.R.*, (1922) 12 J.O.R.R. 151, 153.

132. Under the incentive rate scheme there is a series of rates and minimum weights. The plan, though not the formal title, goes back to the 1920s and probably earlier. For example, on canned goods from British Columbia to certain Prairie points, three sets of rates were published, each subject to minimum weights of 24,000, 40,000, and 60,000 pounds respectively. *Columbia Canners* v. *C.P.R.*, (1932) 39 C.R.C. 284; 21 J.O.R.R. 390. See also *Calgary Livestock Exchange* v. *C.N.R.*, (1923) 29 C.R.C. 207; 13 J.O.R.R. 233. A carrier is not allowed to differentiate in minimum weights on account of the use to which the commodity is put. *Hay & Still* v. *G.T.R.*, (1917) 21 C.R.C. 43; 6 J.O.R.R. 474.

133. *Can. Piano & Organ Mfrs. Ass'n.*, (1911) 12 C.R.C. 22; 1 J.O.R.R. 3.

134. *Re Proposed Classification No. 17*, (1925) 15 J.O.R.R. 177, 199. Prior to 1921 stove and shoe polish moved in carloads at fourth class rates, minimum 24,000 pounds. This was changed to fifth, minimum 35,000 pounds, to add to railway revenue per car and increase the volume of business through reducing the rate per hundred pounds. In 1924 the railways reverted to the old rating and weight. It was shown that even with the old minimum weight, cars had often been loaded to 35,000 pounds so that cutting rates and increasing the minimum had merely reduced railway revenues without adding to the volume of traffic. Manufacturers of floor wax and

metal polish were asking for similar concessions and the carriers feared that their revenues might be lowered. The Board upheld the right of the railways to correct their error in judgment. *Dalley* v. *C.F.A.*, (1924) 29 C.R.C. 232; 14 J.O.R.R. 133.

135. In *Western Retail Lumbermen's Ass'n.* v. *C.P.R.*, (1916) 20 C.R.C. 155; 7 J.O.R.R. 31, objection was made to raising the minimum C.L. weight on brick from 40,000 to 50,000 pounds because many towns in the West were too small to sell the larger amount in one season. The Board stated that the freight rate was only one item in the shippers' costs and a railway was not called upon to adjust its rates so that the shipper could always carry on his business at a profit. Shippers of grain have complained that larger cars put them to additional expense because it is harder for them to stow grain back in the corners and trim it (level off the top of the grain) in the centre of the car behind the grain doors. The Board considered these difficulties were a part of the business and were in no way the responsibility of the railways. The Board was not concerned with equalizing costs of production but with the reasonableness of rates. Hence it refused to change the minima proposed. *Dominion Millers' Ass'n.* v. *C.F.A.*, (1917) 21 C.R.C. 83; 7 J.O.R.R. 28.

136. *Ibid.*, C.R.C. at p. 90–1; J.O.R.R. at p. 32. See also *Battle Creek Toasted Corn Flake Co.* v. *C.F.A.*, (1911) 12 C.R.C. 11: *General Steel Wares* v. *C.F.A.*, (1938) 48 C.R.C. 89; 28 J.O.R.R. 143, 144–5.

137. *Re Proposed Classification No. 17*, (1925) 15 J.O.R.R. 177, 222.

138. Fifty cents prior to April, 1948, and 75 cents to August, 1951. Earlier, the railways had made several attempts to have the minimum increased because they considered it was not adequate to compensate them for the clerical expense, pick-up and delivery, and transportation expenses of small shipments. Also their express departments were capable of handling "smalls." The Board felt that carriage of small articles of freight was of advantage to society and that the charge should not be increased.

138a. *Canadian General Electric* v. *C.F.A.*, (1954) 71 C.R.T.C. 329; 44 J.O.R.R. 271: *Andersen* v. *C.F.A.*, (1963) 85 B.T.C. 185; 53 J.O.R.R. 449.

139. But shippers may not take unfair advantage of regulations to reduce their freight expenses. The C.L. minimum weight for pipe and pipe connections was 36,000 pounds; for barn and stable fittings such as cattle stanchions and litter carriers 30,000 pounds; and for pumps and windmills 26,000 pounds. The C.L. rating on all these commodities was fifth class. Manufacturers of windmills wanted to include the necessary pipes and connections with shipments of their windmills. They could not do so economically because such a practice would raise the minimum C.L. weight from 26,000 to 36,000 pounds. Railways allowed pipe and pipe fittings to be included with windmills at the minimum weight of 26,000 pounds for the mixed C.L. Then manufacturers of pipe began to include a few hundred pounds of windmill parts with several thousand pounds of pipe, thereby reducing the minimum C.L. weight from 36,000 pounds normally applicable on pipe to 26,000 pounds on pipe and windmills. Though legal, the action of pipe manufacturers was contrary to the intent of the original order of the Board. In order to make the order apply, as was intended, to pipe and pipe fittings actually needed in the construction and operation of windmills, the Board amended its order by limiting the weight of the pipe which could be included with

windmills and windmill parts and still obtain the minimum C.L. weight of 26,000 pounds. *Re Classification No. 18*, (1931) 21 J.O.R.R. 120.

140. The Board refused an application for the privilege of mixing flour and feed (in sacks) with baled hay and straw because, in view of the low minimum applying on hay (20,000 pounds) and the higher minimum (30,000 pounds) as well as the higher rating (eighth instead of tenth) on flour, it was doubtful whether the advantage which would accrue to the applicants would be at all compatible with the general disarrangement on the classification. The application, if granted, would be largely a source of trouble to the railway companies with but little, if any, advantage to the shippers. *Central Convention of Farmers' Institutes of B.C.*, (1915) 17 C.R.C. 431.

141. *Re Proposed Classification No. 17*, (1925) 15 J.O.R.R. 117, 190.

142. *Berliner Gramophone Co.* v. *C.F.A.*, (1912) 14 C.R.C. 175.

143. *Re Proposed Classification No. 17*, (1925) 15 J.O.R.R. 117, 237, 245.

144. *Can. Rubber Mfrs.* v. *C.F.A.*, (1918) 23 C.R.C. 50; 8 J.O.R.R. 36. Affirmed in *Muirhead Forwarding Co.* v. *C.F.A.*, (1939) 50 C.R.T.C. 402; 29 J.O.R.R. 461. The Interstate Commerce Commission refused to allow the mixing privilege on paper bags and wrapping paper because this would benefit three companies which produced both these articles and discriminate unjustly against many concerns which made only one of them. *Paper Mills Co.* v. *Pennsylvania Railroad*, (1907) 12 I.C.C. 438.

145. *Re Proposed Classification No. 17*, (1925) 15 J.O.R.R. 117, 194.

146. *Ibid.*, p. 217.

147. *Stationers' Guild* v. *C.F.A.*, (1936) 45 C.R.C. 349; 26 J.O.R.R. 189.

148. *Re Proposed*, see *supra* (note 145) at p. 217. Reaffirmed in *General Steel Wares* v. *C.F.A.*, (1938) 48 C.R.C. 89, 93; 28 J.O.R.R. 143, 145.

Chapter 8: Adjustment of Rates to Distance (pp. 211–225)

1. *Equalization Case*, (1955) 72 C.R.T.C. 1, 54; 44 J.O.R.R. no. 24A, 1, 34.

2. This illustration assumes that the amount of idle time before the empty car is used for another revenue load is no greater in the one instance than in the other. On the average, even when business is good and freight is readily available, about 15 days elapse between the day a car is loaded and the date it receives its next load. Many cars, particularly specialized equipment such as tank, refrigerator, and coal cars, have to be hauled empty back to the point of origin of the original load before being reloaded.

3. I.C.C., Bureau of Accounts and Cost Finding, *Explanation of Rail Cost Finding Procedures and Principles Relating to the Use of Costs* (Washington: The Bureau, 1948). See also Stuart Daggett, "Mileage Rates and the Interstate Commerce Commission," *Quarterly Journal of Economics*, Feb., 1932, pp. 281–315.

4. *Chisholm Saw Mills* v. *C.N.R.*, (1928) 35 C.R.C. 40; 18 J.O.R.R. 400: re-heard and confirmed *ibid.*, (1937) 47 C.R.C. 348; 26 J.O.R.R. 454.

5. *Dominion Sugar Co.* v. *C.P.R.*, (1921) 27 C.R.C. 413; 11 J.O.R.R. 289.

6. *Newfoundland* v. *C.N.R.*, (1951) 67 C.R.T.C. 353, 358; 40 J.O.R.R. 351, 354.

7. *General Investigation, 1925-7*, 33 C.R.C. 127, 282-90; 17 J.O.R.R. 131, 239-45.

8. *Coal Operators* v. *C.P.R.*, (1937) 47 C.R.C. 72; 27 J.O.R.R. 220.

9. *Beachville White Lime Co.* v. *G.T.R.*, (1922) 28 C.R.C. 70; 12 J.O.R.R. 92. See also *Provincial Stone & Supply Co.* v. *C.P.R.*, (1918) 22 C.R.C. 411 and *Crushed Stone, Ltd.* v. *G.T.R.*, (1918) 23 C.R.C. 132: 8 J.O.R.R. 199.

10. *Residents of St. Paul & Heinsburg* v. *C.N.R.*, (1935) 44 C.R.C. 170; 25 J.O.R.R. 219. Almost an identical case arose over a gap of 37 miles between Val Marie and Mankota, Sask. See Canada, House of Commons, *Debates*, 1946, pp. 4945-6. Shippers near Val Marie, and the Saskatchewan Government, asked the Royal Commission of 1951 to recommend that the Railway Act be amended to give the Board authority to order railways to construct new lines when public convenience and necessity required them. The Commission refused since it considered railways to be the best judges of where new lines should be built. Ryl. Comm., 1951, *Rpt.*, pp. 133, 135.

11. Complaint of J. B. Stringer, quoted in *Residents of St. Paul*, C.R.C. at p. 175; J.O.R.R. at p. 222.

12. *Doolittle & Wilcox* v. *G.T.R. & C.P.R.*, (1908) 8 C.R.C. 10, 11; 4 B.R.C. 243. See also *Beachville White Lime*, C.R.C. at p. 72; J.O.R.R. at p. 94: *Spanish River Pulp & Paper* v. *C.P.R.*, (1922) 28 C.R.C. 100, 109; 12 J.O.R.R. 268, 282.

13. "The mileage test which complainant asks to have set up, while showing that the rates from eastern prairie points are proportionately lower than the rates from the Edmonton territory, disregards the fact that the former have been built up under distinctly different conditions." *Chisholm Saw Mills*, C.R.C. at p. 44; J.O.R.R. at p. 401.

14. Most tariffs read to the effect that the rates published therein apply between two points (A to B, and B to A) but a good many tariffs, especially competitive ones, cover traffic only from one station to another (A to B) and not in the opposite direction (B to A).

15. *New Westminster Bd. of Trade*, (1927) 17 J.O.R.R. 303, 408. "There may be, without unjust discrimination, over the same portion of the same line, a difference in rates where the movements are in opposite directions." *Consumers Glass Co.* v. *C.F.A.*, (1931) 38 C.R.C. 77; 21 J.O.R.R. 1.

16. Jackman, *Economic Principles*, pp. 235-6.

17. *Superior Paper Co.* v. *A.C. & H.B. Ry.*, (1916) 22 C.R.C. 361, 367; 6 J.O.R.R. 391, 394. This confirmed *International Paper Co.* v. *G.T.R.*, (1913) 15 C.R.C. 111.

18. The difference in the two rates is not unjust discrimination because the export rate has been virtually statutory since 1925 when the Board decided to apply the Crow's Nest Pass rates on export grain westbound. Crow's Nest Pass rates may not be used for judging the reasonableness of any other rate within Canada.

19. See chapter 2.

20. Export and import rates do not apply between Canada and the United States. They cover only traffic to and from points overseas but apply to this freight whether it is forwarded via ports in Canada or in the United

States. Newfoundland has always been treated as an adjacent country for rate-making purposes even though goods between Newfoundland and the mainland must go upwards of 100 miles by ferry and although until 1949 Newfoundland was not politically part of Canada. *Goodfellow* v. *C.P.R.*, (1937) 47 C.R.C. 160; 27 J.O.R.R. 349.

21. See note 81 in chapter 9.

22. *Re Export-Import Rates*, (1942) 32 J.O.R.R. 123, 125–6.

23. *Associated Growers of B.C.*, (1927) 33 C.R.C. 376; 17 J.O.R.R. 303, 363. Where rates are not published as competitive rates, the tariff contains the rule: "The rates named herein, unless specifically indicated, are maximum rates and must not be exceeded in the same direction from or to any intermediate point in the direct line of transit." Competitive tariffs or competitive rates are specifically indicated either on the front page of the tariff or by symbol and footnote in the succeeding pages. The note on the cover page or the footnote on the inside pages reads: "Rates named herein are competitive and are not applicable from or to intermediate points."

24. *Re Regina Bd. of Trade*, (1927) 17 J.O.R.R. 303, 360–3.

25. *Regina Bd. of Trade*, (1929) 18 J.O.R.R. 397.

26. *Can. Shippers' Traffic Bureau* v. *C.N.R.*, (1928) 35 C.R.C. 168; 17 J.O.R.R. 670.

27. *Lake Lumber Co.* v. *Esquimalt & Nanaimo Ry. (C.P.R.)*, (1920) 10 J.O.R.R. 59.

28. *Guy Tombs* v. *C.N.R.*, (1923) 28 C.R.C. 412; 13 J.O.R.R. 207. "The existence of a rate from a point in the United States to a point in Canada [Suspension Bridge to Sarnia through Hamilton] lower than the rate published between two intermediate points [Hamilton to Sarnia] both of which are within Canadian territory, does not create a violation of the . . . provisions." *Dominion Traffic Ass'n.* v. *C.N.R.*, (1931) 38 C.R.C. 376, 381; 21 J.O.R.R. 81, 83.

29. Two corporations, the C.P.R. and the Kingston & Pembroke Railway, had separate sets of officers but 51 per cent of the common stock of the latter was held by the C.P.R. It was ruled by both the Board and the Supreme Court that they should be treated as one company for the purpose of fixing rates. *Wylie Milling Co.* v. *C.P.R. and Kingston & Pembroke Ry.*, (1912) 14 C.R.C. 5; 8 D.L.R. 949.

30. See "Interchange of Equipment," chapter 11.

31. *Saint David's Sand Co.* v. *G.T.R.*, (1914) 17 C.R.C. 279.

32. *Fonthill Gravel Co.* v. *G.T.R.*, (1912) 17 C.R.C. 248. In the early days of the Canadian Northern, the Board upheld the right of the older roads to refuse to publish joint tolls with the newcomer. The latter was not justified in trying to capture business from carriers which they had spent years trying to develop. *Can. Nor. Ry.* v. *C.P.R. & G.T.R.*, (1908) 7 C.R.C. 289:*ibid.*, (1910) 10 C.R.C. 139: *Grt. Nor. Ry.* v. *Can. Nor. Ry.*, (1908) 11 C.R.C. 424.

33. *Imperial Steel & Wire Co.* v. *G.T.R.*, (1910) 11 C.R.C. 395. But an intermediate carrier has no right to retain the long and profitable portion of the haul to itself and then turn the traffic over to the terminating carrier for delivery by a short and expensive haul. *Branson* v. *C.P.R.*, (1946) 59 C.R.T.C. 211; 36 J.O.R.R. 230. On the complicated question of the Ste. Rosalie, Que., gateway and traffic to Saint John, see Ryl. Comm., 1951, *Rpt.*,

pp. 176–8: *C.N.R.* v. *Nova Scotia*, (1926) 32 C.R.C. 37: *C.N.R.* v. *Nova Scotia & New Brunswick*, (1927) 34 C.R.C. 207; 16 J.O.R.R. 117: *C.N.R.* v. *Nova Scotia*, [1928] S.C.R. 106; 1 D.L.R. 369; 34 C.R.C. 223; 17 J.O.R.R. 423.

34. *Re Joint Freight & Passenger Tariffs*, (1909) 10 C.R.C. 343; 5 B.R.C. 216.

35. *Fullerton Lumber Co.* v. *C.P.R.*, (1914) 17 C.R.C. 79, 84: *Montreal Bd. of Trade* v. *C.P.R.*, (1914) 18 C.R.C. 6, 8. When international traffic is involved, the Board has no jurisdiction over tolls in a foreign country, but it directed that a Canadian carrier should not, as its division of a through toll, exceed its local. Fullerton, *supra*. A complicated problem arose when one carrier refused to accept the former division of revenues from joint traffic. *M.C.R.* v. *Niagara, St. Catharines & Toronto Ry.*, (1916) 6 J.O.R.R. 328.

36. Now section 341 of the Railway Act. Joint rates must be published notwithstanding an agreement between two or more roads to the contrary. *North Fraser Harbour Com'rs.* v. *B.C. Electric Ry.*, (1929) 35 C.R.C. 384; 19 J.O.R.R. 145. "A continuous route in Canada" includes one where a movement by water comes between two movements by rail but not where it precedes a haul by rail. *A.C. & H.B. Ry.* v. *G.T.R.*, (1906) 5 C.R.C. 196; 2 B.R.C. 43: *Dawson Bd. of Trade* v. *White Pass & Yukon Ry.* (1909) 5 C.R.C. 519.

37. *Memorandum*, (1923) 12 J.O.R.R. 372.

38. Ryl. Comm., 1951, *Rpt.*, p. 108.

39. *Ibid.*, p. 107: *Interchange Facilities at Lloydminster*, (1952) 69 C.R.T.C. 141; 42 J.O.R.R. 93.

40. *Almonte Knitting Co.* v. *C.P.R.*, (1904) 3 C.R.C. 441; 1 B.R.C. 71: *Can. Portland Cement Co.* v. *G.T.R.*, (1909) 9 C.R.C. 209: *Fredericton Bd. of Trade* v. *C.P.R.*, (1915) 17 C.R.C. 439; 21 D.L.R. 790: *Hunting-Merritt Lumber Co.* v. *C.P.R.*, (1916) 20 C.R.C. 181; 6 J.O.R.R. 13: *Malkin & Sons* v. *G.T.R.*, (1908) 8 C.R.C. 183; 4 B.R.C. 268: *Two Creeks Grain Growers' Ass'n* v. *C.P.R.*, (1915) 18 C.R.C. 403: *Nova Scotia Apple Shippers Ass'n.* v. *Dom. Atl. Ry.*, (1922) 18 C.R.C. 95; 12 J.O.R.R. 233, which confirmed *Oyer & Hicks & Sons* v. *Dom. Atl. Ry.*, (1916) 20 C.R.C. 238: *Eastern Townships Lumber Co.* v. *Temiscouata Ry.*, (1914) 16 C.R.C. 260. See also *General Investigation, 1925–7*, 33 C.R.C. 127, *passim*; 17 J.O.R.R. 131, *passim*; *Re Edmonton, Dunvegan & B.C. Ry.*, (1915) 19 C.R.C. 395: *Grande Prairie Bd. of Trade* v. *C.P.R. & Edmonton, Dunvegan & B.C. Ry.*, (1924) 29 C.R.C. 324; 13 J.O.R.R. 274: *Drummond* v. *Nor. Alta. Ry.*, (1946) 60 C.R.T.C. 122; 36 J.O.R.R. 322.

41. In Britain it is not uncommon to add constructive mileage for rate-making purposes. An expensive bridge or tunnel a few hundred yards long may be arbitrarily taken as three or four miles for the purposes of compiling tariffs. In the United States an arbitrarily inflated mileage is sometimes added for Mississippi River crossings by ferry or bridge. In Canada a constructive mileage was deducted between Winnipeg and Lakehead with equivalent adjustment for hauls in and out of Vancouver and Churchill. The 124 miles added to the actual mileage in computing rates on export grain from Calgary to Vancouver is another example of constructive mileage.

42. "Where a commodity of general demand produced in different sections is being shipped to a common competitive market, there is not the same

justification for a difference between main and branch line rates." Assistant Chief Commissioner McLean, in *General Investigation*, C.R.C. at p. 192; J.O.R.R. at p. 176. See also *Dominion Millers Ass'n.* v. *C.F.A.*, (1917) 22 C.R.C. 125, 133; 7 J.O.R.R. 290, 294.

43. Ryl. Comm., 1951, *Rpt.*, p. 253.

44. Circular no. 272, (1952) 42 J.O.R.R. 137, 141. Competitive rates could not be reduced, otherwise rate relationships across Canada and the United States might be altered. *Rates on Lumber from British Columbia*, (1953) 70 C.R.T.C. 157; 43 J.O.R.R. 203.

45. Ryl. Comm., 1961, *Rpt.*, vol. II, pp. 220-32.

Chapter 9: Unjust Discrimination (pp. 224–253)

1. Ryl. Comm., 1961, *Rpt.*, vol. II, p. 63.
2. R.S.C., 1952, c. 234, s.s. 317, 319, 320, 349, and 350.
3. Jackman, *Economic Principles*, p. 404.
4. *Western Rates Case*, (1914) 17 C.R.C. 123, 155–6.
5. *Niagara, St. Catharines & Toronto Ry.* v. *G.T.R. (Stamford Jct. Case)*, (1904) 3 C.R.C. 256, 259–60.
6. *Toronto & Brampton* v. *G.T.R.*, (1910) 11 C.R.C. 370, 375: *Spanish River Pulp & Paper* v. *C.P.R.*, (1922) 28 C.R.C. 100, 109; 12 J.O.R.R. 268, 276–7.
7. *Consumers Glass Co.* v. *C.F.A.*, (1927) 34 C.R.C. 56, 75, 76; 17 J.O.R.R. 726, 732–3: *ibid.*, (1931) 38 C.R.C. 77, 80; 21 J.O.R.R. 1, 2.
8. *Cuneo Fruit & Importing Co.* v. *G.T.R.*, (1915) 18 C.R.C. 414, 424.
9. *Western Rates Case* at p. 153.
10. *Calgary Livestock Exchange* v. *C.N.R. & C.P.R.*, (1923) 29 C.R.C. 207, 227; 13 J.O.R.R. 233, 247. See also *Empire Flour Mills* v. *M.C.R.*, (1913) 16 C.R.C. 425.
11. *Toronto & Brampton, supra.*
12. *Wegenast* v. *G.T.R.*, (1908) 8 C.R.C. 42, 45; 4 B.R.C. 245. See also *Paper Mfrs. of Winnipeg* v. *C.P.R.*, (1925) 31 C.R.C. 320; 15 J.O.R.R. 2: *Massiah* v. *C.P.R.*, (1914) 17 C.R.C. 88; 14 J.O.R.R. 106: *Ontario Paper Co.* v. *G.T.R.*, (1919) 24 C.R.C. 177: *Zwicker* v. *C.N.R.*, (1922) 12 J.O.R.R. 152, 153: *Re Telegraph Tolls*, (1916) 20 C.R.C. 1, 23: *Plunkett & Savage* v. *Express Traffic Ass'n.*, (1923) 28 C.R.C. 402; 13 J.O.R.R. 161: *Winnipeg Bd. of Trade* v. *C.P.R.*, (1929) 36 C.R.C. 100; 19 J.O.R.R. 280: *Estabrooks Ltd.* v. *C.F.A.*, (1930) 37 C.R.C. 134; 20 J.O.R.R. 180.
13. Mr. J. E. Walsh, then General Manager of the Canadian Manufacturers Association, stated that he had "worked for the railways long before the Board of Railway Commissioners came into existence. In those days, we were not very much concerned with tariffs. We tried to size up a man to find out how much money he had." Canada, Senate, Standing Committee on Railways, Canals and Telegraph Lines, *Proc.*, 1938, pp. 6–7.
14. S. J. McLean, "Rate Grievances on Canadian Railways," Canada *Sessional Paper* No. 20a, 1902, p. 4: *Sydenham Glass Co. Case*, (1904) 3 C.R.C. 409, 410: *Kennedy* v. *Quebec & Lake St. John Ry.*, (1911) 14 C.R.C. 153 which was confirmed by the Supreme Court of Canada in (1913) 48 S.C.R. 520; 15 D.L.R. 400; 17 C.R.C. 291.
15. *Brant Milling Co.* v. *G.T.R.*, (1905) 4 C.R.C. 259; 1 B.R.C. 72.

16. Under a so-called "traders' tariff" some wholesalers in Winnipeg who were named in the tariff could send goods to smaller centres in the West on the balance of the through rate from Eastern Canada plus the cartage charges in Winnipeg. Other merchants had to send their freight, which was brought in under through rates from the East, to smaller communities at the relatively high local distributing rates. *Winnipeg Jobbers' Ass'n.* v. *C.P.R.,* (1908) 8 C.R.C. 175; 4 B.R.C. 263.

17. *B.C. Coast Cities* v. *C.P.R.,* (1907) 7 C.R.C. 125: *Regina Bd. of Trade* v. *C.P.R.,* (1909) 11 C.R.C. 380.

18. *Consumers Cordage Co.* v. *G.T.R.,* (1912) 14 C.R.C. 222 following *Welland* v. *C.F.A.* (*Plymouth Cordage Case*), (1911) 13 C.R.C. 140.

19. *G.T.R.* v. *Christie Henderson & Co.,* (1909) 9 C.R.C. 502; 5 B.R.C., 320: *Pilon* v. *G.T.R.,* (1913) 16 C.R.C. 433: *Hepworth Brick Co.* v. *G.T.R.,* (1914) 18 C.R.C. 9.

20. *Scobell* v. *Kingston & Pembroke Ry.,* (1904) 3 C.R.C. 412; 1 B.R.C. 68.

21. Even if the agreement is between a municipality and a railway. *Montreal & Southern Counties Ry.* v. *Greenfield Park,* (1918) 23 C.R.C. 106; 8 J.O.R.R. 242. See also *Osoyoos, B.C.* v. *C.P.R.,* (1952) 68 C.R.T.C. 10; 51 J.O.R.R. 171: *Hamilton Radial Electric Ry.* v. *Hamilton,* (1918) 23 C.R.C. 114; 8 J.O.R.R. 250, 253: *Crowsnest Pass Coal Co.* v. *C.P.R.,* (1908) 8 C.R.C. 33; 4 B.R.C. 249; *Lyons Fuel & Supply Co.* v. *A. C. & H.B. Ry.,* (1918) 23 C.R.C. 146, headnote; 8 J.O.R.R. 1: *Superior Paper Co.* v. *Algoma Central Ry.,* (1916) 22 C.R.C. 361, headnote; 6 J.O.R.R. 391: *National Dairy Council* v. *G.T.R.,* (1919) 26 C.R.C. 113, 120, 123; 9 J.O.R.R. 443, 458, 459: *B.C. & Alta. Municipalities* v. *G.T.P.,* (1912) 13 C.R.C. 463: *Re Grand Trunk Pacific,* [1912] 3 D.L.R. 819.

22. *Re Crow's Nest Pass Rates,* [1925] S.C.R. 155; 2 D.L.R. 755; 30 C.R.C. 32.

23. *Montreal Bd. of Trade* v. *G.T.R.,* (1913) 14 C.R.C. 351.

24. *Re Freight Rates on Crude Petroleum Oil, Carloads,* (1934) 42 C.R.C. 287; 24 J.O.R.R. 197.

25. See note 17.

26. *Express Rates on Fish in Carloads,* (1920) 10 J.O.R.R. 446.

27. *Davidson* v. *C.N.R.,* (1935) 43 C.R.C. 207, 213; 25 J.O.R.R. 41, 44. The Board intimated that cottagers and businessmen at Laurentia Beach might, in the long run, suffer from the inauguration of commutation fares as they would attract boisterous "dance hall crowds" instead of the sedate families who had summer residences at Laurentia Beach. No reference was made to the quality of the highways serving the two resorts.

28. *Sask. Co-op. Wheat Producers Ltd.* v. *C.N.R.,* (1935) 43 C.R.C. 284; 25 J.O.R.R. 19.

29. *Midland & Pacific* v. *C.P.R.,* (1934) 42 C.R.C. 245, 252; 24 J.O.R.R. 190, 193.

30. *Canada West Coal Co.* v. *C.P.R.,* (1921) 27 C.R.C. 113; 11 J.O.R.R. 137.

31. *Consumers Glass Co.* v. *C.F.A.,* (1931) 38 C.R.C. 77, 91–2; 21 J.O.R.R. 1, 10. Confirmed in *Fraser Valley-Surrey Farmers' Co-op.* v. *C.N.R.,* (1935) 43 C.R.C. 97, 122; 24 J.O.R.R. 344, 359. See also *Re*

Polymer Corporation, (1950) 64 C.R.T.C. 283: *ibid.* p. 290: 40 J.O.R.R. 1: *ibid.*, p. 4.

32. *Kerr* v. *C.P.R.*, (1909) 9 C.R.C. 207; 5 B.R.C. 207.

33. Inter-line hauls are dealt with later in this chapter.

34. Both the Board and the Interstate Commerce Commission have repeatedly set out that mere "paper" rates under which no commodity is moving are inconclusive. *Spanish River Pulp & Paper* v. *C.P.R.*, (1922) 28 C.R.C. 100, 109–10; 12 J.O.R.R. 268, 279: *Plaunt* v. *A.C. & H.B. Ry.*, (1928) 35 C.R.C. 73; 18 J.O.R.R. 441.

35. *Mount Royal Milling & Mfg. Co.* v. *G.T.R.*, (1910) 11 C.R.C. 347: *Rubber Ass'n. of Canada*, (1921) 11 J.O.R.R. 224: *Dominion Millers' Ass'n.*, (1928) 17 J.O.R.R. 659, 667.

36. *Midland Lumber Shippers* v. *G.T.R.*, (1916) 22 C.R.C. 387; 6 J.O.R.R. 490. No evidence was submitted to show whether there was a difference in water competition sufficient to justify a difference in rates. See also *Re B.C. Lumber Mfrs.' Ass'n.*, (1953) 70 C.R.T.C. 123; 43 J.O.R.R. 40.

37. *Greenwood* v. *C.N.R.*, (1935) 43 C.R.C. 221; 34 J.O.R.R. 408.

38. Complaints regarding blanket rates are particularly frequent in telephone rate-making where the difference in monthly service charges may be $1 or more and the distance between adjacent points in the two rate groups may be only the width of a street. See *Etobicoke* v. *Bell Telephone Co.*, (1938) 48 C.R.T.C. 222; 28 J.O.R.R. 258 and the cases therein cited.

39. *Malkin & Sons* v. *G.T.R. (Tan Bark Case)*, (1908) 8 C.R.C. 183, 185; 4 B.R.C. 268, 269.

40. *Standard Hardwood Lumber Co.* v. *C.P.R.*, (1926) 32 C.R.C. 282; 15 J.O.R.R. 383.

41. *Joliette Chamber of Commerce*, (1927) 33 C.R.C. 375; 17 J.O.R.R. 388, 389–90.

42. *Fullerton Lumber Co.* v. *C.P.R.*, (1914) 17 C.R.C. 79, 87. The Board might have added that a town may be discriminated against in the grouping arrangement applicable to one product and may be favoured in the blanketing of rates on another article. Though in law "two rights do not make up for a wrong," still, when the whole picture is taken into account, a town may not be as badly off as it alleges.

43. *Coal Operators* v. *C.N.R.*, (1937) 47 C.R.C. 72; 27 J.O.R.R. 258: *Great West, Byers Coal Co.* v. *G.T.P.*, (1918) 23 C.R.C. 175, headnote; 8 J.O.R.R. 258; which followed *Galbraith Coal Co.* v. *C.P.R.*, (1910) 10 C.R.C. 325.

44. "When the railways can secure . . . additional traffic which may be handled at less than average unit costs, or without the use of additional transportation facilities, rates substantially lower than those which would be maximum reasonable tolls, but would be reasonably compensatory on the traffic involved, result in some contribution, over and above out of pocket costs, to the general overhead expense of the railway." *Can. Lumbermen's Ass'n.* v. *C.F.A.*, (1935) 25 J.O.R.R. 75, 80.

45. Sometimes the rail rates are two or three cents per hundred pounds higher than the competitive rates by water. The shipper will pay this small differential in order to get more prompt delivery and to be relieved of the necessity of taking out his own marine insurance, and perhaps will get delivery

direct to his warehouse without having to truck from a wharf. "The meeting of competition, generally speaking, under the provisions of the Railway Act or the Transport Act does not involve the publication of rates which are lower than competitively necessary." *C.F.A.* v. *Colonial SS.*, (1939) 50 C.R.T.C. 284, 288; 29 J.O.R.R. 423, 425.

46. *Brock (Western) Ltd.* v. *C.F.A.*, (1931) 38 C.R.C. 326, 332; 21 J.O.R.R. 277, 280.

47. The company's plea "that the greater volume of traffic they give the railway entitles them to a preferential rate is not sound. . . . Were it otherwise, the larger shipper would be advantaged to the detriment, not to say the extinction, of the smaller one in every line of trade." *Lyons Fuel & Supply Co.* v. *A.C. & H.B. Ry.*, (1918) 23 C.R.C. 146, 150; 8 J.O.R.R. 1, 4: *Conrad Mines* v. *White Pass & Yukon R.*, (1910) 11 C.R.C. 138. Although the complaint was based on the unsound claim that rates should be low enough to enable the shipper to carry on his business at a profit, the Board dealt with the case as one of unjust discrimination.

48. See note 85 in this chapter.

49. *Brock (Western) Ltd.* v. *C.F.A.*, (1931) 38 C.R.C. 326, 330; 21 J.O.R.R. 277, 279: *General Investigation, 1925-7*, 33 C.R.C. 127, 135–6; 17 J.O.R.R. 131, 136. Confirmed in *Gainers Ltd.* v. *C.F.A.*, (1935) 43 C.R.C. 309, 313; 25 J.O.R.R. 2, 4.

50. Ryl. Comm., 1951, *Rpt.*, pp. 100–1: Railway Act, R.S.C., 1952, c. 234, s. 337.

51. *The Cast Iron Pipe Case*, (1954) 71 C.R.T.C. 28; 44 J.O.R.R. 1.

52. *Re Agreed Charges on Canned Goods*, (1954) 71 C.R.T.C. 39; 44 J.O.R.R. 33: *Re Agreed Charges on Iron and Steel*, (1954) 71 C.R.T.C. 326; 44 J.O.R.R. 243: *Re Agreed Charges on Wire Rope*, (1956) 73 C.R.T.C. 121; 45 J.O.R.R. 453.

53. Ryl. Comm. on Agreed Charges, 1955, *Rpt.*, p. 45.

54. *Agric. Co-op. Society* v. *C.N.R.*, (1942) 55 C.R.T.C. 44, 49; 32 J.O.R.R. 287, 289–90. The rate from Dolbeau was reduced for other reasons than competition. Strictly speaking, the long- and short-haul clause was not involved in this case although the Board assumed that it was. Only part of the route from Dolbeau to Montreal is included in the mileage between Chicoutimi and Montreal. The case resembled a long- and short-haul one because competion was strong at one point and not at a nearby one.

55. *Bonners' Ferry Lumber Co* v. *Grt. Nor. Ry.*, (1909) 9 C.R.C. 504, 505; 5 B.R.C. 247.

56. *Can. Shippers' Traffic Bureau* v. *C.N.R.*, (1928) 35 C.R.C. 168; 17 J.O.R.R. 670.

57. *Central Alberta Dairy Pool* v. *C.P.R.*, (1936) 46 C.R.C. 10, 13; 26 J.O.R.R. 292, 293. This case was practically a revival of *Central Creameries Ltd.*, (1927) 17 J.O.R.R. 390.

58. *Palisade Coal Co.* v. *C.N.R.*, (1928) 35 C.R.C. 47; 18 J.O.R.R. 404. At the time of this case the Canadian Pacific had to haul coal from Drumheller and Carbon westerly through Irricana, southerly to Bassano and thence to Winnipeg. Since the date of this case the Canadian Pacific has secured running rights over the Canadian National line from Drumheller to

Trefoil and by using its own line thence through Rosemary and Java (Swift Current) to Winnipeg, it can avoid the back-haul formerly existing from Drumheller through Carbon.

59. For example, the former differences in rate levels in Eastern and Western Canada, and the mountain differential.

60. "Strictly speaking, there is no such thing as market competition which is distinct from competition between the lines of transport serving the market. A market can compete only through the agency which transports for it. The carrier makes a rate from a given market, not out of favour to that locality, but because it desires to obtain traffic which will not otherwise come to it. There would seem, therefore, to be little distinction between the competition of markets and the competition of rival roads." *Spokane* v. *Nor. Pac.*, (1911) 21 I.C.C. 400, 411. Perhaps the distinction, if any, lies in whether lower rates are instigated chiefly as a result of pressure from the industry or because the carrier wants more traffic. In any event the term "market competition" is often used in the literature and practice of rate making.

61. Of course, the railways would be no farther ahead if their rate reductions merely displaced one producer with another. Railways gain only if (*a*) lower rates stimulate purchases as a whole, that is, if the demand for the product is elastic; (*b*) if the railways get a longer haul than formerly at the rates which cover out-of-pocket and make a larger total contribution to common costs than before.

62. *Victoria, B.C.* v. *C.N.R.*, (1935) 44 C.R.C. 255, 265–6; 25 J.O.R.R. 399, 405.

63. *Arrow Lakes Lumber Co.* v. *C.P.R.*, (1935) 43 C.R.C. 337, 349; 25 J.O.R.R. 30, 36.

64. *Perrin* v. *Express Traffic Ass'n.* (1923) 28 C.R.C. 389, 392; 13 J.O.R.R. 156, 159. Confirmed *Western Retail Lumbermen's Ass'n.* v. *C.P.R.*, (1916) 20 C.R.C. 155; 7 J.O.R.R. 31. See also *Re International Newsprint Rates,* (1934) 42 C.R.C. 15; 24 J.O.R.R. 65.

65. *United Factories* v. *G.T.R.*, (1904) 3 C.R.C. 424.

66. *International Paper Co.* v. *G.T.R.*, (1913) 15 C.R.C. 111, 115. As no company should ever put in a rate without any regard to the resultant profit, it is suggested that what the Board had in mind was that the carrier paid less attention to immediate than to ultimate profit. The dictum given in the text was repeated in *Superior Paper Co.* v. *A.C. & H.B. Ry.*, (1916) 22 C.R.C. 361, 367; 6 J.O.R.R. 391, 394.

67. *Re Smithers District Bd. of Trade,* (1927) 33 C.R.C. 377; 17 J.O.R.R. 303, 326.

68. *Associated Growers of B.C.,* (1927) 33 C.R.C. 376; 17 J.O.R.R. 303, 363–8.

69. *Chisholm Saw Mills* v. *C.N.R.*, (1928) 35 C.R.C. 40; 18 J.O.R.R. 400: re-heard and affirmed in *ibid.,* (1937) 47 C.R.C. 348; 27 J.O.R.R. 393.

70. *Can. Oil Co.* v. *G.T.R.*, (1911) 12 C.R.C. 350, 357: *Myles* v. *G.T.R.*, (1911) 12 C.R.C. 289.

71. But they must take care not seriously to injure Canadian importers or divert traffic away from Canadian ports.

72. The L.C.L. class rate on this traffic was higher in Canada than in the

United States. *Mount Royal Milling & Mfg. Co.* v. *G.T.R.*, (1910) 11 C.R.C. 347.

73. In *Sydenham Glass Co. Case,* (1904) 3 C.R.C. 409; 1 B.R.C. 67, the Board did order a carrier to set rates to equalize competition between foreign and domestic suppliers but it has since several times reversed its view, viz., *Dominion Sheet Metal Corp. Ltd.* v. *G.T.R.*, (1923) 28 C.R.C. 84; 12 J.O.R.R. 286: *Can. Portland Cement Co.* v. *G.T.R.*, (1909) 9 C.R.C. 209: and *Can. Oil Co.*, *supra*: *Northern Bolt, Screw & Wire Co.*, (1928) 17 J.O.R.R. 632.

74. *Ontario Millers and Farmers* v. *C.N.R.*, (1939) 50 C.R.T.C. 68, 87; 29 J.O.R.R. 141, 152.

75. *Re Freight Tolls, 1922,* 27 C.R.C. 153, 172; 12 J.O.R.R. 61, 73.

76. *Hagersville Crushed Stone* v. *Mich. Central,* (1916) 22 C.R.C. 84, 86; 6 J.O.R.R. 417, 418: *Dept. Highways, Ont.*, (1924) 14 J.O.R.R. 321, 323: *National Dairy Council* v. *C.P.R.*, (1922) 28 C.R.C. 75, 79; 12 J.O.R.R. 144, 147: *Red Deer Valley Operators' Ass'n.*, (1920) 27 C.R.C. 62; 10 J.O.R.R. 66.

77. *Can. Shippers' Traffic Bureau* v. *C.N.R.*, (1926) 32 C.R.C. 3, 17; 16 J.O.R.R. 135, 145. See also note 35.

78. *B.C. Coast Cities* v. *C.P.R.*, (1907) 7 C.R.C. 125, 142–3: *Doolittle & Wilcox* v. *G.T.R.*, (1908) 8 C.R.C. 10; 4 B.R.C. 243: *Can. Oil Co.*, *supra*, at p. 354: *Dominion Sugar Co.* v. *C.F.A.*, (1912) 14 C.R.C. 188: *Hudson Bay Mining Co.* v. *Grt. Nor. Ry.*, (1913) 16 C.R.C. 254.

79. *Quebec Harbour Com'rs.,* v. *C.P.R.*, (1921) 27 C.R.C. 121.

80. *Dominion Sugar Co.* v. *C.P.R.*, (1927) 34 C.R.C. 71; 17 J.O.R.R. 561.

81. *Imperial Rice Milling Co.* v. *C.P.R.*, (1912) 14 C.R.C. 375. See also *ibid.*, (1918) 8 J.O.R.R. 387.

82. *Canada Rice Mills,* (1929) 36 C.R.C. 91; 19 J.O.R.R. 375. See also *Mount Royal Milling Co.*, (1925) 31 C.R.C. 318; 15 J.O.R.R. 44.

83. *Brock (Western) Ltd.* v. *C.F.A.*, (1931) 38 C.R.C. 326, 334; 21 J.O.R.R. 277, 282; confirming *Montreal Produce Merchants' Ass'n.* v. *G.T.R.*, (1909) 9 C.R.C. 232; 5 B.R.C. 224: *B.C. Sugar Refining Co.* v. *C.P.R.*, (1910) 10 C.R.C. 169, 172; 5 B.R.C. 279: *Graham* v *C.F.A.*, (1916) 22 C.R.C. 355; 6 J.O.R.R. 265.

84. *Western Gypsum Products* v. *C.N.R.*, (1941) 53 C.R.T.C. 271, 275; 31 J.O.R.R. 279, 281.

85. *Edmonton Clover Bar Sand Co.* v. *G.T.P.*, (1914) 17 C.R.C. 95: *Re Passenger Tolls,* (1916) 20 C.R.C. 223; 6 J.O.R.R. 92: *Graham, supra.*

86. *Dominion Shuttle Co.* v. *C.P.R.*, (1927) 34 C.R.C. 203; 17 J.O.R.R. 530.

87. *Hudson Bay Mining Co.* v. *Grt. Nor. Ry.*, (1913) 16 C.R.C. 254.

88. *Victoria* v. *C.P.R.*, (1931) 38 C.R.C. 224; 21 J.O.R.R. 231. Freight rates to Vancouver Island are often higher than those to Vancouver, New Westminster, and other points on the lower mainland. On lumber a difference of two cents per hundred pounds was held not unjustly discriminatory against Island shippers. *Vancouver Island Assoc. Bds. of Trade* v. *C.N.R.*, (1922) 27 C.R.C. 129. A differential of 3½ cents per hundred pounds on apples from the Okanagan district for export was not discriminatory.

Victoria v. *C.N.R.*, (1935) 44 C.R.C. 255; 25 J.O.R.R. 399. Neither were higher express tolls on small fruits to Prairie points from Victoria than from Vancouver. *Saanich Fruit Growers' Ass'n.* v. *Express Traffic Ass'n.*, (1935) 43 C.R.C. 362; 25 J.O.R.R. 109, 111–14.

89. *Can. China Clay Co.* v. *C.P.R.*, (1915) 18 C.R.C. 347, 348: *Spanish River Pulp & Paper Mills* v. *C.P.R.* (1922) 28 C.R.C. 100, 107; 12 J.O.R.R. 268, 275.

90. *Lever Bros.* v. *C.F.A.*, (1931) 39 C.R.C. 247, 252; 21 J.O.R.R. 336, 338: *Can. Portland Cement Co.* v. *G.T.R.*, (1909) 9 C.R.C. 209, 211: *Imperial Rice Milling Co.* v. *C.P.R.* (1912) 14 C.R.C. 375: *Hudson Bay Mining Co.* v. *Grt. Nor. Ry.*, (1913) 16 C.R.C. 254, 259: *Western Retail Lumbermen's Ass'n.* v. *C.P.R.*, (1916) 20 C.R.C. 155, 158: *Dominion Millers' Ass'n.* v. *C.F.A.*, (1917) 21 C.R.C. 83, 87: *Roberts* v. *C.P.R.*, (1915) 18 C.R.C. 350, 354: *Waterloo* v. *G.T.R.*, (1918) 24 C.R.C. 143, 147: *Lever Bros.* v. *C.F.A.*, (1931) 39 C.R.C. 247, 252; 21 J.O.R.R. 336, 338. In a broad sense it is doubtless true, as Mr. Justice Holmes said in I.C.C. v. *Diffenbaugh*, (1911) 222 U.S. 42, 46, that "the law does not attempt to equalize fortune, opportunities or abilities."

91. *Can. Oil Co.* v. *G.T.R.*, (1911) 12 C.R.C. 350: confirmed in *Fraser Valley-Surrey Farmers' Co-op.* v. *C.N.R.*, (1935) 43 C.R.C. 97, 116; 24 J.O.R.R. 344, 355: *Brock (Western) Ltd.* v. *C.F.A.*, (1931) 38 C.R.C. 326, 333–4; 21 J.O.R.R. 277, 282.

92. *Cowichan Ratepayers Ass'n.* v. *C.P.R.*, (1915) 18 C.R.C. 395; confirmed in *Sidney, B.C., Bd. of Trade* v. *Grt. Nor. Ry.*, (1918) 23 C.R.C. 173; 8 J.O.R.R. 216: *Hunting-Merritt Lumber Co.* v. *C.P.R.*, (1916) 20 C.R.C. 181; 6 J.O.R.R. 13. Also *Blind River Bd. of Trade* v. *G.T.R.*, (1913) 15 C.R.C. 146. Substantially identical cases in which the same decision was rendered are *B.C. Coast Cities* v. *C.P.R.*, (1907) 7 C.R.C. 125, 129–30: *Plain & Co.* v. *C.P.R.*, (1909) 9 C.R.C. 222; 5 B.R.C. 208: *Can. Oil Co.* v. *G.T.R.*, (1911) 12 C.R.C. 350, 351: *Dominion Millers' Ass'n.* v. *G.T.R.*, ibid., 363, 368: *Can. Lumbermen's Ass'n.* v. *G.T.R.*, (1914) 17 C.R.C. 102: *Dominion Sugar Co.* v. *G.T.R.*, (1913) 17 C.R.C. 231: *Montreal Bd. of Trade* v. *C.F.A.*, (1917) 21 C.R.C. 77: *W. Va. Pulp & Paper Co.* v. *C.P.R.*, (1918) 23 C.R.C. 153; 8 J.O.R.R. 25: *Lakeside Milling Co.* v. *C.F.A.*, (1932) 40 C.R.C. 235, 241, 242; 22 J.O.R.R. 102, 105–6: *Ontario Flour Millers' Ass'n.* v. *C.F.A.*, (1936) 45 C.R.C. 289; 26 J.O.R.R. 198: *Zwicker* v. *C.N.R.*, (1922) 12 J.O.R.R. 151: *Dominion Canners* v. *C.F.A.*, (1917) 22 C.R.C. 312: *Regina Bd. of Trade* v. *C.P.R.*, (1917) 22 C.R.C. 315; 7 J.O.R.R. 78: *Bds. of Trade of Western Cities* v. *C.F.A.*, (1917) 22 C.R.C. 324; 7 J.O.R.R. 321: *Shuswap Lake Lumber Co.* v. *C.P.R.*, (1935) 44 C.R.C. 87, 90; 25 J.O.R.R. 211, 212–13.

93. *Bowlby* v. *Halifax & South Western Ry.*, (1916) 20 C.R.C. 231; 6 J.O.R.R. 367.

94. *Salada Tea Co.* v. *C.F.A.*, (1924) 30 C.R.C. 153, 164: *Midland Lumber Shippers* v. *G.T.R.*, (1916) 22 C.R.C. 387; 6 J.O.R.R. 490.

95. *Mount Royal Rice Mills, Ltd.* v. *C.F.A.*, (1935) 43 C.R.C. 248, 249; 24 J.O.R.R. 325, 326. It can be assumed that a shipper cannot sustain a charge of unjust discrimination because he fears what might happen if and when conditions change. Through rates on chewing gum and confectionery from Buffalo to West Coast Canadian points were much lower than from

Toronto to the same destinations. In both cases the route lay through Canada. No competition actually existed between the two points of origin and British Columbia. As the applicant was fearing a conjectural situation, his application for changing the 'paper' rate from Buffalo was dismissed. *Wm. Wrigley Jr. Co.* v. *C.F.A.*, (1930) 20 J.O.R.R. 269.

96. See above under "Discrimination and the Classification," note 24.

97. *Re Freight Rates on Crude Petroleum Oil, Carloads*, (1934) 42 C.R.C. 287; 24 J.O.R.R. 197.

98. *Consumers Co-op. Refineries, Ltd.* v. *C.N.R.*, (1937) 47 C.R.C. 321; 27 J.O.R.R. 413.

99. See chapter 11.

100. Railways put into effect certain rules governing portable grain elevators. The Board held these rules discriminated against the owners of some makes of these machines. The railway had no right to dictate the means which shippers used to load cars, and they ought not to interfere as long as the method of loading did not delay or hinder the operation of the railway. *Alta. Motor Transport Ass'n.* v. *Ry. Ass'n.*, (1942) 54 C.R.T.C. 165; 32 J.O.R.R. 26: *Ry. Ass'n.* v. *Alta. Motor Transport Ass'n.*, (1943) 56 C.R.T.C. 168; 33 J.O.R.R. 107. It is unjust discrimination for a railway to charge one shipper rent on a private siding and to charge no rent on another siding constructed under a substantially similar agreement. *Buchanan* v. *Dom. Atl. Ry.*, (1946) 59 C.R.T.C. 386.

101. *Wegenast* v. *G.T.R.*, (1908) 8 C.R.C. 42; 4 B.R.C. 245.

102. *Toronto & Brampton* v. *G.T.R.*, (1910) 11 C.R.C. 370.

103. *B.C. News Co.* v. *Express Traffic Ass'n.*, (1912) 4 D.L.R. 239; 13 C.R.C. 176. The Board would not compel the continuance of express car service where it proved unremunerative. *Jordan Co-op.* v. *Can. Express*, (1917) 23 C.R.C. 55; 7 J.O.R.R. 120.

104. *Express Traffic Ass'n.* v. *Can. Mfrs. Ass'n.*, (1911) 13 C.R.C. 169.

105. *London Bd. of Trade* v. *Express Traffic Ass'n.*, (1915) 19 C.R.C. 420.

106. *Guest Fish Co.* v. *Dominion Express*, (1914) 18 C.R.C. 1, 5; 3 J.O.R.R. 50.

107. *Re Joint Express Rates*, (1912) 14 C.R.C. 183. As already pointed out the cost of a two-line haul is higher than a single-line movement in the same general region.

108. *Aylmer Condensed Milk Co.* v. *American Express Co.*, (1914) 17 C.R.C. 100.

109. The Dominion government as owner of the Intercolonial Railway agreed with the G.T.R. in 1898 to charge on all export and import traffic between Halifax and Montreal a rate of one cent per hundred pounds more than the rate prevailing between Saint John, N.B., and Montreal via C.P.R., or Portland, Me., and Montreal via G.T.R. In return the G.T.R. undertook to hand over to the Intercolonial at Montreal all traffic routed through Halifax. When Halifax complained of unjust discrimination because it was charged an extra cent above Saint John and Portland, the Board held that the railways were bound by the agreement which had been validated by special Dominion legislation. *Halifax* v. *G.T.R.*, (1911) 12 C.R.C. 55. The Supreme Court refused leave to appeal. *Ibid.* 58. In 1923, after the G.T.R. was

absorbed with the Intercolonial into the present C.N.R., the contract was abrogated and the statutory discrimination against Halifax removed.

110. *Newfoundland* v. *C.N.R.*, (1951) 67 C.R.T.C. 353, 358; 40 J.O.R.R. 351, 354. See also *ibid.*, 64 C.R.T.C. 352; 39 J.O.R.R. 293.

Chapter 10: Freight Rates and Prices (pp. 254–270)

1. *Re Export-Import Rates*, (1942) 32 J.O.R.R. 123, 134.

2. *Berliner Gramophone Co.* v. *C.F.A.*, (1912) 3 D.L.R. 496; 14 C.R.C. 175.

3. *Dalyte Electric Ltd.* v. *C.F.A.*, (1925) 30 C.R.C. 382, 385; 15 J.O.R.R. 257, 259.

4. *Fitzsimmons Fruit Co.* v. *C.N.R.*, (1928) 35 C.R.C. 34, 36; 18 J.O.R.R. 353, 355.

5. *Stationers' Guild* v. *C.F.A.*, (1936) 45 C.R.C. 349; 26 J.O.R.R. 189.

6. Jackman, *Economic Principles*, p. 380. The same method was followed and the same conclusion reached by Commissioner Stoneman in *Fraser Valley–Surrey Farmers' Co-op.* v. *C.N.R.*, (1935) 43 C.R.C. 97, 161–62; 24 J.O.R.R. 344, 382–83.

7. Jackman, *Economic Principles*, p. 554.

8. *Ibid.*, p. 575.

9. See pp. 183–5.

10. Loans merely postpone the time of payment. In the United States some railway costs have been borne by investors who have not received a fair return on their investment or who have lost their original capital through bankruptcy. In Canada, the Government felt it could not allow the railways to fail and so part of their cost is today assumed by taxpayers. Some of the taxes are borne by the initial payer, others are shifted to customers.

11. I.C.C., Bureau of Statistics, *Freight Revenues and Value of Commodities Transported* (Washington: The Bureau, 1943).

12. D. P. Locklin, *Economics of Transportation* (Chicago: R. D. Irwin, 1947), p. 17, calls attention to an unusual situation. Suppose A's costs are $6 and his freight rate $2; B's are, respectively, $3 and $6 to the same market. A will supply the market and the freight rate will be 25 per cent of the delivered price. If both rates are cut in half, B will supply the entire market. His total costs are $6 compared with $7 for A. B's freight rate is 50 per cent of the delivered price. This illustration also shows that the more distant supplier can penetrate the market or even displace the nearer producer if his other costs of production are sufficiently low.

13. In an elementary discussion of value theory such as this, it seemed desirable to avoid many technical matters of importance, such as extensive and intensive margins of production, reverse demand curves, and so forth.

14. For a good analysis, with graphs, see Locklin, *Economics of Transportation*, pp. 21–42.

15. For any one transportation agency the shrinkage varies with the demand curve for transportation via that agency as compared with its competitors. More specifically, the effect of railway rate increases on railway traffic will depend on the relationship between the new and the higher rates by rail and the tolls by trucks and water-lines.

16. Of course, in the extractive industries some of the elements of decreasing unit costs are also present. Nevertheless the general effect is one of increasing unit costs. Similarly in manufacturing, factors of increasing cost are not entirely non-existent but the trend toward decreasing cost is clear.

17. The theorist will recognize that this statement is not wholly accurate but it is sufficiently correct for all practical purposes.

18. Marketing experts and the more competent business-men prefer taking the gross margin as a percentage of selling price, not of cost. The older, or cost, method is used here because it simplifies the arithmetic.

19. The economist assumes that the costs include a normal profit, i.e. a reasonable rate of return to the owner of the business on the capital he has invested and adequate compensation for his work of management.

20. Locklin, *Economics of Transportation*, p. 39.

Chapter 11: Accessorial Charges (pp. 271–292)

1. *C.F.A.* v. *Winnipeg Bd. of Trade*, (1911) 13 C.R.C. 122, 126.

2. Demurrage Tariff, C.T.C. no. 6, effective Jan. 1, 1966. See also "Demurrage and Weighing," *Certificate Course* (Toronto: Can. Institute of Traffic & Transportation, 1964).

3. No extra time was allowed for fumigating seeds, peanuts, and garden vegetables being imported from abroad. *Canada Seed Co.* v. *Can. Car Demurrage Bureau*, (1920) 10 J.O.R.R. 132: *Commodity Prices Stabilization Corp.* v. *Can. Car Demurrage Bureau*, (1945) 58 C.R.T.C. 245: 35 J.O.R.R. 151. See also *Can. Car Demurrage Bureau* v. *Richardson*, (1933) 41 C.R.C. 260. Where delay is caused by the owner's lack of familiarity with customs regulations, demurrage is also assessable. *Consolidated Rendering Co.* v. *C.N.R.*, (1926) 32 C.R.C. 294; 16 J.O.R.R. 149.

4. R.S.C. 1952, c. 25, s. 71 (2).

5. *C.F.A.* v. *Coastal Elevators*, (1937) 47 C.R.C. 43; 27 J.O.R.R. 193.

6. *Re North-West Line Elevators Assoc.*, (1958) 48 J.O.R.R. 133: *ibid.*, [1959] S.C.R. 239. See also *C.P.R.* v. *Man. Pool Elevators*, (1962) Man. Ct. of Queen's Bench 83; 83 C.R.T.C. 267, and cases therein cited.

7. *Western Produce Co.* v. *Can. Car Demurrage Bureau*, (1937) 47 C.R.C. 128; 27 J.O.R.R. 324.

8. *P.E.I. Potato Growers Ass'n.* v. *Can. Car Demurrage Bureau*, (1942) 55 C.R.T.C. 289; 32 J.O.R.R. 376. Potatoes begin to freeze at 29.6° but with suitable precautions can easily be loaded at slightly lower temperatures.

9. *Ibid.*, affirming *Re Giroux*, (1919) 9 J.O.R.R. 369 and *New Brunswick Farmers* v. *Can. Car Demurrage Bureau*, (1935) 43 C.R.C. 197; 24 J.O.R.R. 431.

10. *Anthracite Sales Co.* v. *Can. Car Demurrage Bureau*, (1945) 58 C.R.T.C. 282; 35 J.O.R.R. 160.

11. *A. R. Williams Co.* v. *Can. Car Demurrage Bureau*, (1924) 29 C.R.C. 306; 14 J.O.R.R. 1.

12. File 1700.407, not reported but referred to in *Alcan Distributors* v. *Can. Car Demurrage Bureau*, (1943) 56 C.R.T.C. 374; 33 J.O.R.R. 291.

13. File 1700.404, referred to in *Alcan Case, supra*.

14. *Ibid.*

15. *Newfoundland Ry.* v. *C.N.R.*, (1942) 55 C.R.T.C. 381; 32 J.O.R.R. 395.

16. *Shipping Federation of Canada* v. *Railway Ass'n. of Canada*, (1943) 56 C.R.T.C. 21; 33 J.O.R.R. 59.

17. *Alcan Distributors, supra.* No extension of free time was allowed where the weather was suitable to permit the unloading of road surfacing material but the consignee postponed unloading until the roads were dry enough to lay the material. *Can. Car Demurrage Bureau* v. *Granby*, (1924) 29 C.R.C. 313; 14 J.O.R.R. 137.

18. *Hedstrom* v. *Can. Car Demurrage Bureau*, (1922) 12 J.O.R.R. 37.

19. *Midland Pacific Terminal* v. *Can. Car Demurrage Bureau*, (1936) 42 C.R.C. 245; 26 J.O.R.R. 295.

20. *Re Demurrage Rules*, (1945) 58 C.R.T.C. 68; 34 J.O.R.R. 249. Subsequently the Board applied the same ruling to private or leased cars handling carbon black. *Goodyear Tire & Rubber Co.* v. *Can. Car Demurrage Bureau*, (1948) 62 C.R.T.C. 145; 38 J.O.R.R. 147.

21. *Re Demurrage Charges incurred on account of Strike Conditions*, (1937) 47 C.R.C. 103; 27 J.O.R.R. 202.

22. As an illustration of individual hardship, a mine screened its coal above railway tracks so that the various sizes such as lump, stove, nut, and slack, fell directly into railway cars spotted on parallel sidings. When a car was filled, it was pulled by means of a steam windlass and cable onto a siding below the tipple whence it was removed on the following morning by a railway locomotive. Often a car was only partly filled at the close of a day's business and if the mine did not work on the following days, demurrage might be charged. At other times the company had loaded cars on hand, because orders from purchasers did not always coincide with the quantity of the various kinds of coal produced. Other, larger companies had storage bins to deal with this situation. This small mine had to pay the demurrage charges legally assessed against it. *Alta. Black Coal Co.* v. *Can. Car Demurrage Bureau*, (1945) 44 C.R.C. 102; 25 J.O.R.R. 213.

23. *Brownlee & Co.* v. *Can Car Demurrage Bureau*, (1926) 32 C.R.C. 291; 16 J.O.R.R. 127. If a carrier tries to charge an unlawful toll and the consignee refuses to unload until such toll is adjusted, demurrage cannot be charged. *Can. Handle Mfg. Co.* v. *Mich. Central*, (1917) 21 C.R.C. 12; 7 J.O.R.R. 113.

24. *Re Canadian Car Service Rules*, (1920) 27 C.R.C. 1; 9 J.O.R.R. 463: *Wallaceburg Sugar Co.* v. *Can. Car Service Bureau*, (1909) 8 C.R.C. 332. Each car must be dealt with as a unit and without reference to other cars. *Anthracite Sales, supra.*

25. Mills can be located with reference to such factors as cost of coal or hydro-electric power, wage rates, size of the local market for flour or wheat by-products such as middlings and bran. For a valuable discussion of stop-offs, interswitching and interchange, see "Transit Privileges," *Certificate Course, supra.*

26. *Sudbury Brewing Co.* v. *C.P.R.*, (1915) 18 C.R.C. 410: *Ont. & Man. Mills* v. *C.P.R.*, (1913) 16 C.R.C. 430.

27. The equivalent poundage for each bushel (60 lbs.) of wheat is 41 lbs. of flour, 12 lbs. of shorts and middlings, 6 lbs. of bran, and 1 lb. of screenings: for one bushel (48 lbs.) of barley it is 36 lbs. of malt, the remaining

12 lbs. being shrinkage. See also *Canada Malting Co.* v. *C.F.A.*, (1958) 77 C.R.T.C. 15, 18; 48 J.O.R.R. 173, 176. On lumber, the deduction for shrinkage from the actual inbound weight ranges from zero when sorted only and 5 per cent when re-sawn or ripped in the rough to 15 per cent when kiln dried. See also *Nance Lumber Co.* v. *C.N.R.*, (1958) 76 C.R.T.C. 332; 48 J.O.R.R. 70.

28. *Dominion Millers' Ass'n.* v. *C.F.A.*, (1924) 29 C.R.C. 339; 14 J.O.R.R. 290. This decision confirmed *ibid.*, (1922) 22 C.R.C. 125; 12 J.O.R.R. 1.

29. *Wylie Milling Co.* v. *C.P.R.*, (1912) 8 D.L.R. 953; 14 C.R.C. 8. Haul out-of-line charges on grain in Western Canada were laid down in *Robin Hood Mills* v. *C.N.R.*, (1952) 69 C.R.T.C. 338; 42 J.O.R.R. 163.

30. *Can. Lumbermen's Ass'n.* v. *C.N.R.*, (1927) 33 C.R.C. 1; 17 J.O.R.R. 31.

31. *Alberta* v. *C.P.R.*, (1921) 27 C.R.C. 317; 11 J.O.R.R. 299. Confirmed in *United Grain Growers* v. *C.F.A.*, (1918) 24 C.R.C. 128 and in *Ross Leaf Tobacco Co.* v. *C.F.A.*, (1927) 32 C.R.C. 320; 17 J.O.R.R. 27.

32. *Alta. Wholesale Implements Ass'n.*, (1927) 17 J.O.R.R. 303, 411–12. Confirmed with respect to twine and flour in *United Farmers of Canada, Sask. Section* v. *C.N.R.*, (1930) 37 C.R.C. 302; 20 J.O.R.R. 213. The Board has no power to order refining-in-transit rates on sugar. *Dominion Sugar Co.* v. *C.F.A.* (1912) 14 C.R.C. 188.

33. *Dominion Biscuit Co.* v. *C.P.R.*, (1933) 40 C.R.C. 373; 23 J.O.R.R. 33.

34. *Shingle Agency* v. *C.P.R.*, (1917) 21 C.R.C. 9; 6 J.O.R.R. 488. But a fabrication-in-transit rate was introduced to allow mills in Toledo to compete with those in Pittsburgh. D. P. Locklin, *Economics of Transportation* (Chicago: R. D. Irwin, 1947), pp. 53–4, 626–9.

35. *Western Livestock Shippers' Ass'n.* v. *C.P.R.*, (1940) 51 C.R.T.C. 321; 30 J.O.R.R. 340. The Royal Commission of 1951 refused to recommend any changes in the law or practice of the Board on transit arrangements. *Rpt.*, p. 113.

36. *United Farmers of Alta.* v. *C.P.R.*, (1930) 37 C.R.C. 290; 20 J.O.R.R. 203.

37. Now s. 315, s.s. 1 (*e*).

38. *Winnipeg & Montreal Bds. of Trade* v. *C.P.R.*, (1921) 27 C.R.C. 138; 11 J.O.R.R. 389.

39. *Columbia Canners* v. *C.P.R.*, (1932) 39 C.R.C. 284; 21 J.O.R.R. 390. See also *British Canadian Canners* v. *G.T.R.*, (1912) 14 C.R.C. 346: *Dominion Millers' Ass'n.* v. *C.F.A.*, (1917) 22 C.R.C. 125; 7 J.O.R.R. 290: *Jas. Goldie Co.* v. *C.N.R.*, (1930) 36 C.R.C. 428; 20 J.O.R.R. 93.

40. *Toronto & Montreal Bds. of Trade* v. *C.F.A.*, (1923) 30 C.R.C. 10; 13 J.O.R.R. 285.

41. But freight may not be billed to one consignee, re-tagged by the shipper or his agent in the railway shed at destination, and then delivered at the railway's expense to a number of persons. Freight forwarders ship carloads of goods belonging to various shippers in their own name and then, at destination, deliver the goods to various consignees by means of their own vehicles.

42. The Dominion Steel and Coal Company owns the Sydney & Louis-

burg Railway. Though the latter is a common carrier operating between Louisburg, Glace Bay, Dominion, Sydney Mines, and Sydney, almost all the traffic it hauls is owned by the Company. From some points of view it is an industrial railway.

43. The Interstate Commerce Commission has held on several occasions that the carrier's obligations are fulfilled if it places the cars on the inter-change tracks with the plant and that it cannot be required to perform the complicated switching operations involved in placing cars for loading or unloading within a plant such as a large steel mill. *Propriety of Operating Practices–Terminal Services*, (1935) 209 I.C.C. 11, 44–5.

44. *Hepworth Brick Co.* v. *G.T.R.*, (1914) 18 C.R.C. 9: *G.T.R.* v. *Christie Henderson*, (1909), 9 C.R.C. 502; 5 B.R.C. 320: *Pilon* v. *G.T.R.* (1913) 16 C.R.C. 43.

45. *Davidson* v. *C.N.R.*, (1921) 27 C.R.C. 343; 11 J.O.R.R. 54.

46. *Fort William Elevator Co.* v. *C.N.R.* (1933) 40 C.R.C. 251; 22 J.O.R.R. 304. Reaffirmed, *ibid.*, (1936) 46 C.R.C. 125; 26 J.O.R.R. 363. Re-hearing refused, *ibid.*, (1938) 48 C.R.C. 197; 28 J.O.R.R. 233.

47. The Canadian National and its predecessor had made no charge for inter-switching between the Dominion Atlantic Railway and certain docks in Halifax but in 1925 it amended its tariffs to add an interswitching charge. The Dominion Atlantic absorbed this charge for four years. Then it assessed the cost against shippers because of its own weak financial position and low freight rates on the traffic concerned. The Board reduced the amount of the interswitching charge levied by the C.N.R., ordered the D.A.R. to absorb half the amount, and assessed the balance against the shippers or consignees. *N.S. Shippers' Ass'n.* v. *Dom. Atl. Ry.* (1924) 28 C.R.C. 95; 14 J.O.R.R. 117, 271. The Board has no jurisdiction over wharfage charges and cannot order a railway to absorb them. *Richardson & Sons* v. *C.N.R.*, (1932) 39 C.R.C. 33; 21 J.O.R.R. 367: *Swift Canadian Co.* v. *C.N.R.* (1952) 67 C.R.T.C. 32; 42 J.O.R.R. 47. But the Board may prevent unjust discrimination in such charges. *Western Grocers* v. *Canada Steamship Lines*, (1951) 67 C.R.T.C. 327; 41 J.O.R.R. 186; re-heard *ibid.*, (1952) 69 C.R.T.C. 56; 42 J.O.R.R. 57. It has also been called upon to interpret a tariff involving cartage charges on export traffic. *Swift Canadian* v. *C.N.R.*, (1954) 70 C.R.T.C. 318; 43 J.O.R.R. 289.

48. The various factors and many of the previous decisions are sum-marized in *C.N.R.* v. *C.P.R.* (*Lulu Island Case*), (1931) 39 C.R.C. 1; 21 J.O.R.R. 313. "The principle which the Board generally follows in applica-tions of this kind is based upon public interest." *Port Dover, Ont.* v. *C.N.R.*, (1949) 63 C.R.T.C. 350; 39 J.O.R.R. 107, 109.

49. Freight between mainland Canada, where railways are standard-gauge (4 feet, 8½ inches), and Newfoundland, with its narrow gauge line (3 feet, 6 inches), has to be trans-shipped. Appearing before the Royal Com-mission of 1951, the Newfoundland government asked for reductions in the transfer charges levied by the Canadian National or for reconstruction of the island railway to standard gauge. Both requests were refused. *Rpt.*, pp. 141–7.

50. The *per diem* charge was 20 cents in 1902; $1 from 1920 to 1945; $1.50 to 1952; $2 to 1955; and then $2.75. In the United States, beginning Jan. 1, 1964, *per diem* rates vary with the age of the car. They range from

$2.16 for older cars which have an assumed value of $1,000 to $7.74 for modern ones which cost roughly $20,000.

51. *Stewart* v. *C.P.R.*, (1910) 11 C.R.C. 197: *Re Cartage Tolls*, (1915) 19 C.R.C. 389: *Port Arthur & Fort William Retail Merchants* v. *C.F.A.*, (1918) 24 C.R.C. 80; 7 J.O.R.R. 469: *Toronto Bd. of Trade* v. *G.T.R.*, (1920) 26 C.R.C. 180; 10 J.O.R.R. 639: *Re Cartage Charges*, (1935) 43 C.R.C. 336; 25 J.O.R.R. 53. The Board lacks authority to order a railway to provide cartage service. *Toronto Bd. of Trade, supra*: *Brade Storage* v. *C.P.R.*, (1934) 42 C.R.C. 261; 24 J.O.R.R. 194.

52. A railway charged two freight forwarders the same tolls on pool cars. In one case it delivered the freight from a team track to the warehouse of the forwarder. In the other it merely shunted the car on the spur track adjoining the forwarder's place of business. As this practice constituted unjust discrimination it was prohibited. *Leonard Warehouses* v. *C.P.R.*, (1928) C.R.C. 196; 28 J.O.R.R. 167.

Chapter 12: *Railway Passenger Services* (pp. 298–308)

1. Passenger Tickets Act, R.S.C., 1952, c. 202, s. 10.

2. *London & Port Stanley Ry.*, (1918) 8 J.O.R.R. 39: *Quebec, Montreal & Southern Counties Ry.*, (1919) 9 J.O.R.R. 26.

3. *Re Inquiry into Cost of Transportation of Coal*, (1927) 17 J.O.R.R. 439, 464. In 1929 the corresponding loss was $10 million. Canada, House of Commons, Committee on Railways, 1930, *Proc.*, p. 6. In 1931 it was $24 million. *Ibid.*, 1932, p. 63.

4. *Twenty-one Per Cent Case*, (1958) 62 C.R.T.C. 1, 64; 38 J.O.R.R. 1, 41: *Seventeen Per Cent Case*, (1958) 72 C.R.T.C. 22; 48 J.O.R.R. no. 16A, 18.

5. D. R. Ladd, *Cost Data for the Management of Railroad Passenger Service* (Boston: Harvard Business School, 1957), p. 280.

6. Ryl. Comm., 1961, *Rpt.*, vol. I, pp. 43–7, 58–60.

7. *Toronto & Brampton* v. *G.T.R.*, (1910) 11 C.R.C. 370, 374–5. See also *Massiah* v. *Can. Nor. Ry.*, (1914) 17 C.R.C. 88, 90: *Brown* v. *Lake St. John Ry.*, (1915) 18 C.R.C. 342.

8. Under s. 350, s. (1), ss. (*b*) of the Railway Act. See also *Re Commutation Fares*, (1950) 66 C.R.T.C. 98, 108; 40 J.O.R.R. 250, 257.

9. *Can. Fraternal Ass'n.* v. *Can. Pass. Ass'n.*, (1912) 13 C.R.C. 178.

10. *Roy* v. *Can. Pass. Ass'n.*, (1915) 17 C.R.C. 320.

11. *Queen's University* v. *C.P.R.*, (1923) 31 C.R.C. 315; 13 J.O.R.R. 191.

12. *National Federation of Can. University Students* v. *Can. Pass. Ass'n.*, (1937) 47 C.R.C. 222; 27 J.O.R.R. 391.

13. *Winnipeg Bd. of Trade* v. *C.P.R. & C.N.R.*, (1929) 36 C.R.C. 100; 19 J.O.R.R. 280.

14. *Associated Can. Travellers* v. *C.P.R., C.N.R. & Can. Pass. Ass'n.*, (1936) 45 C.R.C. 317; 26 J.O.R.R. 131.

15. *Re Independent Commercial Travellers*, (1951) 68 C.R.T.C. 133; 41 J.O.R.R. 315.

16. *Toronto* v. *G.T.R.*, (1920) 25 C.R.C. 409; 10 J.O.R.R. 35, 47.

17. *Ibid.*, C.R.C. at pp. 413–15; J.O.R.R. at pp. 37–9.

18. *Re Commutation Fares*, n. 8: *Can. Pass. Ass'n.* v. *Montreal Suburban Communities*, (1955) 72 C.R.T.C. 72; 45 J.O.R.R. 57: *Increased Commutation Fares*, (1956) 73 C.R.T.C. 193; 46 J.O.R.R. 61: *C.N.R. Commutation Service, Dorval-Montreal*, (1960) 80 C.R.T.C. 241; 50 J.O.R.R. 11: *ibid.*, (1963) 53 B.T.C. 585.

19. *Can. Pass. Ass'n.* v. *Oakville*, (1954) 71 C.R.T.C. 138; 44 J.O.R.R. 203.

20. In 1934 on the Canadian National the cost of food (without taking into account anything for hauling the dining car or its contents, or for interest or repairs but including food for stewards, chefs, and waiters) was $1.08 per revenue meal, and the average meal cheque was 86 cents. The Company tried cheaper meals and lost more money. Canada, House of Commons, Committee on Railways, 1935, *Proc.*, pp. 76, 121. On some trains the Canadian National introduced dinettes where relatively low-cost meals were served at counters. When these proved unsuccessful, it installed some combined news-stands and snack bars. Many travellers still prefer the individualized or luxury service which has been traditional in railway diners. Railways have also experimented with precooked meals like those served on aircraft.

Chapter 13: Merchandise or Express Service (pp. 309–326)

1. Bd. of Ry. Com'rs., *Ann. Rpt.*, 1912, p. 240.

2. *Ibid.*, 1913, p. 281.

3. *Express Traffic Ass'n.* v. *Montreal*, (1919) 25 C.R.C. 61; 9 J.O.R.R. 133.

4. The branch of the Canadian Pacific from Sudbury to Sault Ste. Marie was not included until 1926. For an important discussion of express see C. N. Ham, "Express Service and Rates," in *A Verbatim Report of Lectures on Traffic* (Toronto: University of Toronto Department of Extension, 1945), pp. 256–84. See also "Express", *Certificate Course*, (Toronto: Can. Institute of Traffic and Transportation, 1964).

5. Prior to this decision Vancouver Island formed a distinct zone and its rates are still the lowest in Canada but goods are neither picked up nor delivered.

6. *Express Traffic Ass'n.* v. *Montreal*, (1927) 27 C.R.C. 186; 10 J.O.R.R. 504.

7. (1912) 24 I.C.C. 380, 527.

8. A few places have been arbitrarily translated from one block to another in order to prevent obvious discrimination between two closely adjacent points. Also, in order to line up rates in certain districts where rail lines parallel each other but where there are no transverse rail connections, a number of exceptions were made to the general plan.

9. Daily newspapers shipped to dealers who make their own arrangements regarding delivery and pick-up, are carried at lower rates than magazines and other weekly and monthly publications. Daily newspapers move in volume each week-day to the same consignees. Magazines create peaks in traffic volume and so are more expensive to handle. Weekly editions of news-

papers such as the *Toronto Star Weekly* are classed as magazines. *La Patrie Publishing Co.* v. *Express Traffic Ass'n.*, (1944) 57 C.R.T.C. 214; 34 J.O.R.R. 168.

10. See n. 53, chapter 7.

11. Before 1919 express companies had special rates on books, circulars, calendars, sheet music, and blue prints. These had been introduced to compete with the Post Office but were withdrawn because they did not increase traffic.

12. Up to this time second class rates were called "N" rates. The name was changed to bring Canadian practice into line with American. At the same time the rates on beer and aerated water, formerly called "K" rates, were included in the second class.

13. *Express Traffic Ass'n.* v. *Montreal*, (1919) 25 C.R.C. 61, 98–100; 9 J.O.R.R. 163.

14. *Ibid.*, (1921) 27 C.R.C. 186, 203; 10 J.O.R.R. 504, 516.

15. *Express Traffic Ass'n.* v. *Fisheries Council*, (1951) 67 C.R.T.C. 317; 41 J.O.R.R. 113.

16. Fifty cents up to 1948, when it was raised to 75 cents. As a result of a series of increases the minimum was $2.75 in 1966 except on parcels up to 25 pounds. Smaller parcels are charged substantially the same rates as the Post Office.

17. Bd. of Ry. Com'rs., *Ann. Rpt.*, 1912, pp. 240, 262–7.

18. *Re Increase in Express Delivery Limits in Toronto*, (1919) 22 C.R.C. 375; 9 J.O.R.R. 13.

19. *Express Traffic Ass'n.* v. *Montreal*, (1919) C.R.C. at pp. 112–6; J.O.R.R. at pp. 171–9.

20. The rules are applied regardless of municipal boundaries. For instance, by order of the Board delivery already given in Windsor, Ont., was extended to the adjoining portion of the town of Sandwich. *Sandwich* v. *Express Traffic Ass'n.*, (1930) 37 C.R.C. 139; 20 J.O.R.R. 105. The Board has refused to vary its rules even when the applicants were willing to pay extra for the service. To vary general rules on the application of one locality would immediately duplicate the anomalies and contradictions which existed prior to 1919. *Lancaster* v. *Dominion Express*, (1926) 32 C.R.C. 33; 16 J.O.R.R. 115. The companies are entitled to limit cartage service to certain hours. *Black* v. *Express Traffic Ass'n.*, (1919) 26 C.R.C. 171; 9 J.O.R.R. 323.

21. *Spooner* v. *Express Traffic Ass'n.*, (1922) 28 C.R.C. 62; 12 J.O.R.R. 105.

22. *Re Express Rates on Fruit*, (1921) 11 J.O.R.R. 191.

Chapter 14: Service (pp. 327–351)

1. *Vancouver Island Ratepayers Ass'n.* v. *E. & N. Ry.*, (1952) 69 C.R.T.C. 145; 42 J.O.R.R. 113: *ibid.*, (1957) 47 J.O.R.R. 1: *ibid.*, 275. In *Economics of Canadian Transportation* (Toronto: University of Toronto Press, 1959) the author tried to list all cases on cancellation of passenger service and abandonment of unprofitable branches. These cases have now become so numerous that any listing would clutter up the Notes to this book. Also, they would prove chiefly of historical interest now that the law has

been changed. Hence, only the more significant decisions have been cited.

2. *C.N.R.* v. *Agincourt*, (1961) 82 B.T.C. 321, 335; 51 J.O.R.R. 567, 576-7.

3. *Fredericton* v. *C.P.R.*, (1962) 83 C.R.T.C. 321, 331; 52 B.T.C. 73, 81.

4. *Re New York Central Passenger Service (Malone-Montreal)*, (1957) 75 C.R.T.C. 208; 47 J.O.R.R. 99. Discontinuance of service was allowed by *Order 95597*, Sept. 17, 1958, 48 J.O.R.R. 308: *Truro, N.S.* v. *C.N.R.*, (1938) 48 C.R.C. 30; 28 J.O.R.R. 61. As losses continued, the Board permitted discontinuance of the winter service too. *Ibid.*, (1941) 43 C.R.T.C. 356; 31 J.O.R.R. 351.

5. Ryl. Comm., 1961, *Rpt.* vol. I, p. 60.

6. *Wiarton* v. *C.N.R.*, (1934) 42 C.R.C. 227; 24 J.O.R.R. 185. Deputy Chief Commissioner Garceau dissented because the economies desired by the company would mean a direct loss to labour, necessitate the abandonment of a terminal, involve a change of residence for employees without proper compensation as required by the Railway Act, and reduced employment.

7. *Lake Erie & Northern Ry.* v. *Port Dover, Ont.*, (1950) 65 C.R.T.C. 124; 40 J.O.R.R. 103. Traffic did not develop as anticipated and so abandonment was allowed. *Ibid.*, (1955) 72 C.R.T.C. 290; 45 J.O.R.R. 37. The Board would not allow motor buses to be substituted for electric trains because the former would add to highway congestion and were less likely to adhere to schedules in foggy weather. *Vancouver & Lulu Island Ry.* v. *Richmond*, (1952) 69 C.R.T.C. 220; 42 J.O.R.R. 178.

8. *Maniwaki, P.Q.* v. *C.P.R.*, (1945) 58 C.R.T.C. 65; 35 J.O.R.R. 55. After the war the railway added a train for the lower 25 miles out of Ottawa. In *Train Service, Tignish-Summerside-Borden & Charlottetown*, (1924) 14 J.O.R.R. 209, and in *Eastern King's Bd. of Trade, Souris, P.E.I.*, (1942) 32 J.O.R.R. 353, the Board also rearranged schedules to satisfy certain communities.

9. *Sprague* v. *C.N.R.*, (1928) 34 C.R.C. 113; 17 J.O.R.R. 619. See also *Ste Rose* v. *Quebec Central Ry.*, (1943) 55 C.R.T.C. 398; 32 J.O.R.R. 469: *N.Y.C.* v. *Valleyfield*, (1940) 51 C.R.T.C. 366; 30 J.O.R.R. 223: *ibid.*, (1940) 52 C.R.T.C. 109; 30 J.O.R.R. 277: *ibid.*, (1942) 56 C.R.T.C. 234; 32 J.O.R.R. 105. Also *Abitibi District* v. *C.P.R.*, (1942) 55 C.R.T.C. 338; 32 J.O.R.R. 327: *Torrington* v. *Central Vermont Ry.*, (1949) 63 C.R.T.C. 1; 38 J.O.R.R. 235: *Edmundston, N.B.* v. *Temiscouata Ry.*, *ibid.*, C.R.T.C. at p. 82; J.O.R.R. at p. 219.

10. *Halton County, Ont.* v. *C.P.R.*, (1943) 56 C.R.T.C. 295; 33 J.O.R.R.

11. *Harris* v. *C.P.R.*, (1916) 21 C.R.C. 31; 6 J.O.R.R. 335.

12. *Campbell Township, P.Q.* v. *C.P.R.*, (1932) 40 C.R.C. 355; 22 J.O.R.R. 85. Monetary advantage and the general convenience of residents must be weighed against the additional cost to the railway. *Pointe Calumet* v. *C.P.R.*, (1949) 64 C.R.T.C. 324; 39 J.O.R.R. 221.

13. *Nipissing Central and Temiskaming & Nor. Ont. Ry. Comm.* v. *C.N.R.*, (1943) 56 C.R.T.C. 42; 33 J.O.R.R. 75.

14. *Elgin, Ont., Board of Trade* v. *C.N.R.*, (1955) 72 C.R.T.C. 165; 44 J.O.R.R. 377.

15. *La Tuque, P.Q.* v. *C.N.R.*, (1937) 47 C.R.C. 349; 27 J.O.R.R. 383. The Board had no jurisdiction to order platforms, freight sheds, etc., at

stopping places which are not regular stations or agencies. *Winnipeg Jobbers & Shippers* v. *C.P.R.*, (1908) 8 C.R.C. 151: *Rutter Station Patrons* v. *C.P.R.*, [1912] 8 D.L.R. 711; 14 C.R.C. 1. It had no power to order landowners to rebuild a shelter station which they had erected voluntarily on their own property. Good cause was not shown why the company should be ordered to erect a shelter at its own expense on its own right of way. *Harding* v. *Montreal & Southern Counties Ry.*, (1929) 37 C.R.C. 92; 19 J.O.R.R. 347.

16. *Hartin* v. *Can. Nor. Ry.*, (1916) 21 C.R.C. 437; 6 J.O.R.R. 338. Confirmed in *Grand Piles* v. *C.P.R.*, (1926) 32 C.R.C. 1: 16 J.O.R.R. 99.

17. *Druid Landowners* v. *G.T.P.*, [1912] 7 D.L.R. 884; 14 C.R.C. 20.

18. *Kelly* v. *G.T.P.*, [1912] 5 D.L.R. 303; 14 C.R.C. 15.

19. *Coalhurst, Alta.* v. *C.P.R.*, (1923) 31 C.R.C. 396; 13 J.O.R.R. 259. But the Board did allow the closing of a station at the terminus of a branch 4 miles long. *Ste Angèle-de-Monnoir* v. *C.N.R.*, (1950) 40 J.O.R.R. 109.

20. *United Grain Growers* v. *Donnelly*, (1920) 26 C.R.C. 53: *Sclanders* v. *C.N.R.*, (1923) 28 C.R.C. 433; 13 J.O.R.R. 145: *Willow Creek* v. *C.N.R.*, (1923) 28 C.R.C. 434; 13 J.O.R.R. 141.

21. *Muldoon* v. *C.P.R.* (1927) 33 C.R.C. 13; 17 J.O.R.R. 67: *Dagenais* v. *C.P.R.*, (1950) 66 C.R.T.C. 287; 40 J.O.R.R. 335: *Eby* v *G.T.P.*, (1911) 20 W.L.R. 629; 13 C.R.C. 22: *Forward* v. *C.P.R.*, (1912) 14 C.R.C. 377.

22. *Gainsboro Township* v. *Toronto, Hamilton & Buffalo Ry.*, (1931) 21 J.O.R.R. 117.

23. *Re Agency Stations*, (1951) 66 C.R.T.C. 150; 40 J.O.R.R. 347. See also *Re C.P.R. Place Viger Sta.*, (1951) 41 J.O.R.R. 88. *St Bazile-le-Grand, P.Q.* v. *C.N.R.*, (1933) 40 C.R.C. 334; 22 J.O.R.R. 329: *C.N.R.* v. *Peel County*, (1928) 34 C.R.C. 156; 18 J.O.R.R. 29: *Pere Marquette Ry.* v. *Chatham, Ont.*, (1938) 48 C.R.C. 247; 28 J.O.R.R. 196. In at least one case a railway provided an agent from November to March, not because the volume of traffic warranted it but as a convenience to residents of the community during the winter. *Tway Bd. of Trade* v. *C.P.R.*, (1951) 40 J.O.R.R. 350.

24. *Lardeau, B.C.* v. *C.P.R.*, (1924) 14 J.O.R.R. 257. A similar rule was followed in *St. Laurent, Man.* v. *C.N.R.*, (1945) 34 J.O.R.R. 203.

25. *St. Laurent, supra*: *Oak Point, Man.* v. *C.N.R., ibid.*, 205.

26. *Mallaig* v. *C.N.R.*, (1946) 60 C.R.T.C. 220; 36 J.O.R.R. 285.

27. *C.N.R.* v. *St. Liboire*, (1940) 52 C.R.T.C. 133; 30 J.O.R.R. 329.

28. *C.N.R.* v. *N. Norwich Township*, (1928) 34 C.R.C. 165; 18 J.O.R.R. 35.

29. *Wallace Township* v. *C.N.R.* [1936] Ontario Weekly Notes 431; 45 C.R.C. 370.

30. *Kingston* v. *Kingston, Portsmouth & Cataraqui Elec. Ry.*, (1898) 25 Appeal Reports (Ont.) 462, 469.

31. *Ottawa Elec. Ry.* v. *Nepean Township*, [1920] 60 S.C.R. 216; 54 D.L.R. 468; 27 C.R.C. 32.

32. *Deputy Minister of Justice* v. *Ottawa Elec. Ry.*, (1932) 39 C.R.C. 289.

33. *The King* v. *Ottawa Elec. Ry.*, [1933] 1 D.L.R. 695; 40 C.R.C. 295. The court thought it was not necessary for it to decide whether, where two tribunals had jurisdiction, a plaintiff who had gone before one tribunal was precluded from going before the other.

34. *Goose Lake District Grain*, (1916) 21 C.R.C. 38; 6 J.O.R.R. 1.

35. *Re Coal Transportation Facilities*, (1916) 22 C.R.C. 338; 6 J.O.R.R. 438.

36. *Empire Refining Co.* v. *Pere Marquette R.*, (1910) 10 C.R.C. 158.

37. *Vancouver–Prince Rupert Meat Co.* v. *Grt. Nor. Ry.*, (1911) 13 C.R.C. 15.

38. *Iron Mountain* v. *Grt. Nor. Ry.*, (1913) 15 C.R.C. 311.

39. *Potato Shippers* v. *C.P.R.*, (1917) 24 C.R.C. 46.

40. *Can. Piano Co.* v. *C.F.A.*, (1910) 12 C.R.C. 22: *Okanagan Valley Growers* v. *C.F.A.*, (1918) 24 C.R.C. 55; 8 J.O.R.R. 21.

41. *Brown* v. *C.P.R.*, (1910) 11 C.R.C. 152.

42. *McKenzie* v. *C.P.R.*, (1918) 23 C.R.C. 99; 8 J.O.R.R. 227.

43. *Hunting-Merritt Lumber Co.* v. *C.P.R.*, (1916) 20 C.R.C. 181; 6 J.O.R.R. 13. Regarding horse cars see *Mancell* v. *Mich. Central*, (1914) 19 C.R.C. 246.

44. *Jordan Co-op.* v. *Can. Express Co.*, (1917) 23 C.R.C. 55; 7 J.O.R.R. 120.

45. *United Grain Growers Ltd.* v. *Ry. Ass'n. of Can.*, (1940) 51 C.R.T.C. 103; 29 J.O.R.R. 643.

46. *Rossland Bd. of Trade* v. *Grt. Nor. Ry.*, (1922) 28 C.R.C. 24, headnote; 11 J.O.R.R. 417: *Hunter Bros.* v. *Grt. Nor. Ry.*, (1925) 30 C.R.C. 180; 15 J.O.R.R. 126: *St. Brigid's Parish* v. *C.N.R.*, (1927) 33 C.R.C. 15; 17 J.O.R.R. 63: *Caledon & Albion Townships* v. *C.P.R.*, (1933) 40 C.R.C. 228; 22 J.O.R.R. 292; *C.P.R. Reston Subdivision*, (1941) 53 C.R.T.C. 82, 106; 31 J.O.R.R. 121: *C.N.R.* v. *Deschaillons*, (1936) 45 C.R.C. 356; 26 J.O.R.R. 111. The situation in Great Britain was similar. *Darlaston Local Bd.* v. *London & North Western Ry.*, (1894) 63 L.J.Q.B. 826. The Board has no power to order re-establishment of a line abandoned prior to the legislation of 1933. *C.N.R.* v. *Deschaillons*.

47. (1933) 23–24 Geo. V, c. 47, s. 165A; R.S.C., 1952, c. 234, s. 168. Prior to the amendment "the convenience and the necessities of the public might be entirely disregarded by a railway company which desired to abandon the operation of an unprofitable line. The amendment . . . was intended to remedy this difficulty by providing that the interests of the public should at least be considered." *Vancouver, Victoria & Eastern Ry. & Navigation Co.* v. *Princeton*, (1936) 45 C.R.C. 178, 197; 26 J.O.R.R. 29, 40.

48. *C.N.R.* v. *Tweed*, (1935) 44 C.R.C. 53, 58; 25 J.O.R.R. 159, 161–2.

49. *Ibid.*

50. *Detroit-Toledo & Ironton R. Abandonment*, (1932) 187 I.C.C. 433, 438.

51. See, for example, *Stobie Branch, C.P.R.*, (1935) 44 C.R.C. 405; 25 J.O.R.R. 332: *C.N.R.* v. *Nicolet County*, (1940) 51 C.R.T.C. 299; 30 J.O.R.R. 21: *Calabogie–Snow Road, Ont.*, (1961) 82 C.R.T.C. 336; 51 B.T.C. 491.

52. *C.N.R. Tweed Subdivision (Yarker-Tweed, Ont.)*, (1941) 53 C.R.-T.C. 139; 31 J.O.R.R. 57 was frequently quoted by the Board in later cases and so can be considered as a sort of landmark. In the course of time the Board refined its methods of dealing with abandonment cases, especially by using multiple regression to ascertain operating costs more accurately. A basic case seems to be *Re Minto, N.B., Subdivision, C.P.R.*, (1963) 85 C.R.T.C. 124; 53 B.T.C. 393.

53. *C.P.R.* v. *Grand Forks, B.C.*, (1935) 44 C.R.C. 123; 23 J.O.R.R.

241: *C.N.R.* v. *Algonquin Corp.*, (*Two Rivers–Cache Lake*), (1936) 45 C.R.C. 230; 25 J.O.R.R. 542: *C.N.R.* v. *S. Dumfries, Ont.* (*Paris Jct.– Brant City Siding*), (1935) 44 C.R.C. 41; 25 J.O.R.R. 165: *C.N.R.* (*Lovett-Foothills, Alta.* (1935) 44 C.R.C. 68; 25 J.O.R.R. 195.

54. *C.N.R.* v. *Annapolis County*, (1939) 50 C.R.T.C. 61; 28 J.O.R.R. 428: *C.P.R.* v. *St Eustache, P.Q.*, (1940) 51 C.R.T.C. 401; 30 J.O.R.R. 94.

55. *N.Y.C.* v. *Stormont*, (1939) 50 C.R.T.C. 235; 29 J.O.R.R. 299: *C.N.R.* v. *Wingham*, (1941) 52 C.R.T.C. 261; 31 J.O.R.R. 6: *Wallace Township* v. *C.N.R.* [1936] Ontario Weekly Notes 431. "The fact that subsidies have been paid for the construction of the railway is one element bearing upon the decision, and is to be taken into consideration, but has no controlling or binding effect upon the Board." *C.N.R.* v. *Iberville, P.Q.*, (1935) 44 C.R.C. 269; 25 J.O.R.R. 531. "Regardless of agreements or the payment of subsidies, the Board has absolute jurisdiction to authorize abandonment." *C.P.R.* v. *Mansonville, P.Q.*, (1935) 45 C.R.C. 89; 25 J.O.R.R. 473.

56. See, for example, *C.N.R.* v. *St. Martin's, N.B.* (*Hampton–St. Martin's*), (1935) 44 C.R.C. 334; 25 J.O.R.R. 284: *C.N.R.* v. *Frelighsburg, P.Q.* (*Farnham-Frelighsburg*), (1935) 44 C.R.C. 343; 25 J.O.R.R. 273: *N.Y.C.* v. *Lambton County, Ont.*, (1935) 58 C.R.T.C. 217; 35 J.O.R.R. 139.

57. *C.P.R. Minota & Varcoe and the C.N.R. Rapid City Subdivision* (*MacGregor-Varcoe & Hallboro-Beulah, Man.*), (1941) 53 C.R.T.C. 15; 31 J.O.R.R. 76. One Commissioner dissented saying that while some inconvenience would be suffered, the annual saving was substantial in a territory well served by other railways. See also *C.N.R.* v. *Lena, Man.* (*Louise-Deloraine*), (1940) 51 C.R.T.C. 147; 29 J.O.R.R. 669.

58. *Brandon, Saskatchewan, & Hudson's Bay Ry.* v. *Morden, Man.*, (1936) 43 C.R.C. 188; 26 J.O.R.R. 138: *Vancouver, Victoria, supra*, note 46.

59. Ryl. Comm., 1951, *Rpt.*, p. 223.

60. Ryl. Comm. on Canada's Economic Prospects, *Final Rpt.*, (Ottawa: Queen's Printer, 1957), p. 273.

61. Ryl. Comm., 1961, *Rpt.*, vol. I, pp. 41–2.

62. *C.P.R. McAuley Subdivision*, (1961) 83 C.R.T.C. 91; 51 B.T.C. 579.

63. *C.P.R. Lorraine Subdivision*, (1962) 83 C.R.T.C. 142, 149; 52 B.T.C. 21, 27.

Chapter 15: Railway Labour (pp. 352–383)

1. The percentage varies with hourly and monthly rates of pay, the general level of freight rates and passenger fares, the consist of the traffic, the amount of maintenance undertaken, and the ability of management to keep expense in line with total ton-miles or gross revenue.

2. In 1934 members of railway labour unions constituted 25 per cent of all labour unionists in Canada. As a result of expansion in industry and the growth of organized labour during the war, the steam railway proportion fell to 17 per cent in 1944. In 1928, 57 per cent, in 1943, 70 per cent, and by 1950, over 90 per cent of all railway workers were members of various unions.

3. The number is approximate since some railway employees belong to unions which draw their main strength from non-railway workers.

4. In 1936 and 1948 the top executives from all Canadian labour unions met and negotiated together in the General Conference Committee, a body corresponding to the Railway Labor Executives' Association in the United States. During the strike of 1950 the running trades ceased to operate trains because the danger of accident was greatly heightened when telegraphers and dispatchers were off duty but technically the running trades did not strike either for higher wages or in sympathy with other unions.

5. General Order 806, Feb. 18, 1955, 45 J.O.R.R. 98.

6. *Dominion Joint Legislative Comm., Ry. Train Brotherhoods,* (1939) 29 J.O.R.R. 16.

7. G.O. 522, Nov. 9, 1933, 23 J.O.R.R. 292.

8. G.O. 534, March 27, 1935, 25 J.O.R.R. 57.

9. G.O. 547, Dec. 4, 1935, *ibid.,* at p. 411.

10. *Railway Act,* s. 287.

11. *Canadian National–Canadian Pacific Act Amendment* (1939), 3 Geo. VI, c. 37.

12. See the Board's *Regulations for the Transportation of Explosives and Other Dangerous Articles in Rail Freight and Rail Express Service,* as amended.

13. *Brotherhood of Locomotive Engineers* v. *C.P.R.,* (1945) 58 C.R.-T.C. 200; 35 J.O.R.R. 89. See also *Brotherhoods* v. *Railway Companies,* (1934) 42 C.R.C. 329; 24 J.O.R.R. 217. In an application for an order prescribing the length of sections and the number of employees per section, the running trades joined with the Brotherhood of Maintenance of Way Employees though on the face of it the question directly involved only the latter. *Dominion Joint Legislative Committee* v. *Ry. Ass'n. of Can.,* (1950) 40 J.O.R.R. 275: *ibid.,* (1951) 41 J.O.R.R. 79. See also *Re General, Train & Interlocking Rules,* (1950) 40 J.O.R.R. 187.

14. H. A. Logan, *Trade Unions in Canada* (Toronto: Macmillan, 1948) p. 145.

15. J. L. McDougall, "Progress and the Railway Running Trade Unions: A Case Study," *Queen's Quarterly,* Autumn, 1964, pp. 318–33.

16. Railway Act, s. 179. See also *Brotherhood of Railroad Trainmen* v. *C.N.R.* (*Big Valley, Alta. Case*), (1931) 38 C.R.C. 312; 21 J.O.R.R. 291. But a mere change in the locale for marshalling cars did not constitute abandonment and the Board was without jurisdiction. *Ry. Trainmen* v. *Mich. Central* (*Montrose Yards*), (1932) 39 C.R.C. 239; 22 J.O.R.R. 2. The Royal Commission of 1951 refused to recommend any change in legislation to clarify the law or extend the Board's jurisdiction over abandonment of divisional points. *Rpt.,* pp. 164–5.

17. Issued in 1922 by D. B. Hanna, president of the then Canadian National.

18. Up to 1947 railways insisted they dealt with the men's representatives and not with the union as such. This was subterfuge on the part of railways. Since 1947 "the rates of pay, hours of work and other terms and conditions of employment . . . [on the two major railways] shall be such as are set out in any agreements in writing . . . [between the railways] and the representatives of interested employees" (1947), 11 Geo. VI, c. 28. But Mr.

Justice Wilson in Conciliation Bd., *Rpt.*, 1950, p. 37 stated that there was no real collective bargaining because there were 86 separate contracts between railways and the unions represented before the Board. Each contract was a code covering the wages and working conditions of a group of workers and of grades within that group. Some groups deserved large wage increases or greater reductions of hours than others because of the onerous and unpleasant nature of their work. Yet the revisions of wages and hours were made on the assumption that there was a single contract. As a result, the give and take which is necessary to any kind of bargaining was virtually precluded.

19. (1948) 11–12 Geo. VI, c. 54; now R.S.C. 1952, c. 152. The original legislation was (1907), 6–7 Edw. VII, c. 20.

20. In Canada labour relations normally come within provincial jurisdiction but the Industrial Disputes Investigation Act is *intra vires* the Dominion Parliament in so far as railways are concerned. In "pith and substance" it is railway, not labour legislation.

21. Conciliation Bd., *Rpt.*, 1950, p. 37 (under the chairmanship of Mr. Justice J. O. Wilson).

22. "The tendency, both here and in the United States, is to resolve by government action the stalemate created by the failure of the bargaining process." *Ibid.*, p. 38.

23. In 1918 the government accepted the McAdoo Award on government railways and suggested that private lines should do the same. In 1946 the Canadian National and the provincially owned Ontario Northland granted a wage increase to their employees. The Canadian Pacific pleaded its financial inability to pay higher wages but later in the year it made the same increase. In all other disputes the Canadian National has made common cause with the other carriers. The opinion is often expressed, though without definite proof, that the government orders the publicly owned system to grant part of the increase asked for by the unions and the other systems must follow suit. In 1950, on the contrary, the President of the Canadian National was accused of "carrying the ball" for private enterprise in opposition to another "round" of wage increases.

24. G. M. Rountree, *The Railway Worker* (Toronto: Oxford University Press, 1936) pp. 53–7.

25. *Labour Gazette*, 1926, p. 1059 (Mr. Justice Kelly).

26. *Ibid.*, 1931, p. 1293 (Mr. J. M. Macdonnell). Percentage figures and dates of applicability varied a little from one class of employee to another.

27. *Ibid.*, 1933, p. 478 (Mr. Justice G. F. Gibsone).

28. *Ibid.*, 1937, p. 134 (Mr. Justice A. K. McLean).

29. *Ibid.*, 1947, p. 961 (Professor A. Brady).

30. Holidays with pay were already being allowed some shopmen, freight clerks, etc. According to L. A. Wood, *Union-Management Co-operation on the Railroads* (New Haven: Yale University Press, 1931), p. 249, in 1928 Sir Henry Thornton was forced to put up a grim struggle for vacations with pay which certain Cabinet ministers thought were too revolutionary from an industrial standpoint. Whereas Sir Henry had been ready to accord workers two weeks' holiday with pay, under Cabinet pressure he compromised on one week.

31. *Labour Gazette*, 1948, pp. 571–2, 580–611 (Mr. Justice J. C. A. Cameron).

32. Maintenance of Railway Operation Act (1950), 14 Geo. VI, c. 1.

33. "The Railway Strike of 1950," *Labour Gazette*, 1950, pp. 1638–54; *ibid.*, 1951, pp. 194–226.

34. *Labour Gazette*, 1954, pp. 817–45, 869 (Mr. Justice Kellock).

35. *Ibid.*, 1955, pp. 52–9 (Chief Justice Sloan.)

36. *Ibid.*, 1956, pp. 660–4 (Judge Maybank).

37. Ryl. Comm. on Firemen on Diesel Locomotives, *Rpt.*, reprinted in *Labour Gazette*, 1958, pp. 256–8.

38. *Labour Gazette*, 1958, pp. 1147–58, 1152 (Mr. Justice Thomson).

39. *Annual Vacations Act*, 1958, 6 Eliz. II, c. 24.

40. *Labour Gazette*, 1960, pp. 1030–42 (Mr. Justice J. V. H. Milvain).

41. *Railways Operation Continuation Act* (1960), 9 Eliz. II, c. 2.

42. *Labour Gazette*, 1962, pp. 656–721 (Judge J. B. Robinson).

43. *Ibid.*, 1962, pp. 1181–3; 1964, pp. 1152–79 (Mr. Justice Monroe).

44. The agreement with the Canadian Brotherhood of Railway Employees and Other Transport Workers referred questions of interpretation to the Canadian National Railway Employees Board of Adjustment No. 2, which had only one case, in 1925. Agreements with shópmen were interpreted through direct negotiation between Division 4 and railways.

45. Rountree, *The Railway Worker*, pp. 231–60: S. H. Slichter, *Union Policies and Industrial Management* (Washington: The Brookings Institution, 1941): Wood, *Union-Management Co-operation*.

46. E. M. Fitch and J. M. Gillman, "The Position of Labour" in National Resources Planning Board, *Transportation and National Policy* (Washington, 1942) p. 488; Canada, Senate, Special Committee on Railways, 1939, *Proc.*, pp. 18–77; Twentieth Century Fund, *How Collective Bargaining Works* (New York: The Fund, 1942) pp. 346–51.

47. A day's work for passenger engineers and firemen is a run of 100 miles or less in five hours or less, and for passenger conductors and trainmen 150 miles in 7½ hours or less. Crews of yard locomotives are paid by the hour. Crew members are paid for the time needed at the beginning and end of each run for signing on and off duty, receiving orders, inspecting equipment, and the like. Sometimes they receive "arbitraries" or constructive allowances for rendering services which are not necessarily part of the work to which they are assigned, e.g., switching service performed by road crews.

48. A few employees on premium runs get high remuneration per hour worked. In December, 1947, one passenger conductor actually ran 2,400 miles and was paid for 4.500 miles or $270.73. *Railways' Exhibit No. 24 to Board of Conciliation, 1948*. See also J. L. MacDougall, "The Distribution of Income among Wage Workers in Railway Employment, 1939–47," *Can. Journal of Eco. & Pol. Science*, May, 1947, pp. 248–55. Comparison over time is difficult. In 1939 rail labour was fully organized and had reaped the benefits of organization and of capable union management in a relatively high wage scale whereas other employees were less strongly unionized. Better organization since 1939 has tended to bring up the wages of groups which were formerly paid relatively poorly. The growth of manufacturing during and after the war increased the proportion of skilled, relatively well-paid workers. The wartime practice of extending flat wage increases based on the rise in the cost of living benefited the lower-paid groups by a larger percentage than the higher-paid ones such as rail workers. The practice had the

same effect within the railway industry, e.g., firemen and sectionmen improved their positions relative to conductors and locomotive engineers. Care must be taken in comparing the dollar figures of wages of railway workers with wage earners generally. Women comprise about 50 per cent of the labour force in personal service and about five per cent on railways. Because they are not paid as well as men, the presence of a high proportion of women in an industry pulls down its average.

49. Ryl. Comm., 1931–2, *Rpt.*, pp. 45–6.

Chapter 16: The Canadian Transport Commission (pp. 384–405)

1. Reports upon Railway Commissions, Railway Rate Grievances and Regulative Legislation, Canada, House of Commons, *Sessional Paper no. 20a,* 1902.

2. Actually the Committee was established in 1868 (31 Vict., c. 68) but its jurisdiction was greatly extended in 1888 (51 Vict., c. 29, s. 187) after a report by a Royal Commission under the chairmanship of Sir Alexander T. Galt.

3. Railway Act, 3 Edw. VII, c. 58. Railways fought the establishment of the Board because they feared it would bind them hand and foot. Before long they became its enthusiastic supporters.

4. Originally, members were removable by the Cabinet for cause. The present regulation was introduced in 1905 to protect Chief Commissioner Killam who was formerly a judge, and in 1919 was extended to all Commissioners.

5. 7–8 Edw. VII, c. 62.

6. Since 1918.

7. 11–12 Geo. VI, c. 66.

8. R.S.C., 1952, c. 174.

9. 1 Edw. VIII, c. 34.

10. The Pipe Lines Act, 13 Geo. VI, c. 20; R.S.C. 1952, c. 211.

11. By P.C. 115, Jan. 20, 1923.

12. The former by P.C. 3340, dated July 22, 1948, and the latter by the Terms of Union with Newfoundland. The Board also has jurisdiction over the Quebec, North Shore and Labrador and the Wabush Lake Railways.

13. 23–24 Geo. V, c. 47.

14. Aeronautics Act, R.S.C. 1952, c. 2, s.s. 7–19: National Energy Board Act, 7–8 Eliz. II, c. 46.

15. E. M. M. Hill, *Report on Peace River Pass Route to the Pacific Coast* (Ottawa: King's Printer, 1928): Chignecto Canal Commission, *Rpt.* (Ottawa: King's Printer, 1939).

16. P.C. 2434, dated Oct. 6, 1920, reprinted in 26 C.R.C. 147, 151; and P.C. 886, dated June 5, 1925, reprinted in 33 C.R.C. 127, 131–2.

17. *C.P.R.* v. *Alta.,* [1950] S.C.R. 25; 2 D.L.R. 405.

18. Ryl. Comm., 1951, *Rpt.*, pp. 269, 273.

19. *Ibid.,* p. 273.

20. *Can. Airways* v. *Nor. Alta. Ry.,* (1941) 52 C.R.T.C. 321; 31 J.O.R.R. 56: *Quebec Airways,* (1943) 56 C.R.T.C. 203; 33 J.O.R.R. 143.

21. *C.N.R.* v. *C.S.L.* (1940) 51 C.R.T.C. 185; 30 J.O.R.R. 115.

22. The Governor-in-Council normally refers matters of law to the

Supreme Court. *Employees of Michigan Central* v. *M.C.R.*, (1933) 3 D.L.R. 71.

23. Of the roughly 2,300 formal cases before the Board from its inception in 1904 to 1950, only 79 were appealed to the Supreme Court of Canada and 54 to the Governor-in-Council. The Board's judgement was reversed in 16 cases by the Court and 3 by the Cabinet. In addition, the Board itself referred 7 cases to the Supreme Court. In the 1940s and 1950s two appeals on general rate cases went to the Supreme Court which rejected one on leave to appeal and in *C.P.R.* v. *Alberta*, (1949) 64 C.R.T.C. 129, [1950] 2 D.L.R. 405, S.C.R. 25 scolded the Board for not carrying out its functions as required by law. Almost every general rate case was carried to the Cabinet with varying results as explained in the author's *Economics of Canadian Transportation* (Toronto: University of Toronto Press, 2nd. ed., 1959). By Dec. 31, 1965, the Board had issued Order number 119488, making an average of nearly 2,000 a year since its inception.

24. *Re Railway Freight Rates*, [1933] 2 D.L.R. 209; 40 C.R.C. 97. See also *Manitoba & Saskatchewan* v. *Railway Ass'n.*, (1920) 26 C.R.C. 147: *C.P.R.* v. *Toronto Transportation Commission*, [1930] A.C. 686; 37 C.R.C. 203; 4 D.L.R. 849.

25. The hearings are not open to the general public or to the press but newspapers have, none the less, reported the proceedings in as much detail as if they had been in open court.

26. The Cabinet dismissed the only appeal on abandonment that it seems to have heard. *New Brunswick* v. *C.P.R.*, (1937) P.C. 112; 46 C.R.T.C. 138. Another abandonment case was appealed to the Cabinet but dropped on account of the war. *C.N.R.* v. *Renfrew* (*Arnprior-Eganville, Ont.*), (1940) 51 C.R.T.C. 129; 29 J.O.R.R. 671.

27. Ryl. Comm., 1951, *Rpt.*, p. 80. What is law and what is fact must be decided by a justice of the Supreme Court. Within limits, his decision determines whether an appeal goes to the Supreme Court which under the Railway Act hears appeals only on law or jurisdiction, or whether it will finally be dealt with by the Board as one of fact, subject to further appeal to the Cabinet.

Chapter 17: Government Ownership of Railways (pp. 406–437)

1. "I confess . . . that I never thought that to my suggestion of having the new Transcontinental line reach Quebec, the Maritimes would insist upon adding a second line from Quebec to Moncton." Senator Raoul Dandurand, Canada, Senate, *Debates*, 1919, p. 284. See also A. W. Currie, *The Grand Trunk Railway of Canada* (Toronto: University of Toronto Press, 1957); G. R. Stevens, *Canadian National Railways. II. Towards the Inevitable, 1896–1922* (Toronto: Clarke, Irwin, 1962).

2. Canada, House of Commons, *Debates*, 1914, pp. 1966 ff.

3. In fact there were two other alternatives: to relieve the privately owned roads of their obligations to the government by having the government assume all the interest payments which it had guaranteed, thus giving the lines an opportunity to finance themselves privately; or to allow the lines to be sold to the Canadian Pacific, either before or after bankruptcy. Early in 1917 the Canadian Pacific had offered $25 million for the common stock

of the Canadian Northern but the government, which held most of the shares as collateral for its advances to that company, refused to release its stock and allow the sale to go through. The sale would have been exceedingly unpopular in the West which was fearful of monopoly.

4. Drayton was Chairman of the Board of Railway Commissioners and subsequently Minister of Finance. Acworth was a prominent English economist and railway manager. He was appointed in the place of Sir George Paish, then editor of the London *Statist*, who resigned on account of ill health. The Report might have been quite different if Paish, who was a vigorous proponent of private enterprise, had served instead of Acworth who was later manager of the publicly owned London Passenger Transport system.

5. Quoted by G. P. de T. Glazebrook, *A History of Transportation in Canada* (Toronto: Ryerson, 1938), p. 351. Fifteen years later Sir Joseph Flavelle, then a member of a Royal Commission, declared that, speaking from the most intimate knowledge as a director of the bank concerned and as a former director of the Canadian Northern, there was not a word of truth in the allegation which he had heard hundreds of times.

6. The Chief Justice of Ontario for the Government, a prominent Canadian lawyer for the shareholders, and a Justice of the Supreme Court of Nova Scotia as the neutral chairman.

7. Quoted by Glazebrook, *History*, p. 360.

8. For a complete discussion see Jackman, *Economic Principles*, pp. 696-9.

9. Angry tempers were soothed a little by the government's annual payment beginning in 1926 of 2 per cent interest and 2 per cent sinking fund on the 4 per cent debentures of the Grand Trunk Pacific. These debentures ranked ahead of some of the Grand Trunk securities which were paying interest. The government had a fairly clear moral obligation to pay something on the G.T.P. debentures.

10. The name Canadian National Railways was first used officially by P.C. 3122, Dec. 20, 1918, as a descriptive term for the combined operating system of the Canadian Northern whose directors the government was already appointing, the Intercolonial, and the Transcontinental. In 1919 by 9-10 Geo. V, c. 13, the Canadian National Railway Company was incorporated to absorb all the railways then owned and operated by the government, which abolished the old Board of Directors of the Canadian Northern and set up a new one of from 5 to 15 men. The Grand Trunk Pacific was joined to this group for operating purposes by its receiver under P.C. 1595, July 12, 1920. The government agreed to take over the Grand Trunk by 10-11 Geo. V, c. 13 and assumed control on May 1, 1920. For a time the Grand Trunk was managed by a board appointed jointly by the government and the shareholders but as this was unsatisfactory, the Company agreed to set up a board and head office in Canada, instead of Britain as heretofore. The board consisted of two railway executives from the existing Canadian National Railway Company and three from the Grand Trunk. This board passed out of existence on Oct. 4, 1922, by P.C. 2094. The original members of the Canadian National board were replaced by others who acted in the dual capacities of directors of the Canadian National and the Grand Trunk. Unified operation of both systems began on Jan. 1, 1923, and on Jan. 30,

1923, by P.C. 181 a new board for the Canadian National Railways replaced the existing boards.

11. Ryl. Comm., 1931–2, *Rpt.*, p. 86.

12. "The inspection made in September of last year by members of the Board enables them to assure . . . [the shareholders] that never in the history of the Company has the physical condition of the property been so excellent as it is now. It is largely due to this circumstance that . . . [the] company was able to handle expeditiously a large proportion of the new exceptionally heavy grain crop moved during the latter part of the year." C.P.R., *Ann. Rpt.*, 1923, p. 6.

13. Ryl. Comm., 1931–2, *Rpt.*, p. 13.

14. D'Arcy Marsh, *The Tragedy of Sir Henry Thornton* (Toronto: Macmillan, 1935).

15. Canada, Senate, *Journals*, 1925, pp. 410–12.

16. P.C. 2910, dated Nov. 20, 1931, reprinted in Ryl. Comm., 1931–2, *Rpt.*, p. 5.

17. Chief Justice (Sir) Lyman Duff of the Supreme Court of Canada; Lord Ashfield of the London Passenger Transport Board; Sir Joseph Flavelle, a banker and former railway director of Toronto; Beaudry Leman, a graduate engineer who was general manager of a bank with its head office in Montreal; L. F. Loree, a railway president of New York; W. C. Murray, president of the University of Saskatchewan; and J. C. Webster, M.D., of Shediac, N.B.

18. Ryl. Comm., 1931–2, *Rpt.*, pp. 12–14.

19. *Ibid.*, p. 25. In 1927 the Canadian Pacific deplored duplication of hotels at Halifax. Both railways had been willing to co-operate but the government objected. C.P.R., *Ann. Rpt.* 1927, p. 8.

20. Ryl. Comm., 1931–2, *Rpt.*, pp. 26–7.

21. R. H. Miller-Barstow, *Beatty of the C.P.R.* (Toronto: McClelland and Stewart Limited, 1951).

22. Ryl. Comm., 1931–2, *Rpt.*, p. 43.

23. *Ibid.*, pp. 51, 52.

24. *Ibid.*, p. 49.

25. Later the Royal Commission was criticized for not making greater use of a report prepared for it by Mr. Geo. H. Parker, a transportation analyst practising with the Interstate Commerce Commission. J. L. McDougall. "The Report of the Duff Commission," *Can. Journal of Eco. & Pol. Science*, Feb., 1935, pp. 77–98.

26. Ryl. Comm., 1931–2, *Rpt.*, p. 62.

27. Canadian National–Canadian Pacific Act, 23–24 Geo. V, c. 33; R.S.C., 1952, c. 39.

28. (1936), 1 Edw. VIII, c. 25. For criticism of the trustees by the Minister of Transport see Canada, House of Commons, *Debates*, 1935, p. 2365 and for a gentlemanly defence of his administration by the chairman of the trustees see Canada, House of Commons, Committee on Railways, 1936. *Proc.*, pp. 215 ff.

29. On the non-cumulative preference stock a dividend of 1 per cent was paid in 1936 and 2 per cent in 1937 with the regular dividend of 4 per cent being resumed in 1940. Nothing was paid on the common stock until 2 per

cent in 1942 with 5 per cent beginning in the following year.

30. Before the Royal Commission of 1951, officials of the C.N.R. stated that it was fortunate for the country that none of these lines had been abandoned. All were vital during the war.

31. Canada, Senate, Special Committee on Railways, 1938, *Proc.*, p. 97. See also A. W. Currie, "The Senate Committee on Railways, 1938," *Can. Journal of Eco. & Pol. Science*, Feb., 1939, pp. 56–69.

32. The annual reports of the System in 1934 and 1935 intimated that the tribunal's powers might be made use of. The chairmanship of the Board of Railway Commissioners was vacant for over a year (1933–5) and since the Assistant Chief Commissioner was not authorized under the C.N.–C.P. Act to carry out the duties of the chairman, the tribunal could not have functioned.

33. Jackman, *Economic Principles*, pp. 734–5.

34. Canada, Senate, Special Committee, p. 1387.

35. When Sir Edward Beatty was asked why he did not recommend that the unified road abandon the Prince Rupert line of the Canadian National, he replied: "Nothing, except politics." National defence, a cellulose plant at Prince Rupert, the aluminum establishment at Kitamat, and the spectacular growth of newsprint mills and a refinery at Prince George have justified continuing this line.

36. (1939), 3 Geo. VI, c. 37.

37. Ryl. Comm., 1931–2, *Rpt.*, p. 62.

38. Canada, Senate, Special Committee, 1939, *Rpt.*

39. Ryl. Comm., 1951, *Rpt.*, p. 223.

40. *Ibid.*, pp. 128–30.

41. Canada, Senate, Special Committee, 1938, *Proc.*, pp. 1058, 1068–72, 1081, 1248.

42. C.P.R., *Ann. Rpt.*, 1932, p. 9.

43. Capital Revision Act (1937), 1 Geo. VI, c. 22: R.S.C., 1952, c. 41.

44. Ryl. Comm., 1951, *Rpt.*, p. 195.

45. The Canadian National Railways Capital Revision Act, 1952, 1 Eliz. II, c. 36.

46. L. T. Fournier, *Railway Nationalization in Canada* (Toronto: Macmillan Co. of Canada, 1935).

47. G. V. Ferguson, *John W. Dafoe* (Toronto: Ryerson, 1948), p. 84.

48. Canada, House of Commons, Committee on Rys., 1930, *Proc.*, p. 12.

Chapter 18: Highway Freight Transport (pp. 438–473)

1. S. J. McLean, "National Highways Overland," in Adam Shortt and A. G. Doughty, eds., *Canada and Its Provinces*, vol. X, p. 360: Ontario, Royal Commission on Transportation, *Rpt.* (Toronto: King's Printer, 1939), pp. 36–66: E. C. Guillet, *The Story of Canadian Roads* (Toronto: University of Toronto Press, 1966).

2. The number of licenses issued in Canada (including Newfoundland after 1949) on passenger cars, trucks, buses, motorcycles, service cars, etc., but excluding trailers and temporary licenses for vehicles in transit to dealers has been:

1905	565	1940	1,500,829
1910	9,158	1945	1,497,081
1915	95,284	1950	2,600,511
1920	408,790	1955	3,948,652
1925	724,048	1960	5,256,341
1930	1,232,489	1963	6,074,655
1935	1,240,124		

3. G. P. de T. Glazebrook, *A History of Transportation in Canada* (Toronto: Ryerson, 1938), p. 445.

4. The medieval institution of the King's Highway (so-called even when the reigning monarch was a Queen) was primarily an abstract right of passage rather than a physical roadway. The parishes were expected to keep up the roads but the Crown suppressed banditry along some of them so that judges, pilgrims, ecclesiastics, and merchants might travel in peace.

5. In the larger cities and towns, some streets are practically part of the provincial highway system. They are kept up mainly by the municipality concerned though some provinces make special grants for this purpose. It can be argued that on account of the heavy volume of local traffic on these city streets, the city would need to build and maintain them to about their present standard even though they were not numbered as provincial highways. On the other hand a rural municipality could get along with a road of much cheaper construction if only local traffic needs were considered. In other words, through traffic adds to the costs of roads in townships and small towns to a much larger extent than it contributes to the higher costs of city streets. Therefore provinces are justified in assuming the full cost of the trunk road in the one case and not in the other. Increasingly provincial highways are being diverted around thickly settled communities.

6. In Prince Edward Island there are no municipal organizations except in Charlottetown and Summerside. In some of the Western provinces, counties exist for judicial purposes but are not administrative or spending authorities. Near several large cities suburban roads commissions co-ordinate the highway programmes of various councils.

7. In 1939 the cost of highway transportation of the United States was estimated at $17,500 million of which about one-seventh was for highway facilities and the remainder for vehicle operation. Wilfred Owen, "The Provision of Highway Facilities," in National Resources Planning Board, *Transportation and National Policy* (Washington, 1942), p. 394. The proportion has probably not changed significantly over the years though total costs have skyrocketed. Nevertheless, the emphasis in advertising and designing new vehicles has not generally been on economy of operation.

8. Ontario, Select Committee on Toll Roads, *Rpt.*, (Toronto: Queen's Printer, 1956).

9. Ont. Ryl. Comm., 1939, *Rpt.*, pp. 23, 25; also *ibid.*, pp. 67–84, 169. On February 3, 1948, in a brief to the Ontario government the General Truck Drivers' Union, A.F. of L., stated that transport truck drivers "are being forced to work 16 or 17 hours a day, seven days a week, at starvation pay." A spokesman for a large transport company stated that their drivers worked 50 to 55 hours a week. See also Gilbert Walker, *Road and Rail*

Transportation in Nova Scotia (Halifax: Nova Scotia Economic Council, 1941).

10. *Labour Gazette*, July, 1962, pp. 837–50.

11. *Carpenter Common Carrier Application*, (1937), 2 Motor Carrier Cases 85.

12. See, for example, Rules and Regulations under the Vehicles Act, Saskatchewan Gazette, April 1, 1946, pp. 23–4. Taxicabs are ordinarily controlled by cities.

13. The certificates give the holder a monopoly of common carriage by highway over certain specified mileages. They do not restrict the number of trips or the amount of equipment to be used. For general discussions see George Farquhar, "Public Convenience and Necessity," in John Willis, *Canadian Boards at Work* (Toronto: Macmillan, 1941), pp. 93–112: G. J. Ponsonby, "The New Conditions of Entry into the Road Haulage Business," *Economica*, May, 1937, pp. 184–203. The fee for a certificate has to be nominal. If it were substantial, private carriers who do not need certificates of convenience and necessity would be encouraged while common carriers would be discriminated against.

14. Various jurisdictions interpret the phrase "public convenience and necessity" in quite different ways. For one definition, see Transport Act, 1938, s. 5(1).

15. An Act to Amend the Railway Act, 1955, 3–4 Eliz. II, c. 59: Ryl. Comm., 1961, *Rpt.*, vol. II, p. 112.

16. D. W. Carr, "Truck-Rail Competition in Canada," *ibid.*, vol. III, p. 37.

17. *Ibid.*, pp. 37–8.

18. Quoted by H. E. Stocker, *Motor Traffic Management* (New York: Prentice-Hall, 1942), p. 130. "No one who has experienced several severe rate wars between carriers, or who has studied the history of transportation can fail to believe that regulation is worth all it costs." *Ibid.*, p. 129.

19. See also Arthur Hailey, "An Appraisal of the Motor Carrier Industry," in J-C. Lessard, *Transportation in Canada* (Ottawa: Queen's Printer, 1956), pp. 145–6.

20. Ryl. Comm., 1931–2, *Rpt.*, p. 56: *Rex v. Corry*, [1932] 4 D.L.R. 399: *O'Brien* v. *Allen*, [1900] S.C.R. 340, 342–3: *S. M. T.* [*Eastern*] *Ltd.* v. *Ruch*, (1939) 50 C.R.T.C. 369, and the cases therein cited.

21. *A. G. Ont.* v. *Winner*, [1954] A.C. 541; 4 D.L.R. 657; 71 C.R.T.C. 225.

22. Ryl. Comm., 1951, *Rpt.*, p. 279.

23. Motor Vehicle Transport Act, 1954, 2–3 Eliz. II, c. 59.

24. Owners of abutting land often gain from improved highways because of better access to their property and the possibility of subdividing it for residential or commercial purposes. On this account owners of land which fronts directly on the highway should theoretically pay all or part of its cost. Conversely owners of land farther back from the improved road should pay nothing. Beyond a point, however, property values may decline in consequence of congestion, noise, etc. Moreover, relatively remote landowners may use the road much more than adjacent ones. Then too, in some cases the

cost of the road might exceed the current value of the nearby land. The only highway expenditures paid for directly by abutting landowners are for sidewalks, curbs, sewers, and city streets in residential areas.

25. See Shorey Peterson, "Highway Policy on a Commercial Basis," *Quarterly Journal of Economics*, May, 1932, pp. 417–43: R. C. Breithut, "Literature on Highway Finance," *ibid.*, Aug., 1939, pp. 590–610.

26. Ont. Ryl. Comm., 1939, *Rpt.*, pp. 216–17: *Rpt. of the Conference on Road and Rail Transport* (Salter Committee) (London: His Majesty's Stationery Office, 1932): J. E. Allen, "The Road-Rail Conference Report," *Economic Journal*, Dec., 1932, pp. 661–5: U.S. Chamber of Commerce, *Highway Policies* (Washington, 1944), pp. 7–8: Federal Coordinator of Transportation, *Public Aids to Transportation* (Washington: Government Printing Office, 1940), vol. IV, p. 45: Board of Investigation and Research, *Public Aids to Domestic Transportation*, 79th Cong., 1st sess., House Document no. 159 (1944), p. 283: C. L. Dearing, *American Highway Policy* (Washington: The Brookings Institution, 1941), pp. 158–63, 209–12.

27. Lessard, *Transportation*, p. 98: Ont., Select Committee on Toll Roads, *Rpt.*, p. 26: Canadian Tax Foundation, *Taxes and Traffic: A Study of Highway Finance* (Toronto: The Foundation, 1955).

28. *Ibid.*, Introduction.

29. In 1939, 1949, and 1965 the gasoline tax per imperial gallon was 10, 13, and 19 cents in the Maritime Provinces (except 18 in P.E.I. in 1965); --, 14, and 19 cents in Newfoundland; 6, 11, and 15 in Quebec; 6, 11, and 16 in Ontario; 7, 9, and 14 in Manitoba; 7, 10, and 14 in Saskatchewan; 7, 9, and 12 in Alberta; and 7, 10, and 13 in British Columbia.

30. F. W. Taussig, *Principles of Economics* (New York: Macmillan, 1926), vol. II, p. 505.

31. Lessard, *Transportation*, p. 100. See also Tillo E. Kuhn, *Public Enterprise, Economic and Transport Problems* (Berkeley: University of California Press, 1962).

32. Owen, "The Provision," p. 394.

33. Gasoline is not taxed when it is not used for propelling vehicles along public roads, e.g., in stationary engines, in tractors used on farms, or in trucks using roads built by and reserved for the sole use of logging companies.

Chapter 19: Road-Rail Competition (pp. 474–518)

1. The literature on rate wars is voluminous. The Canadian point of view is presented in A. W. Currie, *The Grand Trunk Railway of Canada* (Toronto: University of Toronto Press, 1957), *passim*.

2. J-C. Lessard, *Transportation in Canada* (Ottawa: Queen's Printer, 1956), Schedule 2 E.

3. *Ibid.*, p. 81.

4. Jackman, *Economics of Transportation* (Toronto: University of Toronto Press, 1926), p. 796.

5. (1932) 182 I.C.C. 263, 301.

6. H. G. Moulton & Associates, *The American Transportation Problem* (Washington: The Brookings Institution, 1933), pp. 523–4.

7. Ryl. Comm., 1951, *Transcript of Evidence*, p. 15584.

8. A. F. Hailey, "An Appraisal of the Motor Carrier Industry," in Lessard, *Transportation*, p. 149.

9. D. W. Carr, "Truck-Rail Competition," Ryl. Comm., 1961, *Rpt.*, vol. III, pp. 15, 29–32, 41–3.

10. *Ibid.*, p. 78.

11. Lessard, *Transportation*, p. 127.

12. *Stewarts & Lloyds* v. *C.N.R.*, (1961) 83 C.R.T.C. 153; 51 C.R.T.C. 597.

13. *Alberta Phoenix Tube & Pipe, Ltd.* v. *C.P.R.*, (1958) 77 C.R.T.C. 40; 48 J.O.R.R. 83: *Page-Hersey Tubes* v. *C.N.R.*, (1963) 83 B.T.C. 354; 53 B.T.C. 359: P.C. 1963–1041, reprinted in 85 B.T.C. 167. Rates on multiple-car shipments were authorized in the United States under *Arrow Trans. Co.* v. *Southern Ry. Co.*, (1963) 372 U.S. 658. See P. W. MacAvoy & J. Sloss, *Regulation of Transport Innovation* (New York: Random House, 1967).

14. *C.F.A.* v. *Elm Valley Coal Co.*, (1940) 52 C.R.T.C. 141, 144; 30 J.O.R.R. 453, 455: *C.N.R.* v. *Lion Oil Co.*, (1939) 50 C.R.T.C. 166: *C.N.R.* v. *Good Rich Oil Co.*, (1939) 50 C.R.T.C. 161; 29 J.O.R.R. 335: confirmed *ibid.*, (1941) 54 C.R.T.C. 140; 31 J.O.R.R. 477: *Imperial Oil* v. *C.N.R.*, (1949) 63 C.R.T.C. 300; 39 J.O.R.R. 1: *Re Agreed Charge No. 48.* (1952) 69 C.R.T.C. 160; 42 J.O.R.R. 12.

15. *C.N.R.* v. *C.S.L.*, [1945] A.C. 204; 3 D.L.R. 417; 58 C.R.T.C. 113.

16. Ryl. Comm. on Agreed Charges, 1955, *Rpt.*, p. 36.

17. *C.S.L.* v. *C.F.A.*, (1956) 74 C.R.T.C. 69; 46 J.O.R.R. 165.

18. *Can. Trucking Ass'n.* v. *C.N.R. & C.P.R.*, (1958) 76 C.R.T.C. 327; 48 J.O.R.R. 65.

19. Ryl. Comm., 1951, *Rpt.*, pp. 47–8.

20. Ryl. Comm. on Agreed Charges, 1955, *Rpt.*, pp. 47–8.

21. *Re "Incentive" Freight Rates in Western Canada*, (1958) 78 C.R.T.C. 85, 89–90; 48 J.O.R.R. 529, 533.

22. *Can. Airways* v. *Nor. Alta. Ry.*, (1941) 52 C.R.T.C. 321; 31 J.O.R.R. 617: *Quebec Airways*, (1943) 56 C.R.T.C. 205; 33 J.O.R.R. 143.

23. Ryl. Comm., 1951, *Rpt.*, pp. 276–80.

24. Ryl. Comm. on Canada's Economic Prospects, *Final Rpt.*, (Ottawa: Queen's Printer, 1957), pp. 284–5.

Chapter 20: Highway Passenger Traffic (pp. 519–533)

1. J-C. Lessard, *Transportation in Canada* (Ottawa: Queen's Printer, 1956), Schedule 2 F; Sun Life Assurance Co. of Canada, *The Canadian Automotive Industry* (Ottawa: Queen's Printer, 1957).

2. By taking good care of one's car, driving as little as possible and then only in good weather and on hard-surfaced roads, one can raise its trade-in or re-sale value above the normal or going amount for that model by perhaps 10 per cent on a model one year old and more on an older car. In this way the annual total of interest and depreciation charges may be reduced. But if only a few miles are run, these charges per vehicle-mile are high. When trading in an old model, a motorist may be able to take advantage of his ability to higgle or the fact that cars generally are hard to get. Thus the timing of

the transaction and the personalities of the participants in the negotiations may be important. Depreciation is heaviest in the first year of operation. A rule of thumb is 25 per cent of original value in the first year, 15 per cent in the second, and 10 per cent thereafter. After the third year or about 50,000 miles, depreciation decreases but repair bills grow. The sum of depreciation charges plus repairs is about the same from the third to the seventh year but repair costs are likely to rise sharply thereafter. After all is said and done, the age of the car, that is, the time element, is the really significant factor in determining depreciation and interest charges per annum. Again, by taking thought, a motorist may keep his repair and tire bills below what they usually are for the mileage involved. But the chances of doing this to any appreciable extent are limited. Conversely a motorist may, in the short run, cut down his out-of-pocket costs by poorly maintaining his car. Without the cost records of thousands of motorists, one is forced to conclude *a priori* that depreciation and interest are related directly to time, and repairs to mileage.

3. Further complications may be added. Some accidents due to negligence may not be covered by insurance. Because urban transit fares are typically on a flat or "postage stamp" basis i.e., they do not vary with distance, the relationship between passenger-car and transit costs per passenger-mile may be quite different for residents in different parts of a city.

4. Car rental, U-Drive, or drive yourself services are in much the same position.

5. Lessard, *Transportation*, p. 19. In the absence of legal restrictions it is easy to enter the taxicab business. Most cities control admission to the industry in order to prevent destructive rate cutting, unreasonably low wages, undermaintenance of cabs, excessive cruising for fares, traffic congestion, and general demoralization of the industry. Cities also set fares and periodically check on the accuracy of meters.

6. Buses are often held up by traffic on congested city streets. Railways have their own relatively unobstructed rights of way, but local trains may be delayed at stops because large quantities of mail and express have to be loaded and unloaded. Buses must wait at rest-stops, and locomotives must be replenished with fuel. A passenger has to travel to and from the railway station at origin and destination. He may or may not find the bus terminal more convenient. Sometimes the route followed by one carrier is more circuitous than that of the other.

7. *Canada Year Book*, 1950, p. 745.

8. These were designed after many years' research by the President's Conference Committee, a group working under the supervision of the conference of presidents of American street railways.

9. In Edmonton investment per seat in 1946 was $450 for trolley coach, $600 for a 50-passenger P.C.C. street car, and $380 for a 44-passenger motor bus. The average life was, respectively, 12 to 15, 20 to 30, and 8 to 10 years. To provide for possible break-downs, a reserve or "spare" of 5 per cent was needed for trackless trolleys and 15 per cent for motor buses. "Operating Costs in Edmonton," Canadian Transit Ass'n., *Proc.*, June, 1946.

10. But one passenger may complain that he pays more and has to stand up during rush hours, while those who travel at lower fares at other hours of

the day get seats. The conflict between cost and value of service crops up in urban transit as in other kinds of transport.

11. The Canadian Northern built a tunnel under the mountain in order to get access to the central part of the city without having to purchase an expensive right of way through thickly built up industrial and residential areas. The tunnel is used for commutation traffic by the Canadian National. For various reasons it cannot relieve congestion in the same way as could a subway of comparable cost.

12. The difficulty was especially serious during and immediately after World War I. The traditional fare was 5 cents and the next highest coin was the 10-cent piece, or 100 per cent more. It is obviously awkward to set the fare at 7 cents or some other combination of silver (or nickel) and copper coins. To get around this difficulty tickets were sold at four for 25 cents with a cash fare of 10 cents. The next convenient "jump" in fares is to three for 25 cents, an increase of 33 per cent. A "jump" to, say, four tickets for 30 cents instead of four for 25 cents is a 20 per cent increase. This may be more in line with the needs of the company but making change is clumsy for patrons and employees.

13. Lessard, *Transportation*, p. 117.

14. N. D. Wilson, "Some Problems of Urban Transportation," in H. A. Innis, *ed., Essays in Honour of W. T. Jackman* (Toronto: University of Toronto Press, 1941), p. 116.

Chapter 21: Civil Aviation (pp. 534–571)

1. J. C. Cooper, *The Right to Fly* (New York: Henry Holt, 1947), p. 240. For some of the material in this chapter the author is greatly indebted to W. H. Merritt, *Government Policy and Commercial Air Transportation in Canada*, an unpublished master's thesis presented at the University of Toronto in 1947. See also Frank H. Ellis, *Canada's Flying Heritage* (Toronto: University of Toronto Press, 1961).

2. *Canadian Aviation*, June, 1939, p. 37.

3. The Judicial Committee of the Privy Council, then the highest court of appeal open to Canadians, interpreted the British North America Act, which is Canada's constitution, to give substantially all control of civil aviation to the Dominion. *Re Regulation and Control of Aeronautics in Canada* [1932] A.C. 54; 1 D.L.R. 58. Some provinces operate their own planes in forestry service.

4. S. E. Veale, *To-morrow's Airlines, Airports and Airways* (London: Pilot Press, 1945), pp. 247–95.

5. Local or "drop" letters and parcel post are exceptions. For a general discussion of the economics of the postal service in Canada, see A. W. Currie, "The Post Office since 1867," *Can. Journal of Ec. and Pol. Science*, May, 1958, pp. 241–50.

6. On Air Canada the percentage of mail compensation to total revenue dropped from nearly 70 in 1939 to less than 25 in the late 1940s and 7 or less after 1959. Figures for other companies are not comparable owing to consolidation of operations.

7. Domestic intercity passenger miles by all modes of travel:

	Canada		United States	
	Total (Millions)	Per capita	Total (Millions)	Per capita
1946	16,800	1,333	344,613	2,444
1951	21,042	1,503	520,336	3,372
1957	34,222	2,063	702,213	4,100

Source: Computed from C.P.A.L., *Submission to Air Transport Board*, 1958.

8. Canada, House of Commons, *Debates*, 1944, pp. 1571-2. As early as March, 1919, the C.P.R. had applied for an amendment to its charter authorizing it to operate commercial air services.

9. Trans-Canada Air Lines Act (1937), 1 Geo. VI, c. 43; R.S.C., 1952, c. 268.

10. A Lockheed aircraft (1939) had 14 seats for passengers; a DC-8 (1960) has 139.

11. The only companies left out were M & C in northern Saskatchewan, Maritime Central, Leavens Bros. of Toronto, and a small concern since abandoned in the Yukon. In 1947 the Saskatchewan government bought out M & C and consolidated it with its other operations in the northern part of the province.

12. 8 Geo. VI, c. 25.

13. 8 Geo. VI, c. 28; R.S.C., 1952, c. 2, s.s. 7-19.

14. Canada, House of Commons, *Debates*, 1944, pp. 2183-2223.

15. Mr. C. D. Howe in *ibid*., 1946, p. 5002. See also C. A. Ashley, *The First Twenty-Five Years: A Study of Trans-Canada Air Lines* (Toronto: Macmillan, 1963).

16. Stephen F. Wheatcroft, "Airline Competition in Canada" (mimeo.; Ottawa: Department of Transport, 1958), pp. 37, 38.

17. *Ibid*., p. 27.

18. *Ibid*., p. 50.

19. *Ibid*., p. 5, quoting *Transcontinental & Western Air, Additional North-South California Services*, Civil Aeronautics Board, *Reports* (1943), vol. 4, pp. 373, 375. The quotation stresses only one of the doctrines of the C.A.B. which also has to concern itself with the present and future needs of the commerce of the United States, the postal service, national defence, and the financial self-sufficiency of airline operators.

20. Wheatcroft, "Airline Competition," pp. 11, 13, 14.

21. For full discussions see Cooper, *The Right to Fly* and *Journal of Air Law and Commerce*, published by Northwestern University.

Chapter 22: Inland Shipping (pp. 572-599)

1. See D. A. MacGibbon, *The Canadian Grain Trade* (Toronto: Macmillan, 1932), pp. 118-42.

2. F. H. Brown, "Canadian Lake Shipping," in H. A. Innis and A. F. W. Plumptre, eds., *The Canadian Economy and Its Problems* (Toronto: Canadian Institute of International Affairs, 1934), p. 88.

3. A one-foot increase in depth has been estimated to represent a gain of over $6 million based on the volume of trade in 1920. R. S. MacElwee and A. H. Ritter, *Economic Aspects of the Great Lakes–St. Lawrence Ship Channel* (New York: Ronald Press, 1921), p. 158.

4. Brown, "Canadian Lake Shipping," pp. 92–3.

5. In 1897 the London *Economist* (p. 1460) commented on the large lake steamers which carried 80,000 bushels and which were replacing older vessels with capacities of 20,000 to 30,000 bushels. It also noted that though Canada had spent about £60 million on canals, the bulk of her wheat was exported via Buffalo and New York.

6. Brown, "Canadian Lake Shipping," p. 92.

7. Inland Water Freight Rates Act (1923), 13–14 Geo. V, c. 49 now R.S.C. 1952, c. 153. A complete and still fairly accurate description of lake shipping is contained in Royal Commission on Lake Grain Rates, *Rpt.* (Ottawa: King's Printer, 1923).

8. Transport Act, 1938, 2 Geo. VI, c. 53, ss. 10–12, 16–34 as amended by (1944–45) 8 Geo. VI, c. 25, ss. 8–11. Provincial governments have control of intraprovincial ferries. See The [Ontario] Ferries Act, R.S.O., 1950, c. 135: and *Owen Sound Transportation Co.* v. *Tackaberry*, [1936] Ontario Weekly Notes 168, 323; 45 C.R.C. 278.

9. Licensing of a ship especially designed for the carriage of automobiles from Windsor to Fort William was unsuccessfully opposed by both railways and Canada SS. Lines. *Re Wilcan Shipping Corp.*, (1956) 73 C.R.T.C. 230; 45 J.O.R.R. 103. Two other applications for licences appear to have been contested, neither very seriously. When application was made to license a vessel which had been converted to a 'tween deck ship in order to replace a vessel lost by fire and there was no question of the quality or permanence of the service to be offered or the financial responsibility of the owners, complete evidence of public convenience and necessity was not required. *Re Canada SS. Lines–Glenross*, (1939) 29 J.O.R.R. 409.

10. This is done when vessels which are primarily carriers of bulk cargoes carry incidental shipments of goods other than their main commodities, provided such other goods are the property of the owners of the vessel and of the main product being transported. See P.C. 1297, June 2, 1939, 29 J.O.R.R. 272 (Canada Cement): P.C. 1309, June 2, 1939, *ibid.*, 273 (Ontario Paper Co.): and P.C. 1641, June 29, 1939; *ibid.*, 274 (Imperial Oil). Exemptions were also granted when vessels subject to regulation competed with schooners and small steamships (under 500 tons) which are not covered by the Transport Act, P.C. 930, April 25, 1939; 29 J.O.R.R. 100: (Dominion Transport Co., Owen Sound to Manitoulin Island, Sault Ste. Marie and Michipicoten Is., also Tobermory to Manitoulin Is.): P.C. 944, April 25, 1939, 29 J.O.R.R. 101 (Canada SS. Lines, Montreal to Quebec).

11. *C.F.A.* v. *Colonial SS. Lines*, (1939) 50 C.R.T.C. 284.

12. Canada Shipping Act, (1934) 24–25 Geo. V, c. 44, ss. 661–5, R.S.C., 1952, c. 29, s.s. 669–73 as amended by (1961) 9–10 Eliz. II, c. 32. See also Ryl. Comm. on Coastal Shipping, *Rpt.*, (Ottawa: Queen's Printer, 1957).

13. Ryl. Comm. on Lake Shipping, 1923, *Rpt.*, p. 53.

14. Canada Shipping Act, s. 673.

15. *Tolls of Licensed Water Carriers within the Mackenzie River Water-*

shed, (1951) 41 J.O.R.R. 33. For a discussion of public convenience and necessity as applied to shipping in the Mackenzie Basin, see *Re Yellowknife Transportation Co.*, (1950) 40 J.O.R.R. 9.

16. Canada Shipping Act, s.s. 243-68.

17. (1948), 11–12 Geo. VI, c. 35.

18. Maritime Transportation Unions Trustee Act, (1963) 12 Eliz. II, c. 17.

19. H. A. Logan, *Trade Union Organization in Canada* (Toronto: Macmillan, 1948), p. 286.

20. Histories of the Seaway include C. P. Wright, *The St. Lawrence Deep Waterway: A Canadian Appraisal* (Toronto: Macmillan, 1935): H. Holgate and T. A. Jamieson, *Rpt. to Montreal Bd. of Trade* (Montreal: Southam Press, 1939): H. G. Moulton, *St. Lawrence Navigation* and Power Project (Washington: The Brookings Institution, 1929): Lesslie Thomson, "The St. Lawrence Problem: Some Canadian Economic Aspects," *Engineering Journal*, April, 1929, pp. 188–304: W. T. Jackman, "The St. Lawrence Waterway Project," in Can. Political Science Ass'n., *Proc.*, 1932, pp. 213–44: A. W. Currie, "The St. Lawrence Waterway," *Queen's Quarterly*, 1951–2, pp. 558–72: Lionel Chevrier, *The St. Lawrence Seaway* (New York: Macmillan, 1959): W. R. Willoughby, *The St. Lawrence Seaway* (Madison: University of Wisconsin Press, 1961).

21. St. Lawrence Seaway Authority Act, R.S.C. 1952, c. 242.

22. D. W. McLachlan and G. A. Lindsay, in Canada, Senate, Special Cttee. on the St. Lawrence Development, 1928, *Rpt.*, pp. 297–338.

Chapter 23: Ocean Shipping (pp. 600–631)

1. *Canadian Annual Review* for 1925–26, pp. 224–5: Canada, House of Commons, Special Committee on Ocean Rates, 1925, *Proc.*

2. Freight should be delivered a few days in advance of the sailing date. Freight must be carefully stowed in order to give the vessel the proper trim and prevent one kind of freight contaminating others or being contaminated by them. If the vessel is to call at different ports, different lots of freight must be stowed away so they will be accessible at the proper time. Even though the ship has empty space, freight arriving at the dock at the last moment before the ship sails sometimes cannot be put aboard because it would pick up or give off odours, "sweat," crush goods piled below it, or shift if the vessel rolled and pitched.

3. The Canadian customs tariff has three columns of rates of duty: the British preferential, which is the lowest; the intermediate, which applies to a great many foreign countries with whom we have reciprocal trading arrangements; and the normal or highest, which currently applies to only a few countries with which our trade is negligible.

4. A. Berglund, *Ocean Transportation* (New York: Longmans Green, 1931), p. 161.

5. The Canadian Maritime Commission Act (1947), 11 Geo. VI, c. 52, s.s. 3 (2) and 8 (b): *ibid.*, R.S.C., 1952, c. 38.

6. Canadian Maritime Comm., *Second Rpt.* (Ottawa: King's Printer, 1949), p. 56.

7. W. Wood, *All Afloat* (Toronto: Chronicles of Canada, 1914): M. J. Patton, "Shipping and Canals," in *Canada and Its Provinces* (Toronto: Glasgow, Brook, 1914), vol. X, pp. 475–624.

8. Bureau of Tr. Eco., *Economic Rpt.*, pp. 17–18: A. L. Lawes, "Ocean Shipping and Canada," *Canadian Banker*, Nov., 1947, pp. 59–70.

9. Maritime Comm., *Second Rpt.*, p. 53.

10. *Ibid.*, pp. 41–3.

11. Ryl Comm. on Coastal Shipping, *Rpt.*, (Ottawa: Queen's Printer, 1957).

12. Sir Alexander Gibb, *National Ports Survey, 1931–2*, Canada, House of Commons, *Sessional Paper*, no. 273, 1932.

Chapter 24: Pipelines (pp. 632–9)

1. Pipe Lines Act, R.S.C. 1952, c. 211.

2. National Energy Board Act, (1959) 7–8 Eliz. II, c. 46. This legislation repealed the Pipe Lines Act. The National Energy Board also took over from the Department of Trade and Commerce the administration of the Electricity and Fluid Exportation Act, R.S.C., 1952, c. 93.

3. National Energy Board, *Ann. Rpts.*, *passim*.

Index